W9-CLG-175

COLLECTED WORKS OF ERASMUS

VOLUME 44

COLLECTED WORKS OF
ERASMUS

NEW TESTAMENT SCHOLARSHIP

General Editor Robert D. Sider

PARAPHRASES ON
THE EPISTLES TO TIMOTHY, TITUS,
AND PHILEMON
THE EPISTLES OF PETER AND JUDE
THE EPISTLE OF JAMES
THE EPISTLES OF JOHN
THE EPISTLE TO THE HEBREWS

translated and annotated by

John J. Bateman

University of Toronto Press

Toronto / Buffalo / London

The research and publication costs of the
Collected Works of Erasmus are supported by the
Social Sciences and Humanities Research Council of Canada.
The publication costs are also assisted by
University of Toronto Press.

ISBN 0-8020-0541-1

Printed on acid-free paper

Canadian Cataloguing in Publication Data
Erasmus, Desiderius, d. 1536
[Works]
Collected works of Erasmus
Includes bibliographical references.
Partial contents: v. 44. New Testament scholarship :
paraphrases on the letters to Timothy, Titus, and Philemon,
the letters of Peter and Jude,
the letter of James, the letters of John,
the letter to the Hebrews /
translated and annotated by John J. Bateman.
ISBN 0-8020-0541-1 (v. 44)
1. Erasmus, Desiderius, d. 1536. I. Title.
PA8500 1974   876'.04   C74-006326-X

Collected Works of Erasmus

The aim of the Collected Works of Erasmus
is to make available an accurate, readable English text
of Erasmus' correspondence and his
other principal writings. The edition is planned
and directed by an Editorial Board, an Executive Committee,
and an Advisory Committee.

Contents

Preface

The nature and scope of the series of volumes to be published as the New Testament scholarship of Erasmus have been described in the preface to volume 42. That volume also provided introductory studies on the origin and nature of the *Paraphrases*, their publication history, and sixteenth-century translations of the *Paraphrases* in English. Those essays should prove useful to readers of this volume. At a later date, a full introduction to the New Testament scholarship of Erasmus will appear in a volume prolegomenous to the series (CWE 41).

This volume (CWE 44) contains the *Paraphrases* on what are commonly called the Pastoral and the Catholic or General Epistles, together with Hebrews. These *Paraphrases* were all published in just a little more than a year (late 1519–early 1521). The *Paraphrases* on the Catholic Epistles and on Hebrews were the last to appear of those on the New Testament Epistles; Erasmus thereafter turned to paraphrasing the Gospels.

The *Paraphrases* translated here add light and lustre to common Erasmian themes. Perhaps nowhere among the *Paraphrases* will one find a fuller definition of 'godliness' than here. In these *Paraphrases* godliness is seen to begin in faith and baptism – though the precise role played by each remains characteristically ambiguous. On the other hand, there is little ambiguity in the representation of the fundamental hostility between faith and philosophy; faith believes, it does not dispute; philosophy, the endless investigation of questions, does not lead to godliness. In the notes, Professor Bateman shows the reliance of Erasmus on Chrysostom in the formulation of this position, and locates in Erasmus' writings elsewhere the antithesis between faith and philosophy expressed in much the same terms as here.

No one, however, is perfectly formed in baptism, and the idea of godliness includes the need for perseverance and growth in good works. Ultimately, claims Erasmus, to be godly is to become like God, and he does not leave his reader without an indication of the 'works' needed to achieve such a happy state. He speaks of self-renunciation, of 'slaying the passions'

– a spiritual substitute for animal sacrifices. He urges upon the reader the extreme application of the Golden Rule; the perfect act is to do good to those who harm us, for in doing so we 'complete the circle of godliness.' Erasmus speaks, moreover, of a 'treasury of godliness': one can hardly be rich and righteous at the same time, but the rich can invest their money in the gospel, and the 'interest' will be paid into the treasury of good works. Money can, in effect, buy righteousness. The idea appears to have been introduced here not as a passing thought, a mere exegetical convenience; it will appear again in the *Paraphrases* on the Gospels – for example, in the explication of the Dominical saying in Luke about making friends 'of the mammon of unrighteousness' (Luke 16:9).

In the course of these *Paraphrases*, Erasmus also touches upon some of the recurring issues in the history of theology, issues he had addressed in his earlier *Paraphrases*. Here, as in the *Paraphrase on Galatians*, he seeks to explicate the economy of salvation: he sees the Old Covenant as a propaedeutic to the New; its dark riddles anticipated the bright light of truth, and its harsh laws restrained a rebellious people until the love of Christ could enter the human heart, leading men and women to do of their own accord more than the Law had forced upon the Jewish race by its requirements (cf CWE 42 113–14). In the *Paraphrase on James* we observe again Erasmus' ambiguity towards the doctrine of 'original sin,' an ambiguity already seen in the *Paraphrase on Romans* (CWE 42 34–6); and the paraphrases on Hebrews 11 go well beyond those on Romans 4 in the vivid images that represent faith as a compelling vision of heavenly realities, a vision so powerful that the Christian becomes insensitive to the values of this world.

Not all in these *Paraphrases* is straightforward admonition for the spiritual life or clarification of theological questions. We also recognize here the author of the satirical portraits of the *Praise of Folly*. The portrait (in the *Paraphrase on Second Timothy*) of the mendicant orders is completed with a few broad strokes: men of 'feigned religion,' 'coarse clothes,' 'sham severity,' and pale features who 'hunt for foolish little women' (p 49). The outline of the ideal bishop-teacher is sharpened by allusions to power-hungry and greedy prelates. Women, always the weaker sex, are characterized as 'flighty,' 'licentious,' given to malicious gossip. A vitriolic attack on the Jews describes them as 'abominable' and 'insubordinate.' But no class of people is portrayed in darker colours than the rich, as Erasmus describes their merciless pillaging of the poor and the folly of their false sense of values – they are, in fact, the anti-Christs who deny Christ by their actions.

Finally, we are able to detect in these *Paraphrases* (with the help of Professor Bateman's notes) some of Erasmus' own personal interests. We can, for example, learn here of his love of pets; or, in a different vein, of his

concern that dowries be provided for unmarried girls from poor families –
and of the provision of a fund for the purpose in his own last will and
testament.

As in the New Testament Scholarship Series generally, the notes in this
volume explain historical allusions and identify the exegetical tradition that
provides much of the literary context out of which Erasmus creates his
Paraphrases. They also address problems in Erasmian scholarship. Indeed, in
the introductory Translator's Note, Professor Bateman has undertaken to
describe, step by step, the genesis of a *Paraphrase*. In a word, this volume
seeks to bring the modern reader into the world of Erasmus and his *Paraphrases*.

RDS

Translator's Note

The translation of the *Paraphrases* in this volume has been made from the text of the Basel 1532 edition of the *Tomus secundus continens Paraphrasim D. Erasmi Roterodami in omneis apostolicas epistolas*, the last edition to appear during Erasmus' lifetime with significant editorial changes.[1] The *Paraphrases* are therefore presented in the order in which the Epistles occur in this edition rather than in the order in which they are found in the New Testament. When questioned on this point, Erasmus replied that the order in which he wrote and first published the *Paraphrases* was a matter of chance and that it simply never occurred to him to arrange them in the canonical order in subsequent editions.[2] The *Paraphrases* on the Epistles to Timothy, Titus, and Philemon were first published by the Antwerp printer, Michaël Hillen, in November or early December of 1519.[3] The *Paraphrases* on the Epistles of Peter and Jude followed some six or seven months later, in the summer of 1520. That, according to Erasmus, would have been the end of his career as a paraphraser had not Matthäus Schiner, cardinal-bishop of Sion in Switzerland, urged him to complete the task of paraphrasing the Catholic Epistles,[4] while other (unnamed) friends argued with him that the Epistle to the Hebrews should not be omitted since he deserved to have the credit for a paraphrase on all the Epistles.[5]

Erasmus set out to comply with these requests sometime in the autumn of 1520.[6] The *Paraphrase on James* was finished and printed in December, and the *Paraphrases* on the Epistles of John and on the Epistle to the Hebrews in January 1521.[7] In addition to completing the *Paraphrase* on the Epistles in this way Erasmus also decided to issue revised versions of the previously published *Paraphrases*. Whether it was his own idea or that of the printer Johann Froben, the new *Paraphrases* together with revised texts of the *Paraphrases* on the other Epistles were issued in a collected edition in March 1521 and reprinted with additional revisions a few months later in July 1521.[8] These two editions are thus the foundation of the subsequent history of the text. Beginning in 1522, Froben issued the *Paraphrases* in two formats: a folio edition comparable in design and size to Erasmus' *Novum Testamentum*, the third edition of which also appeared in 1522, and a smaller octavo edition, divided into sections for separate binding if the purchaser so wished. Froben was in effect issuing a study edition to be read side by side with the New Testament and a 'pocket-book' edition for private reading. This pattern was to be followed in all the subsequent editions of the *Paraphrases* published by the Froben firm until their final publication of a folio edition in 1556 and of the corresponding octavo edition in 1557.

The *Paraphrases* on the Epistles were received at first with general approbation,[9] but starting in 1524 and escalating in 1526, the *Paraphrases* on both the Gospels and the Epistles became the object of a full-scale assault, first from Noël Béda and the faculty of theology at Paris and later from hostile critics in Spain and Italy.[10] Erasmus defended himself and his work vigorously, rarely recanted, but nevertheless began in 1527 to revise the text in preparation for a new edition.[11] This plan was temporarily shelved, however, and the new, revised edition did not appear until 1532.[12] Additional revisions of the text appear in the posthumous folio editions of 1538 and 1540.[13] Though these changes may be due to Erasmus, I have not introduced them into the text but have recorded them in the notes. I have similarly recorded the variants in the first editions and in the Froben editions published before 1532 – not all the variants but only those which would produce a different translation. I have passed over in silence numerous other changes such as transpositions of words, substitutions of one demostrative pronoun for another, replacement of one Latin word meaning 'and' by a different one, and the like, because such alterations of the text would not be reflected in an English translation. Since the Latin text in the Leiden edition of the *Opera omnia* (LB) is the one most likely to be consulted until a new critical edition of the Latin text becomes available,[14] I have listed in the notes all its substantive variants from the 1532 text, except obvious misprints. The reader can thus see how the text of these particular *Paraphrases* was improved and occasionally corrupted both during Erasmus' lifetime and after.[15]

Erasmus' concept of a paraphrase is not easy to describe.[16] On one occasion he defined the paraphrase as a combination of free translation and running commentary in contrast to a literal translation,[17] but it is neither commentary nor paraphrase in the modern meaning of these terms. What he appears to have done is, first, to make a draft or précis of the meaning of the text.[18] This initial draft was made, I believe, with the Greek and Latin text of the two-volume second (1519) edition of the *Novum Testamentum* open before him side by side with the *Annotationes*.[19] The paraphrase itself is based upon the Greek text and Erasmus' Latin version which is printed beside the Greek in the 1519 edition, though cognizance is taken from time to time of the alternative readings of the Vulgate,[20] especially when the latter contains extended phrases or clauses not found in Erasmus' Greek text.[21]

The next step was to read the authorities.[22] For the *Paraphrase* on the Epistles to Timothy, Titus, and Philemon these are chiefly Ambrosiaster, Chrysostom,[23] Jerome, and Theophylact.[24] The controversy with Jacques Lefèvre d'Etaples in 1517 over the Pauline authorship of the Epistle to the Hebrews and the meaning of Hebrews 2:7 seems to have led Erasmus to restudy Aquinas' *Expositio* on this Epistle[25] and also perhaps Nicholas of Lyra's *Postilla literalis*.[26] Evidence of the employment of these two commentaries appears clearly in the *Paraphrase* on Hebrews but not, or at least not to the same extent, in the *Paraphrases* on the other Pauline epistles. However, Erasmus' greater reliance on Aquinas and Lyra in paraphrasing Hebrews may also have been due to the fact that Ambrosiaster did not comment on this Epistle while Chrysostom's commentary on it did not appeal to him.[27] There were no major patristic commentaries on the Catholic Epistles available to Erasmus, apart from Augustine's *Ten Tractates on the Epistle of John to the Parthians* (that is, 1 John), which effectively ends at 1 John 5:3, and some incidental homilies and letters dealing with particular passages. The single most popular commentary on the seven Catholic Epistles was that by the Venerable Bede.[28] This work was extensively excerpted in the *Glossa Ordinaria*[29] but also circulated independently in both manuscript and print.[30] Erasmus seems to have made little use of Bede's commentary on the Catholic Epistles in the first two editions of the *Novum Testamentum*, but his name appears frequently in the annotations in the third edition.[31] In this instance it seems that the reading required for the *Paraphrases* has contributed substantially to the edition of the *Novum Testamentum* rather than *vice versa*.[32]

Having absorbed the content of the commentaries and other authorities,[33] Erasmus turned to the elaboration of the preliminary draft into the actual paraphrase, using his knowledge of rhetoric and his by now highly developed writing skills to create the transitions, emphases, dramatic vignettes, and other devices designed to facilitate the reader's comprehension and aesthetic appreciation of the biblical text.[34] In elaborating a document in this way, Erasmus is adapting to the task of paraphrasing a common practice of sixteenth-century letter-writers as may be illustrated from his own correspondence and from his treatise on letter-writing.[35] A pertinent example is the set of letters to Matthäus Schiner written on 14 Dec 1521. The shorter of the two letters (Ep 1249) contains the text of the letter that was actually sent to Schiner; the longer (Ep 1248) is the version prepared for publication in the first edition of the *Paraphrase on Matthew*, which Schiner had encouraged Erasmus to compose. Comparison of the two letters will show how Erasmus set about the task of elaborating a text.

However, I have not sought to document the literary and rhetorical devices and other procedures which Erasmus employed to develop his paraphrase except in a few places where it was necessary in order to prevent misunderstanding. Instead, I have tried to indicate in the notes, as fully as space permitted, the principal authorities which appear to have been used in the second stage of composition of each *Paraphrase*. English translations exist for the homilies of John Chrysostom on the Pauline Epistles and for the commentaries of Bede; hence I quote or otherwise refer to these translations as well as to the original texts. I have occasionally modified the translation in order to make the relationship of authority and paraphrase clearer and, in a few instances, have silently emended a mistaken translation. Where the texts have not, so far as I know, been translated into English, I have either translated or, as circumstances required, abridged and summarized them. It has not been possible to record or even to refer to every text which is similar to the paraphrase in some respect; nevertheless, I have attempted to provide enough information for the reader to see how Erasmus made use of his reading. Much, of course, was already in his mind as the result of a lifelong study of the New Testament; much was also, no doubt, already at hand in his 'commonplace book,' his theological 'places' (*loci*) or 'nests' (*niduli*) as he calls them in the *Ratio verae theologiae*.[36] To track down all of Erasmus' reading, even if it were possible, would go far beyond the scope of this edition. The same may be said of Erasmus' use of the Bible. The paraphrase on a given text is often permeated with echoes or reminiscences of other biblical texts, chiefly in the New Testament but occasionally in the Psalms and the prophets, especially Isaiah. Explicit allusions and references are identified in the notes. But instead of annotating every reminiscence which I detected I have attempted to incorporate in the translation, in so far as it was practical, the language of the biblical text as a way of imitating the texture of Erasmus' own language.[37]

In other respects, I have generally followed the lead of the translators of the *Paraphrases* on Romans and Galatians in CWE 42, especially in breaking up and rewriting in a more comprehensible form the long complex sentences for which Erasmus has an inordinate fondness in the *Paraphrase* on the Epistles. I also try to retain in so far as the context permits their translations of Erasmus' theological language, although I have in some instances chosen alternative renderings of a few terms. The most important of them is the adjective *pius* 'pious' and its cognates. I prefer to translate it by 'godly' because *pietas* 'godliness' denotes for Erasmus, not a set of

actions or even an attitude, but the condition of a soul in which the emotions (*affectus*) as well as the intellect are infused with the spirit of Christ,
so that all the individual's thoughts, feelings, and consequent actions are
directed primarily towards God through Christ.[38] When Erasmus speaks, as
he often does in the *Paraphrases*, about *pia opera* 'godly works,' he does not
mean pious acts or devotions – these are 'ceremonies' – but prayer, charitable actions and similar activities which proceed from 'faith acting through
love.'[39] With other terms, however, I have found it less misleading to
employ their Engish derivatives, such as 'evangelical' for the epithet *euangel-
icus*, which is often applied to terms like 'faith, spirit, word,' or 'innocence'
for *innocentia*. The latter is Erasmus' recurrent paraphrase for the biblical
term 'justice' or 'righteousness.'[40] Although the *Paraphrases* abound in legal
imagery, 'innocence' is not in my view a forensic term. As used in the
Paraphrase, 'innocence' has both a passive and an active sense. In the former
sense, people are made innocent by having their sins removed, *a priori* by
the death of Christ, *a posteriori* for the individual through faith, itself a gift
of God's kindness (grace), and baptism. On the other hand, if they wish to
be saved, they must persevere in this innocence by remaining in-nocent, that
is, by living harm-less (*in-nocens*), without committing sins, or at least
without committing those sins which would diminish and ultimately
remove the sanctifying grace received at baptism. In this active sense the
noun *innocentia* is frequently modified by the nouns *vitae* 'life' or *morum*
'character'. Christians demonstrate their faith through the innocence of their
lives (or life of innocence as I usually translate this phrase) and through
their moral innocence. The latter is often replaced by the phrase *integritas
morum*, the purity or soundness of a person's character. To be pure is to act
in conformity with the demands of the gospel and with no ulterior motives.
The opposite of *innocentia* then is *vitium*, 'vice,' a fault or flaw in the soul
which produces a 'warped desire' (*prava cupiditas*) that leads to sin (*peccatum*). To live innocently means to remove from the soul the vices and the
evil desires which spring from them so that the soul or mind continues to
be a pure habitation for the Holy Spirit.

In making the apostolic authors speak like Romans (*romane loqui*),[41]
Erasmus has drawn heavily on the diction of Roman moral discourse such
as we find it in Cicero and Seneca. The Romans of New Testament times
knew nothing of sin and grace, and their words *peccatum* and *gratia* did not
have the meanings later given to them by Christians. Erasmus, therefore,
substitutes for 'sin' a variety of terms meaning crime or vice in some form,
and for 'grace' terms like 'benefit' or 'kindness.'[42] Hence mortal sins are
'capital crimes,' venial sins 'trivial faults.' Similarly the corporal and spiritual works of mercy become 'duties' (*officia*) or 'services' (*obsequia*) though

here Erasmus has patristic precedents for such usages. I have by and large rendered this language literally, even though at times it gives a moralistic cast to Erasmus' thought which I doubt that he really intended. But there is one feature of Erasmus' classicizing diction which I have chosen not to imitate. He consistently replaces the ecclesiastical language of salvation with classical equivalents such as *servare* for *salvare*, *servator* for *salvator*, *salus* for *salvatio*. One could concoct English equivalents, but I have preferred to render these terms by the traditional English words derived from ecclesiastical Latin.

Finally, the *Paraphrases* are part of the tradition of biblical commentary, which had a future as well as a past. To establish Erasmus' historical position in this tradition or to assess his achievement as a commentator is not my purpose. Nevertheless, I have not hesitated to refer the reader to various modern commentaries on the individual Epistles where further information, especially on disputed matters, can be found. Of making many commentaries there is no end, and I have made no effort to refer to the most recent or even to the most comprehensive commentaries, but only to those, chiefly in English and French, which contain information that directly elucidates Erasmus' paraphrase in some way. They, together with the patristic and medieval commentaries cited in the notes, are listed among the Works Frequently Cited.[43]

ACKNOWLEDGMENTS

Numerous librarians have assisted my researches on Erasmus over the years but I want to thank in particular Dr J.J.M. van der Roer-Meyers, curator of the Erasmus collection in the Gemeentebibliotheek, Rotterdam; Dr Luc Knapen at the Abbey of Maredsous; Dr Georg Minkenberg of the Domarchiv in Aachen; and Dr Severin Corsten, director of the City and University Library in Cologne. I wish also to thank the General Editor, R.D. Sider, who read the translations in a preliminary version and made many helpful suggestions, and Erika Rummel and David E.G. Smith of the University of Toronto Press, who likewise suggested numerous improvements in both the translation and the notes. I owe a special debt of gratitude to my research assistants, Michael S. Armstrong, Elio A. Colagioia, and Timothy S. Johnson, and to the Graduate Research Board of the University of Illinois at Urbana-Champaign, whose financial support enabled me to employ them. Last but by no means least, my collations of the editions of the *Paraphrases* and the publication of this volume would not have been possible without the generous assistance of the Social Sciences and Humanities Research Council of Canada.

JJB

PARAPHRASE ON FIRST TIMOTHY

In epistolam Pauli Apostoli ad Timotheum priorem paraphrasis

DEDICATORY LETTER

ERASMUS OF ROTTERDAM TO THE MOST EXCELLENT PRELATE
AND DISTINGUISHED PRINCE OF UTRECHT,
PHILIP OF BURGUNDY, GREETING[1]

In these wintry months, my Lord Bishop, though the fields lie bare and barren everywhere, the good corn-land of literature never ceases to bear some kind of crop, nor is midwinter ever so bleak that the harvest-carts of learning cannot come home full. To me it seemed right that some share of this harvest should be set aside for the bishop, as the leader in this sort of husbandry. For when we do our best to aid the business of the Gospel, we in our turn are taking a part of your pastoral burden upon our shoulders. I have done this the more readily because the subject itself invited me to do so; for I have made a paraphrase to explain St Paul's two Epistles to Timothy and one to Titus, to which I have added by way of an epilogue the letter he wrote to Philemon, in order not to leave it out in the cold, last as it is in order, albeit on such a different topic. Not but what in St Paul there is nothing that is not proper to a bishop. In the first three he gives a wonderfully vivid picture of a true and really Christian prelate, the gifts that a man should possess who is to be called to such a high and difficult office, and the service he must render to fulfil the task entrusted to him. How difficult it is to be a bishop beyond reproach, how disastrous the effect on society of a shepherd of the Lord's flock who is not genuine appears, to say no more, from this: on no other subject did Paul ever set down his principles with greater emphasis or more anxious thought. How often he repeats the same precept and underlines it, beseeching, urging, appealing to all that is holy, sometimes with winning words and promises, sometimes with threats, sometimes inspiring by his own example or that of Christ.

Here is Paul then, so anxious for those whom he had shaped by his own teaching and ordained by the laying-on of his own hands, whose faith and honour he had many ways of knowing intimately: far greater the danger today of entrusting so difficult an office unadvisedly to any man! In olden time each individual city was presided over by its own bishop, and in those same cities only a small fraction professed the religion of Christ. I need not add that in those days Christ's blood, so lately shed, was still fervent in men's hearts and the fire from heaven conferred in baptism still glowed; and now both of these seem, I know not how, to have grown cold in our modern way of life. Thus it was that the bishop ruled a flock that was not only smaller than today, but did his bidding of its own accord. And so it seems to me much harder today to be a faithful bishop and uncorrupted, not only because one man has the care of so many towns, but much more because most bishops, besides spreading the teaching of the Gospel, which is the chief and proper function of a bishop, are further burdened by the administration of their secular authority.[2]

Yet it is wonderful to see how ill Christ and the world agree together, how hard it is for heavenly and earthly cares to meet. It is the hardest thing there is to fill either part, that of a good bishop or of a prince who seeks his people's welfare: what a task it must be for a man torn in both directions so to manage his business as to satisfy the demands of both religion and earthly state, to please one's mortal prince without offending that Prince who is immortal, to stand well at court and yet not stand ill in heaven! In olden time the man who took upon himself a bishop's task had forthwith to prepare his spirit to face all the tempests of persecution. I almost think that the tranquillity of our own time, if such it can be called, is more full of dangers than the storms of old.

Yes, things have changed, nor is it possible for the principles which should guide a bishop to be in all ways the same; and we should not condemn out of hand what differs from the pattern of ages past. The cross-currents of human affairs do not always allow a prelate to achieve what he may judge the best result, just as a mariner, however skilled and vigilant, sometimes grasps the wheel in vain when he is carried away in the power of winds and waves. And yet that man will wander less from the true and perfect image of a good bishop, who has Paul's pattern as a target always before his eyes, like an experienced navigator who, though he may be forced to deviate somewhat from his true course, will never take his eyes from the pole-star, so that it may not be his misfortune, as the saying goes, to be the whole wide sky off course.[3] If one cannot keep level with Paul, it is something all the same to follow him as best one can. He who strives for the best will not lack Christ's help; your Highness is his vicegerent, and all mortal endeavour is vain without his help. Farewell.

1519

THE ARGUMENT OF
THE FIRST EPISTLE TO TIMOTHY
BY ERASMUS OF ROTTERDAM

Timothy, whose mother was a Jewish Christian, his father a pagan Greek, had been adopted by Paul into the ministry. He was a young man of good intellect and well educated. Still Paul had to circumcise him on account of the Jews.[1] Since Paul had delegated to him just as he had to Titus the supervision of some churches which he was unable to visit himself, he instructs him in the duties of a bishop and in church discipline and gives him the kind of advice one would give, not to a disciple, but to a son and colleague. To give greater weight to his words Paul asserts his apostolic authority from the very start. He admonishes Timothy to reject those who were introducing Jewish myths and to teach instead the principles of faith and charity. Next, since civil order and public peace depended on the authority of their pagan rulers, Paul will not have Christians reject this authority but even orders them to pray for these rulers. He prescribes the proper behaviour of men and of women in church meetings. He paints a picture of the bishop along with his household. These are the topics, by and large, of the first three chapters.

Next he admonishes him not to accept Jewish myths about discrimination among foods and the avoidance of marriage. Then he instructs him on how to behave towards older men, towards youths, towards older women, towards young girls, towards rich widows as well as poor ones who had to be supported by the church, and towards younger widows who are still at a suspect age. In addition to these matters he gives instructions about what Timothy was to teach to masters and slaves, and to the wealthy, while warning him that he must reject in every way the quarrelsome inquiries of the sophists, which[2] advertise themselves under the false appearance of doctrine.

He writes from Laodicea through Tychicus the deacon.[3]

THE PARAPHRASE OF
ERASMUS OF ROTTERDAM
ON THE FIRST EPISTLE OF
PAUL THE APOSTLE TO TIMOTHY

Chapter 1[1]

Paul, the apostle and emissary of Jesus Christ – let no one suppose that I am engaged in my own or some merely human business.[2] I am not the emissary of Moses or of any other person, but the emissary of Jesus Christ. He too once carried out a mission as the representative of the Father and faithfully executed the wishes of him by whom he had been sent. Moreover, I did not assume this commission on my own authority nor did I receive it from some man; I was called to it by the will of the Eternal Power, and not just called but so compelled by his command and authority that I was not free to decline the office, however arduous, which the authority of God, whom we consider the sole author of our entire salvation, was imposing upon me. For in my view whatever the Son has imposed upon us at the Father's command has been imposed by the Father Himself.[3] Through Christ we owe our salvation also to the Father both when we were redeemed from eternal doom by his death and when we are rescued by his help from the storms of affliction whenever they press upon us. Though it sometimes happens that we are not rescued from affliction, nevertheless we have no reason to be doubtful about our safety so long as we clearly rely upon the help of Jesus Christ whom the Father wanted to be both the example[4] and the source of our surest hope. For as he[5] was scourged, crucified, and suffered death in the body but soon came back to life and to immortality, so will he bring us to life again some day and to the same immortality, even though our present evils may overwhelm us.

Therefore, Paul, an apostle whom the authority of Christ makes brave and invincible, writes to Timothy, a genuine and true-born son[6] whom I did not adopt from some stranger's flock but begot myself from my own heart through the gospel when he was still outside the family of Christ.[7] Timothy in turn so resembles and reflects his parent in the constancy and sincerity of his faith and in the purity of his evangelical doctrine that this very fact declares him to be no supposititious child but my true-born, genuine, and unquestioned offspring. For this reason he is far more dear to me than if he had been engendered out of the substance of my poor body in the ordinary way. That substance gives us life which we are destined soon to lose; through the gospel we are born to immortality. If parents have a deeper and more special love for and recognise as truly their own those children whose features most closely resemble their own, how much more rightly ought I to embrace him whom I begot for Christ through evangelical faith and in whom I see the sincerity of my own faith reborn, as it were? Let the Jews boast as they wish when they have gained some proselyte and have, as they suppose, added him to the family of Moses like an adopted child. I glory because I know I have begotten such a son for the faith of the gospel and for Christ. For the synagogue to be barren henceforth is a good thing. It is the time for the fecundity of evangelical faith to propagate itself throughout the whole world. Just as I can think of many ways of boasting about a son like him, whom I may safely appoint to be a representative of the gospel, so there is no reason, I think, for him to regret that he has me as an apostle and a father. I have transferred a part of my responsibility to him, but since God is the source of my power to do so, Timothy has no reason to distrust the commission I have given him to care for the churches, unless perhaps he distrusts the authority of God.

What should I, a most loving father, ask and pray for a son so uniquely dear? What else than for the goods in which that supreme guide of our life wanted [us][8] to be rich and prosperous in our time here on earth and in which he wishes us to grow a little more each day, until we reach such a measure of maturity[9] that Christ may deem us worthy of recognition as his legitimate brothers? Therefore, I pray for grace that Timothy may understand that for all who truly believe, salvation has been made ready through the free gift of Christ without the aid of the Mosaic law. I pray not only for grace but also for mercy, which can be an ever present help to him, living as he does in the midst of so many worldly dangers. For I know well what great storms surround the life of teachers. Lastly – and this is the special feature of our religion – I pray for peace and concord and I pray that he look for these goods, not from the world (its help is vain); not from Moses (to rely upon shadows now that the truth of the gospel has shone forth leads only to destruction[10]); not from any other mortal, but from God the Father and from his Son, Jesus Christ our Lord. The Father does not abandon those who trust in him, and the Son, who has all things in common with the Father, will for this reason not deprive of his aid those who have once placed themselves wholly in his trust, like trusting servants completely dependent on a master who is both all-powerful and totally good.

My true-born son, you know with how much uproar and risk to life we have gained some small flock for Christ, and you are well aware that false apostles are everywhere on the watch to try to transfer to Moses the still young offspring which we have gathered up for the gospel. They have only one reason for gathering disciples to themselves: to make money and win prestige in the eyes of the crowd. My zeal to extend the boundaries of the gospel's dominion as widely as possible does not keep me in the meantime from watching any less carefully[11] over the offspring which have been already produced. But since I cannot be present in person everywhere, I must complete the remainder of my task partly through the agency of letters, partly through the service of colleagues. It was obviously not my intention to leave the Ephesians with no part of me when the work of the gospel called me back to Macedonia. I left you there like a second self to be my official deputy in charge of a difficult but outstanding province. You see there a class of people with a remarkable propensity for superstition and curious arts, but the glory of the gospel is all the brighter for this fact.[12] As adversaries, moreover, they are as keen as they are numerous and must, therefore, be resisted with both feet on the ground, as the saying goes.[13] Consequently, what I asked you to do when I was leaving, I ask you over and over to do now that I am away. Charge those insincere so-called apostles[14] – I am deliberately suppressing their names to keep their irritation from making them even more shameless[15] – charge them not to subvert and spoil with their new teachings the purity of the evangelical teaching which we transmitted to the Ephesians. Also, admonish beforehand the flock of the faithful lest a dangerous levity on their part leads them to give their attention and a hearing to false apostles of that sort. These men do not teach things which lead to eternal salvation and which are worthy of the gospel of Christ, but press on their hearers some frigid Jewish tales about superstitious and petty man-made regulations which give no impetus to true godliness,[16] and other tales about a complex series of genealogies stemming from remote ancestors on down to great-grandfathers and grandfathers, as if the gift of evangelical salvation trickles down to us through the corporal[17] branches of family trees and was not instead poured out all at once by heavenly kindness on every single person who embraces the faith of the gospel. They do not proclaim these things for the glory of Christ. They want only to raise their own value in your eyes through the respect felt for noble lineage. Secondly, because the teachings of the gospel are plain and straightforward, they want to acquire a reputation for great learning by foisting on

them certain complicated, utterly unsolvable difficulties and verbal laby-
rinths from which there is no way out. They evidently think that anything
which is completely plain and straightforward cannot be completely good.

Evangelical faith brings salvation directly.[18] That wretched man-made
doctrine of theirs creates question after question and not only fails to
reinforce the heavenly godliness which God bestows on us through faith but
subverts the very essence of evangelical religion. Everyone who sincerely
believes has no need of questions. The person who ties and reties one
knotty question after another teaches one thing only – doubt. Curiosity
about questions is diametrically opposed to faith. If they believe God, why
do they go on disputing about his promises? If evangelical faith and charity
produce salvation directly, what is the point of adding man-made regulations[19] about clipping off a little piece of foreskin, about the ritual washing
of hands, about discrimination among foods, about the observance of days?
They trumpet that the Law was handed down to you from God while they,
irksome rather than learned teachers of it, do not understand the essence
and goal of the Law. What is the point of struggling towards salvation
through so many irksome and petty observances when one may pass them
by and fly straight to the goal itself? The person who has grasped the
essence of the Law is sufficiently instructed in the law of Moses.

It is love that directly comprehends and fulfils the entire meaning of
the law of Moses,[20] but this love must issue from a pure heart and from a
mind whose conscience is clear and from a faith incapable of pretence.
Sincere love dictates far more rightly what is to be done than any number
of regulations. If it is present, what need is there for the Law's commands?
If it is not present, what does observance of the Law contribute? Since
ordinary human love is frequently flawed by personal feelings, it is often
found together with an insincere way of life and is sometimes incapable of
complete trust. But evangelical love nowhere deceives, does not hesitate,
cannot falter in the obligations of godliness. For it has no other object than
the glory of Christ and the salvation of a neighbour; it depends on nothing
else than Christ. When people let their attention stray from this target, they
are wont to spread around the empty smoke and fog of Judaic questions in
place of the solid teachings of Christ in order to be thought brilliant teachers
of the Law.[21] They promote themselves with empty talk, though in so doing
they do not understand the very heart of what they are saying. For the
entire law of Moses, varied and diffuse as it is in other respects, is summed
up in Christ alone.[22] Since the Law itself defers to Christ, the person who
interprets it contrary to the intention of Christ is being impudent when he
claims to be a teacher of the Law.

But in no way do we say this because we condemn the law of Moses.

We both know and state that the Law is good unless someone employs it in an unlawful way. To interpret the Law contrary to its own meaning is to misuse it. The ultimate purpose of the Law was to lead us to Christ. Therefore, the person who uses it to call one away from Christ turns the good Law to his own destruction. The person who sees clearly and discerns in what respects the Law, which was given for a limited time, must yield to the gospel and in what it must retain permanent force;[23] who understands how one must adapt its gross letter to the spiritual teaching of the gospel; who understands that those whom the blood of Christ has redeemed from the tyranny of sin and who under the impulse of love willingly do more than the Law of Moses prescribes have no need of either the fear or the admonition of the Law either to be restrained from wicked deeds or to be aroused to do their duty; to this person certainly the Law is good.[24] For he understands that the Law does not pertain to himself since he has learned through the gospel not only to do harm to no one but to do good even to his enemies. Why should a horse that is running readily and willingly need reins or spurs?[25] People who are driven and swept along by the Spirit of Christ take the lead on their own and outstrip all the regulations of the Law. Once they have obtained the gift of righteousness, they shrink from all unrighteousness. Therefore, the Law, which deters from wrongdoing through fear of punishment, was not created for them at any rate. They willingly and gladly do what the Law demands even if they do not keep to the literal words of the Law.

For whom then was the Law instituted? Surely for those who have grown deaf to the law of nature,[26] who have no love in them and, being inclined to every kind of misdeed, are borne along by their own desires unless the barrier of the Law holds them in check. If the Law gives them the occasion to sin with impunity, they return to their native disposition and become openly what they were all along within – namely, unrighteous, rebellious, ungodly, and sinners, irreverent and impure, murderers of fathers and murderers of mothers, manslayers, fornicators, sodomites, kidnappers, liars, perjurers. The threats in the Law were rightly set before the Jews since they were inclined to these evils.[27] The Law was meant to restrain slavish dispositions through the fear of punishment from those misdeeds which I mentioned or from any other kind of wrongdoing opposed to the glorious law of the gospel, which not Moses but God, the Blessed One, has given us through his only Son Jesus.[28] The Jews vaunt the glory of their Law; we have a more glorious Law. They are elated because Moses was its author; we more justly glory because God and Christ are the authors of our Law. They preach the law of Moses which holds certain heinous crimes in check through punishments; I preach the law of the gospel which at one stroke excludes every desire that conflicts with true godliness. I leave it to them to discover the source of their authority to preach the law of Moses. I at least have been entrusted with this truly magnificent and efficacious gospel which has no need of the Law's support. It was not men who entrusted it to me but God himself, not because I think myself in any way worthy of having so great a possession committed to me. This was not due to my merit[29] but to the goodness of God, to whom I am grateful because he has put strength into me – a weak, wretched man and far from being equal to this task – for the glory of Jesus Christ our Lord. As a faithful servant I execute his work faithfully. The only praise I lay claim to from this fact is that as God counted me a trustworthy steward for dispensing the gospel, so I for my part engage sincerely and without deception in the task delegated to me. In no way do I imitate any of those who turn their preaching of the law of Moses into an insult to Christ and serve only their own gain and their own glory, not that of Jesus Christ. I admit that the same blindness held me in the past when I was still possessed by zeal for the law of my fathers. I was a slanderer against the name of Christ. I was so savage a persecutor that I did not refrain even from violence. I kept persecuting the rising glory of the gospel not just with verbal abuse but to the point of using imprisonment and execution. In this respect I count myself no better than they. I am perhaps to be counted better than they on the ground that I did these things in error and ignorance from honest zeal for the Law. I was not yet called to the fellowship of the gospel. They, though they once professed Christ, are nevertheless envious of his glory and too greedy for their own. They impose the useless burden of the law of Moses from stubborn malice. For this reason God had mercy on me in my honest error while they grow blinder every day.

The more passionately I then fought for the Law against Christ, the more spiritedly do I now defend the teachings of Christ against those who assert the claims of the Law. Grace has been exceedingly abundant and has replaced that vehement zeal for the Law, which is being abolished. Confidence in Christ has replaced confidence in the Law. Love for all mortals, love, which we have obtained both by Christ's example and by his gift, has replaced Jewish hatred.[30] The Jews have no reason to protest if I said that with no help from the Law I was turned from an impious criminal into the person I now am by the kindness of God. On the contrary what they think incredible has been put beyond doubt by the surest proofs, and what they reject is to be embraced with all zeal and, as the saying goes, with wide-open arms,[31] to wit, that Jesus Christ, seeing that the Law was inefficacious for complete salvation, became a man himself and came into the world to confer freedom from harm upon us by his own death and to bestow his own righteousness on us by paying the penalties for our unrighteousness. Furthermore, though I was the most tenacious adherent of the law of my fathers, I am so far from excluding myself from the number of sinners that I publicly declare myself to be even the first among them. I do not deny my impurity, for it redounds to the glory of Christ. The less I deserve compassion, the more illustrious his mercy is. I was worthy of punishment. What then was the reason why Christ not only forgave my crimes and showed the utmost leniency towards me but also enriched me with so many freely given gifts? What else than that he might through this remarkable example arouse a similar hope of pardon in all, no matter how soiled by the stains of their earlier life, provided that they abandon their trust in the law of Moses and place all their trust in the goodness of Christ, which never fails us up to the moment of eternal life. The promises are vast but their author is absolutely trustworthy. Whoever reflects that this author is Christ will cease to distrust. But if someone is capable of despising Christ as a mere human and a crucified one at that, let him reflect that the supreme king of the ages, God the Father, immortal, invisible, alone wise,[32] is the chief author of this work and grants all things to us through his Son. Therefore, nothing ought to seem incredible which God, who is so great, promises. Humans can claim no credit for this unique munificence since all honour and glory are owed to God alone and for all time, not for a limited number of years like the glory of the law of Moses. For immortal glory befits him who is immortal. My words are true and confirmed by the facts.

Therefore, just as I perform faithfully the work delegated to me by God, so I give this command especially to you, Timothy my son, to imitate the example of your parent, to fit yourself in all things to the office which you have undertaken. It is God's work that you are performing. You were not elected to it by the votes of the people but by an oracle[33] and command of God. You serve under his banner and will earn the rewards of your virtue from him. You see what forces have been entrusted to your faith; you see with what adversaries you are engaged. There is no place for relaxing your guard, no place for falling asleep. To desert him to whom you have pledged your allegiance and in whose service you have once enrolled is the height of shame and wicked too. He judged that you would be a vigorous and loyal leader. The Spirit of Christ through the power of its inspiration signified this to us when we placed our hands upon you and committed the authority of the bishop's office[34] to you. Therefore, see that you steadfastly live up to God's prior judgment about you and to my own confidence in you, so that he may commend a brave leader and that I may acknowledge my true-born son. The service of which you are now a part is illustrious. Be sure to discharge your duties diligently. You will do this if you keep your faith sincere and unshaken and bring to your faith a good conscience, so that you do not doubt God's promises, while the integrity of your life corresponds to your sincere belief. The purity of your life should be so great that it is not only approved by everyone else but your own conscience is also clear before God. Human questionings[35] cause the strength of faith to slip; human desires sully the conscience when those who appear to be doing the work of Christ are in fact looking in some other direction than at Christ. Moreover, these two are so interconnected that when faith totters conscience too is put in danger. For anyone whose conscience is impure cannot have a pure faith. How can[36] what is dead be called pure? Or how can what lacks life and spirit be lasting? For as a rule people whose consciences are guilty on every score finally cease even to believe what the gospel teaches about the rewards due a life of innocence or of wickedness. We have recently seen an example – only too true, alas – of this result in Alexander and Hymenaeus. When in their preaching the gospel they failed to keep a firm grip on the tiller of a correct conscience, they struck upon the rocks of treachery. Once they were cast out of the confession which brings salvation, they were swept away by the waves of their evil desires into raving against and publicly reviling the teachings of the gospel, so that they were past the point where friendly admonishment might cure them. Therefore, since I judged them to be rotting limbs,[37] I cut them away from the rest of the body of Christ, so that, corrected at least by shame and disgrace, they may learn to refrain from impious abuse and, if they are unable to be good to themselves, they may be less harmful to the rest. People whose impiety has progressed to the point that gentle remedies are no longer effective must be checked by severity. Accordingly, not only God's judgment about your sincerity, not only my own example, not only your own declaration and allegiance to Christ, but also the abominable example of those men ought to inflame your soul to remain steadfast in your office.

Chapter 2

However, it is not enough for you yourself to be blameless. It is the role of a bishop to instruct others as well about what they need to do. These instructions must appear to be worthy of an evangelical mind. Moreover, those who profess Christ must be completely removed from any desire for vengeance, from any urge to do harm, from every form of malevolence. Therefore, be sure to encourage your people to begin their pious devotions and their worship of Christ in this spirit right from daybreak. First, they should pray to God to avert everything which disturbs and upsets the state of religion and the government. Then they should ask him for those things which forward the work of godliness and the tranquillity of the state. Next let them seek his help alone against those who persecute the flock of Christ. Lastly they should give thanks for the things they have obtained from God's kindness and[1] ask in their prayers for what they have not yet obtained. And let these prayers be made not just for Christians but for all men. Otherwise Christian charity may appear limited as though it favoured only its own sect. Instead let it follow the example of God and extend itself far and wide to both the good as well as the evil, just as God, who is perfectly good and beneficial to all so far as he can be, bestows his sunshine on both the just and unjust alike.[2]

God grants[3] us public peace also through pagan officials. It is right then to give thanks for them too. We have no way of knowing whether this or that ungodly worshipper of statues will presently accept the gospel. Hence Christian charity prays for the salvation of all. Jew loves Jew, proselyte another proselyte, Greek loves Greek, a brother loves a brother, a kinsman another kinsman. This is[4] not evangelical love; evangelical love is that love which loves the godly for the sake of Christ and loves the ungodly so that they may someday come to their senses and repent,[5] and be converted to Christ. The pagans sacrifice to demons and invoke evil upon you. You, however, are following closely in the footsteps of Christ who, when he was raised on the cross and had to listen to venomous insults, more grievous even than the punishment of the cross itself, did not hurl back abuse or call down curses but with a loud cry interceded with the Father to forgive them.[6] One must pray for good not only for the whole human race but also for one's rulers, even though they are pagans and estranged from the religion of Christ, and for all who hold some public office in the secular sphere. Do not be moved by the fact that they beat, scourge, imprison, and murder us.[7] One must pity their blindness rather than retaliate with their own malice. Otherwise, they will not become better persons, and we shall cease to be Christians.

This was the approach which Christ adopted as being especially effective, and he wanted all to be drawn to him by its means. But if our love is wasted on some of them, we shall not for this reason cease to be like ourselves. This world too has its own order. It does no good for us to upset public order; our role is to promote peace everywhere. The power and authority of rulers serve divine justice to some extent when they check criminals through punishments, keep the wicked at least partially in line through fear of penalties, repress banditry, protect public peace by their weapons, govern the state by laws.[8] Although they do not do these things from the love of Christ, it is nevertheless unhelpful to the common good for the state of the commonwealth to be disturbed by Christians. Otherwise the teachings of the gospel may be considered seditious and we may soon begin to be hated not because we are Christians but because we are in their view undermining public tranquillity. But if rulers occasionally misuse their powers against us, it is the Christian thing to forget evils and to remember benefits. We owe it to their power, we owe it to their protection and weapons, or rather we owe it to God through their agency that we are allowed to lead tranquil and peaceful lives, secure from public disorder, from acts of banditry, and from wars.

It is worth remembering what a sea of evils the turmoil of war brings with it, what a sea of advantages peace has.[9] The shortage of the necessities of life encourages many evils. Peace brings abundance. Godliness has a place for itself in peacetime; war teaches every kind of ungodliness. Our religion loves chastity. Whose virtue is safe in war? Even if most people employ the benefit of peace to further their own ungodly desires, we must nevertheless employ the public tranquillity to further the worship of God and the purity of our own character. We must in the meantime obey our rulers in everything which they rightly order in accordance with their office or which, while it may cause us pain, does not make us ungodly. They confiscate our money, but our godliness has suffered no loss. They burden us with chains, but they do not thereby drag us away from Christ. They kill our bodies and thereby transport us to the haven of immortality. They would truly[10] harm us only if they were to make us greedy, afraid of death, eager to remain alive, ambitious, vindictive, distrustful of Christ. Therefore, one ought neither to flatter rulers shamelessly nor to fight against them seditiously. If evangelical godliness sometimes requires us to reject their commands, we must do this with such moderation that they understand that we do it not from hatred of them but out of zeal for godliness.

I do not offer this advice because I fear that since we are unequal to the forces of the world, we shall only provoke them to our own despite, but because we should mirror our own ruler Christ through such gentleness. Though he was alone more powerful than all the satraps and monarchs of this world, he nevertheless preferred to claim the world for himself by enduring evils rather than by repelling or returning them. He preferred to conquer with kindness than with punishment. He preferred to heal than to destroy. He preferred to entice than to oppress. This is the way he conquered. Thus did the Father decide that the Son bring back his triumph.[11] We must imitate him if we want our prayers and our offerings to be pleasing and acceptable to God. Christ preferred to be our saviour rather than our punisher. He bore our ungodliness with great gentleness until we should come to our senses and repent.

In keeping with the immensity of his goodness Christ desires that

16

cts
t

e in our case be done if at all possible in the case of
the saviour of all; he excludes no one from salvation;
the gospel to all. Anyone who rejects Christ and hides
.pute this blindness to himself. He who is lost is lost
own fault. What is the physician to do if the patient rejects the
..dicine that will save him?[12] It is certainly not due to Christ that all do
not obtain salvation and fail to thrust aside the darkness of their old life and
come to the light of evangelical truth. Christ is the truth. Whoever acknowledges him will be safe regardless of the kind of life from which one has
come to him. The same salvation is offered to all by him alone and through
him alone. There is nothing here which the Jew can claim as though his
personal property. There is one God. He does not belong to this or that
people but is common to all on the same basis. There is but one reconciler
of the human race to God, Christ Jesus, God and man. For it was fitting that
the one who as the arbitrator[13] of harmony interceded between God and
humanity should have something in common[14] with each party. As God he
interceded before God, as a human he brought all humans back into God's
favour. On what ground can someone say that God belongs to him and him
alone?

If the common Father of all sent Christ to save all, if Christ gave
himself to redeem all, it is proper that we too strive in every way to make
his death equally beneficial to all. But if he died for pagans too, why should
it annoy us to offer up our prayers to God for their salvation? If there was
once a time when it was unclear whether Christ had come to redeem all the
gentiles too, certainly that is now evident and proved by the fact that the
death of Christ concerns the gentiles no less than the Jews. In the past some
concession was made to the stubbornness of the Jews to keep them from
being able to pretend that they had been spurned or rejected. But it was not
long before God wanted it to be completely evident to everyone that there
is absolutely no distinction of race or superstitious belief or social condition
for those seeking refuge in the teachings of the gospel.[15] God wanted me
above all others to be the herald of this fact. He wanted me to perform my
commission for just this purpose since the other apostles[16] were previously
hesitant and reluctant to admit the gentiles to the grace of the gospel. Even
today there is no shortage of persons who would deny any approach to the
benefit of Christ except through the law of Moses. But Christ has committed
to me the office both of preacher and of apostle to preach to all eternal
salvation without the aid of the Law – a salvation which we are to accredit
to Christ alone. I do not assume this authority under false pretences, Christ
himself committed it to me. What I preach is not false. No, the things I say
are true, and I preach them as the teacher of the gentiles. I do not adopt the

pretence of an imposing title as false apostles commonly do. The f̶
themselves have proved me to be the apostle of the gentiles. I do n̶
impose the regulations of Moses on the gentiles like those Judaizers but
evangelical faith. I do not pour over them clouds of empty questions but the
pure and simple truth, teaching as I do things which lead specifically to true
godliness rather than to personal gain or empty ostentation.

To bring my discourse back to its starting point, I want the men to
pray wherever the situation demands it and not just in church. The Jews do
not call upon God except at Jerusalem.[17] The Samaritans pray on mountain-
tops or in holy groves. For Christians every place is pure and holy for the
offering of the sacrifice of their prayers. Christians should believe that there
is no place where there is not a temple sacred to God. No matter where
they are, let them lift up pure hands to heaven as though they were about
to offer a sacrifice. There is no reason for them to feel the need for a mercy-
seat or a Holy of Holies. Wherever they pray, God will hear them. There is
no reason for them to be concerned about the victims, ceremonies, or
sacrifices of Jewish law. In the offering of holy prayer all can perform the
sacrifice by themselves. God does not expect an animal or the smoke of
incense. The sacrifice which pleases him most is a pure prayer which has
issued from a pure heart. The Jews may take as many ritual baths as they
wish, their offerings are still unclean. Even unwashed hands are pure in the
sight of God if the soul is at peace,[18] mindful of no injury, wishing ill to no
one, unstained by any filthy lusts, by greed or ambition. This is the purity
and cleanliness which commend the Christian's offering to the eyes of God.
This is the sacrifice which he desires.

Now let the women pray after the example of the men. If any one of
those feelings which women tend to have is present[19] in their soul, let them
expel it first; let them bring with them moral innocence instead of Jewish
purifications.[20] Let them adorn their souls, not their bodies, for this offering.
Let them not arouse feelings of lust in men through their nudity but let
them cover themselves with the kind of clothing that proclaims the modesty
of its wearer, her sense of shame, and her chastity. Far be it from Christian
women to go to church dressed up the way the crowd of profane women
commonly go out to the theatre or to a wedding.[21] These spend much effort
beforehand adorning themselves in front of a mirror so they can go out
with their hair artfully braided, or in woven gold,[22] or wearing pearl ear-
rings or necklaces, or at the least in a pure silk or purple dress – all to have
this finery commend their beauty to the spectators and at the same time to
disparage by this display of their wealth the poverty of the less fortunate.
On the contrary, let the dress of Christian women correspond to their
Christian way of life and be such as to seem worthy of those women who

profess genuine godliness and the worship of God, not through a display of wealth, but through good deeds, which are the only riches in which God delights. What the world thinks splendid and magnificent is in his eyes only ugly.

This sex, subject as it is to the vice of talkativeness, has therefore no greater ornament than silence.[23] It is appropriate then for the women to make their behaviour match the modesty of their dress; to learn and not to teach when present at an assembly of men; to follow and not to take the lead or to put on a display of authority in the presence of their husbands, to whom they should be subject in every way.[24] Otherwise that assembly of yours where restraint and decorum are most appropriate may be thrown into a confused uproar if, once the reins of modesty have been relaxed, women begin to prattle in a public meeting.[25] Speaking in a meeting is the role of men, especially if they have something to teach which is conducive to godliness. Let each man see for himself how much to permit his wife at home. I do not permit any woman to assume the role of teacher in a mixed assembly, even if she has something to teach. Otherwise once the window is open the weak sex will become overly bold. I do not allow them to practise any authority over their husbands, their love for whom should be mixed with awe and respect. Therefore, let the women keep silent and listen respectfully to what is said by the men. Let them acknowledge the order of nature. As it is the responsibility of the mind to rule, of the body to obey, so a wife ought to hang on her husband's nod. Why do we reverse the divine order? Adam was created first; Eve was then created for his sake.[26] Why should impudence put second what God wanted to be first? Secondly, with regard to the fall, Eve was deceived first when, believing the serpent and beguiled by the enticement of the fruit, she disregarded God's command. The man could not have been taken in either by the serpent's promises or by the allure of the fruit; only love for his wife drew him into a ruinous compliance.[27] How does it make sense that she who was once her husband's teacher in transgression should lay claim to the leading role in the teaching of godliness? Let her acknowledge instead that ancient weakness of her sex. Its traces have not been altogether eliminated even if her offence has been forgiven through baptism. Let her recognize both the dignity and the strength of the male mind and be satisfied that she who was in the past the leader to ungodliness is now the companion on the way to godliness and that she who in the past took the first step towards destruction is now the follower on the way to salvation.

I do not demean the female sex to the point of excluding it from a share in salvation. Woman too has her own function. If she occupies herself in it sincerely, she too will have a share in salvation. There is nothing for her to do in a church meeting. But there is something for her to do at home and in doing it to earn the reward of salvation. Let her by bearing and rightly rearing children[28] make good the wrong that was done in the past in leading her husband astray. This will happen if she strives with all her might to bear again to Christ through faith the children she originally bore to her husband and if she shapes their early life in such a way that they can appear worthy of Christ in their love, their holiness, their chastity, and all the other virtues.[29] If a woman has made herself a good and vigilant mistress of her house, she will have have performed a great deed. What I have said must be considered past doubt.[30]

Chapter 3

These are in general the instructions which you are to give to all without distinction. But there are more important qualifications which you must look for in those who in your judgment ought to be put in charge of the people. It is only right for the one who excels in rank to excel also in virtues. Many seek the prestige perhaps but fail to consider how much responsibility this prestige brings with it. Anyone who desires to become a bishop solely because of ambition, or for the sake of financial gain, or to have dictatorial powers desires his own destruction.[1] He is not paying sufficient attention to the meaning of the word bishop. It is not the name of a rank, but of a function, an office, a responsibility. It means 'overseer' and one who looks out for the advantages and needs of others. Therefore, the man who understands this and is seeking the office of bishop with no other intention than to benefit the largest number of persons is motivated by an honest ambition since he covets the opportunity to exercise his virtue, not the honour of the office. But you will not entrust this honour to him unless you discover that he has the proper qualifications to be a bishop. To give you a firmer basis for making this judgment I shall sketch in a few words a picture of the true bishop.

First, the integrity of his life must be such that no charge of any kind can be brought against him. It is simply incongruous for someone to present himself to the others as their teacher and as one who has the authority to demand innocence from them while failing to practise what he teaches in his own life and behaviour. It is likewise incongruous for someone who, as part of the office which he has undertaken, is obliged to rebuke sinners freely and frankly, to commit a sin for which he himself has to be rebuked. Who believes a teacher whose words are at odds with his behaviour? Who will put up with a castigator whom one sees engaged in the same misconduct as his own or even worse? It is easier to wish than to expect that everyone will be innocent and pure of heart. Certainly it is a matter of great importance that the one person on whose teaching authority[2] the people depend be completely blameless.

Secondly, chastity is an important qualification in the selection of a bishop. Therefore, if a candidate who spurns sexual pleasures completely is not available, then you must certainly make sure that the candidate is or has been married only once. A first marriage may appear to have been undertaken in order to have children, but even among pagans repeated wedlock creates the suspicion that the emotions are out of control. I do not preclude other men from entering a second marriage if abstinence is beyond them. For me to venture to lay this restriction on the entire congregation is too harsh. But it befits a bishop to be so totally free from fault that he cannot even be suspected of having a fault. Furthermore one who stands guard alone over so many people has to be sober and alert. He is the sentry, and danger threatens from every side. In whatever direction he turns his watchful eyes he is not allowed to be careless, lest that one who is ever lying in ambush carry off some prize from the camp of Christ while the leader is asleep.[3] In addition a bishop will display seriousness in the entire conduct of his life, being averse to all that light-hearted and foolish behaviour which lessens and impairs a teacher's public respect and authority. Do not think it sufficient if he is affable and generous towards his own people. He must take care that his guests also experience his courtesy and kindness so that the fragrance of his good reputation spreads far and wide.

While he has these latter virtues in common with most persons, there is a special quality which must be looked for in a bishop. He has to have an aptitude and inclination for teaching – not for teaching Jewish myths or the supercilious, inflated philosophies of this world, but the things which make us truly godly and truly Christian. The first duty in a teacher is to know what is best. The next is that he teach willingly, calmly, diligently, lovingly, without arrogance, in a timely way. For evangelical teaching is such that it wins over by gentleness, not by shouting. If it is provoked sometimes by the sins of the wicked and driven to harsh treatment of them, nevertheless it never forgets Christian charity. Far be it from the evangelical teacher to imitate those who ferociously rave and rant under the influence of wine, or to rage out of control against those who err, or to wound with an abusive tongue the hearts of those whom he ought rather to have healed with fatherly gentleness.[4] In all these situations a bishop must keep in mind the Christian mildness and moderation which is a great deal more effective in correcting people than is harsh treatment. Let him, moreover, shun contention; otherwise his actions may seem to arise from hatred and not from love. Love corrects; contention provokes. Let him shun avarice;[5]

otherwise he may seem to be only pretending godliness for the sake of gain.

Lastly, do you wish to know how he is likely to behave in public affairs? Look at how he takes care of his private property and household. If he is a vigilant head of his own house, if he keeps everything in working order, if he has compliant and obedient children who have been taught in such a way that their natural decency and disciplined character testify to the holy upbringing which their parent has given them, there is a good expectation that, having furnished a singular example of his ability in the management of his household affairs, he will energetically conduct the public affairs that concern all alike. For a home is nothing but a miniature state,[6] the head of a household nothing but the ruler of a tiny community. The wisdom of the world likewise judges men capable of being entrusted with the larger tasks of the state if they have earned praise for their conduct of smaller ones. Moreover, how can you expect a man who does not know how to take charge of his private house to manage well the care of an entire church? How will he take care of so many households when he is not capable of taking care of his own? How will he oversee so large a multitude when he does not know how to oversee so small a number? Will he who treats his own family indifferently take care of strangers reliably? Will he who cannot be useful to a human congregation be useful to the congregation of God?

Now in the selection of a bishop one must look not only at how honestly he has behaved in his private obligations, but also at how long he has been a Christian. Baptism to be sure grafts[7] a person into the body of Christ, but this person does not instantly acquire perfect godliness. Baptism opens the entrance into the church, but it is left to each person at this point to strive vigorously towards the goal of holiness.[8] We are reborn through baptism, but it is still left to us to gain stature and strength over an extended period of time by growing to maturity through daily increases in godliness. Therefore, care has to be taken that a neophyte – I mean, one who has recently enlisted in the fellowship of faith – not be put in charge of so important an office. The seedling is good, but still tender and perhaps unequal to supporting a large burden. There is also the danger that if a new honour is added to someone who is still learning and is insufficiently strong in religion, he may be puffed up with pride and acquire a dangerous self-confidence. He might think that he has been made a member of the flock for the sole purpose of taking charge of its religion. It is not unlikely that, ensnared in one of the nets which the devil stretches out in various guises – and none is more insidious than the guise of ambition – he will behave too proudly in the office entrusted to him and will not escape the slanders of the evil-minded. They will misconstrue his behaviour and say that he sought out the Christians with the aim of becoming pre-eminent among them since he was a lowly figure among his own kind. 'It's a good thing he left us,' they will say. 'He has the reward for his change of religion. He preferred to be a Christian bishop than to live among us as a private person.' He who has given proof of his true godliness and of his own modesty by the passage of time will be safe from such suspicions.

Nor would I heed a candidate if he should say to me, 'What do I care if the pagans disparage me? I'm satisfied to win the approval of my own people.' To my mind that is simply too little to be expected from a bishop. His reputation should be so untarnished and so free from every suspicion of blame that even outsiders approve of him and attest to his reputation. It is not enough for him to have a good reputation only among his own people, to whom he is closer and known like a member of the family. Since outsiders are not in a position to observe his true godliness, they are apt to turn any semblance of evil into a calumny. Therefore, every possible care must be taken to ensure that those who are strangers to our religion are not given a handle for slander or have an opportunity to hurl, I shall not say a criminal charge, but even a false insult with some semblance of plausibility. For the fact that they have a good opinion of us has the benefit of not only enhancing the glory of Christ but also, once they have formed a good opinion of our godliness, of leading them more readily to repent their own ungodliness.

Now since the misconduct of servants brings their masters' authority into disrepute, it will not be enough simply to discover the character of the person you appoint to the position of bishop. The people he has or employs as servants and ministers, who are, so to speak, the bishop's arms and legs, must also match their prelate in every respect. They must be serious and well-behaved in their whole manner of life, and removed from the vices to which the common lot of servants is typically disposed. They are not to be two-faced, addicted to excessive drinking, or panting for petty gains. Their initiation into the mysteries of evangelical faith should be such that their very way of life testifies that they are Christians from a sincere and pure conviction and not just to win favours from their masters – moral innocence is proof of religious sincerity. Nevertheless, I should not want the administration of church business to be put in their hands immediately. Let them be given responsibility for the affairs and property of the church only after you have observed them for a long time and have seen that they have led such innocent lives, long after being baptized, that no charge of wrongdoing can be laid against them.

Furthermore, I require a similar modesty and purity of life from the wives[9] of bishops and deacons because they too have some share in the ministry and their character reflects upon their husbands' character or on the character of whomever they are serving. Therefore, let them be far removed from the vices of typical wives. Let them not be giddy or silly or talebearers or lacking in self-control but sober, not untrustworthy or of questionable loyalty but loyal and steadfast in all things.

Moreover, the chastity of the deacons should match the life of the bishops in this respect: they too are to be married only once, lest a second marriage cause suspicion of a lack of self-control on their part. In educating their children honourably and in administering their own families carefully they too will give a clear indication of the kind of persons they will be in the sacred ministry. Although the office of deacon is inferior to that of priest and apostle, anyone who conducts himself energetically and honestly in this rank is nevertheless taking no small step towards higher duties. His awareness of his godliness increases his faith in his own strength while other persons acquire greater confidence in him from a job rightly done. Consequently when he advances to the higher services of evangelical faith, he outdoes himself in his integrity and vigilance. For the polity of Jesus Christ likewise has, as it were, its grades and ranks of officials. The diaconate is the lowest of these, the elders or bishops[10] come next, and the apostles are at the top. As in the secular state one who has been a vigorous aedile is called to the praetorship and, after having outdone himself there too, is called from the praetorship to the tribunate or consulate,[11] so in the same way a person's worthiness to be a priest or an apostle is revealed by his performance as a deacon.

I am writing these things to you, dearly beloved son, not because I despair of returning to you; on the contrary, my expectation is that I shall revisit your assembly soon. However, if something should occur which compels me to come later than I expect, I want you in the meantime to receive this advice through my letter so that you may know how you ought to behave, not in the temple of the Jews but in the house of God. Why should I not give this name to the Christian church, which has been consecrated and dedicated to the living God? It will never be demolished by any storms of error or of persecution since it is the pillar and foundation of truth. The temple at Jerusalem[12] in the past had its own veneration, it had its own priests, its rites and sacrificial victims. Our temple is much holier than that one. It does not hide its mysteries in shadows and figures. Instead of cherubim, pomegranates, bells, the ark, and similar enigmas,[13] it displays to us solid and genuinely evangelical truth. Do not be surprised, therefore, if you do not hear from me any regulations of the sort Moses prescribed with great zeal to the Levites and priests.[14] There is no reason for us to miss the absence of those shadows because God has revealed to us the purpose for which all those mystical appointments were instituted for a limited time.[15] If the Jews would compare their mysteries to ours, they would have no reason for marveling at the ark or at anything else that was shut up in the Holy of Holies. Let them decide whether their secret objects deserve any special veneration.

Certainly it is beyond controversy that the mystery of evangelical godliness, that mystery which frees us once for all from every superstition is far and away the greatest thing in this temple that stands open throughout the whole world. It is not a table or an ark or a sacrificed animal that is displayed, but it is Christ himself who is displayed and preached. Formerly unknown and unremarked, he has now become so visible that in his human life he was even seen and handled in the flesh by men, while he received so much power in the Spirit that he abolished the sins of all and conferred, and continues to confer, through faith alone the righteousness which the Law was unable to effect. So far was this mystery of ours from being hidden away that it was the object of admiration even to the eyes of angels as they sang 'Glory to God in the highest, and on earth peace, good will to men.'[16] Other mysteries cease to be objects of respect if they are spread abroad. Our mystery has been proclaimed to both Jews and Gentiles alike. Nor was this proclamation ineffective. The simple speech of the gospel, supported by the evidence of miracles, has persuaded the whole world, as no philosophy or human eloquence could have done, of something which would otherwise seem completely contrary to the order of nature.

Lastly, after the punishment of crucifixion Christ came back to life by his own power and with angels visibly waiting upon him he ascended into heaven, thus showing us where all our hope must be directed. What is more holy than this mystery? What more sublime? What more certain? or more clear? If we truly believe it, if we live lives worthy of it, what reason is there to pay any attention hereafter to the petty regulations of Judaism? We possess the mystery of true godliness.[17] Why do we turn aside to things which contain more superstition than godliness? If we are burdened with sins, the surest remission of sins is here. If we feel the need for doctrine, the rule of true godliness[18] is here for us to follow. If we are concerned about our reward, the immortality to which we will be conveyed is before us. Therefore, my dear Timothy, let us be content with this religion and bid farewell to the fruitless regulations of the Jews.

Chapter 4

My zeal in inculcating this doctrine is matched by my fear of the present danger, which is no longer a matter of dubious guesses. For the Spirit himself, knowing the future beforehand, signifies clearly and beyond any doubt through those whom he has inspired that in the last times certain individuals will appear who will abandon the sincerity of evangelical faith and will relapse into a new kind of Judaism. They will make godliness pivot on practices which do not only not promote godliness but are often an actual hindrance to it. They will rebel against the Spirit of Christ and will give heed instead to deceiving spirits. Once they have turned away from the doctrine of the true God, they will give their ears and hearts to the doctrines of devils. Under the guise of a feigned godliness[1] they will say things at variance with evangelical truth. They will use the mask of holiness to ingratiate themselves with plain and simple people although in the sight of God their conscience is impure, foul – stamped and tattooed everywhere with the marks of worldly desires. Inwardly, such men are sodden with envy, hatred, avarice, ambition, and other diseases diametrically opposed to genuine godliness; nevertheless, in order to procure for themselves a reputation for godliness through their 'novel' and 'wonderful' doctrine, they will follow the example of the Essenes and forbid couples from being joined in lawful wedlock, as if a chaste marriage and a stainless marriage bed were not something honourable in God's view.[2] They will demand to be taken for saints because they live in celibacy, though they are infected with the countless other diseases of their vices. In a word they are not free from lust, only from wives. They will go further and try to call people back to a Jewish discrimination of foods as if food possessed some inherent uncleanliness, although God has prepared every kind of food for us to use in moderation to meet the needs of our bodies and to restore our strength when we give thanks to him for his kindness. All of us who have left the Mosaic law to embrace instead evangelical faith and have been brought to the light of truth when the fog of Jewish superstition was dispersed know that everything created by an absolutely good God is inherently good as long as it is used as it should be and for the purpose for which it was created. We know that no kind of food ought to be detested or rejected which, as the gift of a kind God, is received with thanksgiving. To say, 'You shall not eat this food, you shall not touch this body, you shall not wear this clothing, you shall do this or that on this day' is the talk of Jews, not of Christians. For nothing in the created world is impure or unclean if its user's soul is pure and clean. Even if some food should have an element of impurity, what was previously unclean would still be made holy and pure by the holy words and prayers and hymns with which the divine bounty is praised before eating.[3] Such is the smoke of deception poured over the people by those who do the work of Christ dishonestly or rather who are in reality advancing their own interests.

You, however, spurn such dismal rubbish and remind the brothers and sisters of the teachings which you have learned from me. Play the part of the good and honest minister of Christ and with sincere faith dispense his doctrine, which is far removed from their regulations. It is all the more fitting for you to do this because you were not called to the teachings of the gospel at an advanced age when it is normally difficult to turn to new ways. You have been nourished, as it were, from early youth on evangelical faith and sound doctrine so that assiduous study ought to have acquired the force of habit in you and you are unable to be inconstant in that which you have thus far followed unfailingly. Therefore, put before your followers that doctrine which is worthy of the gospel. Reject the frivolous old wives' tales of others. It would be more accurate to call these tales profane, alien as they are to the mysteries of evangelical faith.[4] Let your object be to train yourself for genuine godliness rather than for verbal duels with a class of people whose garrulity is matched only by their obstinacy.

Genuine godliness is located in the mind and cannot be adequately defined or regulated by external and gross material things.[5] Even if, depending on the time or place, fasting, discrimination among foods, or other practices of this kind sometimes appear to have some usefulness because they prepare the body for the duties of godliness,[6] this usefulness is nevertheless neither lasting nor of particularly great moment when compared to the godliness of the mind. On the contrary, it is generally the case that such observances give birth to the destruction of true and genuine godliness. Fasting is sometimes useful, but on other occasions it is destructive.[7] A vigil will be salutary for one person, deadly harmful to another. Sometimes it is profitable to rest through the entire sabbath in quiet. On the other hand, occasions occur when to remain inactive would be ungodly, as when a neighbour's need requires an act of charity.[8] But evangelical godliness, resting as it does on sincere faith and true love, is always useful at every time and in every part of life. It proclaims in brief whatever we must seek in this present life or hope for in the life to come, so that there is no need for us to hunt for help from any other source. What I say is true and not to be doubted; it is manifestly worthy to be accepted by all.

We teach by our actions that we mean what we say and that it is not a piece of fiction. Otherwise what would persuade us to suffer willingly and gladly the hardships of this life, to bear bravely the blows laid on us by the ungodly, the imprisonments, the threats of death, except that we hope for both the help of heaven here on earth and for immortality after this life? We have fixed this hope, not in Moses nor in any other human being who might betray our hope, but in the living God, who can help even the dead and from whom salvation issues, not only for the whole human race, but especially for those who have embraced evangelical faith.

Command and teach these things bravely and steadfastly so that you clearly display the authority of a bishop, since you are convinced that this teaching has issued from Christ himself. There is no reason for you, young as you are and placed in such an important position, to be timorous or to give way before the wickedness of those teaching a different doctrine. There is a place for deference elsewhere. Here where the risk of salvation is the issue, authority must be displayed. You must not look to the number of years you have lived but to the position which you hold. Everyone who displays integrity in his way of life and gravity in his manners is an elder. There is no risk of anyone holding your youth in disrespect if your life and teaching have been such that Christians see in it a model of evangelical godliness. If they see the reflection of a holy mind in all your speech, if they observe modesty and purity in the conduct of your life, if they perceive a love worthy of a bishop in the performance of your duties, if they behold a heart trusting in God in its endurance of evils, if they see you untouched in any respect by human passions, they will readily respect you as though you were their senior.

I am hoping to see you shortly in order to help you not only with advice but also with my services. In the meantime during my absence be all the more vigilant in your office so that you may make up for my being away. You have sacred reading to take the place of my words. Teach according to it if some error arises. Give encouragement according to it if you see anyone faltering. These are the special duties of a bishop. You must be equal to the position which you have taken up. It was not entrusted to you in the casual way that some persons appoint themselves apostles and elders.[9] It was not[10] personal ambition or popular support but the divine Spirit signifying the will of God through the mouths of prophets that designated you for this position. Secondly it was the authority of the elders who, after duly laying their hands upon you, delegated the function of bishop to you. Furthermore, it is a gift of God that you were endowed with the qualities that showed[11] you to be worthy of this honour. Therefore, a twofold care is incumbent upon you, to respond to the kindness of God and to be equal to the authority given to you. This is not a relaxed or comfortable[12] profession; it demands vigilance and application. Therefore, practise these things, give yourself entirely to them, engage in them continuously, so that everyone may see that both your way of life and your teaching alike make the people better. First, you yourself be the kind of person you ought to be. Secondly, a life that is holy will commend your teaching as holy especially if you do it steadfastly and persistently. For truth is lasting, pretence temporary. If you do this, you will win a double fruit. First, by rightly performing the office delegated to you, you will save yourself.

Secondly, you will also save those who heed your teaching. People whose teaching is correct but whose lives are impious may be useful to others; they are certainly destructive to themselves. But a person whose life and teachings are alike insincere is doubly harmful. He brings ruin on himself and leads others into destruction.

Chapter 5

Though one must never deviate from pure and sound doctrine, nevertheless the gentleness[1] with which one teaches or admonishes has considerable effect in the healing of human errors. A bishop's authority must be maintained but in ways which keep it from any semblance of tyranny, and which show that in all his actions he is acting from a desire to help and not because of some dislike. There is no point, therefore, in wounding through harshness someone whom you can cure through friendliness and gentleness. One who perceives that he is loved by his admonisher will obey him more readily. It is a general characteristic of human nature to prefer to be led than to be driven, and more often than not one obtains through blandishment what one could not achieve through brutality. Therefore, the medicine of criticism has to be mixed in accordance with the age and status of each person. It is customary not only among all civilized nations but in churches[2] too for authority to be in the hands of persons of advanced age because of the wisdom and experience that come with age and the need for the old to restrain the wanton behaviour of the young. For this reason if an older man has chanced to commit some wrong, do not thunder at him with wild words based[3] on suspicion or on some secret report, lest the very harshness of the admonition be a barrier to the end sought. For such admonition will be irksome on two grounds: because it is is abusive and because it has come from a younger man. On the contrary, maintain your respect for his age and exhort him as you would want to admonish an erring parent. Being yourself a young man, admonish the young men like brothers, towards whom your criticism should be more candid but still such as to display your love. Admonish the older women in a more respectful and ingratiating way, as if they were your mother. Defer, that is, to their age. Reprimand the young women in a loving manner like sisters. Conduct yourself before everyone in a way that avoids incurring any sinister suspicion of avarice or unchastity or flattery or cruelty.

Now widows too are to have their own special honour, especially those who not only have the name of widow but are truly widowed. I mean women who, deprived of the comfort of husband and children, live the kind of lives which deserve financial aid and support from the church. The church should provide this aid for the alleviation of genuine distress, not to pamper self-indulgence. If some woman has lost her husband but still has sons or grandsons living, there is no reason for her to seek refuge in the church's support as though she were destitute. She has her own family, whose company can mitigate the loss of her husband and to whom she owes her first duty. Therefore, let her not dedicate herself to the service of the church until she has given a sample of her pious devotion to her own family. For her to escape from the debt of nature and the obligation of piety under the pretext of service to the church would be preposterous. Nature dictates that we who received the beginnings of life from our parents should reciprocate and return this devotion to them when they are destitute and worn out with age. But if death has taken them from us, it will be proper to transfer to our children and grandchildren the duty owed our parents. Our children should learn from our instruction that they in turn have a duty to support those who have benefited them. Not only does natural feeling approve this, but it is also[4] pleasing and acceptable in the eyes of God. Widows[5] who neglect their duty sin twice over, since they both rebel against God and are deaf to the common natural feelings which stir even those who do not know God.

But, you will say, who then is a real widow if this kind of widow is not? She who, deprived of husband, children, grandchildren, and all the comforts of this world, has placed all her hope in God. She no longer looks to a second husband and is not pursuing physical pleasures but has dedicated herself wholly to God. Following the example of the widow Anna,[6] she is intent night and day on prayer. She who now has nothing in common with the world deserves to be refreshed by the solace of the church. A widow who refrains from a second marriage so that she may enjoy her pleasures more freely is not even alive. She so lives for pleasure that she is dead to Christ, to whom no one is alive except the one who is alive to godliness. Therefore you will instruct the widows that if they choose to remain widows, their behaviour in widowhood must give no one any handle for evil suspicions. I do not want anyone to think that these widows are avoiding remarriage not because they are in love with chastity but only to be free from a husband's rule so that they can live more loosely and indulge in their pleasures at their own whim. But leave it to the widows' own judgment to decide with what intention each chooses widowhood or how she is to spend her life at home. If anyone[7] takes refuge in the church under the pretext of widowhood and sheds in this way her responsibility to her children or grandchildren or to any other member of her family, I not only do not consider her worthy of the bishop's favour but I think that she should be viewed instead as one of those women who have denied the faith of the gospel and consequently are worse than the pagans. To abandon the commitment which they have undertaken is more grievous than not to have made the commitment at all. Has not she who uses the pretext of faith to do things contrary to the teaching of the gospel denied her faith? Certainly she denies it publicly by her actions. In this particular respect, she ought to be judged lower than the pagan women.[8] Since the latter are strangers to Christ, they take care of their families with nature as their only guide. This Christian woman who, in keeping with the demands of evangelical love, ought to have helped everyone to the best of her ability, withdraws from her own family the duty owed them. Evangelical[9] godliness fails to obtain from her what natural affection obtains from the profane and ungodly. If nature has implanted any seeds of goodness, evangelical doctrine does not remove them; it develops and perfects them.

It is entirely in accord with the gentleness of the Christian religion to foster and nourish in its own bosom those widows who have been bereft of every comfort. But I would not want this support to be given casually or indiscriminately. A double disadvantage could ensue, when the church is burdened beyond its strength and charity is conferred on women who do not deserve it. Two things must be kept especially in view in the process of selection: age and past life. We do not want those who are once admitted to the protection of the church to return to the marriage state; that would result in great scandal. Judgment in the matter of age at least is easy. Do not accept a widow below the age of sixty. This age will not lead people to suspect that the clergy may engage in unchaste acts with such women, but suggests instead the strong likelihood that they will not be touched again by the desire for marriage. And yet not even this age is to be trusted without the proof provided by their past life. Therefore, it is necessary to see whether the widow was content with a single husband. For not even old age extinguishes the passions in some women.[10] Has she everywhere acquired a good reputation from her good deeds? Has she behaved in a good and holy way in bringing up her children? Has she been hospitable towards the saints in so far as her poverty permitted? Did she help them with shelter or wash their feet? Even the poor can provide these services. Did she assist the afflicted and the needy from her own resources? Was she diligent in every good work, neglecting nothing? It is right for the church to receive in turn under its care a woman who has done such good work and has for a long time sought through her good deeds[11] to be enrolled in the permanent ministry of the church.[12]

Do not accept, however, widows who are younger and of an age to invite suspicion. It is better not to undertake the commitment of widowhood than to fail it once undertaken. The vow of continence ought not to be given to a lubricious time of life,[13] especially in this sex. If they want to be chaste, let them test privately in themselves what they are able to achieve. If it proves to be too much for them, they may take refuge in the remedy of marriage with no mark against them. But experience has taught us that sometimes younger widows have given up the right of remarriage, sworn allegiance to the church, and consecrated themselves to Christ as their spouse because of some momentary love of chastity and in pursuit of either leisure perhaps or the honour of the title. After a while their earlier desire begins to itch and they lose control and become wanton. Their behaviour is an insult to Christ, whose yoke they wish to shake off in order to go again under the yoke of matrimony.[14] Meanwhile they bring the stain of this infamy on themselves because they have nullified the pledge of fidelity which they seem to have made with Christ. They deserve censure on two counts. First, they have rashly undertaken the commitment to chastity without having sufficiently explored their own strength; secondly, they have recoiled from this commitment which they have undertaken. But if it should be the case that they do not return openly to the state of marriage, certainly their life in celibacy is such that they are a disgrace to the church. It is better for them to be kept in check by a husband's governance and to be kept busy caring for children than to have a licence to sin under the pretext of widowhood. Idleness teaches them to wander about through the homes of other people since they have nothing to do in their own although it is unseemly for a widow to roam idly through the streets or to loiter in someone else's house. They are now not only idlers but gossips and busy-bodies as well. For gossiping is customarily the companion of snooping. On the pretext of widowhood and through the acceptance given to this position they easily get inside the houses of others and there pry into[15] secrets which they afterwards blab out in other houses, chattering indecently about marriages, quarrels, the sins or domestic scandals of others.

For these reasons I consider it safer for the younger widows to marry. The authority of their husbands will control both their sex and their more susceptible age. I want them to apply themselves to the bearing of children, and to attend to the affairs of their own family rather than in their idleness to disturb the families of others. Respect for a husband curbs the licentious-ness to which women of their age are prone. Likewise, the cares of their own households do not give them the free time to poke into matters which have nothing to do with them. Lastly, let them organize every part of their lives so that there is no occasion for a lapse into open scandal and Satan is given no handle for slandering and besmirching our life before the enemies of Christianity. I am quite ready to appear overly meticulous in this matter; the evil itself teaches us this caution. We would not be so anxious and afraid that any of these things might happen if we had not already seen them happening and not just once. The example of certain women gives us pause. They were co-opted once into the bosom of the church, but to our great shame they were overcome by pleasures and, obeying Satan, slid back into a second marriage. But if a widow whose age requires marriage is prevented from finding a husband by her lack of a dowry,[16] there is no need for her to take the vow of chastity because of poverty. If she has any male or female relatives who are Christians, they are obliged to alleviate her lack of a dowry[17] through their generosity. It is not right for a Christian man or a Christian woman, whose godliness should be a source of help even to strangers, to leave a widowed relative destitute and to thrust her upon the church for support. If the church is burdened with widows of every sort, it will soon exhaust its resources and not have enough to support the real widows to whom this kindness is due and who have no other source of support.

Just as properly deserving widows should receive their appropriate portion of honour, so should support be given and even more abundantly to the elders whom the moral stability and prudence which comes with advanced age as well as the integrity of their life and the authority of their age make effective leaders of the multitude. These are men who truly act like elders. Their age as well as their godliness earn them the right to be free from the injustice of need. On this basis they will preside more calmly over the people, and their authority will not be diminished when they have a regular supply of the appurtenances of a decent life. But this support should be supplied first and foremost to those who not only light the way for the people by the integrity of their life, but also labour in the dispensation of the word of the gospel and of sacred doctrine, because this is their special function and by far the one most profitable to a Christian flock. They are, to be sure, looking towards a higher reward, but in the meantime it is some part of their comfort if some immediate benefit returns to them in the midst of their labours, not in order to become wealthy but to stay alive.[18] It is not right to fail to repay with some portion of that which is transitory and of little value the one who is imparting a share in a far more precious property. The law of Moses forbids the mouth of an ox to be bridled during the time that it is driven around in threshing;[19] this shows how much the one who labours is owed a living. It is surely even more unkind to allow the man toiling in the gospel to be hungry and thirsty. He is not angling for pay, but is a workman so much the more worthy of his hire.[20] If he works for nothing, he will obtain praise for his godliness, while the people will have only blame if they refuse to alleviate the poverty of their benefactor when it is possible to assist him with so little.

You will in addition defer to the authority of the older men[21] by not being overly quick to receive an accusation against them from those who should instead be showing the respect due their elders. We do not want to offer an opening to these persons to make rash attacks on the life of the older men, against whom a sinister suspicion should be received only reluctantly, nor do we want to have their authority diminished. An accuser should not be heard unless he can substantiate his assertions with two or three witnesses. But if the fact that some elders have sinned is too evident and well known to be kept concealed, you will have to arrange for their correction in such a way that you neither hand them over to the cruelty of their accusers nor on the other hand allow the dismissal of the charges against them to serve as a pernicious example to the multitude. Rebuke them vocally in person and in public to ensure that others will be all the more afraid of censure from their bishop when they see through your action that you do not condone even the older men if they have done something deserving reproof.

Secular law uses the bond of religion to keep judges from declaring a wrong verdict under the corrupting influence of their personal feelings.[22] How much greater integrity befits a bishop either in trials or in the appointment of officials! Secular judges are reminded of their oath as they are about to take their seats before the tribunal and are constrained by their religious fear of gods that are, after all, false. But you, Timothy, I charge through God the Father, who is the arbiter and witness of our conduct in office, and through Jesus Christ, whose ministers we are, and through the elect angels, the beholders and spectators of what we do, that you observe in the performance of your judicial duties these instructions which I am giving you and that you come to a judicial inquiry with your integrity uncorrupted. Do not bring into court with you some opinion which favouritism, dislike, anger, or some other passion has instilled into you outside the court, but draw from your knowledge of the facts themselves a correct verdict without being more disposed to one side or the other.

You must display this integrity not only in hearing cases but also in choosing those to whom you entrust the administration of the church. From no other source does such complete ruin arise for the people of Christ than if useless and even pernicious persons should be put into office. Therefore, do not lay your hands on someone hastily. The person to whom you would delegate episcopal authority must be subjected to long and extensive testing and investigation. If his conduct of the office entrusted to him is unworthy, his wrongdoing, whatever it is, will be charged to you. You will seem to have countenanced his vices when, despite what you know about him, you entrust him with such a responsibility. Even if he has deceived you, you will still be unable to escape the blame for negligence when you entrusted so risky a matter to somebody without investigation. It should not be enough in the selection of a bishop that he have a blameless reputation; he must also have an outstanding record of good deeds to commend him.[23] It is not enough for a bishop to exhibit his own innocence, he must also exhibit the integrity of those whom he ordains. In these matters, therefore, see that you keep yourself chaste and pure for the religion which you are administering.

Your temperance is too well known to me to have to recall you from self-indulgence by my admonitions. Nevertheless, you need to be reminded that abstinence has to be tempered lest because of its weakness the body be incapable of performing the duties of piety.[24] A fat and corpulent body often weighs down the mind as it aspires to heavenly things. Likewise poor physical health is too often a hindrance to mental vigour and prevents the mind from freely disclosing and revealing itself through charitable services. Therefore, I think that you have been abstemious enough up to this time. From now on do not drink only water, but instead use a moderate measure of wine. Let[25] the fact that you have abstained from wine up to the present be attributed to the heat of early youth. Now it is time for you to give thought to your health so that you can be equal to performing all the duties of a bishop. The stomach is bolstered by a moderate measure of wine; drinking only water can be very harmful to it. Therefore, to give it some help and to keep yourself from falling ill as often as you now do,[26] allow yourself to use wine as a medicine to avoid the collapse of your strength and the need to call on the aid of doctors.

But to return to the subject I began a moment ago,[27] do not think that all of the sins of your subordinates[28] must be charged to you. The sins of some persons are so manifest that they do not wait for the last judgment of God but spontaneously anticipate judgment. These sins bring condemnation on themselves even before they are brought forward at that final judgment. Both the life of these sinners and their teaching are in open disagreement with the teachings of Christ. In place of evangelical godliness they teach Jewish superstitions while their life is infected with ambition, love of gain, and the other evil passions. You will have to give an account for whatever judgment you may render about them. But[29] God will not hold you responsible for the guilt of those whose wickedness is hidden so that it cannot be apprehended by human judgment, but is reserved for divine judgment when everything will be laid bare. In the same way the good works of some people are so manifest that they do not need the prior approval of men. Therefore, everyone may associate safely with them just as one must withdraw from the company of the openly wicked. But we shall leave it to God

to judge those who so artfully guide their life and so disguise the evil in
their minds under the appearance of godliness that they deceive human
judgment. For Christian godliness does not harbour hateful suspicions.

Chapter 6

It is not our role to attack the lives of those who are strangers to Christianity; it is more expedient to challenge them to a better outlook by our services than to irritate them by our reproaches. We must temper our religion so
that it does not appear to be an occasion or seed-bed of sedition. Let the
pagans see in those dealings which we have to have with them that our
religion has made us more dutiful, not more insolent and troublesome.[1] In
this way they will be more easily moved to join us. Thus any who were in
slavery when they were baptized are to remember that they have been
emancipated from the lordship of sin, not freed from their masters' legal
rights. Therefore, it is inappropriate for them on the pretext of their religion
to refuse to obey their masters on the assumption that they are godless and
unworthy of being served by an initiate of Christ. Let them only remember
that those men are their masters and for that reason let them count their
masters worthy of every honour. Otherwise the name of God and the
teaching of the gospel will be made notorious and will be hated when
people observe that the gospel makes people more troublesome and unre-
strained. On the contrary, slaves should instead add something extra to their
earlier service and be keener to obey. Their service must appear to be
heartfelt. They will thus challenge their masters by their actions and lead
them to accept more easily the preaching of the gospel.[2] It is all the more
necessary, however, that slaves who have Christian masters not hold them
in less esteem because their confession of a common faith has made their
masters into brothers. On the contrary, if they must not withhold the
obedience due pagan masters, they now have two reasons for obeying
masters who are Christians, first, because they are their masters, and secondly because they as masters have replaced arrogance with love in the
fellowship of religion and have begun to be loved instead of feared, to be
kindly instead of menacing. More is to be given to one who deserves well
than to one who demands, to one who loves than to one who commands,
for this is no longer slavery in the usual sense but a reciprocation of duties.
 Teach these things with authority; exhort the faint of heart to follow
them. They are that truly evangelical doctrine which contributes to a godly
life and makes us both pleasing to God and the object of people's love. If
anyone urges a doctrine different from this and does not accede to the most
true words of the[3] Lord Jesus Christ and does not obey that doctrine which

is both consonant with the gospel and summons us to the duties of godliness instead of to superstitious questions, his lack of true knowledge is a
match for his excess of arrogance. As knowledge is a modest thing, so
nothing is more haughty or stubborn than ignorance. The person who is
possessed by this disease becomes hostile to evangelical sincerity, is ob-
sessed with foolish questions and, neglecting everything else in life, engages
in verbal duels which contribute absolutely nothing to Christian godliness
but only cause it to perish. For envy arises from just such quarrelsome
debates when we create authority for ourselves by deliberately diminishing
the authority of others. They also give birth to strife, when in the growing
heat of the quarrel no one wants to yield to another, and give rise to abusive language when the affair ends in a mad rage. Even ungodly suspicions
against God arise when man-made arguments are used to call into question,
as though they were in doubt, matters which should be believed without
inquiry. The contagion infects many when this mange[4] is rubbed off on
them from men whose minds are infected by evil desires. Blinded by these
desires they do not see the real truth of the gospel, nor do they aim their
teaching towards this target, but instead measure godliness and religion by
the amount of their own gain. They do not want people to think that the
highest kind of holiness is that which makes others more acceptable to God;
rather holiness is whatever wins for them the greatest reputation and the
greatest gain. There is no reason for you to expect that they can be overcome by any arguments. Their ignorance is obstinate because even if they
have an absolutely clear view of the truth, they still do not acknowledge[5]
it since it is useless for their own objectives. Therefore, do not debate with
these men in an unsightly fashion and to no avail, but withdraw yourself
from their company.

They may chase after their profits; they may hawk evangelical doctrine
as they wish. For us the gain is great and abundantly so if we grow rich in
true godliness and in the true goods of the soul, content with enough of the
things of this world to meet the needs of our present life as we hasten
towards immortality. It is a grand thing to accumulate those riches which
will never leave us. Does it serve any purpose to be anxious to collect riches
which are not really ours and which we are soon compelled to leave behind
for others?[6] As we brought none of these things with us into the world
when we were born, so shall we take none of them out with us when we
die. To squander wealth on pleasures is a deadly disease; to hoard accumulated wealth is madness. We measure the use of these things by the limits
set by nature.[7] When it supplies us with enough to clothe and feed ourselves, we require nothing more. A modest amount of food and clothing is
readily available anywhere; for food and clothing are not to be employed

for extravagant living, but for daily need. Need is relieved by a small amount, the whirlpool of excess is insatiable. To increase the treasure of[8] godliness by the loss of money is an enormous gain; to lose immortal riches for the sake of a cheap and petty profit is an enormous expenditure.

The pursuit of wealth and the pursuit of godliness can not coexist in the same person. Men whose souls have once been taken over by the desire to become rich are provoked into many shameful acts and fall into a snare and into many desires that are as foolish as they are ruinous. For this particular desire does not come unaccompanied, but brings with it a long train of evils – arrogance, pride, ambition, violence, fraud, injury, debauchery, carnal pleasures, and other plagues of this kind. Their burden gradually sinks a person into death and destruction, and he becomes pestilent and deadly not only to himself but also to the others in his charge. The higher the office one holds, the farther must one stay away from the appearance of this evil. Absolute power requires absolute integrity. But anyone who is motivated by greed can do nothing with integrity, nothing without corruption. Greed is so far from honest goodness that it is the seed and root of all evils even if wealth seems to display a sort of admirable happiness. Enticed by this bait, some in their pursuit of wealth were depraved by desires and strayed from the sincerity of evangelical faith when they placed before their eyes another guide than Christ. While they were foolishly chasing after the sweet life, they entangled themselves in many sorrows, acquiring with a great deal of trouble something which they can safeguard only with anxiety and worry and which, if it should chance to be snatched away, would wound their heart and do a grave injury to their greed. Such are the possessions of those who have dedicated themselves to the god Mammon.[9]

But you who have been consecrated to God shun those things which are unworthy of your profession and pursue only true riches: righteousness, godliness, faith, love, patience, mildness – righteousness to keep you safe from all vices, godliness to make you love God and your neighbour for his sake,[10] faith to keep you from being tormented by worry over such material goods because you rely on God's support, love to make you helpful to everyone, patience to give you endurance in adversity and in the storms of persecution because of your hope for future immortality, mildness to enable you to bear gently the weakness of others. The person who thinks everything must be done from love of wealth is unable to protect this wealth. But you have undertaken a very different course. You have entered an extraordinary contest, a contest in faith, not in greed. No ordinary prize is at stake. For your goal is not to become wealthy here on earth with transitory and false goods[11] but to obtain eternal life. Exerting yourself to the utmost, press on towards this goal, towards this finish. God has called you to it. He is the director of this contest[12] and he cannot deceive. By his own decision he chose you to preside as bishop over the people for the glory of Christ. You professed this, and in the presence of many witnesses, when you undertook the office of presbyter.[13] It is an outstanding profession, but it requires great vigilance for you to measure up to it. If so grand a prize is not sufficient to move you, let the fact that God is a spectator move you, let the expectation of so many people move you, let the holiness of the charge you have assumed move you. Therefore, I command you again and again, and I beseech you by God the Father, who is the author of life to all the living and will recall even the dead to immortality, and by his Son Jesus Christ, who before his judge Pontius Pilate did not fail – even at the cross – the office[14] which he had received from the Father. Carry out the charge delegated to you in such a way as to draw no stain or reproach upon yourself. Do this steadfastly, looking not only to the judgment of men but much more to the coming of our Lord Jesus Christ, whom[15] God will show again in his own time to the world, the Blessed and alone Mighty One, King of those who reign, Lord of those who are lords, who alone of himself has immortality, who alone dwells in unapproachable light, whom no human has yet seen or can see, to whom [be] honour and everlasting power. Amen. Such are the authorities you have for your office; you need have no lack of confidence in your own authority. Such are your spectators and judges; you should do nothing otherwise than you ought. Such are your champions; you need have no fear of the storms of human persecution. Such are the ones who will reward you; you need have no doubts about the promised prizes. The whole glory of the gospel must be attributed to them; no human can claim any praise for himself from it.

I have shown how dangerous the pursuit of wealth is to Christians. If there are among our people, however, any who happen to have received that wealth which leads this world to call them rich and blessed, and to look up to and to revere them like demigods, instruct them that they are not to adopt a haughty attitude because of their confidence in this wealth and that they are not to think that their felicity can be safeguarded by material goods. These goods are, first of all, hollow and meaningless, and, secondly, they are uncertain because if chance does not snatch them away, death certainly does. Let them put their trust instead in the living God who never fails either the living or the dead because he himself is immutable. From his beneficence comes whatever this world supplies in sufficient quantity from the year's produce, which is for our immediate use, not for the accumulation of riches. Let them direct their energy instead to exercising themselves in good works so that they may become truly wealthy and grow rich in good deeds rather than in estates. Let them consider whatever possessions they happen to acquire to belong to all and not just to themselves.[16] For this reason they should be ready to share with the needy and should not treat with disdain the rest of the people who are poor, but should adopt instead a pleasing and mild manner for the meetings and intercourse of social life. Contempt and arrogance are commonly the companions of affluence. Do not let them put their trust in massive foundations of stone,[17] for nothing on earth is permanent, but have them lay down through true virtues a good and solid foundation for the after time so that they may attain true, that is, eternal life. For what else is this life than a race towards death? We must cast off every concern for transitory things and hasten in all eagerness towards this true life.

Oh Timothy, I charge you again and again to keep this doctrine faithfully just as it has been deposited, so that you do not allow it to be contaminated with man-made dogmas. This is not possible unless, as I admonished above, you reject the futile and empty garrulity of those who through their petty investigations and man-made sophistries seek to win for themselves a reputation, false to be sure, for having knowledge. For man-made knowledge which consists only of conflicting opinions does not deserve the name of knowledge. We know nothing truer than what evangelical doctrine and faith have persuaded us of. But some persons in their effort to appear learned and wise through their man-made syllogisms, sophistic debates and novel dogmas which they themselves have contrived have strayed from the sincerity of evangelical faith. Faith believes, it does not dispute, and is not drawn away from God's precepts by man-made decrees.

So that you may understand that this letter is not counterfeit,[18] I shall add these words below in my own handwriting which you know so well,[19] Grace be with you.[20] Amen.[21]

The End

PARAPHRASE ON SECOND TIMOTHY

In epistolam Pauli Apostoli ad Timotheum secundam paraphrasis

THE ARGUMENT OF THE
SECOND EPISTLE TO TIMOTHY
BY ERASMUS OF ROTTERDAM

Since in the previous epistle Paul had led Timothy, his agent in Ephesus, to expect his return and there was now no way that he could do this because he was being held in chains in Rome, he sends a letter encouraging him not to be dejected by the storm of persecutions but following Paul's own example to prepare his soul for martyrdom.[1] Dangerous times were threatening because of certain persons who, under the pretext of godliness, were trying to overturn true godliness and in this way to boost themselves. They thought that Christian godliness consisted in words, not, as is the case, in the purity of the soul. Then, after attesting that the day of his own death was near and that he had now been abandoned by most people, he tells Timothy to come quickly to him in Rome and to bring Mark. He wrote at Rome when he was appearing for the second time before Nero's court.[2]

The End of the Argument

THE PARAPHRASE OF
ERASMUS OF ROTTERDAM
ON THE SECOND EPISTLE OF PAUL
THE APOSTLE TO TIMOTHY

Chapter 1

Paul, the emissary of Jesus Christ, made an apostle by the will of God the Father so that I might reveal how great is the bliss of the life to come, which he promises us through his Son Jesus Christ, lest we make too much of the loss of this present life, to Timothy, his beloved son: Grace, mercy, peace from God the Father and from Christ Jesus our Lord.

I am grateful to God to whose worship I am no recent convert. I have always kept, and continue to keep with a sincere and pure heart his religion, which was handed down from my ancestors. For I now worship as a Christian him whom I worshipped previously, but differently, as a Jew.[1] It is through his kindness that I have found one like you who so imitates me in the preaching of evangelical doctrine that I am able to embrace you as you deserve with feelings no different from those felt for a true-born and natural son. Thus even when you are absent I can never forget you. For you always come to mind in my morning and evening prayers in which it is my habit to intercede with God and commend[2] to him those who are truly dear to me. I am filled with a great longing to see you, most of all when I recall your tears which you shed at my departure.[3] They are the most reliable witnesses of the love and devotion you have for me. For this reason a flood of joy overwhelms and fills me whenever I think of how you resemble me in the genuineness of your faith as a true-born son does his parent. Just as purity in religion has been, as it were, hereditary in me, so does the genuineness of your faith likewise appear to have been transmitted to you directly from your immediate forebears. For it steadfastly dwelt first in your grandmother, Lois, and then in your mother, Eunice. I have no doubt that you, the grandson and son, will match your grandmother's great devotion to religion and your mother's great goodness because you have chosen to take after them rather than after your father's side of the family.

I mention these things so that my own example and the example of your mother and grandmother may make you more eager to stir up by your industry and vigilance the gift of God which you received through the imposition of my hands when you were installed as a bishop.[4] Carry out bravely, and without bending, the task delegated to you. Do not be in the least afraid of the barks of some critics or the savagery of persecutors. It belongs to the Jews to dread the threats offered by this present life. God has given us who have become his sons through evangelical faith a far different Spirit. This Spirit does not make us timid and downcast from fear and diffidence, but brave with heads held high because we have confidence in our innocence and we hope for the immortality promised us. This Spirit makes us free and courageous because of our love which both trusts totally in God's help and is not afraid to undergo danger for a neighbour's sake. Lastly, this Spirit does not allow our minds to be thrown into turmoil but enables us to persevere with hearts resolute and unbroken always. Therefore, since you have received this Spirit, display its power and courageously manifest what you possess. Do not be ashamed of your religion in any way. Through it you proclaim the cross and death of our Lord Jesus Christ. Do not be ashamed to be the disciple of this apostle, burdened though I am with these chains. Nothing is more glorious than the cross of Christ, which has given salvation to the world,[5] has broken the tyranny of the devil, and has made immortality available to us. The cross of Christ is our glory. The chains, which I bear willingly because of my work for the gospel, are not my disgrace, but in fact my glory. Do not shrink then from suffering what Christ suffered and what I now endure for his sake. On the contrary, be ready to share in the tribulations which are inflicted on us because of the gospel of Christ. There is no reason to tremble in the face of any assault. It is not with our own power but with God's protective forces that the battle is being waged. We are weak, but he is strong. He saved us through the death of his Son when we were lost. He abolished the sins of our old life and called us to holiness, not because of any merits on our part,[6] but impelled by his own will and the spontaneous kindness which he lavished upon us. This was no recent plan of his. He had decided from eternity and before all time, before the creation of this world, to confer these benefits upon us through Jesus Christ his Son.

    With God nothing is new, but he has recently manifested to the world what has always existed in the hidden depths of his mind: through the coming of our Saviour Jesus Christ who assumed a mortal body, and through the cross abolished death, and through the resurrection opened the way to life and immortality; through the preaching of the gospel which promises the same reward to those who imitate the cross of Christ. The preaching of this gospel has been delegated to me as the apostle and teacher of the gentiles so that through me they may learn that not only Jews but the whole human race has been called to this gift of God. Therefore, since I have been bound in chains because of the gospel, I am not only not ashamed of this affliction but I consider it even my glory. To suffer because of one's crimes is ignominious, to be afflicted because of Christ's glory is glorious. This tempest does not frighten me at all. Though I myself am weak, nevertheless I know and am convinced that he in whom I have placed my trust is more than able to preserve to the very last day what I have entrusted to him. Through his protection the work of the gospel, my own salvation, and the safety of the Christian flock are secure. If something in this life appears to be lost for a time, nevertheless he will restore it with great gain when that day comes when he will display his magnificence to our world. I have put my life and my salvation in his keeping, while he has entrusted to me the stewardship of evangelical doctrine.[7] If I remain a faithful trustee of what he has deposited with me, he will not deceive our trust in him.

I have in turn entrusted to you what I have received from him. Therefore, since you have[8] a pattern and model of the evangelical stewardship and the pure doctrine which you have learned from me, a pattern which does not depend upon frivolous, perplexing, and trifling questions but upon the faith and love which Jesus Christ has both taught and shown to us, be careful to preserve the deposit which has been placed in your keeping. The doctrine I deposited with you was pure and sincere. See that it is not contaminated through your negligence. I know that many are striving and will go on striving to corrupt the gospel's teachings. But you, relying on the evangelical Spirit which dwells in us,[9] protect bravely and steadfastly what you have received. Made brave through this helper, we shall easily ignore and even overcome any dangers which threaten us. Those who do not have this Spirit are terrified by the storm of evils and abandon the work of the gospel. I think you know that all who at one time had adhered to me in Asia have now abandoned me. Their adherence was only feigned, and when their hypocrisy presently found an occasion for breaking out into the open,[10] they began to shun me in Rome.[11] I do not wish to mention all their names, but Phygellus and Hermogenes are in their number. In both of them their very names reveal their instability. For the name Phygellus is derived from the word 'fugitive,'[12] and Hermogenes is named after the mercurial god Hermes.[13]

It is not in my nature to pray that they receive their just deserts.[14] On the other hand we must pray that God, who is the rewarder of godly deeds and wants to be given the credit for whatever services his servants perform, may bless the household of Onesiphorus. Not only has he often been a

comfort to me on other occasions and a haven of coolness in the heat of my
afflictions, but also at this time he was not ashamed of my bonds. He
understood that it is glorious to suffer for Christ. Fortified by the promises
of the gospel, he was not afraid to associate with me in danger. On the
contrary, when he was in Rome, he not only did not shrink from conversing
with a prisoner, but actually made a great effort to track me down and did
not rest until he had found me. Onesiphorus found material for the exercise
of mercy. May the Lord Jesus grant to him that he in turn find mercy in his
court on that day when everyone without exception will receive the payment which their deeds demand. May he who was eager to be kind to me
in my affliction find God being equally kind to him. I shall not report here
in how many matters he helped me at Ephesus since you know this better
than he himself does. He behaved towards me at Rome, too, just the way
he did there at Ephesus. True love is not frightened by any tempest of
affliction.

Chapter 2

Follow, therefore, the examples of Onesiphorus and myself, and be resolute.
Rely on the kindness which we have from God through Jesus Christ. Thus
fortified and ready for every danger, dearest son,[1] transmit to others the
pure doctrine of the gospel which they are to propagate. I did not transmit
it to you secretly but in the presence of many witnesses. You in turn transmit it not just to anyone but only to those who in your judgment will be
loyal and honest stewards of it and will seem to be capable not only of
themselves following what they have absorbed but also of pouring it
unadulterated into others.

　　You see how soldiers who have taken a military oath, ignoring all
other considerations, do and bear everything in order to perform their
duties commendably. Christ too has his army. You have enlisted in it. You
have sworn allegiance to him. He has put you in command of his camp.
Therefore, as befits a brave general, vigorously oppose all wicked attacks
and in a manner worthy of your commander-in-chief,[2] Jesus Christ, who
persisted in his assigned task all the way to the cross. Do not worry about
ways to support this human life. Leave all that care to the commander-in-
chief. Your only objective should be to carry out energetically the orders he
has given. We must not seem to be slacker in the service of Christ than we
see common soldiers to be in secular service. Which of them worries about
his clothing or daily food when he has once enlisted in the army of a king
or an emperor? The one in command takes on himself the provision of these
things. The soldier does not have to care about anything except to make his

services acceptable to the commander who chose him for this work as a vigorous and loyal soldier. The soldier knows his reward lies ready in the hands of his commander, if only he earns it. Again, among those who have devoted themselves to boxing and wrestling contests, a contestant is not satisfied simply to put on a show. He does everything to win, fully convinced that a trophy is there and waiting, but only for him who has conducted himself energetically and vigorously in the contest. Likewise, when an industrious farmer ploughs, fertilizes, sows, and cultivates, he is totally engaged in his work and does not consider any toil burdensome, because his hopes are in the fruit which he knows the faithful earth will in due course return. All the more should we who are engaged in the work of the gospel do the same, so that, motivated by[3] the reward of immortality, we willingly endure everything here on earth, especially since we have a commander who neither wishes to, nor is able to deceive. Ponder what I mean by these comparisons. May the Lord give you understanding not only in them but in all other things.

There is no loss here; on the contrary, the gain in evangelical salvation increases with the increase in sufferings. This is the way God has decided to manifest his power. We see in the head what we are to expect in ourselves. You must remember what you know, namely that Christ Jesus, after becoming a human being in direct descent from David and thus subject to death, made the glory of the gospel bright in his endurance of insults, and after the punishment of the cross, was borne aloft to the prize of immortality. This is the gospel which I preach constantly to this day, undeterred by either hatred from the Jews or fear of the gentiles. For the sake of this gospel I suffer many evils from both groups, even being imprisoned and shackled like some common criminal. But I do not desist from the preaching of the gospel even in these circumstances. The body has been chained; the tongue that preaches Christ cannot be chained. Though a prisoner, I entice to Christ as far as possible whomever I can. What I suffer is of no concern to me provided that I make some additional gain for the gospel of Christ. Confident as I am in my own salvation, I willingly endure everything for the sake of this gain so that they too whom God has destined for the felicity of this salvation may obtain it through the preaching of the gospel. This salvation is offered to all through Jesus Christ, certainly not through the law of Moses. Just as Jesus suffered for us, so it is appropriate for us in turn to suffer to the full for his gospel and the salvation of our brothers. As he travelled through ignominy and through many kinds of suffering to heavenly glory above, so must we struggle along the same road to the same end.

To many this seems hard and unbelievable, but we must have no doubts about it. For if we have through baptism died together with Christ to the desires of this world or if even those who persevere in their baptismal confession should come to be afflicted by the evils of this world,[4] we are also destined to live with Christ; that is, we who are his fellows in death shall be his fellows in immortality. If we endure to the end with him and for the sake of his glory, we shall surely also reign with him. God is completely just. Those whom he willed to receive their share of evil, he will not allow to be excluded from their share in the kingdom. If we confess Christ here bravely before men, he will acknowledge us in his majesty. But if we deny him – and he who refuses the cross denies him – we shall inevitably hear on the last day those terrifying words, 'I do not know you.'[5] If we have faith in him, we are looking after our own salvation. But if we do not have faith, the loss will not be his. He has neither gain nor loss from our belief about him.[6] He is truthful by nature and cannot be unlike himself. Regardless of whether we believe or do not believe, what he has promised will come to be, immortality for the godly, eternal death for the ungodly.

This is the foundation of evangelical doctrine. Remind everyone of it, not by disputing and debating about it with man-made subtleties, but by invoking the Lord Jesus as the author of this doctrine, as the witness to your reminder, and, if people who have been thus reminded fail to come to their senses and repent, as the one who punishes ungodliness. You will gain more by a dignified and solemn invocation of this kind than by subtle disputations. Do not debate with words like the sophists. Do not collect man-made arguments to support beliefs which must be grasped by faith. That kind of debate is not at all conducive to the advance of godliness. When people hear everything they believe called into question and hear matters, about which it is sinful even to have a doubt, confirmed at one moment only to be destroyed at another by philosophical arguments, their minds are eventually subverted and even those whose faith was firm begin to waver. In this way question propagates question so that there is neither end nor limit to questions.

But you steer clear of such duels. Do your best to show yourself an evangelical workman and not a debater, and a workman approved not by men but by God. Conduct yourself in the work of the gospel in such a way that you need feel no shame before God, who selected you. You will do this if you cut away all superfluous disputations and keep the teaching of the gospel on the direct road of faith and if, once you have cleared away the thicket of perplexing questions, you divide and handle[7] the word of God with right judgment, presenting to the people only those matters which are properly relevant to the work of godliness and salvation. But staunchly reject meaningless verbal disputations.[8] Once such disputations have been accepted, their poison will gradually increase and they will steadily advance to even greater impieties. The situation will finally reach the point where the growing strength of man-made dogmas and dissertations overwhelms, overshadows, overlays, and impairs the vitality of the gospel. The words of such people, once they have taken possession of the ears and minds of simple folk, spread ever more widely, just as a gangrene[9] in the body of a living creature does not stop gradually taking possession of the surrounding parts until it has brought death. Therefore, this evil must be immediately attacked at its very beginnings and, rather than fostered, it must be cut away before it drives in roots.

You may think that I am unnecessarily apprehensive about these things, but we have already seen this fear realized in the case of Hymenaeus and Philetus. While they were handling matters of faith with man-made disputations, they strayed from evangelical truth and went so far as to deny its fundamental point and foundation. They claimed that the resurrection had already been accomplished in Christ and that we were to expect no other resurrection than that in which we are somehow reborn and given new life in the children who resemble us.[10] In the meantime they do not notice that when they remove the expectation of the resurrection, they also remove any fear and hope for the rewards which await the godly and the ungodly.[11] This evil would be more tolerable if they, after subverting themselves, were not also subverting with their teachings the faith of some others. There is, of course, no danger that their perversity will overturn the truth of the gospel completely. Though the tide of human opinion may surge back and forth, certainly faith's foundation, laid and defended by Christ's help, stands firm and is not going to be shaken by any attacks from heretics. Carved into it as into solid rock is the saying, no letter of which can be erased, 'The Lord knows who are his,' and 'Let the one[12] who confesses the name of Christ[13] depart from iniquity.' It is not strange if those whose attachment to Christ was insincere should defect from him. But all who have with pure faith believed once for all in the gospel must shun the doctrine of those men.

Every prayer should express the hope that no hint of such plagues arise in the church. However, in view of our large numbers it is impossible for us not to include some wicked people along with the good. But even their wickedness turns into a good when they provoke the godly to make the steadfastness of their faith all the more evident. Thus one finds in the mansion of a rich man not only gold and silver vessels but also wooden and earthen ones. The former are intended for honourable, the latter for dishonourable uses. Their only difference lies in the material from which they are made, for clay and wooden vessels cannot be turned into gold or silver ones. In matters of faith, since it is not a question of the material but of the intention,[14] one who has by his own vices made himself an ignominious vessel can with God's help make himself again an honourable vessel. Conversely, the cultivator of godliness who has been a golden vessel in the house of God will be a shameful vessel if he relapses into ungodliness through his own fault. Disbelief, ambition, cruelty, lust, and similar diseases of the soul cause a person to be an ignominious vessel. If someone has completely cleansed himself from these vices and has repented and been restored to innocence and godliness, he will surely be an honourable and pure vessel, suitable for glorious uses, always ready for his master as often as the need arises.

I know the young are disturbed by various passions which draw a person towards impurity. But you, who hold the office of an older man, avoid all youthful passions. Pursue instead the things that are worthy of you, righteousness, faith, love, peace with those who confess Christ with a pure heart. Have nothing to do with people like Hymenaeus. Innocence does not sin; faith does not argue; love is not haughty; peace is not contentious. Pay no attention, moreover, to foolish and ignorant questions which possess more ostentation than wisdom. You know well that nothing arises from them other than altercations and quarrels when, as the disputation grows hotter and hotter, the affair finally ends up in mad rage. So unwilling is anyone to yield to another that he prefers to defend with the utmost stubbornness even acknowledged falsehood rather than to be thought less learned than his opponent. Therefore, you will not engage in hand to hand combat with this breed of men since they cannot be defeated.

Christ did not persuade the world in this way; he overcame by modesty and mildness, and his voice was not heard in the streets.[15] It is appropriate, therefore, for the servant of the Lord to follow closely in his master's footsteps and not to be pugnacious but to be calm and gentle towards everyone, for persuasion is easier for one who is commended by his love and his self-control; to be ready[16] to teach rather than to scold, to be lenient and not at all irritable in his tolerance of evils, capable of correcting recalcitrant opponents with dignity rather than with harshness and of showing that he is aiming at nothing else in all these situations except to heal them. For one ought not to give up too quickly in despair over anyone. Through reasonable and friendly correction it is possible that God may make them repent their previous mistakes. After they have dispelled the darkness from their minds, they may acknowledge and accept the truth which they were earlier resisting. Returning to their senses and awakening as it were from the heavy sleep of ignorance, they may shake themselves free from the devil's snare, that is, from the evil desires by which they were formerly captured and driven about at his will even to the point of fighting against evangelical truth.

Chapter 3

Therefore, we must fortify ourselves not only against the persecutions of Jews and pagans, but also against the wickedness of these men. What cannot be avoided must not be covered up but overcome. You can be confident that what the Spirit predicts will come true. In the last days very grievous times will come when, as sincere godliness deteriorates and evangelical love grows cold,[1] men will be lovers only of themselves, devoted to the pursuit of money, boastful, proud, abusive, disobedient to parents, ungrateful, ungodly, without feeling for family and kindred, faithless, false accusers, lacking self-control, unmerciful, haters of the good, betrayers of fellowship and friendship, reckless, swollen-headed, lovers of pleasure more than of God, displaying the appearance of godliness in their titles, garb, ceremonies, and play-acting, but nevertheless denying that which is the essence of true godliness.[2] They are all the more destructive because under the mask of religion they live the most polluted lives and corrupt the purity of evangelical doctrine with Jewish myths and petty, man-made inventions. Even today it is perhaps possible to observe some men with tendencies towards these ruinous habits. Accordingly, turn away from these men too.

To help you do this with greater confidence, I shall sketch an outline of their character for you. To this class belong those who insinuate themselves into the homes of others, using the opening given them by their feigned religion, their coarse clothes, their sham severity, and the artfully induced paleness of their features.[3] Once inside, they first hunt for foolish little women so that through them they may impose more easily on the men just as the serpent deceived Adam through Eve.[4] For in the first place the weaker sex is more susceptible to deception. Secondly, these impostors do not try to trap serious-minded and truly good wives, but flighty, weak ones who, despite their confession of Christ, are loaded down with sins. Because they do not rest on solid godliness, they shift about and are driven around by their various desires. They are not content to have learned once and for all from us what is sufficient for true godliness, but are eager to be ever learning something new. For this reason they attach themselves to teachers suited to their own desires, who teach them to know nothing and do not ever bring them to knowledge of the truth. On the contrary, these men conceal the most impure lives under the pretext of evangelical teaching, and while openly professing Christ secretly teach things which are at variance with, and diametrically opposed to the teachings of Christ.

It should not seem surprising if men are now appearing whose wickedness conflicts with the gospel. There is an ancient example. In Egypt long ago Iambres and Mambres[5] tried through their tricks of magic to destroy belief in the wonders which Moses arranged by the power of God; just so do these men oppose evangelical truth under a false image of godliness. They are hopeless cases because not only are their hearts infected with the foulest desires but they twist even the sincerity of faith and evangelical doctrine to fit their own passions. Up to now they have deceived some people, but hereafter they will by no means be so successful with their deceitful tricks. For the day will come when their mad folly will be visible to everyone, just as the discovery of the magicians' fraud made them objects of contempt and laughter.[6] For the teaching of those whose mind and character are insincere cannot be sincere. Deceptions do not last forever. Time brings out into the open what pretence has temporarily covered over.

But you, who are far different from them, will transfer to others with the same unfailing purity the evangelical doctrine which I transmitted in all its purity to you. You are able to be the best witness to the fact that the character of my life has matched the character of my teachings. You have been with me a long time[7] and have a direct knowledge of everything, including the sincerity of my teaching and the behaviour consonant with it, the zeal of a heart that shuns nothing, the imperturbable strength of faith in the face of every evil, the gentleness towards heretics, the love with which I was eager to be helpful even to enemies, the endurance in the persecutions and afflictions which happened to me in your presence at Antioch, Iconium, and Lystra.[8] You know how heavy the storms of persecution were which I sustained here. They were more than human strength alone could endure, but the Lord rescued me from all of them and through his help I remained unbroken. These things did not happen to me through some destiny peculiar to myself, nor were they inflicted on me because of any wrongdoing on my part. It is because of the sincerity of both my life and my evangelical doctrine that I have been harassed by so many evils. Yes, all who wish to pursue true godliness, following my example and that of Christ, must prepare themselves, following his example and mine, to endure affliction.[9] The world will always have men who, to protect their own fictitious religion, will inflict suffering on others and strive to oppress the practitioners of true godliness. But this suffering will issue in our gain, just as their success will turn into an accumulation of damnation for those deceivers and unprincipled men. They will pay the penalty on two grounds, because they have themselves deserted the truth and because they have involved others in their errors.[10] But leave them to their own punishment if they do not come to their senses and repent.

But as for you, persevere in the things which you have learned from
me and remain steadfastly sincere in the office delegated to you. For you
know that the doctrine and instruction which you possess are not open to
doubt so long as you remember both the source from which they first came
and the instructor from whom you learned them, and so long as you do not
forget the Holy Scripture which you learned from your mother and grandmother long ago in the unformed years of early childhood. Even without
my instruction Scripture, correctly understood, can make you informed in
everything that concerns the attainment of the salvation which the gospel
promises to us, not through the observance of the law of Moses, but
through the faith with which we believe Christ Jesus. What the gospel for
its part teaches has now been fulfilled, this the literature of the Old Testament sketches and predicts will come to be. The Old Testament does not
teach anything different from the gospel but only in a different way. It only
needs to have a reader who is godly and informed. If the books of the
prophets or of Moses are understood spiritually in a way that applies their
content to Christ and to godliness, there is no reason for us to think that
they are superfluous. On the contrary, all of Scripture,[11] which was produced for our benefit, not by mere human talent[12] but by the inspiration of
the divine Spirit, has great usefulness either for teaching things, not to know
which is perilous to salvation, or for refuting those who oppose the truth,
or for correcting and calling back to the path those who are simply straying,[13] or for instruction and learning, not in Judaism or in human philosophy, but in true innocence and soundness of life. Scripture supplies everything conducive to the duties of godliness in such abundance that the man
dedicated to God no longer lacks anything to keep him from being complete
and fully equipped for all the tasks of a Christian life.

Chapter 4

I charge you by God the Father and by Jesus Christ who will judge the
living and the dead and whose verdict no human will escape; I charge you
by his coming,[1] when he who allowed himself to be judged here on earth
will come to judge, no longer lowly but sublime and fearsome; I charge you
by the kingdom of him whom no power will[2] be able to resist, that you
preach the word of the gospel bravely without being deterred by adversity
or seduced by prosperity. Be insistent and urgent in season, out of season.
You will think no time unseasonable when there is hope for some advance
in the work of the gospel. Convict the wrongdoer, exhort the faint-hearted,
rebuke anyone who persists in error. Correct with severity the one whom
quiet admonition fails to correct. But do it in such a way that you blend

every kind of gentleness and teaching with the sharpness of your reprimand. Otherwise you will seem to be hateful if all you do is hurl thunder-
ous abuse, or will seem to be impetuous and quarrelsome if all you do is
issue reprimands completely devoid of instruction. A person is more ready
to be obedient when persuaded and is more willing to obey a friendly
adviser than an unfriendly one.

The need to strengthen in advance the hearts and minds of our people
is all the greater because hereafter there will be, as I said, a grave and
dangerous time when some will abandon their evangelical confession and
will not tolerate the true and healthy teaching of Christ, conflicting as it
does with this world's desires. In keeping with their totally corrupted
passions, and diverse ones at that, they will heap up for themselves diverse
and ever new teachers, not to teach godliness but to titillate their ears with
Jewish myths or with petty human inventions, because they will have ears
itching with the foolish lust to hear subtle novelties rather than useful
teachings. They will turn aside to the fables of these men and will shut their
ears to evangelical truth. With all the more reason then you will exert yourself in the opposite direction. Be watchful, enduring everything for the
gospel's sake. Make yourself truly a herald of the gospel. For those who
teach their own views, though they may be called evangelists, certainly are
not. But you, in the ministry which you are performing in my place, be sure
to conduct yourself in such a way that what you teach is completely persuasive and deeply planted in people's minds, so that they are not easily
shaken by those who will endeavour to teach a contrary doctrine.

You must endeavour to do this all the more diligently because I shall
not be assisting your endeavours any longer. Like a victim destined for
Christ,[3] I myself am already beginning to be sacrificed, and the day of my
death is not far distant. I am sacrificed willingly and gladly. My conscience
is clear about my past life and I am likewise certain about my reward. I
have fought an outstanding fight. I have finished the evangelical race. I
have completed my assigned task with utmost fidelity. I have done my part.
As for what is still left for me, I know that it is secure. I know that the
crown owed to innocence is laid up for me and that the Lord, the commander whom I have served, will give it to me. However, he will not give
it in this life, which is the time for fighting, but on that day on which the
just judge[4] will pay to all of us our reward in accordance with the merits
of our life. For this crown of immortality has not been prepared for me
alone but for all who rely on his promises and keep themselves pure and
unsullied as they joyfully await his coming. I am confident that you above
all[5] will be in their number.

Do your best to come to me as soon as possible. Imprisonment prevents me from walking here or there at will to carry out the work of the gospel,[6] and I have been abandoned by almost everyone. There are some things which I am eager to commit to you orally before my departure. Demas has left me; he prefers to enjoy the delights of this world than to share my sufferings in the expectation of an immortal reward.[7] In this spirit he has taken himself off to Thessalonica. Crescens has been called away to Galatia on business. Titus has gone off to Dalmatia. Luke alone stands by me, the inseparable[8] companion of all my fortunes. When you come, bring Mark along as your companion. I need his services, for I myself have sent Tychicus to Ephesus on a special mission. Bring with you when you come the cloak which I left with Carpus at Troas. It will be useful to me in prison during the winter. Also bring the books, not just the rest of the ones which I left there, but especially the ones written on parchment.[9]

Alexander the coppersmith has not only abandoned me in these storms, but has also done me many wrongs. It is not my place to punish him, but the Lord will requite[10] him as he has deserved. You too beware of him for your own good. For he was so far from standing by me that he even strongly opposed our case.

When I had to plead my case the first time before Caesar's courts,[11] no one stood by me. They were all terrified with fear and forsook me. That is only human[12] and understandable; I would not want it to be charged against them. The Lord, however, did not abandon me, bereft as I was of human help, but stood by me and gave me strength so that the heralding of evangelical faith would be completely persuasive and its fame would reach the ears of all nations. He wanted the teachings of the gospel to be spread far and wide, and it was, I think, with this plan that he drove me hither and yon through different lands and had me carried finally even to Rome. With his help, and he is more powerful than any tyrant, I was delivered from the jaws of the most savage lion. I am confident, moreover, that the same Lord will deliver me also in the future from all the evil actions of the ungodly[13] to keep me from turning aside in any respect on any occasion from the sincere purity of the gospel. Even if death is inflicted in this life, he will nevertheless preserve his servant and soldier for his heavenly kingdom. To him be glory for ever and ever, amen.

Greet Priscilla and Aquila, my hosts,[14] and the family of Onesiphorus, which has done so very much for me.[15] Erastus stayed at Corinth, but Trophimus I have left in Miletus because of unsound health. Do your best to convey yourself here before winter cuts off travel. Eubulus sends his greetings as do Pudens and Claudia[16] and all the rest of the brothers. May the Lord Jesus Christ who has always been with me be with your spirit too. Grace be with you all, amen. I have added this wish here in my own handwriting to ensure greater trust in the genuineness of the letter.[17]

The End of the Paraphrase on the Second Epistle
of Paul the Apostle to Timothy

PARAPHRASE ON TITUS

In epistolam Pauli ad Titum paraphrasis

THE ARGUMENT OF
THE EPISTLE TO TITUS
BY ERASMUS OF ROTTERDAM

The Apostle had placed his disciple Titus, whom he treated like a son, in charge of the most noble island of Crete because of Titus' extraordinary talents, and on his own departure from there had consecrated him an archbishop. He is writing to him from the city of Nicopolis, which is on the coast near Actium.[1] His situation is apparently still fairly peaceful[2] since there is no mention of sufferings or persecutions. Paul advises Titus to finish and complete what he himself had begun in Crete, and to appoint bishops, whom he also calls elders, in the individual cities – the island is said to have had a hundred cities.[3] He outlines for him the pattern[4] of the person suitable to be a bishop. Since the false apostles who were imposing their own Judaism upon everyone had also penetrated into Crete, he encourages Titus to reject and refute them stoutly. Next he prescribes the duties of persons and ages just as he does for Timothy and adds that no one was to use the Christian religion as a pretext to resist rulers or public officials in the performance of their official duties though they were unsympathetic to the faith of Christ. On the contrary, Christians must patiently tolerate them in the hope that some day, perhaps, they too, if God wills it, might come to their senses and repent. Lastly, he tells Titus to come to him in Nicopolis, but not until he himself[5] has sent Artemas or Tychicus to Crete so that the Cretans would not think they had been deprived of the comfort of a bishop.

The End of the Argument

THE PARAPHRASE
OF ERASMUS OF ROTTERDAM
ON THE EPISTLE OF PAUL
TO TITUS

Chapter 1

I, Paul, the servant and devout worshipper no longer of the law of Moses as in the past but of God the Father, who am also the emissary of his Son Jesus Christ – The heart of my mission is this, that I invite to faith, not to the observance of the Law or to a reliance on works, those whom God has elected to receive salvation through the gospel. For faith alone opens to all the entrance to eternal salvation from the freely given kindness of Jesus Christ. And furthermore, I invite them not only to faith but also to the recognition of the truth which, among the pagans, has been buried under the fabrications of human philosophy and, among the Jews, has been concealed under shadows and enveloped in figurative types. This truth, I say, is not that which the philosophers of this world proclaim when they discourse about the causes of natural things, but that which shows in the shortest way[1] on what things true godliness is grounded, the godliness whose goal and prize is the eternal life which will follow upon this temporary life on earth. In the midst of the evils of this present life, no matter how severe they may be, people must hope for that eternal life with all the more confidence for two reasons. First, it was not some mortal, who could be deceived and could deceive in turn, who promised them eternal life, but God, who is no more able to lie than he is able not to be God. Secondly, God did not make this promise of eternal life haphazardly or recently. Even before the creation of the world it was the fixed and determined decision of his divine and immutable mind to do what he is now doing. Nothing new has been added to his decision. But what God wanted hitherto to be kept concealed and hidden for secret reasons known only to himself, he now wants to become manifest to the whole world at this very time – the time which eternal wisdom predestined for this work – and he wants it to be shown not to the Jews alone in enigmatic figures like some sort of obscure shadow, but to be revealed through the public preaching of the words of the gospel to all mortals without any distinction of nation or tongue. This is the essence of evangelical doctrine, the preaching of which was not usurped by me but was given to me as a commission, and a commission not from men but from God our Saviour. He not only called me to the duties of apostolic service, but laid upon me such a command that I am not free to refuse what has been ordered.[2] No one, therefore, may take my authority lightly or the authority of him whom I have commissioned as my successor. I, Paul, therefore, being such a person, write this present letter to Titus, my genuine and true-born son, whom I did not produce through my body but through the faith which I infused into him and in which he so resembles me that I seem reborn in him like a father in his son, for he is no supposititious child. My wish for him is that he receive grace and peace[3] from the One from whom all true goods originate, that is from God the Father, and from Jesus Christ, the sole author of our salvation. Such are the riches in which I am eager for my sons to become wealthy.

To turn my words directly to you, Titus – since I knew the character of the island of Crete and had no doubt that it needed a supervisor who is as watchful as he is faithful, for this reason I left you in Crete as my second self when the work of the gospel called me elsewhere. As my replacement there[4] you are to complete what I had started to set in order.[5] Since you cannot by yourself be equal to the supervision of the many cities in which the island abounds,[6] you will appoint individual bishops in each city as I instructed you on my departure from there. But take care not to appoint anyone too hastily to so important a responsibility. The person whom you appoint to so important a position must be thoroughly tested and be someone not only of known and publicly attested probity but must also be completely removed from every suspicion of crime. To help you make your selection with greater assurance, I shall sketch this person for you in a few strokes. If you know someone whose character and wholesome way of life are such that no criminal charge can be plausibly laid against him, if someone is content with a single marriage and has shown no sign of sexual intemperance, if he has children whose upbringing and education are such that not only their confession of Christianity but also the innocence of their lives is testimony that they are truly Christians – that is, that they are not notorious for dissolute living like the common run of young men and are not disobedient to their parents.[7] For he who is to be considered worthy of an episcopate must be so removed from disgraceful actions and from the suspicion of such actions that he understands that he must also guarantee both[8] the reputation and the integrity of his family. As a rule the sins of children are also laid to the account of their parents. Moreover, anything that harms the reputation of the bishop brings the gospel into ill repute.

Therefore, the person who is in some sense acting as God's surrogate and who, like a special steward, has been entrusted with the treasury of evangelical doctrine must be blameless in every respect and far removed from the vices of the common run of office-holders. Why? – because he governs compliant and willing subjects[9] and should have no other aim than the salvation of the flock entrusted to him; because he should be eager to heal and not to crush, to teach and not to compel, to lead and not to drag by the neck; because he should employ persuasion rather than compulsion and should prevail through acts of kindness and gentleness rather than through the power of his office. A person who has these aims must not be stiff-necked,[10] quick-tempered,[11] sharp-tongued.[12] Men are more quickly alienated than cured by such behaviour. A bishop must not be shamelessly greedy for gain, something which, while both foul and ruinous in a holder of public office, will be much more abominable in a bishop. For he whom the disease of greed has taken possession of does nothing without corruption. A bishop by contrast must be generous and ready to spend even his own property on the refreshment of his guests. In addition, it becomes him to be avid for good things and to be a lover of good men[13] more than of money. He must also be sober-minded, righteous in the innocence of his life, pious in the practice of evangelical religion, subject to no inner passions but superior to all the desires by which the ordinary mass of mortals is driven up and down. But above all he must constantly hold fast to the words of the gospel. They equip him to teach the ignorant what is central and at the same time enable him to exhort the faint-hearted with sound doctrine and to confute those who contradict.

I do not offer this advice casually. There are many insubordinate men, empty talkers, deceivers of minds,[14] who pay no attention to the teachings of the gospel but advance in their place some frivolous and useless fables of the Jews to win gain for themselves and a reputation for learning. Creeping into the minds of their hearers under the cover of religion, they entice a handful of the simple-minded into deception through these tales, so that sometimes they do not corrupt just one or two individuals but subvert entire families through these absurd teachings, which are positively alien to the truth of the gospel. Despite this fact they exploit the respect given to Christ and the gospel to chase shamelessly after profit. Therefore, one must stop up their mouths by sharp reprimands. There are some from among the gentiles who are subject to this evil; however, you will find such persons[15] to be mostly those who have made only a partial conversion to Christ from Judaism. They blend the law of Moses with their profession of the gospel and fail to put their faulty Jewish superstitions totally behind them. It is not surprising to find in Crete the kind of people who feed their bellies from vain talk and dangerous arts since many years ago Epimenides, a Cretan himself, predicted this about his fellow Cretans.[16] His prediction runs as follows: 'Cretans are always liars, evil beasts, idle bellies.' So true is this saying that it could be taken for an oracle. Are they not born liars when they are not afraid to obscure the completely clear light of evangelical truth by their own fables? Are they not harmful beasts[17] when they everywhere breathe their poison on the unwary? Are they not idle bellies when they prefer to use their false doctrine to live in leisure and luxury rather than to go hungry and to suffer evils with us in the defence of the gospel?

Therefore, rebuke them sharply so that they may come to their senses, abandon their confidence in the Law, and embrace the pure faith of the gospel. Cease to give ear to such Jewish fables through which they disregard the commands of Christ and impose the petty regulations of men[18] about new moons, sabbath keeping, circumcision, ritual washing, discrimination among foods, clothing, not touching certain objects, the seven-day impurity of a house, and other things similar to these. God gave these commandments in the past to be observed by the Jews for a limited time, partly to keep in check through a multitude of commandments an otherwise rebellious and unruly people and partly to have these practices, like a prelude, foreshadow the truth. But they have no utility now, and if someone continues to observe them in the fashion of the Jews, there is nothing that can more quickly turn him away from evangelical truth. No nation rebels more stubbornly against the gospel than the Jews, who lack the strength to abandon those trifles. 'This food,' they say, 'is impure. Do not eat it. This body is unclean. Do not touch it.'[19] These distinctions should have no place among Christians to whom, being pure, all things are pure, and who consider nothing accursed which God, who is absolutely good, has created for the use of mankind. As nothing is impure to those who are purely Christian, so nothing is pure to the Jews, who are impure in their hearts, including those very things which the Law permits as pure.[20] The Jews do not have faith in him who, after the revelation of the gospel, did not want all these commandments to be observed in their literal, carnal sense but wanted them to be referred to the activities of the soul. Therefore, what can be pure to a people whose minds are stained with disbelief and whose life is contaminated by dissolute living, ambition, greed, and other diseases of this kind? They hold fast to the Law but do not understand the Law. They have their foreskins circumcised, but their minds uncircumcised.[21] They enter with hands and feet washed, but leave their minds and consciences unwashed. They observe the sabbath rest, but meanwhile they have hearts made restless by hatred, anger, ambition, and the other passions. They are afraid of being polluted if they taste pork, and[22] they think they are still

clean when they greedily drink in an obscene story or a piece of slanderous
gossip. They consider themselves defiled if they have touched a dead body,
and in the meantime do not shrink from touching a whore or stolen property. They believe it sinful to use a garment made of linen and wool
together,[23] and they are not displeased with themselves when they have
their hearts clothed with so many crimes. They are shameless, therefore, in
boasting that they alone know God, though they outdo all other mortals[24]
in denying him by their actions. Do they not deny him when the genuine
filth smeared upon their hearts makes them abominable? when their disbelief makes them insubordinate? when they behave worse than all other
mortals in regard to all the duties of true godliness with which we deserve
well of God and acknowledge him?

Chapter 2

Bid them and their fables farewell. Do not let their wickedness deter you
from remembering your duty and from speaking those things which are
worthy of what the gospel truly teaches – such things, that is, as make us
attractive to God by the purity of our feelings and character and show us
to be disciples of Christ. But, you will say, what are those things? You are,
for example, to admonish the older men to be sober, to be vigilant[1] in the
duties of godliness, and to overcome the sluggishness[2] of their years by the
alacrity of their faith; to be dignified and not to indulge in juvenile foolish-
ness in an unbecoming way contrary to the condition of their age;[3] to be
composed and moderate in their habits in order to receive the respect due
them from the youth; to be self-controlled so that they are not peevish and
easily angered as ordinary old men commonly are; to be approved and
blameless not only in the soundness of their faith but also in their performance of the duties of charity and in their endurance of inconvenience,
especially on account of the gospel of Christ.

You will admonish the older women in the same way to use such
dress and deportment as becomes persons[4] who practise their religion and
are dedicated to God; not to tell malicious stories about other people's lives,
a disease that is especially typical of that sex and time of life; not to be
devoted to much wine though that time of life should be allowed a moderate use of wine;[5] to teach the young women decency, not coquetry;[6] and to
train them to be prudent,[7] to cherish their husbands, to love their children,
to be sober-minded, chaste, industrious at home in the management of their
households. For it is a special praise of women that they be submissive and
obedient to their husbands so that their behaviour does not bring into
disrepute the name of God, whose religion they profess. When we see that

the wives even of the pagans behave well in these duties,[8] what are they likely to say if they see that Christian women, who ought properly to excel in every way, are worse in these same duties?

Now what the older women, following your instructions, are teaching the younger women, you will teach the younger men. Exhort them to be sober-minded and to control their feelings so that the heat present in that time of life does not lead them to act impetuously.[9] In order to be more effective and persuasive in these matters, above all[10] make yourself a model of virtuous action and a model in every duty of godliness. No one persuades more easily than he who unfailingly does what he teaches ought to be done. Therefore, you will teach the young men in such a way that you display in the actual course of your teaching an integrity in your life which is uncorrupted by any vice and a gravity which lends support to the authority of the teacher. Govern all your speech and life in such a way that there is nothing in them which might cause scorn.[11] As a result not only will those to whom you give commands be ready to obey you, but also those who were previously opposed to the gospel will be made ashamed of their evil talk, when they see that everything is so pure and wholesome that, though they look and hunt for something to malign, they can find no good grounds for disparaging you.

Exhort servants to be obedient and subject to their masters in all things, so that the profession of their religion does not appear to make them more troublesome and the sins which they commit through human failings are not charged to the gospel. Exhort them, therefore, not to talk back to their masters and refuse their orders, and not to be pilferers like the common run of ordinary servants.[12] As a result those who profess evangelical faith will show themselves sound and loyal in the performance of every duty for their masters, even if the latter do not deserve it, so that they may commend and adorn the doctrine of God our Saviour by their virtuous conduct. Thus more people will be induced to embrace this doctrine if they see that those who profess it are made easier to love and more useful for life's transactions.[13]

To this end the previously unknown kindness and mercy of God our Saviour[14] was brought to light through the gospel, and brought to light not only for the Jews but for all humans alike, not that we might be freed from the burden of the Law to live in accordance with our own whims. We are taught instead that, once the sins of our past life have been forgiven through baptism and we, swearing allegiance to Christ, have renounced once for all impious religion and the worship of images together with all worldly desires, we are to live thereafter in this world in such a way that we clearly appear to have been truly reborn as different persons. Furthermore, we, who were formerly enslaved to ungodliness, wrongdoing, and the manifold desires which used to entice us into shameful actions, are henceforth to live so temperately that no desire for any human possession can arouse us. We are to live so righteously that we do no harm to anyone but do as much good as we possibly can to everyone. Through the sincerity of our religious commitment and the purity of our lives we are to give now to God the worship which we used to give to demons.

If in the meantime we suffer from poverty, from lack of clothing, from public discredit, abuse, imprisonment, torture, and other such evils, we are not to think that our godliness is fruitless and therefore start to chase after the petty rewards of this world, which are neither important nor lasting. We are to look instead for that surpassing reward of immortality, which will come to us when, at the end of this age[15] in which the members of Christ are still being trained through suffering and ignominy, God the Father will crush all evil and will reveal his glory and greatness before his worshippers. He will then appear no longer lowly but glorious and terrifying to the ungodly.[16] Conspicuous with the same glory, our Lord and Saviour Jesus Christ will appear together with the Father and will impart to his members the same glory of immortality with which he himself shines forth.[17] Let no one give up faith in his promises, for he willingly and knowingly surrendered himself to death and gave himself wholly for us so that, while free himself from every sin, he might redeem us by the price of his blood from the tyranny of the devil to whom our sins made us subject, and might – once the stains of our past life had been washed away – prepare for himself a new and special people which, following his own example, would despise the evils of this world, would trample underfoot the enticements and rewards of this life, and through their good works would strive for the inheritance of immortality, which he promises to all who keep their commitment to the gospel pure and unsullied.[18]

Chapter 3

These are the things, my dear Titus, which you are to say.[1] They are far different from those Jewish fables. Exhort people to them. Refute with utmost authority any who turn away from them so that sharp and stern censure may hold in check those whom teaching does not convince and persuasive exhortation does not move. There are some faults that only sternness can heal. Display the gravity and authority proper to a bishop. Conduct yourself in such a way that no one can have any reason to despise you.[2] Authority is to be employed as often as the situation demands, but there is no room ever for pride and arrogance.

I described above how I expected servants to behave towards their masters even if they are pagans.[3] I would now like you to admonish all Christians to behave in the same way towards those who hold the position of prince or who occupy some other magistracy even though they are unsympathetic to the Christian calling. Every effort must be made to prevent anyone from being able to find in our behaviour an excuse to reject the gospel. For this is precisely what would happen if those who hold public responsibilities should think that we are more uncontrollable and seditious than other people and less law-abiding on account of our religious commitment. They will blame the gospel for this behaviour and will be even further estranged from professing it. Therefore, admonish those who have confessed Christ to remember[4] that they are not on that account freed from the laws of the state and the authority of princes and magistrates. On the contrary, to be law-abiding and obedient subjects and to be prompt and ready for every good work are the appropriate behaviour of Christians, so much so that they should visibly pursue what is right of their own accord and not because they are compelled by any fear of punishment. If those men[5] are ruling rightly, it is wrong, rather it is the worst kind of example, not to obey the power of government. But if their rule is too harsh, if they press too unmercifully, if their demands are too immoderate, a gentle and tolerant response suits none more than the disciples of Christ. Every order which does not in any way diminish our godliness has to be obeyed. They take away our wealth; the treasury[6] of godliness increases. They drive us into exile; Christ is everywhere. But someone might say, 'They're impious, idol-worshippers, stained by their openly heinous actions, enemies of our religion!' So they are, to their own peril. It is not our part to condemn, but, if possible, to correct them. It is better to correct them by obedience and mildness, by the example of a good life than by rebellion or insults. We can leave them to their own judge; for our part let us keep in mind what is worthy of us. Christ interceded even[7] for those who reviled him, so far was he from hurling abuse back at them. How is it seemly, then, for his disciples to be insulting towards someone, to be in love with disputes, and not rather, following the example of him whom they profess, to show themselves courteous and to behave with complete mildness towards everyone, not just towards the good and deserving? Towards the good because they deserve it; towards the wicked so that they may change their attitude and repent. They should not, when understandably annoyed, have their worst opinions about Christianity confirmed. Christian love endures all things, hopes for all things.[8] They deserve our compassion rather than our hatred.

We shall have more reason to do this if we recall that we were at one time just as they are now. We should not shun them because they are ungodly, but should strive to make them cease to be what they are and to begin to be like us. What called us away from our blindness? Was it not God's freely given mercy? The same mercy can transform them too whenever it so wills. Although we who came to the gospel from Judaism did not worship idols, we were nevertheless once subject to faults just as serious. We were foolish, disobedient, deceived wanderers, enslaved to various desires and pleasures, full of envy, full of malice, vying with one another in feuds and hatreds. We were, I say, subject to such great evils even under the law of Moses. But the fact that we are now sober-minded and sane instead of foolish and senseless, mild and manageable instead of rebellious, knowers of the truth instead of lost wanderers, willing cultivators of righteousness instead of slaves to desires and pleasures, honest and kind instead of malicious, charitable instead of envious, wishing well even to those who wish us ill instead of being haters – this fact we do not owe to the Law or to our own merits but to the gratuitous goodness of God. Through his goodness we desire that everyone, if at all possible, rejoice with us in our common salvation and that the truth of the gospel begin to shine on all as it has shone on us. For in the past we dwelt blindly in darkness just like them. But when it had become clear through the light of the gospel just how immense the goodness of God was and how much love God the Father,[9] who is the cause of our salvation, had for all persons, then and only then was the dark mist of our earlier life driven away and we obtained true salvation. This salvation came from God's freely given mercy and not from our observance of the Law which, though it possesses a kind of righteousness, is incapable of producing salvation. For we have been reborn through the holy washing and have been grafted into Christ his Son.[10] Made new through the Spirit of the Son, we have ceased to be carnal and have begun to be spiritual.

Therefore, whatever we are, we owe totally to God, who poured out abundantly on us his Spirit, which the Law could not give, though we had done nothing to deserve it; moreover, he poured it out upon us through Jesus Christ our Saviour, through whom he was pleased to bestow all things upon us. He did this so that, cleansed from our old sins through his kindness, we may strive through good works to be qualified to receive the inheritance of immortal life,[11] the hope of which is made certain for us by the teachings of the gospel. We, such as we were, were once objects of mercy but, freed from our sins only by the mercy of God, we now hope for the crown of eternal life with Christ. Therefore, we must show mercy in turn to others and must strive in every way to have God show mercy to them as well.

A Christian bishop must inculcate these teachings in place of Jewish myths. For they are certain and beyond doubt. Nothing remains for us to do except to respond to the kindness of God by the way we live hereafter. Otherwise our profession of the gospel will be of no use to us. Therefore, I want you to assert and insist upon these things also – they are the heart of the matter – so that all, who have believed once for all that God has redeemed them from sin through his freely given mercy and that he will give the crown of immortality to those who strive with all their might to imitate Jesus Christ in godliness of life, will live out their lives in such a way that they appear not unworthy of their profession and of these great promises. They will show themselves truly Christian, not if they curse or inveigh against pagans or Jews, but if they do good to everyone, and if they are eager to help everyone from their own feelings of compassion. This conduct will adorn and commend their evangelical profession not only as something virtuous in itself but also as[12] a useful way to draw others to Christ and to aid persons hard-pressed by some calamity. To benefit everyone is the essence of Christian conduct. Even wild animals are subdued and made gentle by kindnesses.[13]

You will discourse about these matters, therefore, not as though you were full of doubts like those who, by calling everything into question, seem to have no convictions of their own. Instead let your speech and your expression reveal the greatness of your faith and constancy so that everyone understands that you are yourself absolutely persuaded of what you are persuading others. The fruit of godliness comes from this behaviour. Reject as useless and superfluous for evangelical godliness the foolish and ignorant questions, intricate genealogies, and contentious discourses or, more accurately, battles[14] about the law of Moses which some Judaizers are stirring up for their own glory and gain. How is it any hindrance to godliness if I do not happen to know why Moses' tomb is nowhere to be found or whether or not this is, as the Jews say, to keep magicians from calling him up from the dead? how many years Methusalah lived? how old Solomon was when he became the father of Rehoboam? why Moses forbade the eating of pork?[15] Such queries[16] are only fruitless speculations. What good does it do to investigate why the Jews think a weasel's blood must be expiated with so much care and other inquiries even more foolish than this?[17] What is the point in making the person who is speeding towards the reward of godliness waste time on the explanation of such questions? They should be eradicated rather than explicated. Those who proclaim them as something of extraordinary interest should be rebuked rather than vanquished through disputation. If they are simply going astray, they will, once they are admonished, come to their senses. But if they are sinning with deliberate wickedness for glory or gain or some other disgraceful reason, they will be ready to defend even those things which they know are false. When you have rebuked[18] them once or twice, avoid them as divisive and incurable, lest, when challenged, they do more harm than they do when they are left alone. This will prevent the occurrence of the opposite danger, that those who cannot be cured may draw their admonisher into error.[19] What is the point of applying the medicine of reproof again and again if there is no hope for a cure? Ordinary human error is cured by one or two admonitions. Perversity is incurable and only aggravated by the remedies. Accordingly, leave to his disease the person who, despite one or two rebukes, still continues unchanged; he is hopeless and utterly perverted. You do not have to go to the additional trouble of condemning him since he has been condemned by his own judgment of himself. If he perishes, he perishes by his own fault. For he does not have any pretext to offer such as, 'I was unwittingly in error. No one warned me.' What would you do for a sick person who refuses his medicine? Perhaps if spurned and left to himself he will come to his senses. But if not, at least he will not be breathing the contagion of his sickness on so many people.

I have reasons for wanting to have you with me for a short time. But I should not want this to be done at the expense of the churches in Crete, which have only recently begun to embrace Christianity and therefore have a greater need for a vigilant supervisor to build upon such foundations as have so far been laid.[20] Arrange to meet me then at Nicopolis, but not before I have sent Artemas or Tychicus there to hold my office in your place, so that your departure does not leave Crete abandoned and fatherless. Have no fear that you will come here in vain only to discover that I have gone off somewhere else. I have decided to spend the coming winter in Nicopolis. This is the town in Thrace.[21]

Zenas was once a professor of the law of Moses but is now an outstanding herald of the gospel.[22] Apollos is a man distinguished in evangelical doctrine.[23] Whenever they wish to leave Crete, send them on their way with every care and courtesy. Make sure that they do not lack anything they may need for their departure. If it is an act of courtesy for pagans to escort a well-deserving guest for a part of his way as a mark of honour and to supply him on his departure with travel money and provisions,[24] I think it only right that our people who profess Christ likewise learn to employ such courtesies, but only[25] in order to show their gratitude to those who have benefited them. There is no reason to make them rich from our generosity but only to supply them with the necessities of life whenever there is a need. For Christians to be unproductive and unfruitful towards those from whom they have experienced so much kindness is preposterous when people who are strangers to Christ nevertheless know from nature's teaching how to repay thanks to those who have helped them with a kind act.

All who are here with me send their greetings and prayers for your welfare. You in turn greet in my name all who love us there, not with worldly affection but with the evangelical love which the profession of our common faith obtains.[26] May God's freely given kindness always be present with all of you. Amen.

The End

PARAPHRASE ON PHILEMON

In epistolam Pauli ad Philemonem paraphrasis

THE ARGUMENT OF THE EPISTLE
OF PAUL TO PHILEMON
BY ERASMUS OF ROTTERDAM

According to the Greek tradition[1] this Philemon was a Phrygian by nationality. The unruly and slavish character of this nation is intimated by the
Greek proverb, 'A Phrygian is corrected by blows.'[2] Nevertheless, Paul
counted Philemon among his closest friends because of his godliness and
his services to the saints. Philemon's slave, Onesimus, had stolen something
– a common act on the part of slaves – and had run away to Rome.[3] After
hearing Paul, who was under arrest there at the time, he accepted the
teachings of the gospel and was Paul's servant in prison. Paul, however,
sends him back to his master to keep Philemon from being deeply distressed over the fact that his slave had run away. With amazing zeal and
equally amazing tact Paul reconciles the master to his slave, who was a
runaway and a thief to boot, and offers himself as the guarantor who will
pay for anything which the slave may have pilfered in the course of running away. He writes from prison, moreover,[4] a letter to be carried by the
aforesaid Onesimus, whom he also calls his son.[5]

THE PARAPHRASE OF
ERASMUS OF ROTTERDAM
ON THE EPISTLE OF PAUL
TO PHILEMON

Paul, previously an apostle and servant of Jesus Christ and now even a prisoner for his sake – why should I not glory in being the prisoner of the one on account of whose gospel I am wearing these chains, not as the penalty of a criminal[1] but as the sign[2] of a free and vigorous herald? – and Timothy, a brother together with me in the partnership of evangelical preaching, to Philemon, a brother uniquely worthy of love in the confession of our common faith and not only a brother but also because of his many, many[3] services a sharer with me and a partner in the service of the gospel,[4] and to his wife[5] Appia,[6] a sister most worthy of my love because of our kinship in faith, and to Archippus our fellow soldier, and to the rest of the congregation[7] which is in Philemon's house: Grace to you and peace from God our common Father and from his Son, our Lord, Jesus Christ.

In my prayers, which I regularly offer to God each day, I always give him thanks in your name. For I give God the credit for what I hear voiced abroad by everyone about the sincerity of your faith and the truly evangelical love which you possess for the Lord Jesus, and not only for him but also for all the saints, that is, for his members. He wants any service done for them to be considered as done for himself. I also pray that he will increase his beneficence towards you and that the faith which you have and which is already active in you, will grow ever stronger each day and impel you to aid more and more people ever more bountifully until there is no act of Christian love for which you are not both known and applauded.[8] What you have done so far gives us the confidence to venture to promise ourselves even more abundant benefits from you. For though I think that Christians possess all things in common,[9] I have been filled through and through with an extraordinary pleasure and have taken exceptional comfort in my present sufferings from that love of yours, so bent as it is on doing good to all. Because of it, you have refreshed the hearts of the saints when they suffered from the evils of this world, oh my brother. For by those acts you show yourself to be truly a brother.

Taking heart, therefore, from these numerous instances in which you show that you are a true worshipper of Christ, I am quite confident that if I were only to give the order as a father might to a son or an apostle to a disciple, I would obtain from you what I wish, especially in a matter intrinsically just and in accord with the evangelical doctrine you profess. This doctrine commands that we who have ourselves experienced the Lord's mercy in the forgiveness of a debt are to forgive others too in turn.[10] Yet I prefer that love rather than my authority obtain this request from you and I want to ask as a brother does a brother rather than to order it as a teacher does a pupil. You will not spurn an intercessor like me.[11] How could you refuse the one who makes this request? Will you refuse Paul – when I say Paul I do not imply something paltry to you?[12] Secondly, will you refuse one who is old? Age usually has some allowance made for it. But none of this is new to you. Will you refuse one who is now also a prisoner? In intercessions the very distress of the one who makes the appeal has some weight. Lastly, will you refuse one who is a prisoner for Jesus Christ. Those who profess the doctrine of Christ ought to oblige one who is a prisoner for Christ. You could not refuse one who makes his appeal on so many grounds, even if he[13] should be interceding with you on behalf of some ordinary person. As it is, I am interceding for my son, whom I cherish the more tenderly because I begot him not for Moses, but for Christ, not for the world, but for the gospel, and I begot him while in chains on the verge of my departure from this world. Parents commonly have a deeper love for the children born to them in their extreme old age.

It is Onesimus whom I mean. In the past when he filched his master's property and ran away, he did little to match his name, that is, he was unprofitable and useless,[14] but he has now been changed into the opposite. Consequently, he will be not only useful to you in the future, but he has been useful to me too in prison by his obedient service. Therefore, I am sending him back to you transformed into another person. But if you are the man I believe you to be, and if the recommendation of Paul in old age and in chains has any weight with you, you will receive Onesimus no longer as a runaway slave but as my uniquely dear son[15] and the dearest object of my affections. I am sending him back reluctantly. I should have preferred to keep him with me, if for no other reason than that he might represent you while I am in these chains. I have no doubt that, since your love of the gospel leads you to show so much love towards everyone else, you would, if you were here, expend your charity on me too, in these chains in which I have been shackled because of the gospel. But now one has been found through whom you, though absent, might minister to me. I was unwilling to do this, however, without having asked you first. For, if

I had relied on my authority, as it were, and had usurped this service on my own, even though you would have excused this act of mine, your goodness would nevertheless receive that much less praise because it would appear to have been the result of compulsion. But as it is, I am sending him back so that I may leave you free either to keep him with you or to send him back to me. If you send him back, your act of charity will receive all the more praise because it was not extorted but was free and voluntary.

Put out of your mind the fact that he has run away. He has paid for this mistake by his charity; he has washed it away by his baptism; he has obliterated it by his tears.[16] How do you know whether the mind of God may not have arranged to have it done in this way so that Onesimus' mistake would turn into good both for him and for us?[17] God's judgments are hidden. Perhaps Onesimus was torn away from you for a little while for this purpose, that in place of a temporary slave (slavery after all lasts no longer than life itself) you might receive him back for ever. For whatever the gospel begets is for ever.[18] Moreover, you will be receiving no longer a slave but a very dear brother in place of a slave. At least to me the apostle he is a brother and a very dear brother because of the shared faith which makes us equal in Christ, because of the shared inheritance to which we are equally called, because of the Father we share and the Redeemer we share, in all of which there is no difference between owner and slave, master and disciple.[19] But if for these reasons he is very dear to me with whom he has nothing in common except the kinship of the Spirit, how much the more should he be very dear to you with whom, in addition to the bonds of the Spirit, he has ties based on the flesh as well. You would love a stranger if you were to see that he had become such a person as Onesimus is. Now you will have a greater love for the very reason that a member of your own household has turned into such a person.

If you think me worthy to be counted as a partner in the service of the gospel, you must receive as my second self him whom I take to my heart as my dearest son, as a brother most dear to me, as a sharer of my imprisonment and of the gospel. You must either reject us both or take us both together into your arms. It is not fitting to remember after his baptism what kind of person he was before. Think of him as a new man reborn for you. But if you are distressed by the loss of some piece of property which you want restored before you will consider a pardon, take me as surety for him.[20] Make your demand of me if he has either done any injury or owes anything. I hereby make an agreement with you through this handwritten contract. Look! You have a letter in my own handwriting. If I seem to be a reliable surety, let Onesimus off. Make me liable. I myself shall repay in his place whatever is owed. I should obtain this request, I think, even if I were dealing with a stranger. But in fact I have no wish to remember what I could demand from you in my own right. I shall not mention here that since you became a Christian through my teaching, you owe me not only your goods but even your very self. It should seem to you all the less unjust even if I were to demand that I be forgiven the amount of the damages, whatever it is, that Onesimus owes. But I do not make this demand if you will not remit the debt willingly and freely, not so much to free me from my pledge as to reveal your own love. Oh yes, my brother, Onesimus takes his name from a word which means to enjoy the use of something.[21] Just as he is dear to my heart and I am eager for him to be sincerely acceptable to you, so I hope to have the chance to enjoy you not in the ordinary way a friend is enjoyable to a friend, but in the way an apostle takes pleasure in a disciple whose life is an expression of Christ's teachings.[22] You see how dear Onesimus is to me, and rightly dear on his own account. Refresh my heart by taking him to yourself.

I am not going on at such length in this matter because I lack confidence in your love; I am doing it out of my overflowing affection for my son. Your past services make your obedience so apparent to me that I do not doubt that you will do even more in this matter than I am asking of you. In the meantime welcome Onesimus kindly as a guarantee of me; at the same time prepare a guest room for me in the expectation of my own arrival a little later. For I hope that God, prevailed upon by your prayers, will restore me someday to you. At that time I shall thank you in person for having received Onesimus with forgiveness.

Epaphras, your fellow countryman and my companion in captivity and chains because of his love for Jesus Christ, sends greetings to you. So do my colleagues, Mark, Aristarchus, Demas, and Luke. Think of them all as joining me in my plea for Onesimus.[23] May the grace of our Lord Jesus Christ be ever present to your spirit. Amen.

The End

PARAPHRASE ON FIRST PETER

Paraphrasis in epistolam Apostoli Petri priorem

DEDICATORY LETTER

TO THE MOST REVEREND FATHER IN CHRIST THOMAS,
CARDINAL PRIEST OF ST CECILIA, LORD ARCHBISHOP OF YORK,
PRIMATE OF ENGLAND, AND LORD HIGH CHANCELLOR OF THE
WHOLE REALM, FROM ERASMUS OF ROTTERDAM, GREETING[1]

Often had I looked about me for some offspring of my labours which might
answer to your eminent position, that eminence which hitherto has discouraged me from daring to dedicate to you any of my works;[2] and after all, I
find I have been foolish on two counts. In the first place, how could there
be anything in me, whether in expression or invention, which, even if I
exerted myself to the utmost, could achieve the standard of your greatness,
whether one considers your exalted station, your intellectual gifts which are
so worthy of that station, or the kindness with which your generosity daily
lays under obligation not so much me as our whole programme of studies
in humane letters and in true theology?[3] Secondly, are you the man to judge
the worth of a book by the size of the volume rather than its utility? And
so although, before I had finished the labour of my paraphrases designed
to expound the Pauline Epistles (those at least which are certainly genuine),[4]
I soon had with my already depleted strength to take up arms against my
detractors,[5] yet none the less with levies hastily raised I drove them off, and
at once with the same forces attacked the two Epistles of the apostle Peter
and one of Jude. For at the same time I thought to myself that what is
offered to divine beings or to very great men needs to be not so much
adequate as apt, just as in ancient times it would have seemed absurd for
a man to offer a hundred oxen to the Muses or a chaplet of ivy to the god
of war. And so it seemed to me appropriate first of all that Peter, who was
himself the incomparable head of the Christian religion, should go to such
an outstanding religious leader so that the true and genuine philosophy of
the gospel, which was born and first promoted under his leadership, should
under your pious care, which makes itself felt more day by day, be restored
after its partial collapse.[6] So true is it that human affairs tend always
towards the worse unless we make great efforts in the opposite direction.

And if the difficulty of the work is allowed in some sort to recommend
it, this was a much harder task than the size of the volume suggests. This
is due partly to Peter's style, which is much more complex than Paul's, and

partly to the absence of ancient commentaries which might help us in these Epistles. For the notes supplied nowadays by what they call the *Glossa ordinaria*[7] are taken word for word from the commentary of your country-man Bede,[8] a man who lacked neither learning nor industry by the standards of his time; and this was done with remarkable skill. Part of the notes were withdrawn to the open area of the margins, part were cut down to fit the narrow space between the lines of the Epistle. The attribution to Bede was almost entirely removed, I know not why.[9]

Everywhere there are a number of places which need a careful and attentive reader: in the first Epistle, for instance, the passage about Christ and how he preached in the spirit to the spirits in prison, who had once been unbelievers, and again on the preaching of the gospel even to the dead;[10] in the second, on the demons being reserved unto judgment, on the railing accusation which the angels do not bring against themselves (though I have explained this passage, which was obscured by Bede,[11] differently); on the earth consisting of water and through water, on the heavens and the elements being reserved for destruction by fire[12] – all passages in which some men have found an occasion of error; in the Epistle of Jude, the passage about the condemnation of blasphemy,[13] thought to be taken from the apocryphal book of Enoch, from which a prophecy is quoted a little further on, although we are not told that Enoch wrote anything.[14] This Epistle I have added for this reason, that it shows surprising agreement with the Second Epistle of Peter not only in style and ideas but even in wording, as though it were explaining some passages in that Epistle, as for instance that about the judgment of blasphemy.[15]

On the first Epistle of Peter no doubts have ever been raised; but there are doubts about the second, although it mentions the Lord's transfiguration,[16] at which not more than three disciples were present as witnesses.[17] Hence, if it is not Peter's, it must be by someone who wished to be taken for Peter. The Epistle of Jude was slower in reaching authority, since it adduces evidence from what is called the Book of Enoch, in which there are said to be things out of step with Catholic doctrine.[18] But nothing forbids the use of evidence from apocryphal writings in a suitable place, just as Paul cites a testimony from Epimenides.[19] In any case, since in the first of the two epistles Peter records that he has written by the hand of Sylvanus,[20] and in the second openly records that it is the second, saying, 'This second epistle, beloved, I now write unto you' [2 Pet 3:1], I do not see how the facts can be explained unless either the second epistle is not Peter's or Sylvanus wrote it on Peter's instructions. If it was written by Peter himself, he would seem to have written three, of which the first has perished. Of the time and place of writing nothing is certainly known, though people suppose that the first was written in Rome (which in the conclusion he called Babylon) in the reign of the emperor Claudius.[21]

But my preface must not be longer than the book itself. It is my great desire that this labour of mine, if it in any way deserves it, may be commended by the free and open approval of your Eminence to all who wish to learn. The reason is not that I myself am in pursuit of anything from your Highness – I have never had the right spirit, nor am I now of a suitable age, for ambition – but because the support and approval of those in high estate wonderfully fires and encourages those who are learning. Apart from many accomplished scholars, there are now growing up in your native England, under your generous auspices,[22] many young men of the highest promise, who will one day do greater things and with happier results, if their zeal is fanned by the breeze of your encouragement. Would that henceforward our studies might make this their goal – to attract the minds of men to the best subjects by the charms of a moderate expenditure of time and effort, instead of pretending that all is difficult and lengthy, and thus striving to make ourselves look wonderfully learned, while our noblest minds are discouraged from pursuing the noblest subjects. Many others will achieve this more successfully, I do not doubt, but with more devotion than I have shown there will not be very many. And if your Eminence will continue, as you have begun, to support these most religious endeavours, you will both win God's full approval and leave a most honourable record to posterity. May Christ the Almighty long, long preserve you in health and wealth.

THE ARGUMENT OF
THE FIRST EPISTLE OF PETER
BY ERASMUS OF ROTTERDAM

Peter, like James, writes to Jews who were living dispersed throughout the lands of the gentiles. His letter is truly worthy of the Prince of the Apostles, being full of apostolic authority and majesty. The words are few but packed with meaning. Referring to their hope in the rewards, he urges them to accept patiently the evils which they were enduring as a result of the hatred felt for the gospel. He advises them in addition that because they have been freely called to such a lofty position in accordance with the oracles of the prophets, they should make their lives worthy of their confession. For a Christian life, he says, is not grounded merely in baptism and in the name 'Christian,' but in moral innocence. Besides, the fact that they are being afflicted will not eventuate in the glory of Christ if they appear only to be paying a penalty for their crimes. He goes on to admonish them not to use their Christian beliefs as grounds for refusing to obey the civil authorities on the ground that they are pagans. If the authorities are provoked in this way, they will not be converted and will treat Christians even more cruelly. He likewise admonishes servants not to refuse the service due to their masters because they are pagans; it is the part of Christian goodness to endure everything. Likewise Christian women are not to spurn their pagan husbands but are to strive through their behaviour to arouse them to better things. He advises husbands to respect their wives and to refrain on occasion from sexual intercourse in order to have more time free for prayer. Then he challenges his readers to follow the example of Christ and accept evils patiently and not try to redress wrong with wrong but rather to strive to overcome evildoers through their gentleness and acts of kindness. These are the topics he discusses in the first three chapters and in the beginning of the fourth. After these matters he encourages his readers to pursue their new form of life while discouraging them from the vices of the gentiles. He invites them to sobriety, to vigilance, to constant prayer, above all to mutual love, to hospitality, to the exchange of charitable acts, and once more to the endurance of the persecutions brought on them because of Christ's name.

Next he instructs the bishops and the people subject to them.[1]

At the end he testifies that he has also written a second letter to the same people through Sylvanus. But it is now lost.[2] The present letter appears to have been written from Babylon, for Peter sends them greetings in the name of the church there – assuming that someone[3] does not wish to accept this name as a fiction for Rome.

The End

THE PARAPHRASE ON
THE FIRST EPISTLE OF PETER THE APOSTLE
BY ERASMUS OF ROTTERDAM

Chapter 1

Peter, once the disciple and companion, now the emissary and apostle of
Jesus Christ, to all who dwell scattered here and there throughout the
regions of Asia Minor, some in Pontus, others in Galatia, some in Cap-
padocia and in that part of Asia Minor which belongs to the Ephesians and
has a special claim to the name Asia,[1] others again in Bithynia. Some of you
the storms of war drove hither and yon to that region in the distant past;[2]
others, though innocent, the cruelty of men to whom the name of Christ
was hateful expelled in our time from your ancestral homes and therefore
you now live homeless among foreign peoples as though you were exiles.
The fears of other men have barred you from your native soil, but you are
not for that reason exiled and cut off or disinherited from the gift of the
gospel which God, the ruler of all, though he gave it to the land and nation
of the Jews first,[3] wants to be shared by every person whom he himself has
chosen. For just as those who spurn the teachings of Jesus Christ gain
nothing from being born and living in Jerusalem, so Christians will not be
accused of sin because they dwell among the uncircumcised and unholy
gentiles provided that they cling to evangelical grace in place of the law of
Moses. It is not nationality or place of residence or even the observance of
the law of Moses – over which[4] the commonalty of Jews swells with pride
– that effects true salvation, but the free gift of divine election. He is truly
a Jew who, regardless of the soil he inhabits, regardless of the nation in
which he was born, acknowledges Jesus Christ as the author of true salvation.[5] Jesus did not die for one nation but for the whole world. Moreover,
we do not owe our acknowledgment of Jesus to meritorious observance of
the Law but to the spontaneous goodness of God. He chooses[6] from every
nation and calls to the bounty of the gospel whomever he has decided to
admit. For it was no random or recent thought of his to save the entire race
of mortals in this way, nor is he compelled[7] by our good deeds to repay

salvation to us as a reward for our merits. But God the Father in his eternal wisdom determined to open the haven of salvation not just to the Jews but to all nations, and he did not open it through circumcision or the observance of the sabbath or discrimination among foods or the other ceremonies of the law of Moses which pertain to the body and were given for a limited time, like mere shadows of spiritual realities, but he did it through the true sanctification of the Spirit which the spiritual law of the gospel imparts to us. We are truly cleansed by this law from all our sins, not because we have observed the commands of the Old Law but because we have promptly trusted the promises of the gospel without reservation. We are not cleansed by being sprinkled with the blood of a calf as the rite has been customarily carried out up to now in accordance with the law of Moses,[8] but by the sprinkling of the precious blood of Jesus Christ, a victim without stain and most pleasing to God. His death, undeserved as it was, removes once for all from us all the sins of the old life and restores us through baptism to a new life as people reborn into him.[9]

Since baptism has removed us from this world and placed us in a heavenly city, I shall not pray for the goods whose acquisition and accumulation makes the worshippers of this world think they are happy, but rather for those goods which make us worthy of Christ, our heavenly prince, once we are cleansed of our earthly contagions. These goods are grace, so that without faith in your own merits, without faith even in the ceremonies of the Law you expect true salvation from the spontaneous bounty[10] of God alone and from faith in the gospel; and secondly, peace, so that freely reconciled to God through the blood of Christ you may have concord both among yourselves and with everyone else, not just doing no wrong to anyone but even forgiving the wrongs done by others and returning good for evil. God has given you your share of these goods free of charge. You must accordingly strive through godly endeavours to grow ever richer from the interest earned[11] on good works, not only by persevering in what you have begun but also by progressively improving yourselves day by day until that day comes on which the reward of immortality will be presented. We can claim no credit for this for ourselves; it is from the gospel of Christ that you have absorbed the sure hope of this reward.

The praise for a benefit so immense as this must be given to the kindness of him who is the source through Christ of everything that makes us truly blessed. It is not Moses, but God himself and the Father of our Lord Jesus Christ who has begotten us again to innocence when we were too unhappily born – that is, born to sin, born to death. He has begotten us to immortal life, moved by no merits on our part but spontaneously stirred by his own mercy, because he is totally merciful. He did not do this with the aid of the law of Moses but at the cost of his own Son, Jesus Christ. God wanted him to undergo death so that he might free us, who were otherwise lost, from the tyranny of sin and death. He then called him back from death to life so that we, who are now dead to worldly desires and by following the example of Christ are, so to speak, practising resurrection through our moral innocence, may have for the time being a sure and lively[12] hope that we too shall someday be removed from our present evils and together with Christ shall possess that eternal inheritance. Just as he,[13] our head, attained it, so shall all of us obtain it who have been made members of Christ, and through imitation of him deserve to be called his brothers, and sons of the same father. We are confident that just as we suffer now in common with him, so shall we also receive the reward in common with him. As long as we were sons of the sinner Adam, an unhappy inheritance awaited us.[14] Now that we have become sons of God, we are hastening towards a heavenly inheritance. It is fitting that as children of heaven we look to heavenly things, that as children of God we pursue only divine things.

Soldiers who serve the world seek for transitory rewards and perishable wages. There awaits us after these temporary afflictions that felicitous inheritance whose nature is such that it can neither be corrupted by death nor contaminated by weariness and annoyance[15] nor fade with age and decay. There is no reason for us to fear that someone may defraud us of so rich an inheritance as this; we have a guarantor who is absolutely sure. It is safe for us in his care and is being kept in heaven, but in such a way that in the meantime a sure hope and, as it were, a sort of guaranty are in humanity's possession here on earth; not in every person's possession but in your possession and in that of people like you to whom the Spirit of Christ has been given as a pledge of future payment.[16] You may in the meantime be pounded from all sides by the shifting storm-winds of evil to which human weakness, if left to itself, is completely unequal, but you are being saved by God's help, who is all-powerful. You are not saved by your own merits but by the faith and trust which do not let you doubt that even if God allows you to be overwhelmed for the time being, he will nevertheless bring you forth safe and sound in the last time. From that time onward there will no longer be this present confusion in human affairs, but the wicked, delivered to their own punishment, will be unable to harm anyone, and the good, safe from every evil assault, will enjoy eternal tranquillity. At present the rewards are hidden and those who are really better are commonly judged to be worse off. Those who are completely safe are thought to be perishing and those who are completely lost are thought to be flourishing. The time for the exercise of godliness is in the here and now; the reward has its own time set for it and one ought not to anticipate it beforehand. Let it be enough for us for now that our eternal happiness is in safekeeping. No one, whether human or demon, can steal it away provided that the faith through which we disregard the affairs of mortal men and come to depend wholly upon heaven does not fail us. Let those rebels against God who put their trust in the world's help be savage for now, let them trample on us for now like people[17] vanquished and bereft of help. But when that day comes, the normal course of events will be reversed. They will be the ones to suffer and you will be the victors and will exult.[18] No, you should be exulting right now because of your undoubted expectation of so much happiness. For you ought not to think it a great or grievous matter if you arrive at everlasting and imperishable bliss through short-lived sufferings and troubles which will soon be over. Perhaps there will someday be an end even of these persecutions. But every time they do break out, they must be borne for the glory of God with a heart made courageous and unbroken because of its hope for the future life.

In this way the wisdom of God, which is ever looking out for your best interests, permits the sincerity and constancy of your faith to be tested by a variety of evil attacks. If gold – a perishable substance and one destined by its very nature to perish – is not only tested with a touchstone but is also melted in the furnace and then weighed so that the more exquisitely it has been refined the more valuable it then is, how much more does God want your faith to be proved by various trials! So much honour is due to faith that when it has emerged gleaming brightly from the fires of these evils and sufferings, far more pure and bright than the most purified gold, it is now precious in God's sight. In the end everything will be completely reversed – what seemed in this world destined for disgrace will become an object of praise, what seemed destined for ignominy will be turned into glory, what seemed destined for your dishonour will be turned into an accumulation of honour on that day on which Jesus Christ, whose power now acts in you in hidden ways, will openly reveal himself to all as he rewards all according to their merits.[19] What will be more glorious than that praise from the lips of Christ when you hear the words, 'Come, oh blessed of my Father' [Matt 25:34]? What will be more honourable than to be received by God the Father into a share of the heavenly kingdom together with the Son? But while this glory will belong to all the godly in common, it will be more abundant for those who suffered more greatly on earth for Christ.

If these rewards were evident to all at the present time, a strong faith would not be a source of admiration. As it is, a special source of praise for the good lies precisely in this, that though you have never seen Christ with the eyes of your body, you nevertheless love him whom you see only with the eyes of faith, and that though the pressure of violent pain is felt unmistakably and directly while the rewards which belong to the future are not yet in sight, you nevertheless trust completely in his promises and endure these evils in no different spirit than if the glory prepared for you were present right before your eyes. Not only do you endure this pain bravely, but even in the midst of suffering you rejoice with an indescribable joy, full of glory before God,[20] full, that is, of the conscience of one who has good hopes; full with the certain confidence that by enduring these evils which are beyond anything that you deserve, you will, if God wishes, carry off an abundant and great return from your faith, to wit, the eternal salvation of your souls. For the gain is enormous when the immortal soul is saved by the loss of the perishable body. It is the decision of God's eternal wisdom that humans should obtain salvation in the ways by which even Christ himself reached eternal bliss.

For these events are not chance occurrences. The ancient prophets, who long before us foretold that you would be saved through faith and evangelical grace without the aid of the law of Moses, diligently searched and inquired about that which we see has now been done. They were not content to have only a clouded vision of what was to be, but with pious curiosity they inquired about it from the Spirit of Christ, which was even then signifying to them through its hidden inspiration what Christ was to suffer and to what great glory he was shortly thereafter to be conveyed. They inquired, furthermore,[21] about when or in what circumstances this was to occur, for their minds were possessed by an immense longing for this salvation. It was also revealed to them that those presentiments which they had of the future were not to be fulfilled in their times but in yours, and that they were producing their prophecies for you,[22] not for themselves. They would have wished to see what it has been your lot to see, but their prophecies came first in time so that people would have a surer faith in us, the apostles, who now[23] announce to you that those very things have come to pass which they prophesied would someday happen. So that your doubts would be less, the Spirit of Christ also taught them long ago through secret inspiration what he had determined to do. This Spirit recently swooped down from heaven in tongues of fire and equipped us to be the heralds throughout the entire world of all that has now taken place.[24] For we preach that Christ became a human for the salvation of all of us, that he lived on earth, suffered insults and tortures, was then fastened to a cross[25] and met death on our behalf; that he was thereafter called back to life and was taken up into heaven where he who previously on earth seemed mean and worthless now shines out in majesty and glory with the Father and will convey his own people to the same place. It is not surprising if the prophets

longed to see those things which have been done by the ineffable wisdom
of God since even to the angels themselves it is a very joyful and pleasing
spectacle and their desire to contemplate it cannot be satisfied.[26]

The greater the benefit which is being offered to you, the deeper your
desire ought to be to embrace it, lest it come about through your own fault
that you do not obtain it. The reward is certain, but in the meantime your
task is to conduct yourselves in such a way that you do not appear unworthy of the promises. That last day which will bring the rewards of the godly
and the ungodly into the open, will be here unexpectedly. Whenever it
comes, it will be a joyful and happy day for those prepared to meet it; on
the other hand it will be a terrifying day for those whom it finds slack and
sluggish in their lack of faith.[27] But since Christ wanted that day to be
unknown to us,[28] you must never, never be negligent but must always keep
the loins of your mind girt up like persons prepared to meet the Lord on
his arrival,[29] awake and sober, always standing erect and alert in the sure
and firm expectation of eternal happiness. This happiness is offered now to
all who obey the gospel, but it will be actually possessed only at that time
when our Lord Jesus Christ will openly reveal his majesty to all human
beings as well as to the angels and the demons.

But the only ones to reach this immortality will be those who have
somehow practised it while here on earth and who, following the example
of Christ, have died to the desires of this world, have come back to life with
him for the pursuit of innocence, and have steadfastly persisted in this
innocence as legitimate and true sons who have faith in the promises of
God the Father, obey his commands, and never slide back into the old life,
which was subject then[30] to worldly desires out of ignorance of the teachings of the gospel. For it is fitting that your dispositions and habits be as
different from those of other people as your religion is different from theirs.
The world from which you have long since been separated is evil. You have
been grafted into Christ, who is righteous and holy and sinless; you have
been chosen and called to this same state by the Father, the source of all
holiness, to be as pure, spotless and blameless in your whole life and in all
your actions as you are holy through your profession of faith. The Father
will not acknowledge his children unless they resemble him. This was
doubtless his meaning when he said in Leviticus, chapter 19: 'Be holy,
because I the Lord your God am holy' [19:2]. It will not be enough for you
to satisfy the purity required by the law of Moses, that is, to avoid touching
a dead body, to have your feet washed, to abstain from sexual intercourse.[31]
God wants our whole life and our whole heart to be remote from every
stain caused by any vice. These are the stains which truly make us impure
in the sight of God. Even[32] if you call him Father and implore his aid in all

things, there is still[33] no reason for you to assume, if[34] your life is impure, that he will act kindly towards you or will acknowledge you as his children. He does not judge anyone by his nationality or position in life but only by the merits of his life. He who is born a Jew will not be pure if his life and his mind are alike foul; the uncircumcised gentile will not be impure if he leads a godly and sinless life. It remains, therefore, that you who desire to have God be a kindly father and always have his inescapable judgment before your eyes while you are living in this exile should so guide your lives that the Father has no reason to be offended and to cut you off from the inheritance of your heavenly homeland because you are degenerate and disobedient children.[35]

The higher the price with which Christ redeemed you at no cost to you, the more care must be taken on your part not to turn back to your former servitude deliberately and ungratefully.[36] No slavery is more wretched than to be a slave to one's vices. Those who pay a trifling sum of money to a master to be freed from their slavery and thus to become freedmen instead of slaves are alert in every way to avoid being dragged back, because of ingratitude, into the slavery which they had left.[37] Are you then going to be the cause of your own relapse into the old tyranny and to become slaves again of the law of Moses, preferring to be enslaved to the futile observances handed down to you from your ancestors than to obey the gospel of God – when you know that you have been freed once for all from all those observances, not by the payment of some commonplace substance like gold or silver but by a victim far holier than any known to the law of Moses? You were[38] not purified by the sprinkling of a calf's blood but by the precious blood shed by Jesus Christ who, like a completely spotless lamb,[39] pure and unstained by the filth of any vice, was sacrificed on the altar of the cross for our sins. However,[40] this sacrifice was no chance event. The Son of God was destined for it from eternity and before the creation of the world so that he might reconcile his Father to us through his death. The design and decision of the divine mind, which were unknown to the world for many centuries, have now at last been revealed in these last times. A new sight, though not new in the mind of God, has been shown to the eyes of humanity. It has been shown, moreover, for the sake of your salvation. Christ, who was made man, who died, and who was proclaimed, did this for you so that you, who previously put your trust in the ceremonies of the Law to no avail, may now lay aside all trust in yourselves and may trust only in God the Father. As he wanted Christ to die in order to expiate your sins, so did he raise him from the dead and in return for the endurance of the labours of this life gave him the glory of immortality. He did this so that you, by imitating what you believe was done by Christ, may also hope for the same reward for yourselves. For you rely on God as the source of this reward and believe that what he did in the Son he will undoubtedly do in all whose lives will make them merit being numbered among the members of Christ, into whose body you were grafted after you had been reborn into him through baptism.

In the past you obeyed your desires because you were embracing the carnal shadows of reality instead of true reality. But now you have purified your souls, not by the observance of purificatory rites of the Mosaic law but because through faith you have obeyed evangelical truth, which has cleansed your minds through the Spirit of Christ. Therefore, you must strive both to be like your head, Christ, in the innocence of your lives and to match the concord of the body in the deep, clearly fraternal and completely unfeigned love which you have for one another. As Christ did not cherish you with an ordinary human or carnal love, so must you in turn attend one another with a love that is spiritual. A new relationship demands a new kind of affection. In the past as Jews you cherished other Jews with a physical affection. But now that you have been reborn in a far different way, not from a perishable and earthly seed in a physical way but from an imperishable and heavenly seed through the word of God who lives and abides forever,[41] whose gospel you came to believe, the love[42] you have for your brothers is a heavenly love. The Law was given to Moses for a limited period of time. The word of God has brought for us the evangelical law that will never perish. What has issued from men is temporary, what has come from heaven is eternal, as Isaiah stated beforehand: 'All flesh [is] as grass, and all the glory of man as the flower of the field. The grass withered and its flower fell off, but the word of the Lord abides forever' [Isa 40:6–8].[43] This is the word of God the Father, the eternal word of the eternal God. It was outlined for you long ago[44] by the shadows of the former law, but now[45] it is proclaimed openly through the heralds of the gospel, not only to you but to all who receive Christ with a sincere faith.

Chapter 2

Now that you have completely discarded all the vices of the old life – if there was indeed in it any trace of malice, guile, hypocrisy, envy, slander or cursing – and have been recently reborn by a heavenly engendering through evangelical teaching, be like new-born babes and avidly crave hereafter the milk that nourishes not the body but the soul, the milk of evangelical instruction, a milk which is without deceit and is more suited to the innocent age of your spiritual infancy than to robust adulthood.[1] Evangelical instruction has its own rudiments, its own infancy, its own special food suitable for the weakness of this time of life. It also has its own stages of advancement and finally its own time of maturity. The initial rudiments are to be swallowed eagerly, thirstily, not forced down with a grimace. However, one must not remain in these rudiments but must advance steadily beyond them to ever higher stages of perfection. It would be absurd if a child born in the normal way were to remain always an infant and never to want anything but milk. You too must continue to grow until you reach a mature and perfect salvation.[2] You must not stay forever amid the foundations but must rise up little by little until the construction of the house is complete. For you have followed the advice of the psalmist and have tasted that the Lord Jesus is pleasant.[3] You must be fired by this taste to seek after greater things.

Stones do not change their position in man-made buildings nor do they increase in size.[4] But this building is made from living stones and its keystone, which holds everything together, is the living and everlasting Jesus Christ, rejected indeed by men in accordance with the prophesy of the psalmist (that is,[5] by the Pharisees who, relying on their own temple that was soon to perish, did not know this heavenly building), but chosen by the judgment of God and held in high value. In this building there is nothing to keep anyone from making himself piece by piece into a completely perfect structure.[6] Therefore, placing virtue upon virtue, you must draw near to Christ the living stone, the chosen stone, the stone precious in God's eyes, so that you too, resting upon such a foundation,[7] may yourselves be built up story by story until you are made into spiritual temples far holier than the temple in which the Jews glory.[8] A much holier priesthood is employed in these temples than was the case in that one. For Levites and priests used to sacrifice animals there; in these spiritual temples you yourselves offer spiritual victims which are far more pleasing to God who, as he is spirit and not matter, is accordingly delighted by spiritual victims.[9] To replace any longing you may have for the rites of Moses, which have now been abrogated through the gospel of Christ, you may sacrifice in place of different kinds of animals your brutish and worldly passions such as lust, pride, anger, envy, vengefulness, gluttony, greed.[10] In place of incense you may offer pure prayers soaring to heaven from the altar of a sincere heart. These are the sacrifices which are always made in a spiritual temple and are always pleasing to God. For those sacrifices of the law of Moses have long since turned into objects of disgust, as the prophet Isaiah testifies.[11] The pleasure of these new sacrifices is unceasing through Jesus Christ, through whose commendation the obedient services of Christians are pleasing to the Father.

There is no reason for you to lose faith so long as you remain fastened to your head and resting upon the excellent and unmovable stone, Christ. God said of him long ago through the mouth of Isaiah, 'Behold, I am laying in Zion a stone to be placed at the chief corner,[12] approved,[13] elect, precious, and he who has faith in him will not be put to shame' [28:16]. What Isaiah predicted we see now revealed. That same stone has become precious and a source of salvation to some, to others a deadly destruction. It is rightly precious to you who have faith and rest upon it,[14] kept safe through its protection from every storm and tempest. But it has turned into reproach and ruin for those who preferred to rest upon Moses rather than upon it and who rejected it in their unwillingness to have it placed in the building which they were themselves preparing to build. For God wanted the stone which they did not think worthy of their building to be the 'head of the corner' in his building so that it might connect and hold together each wall, that is, each people,[15] the Jews and the gentiles. Its bulwark would make the structure safe against every insult and would cause all who opposed this new building to stumble and dash against it to their own despite.

All to whom the word of the gospel is an offence stumble and do not believe it, although the law of Moses was meant to prepare them to believe the gospel as soon as that which the law had foreshadowed actually came to be. Therefore, God has in turn rejected those who rejected Christ. But he has made you, whom they reject together with Christ, to be that chosen generation of which Moses spoke long ago,[16] that holy nation, a special people for whom God paid an extraordinary price and made his very own. He has done this so that, as the Hebrew people long ago, freed under Moses' leadership from the tyranny of Egypt and brought through so many perilous events to the long hoped for land, proclaimed to the world God's kindness to them, so you too, mindful of his spontaneous kindness towards you, are to make the marvelous power of God known among all peoples.[17] He has overcome the enemies of your salvation in a new way and has delivered you from the darkness of your ignorance and vices into his marvelous light of evangelical truth through which all the errors of the gentiles and all the shadows of the Jews are alike dispersed. Therefore, the honour which those[18] who were persecuting Christ had promised to themselves has fallen to you, and through a reversal of the normal course of events that which Hosea had predicted would come to be has now happened.[19] The people who were once utterly worthless, inasmuch as they were estranged from God, are now the people special to God. The people whom God had rejected as unworthy of his mercy have now experienced the mercy of God without the aid of circumcision or of the Law, welcomed into the fellowship of the Son of God through evangelical faith alone.[20]

Therefore, now that you acknowledge God's unique kindness towards yourselves – you whom he has redeemed at the price of blood, whom he has reconciled to himself through the death of his Son, whom he has wanted to be members of his only begotten one, whom he has wanted to be living stones of the heavenly building, whom he has adopted into the rights of sonship and has summoned to the inheritance of immortality – I beseech you, dearly beloved, to make the holiness of your lives correspond to your new station and to God's kindness and to the greatness of the reward. You have been reborn for heaven; in this world you are strangers and pilgrims. Hurry towards the place where you have a homeland in which your heavenly inheritance has been reserved for you. Do not let yourselves be called away from this pursuit by earthly and material passions which militate and war with every kind of stratagem against the spirit longing for the things of heaven. Make your life match the religion you profess so that your behaviour may attract to Christ others also whom paganism still possesses and in whose midst you still live. You must not give them any handle for believing that they are right to have a bad opinion of you when they see that you are not one whit better than the rest in the common practices of everyday life. On the contrary, the integrity of your character and your kindness towards one and all should refute the slanders with which they malign you because of their hatred of Christ, whom they do not know, and because of their hatred of your religion, which they consider a criminal superstition.[21] When they learn the facts, they too will change their minds and acknowledge their mistake, inspired by God's mercy whenever he who chose you has determined to attract them also.[22] Thus from your godly works they will glorify him whom in their ignorance they formerly used to curse.

This world too has its own order which is not to be disturbed on religious pretexts in so far as this is possible without injury to the glory of Christ.[23] Christ wanted you to be free from sins, but on the condition that you willingly endure everything, obedient and submissive not only to Christians but also to pagan authorities on account of the work of the gospel. If this authority is a king,[24] obedience must be given to him as the one who is pre-eminent in civil authority. If it is the governors whom the king[25] has sent to a province to administer public affairs on his behalf, they too must be obeyed. Nor should the fact that they are pagans and worshippers of idols move you, but accept their office as necessary to the state, which is composed of diverse kinds of persons and religions. They have authority to govern in order to restrain criminals and dangerous men through fear of punishment and to invite honest men through the use of rewards to do their duty. You who spontaneously do more than human law demands do not require the restraint of fear, nor do you whom the flames of a heavenly reward enkindle require the inducement of men's praise. Nevertheless, you must acknowledge them with the others. For it is the will of God, who is your supreme ruler, that you do not provide their thoughtless ignorance with some handle with which they might plausibly blame the confession of the gospel when they perceive that you are ignoring their authority. What others do because of their fear of the law, you do willingly and sincerely and also in greater measure than they in order to show that you are truly free. The person who does the right thing spontaneously and willingly is free. Far be it from you to misuse the pretext of evangelical freedom as a licence for further sinning.[26] You do not owe servitude to men, but since you are servants of God, you will gladly and willingly submit yourselves to everyone for his glory. Therefore, if some duty or some mark of respect is owed them – either because of the public office they hold or because of some affinity – pay it to all, even though they are pagans, lest they take offence and become more hostile to the confession of the gospel. Nevertheless, it is right to bestow a special love on those whom the common ties of religion have made your brothers. Fear God, whose eyes no one deceives. There is no reason for you to be afraid of the king, who is a source of fear only to malefactors.[27] Nevertheless, recognize his authority in those matters where his demands upon you do not cause any loss of godliness. He asks for a tax, pay it. He demands tribute, give it.[28]

What free men should do for their rulers even though they are pagans, slaves must do for their masters. Baptism does not free slaves from obedience to them. On the contrary, because of baptism they ought to acknowledge their masters with even greater respect, not only if they are good and gentle but even if they are bad-tempered and harsh, lest, irked somehow by overly troublesome behaviour on your part, they inveigh against your religion and become more hostile to it. Instead let your goodness attract and invite them to it. Someone will protest, 'It is hard to bear the tyranny of princes, it is hard to endure the cruelty of masters. The former confiscate, exact, torture; the latter cut the innocent to pieces with whips and blows.' These actions would rightly seem intolerable if they were to be attributed to human agents rather than to God. Because of their ungodliness those men certainly do not deserve to be tolerated; nevertheless, it is God's will that your goodness turn their wickedness into the glory of Christ. It is in just this way that your patience is pleasing to God. Though you are suffering undeservedly, you still endure it calmly not because of any fear of men on your part but because of God's glory. The crowd considers that nothing is more intolerant of insult than is innocence. But the matter is far different for Christians. In their view the better a person is, the more he desires to be

ever more pleasing to God. The more fervently he loves God, the more
eagerly he endures whatever pertains to God's glory. What credit is there
if you endure blows and slaps given you for your misdeeds? A guilty
conscience teaches everybody to bear deserved punishment in silence. But
when you patiently put up with evils returned for benefits, you obtain
favour with God, for whose sake you endure willingly.

Your innocence would have cause to be indignant, were it not that
Christ, though innocent, suffered worse things for us. This is your religion.
These are the terms of your acceptance into the body of Christ: to follow the
example of patience which he left you[29] and, by walking in the same steps,
to advance to eternal glory in the way he reached it. What evil did he not
endure who was crucified with thieves? What was more innocent than he?
He was so far from committing any wicked act that no guile even was ever
found on his tongue. When bitter insults were being heaped upon him, he
did not hurl back abuse, but instead begged the Father to forgive them.[30]
When he was being bound, scourged, crucified, he did not make threats of
vengeance, but left all vengeance to the Father.[31] The Father does not judge
on the basis of feelings[32] but justly; meanwhile Christ plays the role of
intercessor, not of accuser.[33]

As for us, though we now pursue innocence, in the past we deserved
God's punishment because of our wicked deeds. Christ, however, though
he was guilty of no sin, nevertheless, to lighten our load, took upon his own
body the burden of our sins and, like a holocaust, was sacrificed on the
tree[34] of the cross for our wicked deeds. By his own undeserved death he
thrust from us the death which was our due so that we in the meantime
may imitate his death and resurrection and, having died to the old sins and
desires to which we were devoted and enslaved, may henceforth live to the
innocence to which he, the fountain of all innocence, consecrated us. He
transferred our ungodliness to himself in order to confer his righteousness
upon us. We committed the offence; he received the beating. The guilt was
ours; the punishment was cruelly inflicted on him. Therefore, just as Isaiah
had predicted, we have been healed by his stripes.[35] You must, then, give
him the credit for your innocence. That God does not charge your sins to
your past life, you owe to his chains, to his blows, to his wounds, to his
cross, to his death. For in the past like sheep straying without a leader you
wandered in different directions wherever each of you might be led by your
own desires, thinking that you were allowed whatever pleased you. But you
have now left your wandering and have turned[36] to Christ Jesus, the shepherd and guardian[37] of your souls. If you would follow him in enduring
evil afflictions beyond what you may deserve, you will under his leadership
reach the glory of immortality.

Chapter 3

Compliance produces good will in every situation. Just as free men ought to entice princes and public officials to a favourable attitude towards the gospel, so ought slaves to do the same in regard to their masters, or at the least they ought not to irritate them deliberately if they are perhaps incurable. Similarly wives too ought to be obedient to their husbands, and not just to Christian husbands but also to those who have not yet accepted the teachings of the gospel. For it is quite possible that a wife's integrity, godliness, modesty, self-control, chastity, patience may overcome, soften, and in the end gain for Christ men whom our preaching fails to stir. When husbands observe the change in their wives' behaviour after baptism and see in them models of true virtue, perhaps they will be moved (and marital affection is an inducement to this end) to want to be partners in their wives' religion in addition to being sharers of their bed. Pure goodness is an extremely keen stimulus and when observed at close hand often makes carnal love turn into spiritual love. Physical loveliness and a mode of dress which enhances the body's charms arouse the one; the beauty of an immaculate mind, that shines forth and is reflected in moral behaviour, arouses the other. Therefore, wives who have become Christians should not set their hearts on making themselves attractive to men's eyes in the popular fashion by artfully arranging their hair, wearing gold, jewels, or a purple dress, or by using other adornments of the body designed for external show.[1] What else do such actions do except make husbands yearn to use their wives' bodies in lustful ways? Just how important a part of the human being is the body? It should be the goal of wives rather to arouse men by their moral adornments and to make them fall in love with their minds and invisible souls, once they see that their minds are clean and unmarred by the warts of any vice, once they see that, quite unlike the common pattern, there is in them no trace of those feelings women are prone to have – no intemperateness, no angry temper, no jealously, no vanity, no haughtiness, no sauciness – but instead a mild, peaceful, tractable, and gentle spirit.[2] This is a magnificent and splendid style of dress in the eyes of God. This is the adornment that gratifies a husband's mind most of all.

It was by such attractions in the past also that a few holy women, who placed their hopes firmly in God and not in fleeting, transitory things, made themselves attractive to their husbands, not by gold or gems or purple stuffs but by the modesty and compliance which most easily calms the violence of the male nature. This was the way Sarah obeyed Abraham, calling him her lord,[3] though she was his wife and not his maidservant, and subjecting herself to him for modesty's sake. Though it is not fitting for a husband to lord it over his wife, nevertheless he does have an authority with which it is the part of a modest woman to comply even if he abuses this authority in some respect. Moreover, as those who imitate the faith of Abraham are his true-born and genuine sons, so are you daughters of Sarah who reproduce that heroic woman's behaviour and masculine strength of mind when you adorn yourselves with good works and place all your trust in God. When you rely on God's help, there is no reason for you to let the weakness of your sex make you afraid of anything.

Just as it is the duty of wives and mothers to bind their husbands to them with gentleness, chaste obedience, and holy conduct, it is your role, husbands, not to misuse your authority in any way by acting like tyrants towards your wives because they submit themselves to you. On the contrary, be less like lords over them precisely because they make themselves handmaids. They are your partners in all your fortunes and affairs. Let them perceive you as agreeable persons to live with; make your wisdom be a support to the weakness of the female sex. You have greater strength of mind and body and, therefore, should give more assistance to the women's lack of strength in order to improve them through your instruction and guidance and to have them, so to speak, put aside their female sex and become males in the practice of evangelical godliness.[4] For men who take wives only for sexual purposes are not Christian husbands. Instead you must make an effort to have them become your partners in fasting, almsgiving, vigils, and prayers so that they who have also been called to a share in the prize of eternal life may join in your zealous endeavours to hasten towards it. Physical pleasure should have no part or at least only a very small part in a Christian marriage, and piety much the largest part. If you are both like-minded in your piety and abstain occasionally from intercourse, the sacrifice of your prayers which you should offer to God each day will not be interrupted.[5]

Different persons, then, have different duties appropriate to their station in life. Therefore, it behooves each one of us to remember our own duties, the more so because the Christian should excel other people in those duties which pertain to moral goodness. But we all have the same basic obligation to live in concord with one another, just as we have all made the same profession of faith and have been grafted into the same body through baptism. Age, fortune, social condition, or different national origin must not divide you. Such things often supply the seeds[6] of hatred and discord among other people, but you must be completely united. You were reborn to God through the same baptism; you have the same Father in heaven. Dependent, as you are, on your one head, Christ, you are members of the same body; your evangelical profession has made you brothers on an equal basis. For these reasons the heavenly Father has called you all to the same reward of immortality without distinction, regardless of whether you are poor or rich, slaves or masters, husbands or wives, Jews or gentiles.[7] In this respect there is no distinction; therefore[8] there ought to be no dissension or display of arrogance. A submissive Christian love will accomplish much more than imperious authority will. The arrogant, the ferocious, the conceited can never come to an agreement. If the parts in the body of a living creature are meant to assist one another and if something good or bad happens to any one of them, each part considers this to affect itself.[9] People who are united in a family relationship rejoice and grieve in their relatives' gains and losses. How much more appropriate is it for you who are united in so many ways to display this fellow feeling, so that you are no less touched by the goods and ills of others than by your own? You will display a truly brotherly love towards one another if the more successful do not disdain the less fortunate, but grieving at their plight, aid them with all their might; and if those who are pre-eminent in power and authority do not despise and oppress the lower classes, but accommodate themselves to their inferiors in courteous and friendly association with them so that equality exists and Christian love joins together those whom fortune has separated.

Let the passion for revenge be far removed from you. Your task is to nourish concord not only with the godly and with the brethren but also, if possible, with all people. You must vie with the good in acts of charity, challenge the wicked through patience or, better, through kindness. As kindness wins over even wild animals, so it sometimes softens the deplorable wickedness of humans. Have no wish, therefore, to return injury for injury, insult for insult. If you do, by imitating the wicked you will only become wicked yourselves. Instead, repay an injury with an act of charity, a curse with a blessing, so that you conquer and overwhelm their wickedness by your own unsurpassable goodness. God did not call you to defeat others by evil deeds and evil words, but by doing good to everyone and speaking well of all to merit those hoped for words, 'Come, my Father's blessed ones, take possession of the kingdom' [Matt 25:34]. To do wrong to good people is to act worse than a wild animal; to speak ill to those who speak well of you is to play a role lower than a buffoon's. To do good to evildoers,[10] to bless those who slander and revile is the part of Christian virtue.[11] If anyone thinks this hard, let him listen to the author of the Psalms, who, inspired by the spirit of God, teaches the same thing when he says, 'Who wants to love life and to see good days, let him check his tongue from evil and restrain his lips from speaking guile. Let him turn aside from evil and do good; let him seek peace and pursue it. For the eyes of the Lord are on the righteous and his ears are directed towards their prayers. But the face of the Lord is against those who do evil.'[12]

Therefore, if we want God to be kind to us, let us ourselves be kind to all. If we want to escape his vengeance, let us do no harm of any kind to anyone. I do not listen to what human feelings may mutter in opposition here: 'If I do not repel a wrong, my failure to punish will invite a lot of people to start harming me.' On the contrary, nothing will make you safer from wrong than if you either endure it or, even better, repay it with a good service. There is no end to doing harm whenever insult is doubled by insult, wrong by wrong, in a hopeless exchange. If no one fights back, wickedness will grow quiet or at least weary. Who would be eager to harm you if you have striven to do good to everyone, to harm no one? But if any are found so blind that they persecute you out of hatred for virtue or from error, in what real way, I ask, can they do harm? They will take away money, which has to be soon left behind in any case; they will afflict the body;[13] they will kill those who are soon going to die anyway. Since all these injuries are inflicted because of your religion, they not only do not cause you any real loss but produce an even greater profit for you. It is through such evils that the reward of eternal happiness is increased for you. It is through such evils that the reward of eternal happiness is increased for you. But one who is impaired by the loss of a good conscience is truly injured. So long as it remains safe, what the world thinks is loss is really gain; what seems to such people to be a disaster is really a blessing. Therefore, it rests with you to make the violence of evil men harmless to yourselves. God's bounty will restore with immeasurable interest whatever human wickedness has taken away. Consequently, there is no reason for human threats to terrify or the violence of the wicked to disturb those who rely on God. Even when in the center of a tempest of afflictions, do not let yourselves be distressed as if you felt deprived of God's help. Do not revile men who afflict you through ignorance. Instead, glorify in your hearts the Lord God, who turns all things into good for his servants, whether they encounter happy or adverse events.[14] Therefore, he is always to be praised. If this praise cannot always[15] be uttered aloud, it can certainly be expressed everywhere through the feelings in one's heart.

The enemies of God should not be exasperated by insults. Wherever there is some hope that they may be drawn to Christ, be open and prompt to answer everyone who desires to learn what it is that gives you the confidence and hope to scorn the advantages of this life and to accept patiently its disadvantages. And do it, not with a display of indignation or insolence as if you were incensed at them, but with every show of mildness and respect. You may be sure of your good conscience even if you should be unable to persuade them. It is not enough for Christians to speak the truth and in words worthy of Christ, but to speak it in such a way that the very manner of your speech reveals that you are not pursuing your own interests but the glory of Christ and that you have in view the salvation of those to whom you are speaking.[16] This will be a completely certain sign and will put to shame those who slanderously call hypocritical and criminal the way of life which you are living according to the teaching of Christ. Though the feigned appearance of virtue deceives in other circumstances, hypocrisy breaks out and betrays itself in the face of actual suffering. Only a mind that possesses a good conscience and is wholly dependent upon God can bear all things gladly, and be so far from contriving revenge that it tries even to benefit those by whom it is being pained. Do not be moved by the fact that, though innocent, you are suffering the punishments of the guilty. On the contrary for this very reason you must bear the more lightly whatever is done to you. If it is God's will that you suffer these things, it is better for you to suffer doing good rather than doing evil. He who is punished for his evil acts is only paying the penalty he has deserved. Your afflictions lead to the glory of Christ and the augmentation of your own beatitude.

It is glorious for you to imitate your prince. This was the way he made the glory of God the Father clear. Completely[17] innocent, he was arrested, put in chains, scourged, spat upon, crucified, and died for our sins though he himself had no sin. Righteous, he paid the penalty for the unrighteous; guiltless, he paid the penalty for the guilty, gladly obeying the will of the Father in order to present us, who were sinners, pure and unstained to the Father. We too, then, following his example, are to live among the harmful without ourselves doing any harm and, while being good, are to suffer for the salvation of those who are evil. He died only once and was given eternal life in return for temporary suffering so that we who have had our sins removed once for all might not relapse into the same sins. Christ atoned for us. Because of the weakness of the human body which he had assumed he was delivered to death, but he was recalled to life by the power of the Spirit, which could not be overcome by any sufferings. For during the time when his lifeless body was enclosed in the tomb, alive in the spirit he penetrated to the region of the dead. When he was in the body he proclaimed the teachings of the gospel among men encased in mortal bodies. Those who believed it obtained salvation, those who refused to believe it brought the accumulation of eternal damnation upon themselves. In a similar fashion then, after he had laid aside the body, he went to those[18] spirits who had themselves likewise been stripped of their bodies and were residing with the dead, and proclaimed to them that the time was now at hand for them to receive the reward for their godliness. For they had in the past feared the justice of God and had not sought vengeance for wrongs done to them, but, doing no harm themselves, had lived among people who did harm. But to those who did not believe in the days of Noah he announced that they would suffer what they deserved. For during the time the ark was being prepared they had abused God's leniency because they saw that the deluge which God in his anger at the crimes of mortals had threatened to loose was postponed for many years.[19] Therefore, when it did come rushing down, it destroyed everyone with a very few exceptions, namely, the eight who alone followed Noah's counsel, entrusted themselves to the ark, and were not swallowed up by the deluge. Thus even in those times faith did not lack its reward. For God did not allow those who trusted wholeheartedly in him to perish. Nor can those who disbelieve escape the vengeance of God even if you yourselves cannot punish them. It is enough for you to obey God; leave[20] to him the punishment of the ungodly.[21]

What Noah's ark signified for those eight who were saved, baptism now signifies for you. What the flood signified for those evildoers who were destroyed, the everlasting punishment proclaimed for those who do not obey the gospel signifies for the ungodly[22] today. It was enough for Noah to have threatened that the deluge would come, it was enough for him to have shown how people might escape the danger if through their repentance they would only placate God's anger, which they had provoked against themselves by their wickedness. Let your own innocence be enough for you too. Let it be enough to have proclaimed to others what reward is ready for those who believe the gospel, what punishment awaits those who disbelieve. If a few are saved through faith, the credit will not be yours. If a good part of humanity is lost because of disbelief, it is their own fault. God has determined to manifest in this way the distinction between the good and the wicked. Baptism if properly received saves from destruction and washes away filth not from the body but from the soul. Refused, it destroys forever and sinks one in still heavier waves of wickedness. Therefore, that which, when faith is added, is a source of salvation to others brings destruction to the disbelieving and rebellious. However, it is not enough for you that your sins have perished and the warped desires of your old life have perished in the flood of baptism. There must also be present in you a conscience which throughout the whole of your life after baptism continues to respond to God's gift. Christ died, but only once; he rose again never to die thereafter. Through baptism the sins of our past life are destroyed for us once for all through Christ's death, but on the condition that, having been brought back to life again in him for innocence, we never afterwards relapse into sins in so far as it is in our power not to do so. This will happen if we put our mortality aside, as it were, and aspire with our whole heart and soul to that heavenly life whose inheritance awaits those who obey the gospel.

Jesus Christ, when he rose again, did not linger thereafter on earth but withdrew from the fellowship of mortal men to heaven. Enjoying there the glory of immortality, he sits at the right hand of the Father. He has indeed[23] a body but one[24] over which death no longer has any jurisdiction. Death as it tried to swallow the innocent one was completely swallowed, and just as it was promising itself rich spoil was itself the spoils.[25] Christ's victory, moreover, is our victory. The glory which came first in him is held out to us if we will only persevere in what we have begun and follow closely in his footsteps. The sufferings imposed by the wicked had no power over him; on the contrary, by enduring them he conquered and reigns now in triumph, sitting on high in heaven, superior to all the angels or all other powers and authorities there may otherwise be. He has revealed to you the way to heaven so that you too may proceed to the same place by the same way by which he entered it. The inheritance is prepared and certain. He has taken possession of it for you too if only you make yourselves worthy of it; that is, if you join to the innocence which he has given you the zeal to do good to all, even, in so far as it is in your power, to those who are evil and afflict you.

Chapter 4

Therefore,[1] since Christ, your prince and head, did not indulge in the pleasures of this life but reached heavenly glory through the temporary sufferings of the body and, armed with patience, overcame his adversaries, it is right that you who profess yourselves his disciples should arm yourselves with a similar firm purpose in your heart. An innocent way of life is the securest armament. Christian patience is an unassailable bulwark. Whoever has girt himself in this way cannot be harmed by anyone. Whoever has died with Christ in the flesh has so ceased from the sins of his past life that it is clear to all that he has died to human desires. He no longer itches with the craving for fame, is no longer aroused by the lust for revenge; whatever is left of the span of life given in this poor body he lives out entirely for the will of God. He longs to please God alone. It is from him that he expects the reward owed to a good conscience. It is to him that he leaves the punishment of the wicked. Anyone who is prepared for martyrdom is not touched by the pleasures of this world. For he thinks to himself, 'God forbid that once fastened upon the cross with my Christ I should come down from it to the vices I left behind; that once bound for

eternal happiness I should turn back to the delights of this world, as short-
lived as they are insane. The time spent in the past when I was still a
stranger to Christ is more than enough to have spent on the mad pleasures
to which the godless gentiles are shamefully enslaved, addicted and devoted
as they are to licentiousness, lusts, drunkenness, revels,[2] and the impious
worship of images.' We rejoice that thanks to Christ we have left these
things behind us. Whenever we look back at them, we shudder at all the
filth, all the dark ignorance that once existed in our lives. Chastity now
pleases us in place of lust, frugality in place of excess, sobriety in place of
drunkenness, in place of the superstitious worship of images, true godliness
and the devout worship of the living God, to whom the most pleasing
sacrifice is a mind pure and unimpaired by any stain caused by vice.[3]

Those still in the grip of darkness are surprised by this great change
of mind and life in you and become indignant at the thought that their
excesses are condemned by your frugality, and that their way of life, awash
as it is in every kind of self-indulgence, is censured by your wholesome
purity. They would love anyone who shares their vileness. As it is, they
revile you because of the dissimilarity between their life and yours. There
is no reason for you, however, to be aroused by their insults. You are not
to attack them in turn with insults. Let it be sufficient for you to have a
good conscience before God. If you can somehow convert them to better
ways, the attempt must be made, but on the condition that you do not
depart from your own sincerity. If they come to their senses, rejoicing is in
order. If they remain obdurate and assail with abuse even those who wish
them well, leave them to God's punishment. No mortal can escape God's
judgment. He will judge all in his own time, not only the living but also the
dead, the living whom the coming of Christ will overtake alive in the body,[4]
the dead who have already[5] departed from among the living before the
coming of Christ.

But no one is truly alive unless he lives for godliness. Those who are
enslaved to their vices and filthy desires are dead to God. These persons,
who are truly dead, will render an account to this judge if they prove to be
unwilling to change their attitudes and repent of their vices. He will exact
a penalty from them on your behalf and, as he is an absolutely just judge,
he will pay to you in full the rewards due your patient endurance. He
indeed is eager for all to come to life again for the pursuit of evangelical
godliness. For this reason he wanted the grace of the gospel to be preached
not only to the Jews who were living devoutly in accordance with natural
law, but also to those who were dead and buried completely in every kind
of vice. He wanted the light of the gospel to be brought to their darkness.
He wanted them to be taught with all gentleness and patience so that they

too, awakening at last and despising those things in which they now blindly
locate their happiness, may in the eyes of men indeed be held to be no
different from dead bodies because they are not touched by any bodily
emotion, but in the eyes of God they are alive in the spirit. Where the judge
is God, only one who has died in this way is truly alive.[6]

Nothing in this world is lasting and the end of all things will soon be
here. The pleasures of those persons will quickly depart and your sufferings
will presently be at an end. Everlasting happiness waits for you hereafter,
everlasting punishment for them. Therefore, you must be alert in every way
lest that day finds you sleepy and drowsy from drink and indolence.[7]
Instead, keep yourselves permanently prepared against that day by staying
sober and awake in constant prayer. It is the will of Christ that it come
unexpectedly,[8] but if it finds you in the midst of prayer, it can mean for you
only a day of happiness. Sobriety is pleasing to God, to be vigilant is to be
safe. God gladly hears prayers which are commended by abstinence and
vigilance. But much the most pleasing thing of all is for you to embrace one
another in continuous and fervent love as you support one another with
mutual services, so that the more vigilant wakes the drowsy, the more
learned instructs the less learned, the more zealous admonishes the faint-
hearted, the more fervent prods the sluggish, the more advanced makes
allowances for the one wandering in weakness. This burning love for our
neighbour covers a multitude of the sins for which we are liable to God.
The best way to dissolve our debts to God is to invest good deeds in our
neighbour. Let each strive to benefit a brother in accordance with the
resources he has received. The person with property should be hospitable
and give abundantly to the needy, not grudgingly and muttering under his
breath but gladly and eagerly, thinking that when he gives, it is really he
who receives the benefit and that such an expenditure of his resources[9] is
a huge gain in the eyes of God, who returns everything with measures
heaped to the fullest.[10]

Reflect, moreover, that everything you have to spend to help a neighbour is due to God's kindness and was given to you so that from the loan,
so to speak, of this capital you may grow rich from the interest earned from
godly works. God distributes different gifts to different persons.[11] Let no
one take the credit for what he has, but let him consider it to be God's gift.
God wants his gift to be distributed to others through you, so that through
the exchange of mutual services a mutual love cements you more and more
tightly together and the reward of godliness is increased on every occasion
for each person. Let no one be displeased because he has not been endowed
with this or that gift. Let no one be pleased because he excels others in
some gift. Thus did it seem good to a rich and generous God variously to

divide his gifts. No one is the lord of that which he has received; he is only its steward. The property which he administers belongs to the Lord. If he does this faithfully, zealously, meticulously, he is not to expect payment from some man, since[12] he will receive it from God. If it falls to a person's lot to receive sacred doctrine[13] or the gift of a learned tongue, he is not to use it for personal gain or pride or empty glory but for the salvation of his neighbour and the glory of Christ, and his audience should perceive that the words they hear are from God, not from men, and that the one who speaks them is but an instrument of the divine voice. If someone is better at management than at teaching, he should not let his gift for administration be a reason to claim some authority for himself, but he should ascribe the credit to God who supplies him with the power and strength to perform effectively what he does. Thus the result of this variety in the distribution of gifts and in the performance of services will be that God is glorified from every side. All things flow to us as from a spring, and not through Moses but through[14] Jesus Christ through whom, as his only Son, the Father gives us everything that he gives us. Therefore,[15] the one who is aided by the kindness of a brother will give God the credit; the one who rejoices in having aided a brother by his ministry will give thanks to God. The total sum of all glory returns, therefore, from every direction to God, the Father and the Son, to whom belong everlasting glory and dominion that will never end. Amen.

We must not seek glory in this world; we should remember only our duty to please God. Let him in whom we put our faith see to the reward. He will turn the malice of persecutors into your good; he will change your torments to joy, your humiliation to glory. Therefore, dearly beloved, do not be disturbed by the apparent novelty of a situation where you who are to share in the kingdom of heaven are being tested by temporary suffering like gold by fire. What occurred long ago in the testing of the prophets and just recently in the case of Christ should not now appear to be something novel. You ought to bear more lightly what you see you have in common with all the men who have been approved by God. Because you, as disciples and members, resemble your teacher and head Jesus Christ in this respect, you ought even to rejoice and to congratulate yourselves because, just as he now considers you worthy of his wish to have you be partakers of his sufferings, so will you exult in the future when he reveals his majesty to all alike. Then you will exult with an indescribable joy – a joy that[16] can be felt but not expressed in words – while those who made him suffer, and now have made you too suffer because of their hatred of him, will be astonished and put to shame. In the meantime people slander you, not because of any misdeeds on your part, but because of your avowal of Christ. No matter how much you suffer physically, you are blessed because even in the midst of tortures, in the midst of humiliations, that glorious Spirit of God is refreshed in you on account of your innocent mind and clear conscience. It is sweet to suffer with Christ; it is glorious to suffer for Christ. For they insult Christ as best they can, but your innocence, your patient endurance make their insults only enhance his glory.

But God forbid that any one of you is made to suffer because of a murder, or a theft, or abusive language,[17] or from prying into matters which have nothing to do with you. Not the punishment but the reason for it makes one a martyr. However, anyone who suffers on no other ground than that he is called a Christian has no reason to be ashamed of the penalty.[18] To be called a thief is disgraceful, to be called a Christian is glorious. Blessed are they who are allowed even in this way[19] to escape the punishments of Gehenna and are given a passage to everlasting joys through momentary sufferings. God admits to these joys only those who have been tested and approved by much endurance of evils. Someday he will exercise a dreadful judgment when the time of mercy is over and each is given his reward according to his merits. In the meantime his judgment is milder when he uses temporary torments to test us for purity and to make us fit for fellowship with Christ, who will accept nothing unless it is thoroughly purified and refined. Now it is the time for the exercise of that judgment which makes more evident who truly have faith in God and truly love Christ. A prosperous and tranquil life is no proof of true godliness. A hypocrite too can observe the ceremonies prescribed by the law of Moses. But no one bears with equanimity the loss of property, insults, imprisonments, whippings, death, except the person who combines invincible faith with evangelical love. Let those who wish to reign one day with Christ prepare themselves for such afflictions. This judgment will begin from the house of God which is the church. If we who believe the gospel and live lives of innocence need so much purification, what end, what judgment, what penalty awaits those who have no faith in God's gospel and persist in their disgraceful deeds?[20] If this kind of test is made of those who obey the gospel without reservation, who have abandoned the delights of this world and have devoted themselves to the pursuit of godliness, what will it be for those whom the preaching of the gospel has placed in an even worse position? If they who live righteously and are conscious of no evil in themselves do not reach the harbour of eternal salvation without passing through dangers and troubles, with what hope will the ungodly and wicked appear in a court so demanding and so fearsome? Therefore, not only can the wicked have no hope of salvation for themselves in that court but even those who, because of God's will and not because of some crime, are put on

the rack in this world ought not to be self-confident because of their suffering. Instead, by continually doing works of godliness to the best of their
ability they should in this way deposit[21] their souls with God the creator.
His goodness will not let perish what he has created if they are doing good
even as they die and if they put no trust in their own merits but expect
their reward solely from his bounty.

Chapter 5

Make it your aim, brothers, both separately as individuals and all of you
together in common, to follow in the footsteps of Christ and reach your goal
of fellowship with him. But those to whom age lends authority and thus
places in the forefront should also take the lead in the pursuit of godliness.
The rest of the flock depends on their example, their teaching, their authority. By no means is it enough for them to keep their own innocence safe if
they do not also take care of the multitude. Grey hair lends them authority,
experience wisdom, long proved and tested integrity public trust. Therefore,
elders, I call you guardians of the people.[1] I too am an elder and I have
practised in fact and deed what I teach; for I have endured repeated imprisonment and scourging for Christ's name and am ready also to be crucified
whenever God wills it.[2] I also have the highest hopes that the moment that
day arrives on which Christ will reveal his majesty to the world and the
prizes will be brought out because the contest is over, he will welcome into
the fellowship of heavenly glory one whom he considered worthy of suffering on his behalf. I beseech you by the torments endured by Christ on your
behalf, I beseech you by my own sufferings in which I follow my Lord to
the best of my ability, make yourselves truly shepherds of the multitude
which has been allotted[3] to each of you. Be vigilant, make your rounds,
keep your eyes open, take care that the flock for which Christ died lacks
nothing, not holy comfort or saving doctrine or the example of a life lived
according to the gospel. You are called overseers; practise what your title
means.[4] Feed, care for, guide, watch over the flock so that no part of it is
lost, no part wanders off.[5] Do not do this reluctantly as though you were
being compelled by fear, or shame, or the duties of the office, but do it
promptly, gladly, sincerely, having no other standard than what pleases
God.

You are doing God's work and you will receive your wages from him
– wages which are everlasting. Do not ask for a reward in this life. To
oversee the people of Christ just for gain is scandalous. No one receives
praise for this responsibility if one does not do it willingly and freely. He
who seeks to obtain in this world from men the wages of the office forfeits

the reward from heaven. Not very different is the case of the bishop who, though a despiser of money, still desires honour and prestige, who delights in giving orders and in being cultivated by others.[6] There will be no reward for him with God; he has taken his wages here on earth. A bishop's task is far different from lordship. It is not a tyranny but a stewardship. A bishop does not occupy his see just to acquire greater wealth, to reign like a king, and to enjoy greater licence for himself, but to have more opportunity to be of use to others. Therefore, elders, remember your duty. Conduct yourself in all your activities in such a way that your life serves the people as the model of a life lived according to the gospel. Let them learn from your behaviour to pay no heed to money, let them learn to avoid pride, let them learn to expect from Christ the reward for their charitable acts and to have in the meantime as their only motive the thought that to act in this way is right and pleasing to God. In the meantime play the part of good shepherds even without reimbursement, although this work will certainly[7] not be without reimbursement. On the contrary, when the chief shepherd, Jesus Christ – the one who gave all he had for his sheep whose custody he has entrusted to us – appears on the predestined day, then instead of the reward of some cheap and perishable trifle you will receive as the full payment due your office a glorious crown which will[8] never fade. Therefore, do not wish to take for yourselves now what you should be waiting for from your chief; do not wish to anticipate that day about which he wished us to be left in uncertainty.[9]

It is the responsibility of the older men to act like fathers towards the younger men, and these in turn must behave with due obedience and compliance towards their elders. As the elders through the exercise of evangelical love submit themselves to the needs of everyone else in order to be of greater benefit to them, so the young men for their part must not take advantage of their elders' self-restraint and openness. The less the elders abuse their authority, the more readily the young men are likely to obey them. Where genuine love exists, there is no room for authority to display arrogance, nor youth ungoverned wildness. The person who is pre-eminent in status aims only at being useful to others; the one in a subordinate position willingly does more than what the one above him demands. There should be, then, an attitude of modesty and restraint deeply embedded in all. This attitude will keep the cares of their office from being burdensome to the elders and the authority of the elders from being irksome to the young. God detests a wild and ungovernable spirit in people; he is pleased by a submissive and humble heart. He willingly imparts his gifts to those who attribute nothing to themselves; he rejects and turns away the proud[10] as being undeserving of his kindness. He lifts up those who humble themselves; he casts down those who exalt themselves.[11] He considers those who put confidence in their own strength to be unworthy of his help; he cherishes and protects those who have no confidence in their own resources but depend wholly on his will. Humble yourselves, therefore, not because you have any fear of men but because you rely on the mighty hand of God. There is no danger of your being trodden underfoot forever. God will lift you up and carry you aloft when that day of rewards comes. Do not be circumspect, do not be distrustful, do not be afraid that, undefended and neglected, you will be overwhelmed by waves of evil. He who can do everything and see everything has you in his care and he will not allow any part of you to perish.

Youth is a time of life commonly prone to pleasures, to wanton and lewd behaviour. You, however, be sober, keep your minds alert, ever attentive, ever wary. For that adversary of your salvation, who thirsts for people's destruction, does not sleep but walks about like a hungry and roaring lion, trying everywhere to catch someone to devour. He tries every approach against you, sometimes lying in an ambush of pleasures, sometimes making a frontal assault with persecutions.[12] Give him no opening but resist him with spirits unbroken. You may say, 'Where are we to find the strength to resist one so powerful?' He who has you in his care is more powerful. Simply trust in him with your whole heart and your adversary will be powerless. His strength prevails against those who lack faith; against those who have faith his arm is weak. If he were attacking only one or two of you, it would rightly be a grievous affliction perhaps. As it is, he is assailing with undiscriminating hatred the entire flock of the godly. He persecutes Christ in you and begrudges everyone salvation. For this reason the suffering shared by all alike should be born the more lightly and a stand taken with hearts united against the common enemy. These troubles will soon have an end. God from whom all kindness originates will not abandon you in the meantime, but will complete what he has begun in you. He has given you the courage to meet without hesitation the torments you suffer on account of your love for him. He has called you to his everlasting glory through these torments. He will not let you lose the palm of victory. If you contest bravely, he will be with you in the contest. He will support you, strengthen and steady you so that after a short time of suffering you attain the crown of immortality. Through his help we are winning;[13] we shall receive our reward from his bounty. We have no grounds for claiming any praise for ourselves. All glory is due to God alone not only in this world but also through all the ages. Amen.

I shall not discuss these matters further with you at present, for I believe I wrote you recently about this very subject, though briefly, through our faithful brother Silvanus who I have no doubt delivered the letter in good faith.[14] In it I earnestly begged you to persevere in what you have begun and to let nothing alter your intention. You have entered upon the truest road to salvation.[15] Thanks to God you have advanced to your present position. Persist bravely with his help in the contest until you attain the prize of immortal life.

The congregation of Christians in Babylon, which God has chosen for himself along with you, sends you greetings. In the midst of ungodly idolaters[16] it pursues evangelical godliness, in the midst of those whose way of life is thoroughly corrupt[17] it embraces a life of purity. You are not alone. God has his elect everywhere. To be sure they may be few in number, but they are select seeds for propagating the church far and wide some day. Mark, who is like a son[18] to me, greets you. Greet one another not with the everyday kiss of common fashion nor with an insincere one, but with the holy,[19] pure, and truly Christian kiss which is heartfelt, and the truthful sign of one whose love is chaste and sincere.

Now to end this letter on the same note with which I began it:[20] may grace and peace[21] be always with you one and all, who have been placed in the body of Jesus Christ and live in his spirit, grace to bind you to God and peace to fasten you tightly together in mutual concord. May God, all good, all great, bring this to pass.

The End

PARAPHRASE ON SECOND PETER

Paraphrasis in epistolam Petri Apostoli posteriorem

THE ARGUMENT OF THE
SECOND EPISTLE OF PETER
BY ERASMUS OF ROTTERDAM

Peter wrote this letter, it seems, when he was quite old and already close to death, inasmuch as he mentions his own departure. He writes to all Christians without distinction,[1] exhorting them to live pure lives and deterring them from shameful acts by examples from antiquity and by the terror of the last judgment. At the same time he rails vehemently at those who would corrupt the minds of simple people with their perverse teachings when they deny that Christ will come.

The End

PARAPHRASE ON THE SECOND EPISTLE OF PETER THE APOSTLE BY ERASMUS OF ROTTERDAM

Chapter 1

I, Symeon[1] Peter, was once a follower of the law of Moses but am now a servant and emissary of Jesus Christ, whose gospel is a light that shatters and scatters all the shadows of the Old Testament.[2] I write this letter to all without distinction of nationality or religion or sex or status or condition. For we consider most closely connected and related to us everyone who has deserved to be made equal to us in the profession of evangelical faith. Through it we have obtained true righteousness – not through circumcision or the sacrifices required by the Law, but through the goodness of our God and through the death of Jesus Christ our Saviour. Christ freely forgave us our old sins so that we may henceforth pursue evangelical righteousness, which is not based on ceremonies but on true godliness of the mind. Evangelical righteousness possesses something far more perfect than Jewish righteousness, which is only a shadow of true righteousness. I pray that just as you have made great progress up to now in evangelical grace by continually adding each day some small increment to your godliness and by tying ever more tightly day by day the bonds of fraternal concord among yourselves,[3] so God in his goodness will deign to bring his gifts to perfection in you. The more these goods increase in you,[4] the farther you advance in your knowledge of God the Father and of his Son, our Lord Jesus Christ. To have true knowledge of them is eternal life.[5]

To acknowledge[6] the author of salvation is the beginning of salvation. We should not think that any of the credit for our salvation is due to our own merits and powers or to the commandments of the law of Moses. For his divine power[7] has bestowed on us, without any assistance from circumcision but solely through faith, everything which pertains to true life and to true godliness. Through faith we acknowledge God the Father, from whom all things issue, and Jesus Christ, through whom alone all things are given to us. Life and godliness are not the products of our merits but of his freely given bounty which spontaneously called us to the benefit of salvation. We were without glory and were devoid of virtue, but he shared with us both his glory and his virtue so that we, who in our devotion to our vices were like mean and filthy slaves in the service of idols, might be engrafted into Christ and made pure and glorious after the sins which made us filthy had been removed. He transferred our shame to himself so that through his initiative he might co-opt us into the fellowship of his glory. He took our sins upon himself so that we might find joy through his innocence.

Now these goods by themselves are very great, but far greater and more magnificent are the goods which are promised to us in the future, not through the law of Moses, as we have already said several times, but through our acknowledgment of Jesus Christ. What is being promised? This: that though you are not Jews by birth,[8] nevertheless you may be made equally partakers of the divine nature because you have been admitted into the company of God's children and will take possession of the inheritance of immortal life, provided that in the meantime you practise immortality, as it were, here on earth in a life without corruption and provided that you have escaped all the corruption of the vices and desires which infect the soul and direct it towards everlasting death.

God has freely bestowed innocence once for all. It is not enough just to safeguard it. Instead, strive with might and main and labour to become rich in good deeds. Do not let your faith remain idle[9] but let integrity be its companion, so that everything which you say or do is honourable and virtuous. Let knowledge follow upon integrity so that you not only choose what is right but also perceive what is to be done, and where, before whom, to what extent, and in what way. Let self-control accompany knowledge so that[10] the mind, remaining invincible against every enticement from the world, steadfastly follows without deviation that which it has judged to be the best. Let endurance be joined to self-control so that while you are engaged in doing good you bear evils bravely. For sometimes the inability to endure evils breaks those whom worldly blandishments do not soften. Let godliness stand beside endurance so that you give to the glory of God the credit for whatever you do or suffer. Let brotherly affection accompany godliness so that just as you love God for himself, so do you cherish for his sake all who confess God. Let love, which is eager to do good to all, not just to the godly and to Christians, but to the ungodly as well, increase and enlarge brotherly affection.[11]

These are the fruits of evangelical faith. If you possess them, and possess them in abundance, they will ensure that your acknowledgment of our Lord Jesus Christ through faith has not been useless and unprofitable to you even though you are strangers to circumcision. For the sum and substance of Christian godliness is placed in them. If anyone lacks them, he has confessed Christ in vain since he is slipping from evangelical light back into the old darkness. Like a blind man who tests the way with his hand,[12] he is led around in circles through the byways of worldly desires and fails to see the road which he has to take to attain fellowship with Christ. Although he has been cleansed freely from his former sins once for all, he does not thank Christ for this kindness, but, as though he had forgotten this great mercy, he slips back again into the same sins. Therefore, brothers, do not become carefree and slack just because all the sins of your past life have been forgiven and through the goodness of God you, who did nothing to deserve it, have been called to the profession of the gospel. Instead exert yourselves all the more to keep that goodness, through which God called and chose you, from turning into your own ruin and into an increase in your damnation. For that will be the result if you disregard his kindness and relapse into the same condition from which he redeemed you by his death. On the contrary, strive to make it clear through your good deeds[13] that God has not called and chosen you in vain. Some part of this business has been placed also in your hands. For if you think about the state from which God has called you, to what he has called you, what rewards he has held out before you, and if in addition to these considerations you exert yourselves in the ways I showed you just above,[14] you will nowhere slip from the straight course of godliness. For divine aid will be present in abundance for those who exert themselves in this way. God will furnish you his help so that, victorious over this world, you will at last reach the eternal kingdom of our Lord and Saviour Jesus Christ and will possess the goods of heaven with him through love of whom you despised worldly goods on earth. The reward is absolutely magnificent, but it must be sought with the utmost effort.

Therefore, I shall never cease to remind you of these matters even though I know it is not necessary. For you both remember what you have to do and you do it, and you are well established by your extended progress[15] in godliness and by the truth which you have now known for a long time and which, having once embraced it, you follow steadfastly to the present time. Nevertheless, I am mindful of my Lord's command[16] who bade me after my own conversion to strengthen my brothers as long as I dwell with you, a stranger on earth,[17] in the tent of this poor body. I think that it is my role, then, to awaken and arouse in you a zeal for godliness so that you may be ever more watchful in what you have begun. I have even more reason to do this because I know that this poor body in which I reside will soon be stripped away and I shall exchange my exile on earth for the citizenship of heaven. My Lord Jesus Christ, whom I have been serving as

a soldier until now, has made it known to me.[18] Therefore, I shall take pains
now to have these matters so firmly fixed in your minds in the meantime
by repeated reminders that you will be able to remember them even after
my death,[19] when it will no longer be possible to remind you with my own
voice.

Since what you have received from us is absolutely certain, you must
not deviate from it. For our teaching is not like that of the philosophers,
who, with cleverly devised fables and man-made subtleties, try to persuade
people of what they themselves obviously do not understand since they
disagree with one another about it.[20] We have certainly not followed their
course but have revealed to you the power and coming of our Lord Jesus
Christ and we preach to you his majesty, which we have beheld with our
own eyes. For he deigned to display to a few of his followers before his
death a sample, as it were, of the great power and the great glory with
which he will come some day as the judge of the living and the dead, and
to reveal how wonderful is the bliss that he will lavish on those who love
him steadfastly. After God the Father had clothed him with a beauty and
a glory that made his face as bright as the sun and made his clothes surpass
the whiteness of snow – the heavenly spectacle was more than human
vision could bear[21] – the greatest honour of all was added, the witness of
his Father's own voice, borne to him from on high from the magnificent
majesty of the Father. The Father's words were: 'This is my beloved Son
who has delighted my heart. Hear him.'[22] No more complete nor more
magnificent testimony could be produced.[23] And it did not come forth from
some prophet but from the very majesty of the Father. We beheld these
things with our own eyes; we drank them in with our ears when we were
present with him on the holy mountain of Tabor.[24] If the oracles of the
prophets who shrouded their prophecies about Christ in riddles have very
great weight with you,[25] so manifest[26] a proclamation from the Father
himself about the Son ought to have even greater weight. The prophets
concur with the Father's voice provided that one interprets them correctly.
They in a sense prepare the mind for evangelical truth through their promises when they sketch and, as it were, outline what evangelical preaching
portrays completely. Therefore, I fully approve of the way the Jews pay
close attention to the prophets and search in them for the coming of the
Messiah. To believe that Christ will come is to take a step towards evangelical faith. For the one who is already fully convinced that the Messiah will
come is more quick to believe that he has already come. Therefore, there is
good hope for him who, though not yet illuminated by evangelical light,
pays attention to the prophets as to a lamp shining in a dark place. For it
is better to have any kind of light than none at all until the time when, as

the sun approaches and the dawn begins to break to dispel the darkness
completely and to make even the lamplight itself disappear, the morning
star of evangelical preaching,[27] which announces that the sun itself is at
hand, begins to rise in your hearts. The predictions of the prophets will thus
be useful only if those who read them remember that the prophetic part of
Scripture is obscure because of its cloak of figurative speech and can not be
understood without interpretation. This interpretation does not belong to
everyone alike and is not subject to the arbitrary views of any one person.
For the prophets who made these predictions did not make them from their
own understanding and will. Since they were holy men and free from all
human desires, the Holy Spirit inspired their minds and using them, so to
speak, as his organs of speech made his own mind somehow known to us
through them. What men produce from their own human understanding
can be grasped by the human intellect. But what has been produced by the
inspiration of the divine Spirit requires an interpreter who is inspired by the
same Spirit. People who make what is said about Christ fit some king on
earth, or refer what is said about life in heaven to happiness in this world,
or take what is said about the goods of the soul to mean purely material
advantages, go very far astray from the mystic meaning of the prophecy.[28]
They are not easily persuaded that Christ has come, since from a false
interpretation of the prophecy they have imagined for themselves some sort
of earthly messiah whose idea Christ does not fulfil. Therefore, they do not
acknowledge him, not because he is inconsistent with the spiritual likeness
of the prophecy but because he is different from the image created by their
false interpretation.

Chapter 2

Everyone who is moved to utter prophecies on his own initiative is called
a prophet, but wrongly. Everyone who interprets a prophet's prediction in
the light of his own desires is a false interpreter. In the past among the Jews
there were also false prophets who, to win a ruler's favour or to gain money
or to stir up hatred against others, would not prophesy what the Spirit of
God dictated but what they themselves had invented.[1] Passing themselves
off as true prophets they would deceive the foolish and with their lies
clamour against genuine prophets. So too men will arise after my death
who will on false grounds boast themselves to be teachers of the gospel
although they will really be masters of falsehood. They will deviate from
evangelical doctrine and will introduce human fabrications. They will
introduce destructive heresies in place of saving truth as they look to their
own gain or to their own glory and tyranny rather than to the interests of

Christ. They will reach such a pitch of madness that, in their ingratitude, they will not be afraid to deny Jesus, their Lord, by whose blood they were redeemed and to whom they once pledged their allegiance. They are more wicked than even the pagans who have never confessed Christ. They will stir up divine vengeance against themselves by these actions. Not only will they not be helped by their previous profession of Christ, they will even call on themselves swift destruction from a vengeful God. But it would not be enough for those who are already lost if they were to perish alone. They will drag many others down into ruin with them.[2] False teaching will find its disciples, and with their support these teachers will dare to slander the evangelical truth which you have received from us. Their treatment of the words of the gospel will be insincere because they see that these words are not at all conducive to what they desire. Intent on their private gain, they will impose on your simplicity with fictitious discourses. Their object is not to gain you for Christ but to secure from you as much gain as possible for themselves. For they see that those who are captivated by the delights of this world find the teachings of the gospel quite implausible. They see that what we are doing when we steadfastly safeguard the purity of evangelical doctrine against the ungodly in the face of every kind of death is not for the self-indulgent. Therefore, they will adulterate the true teaching of Christ and in place of the truth will teach, not the doctrine which leads to salvation, but pleasantries which will appeal to the sensual minds of their hearers and will win wealth and glory for themselves in the eyes of the world though not in the eyes of God. For the sake of a moment of glory and pleasure they would prefer[3] to prepare[4] everlasting destruction for themselves and for others than to struggle to undying happiness through some momentary sufferings of the body. Do not take them as your leaders unless you wish to go straight off to destruction. Do not be deceived by their proud pre-eminence in this world, by their wealth, by their pleasant way of life. They will not long enjoy the profits of this false felicity.

Just as the godly will soon receive the rewards which God long ago decreed for them, so the punishment of these men which he has likewise decreed is speeding[5] straight towards them. Their ruin does not slumber; it will suddenly overwhelm them in their drowsy, carefree state. They will be able to fool the judgment of men; they will not be able to deceive God. Though men with whom their influence prevails may pardon them, God who fears no one's greatness will not. Why would God spare them now when long ago he did not spare the angels themselves who had sinned, but hurled them headlong from heaven and thrust them into the prison of hell where they are bound with chains of everlasting night and are kept to be condemned at the last judgment and delivered to eternal punishment? Will he who did not tolerate pride in the angels tolerate it in humans and let them go unpunished?[6] Will their actions go unpunished now that the light of the gospel has been shown to all and so many benefits have been freely conferred? God did not spare even the rude and primitive world but, offended by the vices of humanity, brought down the deluge on a world stained by crimes.[7] Out of so immense a multitude of mortals all were destroyed except Noah and seven others whom God wanted to be safe. While the rest of humanity scorned God's leniency, he[8] alone gave evidence through his construction of the ark that he feared the vengeance of the Almighty.[9] Will these men escape his punishment when he has reduced to ashes in a rain of brimstone so many cities and so flourishing a region as that of Sodom and Gomorrah? He overturned them so completely that nothing is now left except a horrible, pestilent lake[10] to give witness to the penalty which awaits those who call forth the anger of God upon themselves by similar acts of shame. Just as it was the ungodliness of the people of Sodom and Gomorrah which led to their destruction, so in the case of Lot it was his innocence which was responsible for his salvation. When lawless men were preparing to do violence to him and were oppressing a chaste and righteous man with their abominable lusts,[11] God rescued him from the society of the wicked, to live in whose midst was most grievous to him. Since he himself was pure and chaste in eyes and ears, it was a heavy punishment for a godly mind to hear daily, to see daily, things which he wholeheartedly detested.

These examples have made it sufficiently clear that God never allows the innocence of anyone to be without effect or the ungodliness of anyone to go unpunished. Even if God is gentle and patient with some for a time so that some day they may change their minds, even if he sometimes allows his own to be tempted for a time, nevertheless, when the proper time comes he knows how to rescue the godly from their afflictions. On the other hand, he also knows how to reserve the ungodly for the day of the last judgment to be punished with everlasting sufferings.[12] No form of unrighteousness will escape unpunished. But those especially will pay the penalty who, as though distrustful of the promises of the gospel, follow in this life whatever pleases the body, enslaved as they are to the foul lusts with which they bespatter their lives from every side. And to make their wickedness even worse they top their foul behaviour with violence and treat with contempt those who have been entrusted with public authority. Bold and headstrong as they are, they are not afraid to assail with abuse men who are pre-eminent in rank.[13] Petty little humans dare these things while angels who are far superior to them in might and strength, though ungodly in other respects, still did not go so far in daring that they presumed to revile God.

While the angels disregarded the will of God in the rest of their behaviour, they were still afraid, out of deference to divine authority, to offend him in this particular.[14] But these men are more wicked than those impious spirits since they are not afraid to revile and curse those placed in authority over them, although they are quite unaware of the reason why they utter their malicious words about them. Like dumb cattle born for no other purpose than to be taken and destroyed, they bring ruin on themselves by their corrupt behaviour, and will, therefore, perish like cattle when they receive the wages their ungodly way of life deserves. They think life is sweet and grand if, after completely shedding every feeling of shame, they indulge in wantonness and foul pleasures, and do so in daylight at that. (Those who do such things only at night possess at least some trace of shame.)[15] Who could trust people like that? They are in truth more like blemishes and stains when, during their foul revels in which, pitiable error, they place the sum total of their happiness, they mock and insult you,[16] and call you insane because you do not enjoy life's advantages here and now. Meanwhile their excesses arouse sexual desires, and when they are soaked with wine, they have eyes full of lust. Their thoughts are on nothing else except adultery and every other kind of disgraceful act. Once they are inflamed with wine and have lost their wits, they do not know how to stop sinning but hurry on from one shameful act to another until finally they are not satisfied to live lives of complete abandon by themselves, but must entice and entrap into their shameless conduct others whose minds virtue has not yet thoroughly strengthened.

Now it would be tolerable perhaps if their sins were the result only of lust and wantonness. But no form of vice is missing. The shameless squandering of their property is matched only by their shameless acquisition of more things to dissipate. They have minds and natures trained for greed, for fraud, for plundering. Everything they do is done for gain. They pray for evils to happen to decent, godly people just so they can make a bit of profit. Corrupted by money they turn aside from the right way and imitate in this respect their father Balaam, the son of Bosor,[17] who, though he knew what was for the best, nevertheless was corrupted by wrongful wages and eagerly sought to curse those whom God favoured.[18] Greed led him to such a height of blindness that he was rebuked by an ass. After he had gone mad and, though a human, had thrown off his human mind, a dumb animal, speaking with a human voice, checked the prophet's insanity. It saw more with its physical eyes than he saw with the eyes of his mind, blinded obviously by his desire for money.

These men, who promise a marvellous and novel doctrine though they offer nothing worthy of evangelical religion, are like waterless springs in

which, if one should run up to them when thirsty, one would find nothing
but mud and dirt. They are like storm-clouds which, driven along in every
direction by the wind, create expectations of rain for the thirsty earth,
though in the meantime not even a drop of the teaching which brings
salvation falls from them. They promise the light of evangelical teaching but
wrap[19] it in the darkness of error; everlasting darkness awaits them in the
nether world.[20] When they have made magnificent claims in lying words
and have enticed and entrapped with these false hopes those who have
started to become aware of a better morality and to repent, they deceive
them and immerse them in the desires of the flesh and the pleasures of this
life. They promise to free others from error while they themselves dwell in
ultimate error. They promise others freedom from vice although they
themselves are slaves of depravity. For a person is rightly said to be a slave
to him by whom he is overcome and at whose will he lives. To have once
been rescued at no cost from the slavery of their vices is of no use to them
if they deliberately slip back to the same place. On the contrary, their
slavery is all the more foul, all the more wretched, because it has been
willingly invited after the taste of freedom. Sins committed before the
gospel was preached to people are ascribed in large part to error and
ignorance. But once the preaching of the gospel has led them to acknowledge our Lord and Saviour, Jesus Christ, and through baptism they have
escaped from the defilements of this world and have promised to lead pure
and heavenly lives, if these persons should be overcome by their desires
and should again wallow in their former filth, not only does their baptism
bring them no help but they are in an even worse condition than they were
before they came to know Christ. The person whose sin is mitigated by
ignorance commits a lighter sin. People who add the vice of ingratitude to
the crime of ungodliness will meet a heavier condemnation. Therefore, it
would have been better for them to have been completely ignorant of
evangelical doctrine, which teaches innocence and purity, than, after having
come to know and to accept it, to abandon the holy commandment that was
once delivered to them. For what else has happened to them than that
which is commonly and truthfully stated in the proverb: 'the dog swallows
again what he has once vomited,' and, 'the sow, having washed, returns to
her wallowing[21] in the mire'?[22] It is futile for a dog to have cleaned out its
stomach by vomiting if it again seeks what it threw up. It is futile for a sow
to wash off her muddy filth with clear water if right after her bath she
returns to the dirt she had left.

Chapter 3

I am schooling you in these matters at such length, dearly beloved, and
reminding you now of this same subject in this second letter, not because

I have any doubts about the purity of your hearts, but so that you will keep
more firmly in mind what you know and understand, and will also be more
eager and steadfast in doing what you do. The wicked teaching of those
men will present less risk if you remember that this risk was predicted long
ago by the holy prophets who warned that one must be on guard against
such people and if you remember that we who are the apostles of the Lord
and Saviour Jesus Christ have commanded this same thing. The Lord
forbade anyone to give a hearing to people who, like them, introduce
destructive teachings in place of evangelical truth. Therefore, know this first,
that one day there will come not preachers but scoffers equipped with tricks
and illusions to deceive the unwary.[1] They will not follow the teachings
which Christ gave us, but will live to satisfy the desires of their own hearts.
Therefore, to accommodate their own lusts, they will teach things which
agree with such a life. Because of their disgraceful manner of life, they
obviously have no wish to see the coming of the Lord. Therefore, they will
convince themselves and try to persuade others that he is never going to
come again. 'Where is the promised resurrection?' they will say.[2] 'Where is
the judgment? Where are the different rewards in keeping with the merits
of one's life? Where is his coming, vainly awaited day after day?' For they
will imagine that what is postponed for some time will never happen. 'What
evidence is there,' they will say, 'for a resurrection? Our fathers met death,
one after the other, and no one has yet come back to life. Just as everything
since the creation of the world has been propagated by things dying and
being born in turn, so the course of nature has remained the same down to
our time.'

Yet it is possible to infer the new world of the future from the change
of the world in the past. Just as that change in the past occurred unexpectedly to those who were living for their own lustful passions, so the renewal
will happen whether we believe or not. For it has escaped them or, as I am
inclined to think, they pretend not to know[3] that the sky was created long
ago and the earth too at the same time[4] when the waters that formerly
covered it left it bare on one side while a large supply of water was similarly suspended far above it.[5] After the human race had been everywhere
defiled by its vices, God was offended and, letting loose the deluge, destroyed the world of that time. Eight only who had cultivated innocence
were saved. God executed that universal judgment at that time by cleansing
and renewing the earth through water. The heavens, however, continue to
the present time to be the same as they were when they were created, since
they are being reserved for the fire through which they too will be cleansed
on the day of judgment when the ungodly will be destroyed by fire just as
they perished long ago by water.[6]

Therefore, since it is absolutely certain that that day will come, it does not make much difference whether it comes sooner or later. The only thing which ought to concern us[7] is that whenever it does come it does not encounter us unprepared. Because of the nature of our minds some things seem long to us, some short. But to God nothing is either short or long. He does not follow our desires in his promises but his own eternal and immutable counsel, to which nothing is either past or future but all things are in the present. Whatever he has promised us he will reveal at the time which he himself has predetermined. In any case it makes no difference to him whether one day intervenes or a thousand years. What he does later, he does with the same reliability as what he does sooner. In so far as he himself is concerned, he has already done whatever he has decided to do. He does not change his mind and in the manner of hesitant humans procrastinate and defer his promises, as some falsely think who measure God by their own behaviour. But sometimes he prescribes a longer space of time for your sake, because in keeping with his leniency and gentleness he, in so far as it rests with him, does not wish anyone to perish, but is eager to have all change their mind some day and repent. Hence those who do perish cannot complain that they did not have the time to change their life for the better. That day will be here unexpectedly and will steal upon mortals like a thief in the night,[8] sneaking up on people asleep. The fire on that day will have so much force that the heavens will pass away with a great rush into a different form and the elements from which this lower world is composed will be dissolved by the heat. The earth and everything contained in it will be burned up by the fire and the whole material universe will be cleansed. But if everything must be so pure then that even those things which do not sin have to be dissolved, how much effort must you make to ensure that that day finds you spotless and cleansed through the complete holiness of your life and the pursuit of every form of godliness? In the meantime, this effort must be made with great speed[9] so that you may always be ready whenever that day of God comes. No one may escape God's exacting judgment. So far is he from tolerating any impurity at all that the heavens must burn and be dissolved and the elements compelled to melt in the heat. After these events we await according to his promise new heavens and a new earth which are to have no corruption, no offence, so that we in whose minds there will be no corruption can enjoy that uncorrupted world.[10]

Therefore, dearly beloved brothers, keep this stern, inflexible judgment always before your eyes and make every effort to have the Lord when he comes find you pure and blameless, not only in the view of men,[11] whose judgments are often deceived, but also in his view. For only the person who is pure when God is the judge is truly pure. If that day may seem late in arriving, do not take this delay to mean that it is somehow not going to come, but consider that this leniency of the Lord's, through which he offers the time for all to repent, is his way of providing for the salvation of all. Our dearly beloved brother and colleague Paul has written to you about these matters, and quite copiously in keeping with the more fertile gift of wisdom which God has given him. In almost[12] every one of his Epistles he encourages the expectation of this day.[13] Sometimes he seeks to give a greater stimulus to godliness by speaking as though the day of the Lord were already close at hand, since that day, precisely because it is uncertain, should be expected as if it were going to come today. However, no one should in fact try to set a specific date for it.[14] In keeping with his sublime wisdom, Paul included these and certain other topics[15] in his Epistles which, although he spoke with complete correctness about them, inexperienced and unstable persons nevertheless distort by their perverse interpretation just as they do the rest of Scripture to their own destruction. As a result, through their own fault they turn what is intended to be a source of salvation for the good into a deadly poison for themselves. Therefore, brothers, you who have been forewarned both by Paul and by me in so many ways, take care not to be misled along with the others by the deceit of the wicked and to fall from the firmness of faith which you have thus far displayed. Take pains instead to continue to grow and advance in the gifts and in the knowledge of our Lord and Saviour Jesus Christ. Glory to him both now in this life and through all time. Amen.

The End of the Paraphrase on
the Second Epistle
of Peter the Apostle

PARAPHRASE ON JUDE

Paraphrasis in epistolam Iudae Apostoli

THE ARGUMENT OF
THE EPISTLE OF JUDE
BY ERASMUS OF ROTTERDAM

Jude rages at some length against those who, blinded by their own desires, were opposing the gospel. This opposition should not, however, be thought to be something novel because the opponents were destined long ago for this end and it was predicted by the apostles that people of this sort would creep into the Christian flock.[1] He arms his readers against them by urging them to be ready either to restrain these men through reprimands or to save them through admonitions. But if his readers are unable to accomplish this, they are at least to get themselves ready for the coming of Christ.

PARAPHRASE ON THE EPISTLE
OF JUDE THE APOSTLE
BY ERASMUS OF ROTTERDAM

I, Jude Thaddaeus, the servant of Jesus Christ and the brother of James,[1] write this letter not only to Jews and their proselytes, but to all alike in common whom God the Father in his spontaneous mercy has sanctified without the aid of the Law,[2] making the ungodly godly and the idolatrous into practitioners of true religion; whom in his divine kindness he saved for Jesus Christ to this end, that they might not depart with the rest of humanity into the abyss of damnation; and whom in his freely given bounty he has now called to evangelical salvation. I could pray for no greater source of happiness in this life than that the goodness of God would always multiply in you his gifts of mercy, peace, and love: mercy, so that every day you may move farther and farther away from the vices of your old life; peace, so that you may nourish by the godliness of your life the concord[3] which you have with God; love, so that you may be of one mind in your mutual concord and may be doers of good to one another.

Dearly beloved, since evangelical love means that everything in life is to be shared, whether it happens to be something good or something evil, especially in those matters which pertain to eternal salvation, my zeal to write to you about your salvation, which is as much a concern to me as though it were my own, was so great and my brotherly love for you so keen that I was quite unable to restrain myself from exhorting you through this letter to contend against false apostles in defence of the purity of the faith which was once for all delivered to the saints by the apostles. Toil[4] not only to persevere in your own faith but also to help others in order to keep them from being led astray by imposters. The treasure[5] of faith is beyond price and you[6] must be all the more alert and watchful to keep it from being stolen from you. Though we have delivered the doctrine of the gospel to you honestly and purely just as we received it from Christ, nevertheless certain ungodly persons have unobtrusively entered your midst under the disguise of religion and have crept like wolves into the Lord's sheepfold. Their appearance of godliness commends them, though they are the enemies of genuine godliness. The apparent novelty of this business may cause your minds some distress, but it was determined by the hidden wisdom of God long ago. It was predicted that men would arise who through their misdeeds were both to trouble your godliness and to invite condemnation upon themselves.[7] They take the spontaneous kindness of our God, through which he freely forgave us our sins once for all and freed us from the harsh severity of the Law, and turn it into an occasion for lewdness.[8] It would have been better for them to be moved by his kindness to protect and adorn[9] with godly pursuits the innocence which he gave them without cost and, inflamed by evangelical love, willingly to make their righteousness more abundant and their justice more exact than the law of Moses had commanded. But as it is, they turn the freedom given to them into a licence to sin and to behave vilely. When they deny God, whom they once confessed and who alone is the master of everything in heaven and on earth, and when they deny even our Lord Jesus Christ, who made us his own at the cost of his holy blood, they deliberately fall back into the old servitude from which Jesus had redeemed them with his own blood. Our redemption will be of no benefit to us if we do not persevere in the things to which we have been called.[10]

Since nothing escapes you, I do not think that you need any additional instruction from me but only a reminder not to forget what you already know, especially the following examples.[11] As a prefiguration of these present times Jesus[12] long ago led the Hebrews from their harsh and wretched slavery to the Egyptians through the Red Sea to freedom, but it was of no benefit to them. He pitied and saved them when they were calling out to him, but he plunged them afterward into worse ruin when they lost faith in the desert and were murmuring against God. Their slavery in Egypt prefigures our slavery to our former vices. What Pharaoh, a hard and unendurable despot, represented to them, the devil, to whose tyranny our vices make us subject, represents to us. The Hebrews trusted in God and escaped unharmed to freedom through the midst of the waves of the sea; we believed the gospel and through baptism escaped from the jurisdiction of Satan. But some of them did not continue to hasten towards the promised land with this same trust. God's kindness was of no benefit at all to them but actually turned into an increase in their damnation. In just this same way it will be of no benefit to us to have put aside our sins once for all in baptism if we do not continue to advance steadfastly towards better things and to head unswervingly towards the inheritance of heavenly life.

I want you also to remember that it was of no benefit even to the angels to have been created to be associates of divinity. As soon as their own depravity led them to alter their completely felicitous nature and to cease to remain in their own station,[13] he sent them headlong from the heavens, deprived them of heaven's light, and condemned them to everlasting darkness in the nether world.[14] There they are kept in unbreakable chains for the day of supreme judgment on which, since they have been found guilty, they will be sentenced to the penalties they deserve.

Now Sodom and Gomorrah and the rest of the cities close to them were flourishing with a wealth of material things,[15] but because they misused God's kindness for dissipation and debauchery when they defiled themselves with wicked and disgusting forms of vile behaviour, they were suddenly destroyed by divine anger, consumed by fire from heaven,[16] doubtless to serve as an example to others who misuse Christ's benefits for their own vile way of life.[17] For those who sin in like manner will not escape a like penalty. Do those not sin in a like manner who, deluded by dreams of imaginary pleasures,[18] not only defile their own bodies but also defy their superiors and others charged with authority and are not afraid to heap abuse on those to whom they owe respect because of their pre-eminence in power?[19] Yet the archangel Michael, though engaged with the devil in a dispute over the body of Moses, was still afraid to say an abusive word openly to him despite his being the most vile demon.[20] Although he could not bear the devil's ungodly language, he moderated his imprecation in this fashion, saying, 'The Lord rebuke you.'

If Michael had scruples about using an abusive word to the devil, how much more insufferable is the action of those who are not afraid to revile people pre-eminent in authority and rank. But so great is the perversity of these men that, although they have no reason to do so, they revile and abuse what they do not understand. They are otherwise so corrupted by dissipation and debauchery that they behave with complete abandon in those activities in which the irrational animals live decently and moderately, that is, in eating, drinking, and copulation. But woe to them. They will be allotted a reward in common with those whose wickedness they imitate. Their model is not Jesus Christ, but the fratricide Cain, whom hateful envy persuaded to commit the first murder;[21] not Christ, but Balaam, who was corrupted by gain and tried to curse the people which God had blessed; not Christ, but Korah, who made a conspiracy and rose against Moses but was annihilated together with his fellow conspirators in a horrifying and exemplary punishment.[22]

Such are the men who, while you are living pure and chaste lives and are espousing evangelical love,[23] are present, disfiguring your flock like blemishes. When you are fasting, they indulge themselves privately in extravagant carousing. Neither fear nor respect for anyone holds them back from their vile licentiousness.[24] They[25] mindlessly pursue whatever has caught their fancy. Through such deeds they proclaim themselves evangelical teachers and guides to true virtue. In truth they resemble clouds which hang high in the sky and seem to promise rain for the thirsty earth but are dry and have no water with which to aid the land. They are carried about here and there mindlessly by their own empty desires. They resemble trees which flower towards the end of autumn and create a false expectation of fruit but soon wither away; they are not only unproductive but twice dead. They themselves do not have lives bent on evangelical godliness and they drag others along with them into destruction.[26] They have been given up for lost like uprooted trees for which there is no longer any hope that they will again be green. Since these persons are restless and seditious, they constantly disturb the tranquil calm of the church with some new uproar.[27] Like relentless waves of the sea lifting themselves on high one after the other, they meanwhile accomplish nothing except to splash others as much as they can with their insults and their shameless acts. They are like stars which with their specious appearance of light give promise of being guides of the way,[28] but only lead the naive and unwary into shipwreck because they are erratic wanderers. They do not steadfastly follow a straight course, but are led away by their feelings sometimes in this direction, sometimes in that. These stars, which now vaunt themselves before human eyes with their false light, will not escape the judgment of God, even if he does not punish them at the present time but saves them for the everlasting darkness of deepest hell.

Although these men have appeared in our day, do not think something novel is happening to you.[29] Enoch, who was the seventh after Adam, prophesied long ago about them and about the punishment which they will some day have to suffer. This is what he says: 'Behold, the Lord has come with a countless multitude of his saints to exercise judgment on all and to convict all of them who are ungodly of all the deeds which they have perpetrated in an ungodly way and of all the words which they have spoken harshly and wildly against him, not only sinners living evil lives but also the impious and the revilers of God.' Since these men measure happiness in this life by the pleasures of the body, they are incapable of enduring any affliction or loss which might befall them. They are not afraid to murmur against God and to complain that he created man to have a short life and to be subject to diseases. They wish this life to be as long as possible and to be as little subject to ills as possible, obviously because they have no faith in a future life. Though they have these mean and despicable feelings in their hearts, their mouths nevertheless utter grandiloquent words and proclaim a wonderful kind of philosophy. They are the most abject slaves not only of pleasure but also of money, something which completely vitiates the teachings of Christ. They do not speak the teachings of evangelical truth but only such words as are welcome and pleasant to those from whom they hope for some profit. They lord it over the poor like tyrants, but play the role of flatterers before the rich.

Their malice will cause you less distress, dearly beloved, if you remember that the other apostles of our Lord Jesus Christ predicted this to you in the past, and in particular Paul and Peter.[30] They said to you that scoffers would appear in the last times who would adulterate the perfectly pure teaching of Christ with their own warped desires, men whose lives most certainly never follow the rule of the gospel but their own ungodly and wicked passions. This is the mark by which one may recognize these men. While the rest live together in harmony because they live according to the Spirit of Christ and in their disdain for earthly things care only for the things of heaven, those men stir up divisions because they are sensual. Serving only worldly passions and devoid of the Spirit, they chase after pleasures, strive for power, and reach out for profit. Men whose minds are bent on these things are incapable of Christian harmony. They prefer to disturb the tranquillity of the flock than to be gathered in orderly ranks.

But you, dearly beloved brothers, who are spiritual, take pains in the building of God's house to be cemented ever more closely together like living stones, resting on the solid foundation of your most holy faith.[31] You have been convinced once for all that however much the godly are afflicted in this world they will not go without their rewards and that the ungodly will not escape the punishment which they deserve. Consequently, you are not to demand your payment in this life nor are you to wish to take the punishment of the ungodly into your own hands. Therefore, keep yourselves in peaceful harmony with one another, love one another, and continually implore God's help in pure and spiritual prayer. For God does not listen to any except those who live in harmony. Do not lose faith if you suffer in different ways in this world on behalf of Christ, but look for the mercy of God which will be shown not in this life but in the everlasting life to come. In the meantime take into account the situation of each person and make every effort to save everyone.[32] Save some by gently and mildly recalling them to a better state of mind, others, however, through the use of fear, snatching them, as it were, from a fire. Do not feel hatred for their persons but only for this body, stained as it is by earthly passions, which, like a dirty garment, burdens and stains the human soul. It is fitting to heal the errors of others all the more mercifully because no one who dwells in this wretched body can avoid being stained, for that is simply not within human power. Therefore, let no one claim any glory for himself, but let all glory, majesty, dominion, and power belong to God alone, our Saviour through Jesus Christ our Lord, not only in this age, but before all the ages and in all future ages forever and ever.[33] For only God can do this for you who are trying to preserve perpetual innocence right to the end. Surrounded as you are by a poor fragile body, the world from every side tries through so many material things to call you away from your devotion to godliness. Preserve your innocence, not just that men may find nothing in your conduct to criticize, but so that you may stand in the presence of the majesty of God with nothing in you which could displease him who sees into the inmost corners of the mind. If you remain innocent, you will exult and rejoice in the coming of our Lord Jesus while the others who seem now to be living such pleasant lives will lament. That you remain innocent should be the object of all your prayers.

The End of the Paraphrase on Jude

PARAPHRASE ON JAMES

In epistolam Iacobi canonicam paraphrasis

DEDICATORY LETTER

TO HIS EMINENCE THE RIGHT REVEREND MATTHÄUS,
CARDINAL-BISHOP OF SION, COUNT OF THE VALAIS,
FROM ERASMUS OF ROTTERDAM, GREETING[1]

I thought I had already reached the end of my race, and was intending to give myself a rest, at any rate from studies of this kind, having now explained all the Epistles which I thought genuinely Pauline. I have added Peter's two and one by Jude to them, because they not only stand close to the Pauline Epistles in the vigour of their gospel teaching but are even more involved in obscurity than Paul's are. As for the so-called Epistle to the Hebrews, not only can it be gathered from many indications that it is not Paul's, but it is written in a rhetorical style unlike the Apostle's,[2] and therefore does not present nearly so much difficulty. The same is true of those ascribed to James and John. John writes with such fullness that he virtually explains himself, and James almost confines himself to commonplaces, for example: For Christ's sake we must bravely endure adversity and therein rely principally on support from God; Men become wicked through no fault of nature or of God but by their own fault, whether fortune be cruel or kind; One should not speak rashly or give rein to one's anger; It is not sufficient to profess the gospel in word alone, unless we express it in our actions and affections; That religion is empty which is combined with lack of control over the tongue; True piety is found in the services whereby in mercy we relieve the needs of our neighbour; No man's worth should be gauged by his external wealth, but by the true wealth of the mind; Profession of the faith is useless, unless it is evidenced by pious actions; No man should take up the task of teaching unadvisedly; The chief plague of life springs from an unbridled tongue, just as on the other hand nothing is more useful than a good and well-governed tongue; There is a great difference between worldly and Christian wisdom; Peace cannot last unless human desires are driven out of the heart; There can be no agreement between this world and God; Those who are elated by their own resources and trust in them are abandoned by God, while he is good to those who distrust themselves and depend upon him; He does wrong to God who condemns and judges his neighbour; Short-lived and fleeting is the felicity of this present life; The powerful, who can do as they please with impunity here, will be bitterly punished hereafter; Revenge for wrongs suffered must be left to God as the judge; Good men's prayers have great weight with God; The virtuous action which most inclines God to forgive our sins is that we should forgive our brother when he sins against us and that when he wanders we should lovingly recall him to the right way – and much else of the same kind, which cannot present very much difficulty in the exposition, though they are most difficult in the performance. And yet there are certain passages which I had to wrestle with, such as the one which puzzles Augustine 'Whoever shall ... stumble in one point, he is guilty of all.'[3]: Again, where he says that faith is of no value without works,[4] while Paul argues on the other side that it happened to Abraham not by works but by faith that he was accounted righteous before God and was called the friend of God.[5] There also seem to be some gaps, so that I have had some trouble in establishing connections.[6]

Be that as it may, when I first took this labour in hand, I did not propose to pay this attention to any except those two great chiefs of the apostles and of the gospel philosophy, Paul and Peter. And behold, as I reach my goal and look forward to my rest, your voice calls me back onto the course, urging me over and over again to leave no portion of this task to others, not only because you judge that this activity will be exceptionally useful to seekers after the gospel philosophy, but also since, though the tooth of slander in these days leaves almost nothing intact, yet this work of mine alone has not yet been bedevilled (so to say) by all the demons of criticism.[7] I obey the summons of your Eminence. It is no secret from me, your heartfelt love of truly Christian teaching, in which you spent not a few successful years yourself; nor your sincere support for me, your perspicacious mind, your clear and independent judgment. If the Catholic church possessed more such men, we should see Christianity far more flourishing and somewhat more peaceful.

What spirit hounds them on, those men who, at the risk of their own reputation and authority and to the detriment even of their sacred duty of preaching, endeavour so persistently to reduce the profit that the studious may hope to find in my work?[8] This question only they can answer. I am myself more swayed by the judgment of other men whose more than common scholarship and high integrity clears them of all suspicion of envy or ill will. I stand in the way of no man's reputation; I chase no man from his professorial chair; I interrupt no man's researches; I seek no promotion; I do not hunt for gain, but what little talent I have, I contribute to the common good. The man who does not like my work is free to leave it alone; I make this gift to the public without reward. Should anyone wish to do

better, I will vote for him with both hands.[9] I have never worn the badge
of any faction, and what I write has left no man blacker by a single hair.

In every age it has been permissible to dissent now and again from the
most eminent authorities. If I disagreed only with Thomas,[10] I might be
thought to have a prejudice against him. In fact, I disagree with Ambrose[11]
and Jerome and Augustine not seldom – always with great respect; towards
Thomas I have a more open mind than commends itself to many excellent
and learned men. But this respect I do not think I owe to Hugh and Lyra
and to all their like, although to Lyra I do acknowledge a debt.[12] In every
generation, however blessed, the best things have always appealed to the
minority. But was there ever a generation that gave more scope to ignorance, effrontery, shamelessness, stupidity, and abusive language? Write
books they dare not, for these must undergo the silent criticism of educated
men;[13] their weapons are words steeped in venom, and their audience the
unlettered multitude and poor credulous women. This innocent credulity
offers them their only hope of winning. What heroes! – these doughty
performers with one single weapon, which they share with fishwives. After
which they think it my fault if their own reputation suffers, if fewer recruits
come forward to join their holy flock,[14] while they themselves make it clear,
even in public, from the facts, how much closer they are to impious black-
mailers than to devotees of true religion. Their nemesis will one day
descend upon them, as they bring disaster upon themselves with their own
horse and cart,[15] and from some source or other will come the proper wedge
to split that knot.[16] Nor do I think it sensible to fight against a conspiracy
of potbellies,[17] without eyes or mind. It is more in keeping for a true Christian to endure mountebanks than to imitate them. For myself, encouraged
by you and others like you, but above all with Christ as my inspiration, I
shall continue by sleepless toiling in this field to urge myself and others on
to better things. Farewell, my most respected benefactor.

Louvain, 16 December 1520

THE ARGUMENT OF THE EPISTLE OF JAMES
BY ERASMUS OF ROTTERDAM

James was the bishop of Jerusalem[1] and in that capacity writes also to the other Jews, who lived scattered among all nations, to instruct and shape their lives through various precepts.

THE PARAPHRASE OF
ERASMUS OF ROTTERDAM ON
THE CANONICAL EPISTLE OF JAMES

Chapter 1

James – once the votary of the law of Moses but now the worshipper and
servant of God the Father, who after the proclamation of the gospel requires
spiritual worship, and of his Son Jesus Christ, our Lord – sends this epistle,
not only to all who are enrolled in the profession of Christ, but most
especially to those from all the tribes of the Jewish nation whom the storm
of persecution which arose after the death of Stephen has variously scattered in every direction.[1] You have been driven forth from your ancestral
home, but you have not been driven away from the fellowship of the
gospel. You have been expelled from your houses, but not from the church
of Christ. I pray for your true salvation, not just your physical salvation,
which the world too might pray for, but also that salvation which Christ
bestows on his own even in the midst of death and destruction.

Since our common confession of the gospel and the same baptism
make us brothers, and since there must be among those who are truly
brothers a fellowship in joys and sorrows alike, that misfortune of yours
would bring intense pain to my heart did I not have such confidence as I
do in your godliness. For I well know that exile is more grievous than death
to those who measure happiness in this life by their prosperity and think
that living in a foreign land, torn away from their dearest ones and
deprived of their possessions, is utter wretchedness. You, however, who
have placed the 'long and short'[2] of your prosperity in Christ alone and
expect to find your own happiness not in this world but in the age to come
should be very far removed from their views. For these disasters are not
being sent upon you by God in anger, but in his very great kindness. His
intention is to make your patience more meritorious and your reward more
abundant through the temporary afflictions which you are undeservedly
suffering. Therefore, whenever you are being pounded from every direction
by the shifting winds of evil, you should understand that you are not to be

dismayed as though you thought that God had abandoned you, but ought rather to be wholeheartedly rejoicing because this is a sign that you are dear to God and objects of his care as he tests your endurance. If you endure steadfastly and do not yield to the assaults of any evil, it will surely be evident that the foundation of your evangelical faith is solid. For had you not been convinced that the reward of immortality has been prepared for those who suffer evils in this life for Christ's glory, you would not now be willingly and eagerly enduring so much evil. God wants our salvation to be attributed above all else to faith. For this reason it contributes to the glory of the gospel that people understand from sure signs that your faith is not an ordinary or vacillating form of confidence but something firm and invincible. Anything which is hollow and weak, a mere facade, is easily shifted from its site when storms of evil assail it, but that which neither exile nor poverty nor humiliation nor imprisonment nor scourging nor even death overcomes and defeats must be solid and true.

Everyone admires the stout-hearted spirit of the person who bears adverse fortune with an unbroken spirit. But when people see you enduring in a spirit of joy and even eagerness things which are in themselves griev- ous and harsh, when they see that you believe the humiliation inflicted because of your profession of Christ to be the height of glory, that you take the loss of your property to be a profitable gain, that you think those torments which trouble the body to be a guarantee of everlasting pleasure, that you consider death, than which there is nothing more frightening, to be nothing else but the threshold and passage to future immortality, then they will surely realize that your hope, on which you base your disdain for these evils, is not some commonplace feeling nor the result of merely human persuasion but a resolve made strong by the inspiration of divine power. But as faith is not yet proved unless it expresses itself through a godly life and charitable acts to neighbours, so endurance will not receive perfect praise unless its constancy in the performance of good works matches its bravery and cheerfulness in the endurance of evil. To suffer evils gladly is an heroic act but only if done for the glory of Christ. To do good when one is being treated badly, and to do it not just to those who deserve it but even to those who are responsible for the affliction, is a perfect act. By doing this, you will as members match your head, as dis- ciples you will match your teacher, as children you will match your father, if, that is, you are perfect and complete in every respect and nothing is missing in you which pertains to the completion of the circle of evangelical godliness.

The law of Moses, I admit, did not make this demand. The wise men of this world even consider it foolish.[3] But the new philosophy which

Christ, the heavenly teacher, brought into the world has taught us this new wisdom.[4] The fact that someone has not yet become sufficiently strong in it is no reason to take refuge with the philosophers of this age. Their teachings are too feeble to effect so great a result. What is required[5] is beyond mere human strength; it needs heaven's help. Therefore, the reward has been prepared in heaven. Whenever those who make the goods and evils of this world the measure of all their actions are hard pressed by evils, they seek advice from and implore help from other men. You, however, must ask God for the aid of heavenly wisdom. He shares it with all, not only with Jews but also with gentiles, and he shares it unstintingly in keeping with his kindness, nor does he make his benefit a reproach to anyone. He does not ask a favour from us in return and has no need of anyone's charity. He is naturally good and willing and eager to benefit all. Whoever asks from him will not ask in vain. He wants to benefit all and can fulfil whatever he wants. He takes no notice of our merits; he requires us only to have trust in him. It is pharisaical[6] to say, 'Lord, do what I ask because I fast twice a week.' One who is truly pious prays, 'I am unworthy of your bounty, I am worthy of your wrath, but nevertheless look upon your servant because you are naturally good and merciful.'

Therefore, if anyone wants to obtain a request from God, let him ask with no doubting, with no wavering.[7] Let him take no heed of the enormity of his afflictions; let him not exhaust his own powers on them; let him only reflect that God on whom he depends is absolutely good and powerful. The one who trusts totally in divine aid is solid and strong, but whoever is hesitant and cautious and qualifies his dependence on God by looking simultaneously for human aid lacks all stability. Such a man does not wholeheartedly believe God's promises but like a person having some doubts uses human arguments to debate with himself about divine matters. As the waves of the sea roll back and forth in this direction and that at the whim of the winds and tide, so this person,[8] off-balance and inconstant, is driven about by human considerations and changing opinions. A man like this is deceived, therefore, if he believes he will obtain anything from the Lord because he has the wrong idea about the one whose help he is imploring. He distrusts him as if his good will towards men or his power or the truthfulness of his promises[9] were all inadequate. Christian trust is unqualified and does not waver at any point. It always looks to him alone who does not abandon anyone who has faith in him, in both life and death. But the person whose soul is divided in two and looks in one direction to God and in the other to the world, is off balance and unsteady not only in his prayers but in everything else he does. He has one thing on his tongue, another in his heart, a creature of circumstance, moved by his feelings now in this direction, now in that.

The Christian should not, as ordinary people do, change his mind in response to whatever direction the winds of fortune may blow. Though lowly and crushed under the weight of his different troubles, let him instead lift up his spirit; let him glory in the fact that though despised by the world, he is not despicable in God's eyes. God is not in the least offended by someone's humble condition or poverty but treats him as worthy of the communion of the saints and does not exclude him from the inheritance of the kingdom of heaven.[10] Let the rich man on the other hand rejoice in the fact that he who was once highly esteemed by the worshippers of the world because of his possession of the false goods of this world is now spurned and despised because of his confession of Christ. Though once swollen with empty goods and driven along by pride, he is now rich in true goods in the eyes of God while in the eyes of men he seems downcast and downtrodden.

Therefore, let neither the man who is poor be dejected by his lowly estate nor the man who is rich be made insolent by his fortune. Let each reflect that neither the evils which burden the needy nor the goods which make the wealthy complacent are lasting, but both vanish quickly like flower blossoms in a meadow. They shoot up suddenly in the springtime dew at the coaxing of the west wind and just as[11] quickly wither and die before the north wind's blast and the heat of the sun. Thus the blossom which is born at sunrise and delights people's eyes with its very pleasing colour is visibly dying at sunset. Because trees rest on deep roots and are supported by solid heartwood, they are green for a long time. Some are even permanently green, and neither injury from the wind nor winter's cold makes them shed the grace of their greenery. But since flowers do not have the same supports, as soon as the sun has become blazing hot, they are deprived of the juices with which they were nourishing the short-lived grace of their blossoms. Therefore, as the stalk grows weak, it no longer nourishes and supports the blossom, but what had delighted people's eyes with so much grace a little while before grows dry and old, dies, and falls over. Therefore, let no Christian glory in things of the present, which are neither solid nor lasting, but let him look instead to those things which are everlasting and delight the eyes of God. Let him strive to be the ever green palm[12] rather than the flower which is shortly going to die from a slight injury. You see the newly born flower? What beauty, what splendour, what charm it has in its colour and fragrance! What a parade it makes of its green leaves! What glow, what juice, what youthful freshness it has! But presently at the blast of the south wind and the heat of the sun what drooping, what decay, what death! The same day sees the flower born, sprouting, reaching maturity, grown old, dead. The happiness of the wealthy is just like that. The man who is now conspicuous in crimson, gleaming with gold, sparkling with jewels, surrounded by a magnificent retinue, carried along stretched out in a litter and worshipped among men like some divinity, if fortune blows the other direction, will go begging into exile stripped of all his goods or will weep in prison or raised on a gibbet will feed the crows, or if none of these things happen to him, certainly an unexpected death will suddenly remove all the noisy stir.[13]

It is the mark of a pagan to measure happiness by goods like those which, besides depending on fortune's whim and being uncommonly quick to desert us at life's end, bring ruin unless they are held in contempt. It is the Christian's role to follow those pursuits which prepare everlasting goods over which neither fortune nor decay nor death has any jurisdiction. For no one is blessed simply because he is rich. He will be blessed only when he has been stripped of his possessions because of his confession of the gospel and when, having spurned the pleasures of this life which he once enjoyed to the full, he suffers tortures and imprisonments for Christ. He will be blessed when, through his love of Christ, he endures unto death in the midst of evils with his heart unbroken, because he realizes in this situation that the greater the number of this world's evils which press on him, the dearer he is for this reason to God.[14] God tests our patience for his own glory, so that whoever worships him may set an example to others of how to despise this world and may himself carry off the palm and crown after he has made a gallant contest and publicly proved his true virtue and faith. The crown is not one of oak or laurel such as they receive who chase after reward and praise from mankind; these crowns wither away.[15] It is the crown of immortal life – promised by God, not by some mortal who might deceive. God has promised it, not to those who have accumulated the most wealth, or have excelled in physical strength, or have routed the most enemies in battle, but to those who from love of him have spurned the goods of this world and have bravely born its evils.

The sincerity of our love for God is tested by the blandishments of this world but much more so by the onslaught of afflictions. However, it is in our power, supported by God's help, to be neither softened by blandishments nor broken by terrors. But if the attractions of the world move someone from a right state of mind, or the burden of afflictions draws someone away from true godliness, there is no reason here to blame God. He who is victorious is victorious through God's help; he who is defeated is defeated through his own fault. God does not offer people the occasion to sin. It is our own mind, corrupted and entrapped by its own passions, which converts into the occasion of its own destruction whatever it is that God in his goodness may provide us to harvest godliness from it. God sometimes gives us material prosperity and the enjoyment of life's advantages to provoke us by his kindness to give him thanks. On the other hand he sometimes allows us to be afflicted by adversity, both to make our godliness more distinguished and to increase our reward. But if the final outcome is just the opposite, it is our fault, not his. For just as God, who is good by nature, cannot be moved by any evil, so he does not move anyone to evil. Whatever turns the good gifts of God into our own evil comes from ourselves. He gives an abundance of food and the juice of the vine so that refreshed in moderation we may exalt their author with praise. Will the person who is made drunk by wine then call God into court? Never! Let him accuse his own soul whose vicious desire enticed and drew him into intoxication.

A certain propensity to vicious behaviour has been implanted in our souls from the vice of our first parents.[16] This propensity is, as it were, the seed of sin. If this seed has been admitted into the soul and taken root, the mind has now, so to speak, conceived sin; and if the vicious desire is not weeded out of the soul, that evil foetus gradually becomes larger and stronger until birth is given to a mortal sin, which in turn begins to reproduce itself when all its parts have reached their full growth. It produces the worst offspring of all, namely, eternal death. This is by far the saddest fruit of that pleasure which, though enticing on the outside and giving promise of something sweet, conceals a deadly hook under the bait of pleasure.

Our souls are like this lower world in which we live.[17] The world contains nothing completely pure and perfect, and the good things in it are flawed by some evil. Happy and sad events intermingle, plague spoils the pure air, sickness and decay attack healthy bodies, darkness interrupts the beauty of the daylight. Similarly during the time our souls are subject to these bodies of ours there is hardly anything in them which is blessed and pure in every respect and is not flawed by the stain of some human passion or by the darkness of error and ignorance. But we must impute whatever evil there is in us to ourselves, not to God. If we kept our feelings pure, if we trusted God wholeheartedly, if we aspired to heaven and eternity with our whole body and soul, whatever this life cast before us, whether something sad or something happy, we would turn it into an increase in our godliness.

Therefore, dearly beloved brothers, do not do as the crowd of foolish people do who, to indulge their own vices, hale into court the creator of nature as the author of sin. You who have learned the philosophy of the gospel should stay far away from this error. God by his very own nature is purely and utterly good, and for this reason he is the source of nothing but good. Accordingly, if any one of the vices occurs in us, we must attribute it not to God but to our own selves. If there is any vestige of goodness, any particle of true light, any trace of unimpaired wisdom, we must assign its source entirely to God.[18] If this material globe has any light, it has it from those bodies in the sky and most of all from the sun. Whatever portion of true knowledge or of pure and sincere emotion exists in us, it does not arise from ourselves – we are otherwise nothing except ignorant sinners – but originates from on high. Whatever is truly good comes from the author of every good. Whatever is legitimate and perfect and such as to make us[19] attractive to God is obtained from the source of all perfection. The Father and Prince of all true light sends to us from himself whatever is truly full of light. He does not impart these gifts because of our merits but bestows them voluntarily inasmuch as he is naturally kind. They are gifts more truly than rewards; it is generosity rather than payment. It is wrong for us, therefore, to take any credit for ourselves from this source; we should ask God for mercy on the evils which are ours alone and should give thanks to his generosity for the goods which are not ours at all. In keeping with the absolute goodness of his nature he cannot give except what is completely good. As he is unchangeable and always self-consistent, so there is nothing in him that can be darkened by any passing cloud.[20] Night follows upon and absorbs our daylight, clouds intervene and overshadow it. Mistaken beliefs overcloud human wisdom, evil passions infect human goodness, but there is no admixture of evil, no alternating periods of darkness in God.

Therefore, we too must strive with all our might towards his perfect simplicity so that by making ourselves through godly practices more and more receptive to his gifts we are, so to speak, transformed into him. It is characteristic of children to reproduce their father's nature. We have to our despite imitated Adam, the originator of this crude and corrupted generation. Overshadowed by the darkness of his sins, he has begotten us subject to darkness. In so far as we disdain heavenly things and gape after earthly ones we reproduce his nature. Our blindness, our delusions, our lapses are due to our earthly parent. But that heavenly Father has given us a new and happier birth, so that like new creations we may now respond to our new origin in the innocence of our life and in our knowledge of eternal truth. Adam, seduced by the serpent's deceptive promises, begot us in darkness. God has begotten us again, not from the corrupt seed of an earthly father but from the most pure seed of the eternal and truthful Word.

The serpent's word was a lie and cast us down from the state of innocence. The word of evangelical teaching is truth. Through it we are co-opted as heirs of immortality and enrolled in the fellowship of Jesus Christ, the Son of God. He was the true light which issued from the highest light.[21] His teaching has enlightened the minds of humans and freed them from the darkness of this world. So efficacious is the heavenly word that it has not only changed us but has transformed us as it were into completely different persons.[22] We now detest what previously we used to love; we love what we previously used to detest. Our heavenly Father thought us worthy of this honour because he was moved not by our merits but by his own spontaneous goodness in which he had decided from eternity to found in an unheard of way a new creation[23] on earth and wanted us who are among the first to be called to the teachings of the gospel, to be, as it were, the first fruits of this new foundation.

Since God, therefore, freely imparted this honour to us, it remains for us in turn to respond vigorously to his munificence. We have been admitted to this felicity without payment. But in the meantime we could lose it through our own fault if we do not strive through godly efforts to protect what has been freely given. Our co-option into fellowship with the Son of God through baptism and our avowal of the teachings of the gospel will be in vain if we do not make the chastity and purity of our behaviour match our avowal. As eternal light illuminated us through the Son of God, so let us make our entire life bear witness that we belong to the fellowship of light.[24] We have once and for all put off the old man with his errors, his passions, his vices;[25] now it is right for us to follow a different course. In the past you preferred to look more like teachers than pupils, because your ambition persuaded you that the person who is the most eloquent was commonly thought the more learned. You preferred to get angry at anyone who gave you good advice rather than to acknowledge your guilt. You preferred to indulge a ruinous lust than to pursue those things which bring salvation. But now, my dearly beloved brothers, let anyone who wishes to be thought a new man be slow to speak, quick to listen, ready to learn from everyone. But let no one assume the role of teacher at random or too hastily. The person who dashes into speech comes close to the risk of a fall, just as the person whose emotions are easily aroused is inclined to commit an injury. The godly must be far removed, not only from every act of vengeance but also from every abusive word. The person who makes no reply is less likely to utter an insult. The one who does not get angry even when injured will do no one a wrong. People are commonly inclined to think a man just when he returns insult for insult, wrong for wrong, but that man is far removed from God's view of justice. He taught us through his Son to bless those who curse us, to wish well to those who wish us ill, to do good to those who do us evil. A man who has anger in his thoughts and loosens the reins on that slippery and quick moving member, the tongue, is not practising these teachings. Such desires overwhelm and choke the seed of the divine word in order to keep it from maturing and bearing fruit.[26] Similarly they prevent it from being able[27] to be planted in the harvest-field of the soul. The seed does not adhere to ground covered with brambles, to marshland or to shifting sand; it requires clean, weedless, and stable soil. Therefore, if you want the seed of the evangelical word, which has been cast only once, to produce fruit in you – I do not mean the transitory or everyday fruit by which the body is temporarily refreshed, but the eternal salvation of your souls – then clear away from the field of your breast not only the tumultuous uproar of cursing and anger but also all the passions with which the human soul is polluted, the thorns of greed, the sand of rashness, the mud of lust, the rocks of pride and obstinacy.[28] For a mind burdened with them cannot contain the word of the gospel, which beats to no purpose on the eardrums if it does not settle deeply into the innermost regions of the heart. If this word has once settled in your souls, it will not be sterile but will emerge and blossom in godly actions. The Jews memorize their law but do not express it in their way of life. Philosophers master the arguments for living rightly and think this is sufficient, but they greatly deceive themselves because human happiness is grounded in life, not in words.[29] It must not be enough for you just to have heard the teachings of the gospel as catechumens, to have been baptized and admitted to the mysteries hidden more deeply in the teachings of the gospel, to have learned thoroughly the entire philosophy of Christ and his whole life, and to have accepted the promise of immortality. What Christ taught must be expressed in conduct, what he did must be imitated by us with all our might. Having died to the passions of this world, we must be buried with him; we must come back to a life of innocence with him; we must be taken with him to heaven; in short we must so live on earth that we appear fully worthy of the rewards of heaven.

Do you wish to hear how the person who listens to the word of the gospel indifferently and thoughtlessly derives no benefit from what he hears? Such a person resembles most closely a man looking at his face in a mirror. He looks, but only looks. He cannot change the face he was born with and he steps back from the mirror no different from what he was when he stepped up to it. No, since he stepped up to it only to see what he looked like, the thought of changing the defects in his appearance does not even occur to him. As soon as he steps back from the mirror, he does not even remember what sort of person he saw. The mirror of evangelical teaching displays not the warts and bumps on the body, but puts all the diseases of your soul before your eyes. Not only does it reveal them, it also cures them. The law of Moses produced evils in the soul rather than healed them.[30] For at the level of the letter the Law was imperfect[31] and deterred people from evil through fear more than it caused them to follow the right on their own initiative. But the law of the gospel obtains more through love from those who are willing and free than the law of Moses tried to twist out. It perfects what it begins while the law of Moses brought nothing to perfection. Therefore, whoever uses this mirror to look carefully at his mind and life and does this persistently, never taking his eyes away from the example and teaching of Christ, that is, whoever does not hear the sacred word so lightly that he soon turns to the concerns of this world and seems to forget what he has heard,[32] but composes his whole life according to its norm and expresses through godly works what has been fixed deep inside the marrow of his soul, this person will be blessed, not because he has heard the word but because he has made it a part of his inmost feelings and character.

You hear from Christ that the punishment of Gehenna awaits anyone who has said to his brother, 'Fool,'[33] but you soon forget what you have heard and are up in arms over a trifling insult. You hear that riches, subject as they are to moths and thieves, are to be disregarded and that true riches are to be stored up in heaven.[34] But you depart from the preacher and go right on heaping up wealth rightly or wrongly with might and main just as if you believed that there were no rewards for godliness after this life is over. Whoever among you thinks he is being exceedingly religious just because he keeps his hands from theft, does not brawl and avoids the other vices, but in the meantime fails to check his tongue from abuse, insults, and obscenities or his heart from foul thoughts, his religion is in truth sterile and useless. The man who only talks of adultery but does not commit it is not punished by human laws perhaps, but in God's eyes he who has committed adultery in his mind is already an adulterer.[35] The man who covets another's property does not pay a penalty to his fellow men in whose view it is permissible to covet with impunity, but in God's eyes the man who has turned only his thoughts to theft is already on trial for it. Since our minds are invisible to other people, we are judged only from our overt actions, but God sees into the innermost feelings of the mind and judges us from them. Furthermore, the thoughts of a corrupt mind are often apt to burst out on the tongue. True godliness is so far from being associated with a shameless tongue that in the Christian view insult is a form of homicide.

To have abstained from actual sin is not enough for Christian religion; there must also be an abundance of good works. Even servants refrain from evil, doubtless from the fear of being punished. Love is the appropriate mark of children. Love is not some idle thing, but is an efficacious and willing expression of itself in every kind of good work. Someone will say here, 'What are those deeds then which make us truly religious?' Those who savour Judaism establish the glory of their religion in cloaks and phylacteries, in discrimination among foods, in ritual washing, in long prayers, and other ceremonies.[36] These ceremonies are sometimes not to be spurned if through these signs we are reminded of the kind of things which are proper to godliness. But they are destructive if someone thinks he is made religious through them; they only turn him more quickly into a hypocrite. Nevertheless, people who mistakenly locate godliness in visible things think that observing and performing ceremonies is the substance of religion. They are perhaps signs of godliness but not its cause since visible things are intrinsically neither good nor evil. They only seem to be such either from common habit or in popular opinion, while genuine godliness exists only in the soul and expresses itself in other, far more certain signs.

Do you want then to hear what true religion is in the eyes of God the Father, who does not judge you in the manner that human beings do? Pure and spotless religion consists in being both compassionate and kind towards our neighbour in the same way we have experienced God's compassion and kindness towards ourselves. We behave this way not from some expectation that a charitable act will be reciprocated, but from a pure and sincere love as we wait for the reward for our charity from no other source than from God. He allows the credit to be given to himself for whatever our love of him has caused us to place in a brother. Among the Jews the godly and pure person is someone who has not touched a dead body or someone who has washed in a running stream. In God's view the one who helps orphans and widows in their afflictions or raises up an oppressed brother or aids the needy with money is godly and pure. To a Jew whoever eats pork is impure. To God anyone is impure whose soul has been tainted and sullied by the passions of this world.

You ask what those passions are? In the world's judgment anyone who is poor is thought to be of no account, while the more wealth a person has, the more respectable he is. For this reason the chief goal of the worldly is to acquire the largest amount of money they can. The person who is wronged but does nothing about it is thought to be cowardly and spiritless; the person who repays an evil act with good is considered foolish. The man who indulges in conspicuous consumption is considered magnificent while the man who follows the course of moderation is thought to be niggardly. A person swollen with pride who looks down from his lofty position on people of lower rank is considered grand. Someone whose affairs succeed to his liking, who is awash in delights and pleasures, who is a slave to his belly and gullet – that one is thought to be happy. But it is such actions that truly make a person's soul ungodly and impure. Only one who is free from them is truly religious in the eyes of God the Father. He has removed us from earthly things and summoned us to heavenly ones, from things which will perish and pass away to eternal things. He has taught us to judge a person's worth by true goods and to have no other object in anything we do than his glory. Recompense for good deeds is to be awaited from him alone. He does not repay the charitable acts of true godliness as this world commonly does with rewards that are transient and soon to perish, but lavishly bestows blessed immortality. The one to whom you extend a charitable service is of low estate, poverty-stricken, unable to repay the favour; nevertheless, it is far better to invest in him than in another rich or powerful person from whom only a worthless and temporary profit can return.[37] For[38] Christ repays with eternal life the assistance given a poverty-stricken brother.

Chapter 2

One who loves his neighbour because of God and loves God in his neighbour does not measure the neighbour by the extent of his power or the size of his wealth or the degree of his nobility, but by the extent to which he abounds in divine goods. Measured by this standard a king or a rich man is no better than someone who is of low estate or poor. Christ died for all men equally and all are equally called to the inheritance of immortality. Therefore, my brothers, if you really have faith in the promises of our Lord Jesus Christ, do not show partiality to persons according to the value of their worldly possessions. By the world's measure Christ was low-born and poor, and yet the Father wanted him to be the prince of all glory.[1] It was not to the rich but to the poor that he promised the kingdom of heaven.[2]

Well then, suppose someone should come into your meeting whose gold ring marked him out or whose splendid clothing made him conspicuous and at the same time some poor man should come in wearing no ring on his fingers and dressed in cheap, shabby clothing. And suppose the rich man immediately catches your eye simply because the splendour of his clothing puts the poor man in the shade, and you take him to the place of honour and say to him, 'Do sit here,' but you say to the poor man, as though he was an object of contempt because of his cheaper clothing and for no other reason, 'You stand over there or sit there[3] below my footstool.' Does not your heart immediately protest, I ask, and tacitly condemn your conduct[4] when out of flattery you attribute to gold and purple the honour owed to virtue but despise the poor person because of his lack of these things? Yet he is far more attractive to God for the true goods in his soul than is that rich man. Do the ring and jewel gleaming on his little finger and the silk wrapped around his body make you attentive to the one, while the sincerity of his faith, the modest attitude, the sobriety, chastity, and other qualities which make the other man truly great and splendid do not lead you to pay attention to him?[5] Why is your judgment at variance with God's judgment?

My beloved brothers, listen with impartial ears to what the facts themselves proclaim to be the absolute truth. However much the world may defer to the wealthy, God himself preferred the poor – poor of course by the standards of this world because they neither have nor desire gold and jewels or high office and kingdoms in this age. God passed over the wealthy in their pride and chose those who are poor in their lack of material goods but rich and powerful in their expectation of the kingdom of heaven and the inheritance of eternity, because they rely on the promise of him who cannot deceive even if he were to wish to, and can fulfil whatever he wishes. To whom did he make this promise of wonderful felicity – to kings and the wealthy? No, to those who truly love him regardless of their condition in life, whether slave or free, rich or poor. And you, when you invited the rich man to the seat of honour and relegated the poor man to the lowest benches, you gave preference to the one who is in God's eyes the more vile and you held in contempt the one who is both rich and respected in the eyes of God. Your respect is paid to that man who prides himself on wealth, which is perhaps the profit of fraud or the product of brigandage; your contempt is given to the one who preferred to be poor than to grow rich at the cost of his godliness, or who, by exhausting his wealth on the support of the poor, deliberately became poor in order to be rich in godliness. Not everyone who is wealthy is impious of course; nevertheless, the rich of this world scarcely ever meet the demands of evangelical piety. It is this class which is most likely to produce the opponents of the gospel of Christ. Who are the ones, I ask, who tyrannize you from their hatred of godliness? Are they not the rich? Who are the people who sue you and drag you off to court? Are they not mostly the rich? Who are the people who blaspheme and curse the holy name of our Lord Jesus Christ through the invocation of which you have obtained salvation[6] and in which you glory? Are they not the rich? Not only do they not have any goodwill towards your profession of Christ but the name, which in your eyes brings salvation and deserves adoration,[7] in their eyes is something deadly and deserving detestation.

However, the confession of this name begins to contribute to your salvation only conditionally; you could through your own fault lose the

salvation promised. The King has revealed the reward, but only for the
person who fulfils the King's law by his actions. No one can plead ignorance of this Law since it was issued in writing long ago.[8] The Law is this:
You will love your neighbour as yourself. Does the person who prefers the
impious rich to the pious poor man love his neighbour in keeping with this
rule? The law of the gospel is the law of love. Whatever is done contrary to
this Law, even if the act is not expressly forbidden, is nevertheless a sin.
You are tacitly convicted by the Law itself which commands everyone of
you to love your neighbour as yourself in every matter. Whoever departs
from this rule is convicted as a transgressor of the Law. Let no one beguile
himself into thinking: it is a trifling sin, the Law is violated only in this part.
On the contrary, the law of the gospel is such that unless it is kept totally,
it seems to be violated totally. Since the sum of the whole Law[9] is contained
in the love of God and of neighbour, whoever is oblivous to love, which is
the root of the whole Law, has surely violated the whole Law and offended
its author. In God's eyes the offender has become to this extent guilty of all
because anyone who has once strayed from the goal of the whole Law –
and it is in his power to do so – seems likely to stray every time the occasion presents itself. For example, when someone is walking in the dark, it
makes no difference whether he goes astray to the right or the left, since he
is certainly liable to go astray somehow once he has left the light. Therefore,
the man who has by his flattery shown a preference for the undeserving
rich man over the deserving poor man is accountable for all the sins which
are usually perpetrated against the love of a neighbour, since he has broken
this part of the law of love. The person who was bold enough to break any
part of God's Law has committed no slight offence against him. He who
gave the commandment of love once and for all has by that very act forbidden once and for all everything contrary to love of neighbour.[10] For the
legislator who said, 'You shall not commit adultery,' also laid it down that,
'You shall not murder anyone.' If you refrain from adultery but commit
homicide, have you not broken the whole Law inasmuch as you have
broken one part of it? The same author forbade both actions and for the
same reason, because each act is opposed to the love of neighbour. But he
forbade not just those acts which are punished by even pagan law, such as
theft, murder, and adultery, but absolutely everything which is at variance
with evangelical love. Though the law of Moses would not punish anyone
who slighted the modest poor man in favour of the arrogant rich one or
who wished ill to his neighbour, the law of the gospel does. Therefore, not
only your deeds must meet its standards but also your speech and the
thoughts in your mind, so that there will never be any discrepancy between
them and neighbourly love. It is the law of freedom, not because it offers

a licence to sin,[11] but because evangelical love secures free and voluntary assent to what man-made laws force from people against their will through fear of punishment.[12] Therefore, fit your whole life to this Law. You will carry off the highest reward if you do what it has prescribed; on the other hand, you will pay the heaviest penalty if you have once departed from that on which the entire Law depends.

You have been freely forgiven the sins of your past life. You have received freely the gift of the heavenly Spirit, through which you have not only been reconciled to God but have also been cemented together in mutual love. This gift was conferred, and conferred freely on you who did nothing to deserve it. All the more severe, therefore, will the punishment be of those who, having experienced so much mercy from God towards themselves, do not show themselves in turn gentle and merciful towards their neighbour. With what cheek will you ask for mercy from God, your judge, when, though a servant yourself, you have behaved without mercy towards your fellow servant?[13] How will you who do not love your own neighbour have the nerve to ask God to love you? If you want to obtain a judgment mitigated by mercy, show yourself merciful to your neighbour whether he is a sinner or someone in need. It is far better for us to turn to this appeal[14] and to rely on mercy rather than on judgment. Since almost everything which we have is due more to God's mercy than to his justice, we must strive to make God merciful to us rather than severe. He saved us because of his mercy. It is right then for us in turn to be more inclined to mercy towards our neighbour than to severity. Leniency, clemency, and kindness gather in far more people than does sternness,[15] so that on this score mercy rightly boasts in its superiority to judgment. For those who would have perished if they had met judgment are saved by mercy and kindness.[16] Everyone of us slips daily and we shall find God, when he condemns our sins, treating us just as we have treated our brothers.

Or is one to think that the profession alone of faith is in itself sufficient for obtaining salvation? But what is faith without love? Love moreover is a living thing; it does not go on holiday; it is not idle; it expresses itself in kind acts wherever it is present. If these acts are lacking, my brothers, I ask you, will the empty word 'faith' save a person? Faith which does not work through love[17] is unproductive; no, it is faith in name only. An example here will make clear what I mean. If someone says blandly to a brother or a sister who lacks clothing or daily food, 'Depart in peace, keep warm, and remember to eat well,' and after saying this, gives him or her none of the things the body needs, will his fine talk be of any use to the ones in need? They will be no less cold and hungry for all his fine talk, which is of no help to their need. He gives them only verbal support, but does nothing in actual fact. A profession of faith will certainly be equally useless if it consists only of words and does nothing except remain inactive as though dead. It should no more be called faith than a human corpse merits the name of human being. Love is to faith what the soul is to the body. Take away love and the word faith is like something dead and inert.[18] It will do you no more good before God to confess in words an idle faith than fine speech benefits a neighbour in need when he must be helped with action. People think they are being mocked when you say to them, 'Keep warm and well fed,' and give them neither food nor clothing. Just so the person who offers no tangible proofs of his faith but repeats every day, 'I believe in God, I believe in God,' seems to be mocking God. A person who gives lip-service to love possesses a fruitless charity. In the same way a person whose belief is only a matter of words possesses a faith that serves no purpose.

Someone will now appear perhaps who, eager to separate things which are by nature most closely joined together and cannot be split apart from each other, might say, 'You have faith, I have deeds. Let each one of us be satisfied with his part. Let your faith be enough for you. I am content to have for my part good deeds.'[19] On the contrary, neither part is sufficient by itself. As for you who boast of faith – if you really have it, you ought to show it by your actions. If the faith you have is dead, the mere fact that you have it is futile. As for you who on the other hand vaunt your deeds – they are not enough by themselves to obtain the crown of immortality unless they issue from love, which is the inseparable companion of saving faith. Loving acts of charity are for us what flowers and leaves are for a tree. If they bloom at the proper time, they show that the roots of the tree are alive and are providing the sap by which the leaves and flowers are nourished. Good deeds are correspondingly beneficial if they are not done for vainglory or for popularity, because of fear or shame, or from hope of gain, but from a living faith which has persuaded us that whatever is done to a neighbour for God's sake is done to God, and that its reward is not to be expected from anyone except God. You are satisfied because you are convinced that God is one while pagans erroneously believe that there are countless gods. You are right to be satisfied, for on this score you do excel them. But your belief that God exists and that God is one is futile unless you believe in such a way that you also obtain salvation from him. But you will not obtain it unless you join love to faith and testify by godly works that you both believe and love. If you believe that God exists, believe also that he is the source of salvation; believe his promises and make your life such that you appear worthy of his promises. He promised mercy, but only to those who practise mercy here towards a neighbour. He promised eternal life, but only to those who spurn the joys of this world. In this way you will not only believe that God is one, but you will be placing all your trust in him alone. Otherwise what will be the profit of your belief? Demons also believe that God exists; they believe that Jesus is the Son of God, and their belief makes them tremble in dread.[20] But because they only believe and do not have love as well, they fear his punishment and have no hope of a reward. They experience God's justice, but they do not deserve to experience his mercy since they are themselves cruel to others.

If you are still so foolish as to be deluded by your futile faith,[21] look, I shall bring out a more familiar and better known example to teach you that a faith which does not work through love is useless and dead. Abraham, in whom we take the greatest pride as the author of our race, merited the chief and special praise of faith before God, who attributed to him the acclaim of righteousness. But faith was by no means sterile in him.[22] He did not merely proclaim with his lips that he had faith in God's promises; for he did not hesitate to lay his only son Isaac on an altar and to sacrifice him at God's command, although in the course of nature he could not expect to have descendants from anyone else.[23] He relied on God's promises, who he knew recalls even the dead to life when it pleases him,[24] and he did not at all delay to carry out what he had been commanded. Therefore, he merited the praise of righteousness from deeds, but deeds which originated from faith. For there are also the works of the law of Moses, but those who have no part in evangelical faith vainly place their faith in them.[25] What would that pre-eminent patriarch not do who so promptly and readily agreed to the sacrifice of his only son Isaac, whom he loved all the more tenderly because he had been born in his extreme old age and because that fruitful line of descendants had been promised in Isaac's name? Abraham was pronounced righteous even before he could sacrifice Isaac,[26] but by God, who knew that the active and living faith of the old man would refuse nothing if the occasion offered itself. Therefore, each thing was an aid to the other. Faith gave him the courage not to shrink from the sacrifice of his son, who he did not doubt would soon be restored to life at God's command, but he added his signal deed, like a colophon, thus showing to men too that the faith of Abraham was neither dead nor commonplace. For a man who does not hesitate to risk his only and uniquely dear son is neither pretending nor having doubts. Would the man who is ready to lead his own son to death, a son dearer to the father than the father is to himself, be reluctant to ignore money for the sake of Christ?[27] On the basis, therefore, of this most remarkable proof of faith it is clear that he was perfected just as Scripture has stated: 'Abraham believed God and it was accounted to him for righteousness' [Gen. 15:6], and he was called 'the friend of God.'[28]

If Abraham had been reluctant to sacrifice his son at God's command, he would evidently have lost the profit of his faith and the acclamation of righteousness. Will someone's faith be of any benefit to him if, despite God's command, he is reluctant to share his clothing with a neighbour who is cold, or is reluctant to share his food with the hungry and his drink with the thirsty, as if he thought God would let anyone who dedicated some part of his own resources to the needs of a brother perish of cold or hunger? If those men and women of old[29] did not receive the praise of righteousness except when actions proved their faith, much less is this praise to be hoped for by those who profess the law of perfect love.

Mercy and kindness towards a neighbour have so much value in the eyes of God that a woman who was a prostitute (and a foreigner at that), commended by her charitable act of hospitality, merited being counted in the register of the godly, in the register of citizens, in the register of the most admirable patriarchs. Rahab was not Jewish; she ran a brothel and supported herself from earnings that certainly do not meet with public approval. Nevertheless, she has merited praise for righteousness in the books of Holy Scripture.[30] For she was convinced that when God is the one who repays, the good deeds of no one are in vain, especially when a deed is performed for good men or at least out of regard for God. Moreover, she took no account of the risk to her own life and thought only of the lives of the spies.[31] She did not want the messengers to die whom the leader of the Jews had sent to spy and so she sent them out secretly by a different route. She could have won considerable favour from her own countrymen if, as it was certainly in her power to do, she had betrayed the spies. But she preferred to serve the will of God rather than her own profit. She was fully confident that he would pay a more bountiful reward than would men. Therefore, just as Abraham did not merit the praise of righteousness from bare faith but from faith confirmed by actions, so Rahab too would have believed in vain that the God of the Jews was the true God if, when the occasion confronted her, she had not shown by her actions that she sincerely believed. Otherwise, as I said, faith which is cold and no longer loving,[32] and fails to display itself when required by the situation, is not even faith; it is only the empty name of faith. For just as a corpse, when the soul abandons it, is dead and useless, so faith in the absence of a love that is not idle is dead and without effect.

Chapter 3

The human tongue has great utility whenever someone is teaching the

elements of true godliness, but to assume the task of teacher[1] is to assume
an office encumbered with risk. It requires a person who is first of all
eminently learned in the content of evangelical doctrine and secondly has
his emotions completely purged.[2] It is not enough for him simply to teach
what is correct; his one and only aim must be the glory of Christ. A teacher
of this kind can have the greatest benefit if he is also in love with what he
teaches. Conversely, there is great loss to the people when someone
occupies the position of teacher whose doctrine is corrupt or whose mind
is corrupted and warped by passions like hatred, anger, revenge, greed,
ambition, or lust. Therefore, my brothers, do not aim indiscriminately at
being teachers. It is safer to be a listener than a speaker, and a small number of teachers is after all sufficient for the instruction of a large number of
people. Therefore, let the man who aspires to the position of bishop and
teacher examine and re-examine himself to see if he is equal to undertaking
the burden. Let him above all reflect on the fact that he is assuming a
responsibility that is subject to immense risk, since he will be rendering the
most exact account to the supreme judge if he should teach otherwise than
he ought. Because the speech of a person with authority has very great
weight, its poison can spread more widely and dangerously. Nothing,
however, is more difficult than to exercise such control over the tongue in
every respect that it never makes a slip. The weakness of our human nature
makes everyone slip every day in many things. Therefore, if someone can
avoid every slip of the tongue, this man might seem to be perfect and
capable of controlling his whole body by the bridle of reason once he has
prevented that most slippery of the members from committing any sin.[3] The
one who prefers to play the role of pupil to that of teacher is farther away
from this risk.

To have complete authority over the belly is an achievement, to control
the eyes and ears is likewise an accomplishment, and it is something again
to keep the hands in check. But to keep the tongue under complete control
is the most difficult of all. The tongue is a tiny part of the body, but all the
rest is virtually dependent upon it. Human speech is an effective and
powerful force for either the benefit or the ruin of the multitude.[4] It pen-
etrates the minds of its hearers; it implants or weeds out pestilent beliefs;
it arouses or calms passionate hatreds; it moves people to war or disposes
them to peace. In sum, the tongue can propel a hearer in any direction at
all. We place bits in the mouths of horses that they may obey us and with
a small piece of iron we drive the animal's whole body around to suit our
own wishes. As the bridled mouth serves the rider, so a tamed tongue
serves its owner.[5]

You see how large a mass a ship makes. Ships with sails unfurled may be carried over the waves by the marvellous impetus of the winds, but they are driven about by a very small rudder in whatever direction the pilot holding the pole intends them to turn. He skilfully pushes on the tiller and that mass for all its great size feels the command of its smallest part. Control of the tongue, therefore, is not to be despised. It is a tiny member, but one that, swollen and boastful, spreads ruin far and wide and stirs up huge uproars if it is not checked by the bridle of the mind. It sets whole peoples, whole kingdoms against themselves.

Let us consider another very similar example.[6] Look at how tiny a fire can kindle a huge a mass of timber.[7] Where did that raging and rapidly spreading fire come from? From a single spark. It could be crushed out at the start with very little trouble; neglected, it gathers strength from all sides and finally reaches a point where it cannot be overwhelmed by any force. Fire has many different uses if it is employed correctly, but it becomes utterly destructive if allowed to wander where it wishes. In the same way there can come from the human tongue both the greatest benefit and on the other hand the ultimate ruin to human life. Do you not see that nature's fabricator signified this very thing when he willed the human tongue to have the appearance and colour of fire?[8] Does it not roll and wheel about just like a flame? However, the evil in this member is not simple and one-sided as it is in most of the other parts of the body. The tongue is a world and collection of all the vices.[9] A small spark is, as it were, the seed from which the whole fire grows. Similarly every evil in life is taken from the tongue as though it were their storehouse. Just as a bit of fire combines with a mound of tinder so that gradually fire mingles with the entire pile, so the tongue mingles with the members of the body in such a way that, if it is not checked, it stains and infects the whole body with its plague and keeps a person's entire life from the cradle to extreme old age ablaze with the fire of every vice.[10] But nature, which by the wall and barricade made by the teeth and the lips reminds us to use the tongue cautiously and with conscious control, did not place the violent power of this evil in the tongue. This evil was inspired from the fire of Gehenna which first infects the mind with evil spirits. This pestilence in the mind breaks out on a larger scale through the organ of the tongue and the person's condition goes from bad to worse.[11] The plague then catches others too with its contagion so that the evil, which is now out of control, cannot be checked by any force or by any reasonable treatment.

But is there anything anywhere so uncontrolled that human attention cannot make it gentle through some kind of treatment? No wild animal is so wild, no bird is so fierce, no reptile so poisonous, no beast of the sea so savage that human ingenuity and kindness do not tame it. Lions are domesticated, tigers and pythons made gentle, even elephants learn to serve. Crocodiles too are subjugated, vipers become mild, eagles and vultures are made friendly, dolphins are even enticed to friendship.[12] Although every kind of animal which earth and sea and air contain has been tamed in the past and is being tamed every day, no method, no art has yet been found to tame the intemperate tongue. Yes, this one evil is still wild and violent, and is not only incapable of being controlled[13] but even drips with a deadly poison.[14] Lions rage with claws and teeth but do not have poison. Vipers are armed with poison, but do not have claws or horns. Only the tongue is doubly baneful with its insuperable ferocity and its deadly poison, which it breathes on anyone it wishes even from a distance – unlike scorpions, which do no injury except to people struck by their tail, or vipers, which cannot harm unless they puncture with their hollow fangs.

The disease would be less frightening if it were simple and harmful in one way only. As it is, the evil takes many different and various shapes in order to injure more grievously and readily, and is often more deadly when it disguises itself under the appearance of good.[15] There is nothing better or more attractive to everyone's eyes than godliness. The tongue does the most harm under the pretext of godliness when it mixes things which cannot cohere. For the person who is cruel and slanderous towards a neighbour cannot be pious towards God. And yet with this organ we praise God, calling him Father, and with the same organ we revile and slander a neighbour created in the likeness of God. We use the tongue to sing to God from whom all blessings flow and we use it also to inflict the worst evils on another person as if the insult done to him is of no concern to God the creator. God's station is neither increased by our praises nor his person harmed by our insults. But a man can be either harmful or helpful to another man, and what we do to him, God reckons to be done to himself as well.[16]

Let no one believe, therefore, that the hymns which one produces with the tongue, not from the heart, are pleasing to God when that same tongue spews the poison of slander upon his neighbour. Can any two things be more opposed than praise and blame? Yet things so opposite proceed from the same mouth. This is common practice among the ungodly. But the same practice ought not to exist among you who have committed yourselves to evangelical sincerity and to whom it is disgraceful to have your tongue utter anything different from what your mind feels.[17] You have learned to love God in your neighbour and your neighbour in God. You have learned not only that you must not injure anyone with the wantonness of your tongue but also that you have in fact a mandate to follow the example of Christ and to bless those who heap insults upon you.[18] The person who is plainly

and undisguisedly evil is a more bearable source of harm. But when someone tries to make slander accepable under the guise of godliness, what else
is it than dosing wine with hemlock to make the poison more deadly by
mixing it with the most wholesome substance? They have in their mouth
'Lord, be merciful,' even as they cruelly rage against a brother with their
tongue. They have on their lips, 'Our Father,' even as they pierce again and
again with the lance of their tongue the neighbour for whose salvation
Christ was pierced. They preach the goodness of God who saved mankind
by his mercy while they themselves are quick to destroy it with the poison
of their tongue.[19] They preach of Christ's goodness to the human race while
contrary to Christ's example they themselves sharpen their tongue against
a fellow Christian. They pour out praise for the gentleness of Christ, who
answered his slanderers calmly, while they themselves assail with lies even
the one who benefits them.[20] They proclaim themselves angels and heralds
of Christ while they are the organ of the devil. They promise the seed of
heavenly doctrine while they sow pure aconite.[21] They not only do such
opposite things with the same tongue but often even from the same pulpit
they begin with the praises of God and then launch into the denigration of
a neighbour. The ruin with which they infect the minds of the audience is
all the greater because under the fictitious appearance of religion they cover
and disguise the deadly poison which they draw forth from their infected
heart through the organ of the tongue. I ask you, brothers, does this not
remind you of some kind of monster?

There are springs which bubble up wholesome water; there are springs
a taste of which is lethal. There are springs which pour out sweet drinking
water; there are on the other hand springs which supply bitter salt-water.
There is nothing strange in this phenomenon since the liquid as it flows
through different veins acquires the taste of lime, alum, sulphur, or another
metal, or of sweet earth. But how can it be that speech, though it originates
in the same heart and comes bubbling out through the same tongue, is so
inconsistent, while among so many different kinds of springs none is found
which simultaneously produces sweet and bitter water from the same
mouth? Does the same tree produce fruit having opposite flavours? Consider, my brothers. Does the fig-tree which is naturally sweet produce the
bitter berries of the olive-tree? Does a grapevine bear figs? Not at all, but
every fruit corresponds to its own tree and reproduces with its flavour the
sap of its root. Does it not then seem to be somehow monstrous for the
same person to be producing from the same heart through the same tongue
godliness and ungodliness, truth and falsehood, salvation and perdition?

Therefore, since nothing is more destructive than a wicked tongue,
nothing more wholesome than a good and well-instructed one, and since it

is rare to find anyone able to control this member in every respect, the person who is to assume the position of teacher must be carefully selected from among a number of candidates. He must be calm-minded and unaffected by the tumult of the passions. His whole life must be remote from any kind of disgraceful behaviour so that he not only teaches those things which belong to true godliness but also teaches them with complete meekness. For a contentious and stubborn style of teaching generates nothing but faction and discord. Among the philosophers of this world the person who is the most obstinate debater and is second to none in the volubility of his tongue holds first place. They do not take this approach so that the listener may go away a better person but to make the winner feel prouder and the loser more downcast. Meanwhile the crowd[22] is distracted every which way by different interests so that there is no solid benefit for either speaker or hearer. Among you, however, who profess evangelical philosophy,[23] anyone who is truly wise and endowed with true knowledge[24] should not make his wisdom evident through pride and a contest in words,[25] but should testify to the kind of person he is by the godliness and integrity of his character rather than by his words.[26] As faith and love which remain at the level of words are alike useless, so a wisdom which does not prove itself beforehand by meekness of character is likewise useless. For this is the sign which allows one to distinguish most easily evangelical philosophy from man-made philosophy. Man-made philosophy produces professors who are captious, obstinate, and ferocious. But the more sincere, the more effective evangelical philosophy becomes, the less it is marked by arrogance. Its special force is located not in syllogistic subtleties or rhetorical trappings, but in sincerity of life and gentleness of character which gives way to the contentious, attracts the docile, and has no other object than the salvation of its hearers. It is a heavenly wisdom. Its teacher must have a mind purged of all earthly passions. Heavenly wisdom must be drawn from a clean vessel.[27]

If, however, you have minds spoiled by bitter rivalry among yourselves, if you have a heart corrupted by contentions or by envy and the stubborn desire to win, give up the role of teacher. Do not lie against evangelical truth by self-seeking and by serving your own glory. No one can communicate evangelical truth sincerely if his mind is not free from all such human ambitions. For this reason, if anyone who comes to this profession perceives that his mind is infected with sensual love or human hate, with envy, with a desire for glory, with a passion for money, with the love of pleasure, let him first purge the innermost parts of his breast so that he may approach the purest of teachings in a state of purity. As for those who prefer to pass by those matters which are actually conducive to godliness and instead throw up a smoke-screen of intricate questions,[28] who speak to win the favour of princes, who speak for monetary gain, who twist the teachings of the gospel to the service of their bellies, who hunt for meaningless marks of human glory, who impose on the shoulders of others a heavy burden which they themselves would refuse to touch with their little finger,[29] who teach ceremonies and petty man-made regulations in place of God's commands, who transmit a new Judaism in place of evangelical philosophy, in sum who really preach themselves rather than Christ – their wisdom is not that wisdom which the Father sent down from on high[30] to us through the Son to call us away from earthly ambitions and to raise us aloft to heaven. Theirs is a gross and earthly wisdom, and for this reason it smacks of the earth. It is a sensual[31] wisdom and for this reason looks more to those things which are conducive to this life on earth than to eternal life. It is a devilish wisdom because it does not come from the inspiration of the divine Spirit but from the impulse of demons, whose[32] promptings are designed to alienate us from evangelical sincerity.

You see how much self-seeking rivalry there is among the professors of worldly wisdom, what fights, what disagreements, what desire to win, how much inconstancy there is in their beliefs and behaviour,[33] and how their life is contaminated in the meantime with every kind of vice. But our wisdom is just the opposite. Issuing on high from the spirit of Christ, it is first of all chaste and pure, unstained by any warped emotions. Secondly, it is peaceable and shrinks from every desire for contention. In addition to these qualities it is modest and not at all grim, tractable moreover and obliging, yielding ungrudgingly to the one who has something better to teach,[34] forgiving and merciful towards those who have erred or fallen and whom it is more eager to save than to destroy, gently tolerant and ready to try everything to have them change their minds, full of good fruits while it never stops doing good to all, converting the ungodly to godliness, calling back those who stray, teaching the untaught, lifting up the fallen, encouraging the faint-hearted, consoling the afflicted. Meanwhile it condemns no one,[35] being more eager to heal than to damn, having no trace of deceit or dissimulation but wishing good to all from a sincere heart. Those who sow the pure and tranquil teachings of the gospel in this way both reap the fruit of eternal life for themselves and attract others to the pursuit of a heavenly life whom they would only otherwise alienate through contentions and ferociousness.

Worldly wisdom also has its fruit, but this fruit lacks substance and can even be deadly.[36] The fruit of righteousness, however, which confers innocence in this life and immortality hereafter, is not sown through contention but in harmony and peace for them who embrace peace. For it is not the part of the good teacher to cross swords in hate with those who appear too obstinate to be likely to obey the teachings of the gospel. It is better to leave them to their own stubbornness if there is no hope that they will change their minds and repent.[37]

Chapter 4

You must strive in every way to live with concord in your hearts. But this is impossible unless you drive worldly passions[1] completely out of your hearts. They are a bane to concord and are the seeds of discord. You say that you are not subject to such passions. Then where do your wars come from? Where do your battles and internal contentions[2] come from? Where do these tumultuous debates and disagreements come from? Christ taught you peace and concord, and where does dissension come from – where else than from the fact that you serve the lust of human desires rather than evangelical love? If these passions were not on active duty and at the head of an army in your limbs, your tongue would not be savaging a neighbour nor your hand be robbing a brother. Remnants of the old life are still to be found in you; you have not yet stripped away all of the old man.[3] One person longs for fame; another pants for lucre. This one is eager for a kingdom; that one hotly pursues pleasure. When you do not obtain what each of you passionately desires, you thrust your competitor aside.[4] You envy him when he reaches his goal; you fight with him when he seems on the point of reaching it. When you are unable to obtain what you are vehemently seeking, your mind is in torment and torn to pieces in a riot of conflicting cares. In these circumstances nobody is at peace with either himself or another. Passions run riot inside your breast. Tongue, hands, and the other members fight and war with the neighbour outside. Meanwhile there is no satisfying your insatiable passions, and you abandon true goods.

If there should be some need or something should be required for true happiness, you must ask God for it. You ask the world for what you ought to ask from God. Either you do not ask from him or if you do, you do not ask for what you ought nor[5] in the way you ought to. For you either ask for something harmful instead of wholesome or you ask without faith or you ask it for an ungodly use. Suppose, for instance, that there is something which you could receive from God's kindness either to support your own daily needs or to relieve a neighbour's want, but you do not ask for it for these reasons but only to spend it on the satisfaction of your own pleasures.[6] When you do such things, what name shall I give you? 'Christians?' Your actions protest. I hear the title, 'Christians,' but I see the actions of adulterers and adulteresses. You were once devoted to Christ, your betrothed; you once swore fidelity to him. He redeemed you from the tyranny of your vices; he made you clean through his most holy blood so that he might display a spotless bride.[7] How can you forget your promise, the kindness of your betrothed, your marital fidelity, and slip back into the adulterous love affairs of this world? Do you not know that God is a jealous lover?[8] He wants to be loved totally. He wants only himself to be loved. He does not tolerate the world, from whose love he reclaimed you at so high a price, as a rival. He is sufficient by himself to supply everything. What reason is there then for you to ask the world for any part of your prosperity? Do you not know that God hates those who limp on both legs?[9] He does not tolerate the servant who is not content with only one master.[10]

What husband is so patient as to put up with a hostile rival for his wife's companionship? Do you think it is possible to please both the world and God at the same time? Do you not understand that just as a wife immediately loses husband's love if she sleeps with an adulterer, so a Christian immediately incurs the hostility of God, who has nothing in common with the world, if he tries to renew his friendship with the world? Therefore, know this for certain that anyone who has been eager to be the friend of this world has on that score made himself unfriendly to God. Light has nothing to do with dark. God has nothing to do with Belial.[11] A human husband does not endure his wife's collusion with an adulterer, he does not allow her marital affections to be divided. And the woman he married brought a dowry, was free-born and an untouched virgin. Will Christ allow his wife to have another adulterous affair with the devil[12] – the spouse whom he saved from destruction, whom he reclaimed from slavery, from whom he washed the filth of her sins, whose naked body he clothed, whom in her poverty he bountifully dowered with so many freely given gifts?

Do you think that there was no reason for writing in the sacred scrolls[13] that 'the Spirit that dwells in you longs after you even to envy?'[14] In the law of Moses some allowance is made for human feelings. In so far[15] as there was no penal act, it was permissible to hate an enemy; it was proper to aim at the acquisition of wealth; it was not considered unjust to meet force with force; to return insult for insult. But the evangelical Spirit which now dwells in you is jealous and, so to speak, envious. He demands more, he wants his love returned passionately even if this means disregarding your wife, your children, your very life. He does not tolerate a dwelling-place stained with worldly passions. He demands purity, he demands heavenly surroundings. He recoils and flees and takes offence if you carry the dirt of this world into his temple.[16] But just as he requires from us a singular kind of love and one far more pure than that expected by the law of Moses, so does he confer a richer grace. It is extremely difficult to do what he requires, but he gives us the strength for this very purpose, to make us able to do it easily. Nothing is difficult for someone in love. This in fact is his gift to us, that we love him or rather that we return his love. He took the initiative in attracting us by his own love and won us over when we were hostile. He will increase his gifts in us if we will only empty ourselves wholly for him, if we depend upon him alone, if we have nothing in common with this world and its prince, the devil. When I say 'world,' I mean precisely those misplaced passions for visible things through which this world promises a kind of false happiness.[17] What the Spirit demands is great, but what he promises is greater yet. He who can bestow boundless benefits can also add strength. He who wants to bestow the highest honours on those who do not deserve them will also deign to add power to the weak. Only let us[18] distrust our own resources and those of this world and place all our hope and confidence in the Spirit. He abandons those who arrogantly trust in their own wealth. He helps those who attribute nothing to themselves, but trust instead in God's goodness. This is surely what the Lord said long ago through Solomon: 'God resists the proud and arrogant, but imparts his favour to the humble and lowly.'[19] God wants you to be united to him as closely as possible. Make yourselves obedient to him just as a bride complies with her husband. But if the devil tries to separate you from God's love, reject the adulterer with his deceits and he will stop annoying you. He will be afraid of you if he sees you firm and steadfast in your love for your spouse. Stay away from him, therefore, whether he tries to frighten or to coax you. Attach yourselves to God through godly pursuits, through chaste and holy prayers, and he in turn will attach himself to you.

Wherever the desires of your heart incline, that is the direction you go. If your feelings are carrying you off towards the good and the heavenly, you are drawing near to God; but if towards the enticements of the flesh, you are speeding to the devil.[20] One must not vacillate, turning now one way, now another, but should hasten steadily onward in the same direction. If you acknowledge Christ as your spouse, you must be pure. Therefore, those of you who are still smeared with the mire of sin, cleanse your hands and refrain from every kind of misdeed. Purify your hearts to keep every trace of ungodly passion from residing there. Those of you who are now double-minded, loving partly the things which belong to God, partly the things which belong to the world, dedicate your whole heart to Christ alone. Why do you look here on earth for the happiness which is promised in heaven? Are you so captivated by the vain pleasures of this age that you ignore eternal joys? If you want to be truly happy, suffer affliction here;[21] if you want to feel everlasting joy, be sorrowful here; if you want to be happy without end, shed tears here. Let your foolish and ruinous laughter be turned into saving sorrow, let your destructive joy be changed into the sadness that brings salvation, let your vain exaltation be converted into humility. Let no one raise himself on high; instead humble yourselves in the sight of God. He will raise up those who humble themselves in this way and make them truly exalted. The less you claim for yourselves on your own, the grander will be the gift that he bestows.

Arrogance has envy for a companion; envy gives birth to detraction. To detract from a brother's reputation in order to make your own more respectable is the wickedest kind of pride. It is like splashing someone else's face with mud to make yourself look more beautiful or putting dirty stains on someone else's clothing to make yourself look more elegant. What is more disgraceful than that a brother detracts from a brother, persons who ought to be sharing everything? Is it any different from the right hand mutilating the left, as if the right hand would be better off if its fellow member were worse off? Yet people who avoid adultery, theft, or perjury do not shrink from detraction as though they thought it a trivial crime. But the more detraction disguises itself under the cover of religion the more pernicious it is. The one who rages against another's vices appears at first to shrink from those vices which he detests in another. Next he pretends that he is being aroused by his zeal for goodness, not by envy or dislike. This poison has a persuasiveness of its own. Reciprocal detraction causes others to have less respect for either participant.[22] No other poison is more efficacious against Christian concord.

Now one who reviles a brother or condemns[23] a neighbour does a wrong not only to the person whom he disparages but also to the Law, which he seems likewise to disparage and condemn. If your brother is innocent and if what he does is not prohibited by the Law, where do you get the effrontery to damn what the law of the gospel does not? But if he commits a sin, why do you disparage with your slandering tongue one who must be punished by the Law? The law of the gospel forbids us[24] to judge one another or to condemn one another,[25] and yet we[26] indulge our personal feelings under the pretext of the Law. The sinner will have his own judge. Why do you pre-empt and usurp this role? Your object is not to see him corrected but slandered. Therefore, whenever someone traduces a neighbour he is either condemning the Law on the ground that it does not correct disgraceful actions or he is disparaging it for being too weak and slow to fulfil the office which he, by disparaging it, tries to usurp for himself.

This world has statutes to restrain crime, but it is the part of Christian mildness to be more zealous to correct than to judge anyone. There is only one lawmaker, who can both save and destroy. Do you think that what each sinner does escapes God? Perhaps he tolerates it when someone sins so that someday this person may come to his senses, or God tolerates him so that in his own time he may punish him more severely. Why do you, who are but a private citizen, claim for yourself the position of judge? Why do you pre-empt the right to pronounce judgment? It is brotherly to admonish, charitable to request, a mark of good will to rebuke, but it is pernicious to slander and arrogant to judge. If you follow the Law, why do you arrogantly usurp the place of the Law? If you take precedence over the Law, you are not an observer of the Law but a judge of it. He who takes precedence over the Law is taking precedence over God, the author of the Law. God alone is liable to no crime. He will not let anything go unpunished. He, who alone is liable to no charge, knows why and to what extent punishment needs to be given. Just who are you, you who judge another? You condemn a brother though you yourself are subject to more serious sins. For you are bent on destroying one whom you do not have the power to save. Finally, you are claiming for yourself jurisdiction over another's servant[27] to the disparagement of the Lord, the master you have in common. Leave him to his Lord, who alone judges justly. You convince yourself that justice is whatever your own ambition or hatred or anger or envy dictates. You are often offended by the speck in your brother's eye though you have a plank in your own.[28] No one drags another's reputation down more venomously than the one who completely refuses to give genuine praise. No one bears another's weakness more lightly than he who has advanced the farthest in the pursuit of genuine godliness.

Now those who neglect the goods of heaven and toil over things which belong to the world ought to be warned even by the brevity and uncertainty of this life that it is madness to place one's happiness in those goods which, granted that they may come to one, nevertheless are sometimes suddenly taken away by fortune's whim; or if fortune does not take them away from their possessor, death snatches the possessor himself from his goods. They learn every day from examples that this is so; nevertheless, like people who have forgotten all of these things they dream of a long life and pile up wealth to sustain their present life as if they thought they were going to live forever.[29] Though the length of their lives is a matter of complete uncertainty while the only certain thing is that they will not live long, they make no provision for the journey to that life which will never have an end. Come now, you foolish people, even though you are uncertain about what tomorrow will bring, do you have the impudence to say, 'We shall depart for this or that city today or tomorrow to live there for one year and to make plenty of money to last for many years'?[30] Life is in itself very,

very short, and so many accidents, so many diseases make it thoroughly
uncertain as well. And here you are, as if you had a treaty with death,
speeding over land and sea to prepare some provision for your old age,
which you will perhaps never reach since no one can guarantee even his
own tomorrow. Why do you put such trust in this life as though it were
something firm and stable? What is that life of yours in fact, which is your
sole concern, the sole object of your toils and exertions? Mere vapour which
appears for a brief moment and soon vanishes. Christians, therefore, should
not mouth words like these: 'We'll go; we'll spend a year; we'll do some
trading; we'll make a profit' – as if the outcome of the future were in your
hands. Live rather day by day, depending on God's will and saying, 'If the
Lord wills,' and 'If he wills our life to go on, we shall do this or that.'
Matters which concern the life of the body, both brief and uncertain as it is,
ought to be taken care of lightly; but every care must be devoted to those
matters which contribute to obtaining immortal life.

While this present life possesses nothing in which you could safely
trust since it is exposed to so many accidents and so many diseases, is
subject to so many tribulations, and is so evanescent and fleeting you still
raise your aspirations just as though you were immortal and you swell with
the confidence of your youth and wealth. It is right to be brave and courageous because you have confidence in divine help; it is godly to be eager
and keen because you hope for heavenly goods. But all that self-satisfied
exultation over goods which are false in the first place and secondly are
soon going to be taken away is not only ungodly but foolish too. Perhaps
this would be tolerable in people who have been convinced by their fore-
fathers that no trace of human existence survives cremation, and the avid
enjoyment of this life would be more excusable in people who do not expect
another life.[31] But evangelical philosophy has taught you that this life must
be disregarded and that one must hasten with every effort towards that life
in heaven, which is not won by riches but by godly acts. But he sins more
gravely who, though he knows from the teachings of the gospel what must
be done, nevertheless under the corrupt influence of his evil feelings pursues the same objects which those pursue who are ignorant of Christ.[32]

Chapter 5

Come now, you rich, who are in a hurry to anticipate in your life here on
earth the delights and felicity which you ought to wait for in heaven where
they are everlasting. Put aside your songs. Give up your physical pleasures
and insane joys. If you have any sense, weep and wail as you think about
those everlasting calamities soon in store for you. Imagine that the time has

already arrived – and it will come very soon – when the wealth in which
you now very foolishly trust will be taken away and you will be wise too
late as you realize that those bright possessions are no longer of any help
to you but that in return for your false happiness genuine and everlasting
calamity now awaits you. Where now is the wealth which was accumulated
rightly or wrongly? Your riches have rotted and your garments have
become subject to moths. Your gold and silver have been spoiled by rust in
the house of your mean and thrifty heir.[1] That rust will testify to your
ungodliness, you who would rather have them perish from decay than
bring them out for the benefit of the needy.[2] You would have been able to
purchase eternal life by the expenditure of that gold and silver. But as it is,
the rust of your buried money will, like a fire, eat away the inmost parts of
your souls. Remorse for having ill-advisedly saved your money will soften
your hearts, but too late and in vain. Your ill-advised saving of your ill-
gotten gains will double your unhappiness. Instead of God's mercy, which
you might have purchased by throwing away your wealth, you have
garnered divine wrath and punishment.[3]

Not only were you grudging to a needy brother, but you also cheated
the pauper of the wages owed him. See how the harvester who sweated to
harvest your crops, cheated of his wages, cries to God and demands vengeance, and such are his cries that their[4] sound pierces the ears of the Lord
of Sabaoth, whom you too ought to fear.[5] They could not punish the powerful. They were not heeded by human judges, who generally favour the
wealthy. They kept silent, but the ungodliness itself shouts out before God,
the judge, who has no fear of the wealthy and considers the wrong done in
the oppression of the poor an offence against himself. But you in the meantime were not disturbed in the least by the misfortune of the hungry and
thirsty poor. You lived from another's sweat. You grew fat from another's
hunger and thirst. Their teeth were clenched;[6] they were freezing; they were
being killed by hunger and thirst. You meanwhile were passing your life on
earth pleasantly and in luxury. You were living riotously, feeding your
souls on every kind of pleasure. Every day you gave banquets no less
splendid than those which others are accustomed to give on holidays, when
an animal has been sacrificed.[7] Not content with having cheated the pauper,
you condemned and killed him, innocent but unresisting. You thought that
you would never be punished for something which humans did[8] not think
deserved punishment. To cheat the poor of their daily food is a form of
murder,[9] but this cruelty did not satisfy your inhumanity. You thirsted for
their blood and fed your souls on the punishments inflicted on the innocent.
Now the tables have been turned.[10] They are enjoying everlasting pleasures;
you are paying for your brief and insane delights with everlasting torments.

Therefore, brothers, do not be disheartened. Do not regret your lot. Do not envy the rich, whose every act here seems to succeed as they wish. Do not wreak any vengeance upon them, but endure until the coming of the Lord. Now is the time for sowing, then it will be the time for reaping. The rewards for your godliness are not yet visible, but they are nevertheless safe and will be given in their own time. Look at the man who tills the earth. How much toil he takes on at his own cost for the time being, expecting no doubt that the land will in due course return with great interest what it has received. And yet the return from the land is not always certain. If the sky should not favour him with a timely rain to moisten the furrowed soil and a late rain to protect the growing crop from the heat, the farmer would lose his work.[11] When you consider that he endures long-lasting toils with good hope for a transitory harvest and does not demand that what he has sown appear immediately, how much more right is it for you to bear patiently the disadvantages of this life in return for the harvest of immortality. Moreover, your reward is safe and sure,[12] provided that you have in the meantime made a good sowing. Following the example of the farmer therefore, strengthen and toughen your minds with a good and certain hope; be neither eager for vengeance nor slack in godly works. The Lord will come both to punish the ungodly and to present you with immortality in return for your transitory afflictions. Nor is that day far off, it will come sooner than expected.

Therefore, my brothers, let no one think himself excessively unfortunate because he is suffering too many evils nor envy the person whose condition is milder. For the one who suffers more grievously has not been abandoned by God but is being trained for higher rewards, and the other is not dearer to God simply because his affairs are more tranquil. Rather God wants some to be present whose piety can alleviate the misfortunes of others. Let there not be among you then that ungodly grumbling, a sign of envy and distrust, lest you be condemned.[13] For such grumblings[14] are the opening notes of a mind verging on despair. Let the very shortness of the time console you. Behold, the judge is standing at the door! The rewards are at hand for each in return for the merits of the life he has lived. In the meantime strengthen your hearts by the example of the holy fathers. If these evils had befallen you alone, there would be perhaps some reason to be surprised. The prophets who published God's oracles to the ungodly suffered more grievous evils. Just as the ungodly rich did not tolerate the predictions of the prophets then, so they do not tolerate the gospel's teachings now, no doubt because they are opposed to and conflict with their own desires.[15] No one, however, deplores the lot of the prophets or judges them unfortunate because they suffered imprisonment and chains or were killed by various tortures.[16] On the contrary, we consider them fortunate and dear to God because they were murdered on account of righteousness. You have heard of Job, the famous example of patience. How much evil did he endure under Satan's attack? You watched him contesting[17] and you also watched him winning with the help of the Lord. And from the goodness of the Lord he received double for each of the things snatched away by the wickedness of Satan.[18] The Lord had not abandoned his contestant, but he wanted his patience to be attested and approved by overcoming so many evil obstacles.[19] The Lord, however, who is compassionate and naturally prone to mercy, turns the wickedness of others into an increase and gain in our happiness.

Your heart should be pure and open and your speech should match your heart. No one should deceive his neighbour with feigned words. But above all, my brothers, do not swear an oath, lest you gradually acquire the habit of swearing falsely. Among the Jews and pagans an oath is employed to obtain mutual trust. Among Christians, who ought neither to distrust anyone nor to wish to deceive, an oath is superfluous. Anyone who acquires the habit of swearing oaths is close to the risk of swearing falsely. You should not only have scruples against swearing by God in profane and trifling transactions, but should also refrain from swearing any kind of oath, so that you do not swear by heaven or by earth or by anything else which is commonly thought to be holy and sacred. Anyone bold enough to lie without an oath will also be bold enough to do it even under oath if he wishes. The honest person trusts even someone who has not taken an oath; the dishonest person distrusts even the one who has sworn. However, there is no place for distrust or for the desire to deceive among you who are endowed with evangelical openness. Let your speech[20] be frank; let it be thought no less truthful and firm than any oath of the Jews or of the pagans no matter how holy. Whenever you confirm something, confirm it sincerely and do in fact what you say. Whenever you deny something, deny it sincerely and do not have something different in your heart from the words on your lips. There should be no pretence in you since you are disciples of truth.[21]

If an affliction has befallen anyone among you, he should not take refuge in this world's remedies such as rings, spells, baths, and the other ways of alleviating mental and physical pain.[22] Let him turn instead to prayer; let him lift up[23] his mind to God with complete confidence, and he will experience immediate relief from his sorrow. On the other hand if someone is cheerful in his prosperity, he should not become proud and overbearing or exult foolishly, but should celebrate with holy hymns the kindness of God, who is the source of his prosperity.

Now if someone is suffering from bad health, he should not take refuge in magical remedies or spend huge sums of money on doctors, whose cures are often such that it is better to depart cheerfully from life.[24] Let him summon instead to his side the elders[25] of the Christian congregation. Let them pour out prayers to God for the sick person and anoint him with oil, not employing the magical entreaties the pagans commonly employ, but invoking rather the name of our Lord Jesus Christ, which is more efficacious than any form of magic spell.[26] Moreover, let confidence be present in their prayers, and God will hear and save the one who is sick. He will not only restore his physical health, assuming that this is to the sick man's advantage,[27] but if he has been guilty of sins (diseases of the body generally arise from evils of the soul),[28] they will be forgiven him in response to the prayers of the elders, so long as their faith commends both those who pray and the person for whom they pray. Further, since humans cannot live without every day committing some slight trespasses,[29] it will be advantageous to employ each day a remedy, namely, that each one of you, acknowledging his or her own offence, should assist one another with mutual prayers. But the remedy will work only if one recognizes the disease and begs for help. The superstitious think there is a secret power present in their own magic spells and entreaties, but in reality it is the intercession of the righteous man that has the greatest effect. It obtains from God through faith everything it asks. Christ has stipulated in the contract which he has made with us that we shall obtain whatever we ask in his name with confidence unless it is such that it would be better not to obtain it.[30] Do you seek proof of this fact? Elijah was a man of purity[31] and a mortal just as we are; nevertheless, in response to his prayers it did not rain on the land for three years and six months. He prayed again to have it rain and soon, as if his prayers had been heard, the heaven gave rain and the earth brought forth its fruit. If the heaven, as though under a spell, obeys the prayers of one godly man, is it strange if God, who is very ready to forgive, is appeased by the prayers of many?[32]

Now, brothers, weigh the following point. If it is an act of piety and Christian charity to alleviate through communal prayer a disease in the body of another person, how much more right is it to aid those who suffer from a disease in the soul? There is nothing grand in bringing it about through prayer that death, which is going to come some day in any case, is postponed a little while for this or that person, but to have forestalled the death of the soul is something grand indeed.[33] Therefore, if anyone has appeared among you who is straying from the truth of the gospel either by still clinging with excessive devotion to the law of Moses or by tenaciously cultivating the pagan traditions of his ancestors, no one should believe that this person must be attacked with insults. One must strive instead with all one's heart to bring him to his senses and to turn him from his error. God does not wish for the death of a sinner, but rather that he be converted and live. Therefore, whoever accomplishes this will be obliging God. The one who saves a soul from death performs a grand deed in freeing a brother from the sins through which he was being held liable to death. Nor will he go without his own reward in the meantime, for Christ in turn will forgive him his own[34] sins too, however many they are, since he has called a brother back from destruction.[35]

The End

PARAPHRASE ON THE FIRST EPISTLE OF JOHN

In epistolam Ioannis primam paraphrasis

DEDICATORY LETTER

TO HIS EMINENCE MATTHÄUS, CARDINAL-BISHOP OF SION,
COUNT OF THE VALAIS,
FROM ERASMUS OF ROTTERDAM, GREETING[1]

I lately offered you James, speaking both in Latin and more lucidly; now I am offering you John. Thus I take my labour in stages piece by piece, and I do not overwhelm your Eminence when you are fully occupied with the business of the empire[2] – if, that is to say, I may assume that you have any time to spare for looking over what I write. My best wishes to your Lordship.

Louvain, 6 January

THE ARGUMENT OF
THE FIRST EPISTLE OF JOHN
BY ERASMUS OF ROTTERDAM

The very character of the language is proof that this Epistle is by John the apostle, the author of the Gospel. It abounds in the mention of light and darkness, life and death, hate and love, and displays his habit of picking up, as it were, and repeating words from preceding clauses. The following specimen of this kind of thing will make my meaning clearer. 'Do not love the world or the things which are in the world. If anyone loves the world, the love of the Father is not in him, for everything which is in the world' – and then – 'is not of the Father, but is of the world; and the world passes away' [1 John 2:15–17]. How often the word 'world' is repeated here! Lastly, John's language throughout lacks concision and is more diffuse than the language of the other apostles.

The Epistle is too lucid to require a résumé. The same is true of the second and third Epistles which are attributed not to John the apostle but to a certain John the Elder.[1]

The End of the Argument

PARAPHRASE ON
THE FIRST EPISTLE OF JOHN
BY ERASMUS OF ROTTERDAM

Chapter 1

We are not writing to you, dearly beloved brothers, about something insignificant or trivial or some novel piece of news, but about something entirely new, which while new to us has been with God from eternity. It is the Word of God,[1] Jesus Christ, both God and man alike, who though he has always been the Son of God wanted to be in our time the son of a virgin. He, who in respect to his divine nature was invisible to human eyes, deigned to assume a human body and to live on intimate terms among men and women so that he might carry us from the darkness of our ignorance into the light of evangelical knowledge and we might thus contemplate with the eyes of the mind him whom we had beheld face to face with the eyes of the body. The disbelief of the human heart demanded that faith be put to crude tests before it would give credence to truth.[2] Christ, however, showed through his own words[3] his preference for the piety of those who believed with absolute conviction that he was the Son of God and the sole source of human salvation, although they had neither seen him with their eyes nor touched him with their hands. It is our task, therefore, to inform others about what our physical senses had convinced us was completely true, since they did not have the same opportunity to see for themselves. Even so, it is profitable to believe that no one should hope for life and eternal salvation except the person who believes the teaching of the gospel of which we are both the witnesses and the heralds.[4] It is not a human word nor one of little moment. It is a divine and heavenly word which brings eternal life to those who will give it an obedient hearing and frees sinners from death regardless of the religion or the way of life from which they will turn away to it. The report which we present is completely reliable, for it is what we, his constant companions, heard with our own ears and saw with our own eyes. It is not something which we saw from a distance or in passing, but we saw it in full view and close at hand. Hearing

and seeing are the two senses which are foremost in commanding faith.
And if this is not enough, we not only heard him teaching, praying, commanding winds and demons, we not only heard the Father, not once but
twice,[5] affirming that he is his Son, we not only saw him producing miracles, dying and rising again, but we even touched him with our very own
hands. For after his return to life from death, to show convincingly that he
was not a bodiless ghost but the same living man whom we had earlier
seen dead, he presented himself to be touched by our hands; he exposed the
scars of his wounds and placed our fingers on them.

The race of mortals was dead; that is, it was subject to vice and sin. He
paid for our wickedness with his death so that thanks to him we may live
now to innocence. Even we ourselves began to lose faith when we saw him
dead and buried, but by coming back to life he brought us the certain hope
of life.[6] Mortals would have no hope of eternal life if he had not thrust
himself before our eyes and removed all hesitation from us through the
most reliable tests. As a man he paid the penalty for our sins, but as God
he bestows immortality on those who have faith in him. He was always
alive with the Father; this life was always determined for us through the
Son. This plan, however, was not yet revealed to the world. The Jewish
nation, and it alone, because of the oracular utterances of the prophets had
a vague and dreamlike expectation of it. Meanwhile, death reigned; life was
in hiding.[7] Some had fixed their hope in Moses, others in the wisdom of the
world,[8] but the salvation and life of all peoples was Jesus Christ, the Word
of God the Father, the teacher of innocence, and the giver of immortality.
For no one is truly alive except the one who lives in a godly way; no one
escapes death[9] except the one who attains to immortality.

He revealed himself at last to the world in his own person by presenting himself to every kind of sense perception and in this way insinuating
himself into human souls. He wanted us to be the spectators and witnesses
of all that he did on earth so that a trustworthy report could be spread
throughout the entire world by our proclamation. We have attained life and
salvation through Jesus himself, provided that we persevere to the end in
the teachings of the gospel. Jesus wanted you, too, to come into fellowship
with us in a comparable way and to share in the same salvation if what you
neither saw nor heard directly from his lips you learned through our
preaching and believed it because of our testimony. We are neither idle
witnesses nor self-motivated ones. He commanded us to be trustworthy
witnesses. Therefore, we testify before everyone at great risk to our lives
and we testify to nothing else except that which we have verified completely through each one of our bodily senses. We whose eyes and ears have
given us faith are fortunate, but you will be no less fortunate if you have

faith in his witnesses. Our faith has cemented us to Christ and made us sons of God and members of Christ. Your faith will make you a part of the same body so that, joined to us by the fellowship of faith, you may constitute one body with us. The result will be that we shall not only be of one mind among ourselves like the parts of one body, but we shall also have peace and a covenant with Jesus, and through him with his Father, God, with whom we were previously at variance. Furthermore, just as the Son is in perfect agreement with the Father and in communion with him in all things, so will our agreement in the confession of the gospel also cement us together in the one body of Christ to be partakers of all the goods of our Head.

I know that you rejoice at so happy an association, but I want to go over these matters again for you in writing so that you[10] may rejoice even more fully, which you will do if each one is not only thankful for his own salvation but is equally filled with pleasure at the happiness of all. Christian love has the effect of making each person rejoice over the goods of another in the same way that he does over his own. The more there will be to share this happiness, the richer will be the joy of each. But unanimity will not exist among us unless the cement of mutual love is present. We cannot have peace with God if we do not conform to our Head, Jesus Christ. Whatever he has he credits to the Father; whatever we have we must likewise credit to Christ. He is the true light issuing from the Father of all light. We cannot be members of Christ unless we are full of light; we cannot have light unless we are transformed into Christ and remain continuously in his company. The light[11] of the soul is truth and innocence; darkness is sin and warped desire. Where there is light, there is life. Where there is darkness, there is death.

What is it that we announce to you so that you may rejoice more fully? It is this, which we heard from Christ himself and communicate to you just as we heard it, namely that God, because he is wholly and of his own nature good, wholly wise, wholly pure, is also wholly light and life. There is no darkness in him. The same is not true of us; we have much darkness from our very nature. If we have any light, we owe this wholly to him through whose spontaneous generosity we have been freed from our past sins. Freed now from the darkness of our former ignorance we have learned through the teachings of the gospel to live in godliness following the example of Christ our Head.

If anyone boasts that he has been made a part of Christ's body through baptism and has fellowship with God the Father through this means, but continues to live in the errors and vices of his past life, he is clearly lying. Since God, as I said, has no association whatsoever with darkness, how can he have anything to do with someone like this, who still lives wholly in error and in his past vices? The person who thinks he can attain innocence anywhere except through Christ is wandering completely off the path. The person who thinks that it is sufficient to have been washed by baptism is likewise wandering in error if he fails to live up to his baptismal promise through the innocence of his life. Anyone who thinks such thoughts errs; anyone who makes such statements lies. Christ is truth, he has nothing in common with liars. To acknowledge one's darkness is the first step towards the light; to acknowledge one's sins is the first step forward towards innocence. Do you want to hear then by what sign we may be able to know that we have a true fellowship with God? It is a sign, if, following the example of God, who is light and wholly without any darkness, we regulate our whole life according to evangelical light and, like God, withdraw from the darkness of all error and vice. It is a sign if, like the Son who has perfect harmony with the Father, we too would[12] live innocently and be of one mind among ourselves. Every one of the offences of our old life has been effaced once and for all by the precious blood of the Son, Jesus Christ. The Father will not lay them to our account provided that, in so far as it is in our power, we refrain in the future from every sin. The blood of Christ washes away all filth and washes it away from all, but it does not wash it away except from those who acknowledge their own evils.

However, if we say that we are not subject to sin, we deceive ourselves; we dwell in error; we live in darkness; and Christ, who is light, who is truth, is not in us. For if he were truly in us, he would scatter this dark cloud of conceited ignorance.[13] But if, once we have received baptism, we chance to slip back into some fault out of human weakness and, as it were, some cloud has cast a shadow on our light, we must take care that conceit does not remove us farther and farther from the light and lead us back to the old darkness. Instead an effort must be made to let self-effacement move us towards the light which will dispel all the dark mist. If a brother does some incidental wrong to a brother, let the one forgive the other the offence so that God in turn will forgive those offences which are being committed against himself. For this is the condition on which God promised that he would remit any offence that we committed against him, namely that we overlook any offence on a brother's part.[14] But God demands his due right to the last penny from the person who, after experiencing his lord's mercy,[15] has shown himself unmerciful to a fellow servant. Though God has freely forgiven once and for all every single one of the offences committed against himself,[16] he obviously judges unworthy of divine mercy the one who refuses to forgive a light offence in another against whom that person himself either sins or might sin every day. The person who recalls[17] the many ways he commits offences against both God and his neighbour will readily pardon the one who commits an offence against him. It is very difficult for a human to avoid committing some sin, but it is correspondingly very easy to heal such offences through mutual forgiveness. Pardon your neighbour and your neighbour in turn will pardon you, and God, so to speak, contracts to pardon both.[18] I am talking about the slips which occur even among people who are good but still human, those mistakes which obscure rather than extinguish the light of evangelical truth. God forfend that murder or adultery or sacrilege occur in the life of those who have once been co-opted among the sons of God.[19] But nothing more invites God's compassion and mitigates his wrath than when someone acknowledges his own sin before God. If even the savage-minded forgive the one who acknowledges his wrongdoing, how much more likely is God to do this who is more merciful than any human? God is by nature prone to compassion and has promised us pardon on this condition: 'Forgive and you will be forgiven' [Luke 6:37].[20] If God should not pardon because he is good, he would pardon because he is just and trustworthy. You need only fulfil the prescribed condition; he will not forget the agreement. If we sincerely forgive a neighbour who offends us, God in turn will forgive us not just one or two wrongs but all our sins, provided that we strive with all our might to be eventually free from every vice. If we cannot fully reach this goal because of the frailty of the human body, God will still supply from his kindness what our own strength lacks and will again cleanse us from our sins.[21] Perhaps it is for this very purpose that he allows some traces of the old life to remain in us so that we may acknowledge our weakness. For God is more pleased by the sinner who is displeased with himself than by the self-complacent righteous man.[22] God wants the credit for the salvation of humanity to be given to his compassion, not to our merits, and he has already affirmed that there is no single mortal on earth who does not slip somewhere.[23] But if we say that sin is not in us, we make a liar of God, who cannot lie, and we contradict him of whom the contradicter, whoever he is, has to be lying.

Chapter 2

It is not my intention in writing these things, my little children, to turn our confidence in God's readiness to forgive into a licence to sin more freely, but to see that no one sins at all in so far as this is in our power. After Christ has once forgiven us our sins, every earnest effort must be made to keep our innocence unimpaired. Still, if it should chance to happen that we slide back into some sin, there is no reason for us to despair of pardon. We have a God who is easily moved by prayer and we have with him a loving and loyal advocate, the Son who obtains everything he asks from the Father. He, who sacrificed himself to save us, sincerely wishes us well, provided that we are completely dissatisfied with our past behaviour from the bottom of our hearts and instead strive for better things. He alone has nothing which has to be forgiven, but he intercedes for the sins of his members and reconciles to us the Father whom we have offended and makes him kindly. And he does this not only for us who have already accepted the teachings of the Son but for the entire human race, provided that they confess with a sincere heart that they are sinners, adopt the intention to live a sinless life, and press on while resolutely holding fast to this intention. For baptism does not free us from the observance of the law of Moses simply that we may sin with impunity thereafter, but to make us tenacious adherents of evangelical love.[1] This love gains more from willing people than the innumerable laws of Moses can wrench from the unwilling. He who commanded us to show towards neighbours the kind of love which he showed to us comprehended a multitude of commandments in one short one.[2] He does not compel one to love him in return, but invites one, arouses one, inflames one to do so. Whoever knows God truly, cannot help loving him deeply. Not every person who confesses God with his lips knows God, but only the one who, kindled by the flame of evangelical love, willingly and gladly does what Christ did first, namely, to do good even to our enemies, to risk our own lives without hesitation for the salvation of a neighbour. Such a person clearly reveals that he knows God. If someone boasts, however, that he knows God because he has learned the mysteries of faith as a catechumen and has professed his name at baptism, but meanwhile does not imitate his love, he is a liar and has not yet learned God fully. God is not known if love does not permeate faith. Christ, who is truth itself, does not reside in anyone who lies, and anyone who does not have Christ abiding in him is not a living member of his body. Faith without love is something empty and dead.[3] Love is not idle; it does not fail to do any of the things which it knows are pleasing to him whom it loves. Christ said that he would not acknowledge the disciple who did not take up his cross and follow him,[4] walking in the path of perfect love.[5]

Therefore, the one who keeps Christ's word declares by this very act that he possesses a perfect and truly evangelical love. By this test we shall know that we are in his body and have deeply imbibed his Spirit. Why do you pride yourself on being a part of Christ's body because you have been received into the Christian flock through baptism? It is not an idle commitment nor an easygoing one. It is not the commitment alone but imitation which makes one a true part of Christ's body. The one who avows with his lips that he is reborn in Christ must walk in his footsteps. Christ did not live for himself. He did not die for himself. He spent himself totally for us. He was one who did good to all. He did not hurl an insult back at anyone, but when fastened to the cross he prayed to the Father for those who were pouring abuse upon him.[6] This is the evangelical and perfect love which those who avow themselves disciples of Christ must emulate by their actions.

Dearly beloved, this commandment about love which I write to you is not a new one. The law of Moses also published it long ago, or rather it was Christ who did so through this Law.[7] Christ renewed his own commandment in the gospel, and he renewed it in such a way as to make it peculiarly his own when he said, 'This is my commandment, that you should love one another, as I have loved you' [John 15:12]. Therefore, the commandment which I am now delivering to you is neither new nor my own nor hitherto unheard by you. It is the very one which we delivered to you on the authority of Christ right at the very beginning. Yet again what I now write you is new. It was old but nullified by human behaviour. The Jews used to memorize, 'You will love the Lord your God, you will love your neighbour,'[8] but each would serve his own private advantage. Christ has renewed it for us, loving us even more than himself and loving not just neighbours but enemies and opponents and men worthy only of evil.

Though I know that you have heard this in the past, nevertheless it must be continually made new through frequent repetition in order to make that which is the very essence of the commitment to the gospel settle ever more deeply in your minds. This commandment was true in Christ, who practised what he taught. But it was not true in you so long as you suffered from hatred of a neighbour and repaid insult with insult, injury with injury. Now it is true also in you after the true light of evangelical teaching arose, dispelled the darkness of your past life, and taught you that no one was pleasing to God except the person who loved good people because of Christ and treated evil people lovingly in the hope that they would be converted to Christ. Those who follow this teaching walk in the light and do not stumble in the darkness caused by evil desires. Hatred of the neighbour pours darkness over the mind. Therefore, the one who has been baptized and has confessed Christ but has not ceased to hate his brother deceives himself in believing that he lives in the light, for he is still in darkness. God does not forgive the sins of the person who does not forgive his brother.[9] It is not enough to have left stealing, adultery, and murder behind in baptism unless at the same time all feelings of enmity are plucked out of the soul and love takes the place of hate. He who persists in love for his neighbour remains in the light, which is Christ Jesus, and does not stumble like

someone walking in the dark. For true love is so far from injuring anyone
that it bears all things[10] and turns them into good. On the other hand one
who hates a brother is still in darkness even though he may have ceased to
sacrifice to idols or may have ceased to be a usurer or a stealer of sacred
property.[11] Obedient to blind desire, he walks in darkness and does not
discern the straight path to salvation although the gospel lights the way for
him. The reason is that the darkness of fraternal hatred has blinded his eyes.
Where hatred rules, there judgment is blind.

My love for all of you is like a mother's, and for this reason I write
partly to congratulate you on your happiness, partly to urge you to continue
to advance towards better things. You are my dearly beloved children,
whom I have borne again to Christ through the seed of evangelical teaching.
For this reason I congratulate you one and all because the sins of your past
life have been forgiven, and forgiven freely, for no other reason than that
you have confessed the name of the Lord Jesus Christ. Therefore, following
his example, each of you is likewise to forgive his neighbour without
charge.

It is not your advanced years but your moral earnestness and godly
concern for your juniors that make you worthy of the name father.[12] Therefore, I write to you to congratulate you, not just for being endowed with the
normal prudence that generally causes old men to be respected for their
experience and to be better able to give sound advice to the inexperienced
young, but for knowing Jesus Christ, the author of salvation, who is not
only old in years but has been with the Father always. You are old in years
and know the Eternal One, and the more fully you know him, the more
diligently you preach him to those who are at a less informed age. Old men
remember and retain many things of an older time; you retain him who was
before all time.

I write to you, young men, who have defeated Satan by the vigour of
your faith despite his persistent and untimely attacks. Ordinary young men
are commonly thought to be fortunate because their physical strength keeps
them from having to yield readily to anyone; you, however, who because
of your strength of mind could not be defeated by either the allure of
physical pleasures or by any of the world's terrors are more fortunate yet.[13]
The virtue of other young men shines out in war. Your virtue has shone out
more brightly against the attacks of demons, the flesh, and the world. I
write to you, children, who, though at your time of life you are not yet wise
through experience in worldly affairs, nevertheless have even now attained
that which can win eternal happiness for you. The first sign of intelligence
in other infants is their recognition of their fathers; you know the Father in
heaven through whom you have been reborn for heaven.

Let each age watch over what it has and advance in that which it has. For this reason I want to congratulate each person and also to remind each rank and station to acknowledge its happiness and to give thanks to God its source. Be mindful of the goal that each of you must reach; continually strive for ever greater perfection. Therefore, I shall repeat myself so that my meaning cannot slip from anyone's memory. I wrote to you, fathers, that you are not to let any longing for this life influence you as you hasten towards eternal life since you know him who has neither beginning nor end. I wrote to you, young men, because you have overcome the suscepti- bilities of youth by your strength of mind and because you have kept with steadfast hearts the word of the gospel and with Christ's help have over- come the devil, the relentless foe of the human race. Persevere in your victory; continue to reject what you have rejected thus far; come to love ever more deeply that which you have fallen in love with.

The world tempts through the deceptive images of transitory goods. It produces fear through the empty deception of apparent evils. As for you, let only those things which are truly evil and have no end cause fear in you. Let what is truly good and knows no end take you captive. Follow the light shed by the gospel and love the heavenly things which the Father in heaven promises. You have been reborn through Christ to him. Shun the darkness of evil desires through which this world baits its traps with feigned goods. It is impossible for you to love both and to serve both at the same time. God and the world have nothing in common, nor do light and darkness. Whoever loves the world loses the love of God the Father. By 'world' I do not mean this world whose creator is God and in which we live whether we wish to or not. I call 'world' those futile desires for the meaningless things in which the common herd of men, oblivious to true goods, place their happiness. No place, however isolated, no special garb or diet or title removes you from this present world.[14] Only a mind free from those desires which I mentioned can do that. What does this world contain that does not lead to destruction? There are three things which most of all deceive the foolish and unwary: the pleasure of the flesh, the incitements of the eyes, the pride and noise of life.[15] The world is a magician, and its tricks are the hollow pleasures through which it caresses the body's senses for a moment so that the soul may be temporarily diverted from its pursuit of heavenly goods. For that heavenly Spirit which God the Father imparts to his children who have been truly reborn through Christ inspires the passion for those heavenly goods.

Satan too has his spirit through which he inspires a baneful love for material things which are neither real nor lasting for those who have devoted themselves to this world. He inspires the evil joys of sexual love which tickle the body's members with a foul and foolish itch. He inspires the fondness for fine food and drink which entice throat and palate. He inspires the comfortable sweetness of relaxation and sleep to make the mind grow more listless from lack of use. He inspires lewd songs and obscene stories with which to cajole the ears. He inspires the allure of beautiful shapes and spectacles of every kind with which to delight the eyes. He inspires the pomp of prestige and the noisy stir of wealth, incitements to ambition. In short, from every side he diverts people's minds from true and everlasting goods to the hollow idols of false goods. Anyone who is captured by a desire for these things should realize that he is not being moved by the Spirit of the Father in heaven but by the spirit of the world.

Inasmuch as the world consists of temporary elements, it offers nothing except that which is destined soon to perish; inasmuch as God is eternal, he bestows everlasting rewards. Therefore, the person who depends upon the support of this world is chasing after a happiness which is evanescent and soon to be removed. Even in this world an unexpected catastrophe often removes happiness, or senility snatches it away. Certainly death, which is destined to come to everyone, dispatches that whole dream of false joy. When the physical basis of a pleasure is removed, the pleasure itself disappears and pain takes its place. When the person himself is removed, everything that was once his is gone and eternal torment takes its place. But the happiness of him who obeys the Father's call to a love of heavenly life will have no end. For the one who bestows this life knows no end. For the time being the goods of this world, which are inherently harmless, are there to be used, but sparingly and moderately to serve natural needs, not the pleasures of some lust. The highest impulse in the soul must be directed towards eternal possessions and must be the standard by which the use of all other possessions is to be measured.

The happiness of the godly is not yet manifest, but it will be revealed at the coming of our Lord Jesus Christ. Meanwhile the ungodly seem to lead pleasant lives here on earth, but eternal ruin threatens them – and soon at that. That last time seems to be near when the universe will be changed, and those who are now suffering on account of Christ will reign with Christ while those who are now rebelling against Christ will be annihilated. You have heard that the Antichrist will come. Armed with all the forces and stratagems of this world, he will wage war against Christ. After the Antichrist has been subdued, the body of Christ will be freed from all evils, and the limbs of the devil will be burdened with every evil.[16] The coming of this Antichrist, which the apostles predicted to you,[17] does not seem to be far off. For this world has grown so strong against the teachings of the gospel that even now several have come into existence who deserve the

name of antichrist. Their life and teaching and their every concern are
opposed to Christ. What else do they seem to be than the forerunners of
that Antichrist and the last prelude before the coming of the storm.[18] For
those who are total strangers to Christ do less harm to the people of Christ
than do these men who, having once lived in his camp and having then
become deserters, are attacking Christ with the weapons and defences of
Christ. They simulate the very things which in Christians reveal the power
of Christ: holiness, teaching, authority, miracles. They went out from us, but
their action need not cause you[19] any distress.[20] They lived in our midst, but
they were not of us. They were enemies of Christ even when they were
active in his camp. If they had really been members of our party, they
would have continued with us without a break. Their garb and title proclaimed them Christians, but in their hearts they were in love with the
world. Consequently, when it came to the point of facing the storms of
persecution and the fires of affliction, they betrayed just what kind of
persons they had really been up to then.[21] By seceding now from us they
relieve us as a discharge relieves a body burdened with evil humours, and
they are less harmful to us as open enemies than as pretended allies. This
was Christ's way of making it evident that not everyone who is baptized in
his name, who confesses his name and participates in the sacraments of the
church, belongs to the body of Christ. A true and steadfast contempt for the
world is proof of the Christian. A mind which stands unbroken and unde-
feated against all enticements and against all wrongs is proof of the Christian. One who abandons Christ's teaching on the spur of the moment was
pretending to be a Christian but was really not one. It is to our advantage
to have them openly separated from us so that they may not do even more
harm to the unwary under the guise of good, although they were not
unknown to you even before they openly withdrew. The anointing from
Christ gives you your name.[22] This anointing, which is the inspiration of the
Spirit of Christ, sufficiently indicates to you just who are truly Christians,
who are not. For he who is spiritual discerns all things.[23] They were not
unknown but were tolerated in the hope that they might perhaps undergo
a change of heart.

What I say is true, and I do not write these things to you as if the
truth were hidden from you who have as your teacher the Spirit of Christ,
which does not let you be ignorant of anything. I am only reminding you
of what you know so that you may cling more firmly to the truth and may
not be distressed at the departure[24] of those evil men. You are fewer now,
but healthier and cleaner and calmer. The body suffers no loss if a boil is
resected or pus has exuded from it. You know that Christ is truth, that
every kind of lie is at variance with him. No hypocrite has any association

with Christ, however much he may confess him with his lips. Lies have many forms. Whoever is a liar in any way whatsoever denies Christ, who is pure truth unadulterated by any lie. Whoever opposes truth, opposes Christ. Whoever opposes Christ is an antichrist. There is no kind of lie more wicked than to deny that Jesus is the Christ. Many false prophets of the Jews do just that, first, by denying that he was the one whom Moses and the oracular utterances of the prophets even long ago promised the world as the vindicator and the author of salvation,[25] and, secondly, by promising some other antichrist in place of Christ. Certainly a liar of this kind is openly an antichrist. On the other hand, there are some people who, though they proclaim with their lips that Jesus is the Christ, live in ways that make both his teaching and the rewards which he promised seem futile and vain.[26] He taught that the poor in spirit are blessed because the kingdom of heaven awaits them.[27] And when someone bends every effort to enlarge his estates, to build a grand mansion, to increase his profits, to fill his chests with coins gained by hook or crook, to prevail through faction, to oppress the poor, to act like a tyrant, does he not protest against Christ whose teaching he turns into a lie in so far as it is in his power to do so? Christ teaches that blessed are they who hunger and thirst after righteousness. And when someone places his happiness in riotous living and in the pleasures of the throat and belly, does he not gainsay Christ? Christ teaches that blessed are the meek because they will possess that heavenly land from which they can never after be expelled. And here is someone who judges himself a success only if he can ground his wealth in the oppression of the poor. Christ teaches that they who mourn in this world are blessed because they are due for eternal refreshment. And when someone chases after the delights of this world in everything, does he not gainsay Christ? He teaches that they are blessed who are merciful to their neighbours. And here is someone who is pleased with himself because he has deliberately done some malicious damage to one better than himself. Christ teaches that those who are harassed with insults and suffering because of their evangelical righteousness are blessed. And here is someone who strives to please the world through every kind of deception and trick. Christ acknowledges the disciple who takes a cross on his shoulders and follows him.[28] And someone else still thinks he is a Christian if he has avoided every tribulation. Christ says to his own, 'In the world you will have torment, in me you will have peace.'[29] And to those men he is a burden, the world a boon. Christ tells us to do good even to an enemy, and here is someone who inflicts an injury even on one who does not deserve it. Does not the person who lives like this gainsay Christ? His lips do not protest, but his life does. Since the Son taught a doctrine very different from theirs, the Father said, 'Listen to him' [Matt 17:5]. But what does this antichrist say? 'Do not listen to him; his teachings are hard; listen to the world.' Therefore, in so far as he resists the Son, he also opposes the Father. So long as he belongs to the world's side, he separates himself from the flock of those whom Christ chooses and sets apart from this world. Christ has nothing to do with this world. The one who cements himself to it opposes Christ and plays the role of antichrist, denying at one and the same time both the Father and the Son. For the fellowship of the Father with the Son is indivisible.

Here the Jew will cry in opposition to me, 'I acknowledge the Father, I do not acknowledge the Son.' Yet whatever wrong you will do to the Son, you will also do to the Father. The Son did not do anything or teach anything except on the authority of the Father. Who detracts from the Son detracts from the Father.[30] Therefore, the person who has estranged himself from the society of the Son does not belong to the body of Christ, which is the Catholic church,[31] and does not have fellowship with God the Father, who agrees with the Son in everything. You see at what great risk they foolishly sever themselves from the Son.

You, therefore, continue in the evangelical truth which you first received from approved apostles. Do not let the lying speech of false apostles lead you astray. If you persist in the teaching which we initially passed on to you, you will abide in the company of God the Father and of his Son Jesus. If to remain in the commitment to the gospel seems hard to anyone because of the sufferings caused by the ungodly, think about the reward. God's demand is arduous, but the reward which he promises is enormous. He does not promise wealth or a kingdom or the pleasures of this world, but eternal life.[32] Whoever purchases this at the cost even of his life purchases it for a small price.

I am reminding you of these things at such length and drilling them into you because of my concern that these ungodly persons who have deserted Christ should not deceive anyone by chance with their tricks. However, even without my reminder the Spirit itself of Christ,[33] which you have in your hearts as a constant adviser and teacher, teaches you sufficiently, I think. As long as this Spirit remains in you, you have no need that anyone should teach you what you must be on guard against. This teacher is hidden but is by far the most sure. Once he has been deeply imbibed by you, he teaches you concerning all things just as the Son promised.[34] For the Spirit is truthful[35] by nature and does not know how to lie. Therefore, persevere in that which he once taught you. You have the correct doctrine in your possession. You remember it.[36] Nothing remains except that you continue in it[37] until the coming of Christ, which I conjecture is not far off.[38]

I beg you again and again, little children, abide in the Spirit's teaching so that when that prince and judge of ours appears, our knowledge that we have lived a good life may give us confidence before him, and we may present ourselves as the kind of persons that he is not ashamed to acknowledge as his disciples and we in turn are not ashamed to come into his sight.[39] With what countenance shall we address him as Instructor and Lord[40] if we have not heeded him in his teaching and have not obeyed him in his instructions? With what countenance shall we call God Father if we have been false to his ordinances throughout our life? It is not baptism by itself but the preservation of our righteousness that makes us children of God. What will they hear who cast out demons in Jesus' name, who predicted the future, who became famous for their miracles? 'I do not know you.'[41] Jesus treats as strangers those in whom he does not see evangelical righteousness. But if you are convinced that God is the author of this righteousness, know this too at the same time, that everyone who practises evangelical righteousness not just in his profession, but in his pursuits, his deeds, his moral conduct, is born of God. Having a good conscience, this person will be able to approach God with the confidence with which obedient children are wont to approach a kindly father. God will acknowledge those like himself, he will not acknowledge those unlike himself.

Chapter 3

Where sincere love exists, trust too exists and fear is absent. See, therefore, how remarkable is the love which he has given to us who abide in evangelical teaching and despise the world with all its attractions and terrors, so that we are not only called faithful servants and friends,[1] but are even named and are[2] children of God. Thus did Christ teach us to call upon the Father in heaven if we should need anything. To be called children of God is the ultimate honour, to be children of God is the ultimate happiness. Since we adhere to him in steadfast godliness and are acknowledged by him, the world does not acknowledge us[3] but shrinks in horror from us and curses us as members of the opposite party. It is hardly surprising that the world does not acknowledge the children of God since in denying his Son Jesus it does not acknowledge God himself. Do not let your hearts be at all distressed, dearly beloved, because the world thinks you mean and despicable. We have even now in God's eyes this extraordinary dignity, that we are children of God. We rejoice inside when we feel in ourselves the spirit not of slavery but of children. This spirit gives us the confidence to cry, Abba, Father.[4] This dignity already exists but it is not yet manifest. It is still the time of battle. The day of victory has not yet come. God will reveal to all how great the dignity is, how great the happiness is of those who have steadfastly shown themselves to be the children of God. What we shall be at the coming of Christ has not yet come to light, but we possess it with a sure hope. The moment he appears to give the rewards to all in accordance with their actions, we, who have been sharers here of the sufferings, shall be partakers also of the joys. We, who have been like him held in contempt by the world, shall be like him as well in the majesty of his glory. We saw him in his suffering in this world; we saw him in his humble estate.[5] Then we shall see him as he is and has always been, exalted and sublime, and on seeing him we ourselves shall be transformed to his likeness – not only our minds but also our bodies.[6] We see him even now, but with the eyes of faith as though through a mist. Then we shall see him in an indescribable way. But in the meantime we must practise to the best of our ability to be now what we shall be in perfection then. In order to be like him then in glory, we must cleanse ourselves in this world from all filth. In order to be able to see him then, we must purify our eyes now so that brilliant though his appearance will be then, it will nevertheless fill us with love, not dread. For the sight of him is not a happy one except to those who are like him. Therefore, everyone who has this confidence in Christ, that he will then be a partaker of his glory, in the meantime purifies himself from worldly feelings through godly pursuits. There was none of the filth of this world in Christ; on the contrary he was wholly pure and heavenly.[7] Therefore, we must strive with all our might to see that no earthly dregs settle in us.[8]

Let no one beguile himself by saying, 'All I have to do to be innocent is not to commit any of the acts forbidden by the law of Moses or punished by the laws of the state, acts such as theft, sacrilege, adultery, homicide.' On the contrary, every kind of sin must be absolutely avoided. Whoever sins in any way, even if he does not sin against the Mosaic commandments, still sins against evangelical law, which is far more holy than the Mosaic law.[9] For this reason Christ came once and for all into the world to point out the way through which his return would become the source of our salvation and happiness. He came to remove once and for all not one or two but all our sins since he alone was subject to no sin. He made us clean once and for all from all sin and without any cost to us in order to make us like himself, something which no law nor any mortal could do. We have been made a part of his sacrosanct body through baptism. But in the meantime it is our task to make every effort not to fall away from our Head. We have been engrafted there through his spontaneous mercy, but we shall fall away if we slip back into our former vices. Everyone who abides in Christ perseveres in innocence and shuns every sin so that he may grow more virtuous day by day and come to resemble Christ, his Head, ever more closely. Everyone who does not refrain from sins has not yet seen Christ fully nor come to know him despite the fact that he has been baptized and has pledged his allegiance to him. If one could see with the eyes of faith how great a disgrace it is to be delivered to the devil to be his child, how great an honour it is to be co-opted into the number of God's children, who could endure to be torn from such a body or to abandon God as one's Father and sink beneath so foul a tyranny, to plunge deliberately from such great rewards into so great a loss?

Little children, let no one deceive you or beguile you into believing that the bare avowal of the name Christian is sufficient for happiness. It is not the one who avows righteousness that is righteous, but only he is righteous who practises righteousness in his life and behaviour in the same way that Christ showed himself an example of complete righteousness in his words and deeds. He who clings truly and totally to Christ avoids to the best of his ability the taint of every vice. The very purity of his character is proof that he is a child of God, who is good by nature and does not know sin. But everyone who sins, even if he has been initiated into the sacraments of Christ, is the offspring of his father, the devil, who is the prince and author of all sin. Whoever imitates him resembles his parent in the very fact that he sins, and shows that he is the devil's child.[10] God does not admit any communion with vice. He sent his Son into this world for this very purpose: to abolish the works of the devil, everything, that is, which conflicts with evangelical love.

We are all born of Adam and subject to sins.[11] We are reborn of God through the seed of evangelical teaching[12]. As long as the force of this seed remains in a man, he does not sin and cannot sin, obviously because divine love forbids it when it carries him away with the impulse to do good and calls him back from every desire to sin. He cannot sin because he is truly a child of God and faithfully resembles the character and nature of his Father and Head. It is not the name 'Christian,' it is not baptism, it is not the sacraments which separate the children of God from the children of the devil, but the purity of their life and the love which reveals and extends itself in good deeds. If love is present, it is not idle. Whoever does not show this love and does not show by his actions that his brother is dear to him is not born of God. If he were a living member of the body of Christ, he would cherish the other members for whom Christ died.

This is the essence of Christian righteousness. This is the message which Christ gave us first and foremost. This is what we have commended to you above everything else, that you show by your love for one another that you are children of God and disciples of Christ. For hatred of one's neighbour is a step towards murder, and envy is diametrically opposed to love. Cain was not a child of God but was the offspring of the devil. Why?

He degenerated, became unlike his good creator, and grew to resemble the devil, who, goaded by envy, had been the first to kill a human being through the inspiration which brought death.[13] Cain reflected the nature of his parent when he killed his brother Abel.[14] What was the cause of his hatred? Doubtless the dissimilarity in their way of life, which also explains why they were of different stock even though their physical propagation made them twin brothers. Each displayed his own parentage. Abel was innocent and aflame with the desire to do good; Cain by contrast when he conceived a hatred for his brother gave no thought to self-correction but only to the murder of his brother. Being ungodly and a child of the devil, he could not tolerate one who was godly and a child of God. So in your case too, brothers, it should not seem strange to you if people who are attached to the world reject you.[15] They hate those who do not deserve to be hated. But let no one of you hate them in return. Since they are dedicated to death and serve the author of death, they contrive death for others. Our part is to pity them, not to do them harm in return. Evangelical love has drawn us away from the desire to do harm and towards the desire to do good. Because we love our brothers, we know from this sign that we are destined for eternal life and are removed from the tyranny of death. He who loves has only good will and does only good.

Breath gives life to the body, the Spirit of Christ gives life to the soul. Where there is no brotherly love, the Spirit of Christ is not found either. Therefore, everyone who hates a neighbour[16] is dead and without inner life. Even if this person has faith, it is a dead faith since love is not present. Or do you dismiss hatred for a brother as a trivial fault? Anyone who hates his brother is a murderer. He has not drawn a blade, mixed poison, made an assault, uttered a curse; he has merely wished him ill. Human law does not condemn him for murder, but he is already condemned for murder before God. He who has once admitted hatred into his heart is a murderer in so far as it is in him to be one. There are many kinds of murder. One who slashes to death with a blade pays a penalty even in secular law. One who kills with poison is punished even by the godless. But one who pierces a brother with the arrow of a poisoned tongue,[17] though he may be acquitted of the crime of parricide by human law, is nevertheless guilty of homicide according to evangelical law.[18] He whom the hater wishes ill is still alive, but the hater himself is already dead. The life of the person hated is unharmed; the hater has lost eternal life, a murderer of his own self.[19]

Do you want to see, brethren, how far we must be from the desire to do harm? Direct your eyes to the example of Christ. He so loved us, who deserved nothing, rather who utterly deserved death, that he paid for us with his own life. How much more ought we to hazard our own lives to save our brothers if the occasion arises, especially those of us who have stepped into the position of Christ the shepherd?[20] He did not entrust his sheep to Peter until Peter had professed his love three times, whereupon he indicated to him the manner of his death so that Peter would understand that he must watch over the safety of the flock entrusted to him at the cost of his life.[21] Will someone who is reluctant to help another with money sacrifice his life for him? Does someone think he has done enough if he does not injure a brother or if he speaks a kind word to him? Christ showed in action how greatly he loved us. If someone has observed his brother in need of food, drink, clothing, shelter, and has the resources to assist his need but is unmoved by compassion and neglects him as a matter of no concern to himself, can anyone believe that the love of God is in this person? Pagan assists pagan, and do you, a Christian, not assist a fellow Christian? You promised to show brotherly love. If it is truly in you, why does it not reach out to a brother who is tormented by need?[22] Do you call him brother and yet produce no evidence of brotherly feeling?

My little children, let us not love one another in words only. Let love be in the heart rather than on the tongue, and let it express itself in actions rather than in words. Let the word 'brother' be part of our everyday language, but on the condition that we are true and that our actions match our speech. Whenever the occasion offers, let us show in action that brotherly love is truly in us. Do not let a brother lack anything that we have in our possession whether he may need clothing, or food, or shelter, or comfort, or teaching, or admonition.[23] If we do this without hesitation, we shall know[24] by this sign that we are children of truth and that our love is not feigned but sincere.[25] Christ himself is truth. We shall make our conscience acceptable to his eyes and thus we shall be acceptable to both God and men.[26] Men will know from our actions that our love for one another is not feigned; God sees the sincerity in the mind directly. We shall assist a brother's need, but only to the point that we alleviate the need and do not encourage extravagance. Our assistance will be heartfelt with no expectation of any reward coming back to us and without regard for empty glory.[27] People do not see the mind but it is aware of itself and is visible to the eyes of God. If people praise us while the mind, aware of its own guilt, condemns us, though we may deceive other people, we shall not be allowed to escape God's judgment. The human heart has its innermost niches and intricate hiding-places, but nothing can be so concealed and hidden away as to keep God from discovering it. He knows all things better than we. He who made our heart knows our heart. He who is present everywhere has eyes everywhere. Dearly beloved, if our heart will not condemn us alone before God, if our mind is sincere and open,[28] if everything we do we do from a pure and unqualified love, God will act towards us just as we have acted towards a neighbour. If we sincerely and willingly forgive a brother his fault, God will readily forgive us too our transgressions.[29] If we give promptly to a brother in need whenever he implores our help, we shall ask God with a sure confidence for that which pertains to our welfare[30] and needs, and he will not deny what we ask. But whenever we say to him, 'forgive us our debts as we forgive our debtors' [Matt 6:12], and we are possessed within by hatred for a brother, will our conscience not immediately contradict us? What effrontery to ask God for what you yourself deny a neighbour! What cheek to demand fulfilment of the covenant when you do not fulfil the condition![31] He promised to forgive us our wrongdoings, but on the condition that we have sincerely forgiven a brother his transgressions. If we say with our lips, 'I forgive,' and nevertheless harbour ill will in our heart, a guilty conscience will deprive us of our confidence in obtaining what we ask from God. If we exchange greetings pleasantly with a brother but are not available at the times when his actual situation demands help, there is no reason to expect God to help us who have failed a brother. If we are deaf to God's commands, he in turn will be deaf to our prayers. It is not godliness but impudence to ask a favour of him whose commandments you disregard. But if we keep his commandments, if everything we do pleases him, and if we do it in such a way that we are acceptable to his eyes who sees through everything, we shall have reason to be confident that we shall obtain our request.

Here the Jew, painstaking observer of the Law that he is, will say to me, 'I observe the Sabbath; I perform my ablutions; I fast; I abstain from forbidden foods; I do not steal. God will hear me.' No, this is not the commandment I am talking about. What is it then? That we place all hope for our salvation and all confidence in Jesus Christ, the Son of God, through whom the Father wanted to give all things to us. Is this now enough? Not at all. We are to love one another following his example. This is what he commanded, but he himself was the first to do what he commanded.[32] One who hates a member of Christ does not yet truly feel affection for Christ. One who wishes another human ill, one for whom Christ died, does not yet love Christ. Therefore, the person who keeps that one commandment of love will thereby keep them all. This is the cement with which we shall be joined to Christ in such a way that he is in us and we in turn are in him.[33] He will dwell in our breast through his Spirit whenever love is hot there. The Spirit of Christ is not the author of hate but the giver of brotherly love. This Spirit is poured into the baptized through the imposition of apostolic hands,[34] but it also recoils and flies away if love should happen to be extinguished. Therefore, if brotherly love has remained in us, we shall apprehend from this sign that the gift of the Spirit which we received in baptism abides in us. To the degree that this love grows cold, to this degree the Spirit will withdraw.[35]

Chapter 4

I have given you a sign, dearly beloved, by which you may discover whether the Spirit of Christ is in you. There are different spirits in people, but they are deceptive and evil. Therefore, do not instantly believe every spirit. Many here and there boast that they have the Spirit of God, but you test whether these spirits have come from God. This world also has its spirit and it counterfeits the Spirit of God. The Spirit of God inspires prophets, but several false prophets have already appeared in the world falsely claiming that they speak under the inspiration of the Spirit of God though they are moved by the spirit of the world. Do you want, therefore, a still more certain proof of the divine Spirit? Listen to him as he speaks, and you will understand. Every spirit which acknowledges the Son of God is of God, that is, which confesses that Jesus Christ, the author of eternal salvation, who was promised long ago, has assumed a human body and has now come just as he had earlier promised through his prophets. On the other hand, the spirit which denies that Jesus has done this is a liar and for this reason is not of God. For no one truly avows the Son unless inspired by the Father. Moreover, not only do those who reject him in words deny him, but so also do those who live as if Christ were not for human beings the model of true godliness or as if he were not the author of perfect salvation.[1] Because his teaching is too much at variance with their own desires they invent some other messiah to wait for. If Christ had favoured the pleasures of the flesh or had promised boundless riches or had made a gift of honours and world empires, they would have long since acknowledged him as their messiah. As it is, since he teaches contempt for these things and invites one to take up a cross and points out that all happiness is to be expected in a future age, they deny that he is the long-promised redeemer of the human race. They bid one to wait instead for a different messiah, one who will promise material welfare and the good things of this present age. It is not enough just to confess Christ unless we should also confess him whole and complete. The person who divides Christ either by taking away his divine nature, which he has identical with that of the Father, or by taking away his human nature, which he received from his human mother, this person is not of God but is the spirit of the Antichrist.[2] You have already heard of this spirit, that it will come;[3] no, it has already come now and is acting in those who have dedicated themselves to worldly delights and fight against the Spirit of Christ.

You have no reason to be afraid of such spirits, little children. Since you are of God and have his Spirit, you have yourselves defeated the antichrists through it.[4] By yourselves you are weak, but the Spirit which dwells in you is greater and is mightier than the spirit which dwells in the world. The devil attacks you through his members,[5] but God protects you by his Spirit.[6] Since they belong to the world's party and have absorbed the spirit of the world, they smack of the world[7] and talk of worldly things. Their teaching pleases those who are themselves too devoted to the world. No one easily believes that which opposes the things he passionately loves. They love earthly things, and their teaching smacks of the earth. But we are of God. The one who knows God – and everyone who loves him knows him – listens to us whose teachings are of heaven and worthy of God. The one who is not of God does not hear us. This person shuns the teachings of the gospel, which tell us to cast riches away, to spurn pleasures, to glory in sufferings, to hold even life cheap compared to righteousness, to await all reward for right actions in the resurrection,[8] which those people either do not believe will take place or would not want to happen. The teaching of the gospel tells us to sacrifice even our lives for a neighbour out of pure love;[9] however, the man of worldly spirit everywhere looks after his own interests even if this means doing wrong to a brother. Through these signs, therefore, one will be able to distinguish the truthful Spirit of God from the deceitful spirit of the world.

Therefore, dearly beloved, seeing that we are of God, not of the world, let us love one another and let each serve the best interests of his neighbour rather than his own, for love is of God. Everyone who is endowed, therefore, with this love is born of God and truly knows God. Everyone who is a stranger to this love does not yet know God because God himself is love. He imparts himself to us whenever he imparts his love. He has shown his love for us so that we in turn might show our own love for a neighbour. But someone will say, 'We recognize the Son's love, but from what do we know the Father's love for us?' From the fact that he sent into this world and surrendered to death his only Son, than whom he has nothing more dear, so that through his terrible death we might obtain eternal life. The wonder of his love is all the greater even and the more remarkable because he showed such remarkable love without having been moved to it by any charity on our part. One who returns another's love is only being gracious; he would be discourteous if he were not to do so. We were in love with the world and rejected God's love. Nevertheless, God first[10] and on his own initiative showed his love for us. He was rightfully offended by our sins and there was no human on earth free from offences who might reconcile us to him, for the one who intercedes for the guilty before the person offended has to be personally acceptable to him. Therefore, he sent his own Son from heaven to sacrifice himself to the Father[11] and through this most pure offering to make him propitious to us. What can be imagined more remarkable, more ardent, more generous than this love?

Dearly beloved, if God, who is in no need of us, spontaneously and willingly loved us so greatly, we too ought to love one another after his example. The Son of God made himself visible to us, but no one has ever seen with his bodily eyes God the Father. Nevertheless, he is perceived through material signs. We feel his anger; we feel his kindness; we feel his absence; we feel his presence. We can give evidence of our mutual love for God by no other sign than if we love one another just as he loved us. If we love one another in this way, God, who, as I said, is love, abides in us. He loved us freely, he loved so that he might save us. While it is characteristic of ordinary human love to show good will to a benefactor, to be affectionate to one who might return a favour, to give evidence of good will through reciprocal services, God's love for us is perfect. He loved spontaneously; he loved those not his own; he loved those from whom no favour could be returned to him; he loved right to the loss of his only begotten Son. If we love our neighbour in a similar way, then God's love is perfected in us because it shows that even God himself is in us. Just as the same spirit unifies the parts of the body and makes them one body, so the Spirit of God somehow cements and ties us together with him and also with one another and gathers us into a unity, as it were. If the Spirit of God which inspires our hearts and minds with love of our neighbour is active in us, by this sign we know both that we abide in God and that God in turn abides in us. Therefore, he who denies that Jesus is the Son of God who sacrificed himself to redeem the race of mortals is an opponent of love.

But we were even spectators at this event. We saw with our eyes, heard with our ears, touched with our hands. We bear witness to the whole world about what we had learned in so many ways, that the Father has sent his Son through whose death the world would be saved if it would only recover from its past errors and adjust its life thereafter to the rule of the gospel.[12] For God did not send him to save the Jewish nation only; he gave him to the whole world to be its saviour. Therefore, everyone who has confessed that Jesus is the Son of God, the one whom the prophets predicted would come, abides in God, and God in him. For this person knows the truth and embraces the love. But the one who does not make this love evident through his love for his neighbour does not acknowledge God's love for him. We, however, know from experience, and believe in our minds, and confess with our mouths, and make evident by our actions the love which God has shown to us. It remains for us to persist in what we have begun and to do nothing to make God sever himself from us or to cause ourselves to be detached from God. As I said before, God is love. Therefore, he who continues in love continues in God and God in turn in him while the divine Spirit remains and ties both together.

Do you want yet another sign to be given you through which you may perceive whether the love of God is perfected in you? It is this, that we have a clear conscience and do not dread that day of judgment on which those who have not imitated Christ will be separated from him. They will tremble when they hear those terrible words, 'Depart from me' [Matt 7:23]. We, however, await that day with confidence, that is, we are fully aware that as he lived in the world, so also are we in the world. He contracted no stain from the world but cleansed it from its filth and, as it was in his power to do, drew it to his own purity. Thus we also to the best of our ability avoid mingling with the world so that we may entice it to Christ through evangelical teaching and the example of our chaste lives.

A bad conscience gives birth to the fear of divine judgment. Fear, therefore, does not square with love. For love adds confidence. If love is perfect, it completely expels all terror from the mind. It feels joy whenever that day of judgment comes to mind, first, because it has the highest opinion of God who is good and, secondly, because it has a clear conscience. Love brings joy; fear brings torment. The person who is afraid shows by this very fact that he has not yet been made perfect in love. In so far as he falls short in love, thus far does he draw closer to fear. He fears that he will find God judging without mercy anyone who has shown himself unmoved by a neighbour's appeals. That day will reveal those who truly showed love in this world. We love God, which is not strange since he loved us first. We could not love him if he were not drawing us to himself by his love. The very fact that we love him is the result of his kindness. Furthermore, by loving our neighbour we testify to the fact that we love God. For it is in him that God wants himself to be loved. If someone says, 'I love God,' yet treats[13] his brother hatefully, he is a liar. Even the godless, most of whom not only do not love God but do not even believe in his existence, still show a neighbour some sort of affection either because he is a relative by blood or marriage, or because he is a close acquaintance, or simply because one human being sees that another is a human too in the same way that each species of animal possesses a natural instinct to love its own kind.[14] How will he love God whom he has never seen when he hates his neighbour whom he does see?[15] Secondly, how does it make sense to say that he who neglects God's commandments loves him? If someone were to say, 'I love

Caesar,'[16] while scorning Caesar's edicts, will he find anyone to believe him? We have this special edict from our own ruler, that one who loves God is also to love his brother regardless of whether the brother is good or evil. If he is good, one should love Christ in him. If he is evil, one should love him in the hope of seeing him converted to Christ.[17]

Chapter 5

Whoever believes that Jesus is the Christ, that is, the one from whom he must seek every source of aid for his salvation, and believes this sincerely, he is born of God and already numbered among the children of God, and he who is a child cannot but love. Moreover, whoever sincerely loves the father who begot him also loves anyone else begotten by his father; that is, he loves the brother with whom he has a father in common. If we sincerely love God himself first, we perceive by this sign that we truly love the children of God. For nothing is truly loved except what is loved for God's sake. Furthermore, it will be evident that we love God only if we keep his commandments and keep them eagerly and gladly. For his commands are not in any case burdensome.[1] What is burdensome to someone who loves? What is burdensome to someone hastening towards such rewards?

The world displays images of terrifying evil: poverty, exile, ignominy, imprisonment, scourging, death.[2] The battle is immense, but victory is at hand. For everything that is born of God overcomes the world. What resources does one have to overcome the world? Money? Troops? Machines of war? Worldly knowledge? Not at all. Only through the confidence with which people entrust themselves wholly to God their defender do they overcome the world no matter how savage it is.[3] Your wealth is confiscated. What does faith offer instead? You have a treasure in heaven.[4] You are driven into exile, but your homeland in heaven is waiting for its citizen.[5] Tortures are applied to the body, but everlasting rewards are purchased with them. Death is threatened, but immortality will follow it. Who is it then that overcomes the world? Not the satrap, not the millionaire, not the philosopher, not the king, but the one, whoever it is, who truly believes that Jesus is the Son of God. Believe in what he promised and no conceivable threat from the world will move you. He overcame the world before us and obtained immortality. He assumed our mortal body and came into this world to overcome it for us, to show us the way to overcome it, to create faith in the rewards.

With what defences was he armed when he came? Jesus Christ came through water and blood: through water to wash away our sins from us, through blood to bestow immortal life on us.[6] Though free from every sin he wanted to be baptized in order to grant us innocence.[7] He wanted to die on the cross in order to open the way for us to immortality. These two were not the only signs through which he gave evidence that he was the Christ and the Saviour, to receive baptism like a guilty person and to die on the cross like a criminal, though he alone of all was free from every sin. The Spirit too, appearing in the form of a dove, gave evidence about him,[8] that he was the one whom the Father had given to be the Saviour of the world. For the Spirit too is truth just as the Father and the Son are. The truth of all three is one, just as the nature of all three is one. For[9] there are three in heaven who furnish testimony to Christ: the Father, the Word, and the Spirit. The Father, who not once but twice sent forth his voice from the sky[10] and publicly testified that this was his uniquely beloved Son in whom he found no offence; the Word, who, by performing so many miracles and by dying and rising again, showed that he was the true Christ, both God and human alike, the reconciler of God and humankind; the Holy Spirit, who descended on his head at baptism[11] and after the resurrection glided down upon the disciples.[12] The agreement of these three is absolute. The Father is the author, the Son the messenger, the Spirit the inspirer. There are likewise three things on earth which attest Christ: the human spirit which he laid down on the cross, the water, and the blood which flowed from his side in death.[13] And these three witnesses are in agreement.[14] They testify that he was a man. The first three declare him to be God.[15]

John also gave testimony.[16] But if we accept the testimony of men, it is right that the testimony of God have more weight with us. For the testimony of God the Father is clear: 'This is my beloved Son, in him I am well pleased. Listen to him' [Matt 17:5]. What could have been stated more openly or more completely? The one who truly believes the Son of God, Jesus Christ, and has stationed in him all the defences of his life so that, relying on Christ's promises, he disdains everything which the world displays, whether it be lovable or frightening, this person has the testimony in himself and bears testimony to the Son of God. For when inspired by the Spirit of Christ he despises out of love for him every kind of death, he produces no light testimony among men that what Christ teaches and promises is not vain. The one who does not believe God but puts his faith in the world makes God a liar in so far as it is in his power to do so. God promised happiness to those who would listen to his Son, Jesus Christ, but this man teaches through his way of life that happiness is to be sought from the world. He thus clings to the good things of this life as if nothing of the human person remained after the death of the body. The Father cries, 'Listen to him,' and the life of the one who does not believe says, 'Listen to the world.' After the Son had prayed to the Father that those should have

eternal life who believed him or would believe him in the future, the
Father's voice was heard like the sound of a trumpet, testifying that the
prayers of the Son would be ratified.[17] The Father has given us, therefore,
eternal life by showing clearly from whom it was to be sought, to wit, from
his Son Jesus Christ. Everyone who accepts the Son's teaching, who imitates
his example and has faith in his promises both possesses the Son and has
life. In the meantime he has the Spirit of God as an earnest of it.[18] This
Spirit gives him the confidence not to be afraid to call God Father.[19] But the
person who is a stranger to the Son is also a stranger to life.

My purpose in repeating these matters at such length and driving
them home in this way is to keep you from being persuaded of the opposite
by anyone else. I want to convince you beyond all doubt that what you
have come to believe is true, that eternal life has been prepared for you
through Jesus Christ, with whom you have been included as co-heirs. You
already have a legal right and an earnest; you will take possession of your
inheritance in due course.[20] Therefore, you who believe the Son of God
make your belief steadfast and your faith in him ever stronger day by day.[21]
He who does not fail you in this life will not deceive you in the promise of
eternal life. For the Spirit of Christ offers you this confidence, that you will
obtain whatever you ask the Father in the name of the Son,[22] provided that
you ask in keeping with his will. This means that you must come to pray
in the state in which he wanted you to come, that is, free from all hatred of
a brother – for the person who does not pardon a neighbour for a trespass
obtains nothing from God – and that you must ask for those things which
are conducive to heavenly life and contribute to the glory of Christ. It is
often the case that we do not know what should be asked from God,[23] and,
if the Spirit of Christ does not suggest to us what it is expedient to ask, we
often ask for harmful things instead of salutary ones. But whenever we ask
in the Spirit of Christ, we are sure that God hears our wishes and are
likewise sure that he will grant us whatever we ask. This is what he promised us;[24] and he can fulfil whatever he promises and he wants whatever
contributes to our salvation.

God, who is ever ready to be moved by our prayers, will not only
increase his goods in us but will also forgive us our daily offences. The
weakness of human nature can hardly go long without committing an
offence. He will not only forgive each one's personal sins if one asks for
pardon, but will also listen to a brother praying for a brother's offences, but
only if the sin is such that, though it may cast a shadow over brotherly love
to some extent, it does not completely extinguish it. There is a sin whose
character does not enable it to be attributed to human weakness nor to be
healed by light and ready-made remedies. Such a sin exists when someone

who has himself confessed Christ persecutes the Christian fellowship with deliberate malice and strives to subvert religion under the pretext of religion.[25] His hopeless perversion does not deserve the intercession of godly people.[26] Yet perfect love prays even for these persons and hopes even for those things which are impossible. No one prays for Satan, whose envy leads him deliberately to oppose the recipients of God's good will. Perhaps one also ought not to pray for those who have crossed over to his side.[27] They are to be shunned to keep them from doing some injury, rather than to be assisted through prayers if they offer no hope of a change of heart.[28] A disease like this requires stronger remedies and is too severe to be removed by the daily prayers which erase the lighter sins that human weakness commits and which are not the product of perversity. Anything which detracts from complete righteousness is a sin, but there are many different kinds of sin. There is a kind of misdeed which though it spoils and diminishes innocence does not totally extinguish Christian love. For example, we occasionally blurt out something against a friend which we regret as soon as we have said it, or a burst of anger has wrenched out of us the kind of word which we immediately wish could be recalled, or captivated by the pleasant taste of some food or drink we take a little something beyond what nature requires. God is prone to forgive these things if intercession is made to him through our prayers for one another. Forgiving parents who would not tolerate more serious wrongdoing generally shut their eyes to such slips by their children. Every sin is evil and something to be avoided by the godly. Unheeded, it draws one on little by little to death. Just as a remedy is to be applied immediately to these lighter sins which can hardly be avoided by human beings, so may God forbid that someone relapse into some capital crime[29] after he has rejected the world once and for all and dedicated himself to God. We are made children of God and members of Christ through our evangelical commitment. It is not fitting for children to be so greatly different from their Father nor members of the body from their Head.

Therefore, he who thoroughly understands that he is born of God keeps himself from shameful acts more than from death itself and keeps himself from associating in any way with that evil lord whom, along with the world, he had earlier served. Christ died and came back to life once and for all never to die again.[30] It is inappropriate, therefore, for one who has once died to the world through baptism and has risen again with Christ to a new state of life again to do that which would require Christ to have to die again. Only those who have not been truly reborn of God and have not received the seed of evangelical teaching everywhere in the inmost reaches of their minds need fear danger to themselves from the world.[31] We know that we are truly of God. Neither the goods nor the evils of this world separate us from Christ. The whole world is seated in wickedness. Wherever one turns, things appear which are meant to call us away from the innocence of our life. But the Son of God has freed us once and for all from this world's enchantments. He came into the world for this very reason, to remove us from the contagion of the world. He dispelled the darkness of our former ignorance and gave us understanding illuminated by the light of the gospel so that we might come to know the true God[32] and the bestower of all righteousness, who alone had no dealings with the world. And we who follow his teachings and promises with a sincere heart are in him, who is true, when we are in his Son, Jesus Christ, whom he sent into the world for this reason.[33] He is the true God, who alone is to be worshipped, and the eternal life, which alone is to be sought.[34]

Little children, if you truly know the true God, avoid the false gods and empty images which the world worships. He whose god is money worships an idol. He whose god is the belly worships an idol. He who disregards God's commandments for the sake of worldly honours worships an idol. There are many kinds of images like these. You for your part avoid them all if you want to remain in the worship of the true God. May he by whose kindness we have been freed from our past errors bring my prayer to fulfilment.[35]

The End

PARAPHRASE ON THE SECOND EPISTLE OF JOHN

In secundam Ioannis epistolam paraphrasis

THE PARAPHRASE OF
DESIDERIUS ERASMUS OF ROTTERDAM
ON THE
SECOND EPISTLE OF JOHN

I, John the Elder, write to the elect Lady and also to her children, whom I love sincerely. I am not alone in this love but all with me who know evangelical truth likewise love. Nor do they love for any other reason except that they understand that the sincerity of the evangelical profession which we follow abides in us[1] and will abide forever. May[2] grace, mercy, and peace be always increased for you[3] by God the Father and by the Lord[4] Jesus Christ as you persevere in the truth of evangelical doctrine and in mutual love.

I rejoiced greatly at having learned that your children, imitating their mother's godliness, persevere in the truth of evangelical doctrine and pay no heed to false teachers who try to turn many away from this truth despite the Father's explicit command to us to be obedient to the teaching of his Son and not to depart from his footsteps. Therefore, Lady, there is no further need for me to instruct your piety with new commandments; we need only[5] continue in the one commandment which has been handed down from the beginning, that we attend one another with a mutual and truly Christian love. The agreement and similarity in our godly lives will secure this good will among us, so that we live with harmonious feelings according to God's commandment.[6] He enjoined on us nothing more diligently than mutual love among ourselves. True love does not exist among those who are neither godly nor like one another. Therefore, I bring no new commandment. I only admonish you over and over to continue in the one which you received long ago[7] and not to let yourselves be severed from it by any craftiness on the part of false prophets.

Many deceivers have arisen in the world[8] who deny that Jesus is the Christ who according to the predictions of the prophets was to come into the world. Whoever teaches this denial is a deceiver and that Antichrist, the adversary of Christ. Let each watch out for himself lest, if he should abandon what he has begun well, he lose all the benefit of the good achievements which he has thus far made. Let us instead take pains to receive the full reward which comes only to those who persevere right to the end.[9] Everyone who turns away from the truth and does not persevere in the teaching of Christ becomes a stranger to the Father too because he has deserted the Son. But he who follows Christ's teaching steadfastly is for this very reason dear also to the Father. Son and Father can be neither had nor abandoned separately from each other. This is that true teaching which you have received from the beginning from the most truthful witnesses.

But if anyone comes to you with a teaching different from this in order to lead you away from evangelical truth, you must not only not listen to him but must not even admit him into your house if he looks for hospitality, nor must you speak a word of greeting to him if you should meet him in the street. There is a risk that he will infect the family by his company and will repay you with wickedness in return for the hospitality of a shared roof, or that a conversation will arise from an exchange of greetings. 'Evil conversations corrupt good habits.'[10] Furthermore, the person who greets and confers with an impostor[11] of this kind appears to be a partner to his evil actions. He gives encouragement to the reprobate when the man sees that he is held in some regard among those whom he is striving to subvert. The greeter also makes a bad impression on others inasmuch as he appears to be favouring the inherent malice of the impostor with whom he is not afraid to associate on friendly terms.

There are many other things which I am eager to write you on these matters, but I prefer to set them out in person rather than to commit them to pen and paper. I hope to visit you shortly and to talk with you person to person so that the joy which I have realized from your steadfast sincerity may become richer and fuller when, face to face, I see in you what I now hear about you from a distance, and you in turn observe with your own eyes my affection for you.

Your nephews, the children of your sister, a Christian woman, send their greetings.[12]

PARAPHRASE ON THE THIRD EPISTLE OF JOHN

In tertiam Ioannis epistolam paraphrasis

THE PARAPHRASE OF
DESIDERIUS ERASMUS OF ROTTERDAM
ON THE
THIRD EPISTLE OF JOHN

The Elder to Gaius, a man worthy of much love, whom I love sincerely.

Dearly beloved, I ask Jesus Christ in my prayers that just as your soul prospers in its perseverance in evangelical doctrine, so with Christ's blessing it may prosper in everything else. For I have received no small pleasure from the statements of the brothers who have come to us and who have given testimony to your sincerity. They are true witnesses just as you are a true follower of evangelical truth, not only in your public confession but also in your desires and in your whole manner of life. For there is not a single thing which brings more joy to my heart than if I should happen to hear that my children whom I begot to Christ through the gospel are following the truth which I transmitted to them.

Dearly beloved, because you are charitable towards any Christians who live there or who may travel there as strangers, your conduct is worthy of one who truly possesses evangelical faith and loves Christ. For men have stood before the whole assembly of Christians and given testimony to your sincerity. Moreover, you have courteously welcomed visitors on their arrival. You would[1] be acting equally rightly if, with the same courtesy, you would send them on their way to their destination, whatever it may be.[2] For this is how those who are doing not their own but God's business deserve to be treated by those who love God sincerely. They have not set out on a business venture to increase their private property but on the work of preaching the name of the Lord Jesus Christ.[3] Though they impart Christ's teaching to the gentiles, they accept nothing in return from them so that they may bring a larger profit to Christ for whom they toil. They wish everything they do to be free from any suspicion that it is done to obtain money.[4] Decency requires us to welcome such people hospitably and to see to it that they lack none of the necessities of life. Thus we too may in some respect share in what they do for the glory of God.[5] Christ promised that he who received a prophet as a prophet would have a prophet's reward.[6]

I wrote earlier to the congregation there, telling them to do the same thing which I am advising you to do. But Diotrephes stands in the way. He refuses to accept our advice and prefers to be the leader among his own followers than to be a humble and pure disciple of Christ. He prefers to be the originator of a new heresy than the sincere adherent of long-standing evangelical doctrine.[7] Consequently, if I come to you, I shall tax him with his actions. He perhaps thinks they escape my notice when, evil man that he is, he prates against us with malicious words to destroy our credit and authority with you when we urge you to persevere in evangelical doctrine. And not content with that, he not only refuses to welcome the brothers, but even prevents those who want to welcome them and thrusts them out of the congregation. So great is the man's perversity!

Beloved brother, do not imitate what is evil but what is good. It belongs to us to tolerate evil persons, not to imitate them. Not all who have received baptism are children of God. He who shows his faith through godly actions is born of God, for he reflects the nature and teaching of his Father. He who behaves in an ungodly way, although he avows God in what he says, does not[8] truly see God. God is seen with the thoroughly cleansed eyes of faith. The darkness of vice makes them blind. Therefore, you will shun the example of Diotrephes and will take Demetrius as your model.[9] Testimony to his godliness is given by everyone. Even if they were silent, the facts themselves testify to the man's virtue. Besides, we also have direct experience of his sincerity. We bear testimony about him, and you yourselves[10] know that we bear true testimony about him.

I also have very many other things which I am eager for you to know, but I do not think it expedient to express them on paper with pen and ink. I hope to come to you very soon. Then we shall say everything more safely[11] and fully face to face.

Peace to you. The friends who are here send their greetings to you. You in turn greet in their name diligently and one by one the friends who are there.

The End[12]

PARAPHRASE ON HEBREWS

Paraphrasis in epistolam ad Hebraeos

DEDICATORY LETTER

TO THE RIGHT REVEREND SILVESTRO, LORD BISHOP OF WORCESTER,
PERMANENT ENVOY OF HIS MAJESTY THE KING OF ENGLAND
TO HIS HOLINESS LEO X,
FROM ERASMUS OF ROTTERDAM, GREETING[1]

It is only right, my Lord Bishop, that for your goodness and your distinguished support of liberal studies your name should be commended to posterity by everyone who writes; not that your modesty cares for any praise from men, but because many will be encouraged to pursue higher studies if they see that eminent persons who have deserved well of the Christian polity are not deprived of the fame which they have not sought and thereby deserve all the more. It was right, in return for all that you have done for me, that there should be no page in my books that does not display the name of Silvestro. So far, however, it has been possible for me to entertain proper feelings of gratitude towards your Lordship, but not to show them. I would have preferred to produce something rather later, provided that it might be on a larger scale; but now that I see myself overwhelmed by a mass of work that increases daily and, as Varro puts it,[2] becoming more like a bubble every day, I thought it right to dedicate this short work to you, not with a view to paying off my debt with this small offering, but as an acknowledgment that I am indebted to you on so many counts that I have no hopes of ever being able to repay you. And yet, if I am hereafter granted life and opportunity, I shall attempt, not to get my name crossed off in your ledger, which I should be sorry to do, since there is no one in whose debt I would rather be, but to escape the stigma of ingratitude.

Here now is Paul,[3] who with my assistance has learned to write at greater length and more clearly and, what is more, in Latin. Not that I have any fault to find with the way he writes; but our sluggish wits could not keep pace with him as he soared upwards. I have certainly made it possible for him to be well thumbed by readers as he never was before. Previously, he was scarcely accessible to scholars and only through hard work; now he is intelligible even to those with only a tincture of learning, provided they are not wholly ignorant of Latin. For this no credit may be due to my brains and none to my scholarship, but I do claim something for my industry.

During the time that I was thus lightening the labours of others by my own, I might have taken my ease. I might have slept or sipped my wine or hunted for promotion or indulged in other avocations. Some men pass their time away in such activities, except for what they devote to criticizing the work of others.

The classical languages and liberal studies have almost reached a stage at which we may hope that their future is secure, though even now there is vehement[4] opposition from the champions of ancient ignorance. If only we had the same hope of seeing the teaching of the gospel restored to its purity and simplicity! But here a bloody battle rages still. Yet we have a good hope of victory, if Christ will help us through you and men like you. And help us he will, if we do his work in sincerity of heart. Towards both ends it will make the greatest contribution if Leo, the supreme head of our religion, works unfailingly for the glory of him whose vice-gerent he is. Farewell, my most distinguished Lord.

Louvain, 17 January 1521

THE ARGUMENT OF
THE EPISTLE TO THE HEBREWS
BY ERASMUS OF ROTTERDAM

No people opposed the gospel of Christ more obstinately than did the Jews.[1] They were likewise hostile to Paul in particular because he proclaimed himself the Apostle of the Gentiles,[2] whom the Jews detested because they considered them profane and ungodly. In their view he was abrogating the Mosaic law,[3] which they held to be sacrosanct and were eager to have spread throughout the whole world in place of the gospel. Even among Jews who had accepted the teachings of Christ there were some who thought that the observance of the Law had to be combined with the gospel. Therefore, the Jews in Jerusalem, who held the powers of the state in their possession and were opposed to the gospel, were inflicting various forms of dire distress on the believers in that city. They threw them into prison; they scourged them; they plundered their property.[4] Paul consoles them, therefore, by speaking on the one hand of their hope for a reward in heaven and on the other hand of the example of the saints of old, most of whom had been tested by similar or even more severe afflictions to make their virtue more evident and beyond doubt, but above all by citing the example of Christ. Next, by recalling many incidents from the Old Testament and accommodating them to Christ, Paul makes it clear that the shadows of the Mosaic law have disappeared in the expanding light of the gospel of Christ. He teaches that it is not from the observance of the Law, given as it was for a limited period of time and imperfect, that salvation is to be hoped for, but from faith, through which even those ancient heroes of tested holiness whose memory was sacrosanct to the Jews had been most pleasing to God. He concludes by offering some precepts which are conducive to the development of a Christian character.

PARAPHRASE ON
THE EPISTLE TO THE HEBREWS
BY ERASMUS OF ROTTERDAM

Chapter 1

God, who in keeping with his devotion to us zealously looks after the human race, often in the past spoke in many and various ways through his prophets[1] to whom he showed himself sometimes in a cloud, sometimes in fire, sometimes in the whistling of a gentle breeze, sometimes in one form and then in another, sometimes speaking through angels, at other times insinuating himself through a secret inspiration of the mind.[2] Finally, in order to declare his love for the race of men through a more trustworthy sign and to make our faith more complete, he has deigned to speak to us in these last times not through an angel, not through a human prophet but through his one and only Son, Jesus Christ, whom in his eternal wisdom he has made the heir and Lord not only of the Jewish race but of the entire world. For as God had previously promised in the Psalms,[3] Jesus is the true and only Son of him to whom everything which has been created in heaven and on earth belongs. It is not strange that he wished the Son to share with him the lordship of the whole world since he created the entire world through him. He created it by his word, and the Son is the eternal Word of the eternal Father. He did not create the world through the Son as though he were an instrument or a minister but in such a way that the power of the Father, who did the creating, and the power of the Son were one and the same.[4] For Jesus Christ is not the Son of God in the way that godly persons are sometimes called sons of God because they obey his commands.[5] He has been truly begotten God by God the Father and begotten in such a way that he has the same nature as the Father. He was (and still is) the eternal brightness of the Father's glory in the way that light emanates from light.[6] He was the express image of his substance,[7] similar and equal in everything to him[8] from whom he is born.[9] He is not only the creator of everything but together with his almighty Father he also governs and moves[10] all creation by his almighty will and command.

And yet you see how much he lowered himself for our sake. He assumed the nature of our human condition, a nature subject to injury. Through his death he sacrificed himself as a victim on the altar of the cross for our sins. Prior to that it had been the regular practice for the priest of the Mosaic law to expiate sins with the blood of cattle. The Son, however, cleansed the wrongdoings of the entire human race by his own sacrosanct blood. He acquired so much glory from this lowering of himself that having returned to life and to heaven he has taken his place at the right hand of the majesty of God the Father in which majesty he had always been equal in respect to his divine nature. But this humiliation of the Son has now made his majesty all the more manifest to the world. He, who earlier was seen to be cast down below the lowest level of humanity, is now held to be and is greater not only than the prophets but even than the angels themselves. He is as much greater as the name 'son' has greater dignity than the name 'servant.' For the word 'angel' means 'minister' and is appropriate to an inferior.[11]

The dignity of the angels, who always stand before the Father, gazing upon his face, is very high indeed, and different ones among them excel the others in dignity. Which of the angels did God ever hold so much in honour that he considered him worthy of the name of son? But he speaks to Christ in a mystical[12] psalm in this fashion: 'You are my Son, today I have begotten you' [Ps 2:7], and again: 'I shall be to him a father, and he will be to me a son' [2 Samuel 7:14]. For he created the angels out of nothing,[13] but he begot the Son from his own substance, similar and equal in every respect. Again, when in a mystical psalm he brings the Son into the world, clothed in a human body, he speaks in this fashion: 'And let all the angels of God worship him' [Ps 97:7]. He means, servants are respected, but the Son, who is equal to the Father, is worshipped. But what does mystical Scripture say when it speaks of the dignity of the angels? 'Who makes,' it says, 'his angels spirits and his ministers a flame of fire' [Ps 104:4]. Angels, because they have been created, are in this respect no different from the rest of the things created by God. Because they have been created spirits and intelligences free from the contagion of the human body and because they continuously burn with God's love and stand ready to be prompt executors of his will,[14] they excel us, of course, in this respect. But how much more magnificent are the things which he says to the Son? 'Your throne, O God, is for ever and ever, a sceptre of righteousness is the sceptre of your kingdom' [Ps 45:6]. You hear the word 'God' applied to the Son,[15] you hear him being given the throne of the kingdom, you hear him being given the sceptre of the kingdom which will never have an end. There follows in the same psalm: 'You have loved righteousness, and you have hated wickedness; therefore, God, your God, has anointed you with the oil of gladness beyond your companions' [Ps 45:7]. You hear how he has been anointed in a quite special way[16] by God the Father above all his companions, whether angels or humans. And again in another psalm see how much authority is given to the Son: 'And[17] you, Lord,' it says, 'in the beginning laid the foundation of the earth, and the heavens are the work of your hands. They will perish, but you remain; and they will all grow old like a garment; and you will turn them around like a cloak,[18] and they will suddenly be changed. But you are always the same, and your years will not fail' [Ps 102:25–27]. To which of the angels were these things ever said? Or this which is read in another psalm: 'Sit at my right hand until I make your enemies your footstool' [Ps 110:1]? Therefore, neither the authority to create nor the majesty of the kingdom is attributed to the angels. No matter how great all the angels are, they remain intelligences appointed for ministry, who are continually sent forth to earth to stand by[19] those who are to be the heirs of eternal salvation. But these heirs are the disciples of Christ.

Chapter 2

The greater is the one whom the Father sent into the world for our salvation, the more attentively are we to listen to what has been said to us through him. That is why I have demonstrated at such length the high position of our Saviour. We must never forget what the Father has proclaimed to us through him. He who sent him is supreme and there is no one greater whom he can send. He wished him to be his last and final envoy. There is no hope at all of salvation if we ignore him the way our ancestors ignored Moses and the prophets.[1] The greater the envoy is and the greater God's kindness to us is, the graver will be the blame we incur for either our stubbornness or our negligence if we do not obey his words. If everything has weight which God commanded our ancestors up to now through the prophets or through the angels who carried his injunctions to Moses,[2] and if everyone who did not obey the injunctions given through them paid a just penalty – because everyone who spurns God's messengers seems to spurn God Himself – how shall we escape punishment if we neglect, not the commandments given to us through Moses, but the salvation given through God's very own Son? a salvation so at hand, so outstanding, so evident? Not Moses, not angels, not prophets, about whom one might harbour the suspicion that they were motivated by vanity, have brought salvation to us but the Son of God.[3] He did not speak to us from afar in a cloud or through a dream or in any of the other ways which might arouse some suspicion of fraud or deception on his part. He was heard from nearby. He was seen and touched.[4] He lived long among men and women, revealing through very many and very great signs that he was the true Son of God and was offering perfect salvation to the entire world through faith in the gospel.

Faith in this great offer had initially been communicated to the world first through the Lord himself, Jesus Christ, who was not only the herald but also the author of eternal salvation. It was subsequently confirmed by those who had been the witnesses of everything which he said and did during his life among men and women. Lest the preaching of these witnesses have too little weight, God himself confirmed their words with many different portents and miraculous signs and other amazing gifts, which that heavenly Spirit distributed to his followers in various ways[5] as seemed to God to be advantageous for the salvation of mankind. From all these things it was abundantly established that the whole of what was being done was not the product of human strength but of divine power and that he who produced these miracles, first by himself and afterwards through his disciples, was not a simple human but God clothed in a human body. Moreover, a mystical psalm declares that he was definitely not an angel when it testifies about Christ as follows: 'What is man that you are mindful of him, or the Son of Man that you have a care for him? You lowered him for a little while below the angels,'[6] then follows:[7] 'you crowned him with glory and honour, and you have set him over the works of your hands. You have put all things under his feet' [Ps 8:5–8a]. Even before the creation of the world, God had already decided in his divine wisdom that whatever was to exist in the world would be placed under the feet of Jesus Christ. But nowhere does it say that dominion over the whole universe in which the angels too[8] are contained has been conveyed to any one of the angels. For he who said that everything was to be made subject left nothing which was not to be subject. The prophecy of this psalm has now been partly fulfilled and will be completely fulfilled in the age to come. For we see that everything has not yet been made subject to him. The ungodly are still in rebellion and there is a severe conflict between the church and the world.[9]

But we do see now that part which has been fulfilled. When Jesus suffered various torments here and subsequently underwent the punishment of the cross, tasting what men judge to be the most bitter taste of all – but only tasting death, not swallowing it – he seemed to have been made lower than the angels who are not subject to death or to any pain.[10] But now he has been crowned with so much glory and honour that the world understands that he, though free from every fault, underwent the punishment of death in keeping with the will of God, who wills only what is best for human salvation. Jesus' death was not the penalty for a wrong which he had committed, but was the sign of God's good will towards the human race, which in his spontaneous kindness he wanted redeemed through the death of his own most innocent Son, Jesus Christ.[11] As he could not raise us up to share with him in his immortality if he were not God, so it would not be appropriate for him who had created all things and now guides everything through his governance to allow what he had created to perish totally. But where would the Son's kingdom be if he alone were with the Father? Therefore, it seemed fitting that the Son, the author and originator of the salvation of all, after being tested and proved by many sufferings, would not only prepare an inheritance of eternal glory for himself, but would also bring with him many other sons who had been reconciled to the Father by his death. For this reason he assumed a human body, so that he as a human might purify all humans. For Christ, the priest who does the purifying, and we, the humans who are being purified, alike take our human origin and nature from the same first parent, just as we both have a common father in heaven. Hence the Son of God is not ashamed in the psalms to call godly people brothers when he speaks thus: 'I shall declare your name to my brothers, in the midst of the church I shall praise you' [Ps 22:22]. Does he not openly call his disciples brothers here? And again in a certain other place,[12] 'And I shall place my confidence in him.' Besides, it is the mark of a tried and true son to trust his father wholeheartedly. But since the Father has promised to put all things under the feet of the Son, there can be no doubt that he will save those too with whom and among whom the Son will reign. Again in a certain other place in the prophet Isaiah the Lord calls his disciples his children when he says, 'I and my children whom God has given me' [8:18]. You hear the terms proper to family relationship.

Therefore, seeing that these brothers and these children of whom he speaks are human beings consisting of flesh and blood, he who was of heaven wanted to assume human flesh and to become in this respect the same as those whom he intended to co-opt to share in his eternal relationship. Thus he would by his own death destroy him who had the power of death, that is, the devil, and would release those who through fear of everlasting death were all their lifetime subject to the bondage of Satan. Through death Satan held sway over the whole race of mortals, for all who are subject to sin are also subject to death.

Christ held none of the angels in such esteem as to assume their nature and to become their brother or relation. But in accordance with the divine promise he took the seed of Abraham.[13] He was born a Jew from Jews. He was born a human from a human. He became subject to all the disadvantages of our nature – thirst, hunger, heat, cold, fatigue, pain, death

– so that this likeness to us would attest that he truly possessed our human
nature, and it would be a guarantee that he would not abandon those for
whom he had undergone so much evil and whom he had bound to himself
with such close ties. It was appropriate, therefore, that in all things he be
made like those whom he wanted to be his brothers. He did this to instill
in them a greater confidence that they would obtain forgiveness, because he
who, to expiate the sins of the whole people, had undertaken the office of
high priest to intercede with God and to reconcile the entire race of mortals
to him, would by this sign seem likely thereafter to be merciful and faithful
to his own. Not only did he share the same nature as they, but it was also
his lot to be tried and tested by the countless sufferings of this world, so
that he might more readily seem likely to aid those who were being harassed by the evils of this world.

Chapter 3

Brothers, you have now been purified by the blood of the Son and have
been called by God's spontaneous goodness to come to share the life of
heaven. Therefore, that you may better respond to his kindnesses, consider
how greatly Christ Jesus, the apostle and high priest of your profession, that
is, of evangelical faith, excels in dignity. Consider also how purely and
faultlessly he acted towards God, by whom he was established in the whole
church[1] just as Moses was praised because he acted as a faithful servant in
God's whole synagogue, which is his house and family. But as greater
honour is owed to the one who has founded the house than to the house
itself, so Christ has merited greater honour and dignity. For every house is
built by someone. But he who created all things is God. Moses, therefore,
so lived in the house that he himself was a part of the house, not its maker,
and the godliness of Moses deserves that he have great authority with us
because he lived in the whole house of God with good faith, but as a
servant and a steward, not as a son. He lived in another's house, Jesus in
his own. Moses offered only types and shadows of those things which
Christ would afterwards explain. But Christ, who is both the founder and
the Son, administered his very own house – whose house we are, we who
are gathered into his church through our commitment to the gospel, if only
we persevere in what we have started; that is, if we continue to remain in
the harmony of the house, and if we hold firm and unshaken right to the
end both the confidence which the spirit of Christ has given us and the
glorious hope with which, as true born sons of God and brothers of Christ,
we expect the inheritance of heaven. To have heard the teachings of the
gospel will be of no use to us if we do not continue to live according to the

teachings of the gospel. On the contrary, the greater is the one who deigned to speak to us in his own person, the more severely shall we be punished.

Therefore, it is necessary to remember what the Holy Spirit says in the mystic psalm[2] when he urges the people to obey the voice of God lest he, being provoked, punish them severely and bar them from the promised rest: 'Today,' he says, 'if you will hear his voice, do not harden your hearts as you did when you provoked God with murmuring and rebellion on that day when he tested your endurance in the wilderness, where' he says, 'your fathers tested me as if to ascertain whether I was the kind of God who was capable of punishing the guilty, and they felt my anger, and those who were unwilling to believe what had been said saw my works, and for forty years too. (That is how long they were driven about in the wilderness when as fugitives from Egypt they were seeking the land in which I had promised them rest.) Therefore, I was displeased with that nation and I said to myself, these men always go astray in their heart, following their own desires, and they have not known my ways. And I was angry on account of this disobedience and I swore that they would never enter the land in which I promised that they would rest from the toils of their journeys.'[3]

Brothers, you have heard God's threats to our fathers, that they would not reach the promised land unless they persevered in their obedience to his commands. We have been freed through baptism from the sins of our past life – we have gone out from Egypt – but we shall never reach the promised immortality with those in heaven unless we persist in the observance of evangelical faith and love. However, if we look back at the Egypt left behind, that is, if we relapse into the desires of our former life, we shall be excluded from our share of life in heaven. See to it, then, that there is in none of you a heart that is so wicked and rebellious against the commands of the gospel or so subject to disbelief that it turns back to the vices which it left behind and to the prince of death, the devil, and thus defects from the living God.

Instead, strengthen and daily exhort one another to endure with perseverance the toils of this life. God uses them to test the sincerity of our faith as long as this life is called 'today'; that is, as long as we wear this mortal body and, surrounded by perils, still travel in the wilderness of this world. Let no one, broken by the evils of this life, be seduced by the attractions of sin from the journey he has begun, as many years ago our ancestors, the Hebrews, weary of the toils of the long journey, longed for the fragrant smell of the pots which they had left behind in Egypt.[3]

We have indeed been grafted into the body of Christ through baptism and our profession of faith, but we can still fall away through our own fault. We shall reach the inheritance of immortality promised to us only if we keep solid and unshattered to the end the initial stage and foundation of felicity which was laid down in us through the gospel. We must continually build upon what has been begun in us, reminded by what we continually hear said to us: 'Today if you will hear his voice, do not harden your hearts as in the provocation' [Ps 95:7–8]. For some, when they heard the Lord's voice but did not obey, provoked him and aroused his anger against themselves.

Not everyone, however, who had set out from Egypt under the leadership of Moses did this. To them at least it was granted to reach the land flowing with milk and honey.[4] Now with whom was he angry forty years? Was it not with those who had sinned? They did not enter into the rest; instead their corpses were laid low in the wilderness. With whom was he so angry that he swore that they would not enter into the promised rest? Was it not those who had disobeyed the voice of God? We see, therefore, that God was truthful on both counts. He fulfilled for the obedient what he had promised and for the disobedient what he had threatened. The former arrived because of their patience, the latter could not enter on account of their disbelief and lack of faith.

Chapter 4

Christ is our leader now as Moses was our ancestors' leader then. They were hastening towards an earthly rest; we are heading to a rest in heaven. Let us fear then to ignore the voice of God which speaks to us daily through the gospel lest,[1] just as the majority of them through their own fault fell short of their expectation of the promised rest, it may likewise happen to one of us to be seen as having fallen short and not to arrive where he had begun to go. For a far more blissful rest has been announced to us than was to them and through a far more trustworthy envoy than the one sent to them. It was, however, of no use to them to have received the promise of rest and even to have heard the very voice of the Lord because they did not believe it when heard. For we who have believed the voice of the Lord are entering the true rest which will be free from every evil disturbance. On the other hand, he says that those who did not believe will not enter, when he says: 'As I swore in my wrath, if they shall enter into my rest' [Ps 95:11]. And yet God's first rest had already occurred many centuries back, that is, when his works in creating the world were completed.

It is in memory of this repose that the Jews celebrate their own sabbath. For Scripture, speaking about the first rest, which occurred on the seventh day after the creation of the world, says: 'And the Lord rested on the seventh day from all his works' [Gen 2:2]. But in the passage which we adduced from the psalm – 'If they shall enter into my rest' – a second rest is mentioned, a rest which was meant to refresh with the hospitality of the land of Palestine the Hebrews who were weary from their long journey. Therefore since it follows from these passages that God first entered his own rest after the creation of the world, that the second rest was entered by only a few persons because of the disbelief of the others, and that the promise will be meaningless unless a people does in fact enter a rest – once we have excluded those first persons to whom a rest had been promised through the prefiguration of the Law, a rest which they to whom it had been promised did not in fact enter – again the mystic psalm designates through the mouth of David, so many years after Palestine came into their possession, a different day, which it does not call the 'seventh day,' but 'today,' as we have already said several times: 'Today if you will hear his voice, do not harden your hearts' [Ps 95:7–8]. If Joshua, the son of Nave,[2] under whose leadership a few did enter Palestine, had given a true rest to the Israelites, God, speaking afterward through the mouth of David, would certainly not have mentioned another day. Otherwise people could say, 'What new rest are you proposing to us since we now rule the land of Judaea and possess the promised rest?' Therefore, there remains some other sabbath rest for the people of God; there remains another rest, not in Palestine, but in the homeland of heaven, to which we are hastening under the leadership of Jesus Christ. But we shall not reach it if we do not celebrate in purity here an evangelical sabbath rest by abstaining from the works of this world.[3] Whoever has entered this true rest has also himself rested from his works just as God rested from his after the creation of the universe. For he has been conducted to that life which is undisturbed by toils and pains.[4]

Therefore, while we are still journeying in the wilderness of this life, let us not lag behind; let us not look back, but let us hasten on with incessant effort and ardent prayer to that true rest to which our leader Jesus calls us. Let no one of us cause another to fall on the way as the Hebrews fell. If we give a similar example of sin, the penalty will be no lighter for us. The threat made by the Word of God, Christ Jesus,[5] must not be ignored. For he is alive and active and more penetrating than any two-edged sword. He cuts not only into the parts of the body, but also into the emotions deep within the mind where he can sever the soul from the spirit, can sever all the joints and marrow of the mind; he discerns the hidden thoughts and intentions of our heart. So far is any human thought from deceiving him that no creature exists anywhere at all either in heaven or under the earth which is hidden to his eyes. All things are naked and laid open for scrutiny[6] to the eyes of him to whom we must give an account of our life. Just as God was not deceived in the past by the murmuring of the Hebrews and had no need of any other sword to destroy them than his divine command, so Christ will not be deceived now by the person who professes to live according to the gospel but is secretly in love with what belongs to the world and does not hasten in all sincerity towards the promised rest.

We have, then, a high priest who is truly great, Jesus Christ, the Son of God, who, after completing the sacrifice required for our reconciliation, did not enter the inner shrine of a temple built by hands but penetrated the heavens to make the Father propitious to us; therefore, let us persevere in our confession as we follow the way which he showed us and hasten towards the things which he promised. Do not let his majesty deter us but rather let his mercy give us courage. He abides in the heavens, but formerly he lived as a man on earth. Let us not imagine then that we have a high priest who is unaware of our weakness and unable to be touched by it. He was assailed by every kind of evil to which our life is subject, but he returned to heaven victorious. Through his help, therefore, we shall not grow weary in our affliction, but with spirits unbroken shall win through to that everlasting and blissful rest which he has reached. He was afflicted; he was scourged; he was spat upon; though completely guiltless he was crucified like a criminal for no other reason than that he might cleanse us who were truly guilty from all our sins. He has not changed his feeling for us provided that we do not alienate him by our perversity. Relying then on his mercy, let us approach his throne, a throne which arouses not fear but calm and is ever ready to help, not to destroy. Let us approach it then with confidence, without hesitation, to obtain mercy, which forgives us our sins, and grace, which equips and enriches us with the goods of heaven whenever our situation requires it.[7] For we must not ask for help from any other source than from whence we hope for the reward.

Chapter 5

It is the custom among the Jews for every high priest, chosen as he is from the midst of humanity, to be appointed to intercede on behalf of humans in those transactions which take place between God and human beings. He is, as it were, an intermediary between two parties, so that if God has been offended in some respect by the sins of mortals, the priest may reconcile him with gifts and duly offered victims. Although the authority of his priestly position gives him stature in the eyes of God, he nevertheless retains his full share of human weakness. It is precisely because he has the nature common to all human beings and is therefore subject himself to the same weakness as they, that he can be quicker to forgive those who have sinned through ignorance or error. For those who have been taught compassion through a similar experience of evil are quicker to feel grief at the evil of others. He who himself sometimes slips or is at least not far from the risk of slipping brings help more readily to the errors of others. For this reason the Mosaic priest is obliged to sacrifice a victim also for his own sins just as he sacrifices for the sins of the people. Christ, who shared our common nature, which is necessarily subject to pain and death, nevertheless had no share in any sin. Without knowing sin he shared the punishment.

Furthermore, in keeping with Mosaic ritual no one on his own initiative claims or usurps the honour of the office of high priest, but he alone takes it to whom it is assigned by divine command just as it was assigned to Aaron.[1] He who seeks the position out of pride is thought unworthy of the honour while he who thrusts his way into it on his own is unqualified for the office. In this respect too, Christ furnished the example of the legitimate high priest. For he did not on his own initiative lay claim to the glory of the high priest's position; he was approved by the Father, who acknowledged Jesus as his true Son when he said, 'You are my Son, today I have begotten you' [Ps 2:7]. Next he made him a true and legitimate priest when he said, 'You are a priest forever according to the order of Melchizedek' [Ps 110:4].

You understand the manner of his ordination. Now see how he was tempted and tested. While he was still wearing his mortal body on earth, he offered prayers and supplications to God the Father, who could have saved him from the punishment of the cross if he had not preferred to provide for the salvation of mortals by the death of the Son. Moreover, he offered them with deep feeling, with vehement cries and much shedding of tears, and, in keeping with both the love and the position which he holds with the Father, he was heard.[2] He gained what he wanted, for he wanted not to escape the punishment of the cross but to obtain our salvation through his own death.[3] He felt the dread, he felt the agony of death,[4] but his love for the human race prevailed. He was the Son, and he would have obtained everything from the Father if he had but asked, but our salvation was deemed to require instead that, suffering every evil even to the punishment of the cross, he present to his followers the model of perfect obedience. You ask what this endurance in our priest accomplished? Having been thus tested and having proved in every way that nothing was found lacking in him, he not only saved himself but was the cause of salvation for all who imitate this example of obedience. For he obtained his request from the Father that those who would have joined with him in sharing his sufferings would also join with him in sharing his kingdom. Because this sacrifice was duly carried out, he was designated by God a high priest according to the order of Melchizedek.

It would take many words on our part to tell who Melchizedek was and to show the similarities in which he prefigured the Son of God. It would also be very difficult to explain it to you point by point because your ears are incapable of taking in such an account and are too weak to be able to endure so arduous and lengthy a discourse. In this respect I am forced to find your interest and ardour for advancement lacking. Many years have passed since you first confessed Christ and in view of this length of time you ought to be teachers of others. Instead you still need us to teach you the first rudiments of divine Scripture, that is, the things commonly taught those who are being reborn to the gospel through baptism in the way that children are taught their ABC's. At this point in time you should be hardy and robust students of evangelical philosophy; however, instead of being ready for the solid food of higher learning, like tender infants you still need the milk of elementary instruction. You still cling to and creep along, as it were, in the literal meaning of divine Scripture; you do not yet rise to the higher meaning hidden within it. But a person whose condition is such that he still needs to be nourished with milk is unformed and not yet strong enough to be instructed in evangelical righteousness, which is not found in the literal meaning but in allegories.[5] He is unable to grasp the word which transmits perfect righteousness to us because he is still an infant in Christ, newly placed in Christ's body in the expectation that he will proceed step by step towards higher things. The solid food of the higher meaning belongs, however, to the mature and perfected, namely, to those who by long and persistent meditation have their senses exercised to discern good and evil. One who is a child and nurtured on milk keeps himself alive, but has not yet acquired from age and experience the strength and ability to select by himself the best from everything available. He must wait for someone else to put in his mouth milk or a piece of prechewed food suitable for children.

Chapter 6

Therefore, let us who ought by now to have ceased to be children in the philosophy of Christ leave the discussion of the elementary matters with which the unskilled are first instructed and let us progress towards perfection. Let us not remain stuck in the task of laying the foundation of repentance over and over again. For to repent our past life and to withdraw from sin is the very first step on the way to the practice of Christianity. The next step is to learn that true innocence and salvation must be hoped for only from God. The third is to be cleansed by holy baptism from the filth of our vices, to be restored to innocence, and thereafter[1] to receive the Holy Spirit through the laying on of the hand[2] and to believe in the future resurrection of the dead and with it that last judgment, which will sentence some to eternal happiness, others to eternal torment. To have learned these things once is sufficient; to have professed them once is sufficient; to have believed them once is sufficient. It would be an absurdity if, after we have received these teachings, we continue to act in such a way that we have to be taught over and over the teachings which were given to us to be the foundation on which the rest of the building was to be constructed. Instead, once these elementary matters have been learned, we must strive with burning zeal to grow each day in godliness until we are mature and perfect. We must make every effort to use the gold and silver and precious stones[3] of virtues and godly deeds to erect a noble structure, from the initial foundations right up to the peak of the highest roof.[4]

It is our role to strive to perfect what we are attempting if God should prosper, favour, and assist us in our attempts. Without his aid human effort can do nothing. After we have once entered this course, there must be no stopping, no looking back, no returning to what has been left behind, but only continual advance towards better things. It would be the height of folly to run back to that which neither can nor ought to be repeated. For when people have been enlightened by the teachings of the gospel and have once and for all left the darkness of their earlier life behind; when, after their sins have been forgiven through baptism, they have felt God's spontaneous generosity and have received the heavenly gift through which he removes every vice once and for all and bestows innocence; and when they have then through the laying on of the priest's hand become partakers of the Holy Spirit, through whom they began to have faith in the blissful promises of eternal life[5] and to have, as it were, a foretaste now of the powers of the age to come, it is afterwards impossible for them to be renewed again through repentance if through indifference they slide back into the shameful state of their earlier life. For this renewal is made once and for all in baptism, in which the old man with his acts is put off once and for all and a new creature comes forth from the baptismal font. For those who ask to be made new again through baptism when they have repeatedly slid back into their old life – what else do they do except to crucify the Son of God again for themselves and again to expose him, as it were, to public shame?[6] He died for us just once. We died with him in baptism just once. He rose again just once and will never die again. We too must rise again with him into a new state of life in such a way that we do not relapse into the death of the life left once and for all behind and thus arouse in God a wrath as fierce as his generosity was abundant towards us. We must make our industry match God's kindness to us. He puts, as it were, seeds of godliness in us; these we must in turn tend in order to make them grow to maturity. For the earth which drinks in the rain that often comes upon it, and bears herbs useful to those who cultivate it, is praised by God because it is not sterile and does not suppress and choke and cause the seed which is sown in it to be without fruit. But that which produces thorns and briars after receiving good seed is rejected and near to receiving God's curse; its end is to be burned, not harvested.

Dearly beloved, we say these things to encourage you, not because we think these words about sterile earth fit you. On the contrary, we are convinced of better things concerning you, which, if God aids you, promise to be your salvation rather than your destruction. Even so, we have constructed this comparison in order to sharpen in you the desire for evangelical godliness. We do not want you to grow slack and gradually descend into the extreme of evils. God will be with you as you strive towards better things. He is not so ungrateful or so unjust as to forget your good deeds and the labour which you have undertaken, not for glory or for gain, but for love of his name. You have shown this love by your actions both in the past, when you used your personal property and services to minister to the saints through whom the name of Christ is preached, and now in the present as you continue to minister to them in this way.

We have made this point because we are eager that each one of you continues to persevere in what you are now doing, for some among you are more sluggish than I could wish. We are eager for you not only to persevere, but also to advance farther and farther every day until you arrive at perfection. You will make me all the more confident in the good hopes which I now have of you when I see that you are continually moving forward into something better and are far removed from the danger of those who grow lazy and gradually slide back into their old life. Unlike them you are walking in the footsteps of those who, trusting in Christ's promises and with a tenacious hope for their rewards in heaven, reach their inheritance of immortal life in the kingdom of heaven which he promised to his followers.

Those who distrusted God's promises and kept looking back towards the Egypt they had left behind did not reach the promised land.[7] Abraham, however, had a steadfast faith in God's promises even when nature was opposed; therefore, he obtained what he had expected. To make the faith of his promise more reliable God interposed an oath, something which humans customarily consider the most reliable pledge.[8] He swore by himself because he had no one greater than himself by whom to swear. He swore in this fashion: 'By myself I have sworn because you have done this thing, and have not spared your only begotten son for my sake. Blessing I shall bless you and multiplying I shall multiply your seed as the stars of the heaven and as the sand which is on the seashore' [Gen 22:16–17]. Therefore, when God saw the steadfastness of the old man who did not hesitate to kill even the son in whom all hope of descendants seemed to be placed, he confirmed with an oath what he had promised earlier.[9]

God imitates human customs when he is dealing with human beings. For we swear through one who is greater in order to make the oath more weighty, and if something is in doubt or dispute, it is resolved and ended for us if the confirmation of an oath is added. It was for this reason that when God wanted to make strikingly clear to the heirs of the promise the firmness of his purpose, he interposed an oath. No one could then suspect that God would prove false when he had pledged his faith with the double bond not only of a promise but also of an oath. Because we have here a sure basis for our confidence, we also have a strong source of consolation in the midst of this world's storms. We have not placed our happiness in the goods of this life, but have found refuge in the belief that in the age to come we shall take possession of the hope placed before us. Meanwhile in the tempests of the world we hold on to this hope as an anchor of the soul, both sure and steadfast, because it has been made fast for us not in transitory things but in heaven; that is, it stretches all the way to those things which are behind the veil where change does not exist, but all is eternal and secure. This is that inner part of the temple which Jesus Christ, our forerunner and revealer of the way, has entered to intercede for us with the Father, having become, as I said earlier, high priest forever according to the order of Melchizedek.

Chapter 7

Now seeing that the course itself of our talk has brought us again to the mention of Melchizedek, let us contemplate his special features and the ways in which he was the type of our own priest. This Melchizedek, king of a city named Salem, is called in Scripture the high priest of the Most High God. He met Abraham returning from the slaughter of the three[1] kings and blessed him for his brave exploit. Abraham then gave him a tenth part from all his goods.[2] First, his name 'Melchizedek' means literally 'king of righteousness'; secondly, he is given from the name of his kingdom the title 'king of Salem,' that is, 'king of peace.' He was said to have neither a father nor a mother nor a genealogy, having neither a beginning of days nor a destined end of life. What it does say of him – and this truly fits the Son of God – is that he remains a priest for eternity. So far every one of these features fits Christ, our high priest, who established the kingdom of righteousness, who is the Prince of Peace, who in respect to his divine nature had neither father on earth nor mother,[3] whose genealogy cannot be expressed in human language,[4] who neither began to exist nor will cease to exist, whose priesthood remains for eternity, purifying until the end of time all who believe in him.

Let us now examine the high position of Melchizedek and the great distance between him and the priests of the Mosaic law. Abraham, though a great patriarch, not only deigned to receive a blessing from him after he had carried out the slaughter of the kings, but even gave him a tenth of the spoils. The law of Moses ordained that the descendants of Levi were to succeed to the office of the priesthood and to receive the tithe, but only from their brethren, that is, from the descendants of Abraham.[5] The rights and the status of the Levites extend no further. But Melchizedek though he did not belong to the Jewish race received a tithe from the very founder of the entire race, Abraham, and blessed him from whom according to God's promise the nation of the Jews was to spring. It is beyond dispute that what is inferior receives a blessing from what is superior. Whoever has given a blessing approves, as it were, on his own authority what has been done. Moreover, the right of approval customarily belongs to a superior, not to an equal or an inferior. Furthermore, in the family of Levi the tithe was received by those who are both mortal themselves and at whose death the right passes to others. But it was said of Melchizedek that he lives and remains for eternity, pre-eminent in an everlasting priesthood. Finally, since the right to exact tithes came to the priests from their originator Levi, Abraham's act in paying a tithe to Melchizedek makes Levi himself appear to have become subject to the payment of tithes though he is accustomed to receive them from others. Therefore, as they who pay tithes to Levi are viewed as lower in status, so Levi too was inferior to Melchizedek, to whom he gave a tithe. Someone will object, 'How did he who was not yet born at the time when Melchizedek met Abraham give a tithe?' But since descendants are judged to exist somehow in the source of the race, therefore on this ground I said that Levi gave a tithe to Melchizedek in the person of Abraham.

If perfect religion depended, as the Jews like to think, upon the Levitical priesthood just because the law was given in the time of Aaron who was a member of the tribe of Levi,[6] what further need was there that another priest should rise who, in the words of the mystic psalm, was to be appointed, not according to the order of Aaron, but according to the order of Melchizedek?[7] Since the nature and authority of the law are tied to the nature of the priesthood, of necessity when the priesthood is changed to a different form, the form of the law too is changed. For the change in tribe makes it sufficiently clear that the nature of the priesthood has also to be changed. For he of whom the prophecy in the psalm speaks did not belong to the tribe of Levi, but was from that tribe from which no one had as yet officiated at the altar, because it is evident that our Lord Jesus came from the tribe of Judah. But when Moses instituted the rite and law of the priesthood, he made no mention of this priesthood which was to be connected with the tribe of Judah. That the priesthood about which the psalm speaks does not have the same nature as the Mosaic priesthood is even more evident from the addition which the prophecy plainly makes, 'according to the order of Melchizedek,' obviously referring to a priest unlike Aaron and like Melchizedek, so that we may understand that there is no less a difference between the two persons than there is between the rites and meaning of the two priesthoods. What do the words 'according to the order of Melchizedek' mean? They describe one who would not sacrifice the animals which the crude and carnal Law prescribes, but who would be able to bring people to eternal life through heavenly grace.[8] The Old Law would purify the flesh by washings and various lustrations. The New Law purifies souls by a more efficacious victim. Just as Aaron does not remain forever, so the order of his priesthood was not eternal; and just as Melchizedek was said to remain forever, so the order of his priesthood will have no end. The mystic psalm shows that these elements truly fit Christ when it says, 'You are a priest forever according to the order of Melchizedek' [Ps 110:4]. The temporary priesthood gives way to the everlasting, and the mortal high priest to the immortal. As the more imperfect priesthood yields to the more perfect, so the imperfect Law gives place to the more perfect law of the gospel through which the Mosaic ordinances of the Old Testament are in effect repealed because they lacked sufficient power and did not provide the usefulness which they ought to have provided. God wanted us to be made perfect, but the Law brought nothing to perfection and was not given for this purpose. Nevertheless, it was not given in vain, but was given for a period of time to be a stairway designed to take us ultimately up to a better hope. It promised a fruitful land in which those who had kept the commandments of the Mosaic law might lead a tranquil life.[9] The Law was crude,[10] the reward crude, but care was being taken in this way to make the crude minds of humans gradually become accustomed to move from the things of the senses to the things of the mind.[11] The commandment was given that they were not to kill; they were not to steal; they were to use certain rituals to cleanse any contact with a dead body.[12] A land was promised in which they might pass a few years in quiet, but we are promised heaven, in which we are to live happily always. In the meantime we are commanded to love even our enemies. When their priest conducted with utmost care the sacred rites in order to intercede with God for the people, he withdrew to the inner area behind the veil.[13] But our priest passed through even the heavens themselves to plead our case with God the Father, into whose presence we are brought through our representative[14] Jesus Christ, who is the head of the church. Where the head is, the body cannot be absent.

With this kind of high priest our hope is therefore more certain than the Jews' hope could be through their priests, because their high priests were appointed without an oath, ours with an oath. God wanted this oath to intervene so that because of it we would have a surer confidence in the promises if the priest, through whose intervention we hope for the promised happiness of immortality, is attested eternal high priest by an oath, and this by God who is utterly incapable of lying. For this is what he says in the prophetic psalm: 'The Lord has sworn and will not relent, "You are a priest forever according to the order of Melchizedek"' [Ps 110:4]. Just as there is a difference between heaven and earth, the everlasting and the temporary, immortality and mortality, the divine and the human, so the covenant of which Jesus, our high priest, has become the surety is so much better, and just as in the human world a promise confirmed by an oath is more trustworthy than a simple promise, so is he that much more trustworthy. Furthermore, because it was necessary under the Mosaic law for several priests to be appointed either so that they might perform their priestly duties in stated turns[15] or because death did not allow the same men to remain permanently in office, the repeated change[16] of the surety brings with it an element of uncertainty. But our high priest stands alone on behalf of all and does not need a successor. Because he remains forever, he has an everlasting priesthood. Therefore, he can bring to perfect salvation those whom he has begun to save because they always have a saviour at hand through whom they may come to God. For Christ ever lives to intercede with God on behalf of his own whenever there is need.[17] For Christ did not sacrifice a victim just to help a few for a short time, but to placate God efficaciously for all persons and for all time.

Therefore, since this Law was perfect and heavenly, it was fitting that its high priest likewise be such, godly, without guile,[18] undefiled, far removed from the company of sinners, elevated above all the heavens, who does not need, as did the Mosaic priests, to offer up sacrifices daily for his own sins and then for the misdeeds of the people. What kind of reconcilers were they who themselves needed reconciliation with him before whom they were asking pardon for the offences of others? What kind of sacrifice was it which had to be continually repeated for one set of sins after another? Our high priest, who had no sin of his own, transferred to himself the sins of the whole world and offered up once and for all a victim on behalf of all, not an animal but himself. For in keeping with its weakness and imperfection the Mosaic law appointed high priests subject to weakness. But the word of the oath, which we have reported above and which clearly shows that a better Law will succeed the Old Law, appoints not some man but the very Son of God a priest forever, always ready and able to intercede for us because death cannot cut him off and no infirmity hinders him from being an able and perfect pleader on our behalf.

Chapter 8

Now the main point and substance of what we have been discussing at such length is this, that we have no reason to admire hereafter the high priest of the Mosaic law because we now have a high priest so excellent in every respect that he sits on the right hand of the majestic throne of God in the heavens, duly to perform the true and heavenly rites, not the shadows of them which Moses prescribed, and to dwell within the tabernacle, not within that shadow-like reflection of the tabernacle which a human being had erected, but within the inner shrine of the true tabernacle which God, separating the things of heaven from those of earth, erected.[1]
    Since it is the custom that every high priest be appointed to offer gifts and sacrifices to God, it would be impossible for one who does not have something to offer to be a legitimate high priest. But if a high priesthood of the earthly kind had been given to Christ, he would not even be a priest since he never offered and does not now offer any of those victims which according to the Law's command are customarily offered by other priests. Those practices are only shadows and types, as it were, of the heavenly temple and of heavenly victims. Since everything which Christ did even on earth was not done according to the flesh but according to the spirit and, having originated in heaven, was directed towards heaven, it is rightly called heavenly when compared to the coarse nature of the Mosaic priesthood. For this seems to be the significance of God's words when, instructing Moses about the form of the temple which he was to build, God spoke as follows: 'See that you make all things according to the pattern which was shown to you on the mountain' [Exod 25:40]. For Moses had seen with spiritual eyes another kind of temple and another kind of priesthood and victims. Using them as a pattern he was to create for the time being a crude image and shadow of their reality until the time should come at which it had been determined that shadows should give way to true realities.

Well then, this time is now at hand. We[2] have a heavenly high priest and a priesthood worthy of him, a priesthood better in every respect as the evangelical covenant is better than the old one of Moses and as the promises of the new covenant are grander than those of the old. In the old covenant, bodies were purified by the blood of cattle; in the new covenant, souls are purified by the blood of Christ. In the old one, a land is promised; in the new one, rewards in heaven are promised. And in the new covenant, our heavenly high priest intercedes in a heavenly ritual between mankind and God. But if that earlier covenant had been such that, as the Jews like to think, nothing was lacking in it, there would certainly have been no need to find room for a second covenant. For it would be superfluous to add anything to something which is already perfect. But as it is, God complains that that earlier covenant was useless[3] and promises another more effective and better one, when he speaks in the following way in the prophet Jeremiah:[4] 'Behold, the days are coming, says the Lord, I[5] will make a new covenant with the house of Israel and with the house of Judah, not according to the covenant that I made with their fathers in the day when I took their hand to lead them out of Egypt; because they did not continue in my covenant and I in turn held them in disregard, says the Lord. For this is the pact that I will make with the house of Israel,[6] says the Lord, when I will not inscribe my laws on stones or sheets of paper as was vainly tried in the past,[7] but I will put them in their minds and will write them on their hearts. And I will truly be their God and they in turn will truly be my people. Nor will they pass them from one to another by hand so that each one is compelled to teach his neighbour and each one his brother, saying, "Know the Lord." For now not merely a few Jews but everyone everywhere will know me,[8] from the least to the greatest, because, when their crimes and sins have been forgiven,[9] I will be made propitious through the intercession of the Son and I will remember their lawless deeds no more.' You have heard the words of him who is promising a new covenant because the old one had been useless. That it is called new, that is, spiritual, signifies that the old, that is, the carnal covenant, was to be cancelled; otherwise, this covenant could not be called new unless that which preceded it was becoming obsolete and was growing old. But what is becoming obsolete and growing old is ready to vanish away, that is, it is verging little by little on extinction.

Chapter 9

Someone might say, 'Was the religion of the old temple futile then?' Not at all. Even that old temple, whose religion has disappeared now that evangelical truth has succeeded it, once had certain rituals and established ceremonies,[1] ablutions and animal sacrifices. The observance of these rituals had the appearance of justifying and purifying,[2] as they displayed to the eyes of men through external and visible things a pattern of loftier and spiritual things. These rituals were performed mostly in that part of the temple which Scripture calls the secular or worldly sanctuary because admission to it was open to all alike, whether Jews, proselytes, or gentiles.[3] For the structure of the temple like that of the tabernacle was such that each successive part of it was considered more sacred than the preceding part until one came to the part that was believed to be the holiest. For a tabernacle was made in front in which were kept with great religious veneration the lights,[4] the table, and the seven[5] sacred loaves of bread which are called 'the shewbread' because they are accustomed to be shown on the sacred table. They name this part of the temple simply the 'Holy Place,' because while distant from profane things it was still a considerable distance from those things to which special holiness was attributed. Moreover, behind the second veil which separated this part of the temple from the rest was another tabernacle which was called the Holy of Holies because of its religious pre-eminence. It held certain more sacred commemorative objects[6] – the golden censer[7] and the ark of the testament, as they call it,[8] which was covered on all sides with gold leaf and held the golden pot which contained manna, a memorial of the ancient miracle when a new kind of food rained down from heaven because the Hebrews were suffering from hunger;[9] and Aaron's rod which, an unheard of wonder, had leafed out and burst into flowers from its swelling buds though it had been cut away from its trunk, and the flowers then became almonds.[10] The ark also held the tablets of the testament as they call them because they had on them the ten commandments carved by the finger of God.[11] Above the ark were winged images of cherubim, representing the divine majesty and glory, which overshadow the mercy-seat. Each of these items has some kind of signification for the more sacred things which the gospel revealed later, but to discuss their meaning in detail would be a prolix undertaking.[12] It will be enough for us to note that the sum and substance of this entire matter refers to the priesthood of Christ.[13]

Now, with the temple being divided in this fashion and the sacred memorials arranged in their places, the ordinary priests would go into the first tabernacle everyday to perform the sacred rites. But the high priest, who had the foremost position among the priests, went alone into the more sacred second part only once each year, taking with him the blood of the animal which he was offering there, first for his own offences and then for the offences of the people which they had committed through error and ignorance.[14] The Holy Spirit was signifying by these actions, as if through riddles of some sort,[15] that access was not yet at that time open to those places which are truly holy and have no trace of worldly contagion. For so long as the high priest alone entered the more secluded shrine from which everyone else was excluded and so long as that first tabernacle still remained which was the image of those days[16] when people were somehow retained in the Jewish religion by certain crude ceremonies to keep them from slipping into worse practices, certain crude and popular rites used to be performed in this tabernacle by ordinary priests. Gifts were offered; victims were sacrificed; animals were slain as offerings. These acts gave the appearance of purification but could not make those who performed them completely pure in their conscience and heart. For God judges us by the purity of our hearts and consciences even if in respect to the body and in the judgment of human beings those actions were thought to add some element of purity. For everything that was done in the tabernacle pertained chiefly to the body since it was a matter of various ablutions, other cleansings of the flesh, and discrimination in food and drink, despite the fact that food does not in reality either pollute or purify the heart.[17] These rituals were not instituted to confer perfect righteousness[18] on people but to make them by means of these rudiments become gradually accustomed to true religion, to bring them to the truth through shadows, and to make them capable of grasping the superior realities which the teachings of the gospel would disclose in its own time.[19]

You see here the essence of the whole religion which satisfies the Jews so deeply. Now let us compare with their rites the dignity and status of our high priest. For Christ the high priest is the guarantor and source not of bodily purification nor of the perishable goods of this age but of eternal and heavenly goods. He did not enter through a veil woven by human hands but through a different tabernacle which was not made with hands, that is, not of this building[20] which men erect and can therefore demolish. He entered through heaven itself into places truly holy and truly removed from every trace of mortality, bringing with him not the blood of goats and calves with which to placate God but his own blood, which he had shed for us on the altar of the cross and with which he freed not one people but the whole human race from all its sins. He did not do this for only a single year but for all time until the end of the world, so long as people repent of the offences of their past life and acknowledge and imitate Christ to the best of their ability. What comparison is there between a dumb animal and Christ,[21] between God and man? If the blood of bulls and goats or the ashes of a burned calf, sprinkled on the unclean, cleanse them in respect to some carnal and shadowy holiness, how much more will the blood of Christ purify not your bodies but your consciences from those works which truly bring death to the soul?[22] He did not make his offering through material fire[23] but through the eternal Spirit, which thirsted for the salvation of humanity; he did not offer to God the Father a brute animal but himself, a victim pure and stainless.

His death frees us from everlasting death; his most pure Spirit purifies our formerly unclean spirit. In both rites there is blood, but there is an enormous difference. In both rites there is death, but an unequal one. In both rites there is spirit, but one completely dissimilar. For what was done in the temple through reflections and shadows, as it were, Christ did in reality. Because in the old testament the person who interceded as a mediator between God and men did not bring perfect righteousness, Christ has therefore replaced him as the new interceder of the new testament. His death removed the sins which could not be removed through that former testament and which kept God estranged from us. As a result of his death, not only the Jews but all who have been called to the company of Christ may now receive the promise and hope of eternal inheritance through the teachings of the gospel. For where the word 'testament' is employed, the death of the testator must necessarily intervene. Otherwise it would not be a testament or, if it were, it would not be valid. For the death of the testator validates a testament, which does not yet have binding force as long as its maker is alive because if he wishes to change it he is free to do so. Therefore, since the old one was also called a testament,[24] it too was dedicated with blood and death, but that of an animal which was doomed to die in any case. As you may read in the book of Exodus,[25] after Moses had read aloud the entire law of God to the people and had explained what reward they might expect from observing it, what penalty they should fear from neglecting it, to validate the contract between God and the people, he mixed the blood of calves and goats in a bowl together with water[26] and sprinkled with scarlet-dyed wool and hyssop both the book itself, from which he had read aloud the commandments of the Lord, and the whole people, saying: 'This blood is the witness and ratifier of the testament which God has commanded you to observe.'[27] Not content with this, he similarly sprinkled blood over the tabernacle and all the sacred vessels in it which they used in sacrifices. Furthermore, in the other rituals everything which was purified according to the instructions of the Mosaic law was likewise purified with blood, and no remission of sins was made except through the shedding of blood.

It was, therefore, quite appropriate that those things on earth which represented the reflection and shadow of things in heaven be performed with such crude purifications. But when the light of truth had dawned, it was fitting that the heavenly rites themselves be performed with better victims and that they confer a truer purity. For, as I said above, everything that Christ did on earth is also heavenly. For Christ did not enter the Holy Place which was made by human hands. It is holy only because people believe it to be holy rather than because it really is, and it can be profaned.[28] For that Holy Place was only a shadow of the things that are truly holy. He has entered into heaven itself, where God immortal dwells with the ethereal minds.[29] As a legitimate high priest he asks in God's own presence pardon for the sins of the whole world, making himself acceptable through his own blood, which he shed for us out of his pure and spontaneous love. He made this plea with a victim so efficacious that there was no need to repeat it every year as the high priest of the old testament did who used to enter the more secluded shrine each year. It is not surprising that the victim of the latter was not completely efficacious since he was himself liable for his sins and was offering blood which was not his own but that of an animal. If Christ had been a high priest of this kind, it would have been necessary that he sacrifice a victim as frequently as the priests of the old covenant used to do because there were so many recurrences of ages and years since the creation of the world. But as it is, his nature was such that it was sufficient to sacrifice himself just once and, by a single sprinkling of his blood, to remove the sins of all the ages until the end of the world. And this did not take place at the beginning of the world but as the end was approaching when it was manifest to all that everything was vitiated by sins and there was no remedy except from God. It would thus be evident how efficacious a priest he was who could expiate with a single victim so vast a heap of sins. The remedy which was at hand and was easy to apply[30] was rejected so that one and the same victim might give satisfaction through the countless years for all who did not make themselves unworthy. He transferred to himself not only the sins of those who had placed their hope of salvation in him many years before but also the sins of those who would believe his gospel for many generations afterward. Therefore, the world has no reason to wait for another priest or another victim for the expiation of sins.

It is appointed for all men to die once, with no hope of returning to this life in which we lapse repeatedly and are expiated repeatedly. Nor is there anything for each of us to await after death except that last judgment which is to determine the eternal rewards of both the godly and the ungodly. Thus Christ, in dying once, was offered for all and transferred the sins of all to himself, as it was in his power to do, in order to pay the penalty for all. He intended nothing to be left except the last judgment when he will again appear to mankind, not as before, like an appointed victim, like a criminal deserving punishment, but as one glorious and innocent of every sin.[31] Then, to those who have been purified through his death and have persevered in a life of innocence until he comes a second time, he will appear as the bringer of salvation and beatitude, not as a sacrificial victim but as a judge such as the godly hope for and the ungodly dread.[32]

Chapter 10

The reason the high priest of the old covenant did not have the same power[1] as Christ is this. Because the Law did not possess a living and true image of the good things but only the kind of shadow that produces an outline sketch, rather than the complete picture of anything, it could never with the sacrifices of ordinary animals, even though they were offered continually year by year by those priests, make perfect those who approach God for reconciliation. For the priests were weak and the sacrifices were ineffective. If this perfection had been possible, would not the sacrifices have ceased to be repeated after they had once been offered? And yet whenever these sacrifices are repeated, mention is again made in them of past sins, a fact which proves that the people had no faith in a single sacrifice. What was the point in redoing the rites year after year if a single offering would have so cleansed them of all their sins that those who had sacrificed once and had once been cleansed were no longer at all aware of their offences? Since sin is a defect of the soul, not of the body, a crude and material thing like the blood of bulls and goats cannot eliminate a disease of the mind.[2] This can only be done completely by the heavenly and spiritual sacrifice of Christ, which through faith and baptism so thoroughly erases all the faults of the earlier life, regardless of how many or how atrocious they may be. Hence no particle of fear or remorse resides in our conscience thereafter so long as we take care not to relapse into our former misconduct.

So far was God from being propitiated by the multiple sacrifices of the old law that he was actually offended and desired a single, efficacious, and permanent sacrifice. For the Son, when he was about, so to speak, to step into the world to make the Father propitious to the human race through the sacrifice of his own body, speaks to him in the mystical psalm like this: 'Sacrifice and offering you did not want, but you have equipped me with a body; you did not approve of burnt offerings and the other sacrifices accustomed to be offered for the expiation of men's sins. Then I said: "Behold, since the head of the book appoints me to be the victim,[3] I am here myself to obey your will, O God"' [Ps 40:6–8]. Therefore, when he says in these words: 'You did not want sacrifice and offering, burnt offerings, and offerings for sin, and you did not approve of any of the offerings which are accustomed to be offered according to the Old Law,' and then adds: 'Behold, I am here to obey your will, O God, and to offer a sacrifice which can be pleasing to your mind,'[4] he abolishes that first priesthood as displeasing God in order to establish the second, with which he would satisfy the divine will. What was that will of God who was rejecting the lawful sacrifices of the old testament and demanding a new kind of sacrifice? It was doubtless this: in his spontaneous goodness he had decided that the heavenly Son, that is, Christ, should put on a human body and by dying for the sins of all should through a single sacrifice, made just once and in the proper form, cleanse them of all their sins so that afterwards there would be no need for any further blood offerings.[5]

Every priest of the old testament is required to officiate at the sacred rites daily, continually repeating the same sacrifices, which, regardless of how much they are multiplied, can never take away sins completely. Thus the business never ends for both parties, the one who makes the offering and the priest through whom he makes it. But Christ, after he had offered once and for all a single sacrifice for the sins of all who did believe, do believe, or will believe his promises, now sits at the right hand of God the Father, waiting for nothing else except what alone is left – the gathering of all the members of the body into one and the final fulfilment of the promise made in the psalm that his enemies, those who rebel against the gospel, will be made his footstool.[6] There is absolutely no need in the meantime for him to sacrifice himself again for us because by a single offering he has made completely perfect for all time all who through their faith have merited sanctification so that not one of our past crimes is imputed to us. The Holy Spirit himself also testifies to what I say, speaking through the mouth of the prophet and predicting long ago the future which we see has now taken place: 'This,' he says, 'is the testament that I will make with them after those days, says the Lord. When I have put my laws into their hearts and have written them on their minds, I will remember no more their sins or[7] their iniquities, so far am I from wishing to punish.'[8] But after every sin has once and for all been forgiven and forever, why is there any need for the sacrifices which the Jews used to make for the expiation of sins?

Therefore, brothers, now that the awareness of sin which deterred us from calling on God has been removed and we have been given the confidence[9] to enter the Holy Place, let us rely on the blood which Jesus shed for our reconciliation and through which he opened a way and approach for us far different from the old way. For it is a fresh and new way, a living and permanently efficacious way which, once opened, cannot afterwards be closed. He inaugurated this way for us, entering – the first one of all to do so – through the veil, that is, his flesh, which covered his divinity during the time he was among human beings.[10] Now that it has been taken up into heaven, heavenly things have been opened.[11]

We have a high priest promised by God according to the order of Melchizedek. God has placed him over his whole house, that is, the Catholic church, which he governs, not as its servant but as its creator and lord.[12] In the meantime let us too go for this reason towards that same place to which Christ has opened the way for us. Let us not go, however, with the feet of our body into a temple of stone; let us enter instead with pure hearts the heavenly temple, completely confident that we shall obtain what we ask. For our bodies have not been sprinkled beforehand with the blood of an animal, but our minds and spirits have been sprinkled with the blood of Jesus Christ. This blood has removed from us the awareness of our old sins; furthermore, baptism has washed our bodies with the pure water which also cleanses all filth from the soul.[13] It only remains for us to persevere in that which we have once begun, and, without wavering at any point, to hold fast to the hope of immortal life which we professed at baptism.[14] We are to rely on one thing and one thing alone, that God, who made the promise, is completely faithful and, even if he wanted to deceive, cannot. We have only one condition to fulfil, to continue in our faith.[15]

We have become, moreover, members of the same body; let us cling together, therefore, in mutual love and concord, taking into consideration how much each of us has advanced in his evangelical profession, not to envy the one who has outdistanced us nor to spurn the one who has been left behind, but to arouse one another to love and godly works through mutual example and through mutual encouragement . We will do this if the advance made by a brother stirs us to an even more ardent pursuit of godliness and if we with brotherly concern stimulate to better things him whom we see starting to falter, congratulating those in front and supporting those struggling along at our side. Let us not do anything to cause someone to be left alone and lost from our flock as sometimes happens to those who are in the habit of making a good beginning but then give it up at the first chance. Let us instead stimulate and inflame one another in every possible way to continue to the end in what we have begun. You have all the more reason to do this because you see that the day of the Lord is imminent. On that day each of us will receive the rewards due our actions. We will no longer have an opportunity to heal what we have done wrongly, but every deed will be carefully weighed with exact judgment.

Those offences which are committed through error or human weakness are readily pardoned. But through the gospel we have come to know the truth and we have been thoroughly instructed about what we are to expect[16] or to avoid and what rewards await both the godly and the ungodly. Therefore, if we willingly and knowingly fall back into capital sins,[17] no sacrifice is left which might once again freely pardon through baptism the sins of those who have relapsed into their old life.[18] For Christ washed away those sins with his blood, once only, since he died but once and will never die again. What is left then? A certain fearful expectation of the last judgment and then the fierce and deadly fire which will devour the adversaries to punish their scorn of divine goodness. Do you think that if someone has despised the law of the gospel he will go scot-free? The more merciful and the more beneficial it is, the more severe will be the penalties paid by the one who wilfully and knowingly makes a mockery of it.[19]

That is what the person does who wilfully casts his lot with the servants of the devil after he has once been admitted into the number of the sons of God. So severe were the punishments exacted among the Jews that anyone who had disobeyed a priest propounding the commandments of the Mosaic law, that is, anyone who had been told to abstain from the flesh of pigs[20] but ate it out of wilful disobedience was executed immediately without mercy after being convicted by the testimony of two or three persons.[21] How much more severe a punishment will he deserve who has trampled underfoot not some priest but the Son of God, Jesus? – for he tramples Jesus underfoot when he rejects his great act of kindness. Or he who has considered not some animal's blood to be profane but that sacrosanct blood with which the new testament was dedicated and by which he himself was once cleansed from all the sins of his past life, or has treated contemptuously the Spirit through which he obtained the grace of the gospel – for he betrays the temple[22] of God to the devil when through his vices he expels the Spirit from it. Do we promise ourselves impunity because those who defect from the sincerity of evangelical life are not immediately punished by their fellow men? We know him who said, 'Vengeance is mine, I will repay, says the Lord' [Deut 32:35]. And again in another passage, 'The Lord will judge his people' [Deut 32:36]. Let no one who is guilty congratulate himself if he escapes the hand of a human avenger; no one can escape the hand of God.[23] Yes, it is a fearful thing to fall into the hands of the living God.

When you first made your evangelical profession, you received very great acclamation, but greater still will be your disgrace when you fall back into your former life. To keep this from happening, recall to mind and remember those times in the past when, after you had been illuminated through evangelical teaching and faith, you bravely endured, because of your hope of a future life, a twofold struggle with sufferings. Visited with both reproaches and tribulations, you became on the one hand an object of ridicule to all who curse the teachings of Christ and on the other hand your evangelical love led you to share in the reproaches and sufferings which were being visited on other Christians or on the apostles[24] who rejected the world to follow the rule of the gospel. For you were willing partakers of the suffering and reproach which you incurred in the eyes of men because of my chains. You felt pain at another's pain and considered the insult done to another to be an insult done to you. Nor did you show yourselves genuine Christians just this far and no farther, but you accepted joyfully even the plundering of your goods. In so doing you clearly showed that you know and believe that you have better and more desirable riches set aside in heaven which neither the sneak-thief nor the violent highwayman can snatch away.[25] On the contrary, the loss of the possessions of this world, which we suffer on account of Christ's name, only increases our riches in heaven. Those acts rightly added to your confidence in obtaining Christ's promises. For the highest rewards are owed to such invincible faith and will undoubtedly be paid by a just and generous God, though in his own time. Now is the time for contesting; the crowns will be distributed later.[26] In the meantime you have need of patience so that after you have obeyed the will of God with steadfast hearts, you may as victors carry off the promised crown of eternal glory. That day does not yet appear when the contest will be over and the prizes will be awarded. However, the day is not far off when our commander – who,[27] as he was about to ascend into heaven, promised that he would return to us again[28] – will come and will no longer tarry. In the meantime the righteous one will live from his faith.[29] No matter how much he is afflicted, how much he is mocked, no matter how much he is extinguished, he will nevertheless sustain his courage from the expectation of the promises. But if he does not continue in faith, if he is broken by despair and withdraws from his evangelical commitment, 'my soul will have no pleasure in him.'[30] But God forbid that after a good beginning we draw back to perdition because of our lack of faith. On the contrary, we have confessed faith and we shall continue in it in order to gain life and the salvation of the soul, following the advice of Isaiah[31] who says, 'The righteous one will live from faith.'

Chapter 11

Nothing makes the godly more attractive to God than to have a sure confidence[1] about him. For to have no doubts about God's words is evidence of a mind that holds only the best thoughts about him, since the things of which he speaks are nowhere apparent to the human senses and cannot be proved by human arguments. There are things which the mind conceives of only through hope, since they do not exist anywhere in any physical way. Most people believe that such conceptions are insubstantial and no different from dreams. They think it foolish to believe something to be true which cannot be shown to the eyes. And yet this faith through which the righteous man will save his life when others perish is not some vulgar credulity; it is the solid and firm foundation[2] of those things which can be apprehended neither by the senses nor by man-made arguments. Firm hope makes them so present to the mind that they appear to be held in the hands right before the eyes. Hope does not persuade through man-made proofs but through a sure confidence in God their source that those things which cannot be seen in themselves are absolutely sure. The Jews have faith in their own works, but our confidence in God is the one thing which makes us pleasing and dear to him – and not only us; anyone who reviews the history of the world, starting with the creation, will find that it was above all on the grounds of their faith that all those ancestors of ours who are renowned and remembered for their godliness deserved what they attained.

First, do we not owe to faith our understanding that this whole world and everything it contains were created by the word of God and the mere command alone of its creator? For otherwise who could persuade us that things which are seen come into existence from things which are not seen or that what exists is made from what does not exist? Philosophers following human reasoning think that the universe is uncreated and no more had a beginning than did its fabricator.[3] As for us, however, we believe just as if we had actually seen what could never in fact have been seen and cannot be inferred by the reasoning power of the human mind, and we base our belief on the divine books which tell how the world was created by the command of God who we know is all-powerful and cannot lie.

Abel was the first human being to deserve the epithet 'righteous.' He is all the more praiseworthy because it was entirely on his own and without the stimulus of someone else's example that he behaved as one who is innocent and trusting in God.[4] But what caused him to be more dear to God than his brother Cain was? Clearly it was the faith with which he depended totally upon God, while Cain by ploughing up the land showed that he lacked faith and was not satisfied with those things which the ground poured forth spontaneously to nourish life without harm to anything.[5] Each offered sacrifices to God from his own acquisitions. But the sacrifice of Abel alone was pleasing to God because innocent man that he was he had a completely sincere faith in the goodness of God and did not look about for the benefits of this world, but looked for the reward of his godliness in heaven. Therefore, it was from his faith, not his offering, that he earned the favour of God's own testimony to his righteousness when God sent fire down from heaven and embraced his gifts.[6] Because of this most beautiful expression of approval he so dwells in the mouths of men after so many thousands of years that though dead he seems still to be alive and speaking.[7] After he had been killed despite his innocence, he was dead so far as his brother was concerned, but he was not dead where God was concerned to whom his blood still cried from the earth.

That Enoch was the offspring of an ungodly father was no hindrance.[8] Divine Scripture testifies in his favour that even while he was living on earth he dwelt with God.[9] This means that because of faith he pursued not those things which are seen but those which are not seen, that is, eternal and heavenly things, and for this reason he was carried still living to those things which he had loved, and he was removed from death. For his life before he was taken up from human society was such that he seemed to be living in heaven rather than on earth, and he who had committed no act worthy of death seemed unworthy of death. This was done so that men and women might thereafter learn from his example that the way to immortality lay open through faith and through the innocence of one's life. Therefore, he was taken up because he had pleased God. But he pleased most by his faith, without which no one pleases God, however abundant he may otherwise be in deeds. For whoever wants to be acceptable to God must believe, first, that God exists, is omnipotent, and wills only what is best; secondly, that God oversees human affairs and that through his agency the godly, who neglect the visible goods of this world and seek the invisible God, are not cheated of their rewards, however much they may suffer in this life, while the ungodly on the other hand will not fail to receive their due punishment even if they seem to sail along with fair winds in this world.[10] Therefore, whether one thinks of it as glory or as felicity, it was because of his faith that Enoch was taken from the company of men and lives with God.

Noah provides an example of confidence in God that is more remarkable even than Enoch's. Noah had been warned by an oracle that a deluge would destroy the entire race of creatures living and breathing on earth.[11] But when the sky remained clear and no signs appeared in it to lend support to the prediction made in the oracle, men ignored it and went on living as usual. Their banquets and celebrations of marriage made a mockery of the oracle's threats.[12] Noah, however, had absolutely no doubt that what God had predicted was going to happen would in fact come to pass and, therefore, he prepared the ark, with which he both saved his own family and condemned the rest of humanity. They had so little faith in the divine word that they even mocked Noah as mad for fitting out a device against the future flood. Not only was he saved from the deluge, but he also obtained the same praise as his ancestors, Abel and Enoch, who are famous for the righteousness which, through true faith, makes one acceptable to God.

Now how many times did Abraham give proof of his extraordinary confidence in God? First,[13] though a man has nothing sweeter than his native soil, nevertheless when he was told by God to leave his native land and dear ones behind and to emigrate to an unknown land, he obeyed the divine voice without hesitation, without the stimulus of anybody's example, without having any plausible proofs to make him hope that he would be coming into the hereditary possession of some land, of which up to that time he knew neither the name nor the location. So sure was his confidence that God would fulfil whatever he promised. It was from the same confidence that, no matter what happened, Abraham was never led to lose faith in God, who had promised the land. Although he had come down into the land promised by God, affairs did not proceed as he wished either for himself or for his son Isaac or for his grandson Jacob.[14] The inheritance of the land had been promised not only to Abraham but also to his descendants; nevertheless, he himself was compelled repeatedly to engage with enemies, while the Philistines kept harassing and troubling Isaac. Jacob meanwhile had been driven off to Mesopotamia through the agency of his brother Esau, and when he returned from there he was forced to buy a tiny piece of land on which to pitch his tent. Despite all this Abraham did not complain that he was being treated as an exile and not as an heir, nor did he divert his attention to those things which were visible on earth but kept it fixed on heavenly things which are perceptible only to the eyes of faith. For he was aware that this was not the land which the divine promise had meant. So small was the value which he placed on the land that he did not even dream of constructing some building or town there, but like a guest who was presently going to move some place else, he kept himself and his whole family in tents. What could he have been waiting for when he saw that this did not appear to be the promised land? Obviously he was waiting for another city, a stable and lasting one, from which he would never be expelled, a city whose builder and maker was God, a city far different from the cities on earth which men build and then demolish.

Furthermore, his wife Sarah, though she had an elderly husband and had herself reached that time of life when the native power of her womb to draw in and retain the male seed had failed, nevertheless conceived and gave birth to Isaac. She had no faith in her natural powers but had faith in God who, through the angel, had promised Abraham that a male child would be born the following year. She did not heed the voice of nature, which was against it; she was completely convinced that God could not lie. God had promised Abraham a posterity equal to the number of the stars and equal to the sand on the shore. Nature gave no hope of offspring; nevertheless, he did not lose faith.[15] For this reason, from one aged man, quite worn out in years, were born descendants as numerous as the stars of the sky and as the sand on the seashore. For the children and grandchildren whom he was expecting were not to be descendants through blood but through imitation of his faith.[16] It is on this basis that all of us who have faith in the promises of the gospel are descendants of Abraham.

Therefore, the confidence not only of Abraham but also of his true-born descendants was so steadfast that not even death took it away from them.[17] For these all died, though they did not yet have the promises but saw them from afar with this faith and believed, and in their deep longing hailed them. So far were they from having faith in this land, in which no one is allowed to live long, that they confessed that they were strangers and sojourners not only in Palestine but in the whole world. For they often call this present life a sojourning and a residence in a strange land, and in the mystic psalm David proclaims himself a sojourner in the land just as all his fathers had been[18] – and this despite the fact that he was the king in Palestine and had founded the state. The region itself was circumscribed by quite narrow borders and in large part did not yield to the Hebrew descendants of Abraham, for they were unable to drive the original possessors from their positions.[19] Not even Moses entered it, but only greeted it when he was on the point of death and saw it from a distant mountain;[20] nevertheless he did not despair of the promises. Therefore, when they admit that they are sojourners, they declare plainly enough that they are longing for a homeland.

But what homeland do those seek to whom this entire world is a place of exile? They had left their Chaldaean homeland. If longing for it had tortured them, it was not so far away that they could not conveniently return there. Therefore, they were not longing for that homeland but for another better one in which it would be possible to live forever, completely removed from all pain and trouble. It was to this heavenly homeland that God had summoned them. He wanted them to have such love for it that they would live in this world as though they were not in the world. For this reason, though God is the creator and ruler of all, he calls himself in a special way the God of Abraham, Isaac, and Jacob.[21] For he is properly the God of those who have placed in him all their confidence and make him the sole basis of their happiness. And he has prepared for such people a city, not on earth but in heaven, in which they are happy for ever, ruling with God, for love of whom they disdained all else.

Was it not also an outstanding proof of Abraham's faith that when, to test the sincerity of his faith in him, God told him to sacrifice his son Isaac, without a moment's delay he started to do what he had been told, although Isaac was his only son and it was in his name that the descendants had been promised? For the words of God's promise were, 'In Isaac your seed shall be called' [Gen 21:12]. Abraham did not start arguing with himself: 'Where will my descendants come from if I kill him in whom my hope of descendants exists?' Instead he carefully weighed in his mind the fact that God, who had made the promise, could not lie and, if it should so please him, was able to raise up, even from the dead, his lifeless son to be the propagator of the race. Abraham believed in the resurrection of the dead,[22] and for this reason it was granted to him to bring back home his lifeless son restored to life – restored, that is, because it had been in Abraham's power to kill him.[23] For this reason Isaac was even then an image foreshadowing the future resurrection of Jesus Christ.[24]

Now it was also a clear proof of a mind which trusts God completely that, when Isaac was on the point of death,[25] he ventured to promise to his sons Jacob and Esau the happiness which God had promised, even though Isaac himself had not yet received it. Foreseeing the life of each and the different reward of each, he nevertheless blessed them both. Such is the vision of faith that it sees that which is remote and physically imperceptible as though it were immediately present. It was due to this same confidence that Jacob, when he was dying, blessed each of the sons of Joseph. Completely aware of what was to be, he crossed his arms and placed his right hand on Ephraim, who was on his left, and his left hand on Manasseh who was on his right.[26] He had no doubt that what the Spirit of God had signified to him was to happen would someday come to pass. But the faith of the old man saw even farther ahead when, kissing the top of his son Joseph's staff, he venerated in it Christ, who was to be the ruler of all.[27] Joseph, who was informed against and betrayed by his brothers, was the type of Christ.

Nor did Joseph degenerate from the faith of his ancestors. For when he was on the point of death in Egypt, he foresaw, with divine help, that the Israelites – and at that point of time it hardly seemed likely – would emigrate from Egypt in order to reach the land promised by God. Joseph was so far from having any doubts about this event that he gave instructions to have his own bones transferred there at the same time.[28]

It was, moreover, the faith of Moses' parents that saved him right after he was born.[29] The king had issued an edict that every Hebrew child of the male sex should be immediately killed. But as soon as the parents of Moses saw their child, whose beautiful face was an immediate sign of something grand in store for him, and realized that it was God's will that the infant be saved for the public good of the people, they ignored the king's edict and hid the boy in their house for three months. Then, enclosing him in a little box, they exposed him on the river bank, confident that God would save the boy on whom he had poured so much grace. They were more afraid to offend God than the tyrant, obviously because they understood that those who cherish godliness cannot be deprived of their reward regardless of how human affairs may turn out.

While Moses' parents duly deserve this praise, it was to Moses' own credit that, after he had grown up and had been adopted by Pharoah's daughter, he rejected the honour of being a member of the king's family. Having proclaimed publicly that he was a Hebrew, he chose to suffer evil affliction in common with the people of God rather than to maintain an impious pretence and secure the advantages of a life at court.[30] In his judgment, to bear the reproaches of evil men in return for saving his people was wealth more felicitous than all the treasures of the Egypt. For he was even then the type of Christ, who was one day to suffer much more severely for the salvation of Moses' own race.[31] Moses disdained what was in his possession and turned the eyes of faith to those things which were far distant from the senses, relying on God who does not allow the godliness of men to be cheated of the rewards it has earned.

Because Moses relied on God's support, he dared even greater things than these. He was not afraid of the wrath of a savage tyrant and did not hesitate to labour to bring about the flight from Egypt and to lead the people out with him.[32] He disdained the king, whom he beheld with his eyes. He ignored the threats of so grand a prince, whom he saw armed and threatening the necks of his people. With an unbroken spirit, he had faith in the invisible aid of the invisible God just as though he saw him face to face with his own eyes. It was due to the same confidence that while he understood that the avenging angel would walk through the whole of Egypt and would kill every one of the first-born, he had no fear at all for his fellow Hebrews. Instead he instituted for them at that time, shortly before the departure, the yearly ritual of eating the paschal lamb with whose blood they sprinkled the threshold and the lintel as well as both doorposts of their houses.[33] Relying on this sign, they were not afraid for themselves in the midst of the slaughter of the Egyptians. Later[34] when the Red Sea stood in the way of their flight and at a blow from Moses' staff was divided into two parts, leaving a passage in the middle through which the Hebrews might pass as though along a dry road, the whole people, relying on God with the same confidence, escaped unharmed. But when the Egyptians impulsively entrusted themselves in their anger to the same sea, they were drowned as the waves soon came back together.

What[35] caused the walls of Jericho once upon a time to collapse suddenly on the seventh day after the Hebrews marched around them seven times? For they were not being battered in by any machines, but at the sound of the priests' trumpets and the shout of the people an entrance was given at the point where each of the Hebrews had taken his position in their ring around the city. Was it not the faith of the people and of Joshua the leader? Joshua was convinced that God could do everything and that what he had promised to do would undoubtedly be done. Furthermore, it was no slight proof of faith that the harlot Rahab had from the first given a hospitable reception to the spies on their mission and, realizing that that people was dear to God, preferred to look out for the interests of the spies at the risk of her own life than to win favour with her ungodly fellow citizens. She carried off the reward for her faith when she and her family were alone saved from perishing together with all those who, confident in their own powers, had not believed that God would overthrow their city whenever he wished.

Since among so many extraordinary deeds of our ancestors not a single outstanding exploit was performed without the aid of faith, what point is there in continuing to review them one by one? Time will fail us more quickly than examples if I go on to speak about the commander Gideon who, relying on God's aid, dared with three hundred men to attack the forces of the Midianites, though completely equipped with men, arms, and the rest of the materials of war. He routed the huge multitude and put it to flight with the blare of trumpets, the crashing of jars, and the miracle of the lamps so that the enemy themselves slew one another with mutual slaughter while the Hebrews did not even draw a sword.[36]

Or about Barak? Relying on the prophecy of the woman Deborah, he engaged in battle the thoroughly equipped regiments of General Sisera, cut them to pieces in a massacre, and put to flight King Jabin, who was shortly afterwards pierced and killed by the hand of a woman.[37]

Or about Samson? With the support of God's help he performed many, well nigh miraculous deeds against the Philistines on behalf of his people, deeds which could not be performed either by a multitude of men in concert or by the physical strength of any human body.[38]

Or about Jephthah? Though he was illegitimate and the humblest member of his kindred, nevertheless, relying on God's assistance, he won the most splendid victory over the Ammonites, the enemies of his people.[39]

Or about David? Not to mention the many victories won with God's assistance, the many dangers avoided when God saved him, did he hesitate, despite his youth, to engage unarmed the fully armed Goliath?[40] He laid him prostrate with a blow from his sling, so that the glory of the victory would belong to God and not to human effort.

Or about Samuel? He did not protect himself with some large retinue but governed the people of Israel for many years, administering the office of judge and ruler without payment, convinced, obviously, that God would in turn reward anyone who has carried out his office correctly.[41]

Time, I said, would fail me if I continue to review all the examples of this kind. I may pass over in silence for the moment the many outstanding prophets[42] who, relying on God, counted the threats of tyrants as nothing, or about the many men renowned for their religious devotion who, without human resources, but with the support of God, in whom they had placed total confidence, performed wonders and left to posterity a memory of themselves from their outstanding deeds. For, omitting the names of the authors of the deeds and touching only on the chief points in their history, their faith must be given the credit for what they did. Unequal to their enemies in all but one thing, namely that they had God as their helper, they defeated the richest kingdoms. Because they expected their reward to come from God, they could not be induced by any terrors to give up the observance of the Law handed down to them. Since no delay of the promises diminished their confidence, they too at last become possessors of those things which God had promised their ancestors. They obtained from God through prayers of faith what was impossible in the normal course of nature. With God as their saviour, they were rescued from extreme dangers. They either overcame or at least received no injury from lions whose savagery towards others was irresistible. It was as though the lions were incapable of injuring those whom God wished to be unharmed because their jaws were stopped or their claws tied together.[43] Cast into the midst of fire, they nevertheless remained unharmed as though they quenched the native violence of the fire with their own bodies.[44] With God as their protector, they escaped unharmed from the midst of the swords which their enemies had drawn against them. With God renewing their courage, they drew the utmost strength of mind from the utmost despondency in the face of events so that taken shortly before for dead, they suddenly bore themselves valiantly in war and vigorously repulsed their enemies' invasions.[45]

Why, the confidence of women even brought it about that mothers saw their dead children called back to life![46] Men, stretched on the rack and half-dead from different kinds of torture, preferred to expire in pain than to obey the ungodly commands of princes[47] and thus be removed from their torture. With great confidence they gave up for God the life which they knew they would receive back with interest in the resurrection of the dead. In their judgment, to acquire immortality through the loss of this brief life was a much better contract than to lose eternal life just to gain a small amount of time. Still others because of their tenacious zeal for truth and righteousness were objects of ridicule to people who derided and slandered them as madmen and criminals.[48] Not only were they visited with reproaches because of the confidence which they had in God, but their sincerity was also tested by scourgings as well as by chains and imprisonment. They were stoned to death. Their bodies were pulled in different directions in a horrible punishment as they were cut apart.[49] With what kind of evils were they not tempted?[50] They fell, slain by swords, convinced that not even death could tear the godly away from God. But to those for whom death did not chance to end their torments, life brought nothing except a long and painful martyrdom. They were cast out of their own homes and exiled from their towns. They wandered over the desert like wild animals, covering themselves as best they could with goatskins and sheepskins, suffering from the lack of necessities, hard pressed on all sides by the savage threats of their persecutors, and afflicted by the varied ills of this life. Not only did they not deserve such evils, the world itself did not deserve to have in it men so holy. One might think that God removed them from the company of men so that people so pure and chaste did not have to live out their lives among the polluted and the stained. Therefore, having no fixed abodes, they wandered through the trackless mountains, using caves and caverns in the earth for shelter.

Although all these have not yet obtained the reward promised for godliness, which will occur in the resurrection of the body, nevertheless they have earned everlasting praise for their steadfast confidence. Someone may say, 'Why is each one not given his or her reward immediately after death?' Evidently God has decided that the entire body of Christ will receive the glory of immortality at the same time.[51] For we are all members of the same body and those who have gone before us are willingly waiting so that together with their physical bodies and the whole company of their brothers all will come equally into the inheritance of eternal glory and will be joined at the same moment to their Head.[52]

Chapter 12

Therefore, since we are surrounded by so great a crowd and, if I may so speak, a cloud, of those who through the endurance of such evils have given testimony even[1] in the Old Testament that they put their faith wholeheartedly in God's promises, let us ourselves, encouraged by their example, be likewise concerned to cast aside the weight and burden of material goods and desires[2] which hold back the care-laden mind in its quest for heaven and to shake off the sin which attaches itself to us from all sides.[3] Inflamed by the hope of heavenly things, let us run vigorously in the race that is set before us. Let no afflictions or distractions slow us down in the course we have undertaken. Let us instead keep our eyes steadily fixed on Jesus Christ. As he is the author of this confidence which we have conceived about God, so will he finish in us what he has begun. Let us keep in view the course he took and the destination he reached. Though it was possible for him, innocent as he was, to escape death and to be as far from every agony as he was from every sin,[4] he nevertheless rejected the joys of this life and underwent death, and to make the evil more grievous through the addition of humiliation, he underwent death on the cross, for men are wont to endure death more readily when it is a glorious death. You see where he began his journey. Now where did he end it? By despising this life he obtained immortality; by despising public humiliation he obtained eternal glory in the heavens where he now sits at the right hand of the majestic throne of God the Father. You are speeding over the race-course of humiliation through every kind of pain and suffering towards your share in this glory. Never grow weary and broken-hearted in the race set before you, but reflect within yourselves that your leader endured so many reproaches, so many humiliations, so many accusations to the point that he even allowed himself to be reduced to suffering the punishment of a criminal's death on the cross. Though without any sin, he endured all these things so that we might have a model of true patience. You who, though not free from any sin, are enduring lighter sufferings ought not to be downcast. It is better to die a thousand times than to lapse back into the old life.

While you have been visited up to now by lighter evils, you have not yet resisted sin to the point of bloodshed. Sin attacks you fiercely when you rebel against it, and you immediately begin to think[5] that you have been abandoned by God. It does not occur to you to ask why in the mystic Proverbs a kindly Father speaks to you as sons, consoling you and quietly goading you into being courageous. 'My son,' he says, 'do not despise the chastening of the Lord, nor become despondent whenever you are rebuked by him. For whom the Lord loves, he chastens with the evils of this life and scourges every son whom he receives.'[6] But if you bear such chastisement patiently,[7] God acknowledges his sons and shows himself a kindly and loving father to them in turn and does not exclude them from the inheritance of heavenly life. Do you think you are hated and neglected by God just because you are being afflicted by the evils of this world? On the contrary, this very fact should serve as a sign that you have been destined for a paternal legacy. What father is there who does not sometimes chastise his son, whom he acknowledges as true-born? Since all the godly who are and have been dear to God have been trained to true godliness through temporary sufferings, if you are let off from such fatherly chastisement, it is obviously a sign that you are illegitimate and not true sons.

Our parents are the cause of our physical existence. There was a time when we not only put up with them but even revered them when, by scoldings and whippings, they trained us in the common customs and practices of society. We did not struggle against their authority but understood their actions to mean that, regardless of the way they were treating us, they were doing it with friendly intentions. Once we have persuaded ourselves that the Father in heaven has a like interest in providing for our salvation, regardless of the ways he allows us to suffer, shall we not much more readily be in subjection to him and entrust ourselves to him who is the creator not of our bodies only but also of our spirits?[8] Just as a human father does not treat his son cruelly in order to kill him but to save and improve him, so God chastises us in this world so that we may live forever. They indeed, our parents, disciplined us at their pleasure, sometimes misusing their authority, and they disciplined us for a short time in matters that were transitory and soon to perish – I mean in those things which pertain to the acquisition and preservation of the family's property – and sometimes they were looking out for their own personal advantage in getting the benefit of our obedience. But our heavenly Father, who does not need our help, is always looking out for our best interests, and these are not your everyday interests. For he does not aim to make us rich with earthly wealth, or to see that we inherit a few acres of land; he wants to give us a share of his heavenly goods, that is, holiness in this world, eternal happiness in the age to come. The person who calculates in his mind what an exceptional profit this is will easily endure the temporary troubles of this life. When human parents discipline their children, this chastisement does not bring pleasure but vexation at the time. But when the children are older and begin to realize how much that pain was for their own benefit, they are very glad that they were whipped and scolded, and they smile and thank those before whom they once stood in tears. Similarly when a disaster in this world looms over and threatens these mortal bodies, it is very painful to our senses during that time. But this pain, the uproar which disturbs even our mind because of its connection with the body, yields the serene and sweet fruit of righteousness in its own time.[9] Suffering teaches godliness; godliness produces the joy of a good conscience; a good conscience gives birth to immortality.

Therefore, let no one's heart falter in this most beautiful contest. The effort required is enormous, but the prizes are exceptional, the director of the contest trustworthy.[10] Imitate courageous athletes and sturdy runners. Hold up your drooping hands. Lift up your weak and tottering knees. Hurry in a straight course towards the finish line before you. Do not let your feet turn aside and stray from the straight path to one side or the other. On the contrary, if the urge arises to turn aside or to falter, remedy it with a new burst of energy.

It is not enough for you that each runs his own race with no regard for others. No, peace and concord should so join and fasten you all together that everyone is concerned with one mind about everyone else and takes care that no one falls from God's grace in the race which all are running. Let it be your concern that no one lose the holiness which befits the members of Christ and without which no one will see God, and thus become a burden to the body and unworthy to take possession of the prize set before you. Take care that, as you hasten towards heavenly things, some root of bitterness does not spring up, put forth shoots, disturb the godly efforts of the others, and, as it spreads out ever more widely, begin to defile many with its contagion. Take care that no one among you is a fornicator or a profane person, devoted to gullet and belly. Such desires hinder your running and turn it away from the straight path. They cause you, while you are looking back towards false goods like these, to lose that supreme and eternal trophy. This is what happened to Esau. Famished, he sold his birthright because of the pleasure of a single meal and bought permanent regret at the price of a moment's pleasure. For you should remember – and let this be an example to you – that afterwards when he tried to have his birthright restored through his father's blessing he was rejected, and his regret, coming too late, was of no use to him though the tears he shed in profusion were evidence that what he had done was painful to him.[11]

Bitterness, which arises from hatred, envy, and pride, destroys brotherly concord; lust, wantonness, and the other desires which lead to sordid acts destroy the purity and holiness of one's life. You, on the other hand, must preserve purity and concord among yourselves. One does not exist without the other. For concord which is pleasing to God does not exist among the impure, and true moral integrity cannot exist wherever discord reigns. Therefore, we too must take care not to exchange most foolishly our heavenly inheritance for the delights of this world. The things towards which we are hastening are heavenly. We must be pure as we approach them. We must dwell in the light of the gospel. We must make the holiness of our life match the holiness of our profession. You must correspond to your high priest and to his Law. For you have not come, as your ancestors did long ago when Moses was promulgating the Law, to Mount Sinai, which can be physically touched, and to a burning fire, which is perceived by the human senses, and to a whirlwind[12] and darkness, and to a storm and the sound of a trumpet, all of which are perceived by the ears and eyes; or to a voice whose words, though they could be felt by human ears from the beating of the air and had only the barest resemblance to the true voice of God, nevertheless were so majestic that the people who were listening were terrified by the dreadfulness of the voice and begged that God not continue to speak but that Moses himself pronounce with his own voice what God had commanded.[13] That voice was simply too terrifying for the weakness of human ears to be able to bear it. Those events, which were only types of the law of the gospel,[14] possessed so much religious awe and fear that the people were kept at a distance from contact with the mountain, and an edict was issued that a beast which had touched the mountain should be stoned or struck down with a javelin.[15] So terrifying was the appearance of the things which were being displayed to the physical senses that Moses himself was frightened and trembled at the horror of the spectacle.

You have not come then to a spectacle which is perceptible to the senses like that at Sinai, which was an adumbration and a type of far better things. The things to which you have come are more real than that spectacle because they are not perceived by the physical senses, but by the mind. You have come to the spiritual Mount Zion which is touched by the spirit, not by the hands; to the city of the living God, the heavenly Jerusalem, where peace is eternal;[16] to the innumerable concourse of angels who are the native inhabitants and leading citizens of this city; to the assembly of the sons of God who have not, like Esau, lost the right of the first-born, but by adhering to Christ have deserved to become citizens of the same city and to be registered in heaven; to God the Judge of all, the Prince of that state; and to the spirits of righteous men whom perfect godliness has united to the heavenly company and made assistants[17] to the Judge; to the high priest of the new testament, Jesus, who does not destroy but reconciles, and to his blood, by whose sprinkling souls are made clean and which speaks much better things than the blood of Abel. For the latter demanded vengeance, the former obtains forgiveness.[18]

The more mercifully and lovingly his blood speaks for us, the more must we take care that we do not spurn Christ speaking to us in this way.[19] For if they who turned away from the man, Moses, speaking on earth, did not escape punishment for despising his words, much more severe will be the penalty that we shall pay if we turn away from Christ, speaking to us from heaven. His voice shook the earth then to fill the people with fear and deter them from sinning. But what does he now threaten from heaven to do, speaking through the prophet Haggai? 'Yet once more,' he said, 'and I will shake not only the earth, but also heaven' [Hag 2:6], so that not only men on earth but the heavens too may be terrified. Now this phrase, 'yet once more,' indicates the removal of those things that are being shaken, as of things that are made by human hands such as the temple and the city of Jerusalem, so that those things may remain which were not made by human hands and cannot therefore be shaken since they are eternal. The Jews glory in their temple. They glory in the holy city, but someday these will not exist. They are waiting for a kingdom; we see that it has been removed to another place. Therefore, let us, who have begun to strive for a heavenly kingdom such as cannot be toppled and who do this through the benefit of the divine Spirit, persevere in this benefit from God.[20] Let us dwell then in this heavenly temple, worshipping God with such reverence and awe that we please by the purity of our minds him who requires no other kind of sacrifice than this. If religious scruples in the past did not allow in the performance of a sacred rite anything which might offend the eyes of men, how much more observant must we be in spiritual offerings that there be nothing in them to offend the eyes of God? If it was dangerous in the past for someone to approach religious places improperly, how much more dangerous will it be for us if with minds insufficiently pure we approach God himself? He is not some material fire which can be ignited or extinguished at will; he is a fire capable of completely annihilating whatever he wishes.

Chapter 13

Let brotherly love continue among you since you are members of the same body.[1] Enfold in your love not only those who live with you permanently but also those who lodge with you as guests. For not slight is the approval hospitality has in God's eyes. Through it Abraham had the merit of entertaining angels, though he did not know it but thought he was offering this charitable service to men.[2] Christian charity demands that the misfortune of those who are in chains because of their profession of Christ stir you just as if you yourselves were in chains. It demands that the torments of those who are being afflicted with various evils in other circumstances touch you too. It will thus be evident that you remember that you have a body liable to the same evils and also that you are not insensitive to the pains which the members of the same body are suffering.[3]

Marriage, which when preserved as it should be is held in honour even by pagans,[4] should be likewise honourable in your eyes, and the marriage-bed should not be defiled by any kind of illicit intercourse. God will judge fornicators and adulterers. There should be no covetousness in your conduct. Be content then with such things as you have, living as it were from day to day without concern for the future.[5] For it was with this intention that God himself promised Joshua and likewise all who have faith in him, 'I do not forsake you or abandon you,'[6] so that relying on this promise we may now say with confidence what the prophet says in the mystic psalm: 'The Lord is my helper, I will not fear what man will do to me' [Ps 118:6].

Have due regard for those who are in charge of you. For you have not received man-made teachings from them but the words of the Lord. Take care, therefore, that they do not lack any of their daily needs.[7] Just as you believed their words in the beginning, so keep your gaze fixed on their life as though it were a target. Imitate their faith, observing the constancy with which they persevere in their evangelical profession right to the end of their life.[8]

Once the gospel has been correctly communicated, it must always be kept with complete steadfastness. For as Jesus Christ was yesterday and is today and will always be for all time and will never be changed, so will his teaching remain always. Therefore,[9] stand fast in it, steady and firm, and do not be carried about by ever new and various doctrines as though you were resting upon a shifting foundation. The Mosaic law did not teach something different from what the gospel teaches but only in a different way. However, it is foolish to stay with shadows when the light of truth has dawned. Nevertheless, there is no shortage of people who would renew the old and now obsolete Judaism, basing godliness on foods and bodily nourishment.[10] But those who are superstitiously occupied with the observance of such things have not received the fruit of righteousness from them. Anyone who wants to attain a solid and true godliness, which does not hold the mere shadow of righteousness but strengthens the mind itself with a good conscience in the eyes of God, must stand firm in grace and faith.[11] He must rest upon this foundation which Christ has laid. Then he will not shift back and forth under the influence of Jewish superstitions. Let the Jews, not you, make abstinence from certain foods, including sacrificed foods, a matter of religion.[12]

We have an altar and a much holier one from which the right to eat does not exist for those who still adhere to the ceremonies of the law and do not know evangelical grace, the bestower of true salvation. For in accordance with the commandment of the law, the bodies of the animals whose blood is customarily offered for sin by the high priest in the tabernacle called the Holy Place were ordered to be burned outside the camp.[13] It was evidently thought that the blood possessed some element of the sacred, while the bodies, which are thought to be polluted, are carried outside to be burned in profane places. For this reason they abstain from these bodies as being, in their view, unclean food. They have the shadow, but we embrace that which the shadow signified. Their conscience was not one whit holier after they had been sprinkled with blood nor, since their souls were steeped in vice, were they any purer because they abstained from eating the bodies.

We accept Jesus as our offering and our high priest. He, as though playing upon the image of the Law, wanted to be crucified outside the gate of the city of Jerusalem to cleanse his people with his own blood. We must imitate his example scrupulously but not superstitiously. We shall do this if we too take up our own cross and follow him in the way he departed from the company of men like a criminal. Let us too depart from the traffic of this world and let us consider it a sweeter thing to undergo reproach for Christ than to enjoy the glory which the world bestows.[14] Let us say fare-well to this earthly city. We do not have here a lasting city, but we long for the one to come, heavenly and everlasting. Everyone who casts off the desires of the flesh and bends every effort to the practice of heavenly things is going forth from the city. Our offering is not sacrificed inside the walls, but we too, going out with our high priest, Christ, continually offer a victim pleasing to God through him. We do not offer some animal or the produce of the fields, but the fruit of our lips, and by lips I mean not so much the lips of the body as of the mind. With them we acknowledge God's kindness to us and, commemorating the cross of Christ, give thanks for the forgive-ness of sins and for so many gifts. The Jews are not partakers of this altar; remaining inside the walls, they care for nothing except that which belongs to the flesh.[15]

Now learn also about another kind of sacrifice worthy of the gospel. One should be constantly offering it to God. A neighbour must be helped with kindness and if he should be in need he must be assisted with material support. For God is conciliated more quickly by such sacrifices than by the trivial observances the Jews perform when they have neglected a brother.[16]

Obey those in whose charge you are and submit to them even if they are wicked,[17] provided that they do not drag you into ungodliness. For in the performance of their office they watch out for your souls and look after your salvation. They do this at their own risk in that they will render an account to God from whom all power derives. You will lighten their burden in some part if you show yourselves compliant and obedient[18] so that they may do what they do with eagerness and joy rather than with grief. For this is as vexatious to them as it is unprofitable for you. Toil undertaken to no purpose only makes them hostile and there is no gain for you in provoking God's anger against yourselves because of your disobedience.

Brothers, commend us too to God in your prayers, for I think I deserve to be counted among those who preside over you well. I do not know whether I meet with the approval of everyone.[19] I am confident at least that I have behaved sincerely and with a good conscience in front of all who are eager to live according to the standard of the gospel. I pray all the more earnestly that you do this so that I can be restored to you the sooner. Meanwhile[20] I in turn pray for you that God, the author of peace, who called back from the dead that supreme[21] shepherd of the sheep, our Lord Jesus Christ, who, restored to life, entered heaven through his blood to intercede for us with the Father, the blood with which he consecrated the new and everlasting covenant – may God, I pray, make you perfect and complete in every good work so that you may be capable of satisfying his will, and that he also make all your actions pleasing in his sight, and this through Jesus Christ who is always present making our sacrifices acceptable, to whom is due all glory not only in this life but for all time. Amen. There is nothing which we may claim as our own from our good deeds. Everything we do that is such as to please the eyes of God is a gift from him.

I have written these things to you for exhortation. Please take in good part what we have done with good intentions. I have written in few words because I expect to see you soon in person.[22] I want you to know that Timothy is not with me at the present time but has been sent away elsewhere.[23] If he returns shortly, I shall visit you in his company. Greet in my name all who are in charge of you but also the entire flock of the saints with them. The Italians greet you. May the grace and favour[24] of God be always with you all. Amen.

The End of the Paraphrase on the Epistle to the Hebrews
by Erasmus of Rotterdam, Professor of Theology[25]

Notes

Translator's Note

xiii

1 An edition of the complete *Paraphrase* on the Gospels, Acts of the Apostles, and the Epistles appeared in 1534, but in so far as the Epistles are concerned, it is a reprint of the 1532 edition. See CWE 42 xxxv.

2 See *Elenchus in N. Bedae censuras* LB IX 511B–C.

3 See Allen Ep 1043 introduction.

4 See the dedicatory letter in the *Paraphrase on James*.

5 See the *Elenchus in N. Bedae censuras* LB IX 511B–C. In Erasmus' view, or so he states, the Epistle to the Hebrews did not present much difficulty to the reader, compared, that is, to the genuine letters of Paul and the letters of Peter, and hence did not really need to be elucidated by a paraphrase.

6 It is not known when or where Schiner urged Erasmus to paraphrase the remainder of the Catholic Epistles. Allen Ep 1171 47n surmised that the occasion may have been a dinner which Erasmus attended with Schiner in Cologne shortly before 8 November, but it seems unlikely that Erasmus would have had time to make all the preparations for the new edition as well as to write the three new *Paraphrases* between the time of his return to Louvain (after 19 November) and the writing of the dedicatory letter to Schiner on 16 December. Schiner joined the court of Charles V in Brussels on 2 September 1520, so that he could have had numerous opportunities for meeting and talking with Erasmus in Brussels, Antwerp, Mechelen, and even Louvain, before the dinner in Cologne.

7 In a letter dated 31 December 1520 (Ep 1177:48–52) Erasmus states that he has completed *Paraphrases* on all the Epistles except Hebrews.

8 To facilitate the use of the *Paraphrase* as a running commentary on the biblical text Erasmus placed in the margins of the March 1521 edition an almost sentence by sentence series of two or three-word citations from the Vulgate. These citations are not included in the CWE translation but are replaced by modern verse numbers in the running titles. A few of the side notes, however, offer additional comments on the biblical text. These are translated in the notes.

xiv

9 See the letter to Matthäus Schiner at the head of the *Paraphrase on James*.

10 See Rummel *Critics* II 29–55, 81–134.

11 See Allen Epp 1672, 1746, and especially 1804.

12 See Allen Epp 2094 and 2095.

13 Octavo editions appeared in 1534 and 1539, but they are by and large reprints and do not contain new information about the text of the *Paraphrases* on the Epistles. The text of the 1539 edition is remarkedly corrupt; therefore, I have omitted it from the list of early editions.

14 To appear in three parts as ASD VII-4, 5, 6

15 For a list and brief description of the editions of the *Paraphrases* through 1680 see CWE 42 xx–xxix. To this list may be added the series of textbooks published between 1795 and 1802 for students at the school of the Benedictine abbey of the Assumption of the Blessed Virgin Mary in Salzburg: Ephesians 1795; Galatians and Colossians 1796; 1 and 2 Timothy 1797; Romans 1798; 2 Corinthians and James 1801; 1 and 2 Peter, Jude 1802.

16 See CWE 42 xv–xviii.

17 Cf Ep 1274:36–43.

18 See Irena Backus 'Deux cas d'évolution théologique dans les *Paraphrases* d'Erasme' in *Actes du colloque international Erasme (Tours 1986)* Travaux d'Humanisme et Renaissance 239 (Geneva 1990) 141–51.

19 I make this assumption because in numerous places what at first sight could seem to be a paraphrase of an individual word or phrase in the biblical text is in fact an alternative translation which Erasmus had found in one or another of his patristic authors and had recorded in an annotation. I do not as a rule comment on these annotations unless the original author is being cited for some reason.

xv

20 By 'Vulgate' I mean the text in circulation in Erasmus' time. What actual edition or editions he may have had, either before his eyes or in his memory, is unknown. A text of the Vulgate is printed beside Erasmus' Latin version in the fourth (1527) edition of the *Novum Testamentum*, but it has variants which suggest that it was not 'his own' text. In any event Erasmus' Vulgate is based upon the recension of the text made in Paris in the thirteenth century, which underlies the later Sixtine and Clementine editions. Unless stated otherwise, the term Vulgate in the present volume always means the Clementine Vulgate.

21 For the convenience of the reader individual annotations are cited from the Leiden edition of the *Opera omnia* (LB VI) and are identified by the Latin lemma from the Vulgate which precedes each annotation in that edition.

22 Cf Beatus Rhenanus *Compendium vitae Erasmi* CWE 4 301–7: 'It is doubtful whether the favorable reception [of the *Paraphrases* on Paul and the Gospels] by students everywhere or his own enthusiasm in writing them was greater. "Here," he said, "I am in my own field." And this was true. He used to look in the ancient exegetes above all, among the Latin ones, Ambrose [ie Ambrosiaster], Jerome, Augustine, Hilary; of the Greeks Chrysostom and his imitator Theophylact. He furnished only the appropriate style.'

23 In a Latin translation; see Allen Epp 1858 and 2648.

24 Erasmus knew Theophylact's commentary from a Latin translation falsely

ascribed to Athanasius (see Ep 846 n9) and in Greek from the commentary
in the margins of Manuscript 2ap (Basel A.N. III. 15) which he used for the
first edition of the *Novum instrumentum* in 1516. He appears to have made
numerous excerpts from this commentary which subsequently appear in the
second edition of the *Annotationes,* where they are cited from 'Vulgarius.'
The erroneous name is corrected to Theophylactus in the third edition of
1522; see Rummel *Annotations* 37.

25 There is a substantial increase in the number of citations from Thomas in
the third edition (1522) of the *Annotationes,* which may reflect the use made
of it for the *Paraphrase.*

26 In the dedicatory letter for the *Paraphrase on James,* Erasmus admits that he
owes a debt to Nicholas of Lyra; cf 134 below.

27 Erasmus may have already considered it spurious; see Allen Ep 2253:17–18.
He evidently preferred Theophylact's much more succinct commentary on
Hebrews. He had apparently not yet realised that Theophylact's commentaries on Paul were largely derived from Chrysostom; see Allen Ep
1790:17–20.

28 Bede (c 672–735) began his works on the Bible with commentaries on Acts,
the Catholic Epistles, and Revelation. They appear to have been written
between 709 and 716; see the *Theologische Realenzyklopädie* 5 (Berlin-New
York 1980) 397–402 and the essays by M.L.W. Laistner on 'Bede as a Classical and a Patristic Scholar,' 'The Library of the Venerable Bede,' and 'The
Latin Versions of Acts Known to the Venerable Bede' in Chester G. Starr ed
*The Intellectual Heritage of the Early Middle Ages: Selected Essays by M.L.W.
Laistner* (reprinted New York 1966) 93–164. In addition to being incorpor-
ated wholesale into the *Glossa ordinaria,* the commentary on the seven Catholic Epistles circulated separately and continued to be copied in manuscript
form into the sixteenth century. See M.L.W. Laistner *A Hand-List of Bede
Manuscripts* (Ithaca, NY 1943) 30–7, who remarks that 'This work, to judge
by the number of extant MSS, was the most popular of all Bede's theological
expositions' (30). In making his comparison of the complete commentary
with the excerpts in the *Glossa ordinaria* Erasmus may have used a manuscript in the library of the Franciscan convent in Antwerp; see the annotation on 1 Pet 2:1 (*rationabile sine dolo lac*) LB 1045C, where Erasmus refers to
this manuscript in a comment about Bede which he added to this annotation in the 1522 edition of the *Novum Testamentum.* He later employed the
edition by Josse Bade and Jean Petit (Paris 1521), a copy of which was in
his library (see Fritz Husner 'Die Bibliothek des Erasmus' in *Gedenkschrift
zum 400. Todestage des Erasmus von Rotterdam* [Basel 1936] 240 no 160). The
annotation on Acts 1:14 (*cum fratribus eius*) LB VI 437F suggests that Erasmus
had some reservations about this edition; see the article by de Jonge cited in
the following note. A critical edition of the Latin text of Bede's commentary
on the Catholic Epistles and an English translation are now available, both
by David Hurst OSB.

29 *Glossa Ordinaria* was the name given in the thirteenth century to the compi-
lation of interlinear and marginal glosses or comments that formed the
major commentary on the Bible during the early Middle Ages. See Beryl
Smalley 'Glossa ordinaria' *Theologische Realenzyklopädie* 13 (Berlin-New York
1984) 452–7 and Guy Lobrichon 'Une nouveauté: les gloses de la Bible' in *Le
Moyen Age et la Bible* sous la direction de Pierre Riché et Guy Lobrichon

(Paris 1984) 95–114. The history of the work in the late Middle Ages and of the manuscripts in which it circulated is still obscure. The first printed edition is attributed to Adolph Rusch (Strassburg 1480 or 1481), which is probably the edition that Erasmus was using at this time; see H.J. de Jonge 'Erasmus und die Glossa Ordinaria zum Neuen Testament' *Nederlands Archief voor Kerkgeschiedenis* 56 (1975) 51–77, though the evidence cited by de Jonge for this assumption belongs to the following year (1521). Erasmus' attitude to this piece of 'patchwork' was generally unfavourable; nevertheless, he appears to have made substantial use of it in a variety of ways both in the Annotations to the *Novum Testamentum* and in the *Paraphrases*. It is not always possible to determine whether Erasmus consulted Bede's commentary directly or through the excerpts in the *Gloss*. To simplify matters for the reader I refer only to Hurst's edition of Bede's Latin text and his English translation and for the most part ignore the excerpts in the *Gloss*.

30 The *editio princeps* appeared in Venice in 1506, but Erasmus does not seem to have known or used this edition.

31 See Rummel *Annotations* 69–70.

32 Erasmus (Allen I 14:20–1) remarks in connection with the publication of the fourth edition (1527) of the *Novum Testamentum* that while writing the *Paraphrases* he had caught many things which had previously escaped him.

33 Erasmus does not in the manner of the medieval commentators actually quote the patristic commentaries. That would be anachronistic and would disrupt the fiction that the paraphraser is the apostolic author. My impression is that he works from memory rather than from an open text, except perhaps in the case of Ambrosiaster, whose translations as well as interpretations of the biblical text appear frequently in the *Paraphrases* on the Pastoral Epistles.

34 For Erasmus' 'imaginative' paraphrases see Roland H. Bainton 'The Paraphrases of Erasmus' *Archiv für Reformationsgeschichte* 57 (1966) 67–75 and John N. Wall jr *The First Tome or Volume of the Paraphrase of Erasmus upon the Newe Testamente* (Delmar, NY 1975) 3–9; and for Erasmus' employment of the art of rhetoric in the *Paraphrases*, Jacques Chomarat *Grammaire et rhétorique chez Érasme* 2 vols (Paris 1981) chapter 4 'Les paraphrases.'

35 See *De conscribendis epistolis* CWE 25 14–5 and 74.

xvi

36 See the *Ratio* Holborn 291:13–34.

37 For this purpose I have used the Authorized Version and in more modern dress the New King James Version as the translations closest to Erasmus' Greek text. His Latin translation, or, as I prefer to call it, his Latin version, is actually a revision of the Vulgate designed to bring it closer to the Greek text and (in the second edition of 1519) to the standards of classical Latin; see H.J. de Jonge 'The Character of Erasmus' Translation of the N.T.' *Journal of Medieval and Renaissance Studies* 14 (1984) 81–7. For the Vulgate I have used the Challoner revision of the Douay-Rheims translation, and where that was too archaic, I have resorted to the Knox translation. Occasionally Erasmus' Latin version has a different nuance from the standard versions and I have then made my own translation. Quotations from the Bible in the notes are generally from RSV in accordance with the editorial policy of CWE.

Other English translations are referred to from time to time, primarily to illustrate the difference of opinion among scholars about the meaning of the original text.

xvii

38 See the editor's introduction in CWE 66 ix–xxv.

39 Cf the paraphrase on 1 Pet 1:3–4.

40 See the translators' note CWE 42 xxxv–xxxviii. The term *innocentia* is itself a paraphrase, that is, a 'free translation' or rather an explication of the significance of the Greek word δικαιοσύνη, 'righteousness' in the standard English translations, which is commonly translated *iustitia* 'justice' in the Vulgate. For Erasmus' essentially medieval view of righteousness see C.A.L. Jarrott 'Erasmus' Biblical Humanism' *Studies in the Renaissance* 17 (1970) 128–35.

41 Cf the final sentence of the *Argument of the Epistle of Paul to the Romans* CWE 42 14. The object in making the authors of the Epistles 'speak classical Latin' (*romane loqui*), as Erasmus explains in numerous places, was to arouse an interest in the New Testament on the part of the 'fastidious' reader who might otherwise refuse to read it because of the barbarous Latin of the Vulgate.

42 The matter is, to be sure, a good deal more complicated than I may seem to suggest. See Robert D. Sider '"In Terms Quite Plain and Clear": The Exposition of Grace in the New Testament Paraphrases of Erasmus' *Erasmus in English* 15 (1987–8) 16–25. Erasmus was later criticized for his failure to employ correct theological language, but he replied that to do so would be anachronistic.

xviii

43 In citing the medieval commentaries, Aquinas apart, I have as a rule not given specific page references, except when a comment might extend beyond one page. Early editions of the *Glossa ordinaria*, and the *Postillae* of Hugh of St Cher and of Nicholas of Lyra are printed with the biblical text, and the reader will usually find the cited comment adjacent to the verse under consideration.

PARAPHRASE ON 1 TIMOTHY

Dedicatory Letter

2

1 The translation of the dedicatory letter (Ep 1043) to Philip of Burgundy is by R.A.B. Mynors with modifications and notes by the translator of the present volume. Philip, a natural son of Philip the Good, duke of Burgundy, was born in 1464 and died in 1524. After a varied career in military service and in the priesthood serving, first, the emperor Maximilian and then his successor Charles of Hapsburg, later Charles V, he was elected prince-bishop of Utrecht in March 1517, on which occasion Erasmus dedicated to him his *Querela pacis* (cf Ep 603). Although maintaining a corre-

spondence with the bishop, both directly and through Philip's secretary, Gerard Geldenhouwer, Erasmus did not actually meet him until March 1519. Later that year in August Erasmus made a special trip from Louvain to Mechelen to greet the bishop (Ep 1001). These meetings, together with long-standing ties with other members of the bishop's family, may have prompted Erasmus to dedicate the *Paraphrases* on this set of Epistles to a prelate whom he respected both as a churchman and a patron of learning. See the article on Philip in CEBR I 230–1, and also those on Adolph of Burgundy (ibidem 223–4) and David of Burgundy (ibidem 226–7).

3
2 For Erasmus' view of the role and function of the bishop in the church see José Ignacio Tellechea 'La figura ideal del Obispo en las obras de Erasmo' *Scriptorium Victoriense* 55 (1955) 201–30.
3 See *Adagia* I i 49.

Argument

4
1 Cf the *Paraphrase* on Acts 16:3 LB VII 730B–E.
2 which] The two 1520 editions and the 1538 edition, followed by the 1540 edition and LB, correct to 'who.'
3 The statement that the letter was written from Laodicea, a town close to Colossae in southwest Turkey, is printed at the end of 1 Timothy in Erasmus' *Novum Testamentum*. It comes from a subscription found in several Greek manuscripts; see Metzger *Textual Commentary* 645. Tychicus was one of Paul's close associates (Acts 20:4) and letter-carriers (Eph 6:21–2, Col 4: 7–8). This latter fact, coupled with the mention of him in 2 Tim 4:12, probably led to the inference that he carried the present letter to Timothy.

Chapter 1

5
1 I have added the heading for chapter 1. The heading for chapter 1 is omitted in the *Paraphrase* on each of the Epistles.
2 Chrysostom *Hom in 1 Tim* 1 (on 1 Tim 1:1) PG 62 503 / NPNF 408a observes, 'Everywhere in his writings Paul adds the name of Apostle, to instruct his hearers not to consider the doctrines he delivered as proceeding from man. For an Apostle can say nothing of his own, and by calling himself an Apostle, he at once refers his hearers to Him that sent him.'
3 Chrysostom ibidem / NPNF 408b comments, 'It does not appear that the Father anywhere commanded him. It is everywhere Christ who addresses him. But whatever the Son commands, this he considers to be the commandment of the Father.'
4 Ambrosiaster *Comm in 1 Tim* 1:2 CSEL 81/3 252:2–3 sees in the resurrection a similar example of hope, 'No one should doubt that the hope is in Christ Jesus who they know gave an example of this hope through his resurrection from the dead.'

5 he] *ille*. The 1540 edition and LB read *ipse* 'he himself.'

6 Cf 1 Cor 4:17.

7 The appellation 'son' was thought to be a metaphor for convert; cf 1 Cor
  4:17. Aquinas *Exp in Epist 1 ad Tim* lect 1 (on 1 Tim 1:2) 586b comments:
  '"Son in faith," that is, converted by him.' Using the device of paraphrasing
  through the opposite, Erasmus contrasts Timothy's pre-conversion state
  with his new sonship in Christ.

6

8 us] I have supplied the pronoun required by the syntax. It is omitted in all
  the editions except the 1520 editions, which read *suos* 'his own.'

9 Cf Eph 4:13.

10 This contrast between the 'shadow' of the Law and the 'light' of the gospel,
   which goes back to the church Fathers, recurs repeatedly; see the paraphrase on Gal 5:3-7, CWE 42 122–3.

7

11 Any less carefully] Added in 1532

12 By 'curious arts' Erasmus seems to mean magic. He is creating his portrait
   of the Ephesians from Acts 19:18–19 and 28–34; cf also 20:29–31.

13 Cf *Adagia* III i 34.

14 The belief that the opponents were apostles and Judaizers is found in
   Chrysostom *Hom in 1 Tim* 1 (on 1 Tim 1:3) PG 62 506 / NPNF 410a, who
   ascribes to them the motives of vainglory, profit-making, and the desire to
   have disciples.

15 This thought is likewise found in Chrysostom ibidem: 'He does not mention
   the persons by name, that he might not, by the openness of his rebuke,
   render them more shameless.'

16 This interpretation of the term 'fables' (NKJ; 'myths' RSV) is made by Ambrosiaster *Comm in 1 Tim* 1:3 CSEL 81/3 252:24–5 and Chrysostom *Hom in 1
   Tim* 1 (on 1 Tim 1:3) PG 62 506 / NPNF 410a. It recurs in Theodoret, Theophylact, the *Gloss*, Hugh of St Cher, Aquinas, and Nicholas of Lyra. Theophylact (implicitly) and the medieval commentators explicitly refer to Matt
   16:6, 'Thus you have made the commandment of God of no effect by your
   tradition.'

17 corporal] Added in 1532. Erasmus evidently wants to emphasize that salvation does not come from being a physical descendant of Abraham as the
   Jews claimed (Luke 3:8; Rom 4:1; etc), but a spiritual descendant through
   faith as Paul stated (Gal 3:7). The language, and in particular the words
   'through branches' (*per traduces*), is used by Ambrosiaster CSEL 81/3 253:2.

8

18 'directly' – literally 'through a short cut' (*compendio*). Ambrosiaster *Comm in
   1 Tim* 1:3 CSEL 81/3 253:3–4 employs the term in his comment on this verse:
   compendio per fidem salutem quaerere 'to seek salvation directly through faith';
   however, the word is a favourite with Erasmus and appears, for example,
   in the title of the *Ratio seu Methodus compendio perveniendi ad veram theologiam* which was published shortly before the *Paraphrases* on the Epistles to
   Timothy, Titus, and Philemon. See the paraphrase on Titus 1:2.

19 A recurrent complaint; cf 4:3 below and the paraphrases on Gal 4:10 and 5:3 (CWE 42 116 and 122), Phil 3:18, Titus 1:14, and *Ratio* Holborn 297–304.

20 Cf Matt 22:34–40

21 Erasmus is paraphrasing the literal meaning of *mataeologia* 'empty' or 'meaningless talk' (RSV) in 1 Tim 1:6. Elsewhere he puns on *mataeologi* and the similar sounding *theologi*, the spouters of meaningless theology; see *Ratio* Holborn 301:1–9 and Rummel *Annotations* 142–6.

22 Alluding to Rom 10:4

9

23 Cf Ambrosiaster *Comm in 1 Tim* 1:11 CSEL 81/3 254:11–12: 'He uses the Law lawfully who can discern those things which were given for a limited time from those which are everlasting.'

24 The contrast between the the gospel as the law of love (*lex amoris*) and the Mosaic law as the law of fear (*lex timoris*) goes back to Augustine, if not earlier (cf eg *Contra Adimantum* CSEL 25 166:28) and is ubiquitous in medieval exegesis.

25 The comparison appears in Chrysostom *Hom in 1 Tim* 2 PG 62 511 / NPNF 414a.

26 Ambrosiaster *Comm in 1 Tim* 1:11 CSEL 81/3 254:20–8 makes this point.

27 Erasmus probably follows Chrysostom here, who believed that this verse referred to the Jews (*Hom in 1 Tim* 2 PG 62 511 / NPNF 414a).

28 Cf the paraphrase on Gal 3:23 (CWE 42 113).

10

29 This point is made by Chrysostom *Hom in 1 Tim* 2 (on 1 Tim 1:12) PG 62 515 / NPNF 416a, who sees here evidence of Paul's humility. But Erasmus may also have had in mind texts like 1 Cor 2:3 and Gal 4:13; cf the paraphrase on the latter verse (CWE 42 117).

30 Non-Jews in antiquity believed that the Jewish way of life, which kept them from intimate association with gentiles, was motivated by the Jews' hatred of other nations. See the Argument of Hebrews, n6.

31 Cf *Adagia* II ix 54.

11

32 Erasmus follows his Greek text here, which he thought was supported by the commentaries of Chrysostom *Hom in 1 Tim* 4 (on 1 Tim 1:17) PG 62 523 / NPNF 421b and Theophylact PG 125 26A. However, he had doubts about the correctness of the text and would have preferred to omit the epithet 'wise'; see the annotation on 1 Tim 1:17 (*soli deo*) LB VI 930C.

33 Erasmus uses the word *oraculum* to describe an OT text which was interpreted as a prophecy of some future event in the life of Christ or in salvation history. Erasmus appears to take the prophecies mentioned in 1 Tim 1:18 to be the same as those in 4:14 and thus to refer to Timothy's consecration as bishop.

34 'Bishop's office' is my paraphrase of the term *presbyterium* which Erasmus, following 1 Tim 4:14, employs in the paraphrase on 1:18. Modern translators and commentators generally take the term in 4:14 to denote some kind of 'council of elders' (RSV; see Spicq *Epîtres pastorales* 517–18). Erasmus,

however, thought the term 'presbyter' was the title of an office; see his annotation on 1 Tim 4:14 (*manuum presbyteri*) LB VI 938F where he observes that in antiquity there was no difference in meaning among the words *presbyter* 'elder', *sacerdos* 'priest', and *episcopus* 'bishop.' The *presbyterium* was thus the office of bishop, which was conferred on Timothy through the threefold action of the gift of the Spirit, the prophecies, and the laying on of hands. For a modern argument in support of a similar interpretation see Kelly *Pastoral Epistles* 107–8.

12

35 The motif comes from Chrysostom *Hom in 1 Tim* 5 (on 1 Tim 1:19) PG 62 527 / NPNF 424b who, anticipating the image in 1:20, says: 'And some turn aside from the faith, who seek out everything by reasoning; for reasoning produces shipwreck, while faith is as a safe ship.'

36 How can ... be lasting?] Added in 1532

37 The comparison is with gangrenous parts of the body which must be amputated; cf 2 Tim 2:17.

Chapter 2

13

1 and ... obtained] Added in 1532

2 Cf Matt 5:45. The same reference is found in Chrysostom *Hom in 1 Tim* 6 (on 1 Tim 2:1) PG 62 531 / NPNF 427a): 'For we must give thanks to God for the good that befalls others, as that he maketh the sun to shine upon the evil and the good, and sendeth his rain both upon the just and the unjust.'

3 God grants ... the salvation of all.] Added in 1532

4 This is ... love is] 1532. The earlier editions read 'Evangelical love is not this but that love which' etc.

5 Erasmus' favourite term for repentance, used here and elsewhere, is *resipiscentia*. In classical Latin the verb *resipiscere* means 'to come to one's senses, to see reason'; in ecclesiastical Latin it is used to translate the Greek verb μετανοεῖν 'to repent.' Erasmus preferred to emphasize the mental action or change of attitude implied by the Greek and Latin verbs rather than the element of satisfaction, the outward penance which compensated for the sin. As he explains in his annotation on Matt 3:2 (*poenitentiam agite*) LB VI 17E–18B repentance is a three-stage process in which a person becomes aware, first, that he has done something wrong and, secondly, regrets what he has done. This change of mind and feeling of regret are then followed by some form of compensation for what has been done. A bad conscience leads to contrition which in turn is followed by penance. See Payne *Theology* 195–209.

6 Cf Luke 23:34.

7 The disciple must imitate the Master; see Luke 22:63–5.

8 Chrysostom *Hom in 1 Tim* 6 (on 1 Tim 2:2) PG 62 531 / NPNF 426b makes a similar point, though relating it to his own historical situation. The topic, however, had already appeared in the paraphrase on Rom 13:1–7 (CWE 42 73–5).

14

9 Ambrosiaster *Comm in 1 Tim* 2:2 CSEL 81/3 260:11–15 remarks that peace
(*quies*) is necessary for the preservation of piety and chastity, but the comparison of the disadvantages of war with the advantages of peace was a
subject of lifelong and passionate interest to Erasmus. See Robert P. Adams
*The Better Part of Valour: More, Erasmus, Colet, and Vives on Humanism, War,
and Peace, 1496–1535* (Seattle 1962).

10 truly] *vere*, 1519–1534. The 1538 and 1540 editions and LB read *vero* 'however.'

11 In Col 2:15 Christ is depicted as a warrior who despoils Death and cel-
ebrates a triumph. Prudentius *Liber Cathemerinon* 9:104–5, in language similar to that used by Erasmus, likewise depicts the victorious Christ 'carrying
back' (*reportans*) to heaven the glory of the passion. The image of the victor
carrying off his prize recurs in the paraphrase on 1 Pet 1:9, where it
describes the Christian who carries off the fruit of his faith, that is, the
salvation of his soul, and in the paraphrase on Heb 10:36, where the victor
'carries home the promised crown of eternal glory.'

15

12 The example is taken from Ambrosiaster *Comm in 1 Tim* 2:4 CSEL 81/3
260:26–261:4), who also makes the point that the person who refuses salvation perishes through his own fault.

13 arbitrator] *arbiter*. The term is used by Ambrosiaster *Comm in 1 Tim* 2:5 CSEL
81/3 261:16–17: *missus enim a patre factus arbiter reconciliavit deum et homines*
'sent by the Father he became the arbitrator and reconciled God and
humanity.' For the concept of Christ as arbitrator between God and men see
A.T. Hanson *Studies in the Pastoral Epistles* (London 1968) 56–8.

14 This point is made by Chrysostom *Hom in 1 Tim* 7 (on 1 Tim 2:5) PG 62 536
/ NPNF 430b.

15 Cf Gal 3:28.

16 Cf Gal 2:7-10, Acts 11:1-3, and Chrysostom *Hom in 1 Tim* 7 (on 1 Tim 2:7)
PG 62 537 / NPNF 431a.

16

17 The contrast between Christian and Jewish prayers is made by Chrysostom
Hom in 1 Tim 8 (on 1 Tim 2:8) PG 62 539–540 / NPNF 432b. But in what
follows Erasmus seems to have John 4:20-4 in mind.

18 Cf Ambrosiaster *Comm in 1 Tim* 2:8 CSEL 81/3 262:22-4: 'The soul must be
at peace when praying so that the prayer may become effective. For hands
are holy when the heart is pure.'

19 is present] *est*, added in March 1521. The verb is omitted in the first edition.
The 1520 editions add *haesit* 'has stuck fast in.'

20 Cf eg Lev 12:2-8 and 15:19-30.

21 Erasmus draws on a traditional theme of satire which he had earlier employed in his *Moriae encomium* (ASD VI-3 90-1); cf also the paraphrase on 1
Peter 3:3. For similar treatments in patristic literature cf eg Chrysostom *Hom
in 1 Thess* 5 (on 1 Thess 4:7-8) PG 62 427–428 and M.L.W. Laistner *Christianity and Pagan Culture in the Later Roman Empire* (Ithaca, NY 1951) 85–122;
Jerome *Ep* 107.5 CSEL 55 296:7-9.

22 The Latin *auro intertexto* means 'with interwoven gold,' but it is not clear
whether Erasmus is thinking of some kind of gold ornament for the hair
such as the ancient *stephane* or the hairbands which women commonly wore
in his own time, in which case the phrase would presumably mean 'artfully
braided hair with interwoven gold'; or whether he understands the Greek
to refer to some kind of gold jewellery or to clothing embroidered with
gold. The NT text is itself vague, and ancient customs would permit any one
of these interpretations; cf Spicq *Epîtres pastorales* II 377.

17

23 The point occurs in Chrysostom *Hom in 1 Tim* 9 (on 1 Tim 2:11) PG 62 544 /
NPNF 435b), but the theme is ubiquitous in classical and later literature.
24 Cf Eph 5:24 and 1 Cor 14:34–5.
25 That is, in church; Chrysostom *Hom in 1 Tim* 9 (on 1 Tim 2:11) PG 62 543 /
NPNF 435a complains bitterly about this habit.
26 Cf 1 Cor 11:9.
27 In his *Ecclesiastes* (LB V 1043E) Erasmus calls this way of interpreting the Fall
an 'allegory or tropology.' In traditional allegorical exegesis Eve represents
the weak flesh and is thus prone to sin; Adam represents the rational mind
and in his prelapsarian state could not be deceived. Therefore, he does not
sin in the same way that Eve does. Chrysostom *Hom in 1 Tim* 9 (on 1 Tim
2:14) PG 62 544–545 / NPNF 435b–436a offers a similar argument, and
Erasmus may be drawing upon his commentary here. The allegorical interpretation of Gen 3:1–6 has a long history; see Joseph Coppens *La Connais-
sance du Bien et du Mal et le Péché du Paradis: contribution à l' interprétation de
Gen II–III* Analecta lovaniensia biblica et orientalia series II fasc 3 (Louvain
1948), and Payne *Theology* 43–4.

18

28 This interpretation of the term 'childbearing' is advanced by Chrysostom
Hom in 1 Tim 9 (on 1 Tim 2:15) PG 62 545 / NPNF 436.
29 Erasmus' exegesis is based on Chrysostom (see the preceding note) and
Jerome *Adversus Jovinianum* 1.27 PL 23 248B–249A.
30 Erasmus is probably following Chrysostom *Hom in 1 Tim* 9 (on 1 Tim 3a) PG
62 546 / NPNF 436b who takes the phrase 'This is a faithful saying' to refer
backward, not forward. Erasmus places the verse in chapter 3 in his Latin
version and in the *Annotationes*.

Chapter 3

1 Cf Chrysostom *Hom in 1 Tim* 9 (on 1 Tim 3:1) PG 62 547 / NPNF 437b–438a,
who makes the same contrast between good and bad ambitions in a bishop
and remarks: 'For the Episcopate is so called from having the oversight of
all.' The word 'bishop' is derived from the Latin *episcopus*, itself a transliteration of Greek ἐπίσκοπος which means literally, as Erasmus points out,
'one who watches over,' an over-see-er.

19

2 'Teaching authority': *magisterium*. Although this word is classical and
denotes the office of the *magister* or teacher, Erasmus is probably using it in

this context in its theological sense to designate the teaching authority of the bishops.

3 Chrysostom *Hom in 1 Tim* 10 (on 1 Tim 3:2) PG 62 548 / NPNF 438a, commenting on the word νηφάλιον 'temperate,' compares the bishop to a general who must go about the camp day and night in the performance of his duty.

4 This interpretation of the word 'violent' is found in Chrysostom, *Hom in 1 Tim* 10 (on 1 Tim 3:3) PG 62 548 / NPNF 438b and in Jerome, who gives a similar interpretation of the word in his commentary on Titus 1:7; cf the paraphrase on this verse.

5 'Let him shun avarice' is a paraphrase on the Greek adjective ἀφιλάργυρον 'not a lover of money' (RSV) in 3:3. In his Latin version Erasmus translated *alienum ab auaritia* 'free from avarice.'

20

6 Chrysostom *Hom in 1 Tim* 10 (on 1 Tim 3:5) PG 62 549 / NPNF 439a, after noting that men who manage their households well are likely to manage public affairs equally well, compares the church to a house.

7 Latin *inserit*. Erasmus repeatedly uses this metaphor, derived from Rom 11:17–24, to describe membership in the body of Christ.

8 Erasmus uses the noun *sanctimonia* here as a classicizing equivalent of the theological term *sanctificatio* 'sanctification.'

21

9 The interpretation of the word γυναῖκας 'women' in 1 Tim 3:11 is a vexed question; see Spicq *Epîtres pastorales* I 460–1. Erasmus translated the Greek by *uxores* 'wives' and explained that he believed that Paul was describing in this part of the Epistle the character and duties of all the members of a bishop's household, including wives, children, and servants (deacons); see the annotation (*mulieres similiter pudicas*) LB VI 935F. The translation was criticized by Edward Lee (LB IX 232E) and Zúñiga (ASD IX-2 226:6–16).

22

10 Without arguing the point, Erasmus tacitly asserts that priest (*presbyter*) and bishop (*episcopus*) were one and the same office in New Testament times.

11 Erasmus has confused the order in which these offices were normally held since the tribunate usually preceded the office of praetor. Of greater interest, however, is the suggestion, implicit in this comparison, that the historical development of the hierarchy and the governance of the Catholic church followed the model of the Roman government.

12 This contrast between the temple and the church is taken partly from Chrysostom *Hom in 1 Tim* 11 (on 1 Tim 3:16) PG 62 554 / NPNF 442a, and partly from Theophylact, PG 125 49B–C. The latter provides the details on the contents of the Holy of Holies; cf on Heb 9:4 below.

13 The pomegranates and bells were part of Aaron's robe (Exod 28:33–4). Erasmus evidently thought that the robe was preserved in the Holy of Holies together with Aaron's rod. By 'enigmas' he means that the appearance and contents of the Holy Place and the Holy of Holies were shadows or figures of the gospel and required allegorical interpretation in order to

be understood, a procedure which he for the most part eschews in the *Paraphrases* on the Epistles.

14 Chrysostom *Hom in 1 Tim* 11 (on 1 Tim 3:16) PG 62 554 / NPNF 442a makes this point.

23

15 By using the epithet mystical Erasmus implies that the OT texts which mention the two sanctuaries and their contents must be interpreted figuratively, that is in their spiritual meaning, if they are to have any significance for Christians. See the paraphrase on Heb 1:5.

16 good will to men] March 1521, following the reading of Erasmus' Greek text of Luke 2:14; the 1519 and 1520 editions read 'men of good will,' the text of the Vulgate. Edward Lee criticized Erasmus for failing to indicate in his *Annotationes* that the reading of the Greek manuscripts was not supported by patristic commentators. Erasmus defended himself vigorously; cf *Responsio ad annotationes Lei* LB IX 146E–148D and the annotation on Luke 2:14 (*hominibus bonae voluntatis*) LB VI 231F. On the textual question see Metzger *Textual Commentary* 133.

17 the mystery of true godliness] Here and below in the phrase 'the rule of true godliness' the first edition reads *vere* in both places. This word could be taken as either the adverb *vere* 'truly' or the adjective *verae* 'true' since the two words were pronounced alike and in Erasmus' own practice were both written *vere*. The adverb *vere* would in each sentence modify the verb: 'we truly possess,' 'the rule of godliness is truly here.' The Basel editions, however, vary between the two forms. The 1532 edition reads 'the mystery of true godliness' but 'the rule of godliness is truly here.' The 1520–1522 editions and the 1523 folio edition have the adverb in both places; the 1523 and 1534 octavo editions have the adjective in both places as do the 1540 edition and LB. Erasmus' usage elsewhere (cf eg the Argument of the Second Epistle to Timothy below) suggests that the adjective *verae* should probably be read in both sentences, and I have translated accordingly.

18 'The rule of true godliness': *regula verae pietatis*. The phrase, if textually correct (see the preceding note), seems to be modeled on the patristic slogan, *regula fidei* 'the rule of faith' (cf Bengt Hägglund 'Die Bedeutung der "regula fidei" als Grundlage theologischer Aussagen' *Studia Theologica* 12 (1958) 1–44). Godliness (*pietas*), as Erasmus understands this concept, is the standard by which to test theological conclusions; cf CWE 66 xv–xxi.

Chapter 4

24

1 feigned godliness] 1532. The earlier editions read 'the feigned guise of godliness.'

2 Mention of the Essenes is made in Erasmus annotations on Jerome Ep 22 'To Eustochium' CWE 61 191, first published in 1516; in the *Encomium matrimonii*, first printed in 1517 or 1518 (CWE 25 137); in the letter to Paul Volz written as a preface for the revised edition of the *Enchiridion* 'Ep 858:

519–21); and in the dedicatory letter to Erard de la Marck in the *Paraphrase on the Epistles to the Corinthians* (Ep 916:303–7; cf also Ep 901:10–17). Erasmus drew his knowledge of the Essenes from Pliny the Elder *Naturalis historia* 5.73 and 104, where the celibate life of the Essenes is described as an unnatural wonder, from Josephus *Jewish War* 2.8.2 and *Jewish Antiquities* 18.21, and indirectly from Philo's *Apology*, which he knew of from Eusebius *Praeparatio evangelica* 8.11. These texts were our major source of information about the Essenes prior to the discovery of the Dead Sea Scrolls. Whatever Erasmus actually knew about the Essenes, they appear in the three works mentioned above either as the representatives of an extraordinary and dubious way of life (*Encomium matrimonii* and the letter to Paul Volz) or as the originators of a heresy whose vestiges still remain in Christianity (letter to Erard de la Marck). Erasmus does not say explicitly what these heretical vestiges are, but he evidently associates them with the commitment to what he calls Jewish ceremonies. In this respect Essene is a synonym for monk; see E.V. Telle *Erasme de Rotterdam et le septième sacrement* (Geneva 1954) 121 and *passim*. The identification of the anonymous heretics 'who forbid marriage' in 1 Tim 4:3 with the Essenes, an identification which Erasmus seems to have been the first to make, may thus be a reflection of his views about monasticism rather than evidence of his historical interests. This identification, which has apparently left little trace in later commentaries, has been revived recently, though without reference to Erasmus, by Constantin Daniel in his article 'Une mention paulienne des Essénes de Qumràn' *Révue de Qumràn* 20 (1966) 560–7, especially 560–2.

3 before eating] Added in the 1532 edition

25

4 Erasmus is engaging here in a kind of double paraphrase, explicating the Greek adjective βεβήλους, which means 'profane,' and the translation in the Clementine Vulgate by the Latin word *ineptas*, which means 'silly' or 'frivolous.' He makes a similar double paraphrase when he renders the Greek verb ὑποτιθόμενος 'put before' in 4:6 by 'remind,' which is what he thought the verb meant in this verse, and then paraphrases it again at the beginning of 4:7 with the words 'put before,' which is the rendering in the Vulgate (*proponens*) and in most modern translations.

5 This is an axiom of Erasmus' 'philosophy of Christ.' Cf *Ratio* Holborn 249–51 and the *Enchiridion* CWE 66 65–84.

6 By duties of godliness Erasmus probably means saying mass and similar divine services for which the priest prepared by fasting and prayer.

7 Cf the colloquy 'A Fish Diet' in Thompson *Colloquies* 348–9.

8 Cf Luke 13:10–17 and 14:1–6.

26

9 Erasmus uses here and just below the word *presbyterus*. He seems to consider the *presbyterion* ('presbytery' in NKJ, 'council of elders' RSV) to have been some kind of council of bishops or persons having the status of bishop in the early church; cf note 34 on 1:18 above and the paraphrase on 3:13, where 'elder' is glossed by 'bishop,' and on 6:12, where Timothy's consecration as bishop is described as the undertaking of the office of presbyter.

10 It was not ... prophets] 1532. The earlier editions read 'Prophecy designated you' etc.
11 showed] The 1538 and later editions read 'show.'
12 or comfortable] Added in 1532

Chapter 5

27

1 See the paraphrase on Titus 3:2 below and the *Ratio* Holborn 225–7, where Erasmus presents a collection of texts on Paul's display of gentleness while teaching.
2 churches] 1532. The earlier editions read 'the church,' perhaps because the singular is used in Ambrosiaster *Comm in 1 Tim* 5:1 CSEL 81/3 278:5–7: 'Old age receives respect everywhere among all peoples; hence both the synagogue and afterwards the church had elders, without whose counsel nothing was done in the church.'
3 based ... report] Added in March 1521

28

4 also] Added in 1532
5 Widows ... know God] Added in 1532
6 Cf Luke 2:36–7. Ambrosiaster *Comm in 1 Tim* 5:3 CSEL 81/3 278:28–279:2 cites the example of Anna.
7 The Vulgate takes this pronoun to be masculine gender 'any man' (DR). In his annotation on 1 Tim 5:8 (*si quis autem suorum*) LB VI 940D (first in the 1519 edition of the *Novum Testamentum*) Erasmus argues that Paul is talking about the widow and cites in support of this interpretation of the Greek indefinite pronoun τις the 'Greek Scholia' (by which he means, I think, a catena or a commentary like that of Oecumenius found in one of his Greek manuscripts; cf the note to the Argument on Philemon below) and Ambrosiaster *Comm in 1 Tim* 5:8 CSEL 81/3 280:19–23.

29

8 Erasmus follows Aquinas here. In answering the question, how can one of the faithful be worse than an infidel, Aquinas *Exp in epist 1 ad Tim* lect 1 609b argues that a distinction must be made in terms of 1/ their absolute state of sin and 2/ their state in respect to a particular sin. In absolute terms a believer is better, not worse, than an unbeliever, but if they both commit the same sin, the sin of the believer is the more grievous because it is also an injury to faith. Erasmus summarizes Aquinas' discussion in his annotation on 1 Tim 5:8 (*fidem abnegavit, et infideli deterior est*) LB VI 940D and then adds a personal comment, 'Today in the judgment of some persons it is considered the height of piety if someone abandons his wife and children or even his aged parents and goes off to Jerusalem or hides himself away in a monastery to live for himself, or perhaps just for his belly.'
9 Evangelical] Added in 1532
10 Compare the lecherous old women in the *Moriae encomium* ASD IV-3 108: 688–110:705 / CWE 27 106.
11 through her good deeds] Added in 1532

12 Cf Ambrosiaster *Comm in 1 Tim* 5:10 CSEL 81/3 281:7–9: 'Having immersed herself in charitable activities and wearing her life away in them she deserves to be received into the bosom of the church to which she has long since devoted herself in her lawful services.'

30

13 The phrase 'lubricious time of life' (*lubrica aetas*) occurs in Ambrosiaster *Comm in 1 Tim* 5:12 who is probably Erasmus' immediate source for the interpretation of verses 11-15; cf *Comm in 1 Tim* CSEL 81/3 281:22–282:4. However, Jerome in Ep 123.2–6 gives a similar exposition of this passage. Erasmus refers to Jerome's exposition in his annotation on 1 Tim 5:11 (*quum enim luxuriatae fuerint in Christo*) LB VI 940F and may have had it in mind while writing the paraphrase on this verse.

14 Erasmus remarks in his annotation on 5:11 (*quum enim luxuriatae fuerint in Christo*) LB VI 940F that the verb στρηνιᾶν 'to grow wanton' is a metaphor drawn from the behaviour of pack-animals which grow restive and break away from their halters to roam wild. He refers to Jerome Ep 123.2 for the view that this behaviour on the widows' part is an insult to their bridegroom, Christ.

15 pry into] First in 1532; the earlier editions read 'get to know.'

31

16 Erasmus has his eye on contemporary conditions rather than the exegesis of the text, which contains no such suggestion. One of the bequests made in his own last will and testament was the provision of a fund to provide dowries for unmarried girls from poor families. See Allen XI 365:45–50 and Carl Roth 'Das Legatum Erasmianum' in *Gedenkschrift zum 400. Todestage des Erasmus von Rotterdam* (Basel 1936) 282–98.

17 her ... dowry] The 1519–1523 editions read *inopia horum* 'the lack of these things,' that is, the dowry and other property which a bride was expected to bring to her new household. In the 1532 edition the *horum* is changed to *harum* ('their,' that is, the widows' lack of a dowry), but this change introduces a plural pronoun which conflicts with the singular subject in the 'if' clause and in the preceding sentence. I suspect that the change in the 1532 edition is a typographical error and I have, therefore, retained the reading of the earlier editions.

18 The paraphrase follows Ambrosiaster *Comm in 1 Tim* 5:17 CSEL 81/3 284: 9–15: 'Good and faithful stewards ought to be judged worthy of honour not only on high but also on earth so that they are not worried by a lack of funds but may rejoice rather because of their faith and teaching. For he becomes more impressive if he is not humiliated by need, and a feeling of authority grows in him when he sees that even in the present time he is receiving the fruit of his labour, not so that his reward may be bountiful but so that it may not be completely negligible.'

19 Cf Deut 25:4.

20 Cf Deut 24:15.

32

21 Erasmus was in doubt whether 'elder' in 5:19 denoted an older person or

an officer of the church. Patristic authority seemed to him to favour the former view and that presumably accounts for the paraphrase; cf the annotation on this verse (*adversus presbyterum*) LB VI 942E.

22 Athenian jurors, before being assigned to individual cases, swore an oath to hear both parties impartially. A purported text of this oath is found in Demosthenes *Against Timocrates* 24.149–51. Roman jurors in criminal cases, and perhaps also the judge in a civil case, likewise swore an oath on being seated; see A.H. Greenidge *The Legal Procedure of Cicero's Time* (Oxford 1901) 270 and 474.

33

23 Cf Ambrosiaster *Comm in 1 Tim* 5:22 CSEL 81/3 286:3–5: 'It is not sufficient that he have no charge against him – he must show the merits of his good works if he is to be considered worthy of ordination.'

24 Cf Ambrosiaster ibidem 286:9–18: '[God does not want those who serve him] to become feeble because of their excessive zeal and then require the services of doctors. Temperance is necessary so that, if possible, the service which one has once begun may gradually improve, not be diminished through lack of care. Intemperance causes unease in the soul so that when it frets about its infirmities it is insufficiently devoted to divine services. Therefore, lack of prudence brings a loss. For a tranquil soul raises the entire heart to God as it prays with sound mind for what must be asked.'

25 Let ... be attributed] 1519–1534. The 1538 and later editions read 'has been attributed.'

26 as often as you now do] Added in 1532

27 The reference is, I assume, to the paraphrase on 5:17–22 dealing with the 'elders,' the bishops and other clergy subordinate to Timothy in his capacity as archbishop. But Erasmus' language is vague, and he could just as well be talking about the sinners and the godly in general in Timothy's congregation. Both views of these verses have been advanced by commentators; cf Kelly *Pastoral Epistles* 124–30 and Fee *1 Timothy* 133–5.

28 'Your subordinates': *tuorum*. The Latin could equally well mean 'your people' in the sense of your congregation.

29 A clause, 'because you cannot know,' found at this point in the editions of 1519–23, is omitted in the 1532 edition, perhaps accidentally, since the clause does not seem to have been the object of criticism.

Chapter 6

34

1 Cf Chrysostom *Hom in 1 Tim* 16 (on 1 Tim 6:1) PG 62 588 / NPNF 465a.

2 This motive appears in Ambrosiaster *Comm in 1 Tim* 6:1 CSEL 81/3 287: 18–20: 'Since it is through God's discipline that they have shown loyal service to their masters, perhaps the masters too will subject themselves to this discipline.'

3 the] LB reads the customary 'our.'

35

4 This term is a paraphrase on the Greek word παραδιατριβαί 'wranglings'

(NKJ) in 1 Tim 6:5. In his annotation on this verse (*malae conflictationes*) LB VI 944C–E Erasmus reports that the Greek Scholia, Chrysostom (*Hom in 1 Tim* 16 [on 1 Tim 6:5] PG 63 592 / NPNF 568a), and Theophylact (*Exp in Epist 1 ad Tim* 6:5 PG 125 78D) state that the word is a metaphor from the action of sheep which rub their mange on to one another.

5 do not acknowledge] 1532. The 1519–23 editions read 'will not acknowledge.'

6 Cf Matt 6:25 and Luke 12:22.

7 The paraphrase suggests that Erasmus has Job 1:21 in mind, a verse which Ambrosiaster quotes in his commentary on 6:9 (CSEL 81/3 289:5–290:18). However, the idea that the riches which we accumulate will only benefit others, that is, our heirs, is common in classical authors, especially Horace (cf eg *Odes* 2.3.17–20 and 2.14.21–8). Equally common is the belief that nature sets limits on the use of material goods; cf Kelly *Pastoral Epistles* 137.

36

8 the treasure of] Added in 1532. The 'treasure of godliness' is the accumulation of merit in heaven. Erasmus is alluding to Luke 12:33–4.

9 This deification of Mammon, which is also developed in the paraphrase on Matt 6:24, may have been influenced by classical examples such as the deification of wealth in Aristophanes' *Plutus*; cf the annotation on Matt 6:24 (*et Mammona*) LB VI 38D. There was no ancient god actually named Mammon and the Latin could be translated 'to Mammon as their god.'

10 and your neighbour for his sake] Added in 1532

11 here on earth with transitory and false goods] Added in 1532

37

12 'Director of this contest': *agonotheta*. The athletic contest is a common metaphor for the life of the godly both in the New Testament and in patristic literature. The term agonothete or supervisor of the contest does not appear in the NT but is frequent in both Greek and Latin patristic literature. Cf eg Chrysostom *Homily on the Holy Maccabaeans and Their Mother* PG 50 618–619; Clement of Alexandria *Stromata* 7.3 and *Protrepticus* 96.3; Tertullian *Ad martyras* 3. Jerome *Adversus Jovinianum* 1.12 PL 23 228A states: 'The agonothete proposes the prize, invites [you] to the race, holds the trophy ... in his hand.' Jerome's text was certainly familiar to Erasmus though not necessarily in his mind here.

13 The reference of the 'this' is obscure, but Erasmus seems to mean that at his consecration Timothy promised to make salvation in heaven, not earthly wealth, the object of his office as bishop. That the 'good confession' in 6:12 refers to Timothy's consecration as bishop is the view found in the interlinear *Gloss*, Hugh of St Cher, Aquinas *Exp in epist 1 ad Tim* lect 2 617b, and Nicholas of Lyra. Patristic commentators – Chrysostom *Hom in 1 Tim* 17 (on 1 Tim 6:12) PG 62 594 / NPNF 469a, Theophylact PG 125 81D, Ambrosiaster *Comm in 1 Tim* 6:12 CSEL 81/3 291:13–15 – refer the confession to that made by Timothy at his baptism, which is the position taken by most modern commentators (see Kelly *Pastoral Epistles* 142, Spicq *Epîtres pastorales* II 569). Why Erasmus should have abandoned his patristic sources for the medieval commentators at this point is not evident.

14 the office] *functioni* 1532. The 1519–23 editions read *suum mandatum* 'his mandate.'

15 The Latin relative pronoun *quem* in the Vulgate version of 6:15 could have either *adventum* 'coming' or *Iesu Christi* as its antecedent. In his annotation on 1 Tim 6:15 (*quem suis temporibus*) LB VI 945E, Erasmus points out that the Greek clearly shows that the antecedent of the relative pronoun is the noun *adventum* 'coming,' not 'Jesus.' However, the insertion of the adverb 'again' with the verb 'manifest' suggests that in the paraphrase Erasmus intends the relative pronoun to refer to Jesus, contrary to what he says in his annotation.

38

16 Cf Acts 2:44–5 and *Adages* I i 1.

17 Another motif from Horace; cf *Odes* 3.1:33–7.

18 Cf Ambrosiaster *Comm in 2 Thess* (on 3:17) CSEL 81/3 248:18–22 on this explanation of the Pauline ending, 'Grace be with you.'

19 Cf 1 Cor 16:21, Gal 6:11, and Erasmus' annotation on 1 Tim 6:21 (*gratia tecum*) LB VI 948C, where he attributes this idea to Ambrosiaster. For the ancient practice of adding a word or two in one's own handwriting at the end of a letter written by someone else see Gustav Adolf Deissmann *Light from the Ancient East* (New York 1927) 171–2.

20 You singular (*tecum*) is the reading of Erasmus' Greek text and of the Clementine Vulgate. See Metzger *Textual Commentary* 644.

21 This 'liturgical' Amen is found in the Greek and Latin manuscripts used by Erasmus for his edition of the New Testament and hence in the *Paraphrases* on each of the Epistles except 2 and 3 John. See Metzger *Textual Commentary* 645, 651, 658, 677, 686, 698, 707, 718, 720, 722.

PARAPHRASE ON 2 TIMOTHY

Argument

40

1 This motive appears in the Argument of Ambrosiaster's *Comm in 2 Tim* CSEL 81/3 295:3–7.

2 The belief that the imprisonment implied by this Epistle is different from and later than the one referred to in 1 Tim 4:16, and that Paul was tried twice by Nero is found in Eusebius *Historia ecclesiastica* 2.22.2,3; in the subscription at the end of 2 Tim in several Greek manuscripts (see Metzger *Textual Commentary* 651–2); and in Erasmus' edition of the Greek text LB VI 961C.

Chapter 1

41

1 In the *Ratio* Holborn 250:3–7, Erasmus says, citing Rom 1:9, 'Paul, when still

living as a Jew, worshipped God, but with periodic fasts, with observance of the new moon, with keeping the sabbath, with ritual washings, with discrimination among foods. Now, having accepted a different kind of worship, he adores the Father, neither on a mountain [that is, like the Samaritans] nor in Jerusalem. For God rejoices in those worshippers who worship him in the spirit.'

2 Cf 1 Tim 2:1.

3 Cf Ambrosiaster *Comm in 2 Tim* 2:4 CSEL 81/3 297:6–7: 'On account of Paul's recollection of the tears which Timothy had shed out of love for the apostle when he was departing.'

42

4 Ambrosiaster ibidem 297:16–22 makes the point that Paul mentions Timothy's mother and grandmother in order to arouse his zeal for his work as bishop.

5 Cf Chrysostom *Hom in 2 Tim* 2 (on 2 Tim 1:8) PG 62 607 / NPNF 479b–480a.

6 The translation *merita nostra* 'our merits' appears in several manuscripts of Ambrosiaster *Comm in 2 Tim* 1:9 CSEL 81/3 298:27. The Vulgate has *opera nostra* 'our works.'

43

7 The words 'my deposit' in this verse are ambiguous and could refer to something which Paul has entrusted to God or which God has entrusted to Paul. See Fee *2 Timothy* 231–2 and 234 or Kelly *Pastoral Epistles* 165–6. The paraphrase combines both interpretations. The explanation of the deposit as Paul's salvation (*salus*) occurs in Ambrosiaster *Comm in 2 Tim* 1:12 CSEL 81/3 300:16.

8 Erasmus appears to be following a text of the Vulgate or of Ambrosiaster which had the participle *habens* 'having' instead of the imperative *habe* 'have, hold.' His Greek text and his Latin version both have the imperative.

9 The paraphrase of 'Holy Spirit' by 'Spirit of the gospel' (*spiritus evangelicus*) suggests that Erasmus takes spirit here to mean specifically Christ's Spirit, which is communicated in and through the gospel. Cf Rom 8:9.

10 This idea was probably suggested by Ambrosiaster *Comm in 2 Tim* 1:15 CSEL 81/3 301:1–4: 'They pretended to be friends of the apostle so that by sticking close to him they might find grounds for false accusations either on their own part or contrived through others. After they saw that they were discovered, they withdrew from him.'

11 Chrysostom *Hom in 2 Tim* 3 (on 2 Tim 1:15) PG 62 613 / NPNF 484b remarks: 'It seems that there were then in Rome many persons from the regions of Asia.' This view is accepted by some modern scholars, rejected by others; see, for example, Spicq *Epîtres pastorales* 731–2, and, in contrast, Fee *2 Tim* 235–6 or Kelly *Pastoral Epistles* 169.

12 That is, from the Greek word φυγή 'flight'

13 Erasmus wrote *Mercurius* 'Mercury,' but I have substituted the Greek equivalent, Hermes, in the translation to make Erasmus' point clear.

14 Cf the comment of Chrysostom *Hom in 2 Tim* 3 (on 2 Tim 1:15–18) PG 62 614 / NPNF 484b: 'Observe the philosophy of [Paul's] soul. He only mentions their conduct, he does not curse them, but he praises him that showed

kindness to him, and invokes a thousand blessings upon him, without any curse on them.'

Chapter 2

44

1 dearest son] Added in 1532
2 'Commander-in-chief': *imperator*. The Latin word can also mean 'emperor.' LB distinguishes between the two meanings by capitalizing when it assumes the word means 'emperor.' Erasmus, however, does not seem to make any distinction between the civil and military meaning when he characterizes Christ variously as *imperator* 'general,' *dux* 'leader,' *princeps* 'prince, head' etc. See Payne *Theology* 69–70. The titles, while traditional, are part of Erasmus' view of the church militant as the body of Christ; cf eg the *Enchiridion* CWE 66 29–30.

45

3 motivated by] Added in 1532. The 1519–23 editions read 'because of the reward.'

46

4 For this twofold interpretation of the clause 'if we died with Him' cf Chrysostom *Hom in 2 Tim* 5 (on 2 Tim 2:11) PG 62 625 / NPNF 492a.
5 Cf Matt 25:12 and Luke 12:8–9. Ambrosiaster *Comm in 2 Tim* 2:12 CSEL 81/3 305:3–6 and Aquinas *Exp in epist 2 ad Tim* lect 2 629a make the same reference to Matt 25:12, but the phrase 'those terrifying words' seems to be influenced by Chrysostom *Hom in 2 Tim* 3 who, moralizing on 2 Tim 2:13–18 in a catena of these dominical warnings from Matthew and Luke, calls Matt 7:23 'that awful sentence' and Matt 25:40 'that fearful word.'
6 Cf Chrysostom *Hom in 2 Tim* 3 (on 2 Tim 2:13) PG 62 625 / NPNF 492b: 'If we believe not that He rose again, He is not injured by it. He is faithful and unshaken, whether we say so or not. If then He is not at all injured by our denying Him, it is for nothing else than for our benefit that He desires our confession.'
7 and handle] Added in 1532. The verb is taken from the Vulgate which translates the Greek verb ὀρθοτομοῦντα by *recte tractantem* 'rightly handle.' In his Latin version Erasmus had translated the Greek literally by *recte sectantem* 'rightly dividing,' which he paraphrased in the 1519–1523 editions by 'you divide ... with right judgment.' His literal translation was severely criticized, chiefly by Zúñiga; see the annotation on 2 Tim 2:15 (*recte tractantem*) LB VI 955D and *Apologia ad annotationes Stunicae* ASD IX-2 230–3. The addition in 1532 was probably influenced by this criticism.
8 Paul urges Timothy to avoid profane and empty talk ('godless chatter' RSV). Specifying this chatter as disputations (*disceptationes*) is congruent with 1 Tim 1:6–7 and 6:20, where the *Paraphrase* defines this kind of talk as meaningless speculation and condemns the interpretation of Scripture through philosophical or dialectical arguments of the kind developed in the medieval universities. Cf Kelly *Pastoral Epistles* 184 who similarly takes the adjective βεβήλους 'profane, godless' in 3:16 to be the equivalent of 'substituting human speculation for divine revelation.'

47

9 Erasmus translated the Greek word γάγγραινα 'gangrene' in 2:17 by the Latin word *cancer*. Calvin later criticized him for confusing gangrene with cancer (cf Spicq *Epîtres pastorales* II 756). However, the Latin term *cancer* was used not only to denote cancer, but also gangrene, canker, and similar ulcerous infections, so that it is not really clear whether in using the word *cancer* Erasmus meant 'gangrene' or 'cancer,' if we may assume that he was aware of the difference. Since he has just compared verbal disputation to a spreading poison, I have given him the benefit of the doubt. As he remarks in his annotation on 2:17 (*ut cancer serpit*) LB VI 956E, 'The disease feeds on the place it has occupied and must, therefore, be immediately checked.'

10 Hymenaeus is mentioned in 1 Tim 1:20, Philetus only here in 2:17. We know nothing of either individual or of their teaching beyond what is said in 2 Tim 2:18, the interpretation of which is itself unclear. Fee *2 Timothy* 257 and Kelly *Pastoral Epistles* 185 assume that by 'resurrection' Paul means the mystical death and rebirth experienced in baptism, a doctrine which he himself proclaimed (cf Rom 6:1–11). Erasmus' interpretation probably comes from Ambrosiaster *Comm in 2 Tim* 2:18 CSEL 81/3 307:6–7: 'They ... said that the resurrection was made in (one's) sons.' The origin of this belief is obscure but it already existed in the second century; see Walter Lock *A Critical and Exegetical Commentary on the Pastoral Epistles* (New York 1924) 99–100 and Fee *2 Timothy* 259, who cite as evidence *The Acts of Paul and Thecla* 14, a work which Erasmus did not know.

11 This point is made by Chrysostom *Hom in 2 Tim* 5 (on 2 Tim 2:18) PG 62 626–627 / NPNF 493b.

12 The word 'everyone' in the biblical text of 2:19 (*omnis* in Latin) is omitted here in the paraphrase, either by Erasmus when writing it or by the typesetter of the first edition. The 1538 edition, incorrectly, changes the verb to the plural, 'who confess.'

13 'Christ' (Χριστοῦ) is the reading of Erasmus' Greek text in 2:19; however, he knows that other Greek manuscripts had the reading Κυρίου 'Lord,' which he in fact preferred. See the annotation on 2:19 (*qui invocat nomen*) LB VI 957C.

48

14 Cf Chrysostom *Hom in 2 Tim* 6 (on 2 Tim 2:21) PG 62 630 / NPNF 496a–b, for the contrast between the material of the vessel and the intention of the person.

15 Cf Isa 42:2 and *Ratio* Holborn 223.

16 to be ready] 1519–23. The 1532 edition reads 'is ready,' but it is evident that all of the adjectives in this sentence – 'pugnacious, calm, gentle, ready, lenient, irritable' – should modify the noun 'servant,' and I have emended the text accordingly.

Chapter 3

49

1 Cf Matt 24:11–22 and *Ratio* Holborn 201.

2 This description is a recurrent feature of Erasmus' view of the mendicant orders in his own time. See, for example, *Ratio* Holborn 256 where Erasmus applies the parable of the blasted fig tree (Matt 21:19) to those 'who under the pretext of piety are in fact impious and while using their titles and garb as evidence of their religion live irreligious lives'. In *Ratio* Holborn 250–1, after quoting 2 Tim 3:2–6 as evidence of how destructive the false pretence of godliness or piety is to genuine godliness, Erasmus goes on to say, 'I ask you, dear reader, do you not think that [Paul] is pointing his finger directly at certain members from the orders of those who, though totally caught up in the affairs of the world, call themselves monks and throw a cloak of mendicancy over their avid pursuit of regal luxury, glory, and tyranny?' Two side-notes in Greek were added to the March 1520 editions opposite the paraphrase on verses 6 and 8: 'Hearken, beggar-tyrant' and 'Beware, beggar-tyrant.' These side-notes were probably written by Erasmus for inclusion in the second edition (they do not appear in the March 1521 and later editions); even if they are not from his hand, they nevertheless indicate that contemporary readers understood the point of his description. See also the satirical description of the monkish concern with dress and titles in the *Moriae encomium* ASD IV-3 160:538–56 / CWE 27 131.

3 The punctuation in the 1519–1523 editions require the phrase 'of their features' to be taken with the noun 'severity'; the punctuation is changed in the 1532 edition to make the phrase go with the following noun 'paleness.' This change is clearly an error, whether made by Erasmus or the typesetter; it is corrected in the 1538 and 1540 editions.

4 Cf Chrysostom *Hom in 2 Tim* 8 (on 2 Tim 3:6) PG 62 644 / NPNF 505b for the characterization of women who are always in pursuit of some novelty, and Ambrosiaster *Comm in 2 Tim* 3:6 CSEL 81/3 312:4–15 for some of the details in this portrait of the sham teachers. In Ambrosiaster these pseudo-teachers are Manichees, but Erasmus avoids this kind of anachronism.

50

5 Iambres is the spelling found in the Greek text, Mambres in the Vulgate, of the second name in the series 'Iannes and Iambres.' The peculiar combination found in the *Paraphrase* is the reading of the first edition. It was corrected to 'Iannes and Iambres,' following the Greek text, in the 1520 edition, but was evidently overlooked when the text of the first edition was being corrected for the March 1521 edition. It was then left unchanged in all subsequent editions. In his annotation on 3:8 (*Iamnes et Mambres*) LB VI 959D Erasmus commented that the two forms 'Iambres and Mambres' apparently have the same meaning. This combination of the two names in the annotation may have led him inadvertently to use it in the paraphrase. His belief that the two Hebrew words, Iambres and Mambres, had the same meaning was to be attacked later by Zúñiga (cf *Apologia ad annotationes Stunicae* ASD IX-2 234), but this seems an unlikely reason for Erasmus to have left the text unaltered. The reading 'Iambres and Mambres' in the 1521 and later editions is probably an unnoticed error.

6 Erasmus thought the term 'folly' in 3:9 denoted a form of mental illness; cf the annotation cited in the preceding note. Nothing is known of the fate of the magicians who opposed Moses, either from the OT or elsewhere, so that

Erasmus' description is only surmise, motivated perhaps by Chrysostom's observation that all such trickery is eventually exposed (*Hom in 2 Tim* 8 (on 2 Tim 3:9) PG 62 644 / NPNF 506a).

7 This is a paraphrase on the word παρηκολούθησας 'you have carefully followed' (NKJ), 'observed' (RSV), which Erasmus thought implied that 'you were present with me from the beginning to the end and are an eyewitness of everything'; cf the annotation on 2 Tim 3:10 (*assecutus es*) LB VI 959E.

8 Cf Acts 13:50, 14:5 and 19.

9 Cf 1 Cor 11:1, but Erasmus probably has 2 Cor 11:12–15 and 23–9 in mind.

10 For this interpretation see Ambrosiaster *Comm in 2 Tim* 3:13 CSEL 81/3 314:8–10): 'The deceivers will be punished not only because of their own errors but also because of the errors of those whom they ruin by their example.'

51

11 'All of Scripture': *tota Scriptura*, which Erasmus in his annotation on 3:16 (*utilis est*) LB VI 959F calls 'canonical Scripture,' meaning, presumably, the entire Bible

12 This is not a rhetorical flourish. Erasmus explains in his annotation on 3:16 (*utilis est*) LB VI 959F that the phrase 'given by inspiration of God' contains an implicit argument in which divine inspiration is contrasted with 'man-made doctrine.' Human speech is ineffective compared to the efficacy of the word of God.

13 'Simply,' because they do not have the ulterior motives of the false teachers

Chapter 4

1 In the phrases 'by his coming' and, below, 'by the kingdom' Erasmus follows the Vulgate rather than his Greek text and Latin version of 4:1, in which the phrases 'at his coming' and 'at his kingdom' both modify the verb 'will judge.' Compare DR with AV.

2 will be able] *poterit* 1519–1538. The 1540 edition and LB read *possit* 'might be able.'

52

3 Cf Ambrosiaster *Comm in 2 Tim* 4:5 CSEL 81/3 316:19–21: 'Paul calls his suffering an offering (*delibatio*); for he who suffers for God's righteousness is being sacrificed (*immolatur*) to him.' Erasmus' use of the term *immolari* 'sacrifice' as a translation of the Greek verb σπένδομαι 'pour out in a libation' was called into question by Zúñiga; see *Apologia ad annotationes Stunicae* ASD IX-2 234–6. But neither Zúñiga nor Erasmus appear to be familiar with the actual ritual of the libation.

4 'The just judge': *iustus iudex*. The term 'righteousness' in the phrase 'crown of righteousness' (NKJ) is, as usual, paraphrased as the 'crown owed to innocence' (*innocentia*).

5 This point is made by Chrysostom *Hom in 2 Tim* 9 (on 2 Tim 4:8) PG 62 653 / NPNF 512a): 'Here also [Paul] uplifts him. If "to all," much more to Timothy. But he did not say "and to thee," but "to all"; meaning, if to all, much more to him.'

53

6 Chrysostom *Hom in 2 Tim* 10 (on 2 Tim 4:9) PG 62 655 / NPNF 513a suggests this as one of the reasons why Paul sends for Timothy.

7 This explanation likewise occurs in Chrysostom ibidem.

8 Chrysostom *Hom in 2 Tim* 10 (on 2 Tim 4:11) PG 62 655 / NPNF 513b observes: 'For [Luke] adhered to him inseparably.'

9 The meaning of the Greek in 4:13 is obscure, but Erasmus' guess may be correct; cf Fee *2 Timothy* 295. This verse triggered one of Erasmus' typical outbursts: 'Behold the furnishings of the Apostle! A cloak to keep off the rain and a few books, holy ones no doubt. Nowadays what a train of horses, cannons, and other things I am reluctant to mention [accompany a bishop]' (see the annotation on 2 Tim 4:13 [*et membranas*] LB VI 962D).

10 Erasmus adopts the future indicative found in the Vulgate (and in the better Greek manuscripts) in place of the optative mood which he found in his Greek text of 4:14; compare 'May the Lord repay' NKJ with 'The Lord will requite' RSV. He does not explain why. A possible reason is that he wanted to avoid the implication that Paul might wish ill to an opponent; cf the annotations on 2 Tim 4:14 (*reddet illi dominus*) LB VI 962E and on Acts 23:1 (*percutiat te deus*) ibidem 521E. That Paul might curse an opponent would contradict the assertions about Paul's character made in the paraphrase on 1:16 above.

11 In Rome, after the journey narrated in Acts 27–8; see the Argument on 2 Timothy n2.

12 Ambrosiaster *Comm in 2 Tim* 4:16 CSEL 81/3 318:21 calls desertion of this kind *consuetudo* 'customary behaviour.'

13 of the ungodly] Added in 1532

14 Cf Acts 18:2–4.

15 Erasmus applies to the household of Onesiphorus what he says of the man himself in the paraphrase on 1:16–17. Modern commentators assume that Onesiphorus was dead at the time this letter was written; see Fee *2 Timothy* 237–8 and Kelly *Pastoral Epistles* 171.

16 Linus (4:21) is omitted, probably through an oversight on Erasmus' part, since there does not appear to be any reason for a deliberate omission.

54

17 See the paraphrase on 1 Tim 6:21.

PARAPHRASE ON TITUS

Argument

56

1 Cf chapter 3 n21 below.

2 Chrysostom *Hom in Titum* 1 (on Titus 1:1–4) PG 62 664 / NPNF 519b–520a observes that Paul's failure to mention any of his trials implies that he was at liberty and not in prison, while the intention to spend the winter in Nicopolis suggests that the Epistle to Titus was written before the Second Epistle to Timothy.

3 Cf Homer *Iliad* 2:649.
4 'Pattern' (*formam*) is the word used by the Vulgate to translate ὑποτύπωσις in 2 Tim 1:13.
5 he himself] *ipse* 1532. The earlier editions read *Paulus* 'Paul.'

Chapter 1

1 'Shortest way': *compendio*; cf the *Paraphrase* on 1 Tim 1:4 n18.

57
2 Cf 1 Cor 9:16–17.
3 Erasmus probably omits the word 'mercy' deliberately. It is found in his Greek text (cf AV), but not in the Vulgate. He considered it to be a later addition to the text; see the annotation on Titus 1:4 (*gratia et pax*) LB VI 966B.
4 there] Added in 1532
5 The inference that Paul had already initiated the mission in Crete is drawn from the prefix ἐπί in the verb ἐπιδιορθώσῃ 'you should set in order.' In the annotation on Titus 1:5 (*quae desunt corrigas*) LB VI 966C, Erasmus comments on this verb, '[Paul] means that he set some things in order first; he tells Titus to set in order these same things which have not yet been completely set in order,' and cites Jerome *Comm in Titum* (on Titus 1:5) PL 26 561C–562A to support this view. (Erasmus also claims that Chrysostom's exegesis of 1:5 [*Hom in Titum* 2 PG 62 671 / NPNF 524a] agrees with this interpretation of the prefix, but the claim is questionable.)
6 Cf the Argument n3.
7 The anacoluthon is due to Erasmus. He is following the sentence structure of the original closely.
8 both] Omitted in the 1540 edition and in LB

59
9 Cf the Argument of 1 Timothy 4 above. Chrysostom *Hom in Titum* 2 (on Titus 1:7) PG 62 672 / NPNF 525a thought that a bishop should rule with the consent of his flock and share his counsels with them.
10 'Stiff-necked' (*praefractus*) is Erasmus' translation of αὐθάδης 'self-willed' which the Vulgate renders by *superbus* 'proud.' The translation was criticized by Zúñiga, but Erasmus defended it, arguing that 'a person who is overly pleased with himself and holds to his own point of view more than is right is called αὐθάδης. The *praefractus* does not listen to what other people have to say' (*Apologia ad annotationes Stunicae* ASD IX-2 236:179–92; cf also the annotation on Titus 1:7 (*non superbum*) LB VI 966E).
11 The requirement that the candidate be *non vinosum* 'not given to wine' is omitted in the paraphrase, probably by an oversight on Erasmus' part.
12 Jerome *Comm in Titum* (on 1:7) PL 26 567B–C argues that the word πλήκτην (a 'striker' AV, 'violent' RSV, that is, a person given to using his fists) referred to tongue-lashing, not physically hitting someone. See the paraphrase on 1 Tim 3:3, Erasmus' annotation on this verse (*non litigiosum*) LB VI 934E and his annotation on Titus 1:7 (*non percussorem*) LB VI 966E.
13 and to be a lover of good men] Added in 1532. Cf the annotation on Titus

1:8 (*benignum*) LB VI 967C where Erasmus offers alternative translations of the adjective φιλάγαθον 'a lover of what is good' (NKJ), 'a lover of goodness' (RSV): *studiosum bonarum rerum* 'a pursuer of good things' and *amantem bonos* 'one who loves good persons.' He adopts the former in his Latin version, but combines both meanings in the revised paraphrase.

14 'Deceivers of minds': *mentium seductores.* Jerome *Comm in Titum* 1:10 PL 26 570B translates the word φρεναπάται by *mentium deceptores* 'deceivers of minds,' which Erasmus cites in the annotation on this verse (*seductores*) LB VI 967F. The paraphrase combines the translation *seductores* of the Vulgate with Jerome's rendering of the Greek.

15 such persons] 1532. The earlier editions read 'them.'

60

16 This identification of the anonymous prophet is made by Chrysostom *Hom in Titum* 3 (on Titus 1:12) PG 62 676 / NPNF 528a and Jerome *Comm in Titum* PL 26 571C–572A. Jerome says, 'This verse is said to be found in the oracles of the Cretan prophet Epimenides whom [Paul] called a prophet ... because he wrote about oracles and responses (from the gods) of the kind that announce in advance the future itself and predict long beforehand that which is going to come.' Jerome goes on to say that the title of Epimenides' work was *Oracles*. Erasmus' use just below of the word oracle suggests that he is drawing upon Jerome directly though the identification also appears in Aquinas *Exp in epist ad Titum* lect 3 648b and the other medieval commentators who, along with Jerome, seek to explain why Paul called Epimenides a prophet; cf Fee *Titus* 179–80 and Kelly *Pastoral Epistles* 235. For a complete study of these texts see Felix Jacoby *Die Fragmente der griechischen Historiker*, Dritter Teil, b, Kommentar zu Nr 297–607 (Leiden 1955) No 457, 308–30, especially 321–2.

17 'Harmful beasts': *noxiae bestiae.* In the annotation on Titus 1:12 (*malae bestiae*) LB VI 968D Erasmus comments, 'The Greek word θήρια does not mean simply 'beasts' but 'wild and poisonous beasts.' To support this interpretation of the word, he cites the title of Nicander's *Theriaca*, a poem about poisonous snakes, scorpions, spiders, and the like.

18 Erasmus follows Jerome *Comm in Titum* PL 26 575 in alluding here to Matt 15:1–11. The list of Jewish carnal practices recurs elsewhere. Cf eg the paraphrases on Gal 4:10 and 5:3 (CWE 42 116–7 and 122), Phil 3:18 (LB VII 1000F–1001A), and on 1 Tim 4:3 above. However, the addition of the 'seven-day impurity of the house' (Lev 14:33–40) suggests that Erasmus is in part following Ambrosiaster *Comm in Titum* 1:14 CSEL 81/3 326:14–6 whose list includes 'foods, spouses [that is, the regulations on intercourse, menstruation, childbirth etc.], new moons, weasel's blood, the house unclean for seven days.'

19 Jerome *Comm in Titum* 1:13–14 PL 26 575 cites Col 2:21 and makes the same contrast between Jewish shadows and evangelical truth.

20 The identification of the 'defiled and unbelieving' in Titus 1:15 with the Jews and the paraphrase on 1:15–16 follow for the most part Chrysostom's explication of these verses (*Hom in Titum* 3 PG 62 679–680 / NPNF 529b–530b). Erasmus' attitude towards Jews and Judaism ranged from indifference to the outright dislike which appears in passages like this one.

Modern assessments of his attitude vary; see Guido Kisch *Erasmus' Stellung zu Juden und Judentum* Philosophie und Geschichte 83/84 (Tübingen 1969), Harry S. May *The Tragedy of Erasmus: A Psychohistoric Approach* (Saint Charles, Mo 1975), and Shimon Markish *Erasmus and the Jews* (Chicago-London 1986; first published in Russian in 1971 and then in French in 1979). For Chrysostom see Robert L. Wilken *John Chrysostom and the Jews: Rhetoric and Reality in the Late 4th Century* (Berkeley 1983).

21 Cf Rom 2:29.
22 and] Added in 1532

61

23 Cf Lev 19:19.
24 mortals] Added in 1532

Chapter 2

1 Jerome *Comm in Titum* 2:2 PL 26 578B observes that the Greek word νηφαλίους can mean either 'sober' or 'vigilant.' His observation is cited in Erasmus' annotation on this verse (*sobrios*) LB VI 968F. The paraphrase incorporates both meanings.

2 Chrysostom *Hom in Titum* 4 (on Titus 2:2) PG 62 681–682 / NPNF 531 lists among the typical characteristics of old age slowness, timidity, forgetfulness, insensibility, and irritability, in a passage which Erasmus summarizes in his annotation on the word σώφρονας (*prudentes*) in this verse LB VI 969B.

3 The Vulgate translates the adjective σεμνός 'dignified, serious' in the Epistles to Timothy and Titus by *pudicus* 'modest, chaste' and its corresponding noun σεμνότης by *castitas* 'chastity.' This sexual interpretation of these words is also advanced by Jerome; see eg his *Comm in Titum* 2:2 PL 26 578B. Hence while Erasmus' paraphrase could describe any kind of youthful behaviour which is unseemly in an older person, he probably expected his reader to understand it as unseemly sexual activity. For his view of 'May-December' marriages see the colloquy, 'A Marriage in Name Only, or, The Unequal Match' in Thompson *Colloquies* 401–12.

4 persons] The 1520 editions correct this to 'women.'

5 Chrysostom *Hom in Titum* 4 (on Titus 2:3) PG 62 683 / NPNF 532a, after describing the deleterious effects of wine on the brain of the elderly, remarks, 'Because of the weakness of this age wine is necessary to it, but not much is required.'

6 By coquetry (*lenocinium*) Erasmus means apparel, cosmetics, and behaviour designed to attract the notice of men; see the paraphrase on 1 Tim 2:9 and his annotation on Titus 2:3 (*bene docentes*) LB VI 969C: 'I think [Paul says this] because some women at that age are procuresses, servants to another's wickedness.'

7 to be prudent] The 1520–1522 editions read 'to be sober-minded' at this point and omit this phrase later in the sentence. The March 1521 edition, following the order in the NT, inserts 'to be sober-minded' at the correct place in the sentence, but leaves the first occurrence of the phrase before 'to cherish their husbands.' Instead of deleting the first occurrence of 'to be

sober-minded' to avoid the repetition, it was emended to 'to be prudent' in the 1523 editions. If this change was made by Erasmus, as seems likely, then he was evidently correcting the *Paraphrase* without reference to the original text of the New Testament.

62

8 The comparison is made by Jerome *Comm in Titum* 2:5 PL 26 582B: 'Even pagan women serve their men under the common law of nature.'

9 Cf Chrysostom *Hom in Titum* 4 (on Titus 2:6) PG 62 684 / NPNF 532b–533a: 'For nothing is so difficult for that age as to overcome unlawful pleasures. For neither the love of wealth, nor the desire of glory, nor any other thing so much solicits the young, as fleshly lust.'

10 The phrase 'above all' and the adjective 'every' in 'every duty of godliness' are apparently intended to paraphrase 'in all things' in the original text of 2:7. Erasmus follows Chrysostom *Hom in Titum* 4 PG 62 684 / NPNF 533a in construing this phrase with 'showing yourself' rather than Jerome *Comm in Titum* 2:6 PL 26 582C who takes it with 'to be sober-minded.'

11 The adjective ἀκατάγνωστον in 2:8 has two meanings, 'cannot be censured' (RSV) or 'cannot be condemned' (NKJ, NIV), and 'cannot be despised.' Erasmus, following the Vulgate, adopts the former meaning in his Latin version, which is also the interpretation found in modern translations and commentaries. In the *Paraphrase* he adopts the latter meaning, probably following what he says about the Greek word in his annotation on it (*irreprehensibile*) LB VI 970B: '[This word] can also mean "such that he cannot be despised," that is, that Titus teach with authority.'

12 This jaundiced observation may be an allusion to the case of Onesimus (see the Argument of the Epistle to Philemon), a reflection of the portrait of servants in Greek and Roman literature, especially in comedy, or simply Erasmus' personal view of household servants.

13 This point is made by Chrysostom *Hom in Titum* 4 (on Titus 4:10) PG 62 685 / NPNF 533b: 'When therefore it is seen that the power of religion, imposing a restraint upon a class naturally so self-willed, has rendered them singularly well-behaved and gentle, their masters, however unreasonable they may be, will form a high opinion of our doctrines.'

14 'God [and] Saviour' *Dei [et] salvatoris* is the reading of the Vulgate, Ambrosiaster *Comm in Titum* CSEL 81/3 329:27 (Erasmus apparently had a text which read *salvatoris* rather than *salutaris*), and Jerome *Comm in Titum* PL 26 586B–C in 2:11. Erasmus' Greek text reads 'the grace of God that brings salvation.' In following the Vulgate in the paraphrase rather than his Greek text Erasmus may be seeking to avoid unnecessary conflict with critics, Lee in particular, who asserted (wrongly, in fact) that Erasmus' Greek manuscripts were corrupt in this verse; cf the annotation on Titus 2:11 (*dei et salvatoris*) LB VI 970E and the *Responsio ad annotationes Lei* LB IX 228D–E.

63

15 when, at the end of this age ... shines forth] March 1521. The 1520 editions, and presumably the missing part of the first edition, read 'when God and our Saviour Jesus Christ will appear, no longer humble but glorious.'

16 This attribution to the Father of the humiliation undergone by the Son is

probably not deliberate, but the result of careless rewriting of the original sentence. See the preceding note.

17 Erasmus follows Ambrosiaster, who virtually alone among the early church Fathers understands the phrase 'our great God and Saviour Jesus Christ' to refer to the Father and the Son separately and not just to Jesus. This position involved Erasmus in endless controversy, especially with Lee, Sancho Carranza, and a group of Spanish monks; cf the annotation on Titus 2:13 (*magni dei et salvatoris*) LB VI 971C; *Responsio ad annotationes Lei* LB IX 273B–274B; *Apologia ad Carranzam* LB IX 411D–412C; and *Apologia adversus monachos* LB IX 1043C. Modern scholars are equally at odds over the meaning of the phrase; cf Fee *Titus*, Kelly *Pastoral Epistles*, and Spicq *Epîtres pastorales* on 2:13, and Murray J. Harris, 'Titus 2:13 and the Deity of Christ' *Pauline Studies: Essays Presented to Professor F.F. Bruce on His 70th Birthday* edited by Donald A. Hagner and Murray J. Harris (Exeter and Grand Rapids, Mich 1980) 262–77.

18 Cf Ambrosiaster *Comm in Titum* 2:13 CSEL 81/3 330:23–5: 'Christ redeemed us to this end, that pursuing a pure life and filled with good works we can be heirs of the kingdom of God.' Cf also 3:7 n11 below.

Chapter 3

1 The paragraphing of the Byzantine Greek manuscripts places 2:15 with 3:1 rather than with 2:14, and this arrangement, which also appears in Chrysostom *Hom in Titum* 5 PG 62 697 / NPNF 537 may have led Erasmus to place the verse in chapter 3 in the *Paraphrase*. In the *Novum Testamentum* it is placed with chapter 2 as in the Vulgate and the earlier Greek manuscripts.

2 Cf Jerome *Comm in Titum* 2:15b PL 26 589–590, summarized in part in Erasmus' annotation on this verse (*nemo te contemnat*) LB VI 972C. Jerome's point, and probably Erasmus' also, is that good order in the laity depends upon good order in the clergy. Misconduct on the part of the clergy produces contempt in place of respect and deference.

64

3 See the paraphrase on 2:9 above.

4 to remember] Added in 1532. The 1520 editions read 'to understand.' The 1521–1523 editions, and presumably the first edition, omit the infinitive and read 'Remind those ... confessed Christ that...'

5 those men] 1532. The earlier editions read 'they.'

6 the treasury] 1532. The 1520–1523 editions read 'but the treasury.'

7 interceded even] 1532. The 1520–1523 editions read 'even interceded.'

8 Cf 1 Cor 13:7.

65

9 the Father] Added in 1532. In his annotation on Titus 3:4 (*et humanitas*) LB VI 972D Erasmus stated that the words 'God our Saviour' in this verse referred to the Father rather than to the Son. Edward Lee took exception to this comment and insisted that the reference was to the Trinity. Erasmus, fol-

lowing the lead of Ambrosiaster *Comm in Titum* CSEL 81/3 332:4–6 and Jerome *Comm in Titum* PL 26 593C who argued that all three persons of the Trinity were referred to in these sentences, responded that the sequence of the thought in 3:4–6 with the mention, first, of God, and then of the Son and the Spirit required a threefold distinction between Father, Son, and Holy Spirit; cf the *Responsio ad annotationes Lei* LB IX 238E–239B. The addition of the words 'the Father' here and 'his Son' below are evidently designed to make this interpretation clear.

10 his Son] Added in 1532. See the preceding note.

11 Ambrosiaster *Comm in Titum* 3:7 332:4–8 says in effect that we are reborn and receive the Holy Spirit in order to obtain the inheritance of the kingdom of heaven through the support of good works (*bonis operibus inniti*) and the aid of Christ. Cf his comment on 2:14, cited in chapter 2 n18 above.

66

12 as] The two 1520 editions do not have this 'as' and read instead 'but will also be useful.'

13 Cf the paraphrase on James 3:7.

14 or, more accurately, battles] 1532. The 1520 editions read 'and empty battles'; the 1521–1523 editions 'and battles rather.'

15 The examples of Moses' tomb and, below, weasel's blood appear in Ambrosiaster *Comm in Titum* 3:9 CSEL 333:5–6, Methusalah's age and Rehoboam's birth in Jerome *Comm in Titum* PL 26 596B. The prohibition against eating pork is Erasmus' own contribution to these lists; it is a specific example of what he usually refers to as 'discrimination among foods.' The prohibition against eating swine's flesh seems to have been especially obnoxious to him; see the paraphrase on Hebrews 10:28. Similar lists of 'curious questions' pursued by later theologians occur in a lengthy annotation on 1 Tim 1:6 (cf Rummel, *Annotations* 143–6) and in the *Ratio* Holborn 297:12–301:9. At one point in the latter work Erasmus remarks, 'It often happens, when someone is investigating everything speculatively (*curiose*) rather than piously, that arguments occur to him which to some extent undermine and rock the strong foundations of faith' (299:12–14). The entire approach and the assumptions on which it rests are satirized in the *Moriae encomium* ASD IV-3 146–50; see especially the citation from Lister's commentary on 146 n395. For the criticism of such *curiosa* or fruitless speculations in late medieval theology see H A. Oberman 'Contra vanam curiositatem. Ein Kapitel der Theologie zwischen Seelenwinkel und Weltall' *Theologische Studien* 133 (Zürich 1974).

16 Such queries ... to investigate] Added in 1532. This correction of the text is referred to in the *Loca quaedam in aliquot Erasmi lucubrationibus per ipsum emendata* (Basel: Hieronymus Froben, Johann Herwagen and Nicholaus Bischof 1529) 320, where Erasmus remarks that it was made 'on account of slanderers,' by which he evidently means one or more of his critics.

17 Cf on 1:14 above.

67

18 Erasmus follows the rendering of the Vulgate *correptio* 'rebuke, censure,'

though he points out in his annotation on Titus 3:9 (*et genealogias*) LB VI
973C that 'admonition' is a better translation, an opinion which he probably
took from Jerome; see *Comm in Titum* 3:11 PL 26 597C.

19 This point occurs in Jerome *Comm in Titum* 3:11 PL 26 597D who observes
that the person who thinks that it is really his own corrector who is in error
gets himself ready for a battle of words and wants to win his teacher over
to his own side.

20 This explanation likewise occurs in Jerome *Comm in Titum* 3:12 PL 26 598B,
as does the image of the abandoned and orphaned Crete in the next sentence.

21 Jerome in the introduction to his *Commentary on Titus* PL 26 556A and in his
comment on 3:12 ibidem 598C says that this Nicopolis was the city which
Augustus founded in the district of Epirus in western Greece to commem-
orate his victory over Mark Antony and Cleopatra in the battle of Actium
in 31 BC. The Greek tradition, however, beginning with Chrysostom *Hom in
Titum* 6 (on Titus 3:12) PG 62 696 / NPNF 541a, locates Nicopolis in Thrace
in northeastern Greece. Chrysostom probably means Nicopolis on the
Nestos in southeastern Bulgaria near modern Nevrokopion. Theophylact,
however, identifies it with the Nicopolis on the Danube (modern Nikopol
in Bulgaria). Erasmus' identification of Nicopolis here as a city in Thrace
thus comes either from Chrysostom or from Theophylact. He has either
forgotten that in the Argument he followed Jerome or he may have thought
that Illyria was part of Thrace. In an annotation on 3:12 (*Nicopolis*) LB VI
974D, added in the 1522 edition of the *Novum Testamentum*, after citing
Chrysostom's opinion, Erasmus states: 'Nicopolis, a city of Thrace, [named]
from the victory which Augustus won over Cleopatra, as Jerome indicates.
Theophylact wrote that it was on the Danube river.' The geography is corrected in a revised version of this annotation in the 1535 edition of the
Novum Testamentum, but Erasmus refrains from trying to choose among the
three locations. Modern commentators are inclined to agree with Jerome;
see Spicq *Epîtres pastorales* II 690.

22 This interpretation of the term 'lawyer' in 3:13 is found in Ambrosiaster
Comm in Titum 3:13 CSEL 81/3 334:13–15, Chrysostom *Hom in Titum* 6 PG 62
696 / NPNF 541a, and Theophylact *Exp in Titum* PG 125 170B. Erasmus fuses
it with the view of Jerome *Comm in Titum* PL 26 598D that Zenas was carrying out the same task as Apollos, to edify the churches of Christ. Nothing is
known about Zenas, and modern scholars are inclined to think that he was
more likely a practitioner of Greek or Roman law than an expert in the law
of Moses; cf Fee *Titus* 215 and Kelly *Pastoral Epistles* 258.

23 Cf Acts 18:24, 'an eloquent man, and mighty in the Scriptures.'

24 Cf the *Paraphrase* on Acts 15:3 LB VII 726C, where Erasmus explains the
words 'being sent on their way' as referring to an escort done 'for the sake
of respect (*honor*).' Cicero *De senectute* 63, though not referring specifically
to escorting arriving or departing travellers, calls such activities 'marks of
respect' (*honorabilia*).

25 but only] Added in the 1532 edition. Jerome *Comm in Titum* PL 26 599 uses
Titus 3:14 as a proof-text for the obligation of the laity to support the
clergy, and is followed in this interpretation by the medieval commentators.
While not explicitly rejecting this use of the text, Erasmus evidently wants

to suggest that there are limits to what is due to the clergy. Cf Aquinas *Exp in epist ad Titum* c 3 lect 2 660.

68

26 Jerome *Comm in Titum* 3:15b PL 26 600A–B develops this antithesis between worldly and evangelical love at some length.

PARAPHRASE ON PHILEMON

Argument

70

1 In a paragraph added to the annotation on Philem 19 (*ego reddam*) LB VI 979C in the 1519 edition of the *Novum Testamentum*, Erasmus identifies the 'Greek Scholia,' and specifically Theodoret, as a source of this information about Philemon. The 'Scholia' evidently contained excerpts from Theodoret's *Interpretatio in xii epistulas sancti Pauli*, a work that Erasmus does not seem to have known in its complete form. The reference cited occurs in the Argument of the *Interpretatio epistulae ad Philemonem* PG 82 872A.

2 Cf *Adagia* I viii 36.

3 Cf Jerome *Comm in Philem* 18 PL 26 614C, Theodoret (see n1), and the Argument of Chrysostom's *Hom in Philem* PG 62 701 / NPNF 545 make this inference about Onesimus as do most modern commentators. It is an ancient figment which has become firmly embedded in the commentary tradition.

4 moreover] This is the reading of the 1520 and 1532 editions; the 1521–1523 editions read 'For he writes,' which is the text of the Argument in the editions of the *Novum Testamentum*. The sentence itself is a paraphrase on the subscription found in Erasmus' Greek manuscripts and appears at the end of the letter in the *Novum Testamentum*: '[The letter] was sent from Rome through Onesimus the slave.' See Metzger *Textual Commentary* 658. That Onesimus carried the letter to Philemon is quite likely.

5 In verse 10 the Vulgate and Erasmus translate τέκνον 'child' by *filius* 'son.'

Philemon

71

1 Cf the paraphrase on 2 Tim 1:8 and Ambrosiaster *Comm in Philem* 1 CSEL 81/3 337:14–16: 'Just as it is a scandal to be put in chains because of wrongdoing, so it is on the other hand the greatest glory to wear chains on behalf of Christ.'

2 sign] *insigne*. The 1520 editions read *insignia* 'insignia.' It is impossible to know whether the first edition, which is no longer extant for the *Paraphrase on Philemon*, read the singular *insigne* or the plural *insignia*; that is, to know whether an original plural was changed to the singular in the March 1521 edition or an original singular to the plural in the March 1520 editions. The singular *insigne* is used by Jerome *Comm in Philem* 1 PL 26 601C in reference

to the dove descending upon Jesus at his baptism as the special mark or sign that the Holy Spirit was in him. If Erasmus is using the word 'sign' in this sense, then he means that chains, that is, suffering for Christ, are the special sign of an apostle. The paradox that the imprisoned apostle is nevertheless free is consonant with Erasmus' conception of the philosophy of Christ in which what is folly in the eyes of the world is wisdom to God, but the paraphrase may also reflect Acts 28:31 where Paul is described as 'preaching the kingdom of God and teaching about the Lord Jesus Christ quite openly and unhindered.'

3 many, many] *pluribus* is the reading of the 1532 edition. The earlier editions read *suis* 'his.' The phrase *pluribus officiis* is also brought to the head of the clause in the 1532 edition, which gives it more emphasis; hence my translation.

4 'The service of the gospel' (*evangelica functio*) appears to mean the office of evangelist or preacher of the gospel. Erasmus views Philemon as a convert and co-worker, like Timothy and Titus, in the service of the gospel; see the paraphrase on verses 16-20, and the statement in the Argument that he was one of Paul's closest friends. There is, in fact, no evidence either in the Epistle or elsewhere that indicates where, when, or how Paul came to know Philemon; see F.F. Bruce *The Epistles to the Colossians, to Philemon, and to the Ephesians* (Grand Rapids, Mich 1984) 206.

5 This is the view of Chrysostom *Hom in Philem* 1 (on verse 2) PG 62 704 / NPNF 547b and of Aquinas *Exp in epist ad Philem* lect 1 662. Jerome *Comm in Philem* PL 26 607C seems to take the word 'sister' in its literal sense – 'to Appia, who has no trace of a false or feigned sisterliness (*germanitatis*) in her.' Erasmus combines the two interpretations of 'sister,' just as he combines his Greek text, which reads 'to our beloved Apphia' (AV) and the Vulgate, which reads 'our dearest sister' (DR).

6 Appia is the orthography of the Vulgate; Erasmus' Greek text and his Latin version have Apphia.

7 In his annotation on Philem 2 (*quae in domo tua est ecclesia*) LB VI 977D Erasmus comments, '[Paul], I believe, is thinking of the household; therefore, I have translated ἐκκλησία by *congregatio*. Chrysostom makes this clear in his explication.' (Chrysostom *Hom in Philem* 1 PG 62 705 / NPNF 547b explains the 'church' as the assembly of both slaves and masters in the house of Philemon.) 'Congregation,' therefore, means for Erasmus a small or house church, while *ecclesia* denotes the church of a city or the whole church; cf also the annotation on Col 4:15 (*et quae in domo eius est ecclesia*) LB VI 897D.

8 Erasmus means, 'I pray that God will increase his grace in you so that your faith may issue in even more and greater works of charity.' He has Gal 5:6 in mind and perhaps James 2:20.

9 Cf Acts 2:44 and *Adagia* I i 1: 'Friends have everything in common.'

72

10 Cf Matt 18:35.

11 Cf Chrysostom *Hom in Philem* 2 (on verse 9) PG 62 709 / NPNF 551a: 'How many things are here to shame him into compliance! – Paul, from the quality of his person, from his age, because he was old, and from what was

more just than all, because he was also "a prisoner of Jesus Christ."' Chrysostom, however, says nothing about the meaning of Paul's name but describes him as 'a combatant who has won a crown.' The focus on the name may have been suggested by Jerome *Comm in Philem* (on verse 1) PL 26 603–605 who offers there an elaborate analysis of the significance of the change of the apostle's name from Saul to Paul and contrasts the absence of the designation 'apostle' – a term of authority – found in the other letters with the seemingly shameful epithet 'prisoner' used in the salutation of the letter to Philemon.

12 Erasmus puns on the name *Paulus* and the Latin adjective *paulus* (little, small). In the annotation on Rom 1:1 (*Paulus*) LB VI 553A–C, Erasmus surveys the discussion of the meaning of the names Saul and Paul in Hebrew and Greek found in Ambrosiaster, Chrysostom, and Jerome, in the course of which he remarks that the Latin cognomen *Paulus* means 'small.' See the *Argument of the Epistle of Paul to the Romans*, CWE 42 6–7.

13 he] March 1521 and all subsequent editions. The March 1520 editions read 'I.'

14 The name Onesimus means 'useful, profitable.'

15 In an annotation on verse 12 (*illum ut mea viscera*) LB VI 978E added in the 1522 edition, Erasmus says, 'The addition, "my most dear son," made in many Latin manuscripts is not found in the Greek manuscripts, nor is there anything in Jerome's commentary from which one might conjecture that he read "most dear son." Perhaps the words were added by someone who wanted to explain the meaning of "that is, my own heart."' As elsewhere the *Paraphrase* combines the readings of both the Greek text and the Vulgate.

73

16 In effect, Onesimus has confessed his sin (*error fugae*), had it forgiven through baptism, and has made a good act of contrition. Paul will himself complete the required penance or satisfaction by offering to compensate Philemon for his financial loss.

17 Jerome *Comm in Philem* 15 PL 26 613C–614B develops an extended commentary on the thought, 'Sometimes evil is the occasion of good, and God turns the wicked plans of men into what is right.' Cf also Rom 8:28 and 11:33.

18 Jerome ibidem 614A remarks: 'No one is an eternal owner of his slave; for his power and the status of both persons are terminated by death. But Onesimus, who has been made eternal from his faith in Christ, after receiving the spirit of freedom, begins to be no longer a slave, but a brother in place of a slave, a most dear brother, an eternal brother of Philemon, who is also eternal because he too believed in Christ.' Chrysostom *Hom in Philem* 2 PG 62 711 / NPNF 552a, by contrast, interprets the words 'for ever' in verse 15 to mean that Onesimus will be a brother for the rest of his life and will not run away again.

19 Cf Gal 3:28.

20 As in the Argument Erasmus follows the interpretation invented by Jerome and Chrysostom (or their common source), but he ignores their more picturesque details such as that Onesimus had already squandered what he had stolen and consequently Paul had to promise to make it good rather than simply return the stolen property. The psychological touch – Paul's

suspicion here that Philemon is distressed – is a recurrent feature of the *Paraphrases*.

74

21 That is, the verb ὀνίνημι, 'to profit (from)'; cf verse 11. Erasmus may be the first commentator to see a pun between the name Onesimus and Paul's use of this verb; see the annotation on verse 20 (*ita frater*) LB VI 980B–C. Modern scholars dispute the existence of word-play here; see Friedrich Blass, Albert Debrunnner, Robert A. Funk *A Greek Grammar of the New Testament and Other Early Christian Literature* (Chicago-London 1961) §488 (259.1b), followed by Eduard Lohse *Colossians and Philemon* (Philadelphia 1971) 205. On the other hand, F.F. Bruce *The Epistles to the Colossians, to Philemon, and to the Ephesians* (Grand Rapids, Mich 1984) 221 believes that there is a deliberate pun. Bruce bases his argument in part on the appearance of what looks like a similar pun in Ignatius of Antioch, *Letter to the Ephesians* 2.2, where Bruce believes that Ignatius has *Philemon* 20 in mind. However, other scholars doubt this connection between the two letters; see William R. Schoedel, *Ignatius of Antioch: A Commentary on the Letters of Ignatius of Antioch* (Philadelphia 1985) 45. The first person singular, optative mood of the verb ὀνίνημι, meaning 'may I enjoy, let me enjoy,' was a conventional way of expressing polite interest, and was employed in ancient letter-writing (six times, for example, in the letters of Ignatius) and in other Greek literature, often with an ironical tone. Even though Paul employs the formula, he could still be making a play on the word, just as he does in verse 10 with the meaning of the name Onesimus. But whether it is a play on words or not, the addition of the phrase 'in the Lord' gives the formula a distinctly Pauline slant; see the following note.

22 Cf Jerome *Comm in Philem* 20 PL 26 615B: 'The Apostle enjoys only him who has in himself many, coherent virtues and all that Christ, for various reasons, is called – wisdom, righteousness, continence, gentleness, self-control, chastity ... And lest one think that he means that enjoyment with which we mutually delight one another, he has added "in the Lord," to make it clear that the enjoyment which someone has without the Lord is a quite different kind of enjoyment.'

23 Chrysostom *Hom in Philem* 3 (on verses 23–4) PG 62 716 / NPNF 556a likewise sees a rhetorical function in the addition of these names, but with a different focus: 'And from these he salutes him [that is, Philemon], urging him the more to obedience, and calls them his fellow labourers, and in this way shames him into granting the request.'

PARAPHRASE ON 1 PETER

Dedicatory Letter

76

1 The dedicatory letter (Ep 1112) is translated by R.A.B. Mynors, with minor revisions by JJB.

2 Erasmus had in fact dedicated to Wolsey in 1514 a translation of Plutarch; see Epp 284 and 297. On Erasmus' relations with Wolsey a few years before the present dedication see Cecil H. Clough 'Erasmus and the Pursuit of

English Royal Patronage in 1517 and 1518' *Erasmus of Rotterdam Society Yearbook One* (1981) 126–139.

3 Cf note 22 below.

4 That is, all except the Epistle to the Hebrews

5 Chiefly Edward Lee, whose *Annotationes in annotationes Noui Testamenti Desiderii Erasmi* appeared in February 1520. Erasmus responded immediately, first, with the *Apologia qua respondet invectivis Lei* (March 1520), and then with the *Responsio ad annotationes Lei* in two parts (April and May 1520). See *Opuscula* 225–34, the introduction to Ep 1080 in CWE 7 226, and, for details of the entire controversy with Lee, Rummel *Critics* II 98–9.

6 For this notion about the partial collapse of true religion, supported by the same appeal to the natural tendency of human institutions to deteriorate, see Ep 384:27–9, to Leo X, which serves as the preface to the *Novum instrumentum* of 1516.

77

7 See the translator's note xv n29.

8 See the translator's note xv n28.

9 The Latin means literally: 'The title (*titulus*) was almost entirely removed.' There is, strictly speaking, no actual title for Bede's commentary, which in the manuscript incipits to the different Epistles is variously called the *Expositio*, *Expositum*, *Tractatus*, or simply *In epistulam*. Even the prologue to the whole work seems to lack Bede's name, which thus appears only in the incipits and explicits. These, and the *Prologus*, are omitted in the *Glossa ordinaria* and with them all indication that Bede is the author of the excerpts taken from his commentaries. It is presumably this omission of any reference to Bede which Erasmus has in view here. Erasmus himself cites the commentaries in his annotations to the New Testament simply as 'Bede.'

10 1 Pet 3:19–20, 4:6

11 The passage in question is 2 Pet 2:11. In his commentary on this passage Bede *Exp 1 Pet* CCL 121 273:164–72 / Hurst 141 states that the word 'where' (*ubi* 'whereas' RSV) at the beginning of the verse implies that the angels 'in so far as they despise authority, are bold, pleasing themselves, create heresies (that is sects), and blaspheme. For by doing these things the angels deserved to become demons and to pay the penalty for their pride. For their spiritual nature did not allow them to be defiled by the impurity of bodily concupiscence, except perhaps that [Peter] implies that they are also to be judged for this when they entice human beings to it, just as also for the other evils they persuade humans to do.' See Bauckham *2 Peter* 261–3 for an elucidation of the difficulties of this verse.

12 2 Pet 2:4 (demons), 2:11 (accusation), 3:5 (earth consisting of water), 3:10 (destruction by fire)

13 Jude 9 and 14–15

14 Erasmus means that in Gen 5:18–24 nothing is said about Enoch being an author. Erasmus did not know *1 Enoch* directly and his information is derived from patristic commentaries; see the annotation on Jude 10 (*imperet tibi deus*) LB VI 1090E. For information about *1 Enoch* and *2 Enoch* see George W.E. Nickelsburg *Jewish Literature Between the Bible and the Mishnah* (Philadelphia 1987) *passim*.

15 Cf Jude 9 and 2 Pet 2:10–11. The literary relationship of the two Epistles has long been problematic. The current consensus is that Jude is prior to 2 Peter; see Bauckham *2 Peter* 138–43 and *passim*.

16 2 Pet 1:16–18

17 Cf Matt 17:1; Mark 9:2; Luke 9:28.

18 Jude 14–15. Doubts in antiquity about the canonicity of Jude are mentioned in Jerome *De viris illustribus* chapter 4, and Bede *Exp Iudae* CCL 121 340:219–341:233 / Hurst 249–50. Actually Jude was accepted in the late second century as an approved work and came under suspicion only later in the fourth century; see Harry Y. Gamble *The New Testament Canon* (Philadelphia 1985) 47–8 and 53, and for a detailed presentation of the evidence, J. Chaine *Les épîtres catholiques* (Paris 1939) 263–67.

19 See the paraphrase on Titus 1:12 n16.

20 Cf 1 Pet 5:12. In his annotation on this verse (*per Sylvanum*) LB VI 1056C Erasmus points out the words 'through Sylvanus' are ambiguous and could mean either that Sylvanus wrote a letter at Peter's direction or that Sylvanus carried the letter to the addressees. See Michaels *1 Peter* 306–8 for a discussion of modern attempts to deal with this phrase. Erasmus creates an additional, and probably unnecessary, difficulty by taking the Greek aorist ἔγραψα (*scripsi* in the Vulgate) to be a genuine rather than an epistolary past tense – that is, 'I wrote [a letter]' rather than 'I have written [the present short letter]' – and construing the clause 'as I consider' (NKJ) with the verb 'wrote' instead of with the words 'our faithful brother.'

78

21 1 Pet 5:13. Erasmus doubted this assumption, which is found as early as Papias and appears to have been accepted unanimously by later commentators; cf Selwyn *First Peter* 243–4 and 303–5. In the 1522 edition of the *Novum Testamentum* Erasmus added to his annotation on this verse (*in Babylone collecta*) LB VI 1056D the statement: 'Some take Babylon here to mean Rome, which to me at least is not entirely probable. I am inclined to think that Peter at that time really did live in Babylon.' This comment was criticized on various grounds. Erasmus was provoked into an extended reply in the 1535 edition of the *Novum Testamentum* and made a complete survey of the ancient evidence. He seems to have felt that a letter from Babylon was more congruent with the assumption that Peter evangelized the regions of Asia Minor mentioned in 1:1 than a letter from Rome would be. He also observes, correctly, that while 2 Peter 1:14–15 indicates that Peter is old and near death, there is no internal evidence for the date of 1 Peter.

22 Erasmus is probably referring to the six readerships in the Humanities established by Wolsey in 1518 at Oxford. Among the first holders of these positions were John Clement, a protégé of Thomas More, whom Erasmus had probably met five years earlier (see CEBR I 311–2), and Thomas Lupset, who was a good friend of Erasmus (see Ep 1087 and CEBR II 357).

Argument

80

1 subject to them] LB reads 'the subject people in their midst.'

2 Cf the dedicatory letter to Wolsey 77 n20.

3 that someone ... Rome] Added in the March 1521 edition; cf the annotation on 1 Pet 5:13 (*in Babylone collecta*) LB VI 1056D. The 'someone' is Erasmus himself. Whether or not this was his intention, his interpretation undercut one of the proof-texts for Peter's presence in Rome and thereby for the primacy of the Pope; cf CWE 7 425 n16.

Chapter 1

81

1 Ephesus was the chief city of the Roman province of Asia, which was only one part of the much larger area of Asia Minor.

2 The reference is not clear. Erasmus may have had in mind Nebuchad-nezzar's capture of Jerusalem (2 Kings 24:10–25:21) or the expulsions mentioned in 1 Macc 1:20–32 and Tacitus *Historiarum libri* 5.8. The second group, the others who were expelled 'in our time,' refers to the persecution which followed the death of Stephen (Acts 8:1); cf Bede *Exp 1 Pet* 1:1 CCL 121 225:22–4 / Hurst 70.

3 Cf Rom 1:16.

4 over which ... pride] Added in 1532

5 Cf Gal 3:7–14.

6 chooses] The 1538 and 1540 editions, followed by LB, read 'has chosen.'

7 nor is he compelled] LB reads 'as though he were compelled.'

82

8 Cf Heb 9:10–14 and Bede *Exp 1 Pet* 1:2 CCL 121 226:40–6 / Hurst 70–1.

9 'Reborn into him' (*in ipsum renatos*), that is, as members of the mystical body

10 bounty] *munificentia*, 1532. The earlier editions read *beneficentia* 'kindness.'

11 Cf Matt 25:27.

83

12 and lively] Added in 1532 to paraphrase the adjective 'living' in 1:3

13 he] *ille* 1532, probably to avoid using the name 'Christ' three times in close proximity. The early editions read *Christus* 'Christ.'

14 Cf Rom 5:12–19; Bede *Exp 1 Pet* 1:2 CCL 121 226:43 and 62 / Hurst 70–1 likewise alludes to this passage in Romans.

15 This paraphrase on the adjective 'undefiled' (RSV) may be influenced by Bede's comment on the adjective 'unfading' *Exp 1 Pet* 1:4 CCL 121 227:72–6 / Hurst 72: '... *unfading* because the heavenly way of life cannot at last become worthless in the minds of the blessed from long use, as the luxuries and delights of the present time sometimes become a cause for revulsion through daily habit and use.'

16 Cf Eph 1:13–14.

84

17 like people ... help] Added in the 1532 edition

18 The future tense follows the text of the Vulgate. The correction made in the

next sentence reflects the present tense in the Greek text. In his Latin version Erasmus takes the Greek verb in 1:8 to be a present indicative but points out in his annotation on it (*exsultabitis*) LB VI 1042D that it could also be an imperative. The paraphrase thus takes into account all three possibilities; cf Selwyn *First Peter* 258–9 and Michaels *1 Peter* 34.

19 Cf Bede *Exp 1 Pet* 1:7 CCL 121 228:115–28 / Hurst 74 who likewise cites Matt 25:34 in his commentary on 1:7.

85

20 full] *pleni*, 'full' modifying the subject 'you,' is the reading of the 1523, 1532, and later editions; the March 1521 edition reads *plenique* 'and full.' All the other editions have the adjective 'full' modifying the noun 'joy' and read *gaudio pleno gloriae* 'joy full of glory,' which is in fact closer to the text of 1:8 – *gaudio ... glorificato* – in Erasmus' Latin version.

21 furthermore] Added in the 1532 edition

22 Erasmus' Greek text has 'to us' whereas the Vulgate reads 'to you.' Thus the paraphrase at this point follows the Vulgate while the 'to us' of the Greek text is paraphrased in the next sentence by 'us, the apostles.'

23 now] Added in the 1532 edition. The word order of the Latin suggests that the adverb modifies the verb 'announce,' but it might conceivably have been intended to modify the verb of the indirect statement clause so as to mean 'have now come to pass.'

24 Cf Acts 2:1–4. This interpretation of the phrase 'sent from heaven' in 1 Pet 1:12 appears in the commentaries of Hugh of St Cher and Nicholas of Lyra on this verse, but not in Bede's commentary (he has a quite different point to make) nor in the *Gloss*. It is clear from Nicholas of Lyra's commentary that Erasmus' words 'throughout the entire world' are a paraphrase on 'they began to speak in other tongues,' (which is taken to mean in other languages).

25 fastened to a cross] *cruci suffixum*. LB reads *crucifixum* 'crucified.'

86

26 Bede *Exp 1 Pet* 1:12 CCL 121 229:169–74 / Hurst 76 and the medieval commentators understand the object of the angels' desire to be the beatific vision. Erasmus evidently rejects this interpretation and, with modern commentators, prefers to understand the object of their desire to be the events of salvation history.

27 'Lack of faith' is an echo of Eph 5:6 where the Vulgate translates τῆς ἀπειθείας 'disobedience' (NKJ) by *diffidentiae* 'unbelief' (DR).

28 Cf Matt 24:36 and 42.

29 Like the wise virgins in Matt 25:10

30 then] Added in the 1532 edition

31 These so-called 'requirements' of the Mosaic law are only generalizations on Erasmus' part. They are not prescribed in the unqualified way that he implies and for the most part they pertain only to the priests. For the avoidance of dead bodies see Lev 21:1–12, Num 19:11–13; for washing the feet Exod 30:17–21. There was no requirement to abstain from sexual intercourse but only with certain persons and at certain times; see eg Lev 18:1–23.

32 Even] Added in the March 1521 edition

87

33 still] Added in the March 1521 edition

34 if ... impure] Added in the 1532 edition

35 Cf Bede *Exp 1 Pet* 1:17 CCL 121 231:226–7 / Hurst 78: '[God] utterly disinherits his sons for ever for the fault of disobedience.'

36 Cf Bede *Exp 1 Pet* 1:18–19 CCL 121 231:234–6 / Hurst 78: 'The greater the price is with which you were redeemed from the corruption of your carnal life, the more you ought to fear that you may perhaps offend the sensibilities of your redeemer by returning to the corruption of vices.'

37 It is not clear just what ancient texts Erasmus may have had in mind, but see, for example, Plato *Laws* 915A: 'Any man may also carry off [ie return to slavery] a freedman, if he does not pay respect or sufficient respect to him who freed him,' and Suetonius *Claudius* 25: '[Claudius] reduced to slavery any [freedmen] who failed to show due gratitude or about whom their former owners had cause for complaint.' See William L. Westermann *The Slave Systems of Greek and Roman Antiquity* (Philadelphia 1955) 25–6 and Thomas Wiedemann *Greek and Roman Slavery* (Baltimore-London 1981) 53–6.

38 were ... purified] Added in the 1532 edition. In the earlier editions this sentence lacks a verb.

39 Cf Exod 12:5, *agnus absque macula* in the Vulgate.

40 However] First in 1532. The earlier editions read 'For.'

88

41 The antithesis occurs in Bede *Exp 1 Pet* 1:24–25 CCL 121 232:256–9 / Hurst 79.

42 the love ... heavenly love] Added in the March 1521 edition

43 Erasmus follows the rendering of 1 Pet 1:24–5 in the Vulgate except that the phrase 'of man' comes from his Greek text and 'as the flower of the field' from Isa 40:6.

44 long ago] Added in the 1532 edition

45 now] Added in the 1532 edition

Chapter 2

1 Cf 1 Cor 3:1–2; Heb 5:12–14.

89

2 The word salvation and the idea of growing up to it are not in Erasmus' Greek text but are taken from the Vulgate; cf DR, RSV with AV, NKJ. In his annotation on 1 Pet 2:2 (*crescatis in salutem*) LB VI 1045D Erasmus contends that the notion of growing up to salvation does not fit the context since, though infants in faith, the addressees are already saved. The paraphrase follows the Greek text in emphasizing the need to become mature Christians, perfect in Christ, while taking over from the Vulgate the idea that the goal of this growth is salvation.

3 Cf Ps 34:8.

4 The antithesis between the stones of man-made buildings and the living stones of the church, though an easy one, may have been suggested by Bede *Exp 1 Pet* 2:4 CCL 121 233:39–44 / Hurst 82.

5 that is] Added in 1532
6 For the imagery cf 1 Cor 3:1–14, Eph 2:19–22 and 4:12–16.
7 Cf 1 Cor 3:11, quoted by Bede *Exp 1 Pet* 2:5 CCL 121 234:54–5 / Hurst 82.
8 Cf 1 Cor 6:19 and Erasmus' annotation on 1 Pet 2:5 (*in sacerdotium*) LB VI 1045E.
9 Cf John 4:24. The contrast between the carnal sacrifices and cult of the Old Law with the spiritual sacrifices of the New Law occurs in Bede and the medieval commentaries. This is a recurrent feature of Erasmus' exegesis; cf eg the paraphrases on John 2:11, 4:24, and 7:21–4 (CWE 46 40–1, 58, and 96–7).
10 See the paraphrase on Rom 12:1–2 (CWE 42 69) for this notion of sacrificing the passions. The particular passions listed produce the seven capital or deadly sins; cf the *Enchiridion* CWE 66 113–26. Erasmus regularly substitutes vindictiveness or the desire for revenge (*cupiditas vindictae*), as he tends to call it, for spiritual torpor (*acedia*) in the traditional list of the seven capital sins. Vindictiveness was usually listed as an alternative to anger; see *Dictionnaire de théologie catholique* 12 (Paris 1933) 210–12 or *New Catholic Encyclopedia* 13 (New York 1967) 253–5 and the bibliography listed at the end of the article.
11 Erasmus is apparently alluding to Isa 66:3–4.

90
12 In his Latin version Erasmus translates the Greek adjective ἀκρογωνιαῖον in 2:6 by *in summo ponendum angulo* 'to be placed in the chief [or topmost] corner.' He retains the same translation in the paraphrase but replaces the verb *ponendum* with its synonym *collocandum* 'to be located, stationed.' Neither in the translation nor in his annotation on it (*summum angularem* LB VI 1045F) does Erasmus make it clear whether he intended the adjective *summo* to mean 'topmost' or, as in AV, 'chief'; that is, whether he intended his Latin to mean 'to be placed at the top of the corner' or 'to be placed at the chief corner.' There is in any case some question about the exact meaning of the Greek word; cf Selwyn *First Peter* 163 and Michaels *1 Peter* 103.
13 The adjective 'approved' (*probatum*) is taken from the Vulgate; it is not in Erasmus Greek text.
14 The verb 'to rest upon' (*inniti*) is a paraphrase on the verb 'to have faith' (*fidere*); cf *Declarationes ad censuras Lutetiae vulgatus*, LB VII 890B: 'For me [that is, Erasmus] *fidere* ['to have faith'] means first and foremost *inniti* ['to rest upon'].'
15 that is, each people] 1532. The earlier editions read 'each race' without the 'that is.' The same interpretation of the function of the cornerstone occurs in Bede *Exp 1 Pet* 2:7 CCL 121 236:146–7 / Hurst 86, who refers to Eph 2:14–16.
16 The phrase 'chosen generation' does not occur in Exod 19:5–6 but comes from Isa 43:20. Cf Bede *Exp 1 Pet* 2:8 CCL 121 237:164–238:199 / Hurst 87–8, who comments on each term in 2:8 as though it came from the Pentateuch. Bede ibidem likewise views the exodus as a foreshadowing or type of the redemption. It is likely then that Erasmus' statement in the paraphrase that God 'has overcome the enemies of your salvation in a new way' is a description of the incarnation and redemption.
17 Cf Matt 28:19–20.

18 those] *illi*, added in 1532. Erasmus means 'those Jews.'
19 Hos 1:6, 9, 10 and 2:23
20 Cf Gal 5:5–6; Rom 9:30–3.

91

21 Cf Pliny the Younger *Epistulae* 10.96.8; Tacitus *Annales* 15.44.4, Suetonius *Nero* 16.2.
22 The clause 'Whenever ... them also' is an explication of the words 'in the day of visitation' in 2:12; cf Erasmus' annotation on this verse (*in die visitationis*) LB VI 1046F. Erasmus follows the medieval commentators. The *Gloss*, for example, states: 'Visitation: when the Lord will visit them by converting them.' Similar comments occur in Hugh of St Cher and Nicholas of Lyra, though Hugh, in keeping with the nature of his *Postilla*, also lists several alternative interpretations. Selwyn *First Peter* 171, Kelly *Peter and Jude* 106, and Michaels *1 Peter* 119–20 illustrate the range of modern opinion about the meaning of the word 'visitation.'
23 The paraphrase on 2:13–17 may be usefully compared with that on Rom 13:1–7 CWE 42 74–5.
24 'If ... a king' (*sive rex sit ille*). The Latin can also be translated, 'if it is *the* king,' that is, the Roman emperor, which is the way modern scholars generally understand the word 'king' in these NT contexts (cf eg Selwyn *First Peter* 172, Michaels *1 Peter* 125) – as does Erasmus himself; cf the annotation on 1 Pet 2:14 (*sive ducibus, tanquam ab eo missis*) LB VI 1046F. But in the *Paraphrase* he seems to take verse 13 as a general mandate: on the Lord's account be subject to every human being, whether a king or a king's ministers; and I have translated accordingly. The generalization better fits, of course, the circumstances of his own day.
25 the king] Added in 1532. The earlier editions read simply 'he.' In the annotation on 2:14 cited in the preceding note Erasmus points out that the word 'him' in the phrase 'sent by him' is ambiguous and could mean either the king, that is, the Roman emperor, or God, as the *Gloss* interprets the pronoun. The addition made in the 1532 edition is apparently intended to eliminate the ambiguity.

92

26 Bede *Exp 1 Pet* 2:16 CCL 121 241:295–9 / Hurst 92 argues that freedom from sin and servitude to the devil does not give us a licence to sin; quite the contrary, sin leads to the loss of liberty and a new servitude. Bede goes on to say, lines 299–301: 'St Peter wants us to be free from the servitude of guilt so that we may be able to remain loyal servants of our good creator.'
27 Cf Rom 13:3.
28 The reference to Matt 22:21 is made by Bede *Exp 1 Pet* 2:17 CCL 121 241:303–5 / Hurst 92), and following him, by Hugh of St Cher and Nicholas of Lyra. Cf also the annotation on 1 Pet 14 (*sive ducibus, tanquam ab eo missis*) LB VI 1046F, where Erasmus observes that the command 'be subject to' in verse 13 means to accept patiently the legitimate acts of pagan magistrates such as levying and collecting taxes.

93

29 The pronoun may come from the Vulgate which has second person plural

pronouns in 2:21 whereas Erasmus' Greek text has first person pronouns. On the other hand, Erasmus may be simply adjusting the pronoun to the paraenetic context.

30 Cf Luke 23:34.

31 Kelly *Peter and Jude* 121 likewise comments: 'The point [in the words 'he trusted to him who judges justly'] is, not that the Lord was concerned about His own fate, but that, confident though He was of His righteousness, He preferred to leave its vindication to God than to take action Himself against His enemies.'

32 Cf 1:17. The thought is: Unlike human beings whose judgments are usually motivated by their emotions, God judges impartially.

33 'Accuser' (*instigatorem*), the person responsible for bringing a lawsuit. Christ by contrast is the paraclete or advocate who speaks on behalf of the defendant (cf 1 John 2:1). See the paraphrase on Rom 8:34 CWE 42 51.

34 'The tree': *in ligno*. The word *lignum*, which means 'wood,' is the translation in the Vulgate, so I have kept the translation of DR.

35 Isa 53:5

36 'Have turned': *conuersi estis*, which should perhaps be translated 'you are converted' (DR) in view of the contrast between the old life and new.

37 'Guardian': *curatorem*. Erasmus uses this word in both his Latin version of 2:25 and in the paraphrase to make it clear that ἐπίσκοπον (*episcopum* in the Vulgate) in this verse does not mean bishop (cf DR).

Chapter 3

94

1 Cf the paraphrase on 1 Tim 2:9. The purple dye made from the murex was extremely expensive in antiquity and garments or other materials dyed with purple were a symbol of great wealth. Cf Luke 16:19 where the rich man 'was clothed in purple and fine linen.' The combination of gold and purple occurs repeatedly in Roman literature to denote the magnificent appearance of some individual (cf eg Virgil *Aeneid* 2.163). The threefold combination of gold, gems, and purple is used by Horace as an image of unsurpassable wealth in *Odes* 2.16.7.

2 Cf the *Enchiridion* CWE 66 45.

3 See Gen 18:12, but the paraphrase suggests that Erasmus has Gen 12:11-16 also in mind.

95

4 For a detailed development of these ideas see the *Institutio christiani matrimonii* LB V 690F-692D.

5 This interpretation of 3:7 in the light of 1 Cor 7:5 is made by Bede *Exp 1 Pet* 3:7 CCL 121 244:37-43 / Hurst 96: 'If we abstain from sexual relations, we accord honour [to the weaker womanly vessel]; if we do not abstain, it is evident that sleeping together is contrary to honour.' The medieval commentators follow Bede's interpretation, except for Nicholas of Lyra, who strongly opposes it as inappropriate to the context. Cf Erasmus' annotation on 3:7 (*honorem impartientes*) LB VI 1049D and his *Responsio ad annotationes Lei*

LB IX 242C–243E. However, it is not entirely clear from these two texts whether Erasmus himself accepted this interpretation, which goes back to Jerome.

6 seeds] 1532. The earlier editions read the singular, 'seed.'

96

7 Cf Gal 3:28.

8 therefore] 1532. The earlier editions read 'and therefore.'

9 Cf 1 Cor 12:26.

10 To do good to evildoers] First in July 1521. The earlier editions read 'to do evil to doers of good'(!).

11 Cf Luke 6:27–8.

97

12 Erasmus takes this translation of Ps 34:12–16 largely from the Vulgate but modifies it partly from his own Latin version of 1 Pet 3:10–12, partly by paraphrasing.

13 By torture, cf Bede *Exp 1 Pet* 3:13 CCL 121 245:70–1 / Hurst 98.

14 Cf Rom 8:28 and the paraphrase on this verse CWE 42 50.

15 always] Added in the 1532 edition

98

16 of those to whom you are speaking] 1532. The earlier editions end the sentence with 'their salvation,' which leaves the reference of the pronoun unclear.

17 Completely] Added in the 1532 edition

18 those] Added in the 1532 edition

99

19 This notion appears to be an inference from Bede's belief that it took Noah one hundred years to build the ark (cf Bede Hurst 121 n11). The *Gloss* comments on 3:20: 'Although the patience of God invited them to repentance by sparing them during the one hundred years that Noah was building the ark, through which what was in store for the world was being revealed, they did not use God's patience to repent but awaited it as though it was going to last forever.'

20 leave] 1532. The earlier editions read the participle 'leaving.'

21 Cf the paraphrase on 4:5 below.

22 the ungodly] March 1521. The first two editions read 'to you.'

100

23 indeed] Added in 1532

24 but one ... jurisdiction] The 1523 folio and later editions. The 1523 octavo edition and the earlier editions read 'but such that death can no longer have' etc.

25 Erasmus is paraphrasing a clause 'swallowing down death, that we might be made heirs of life everlasting' (DR), which occurs in the Vulgate but is not found in the Greek manuscripts. See Metzger *Textual Commentary* 693–4. In his annotation on 3:22 (*qui est in dextera dei*) LB VI 1051E Erasmus notes

the difference between the Greek and Latin texts, but does not otherwise comment upon it. The language he employs in the paraphrase shows that he has 1 Cor 15:54–5 in mind and is therefore probably following Bede *Exp 1 Pet* 3:21–2 CCL 121 250:272–251:284 / Hurst 106.

Chapter 4

1 The paraphrase follows Bede *Exp 1 Pet* 4:1–6 CCL 121 251–3 / Hurst 107–9.

101

2 revels] The phrase, 'drinking-parties,' which follows the word 'revelries' in 4:3 (cf NKJ), is read in the 1520 editions and in the 1521, 1522, and 1523 octavo edition. It is omitted in the February 1522 edition, the 1523 folio edition, and consequently in the 1532 and subsequent editions. Since the February 1522 edition is full of typographical errors, it is likely that the omission was an accident rather than a deliberate revision.
3 See the paraphrase on 2:5 above.
4 in the body] Added in 1532
5 already] Added in 1532

102

6 Cf the paraphrase on Romans 6:10–11 CWE 42 38.
7 Cf Luke 21:34–6.
8 Cf Matt 24:36 and 42; Mark 13:32–7.
9 resources] *facultatum* 1532. The earlier editions read *rei* 'property.'
10 Cf Luke 6:38. Bede *Exp 1 Pet* 4:8 CCL 121 254:92–5 / Hurst 110 likewise alludes either to Mark 4:24 or to the parallel in Luke, but Erasmus seems to have the Lucan text in mind.
11 Cf Rom 12:6–8, and for spiritual gifts 1 Cor 12:4–10 and 28–30.

103

12 since] *quum* in all editions except LB which reads *quam* 'which'
13 'Sacred doctrine': *doctrina sacra*. Erasmus probably means biblical learning, the ability and knowledge required to interpret Scripture. In the paraphrase on Rom 12:7 those who receive the 'gift of teaching' should impart their learning to the unlearned without disdain or contempt (CWE 42 71). In the paraphrase on 1 Cor 12:28 the 'teachers' (*doctores*) are endowed with a knowledge of letters and disciplines which they contribute to the common good (LB VII 900B).
14 through] 1532. The earlier editions omit 'through' before 'Jesus Christ.'
15 Therefore] Added in 1532
16 a joy that ... words] Added in 1532

104

17 Abusive language (*convitium*) is a paraphrase on the adjective *maledicus* 'speaker of evil,' which is found in the Vulgate version of 4:15 and was in Erasmus' opinion a mistranslation of the Greek word for 'evildoer.' Cf his annotation on 1 Pet 4:15 (*aut fur*) LB VI 1054C.

18 Erasmus uses legal terminology here and may be thinking of the situation described by Pliny the Younger *Epistulae* 10.96.2: 'Is the name itself, even without any specific crimes, subject to punishment, or only the crimes attached to the name?' See Kelly *Peter and Jude* 190–2 for a discussion of the problems posed by 4:16.

19 It is not clear precisely what Erasmus means by the words 'even in this way' (*vel sic*). Perhaps he means that a martyr is translated immediately to heaven without suffering any temporal punishment in purgatory.

20 Cf Bede *Exp 1 Pet* 4:17 CCL 121 255:148–56 / Hurst 113: 'If the sons are scourged, what must the very wicked servants to hope for?'

105

21 'Deposit' (*deponant*) is Erasmus' translation of παραθέσθωσαν 'let them entrust for safekeeping'; cf the paraphrase on 1 Tim 1:12.

Chapter 5

1 In this paraphrase on 5:1 Erasmus adopts the translation of the Vulgate, *seniores ergo* ('ancients' in DR), substituting *itaque* for *ergo*. In his Latin version he used the Graecism *presbyteros* 'elders,' which he says in his annotation on this verse (*seniores ergo*) LB VI 1054E is a superior translation (cf also the annotation on 1 Pet 5:2 (*providentes*) LB VI 1054F). That Erasmus believed that by 'elders' Peter meant bishops and not simply elderly persons is evident from his annotation on 1 Pet 5:3 (*non dominantes in cleris*) LB VI 1055C and from the general thrust of the paraphrase on 5:1–4. Cf Martin Luther *Commentary on Peter and Jude* (Grand Rapids, Mich 1982) 202–3.

2 This explanation of the phrase 'witness of the sufferings of Christ' in 5:1 by reference to Peter's own sufferings and future death by crucifixion is made by Bede *Exp 1 Pet* 5:1 CCL 121 256:2–5 / Hurst 114. Kelly *Peter and Jude* 198–9 presents a modern argument in support of this view.

3 has been allotted] 1532. The earlier editions read 'has chanced to fall.' The change to 'has been allotted' may reflect the assumption that elders were selected by lot as Matthias was in Acts 1:26.

4 That is, *episcopi*, which should perhaps be translated 'bishops' in view of what follows; cf the annotation on 5:2 (*providentes*) LB VI 1054F, where Erasmus, following Jerome, points out that the Greek verb – ἐπισκοποῦντες 'serving as overseers' (NKJ; the participle is omitted in RSV [see marginal note on 5:2 and Metzger *Textual Commentary* 695–6]) – denotes someone who not only exercises oversight but also looks out for the material needs of others. Contrast the use of *curator* in the paraphrase on 2:25 above.

5 Cf Matt 18:12 and Luke 15:4. In his annotation on 5:3 (*non dominantes in cleris*) LB VI 1055C Erasmus recommends that these words of Peter 'be inscribed in letters of gold in the palace of every single bishop.'

106

6 Erasmus concludes the annotation, cited in the preceding note, on the words 'nor as being lords' (NKJ) in 5:3, with the observation: 'Nowadays the common run of bishops hears nothing from their learned flatterers except

lordship, jurisdiction, the sword, the keys, power – hence that pride exceeding the pride of kings, that savagery exceeding that of tyrants.

7 certainly] Added in 1532

8 will ... fade] LB reads the present tense, 'fades.'

9 Cf the paraphrase on 1:13 above which alludes to Matt 24:36 and 42.

10 the proud] 1532. The earlier editions read 'the former.' For the thought cf James 4:6.

107

11 Cf Matt 23:12.

12 The shift in metaphor from a raging lion to an enemy probing for weak spots in the Christian defences appears in Bede *Exp 1 Pet* 5:8 CCL 121 258:81–98 / Hurst 117–18 in a quotation from Cyprian's *De Zelo* 10.2–3. Of the eight means of attack listed by Cyprian, Erasmus selects only two, pleasure and persecution.

13 We are winning] *vincimus*. The present tense, instead of the expected future *vincemus*, is the reading of all the editions.

108

14 Cf the dedicatory letter to Wolsey 77 n20.

15 This interpretation of the word grace, though not the journey metaphor, occurs in Bede *Exp 1 Pet* 5:12 CCL 121 259:112–14 / Hurst 118, who also cites Acts 4:12 in this context.

16 Cf Bede *Exp 1 Pet* 5:13 CCL 121 259:120–2 / Hurst 119. According to Jerome *Liber interpretationis hebraicorum nominum* 3:18 CCL 72 62 the name 'Babylon' means a place full of confusion. Cf Luther's comment on the significance of the name, which he relates to the behaviour of the gentiles described in 4:3–4, *Commentary on Peter and Jude* (Grand Rapids, Mich 1982) 226.

17 Cf Rev 17:4–5.

18 Bede *Exp 1 Pet* 5:13 CCL 121 259:131–230:1 / Hurst 119, followed by Hugh of St Cher and Nicholas of Lyra, takes 'son' to be a metaphor for convert or godson. Michaels *1 Peter* 312 maintains this interpretation; other commentators, however, agree with Erasmus in taking the term 'son' to be simply a sign of personal affection (cf eg Selwyn *First Peter* 244 and Kelly *Peter and Jude* 220). All believe that this Mark is the John Mark first mentioned in Acts 12:12 and the putative author of the Gospel bearing his name. Bede ibidem 260:133–8 / Hurst 119 repeats the story that Peter sent Mark from Rome to Alexandria to evangelize that city and infers from this mention of him in 5:13 that Peter wrote the epistle in Rome during the reign of Claudius; that is, some years before his supposed martyrdom during the reign of Nero.

19 The Vulgate reads 'the holy kiss'; the Greek text has 'the kiss of love.' The paraphrase combines both readings. Bede *Exp 1 Pet* 5:14 CCL 121 260:139–40 / Hurst 120 makes the point that a holy kiss is sincere and unfeigned.

20 This reason for the repetition of grace and peace in the conclusion of the letter appears in Bede *Exp 1 Pet* 5:14 CCL 121 260:145–6 / Hurst 120.

21 'Grace' is the reading of the Vulgate, 'peace' of the Greek text and the better manuscripts of the Vulgate. Erasmus combines the readings of the two traditions, and thus reinforces the inclusion or reference back to the opening of the Epistle.

PARAPHRASE ON 2 PETER

Argument

110

1 By contrast, Bede *Exp 2 Pet* 1:1 CCL 121 261:4–6 / Hurst 123, the *Gloss,* and
Nicholas of Lyra believe 2 Peter to be written to the same recipients as 1
Peter. Hugh of St Cher in his introduction to 2 Peter, like Erasmus, views it
as written to all the faithful.

Chapter 1

111

1 Symeon] The reading of all the editions except LB which changes Symeon to
the traditional 'Simon.' Symeon is the form of the name found in several of
the major Greek manuscripts and in Erasmus' edition of the Greek text and
his Latin version, both here and in Acts 15:14; see Metzger *Textual Commentary* 699. The manuscripts and editions of the Vulgate, however, uniformly
read 'Simon.' In the annotation on Acts 15:14 (*Simon narravit quemadmodum*)
LB VI 491E Erasmus notes the two different spellings of the name (or rather
three, since his Greek text has Σιμεών, which he transliterates *Simeon*) and
comments: 'I do not know whether [Simon] was written wrongly through
error or whether the Hebrew form *Symeon* was given the Greek inflection
Simon, as in the case of *Saul Saulus* [sic].' In his annotation on 2 Pet 1:1
(*Simon Petrus*) LB VI 1057A Erasmus comments that the Greeks pronounce
the name in different ways, but does not indicate what these might be, nor
does he say anything about different spellings, though that may be what he
means by different pronunciations.

2 The antitheses, familiar from Paul, between the law of Moses and the gospel of Christ in this sentence and between circumcision and grace in the
third sentence, are employed by Bede *Exp 2 Pet* 1:1 CCL 121 261:7–20 /
Hurst 123. Erasmus, however, ignores Bede's interpretation of righteousness
(*iustitia*) as works (*opera*) which lead to salvation.

3 Cf Bede *Exp 2 Pet* 1:2 CCL 121 261:23–6 / Hurst 124, who notices that in 1
Pet 1:2 Peter had written 'be multiplied' whereas here in 2 Pet 1:2 he wrote
'be fulfilled,' and infers from the use of the different verb that the first
letter was written to beginners, the second to persons more advanced in
knowledge and faith.

4 you] LB reads 'us.'

5 Cf John 17:3, quoted by Bede *Exp 2 Pet* 1:2 CCL 121 261:27–30 / Hurst 124.

6 Here and throughout the paraphrase on verses 2 and 3 Erasmus uses the
verb *agnoscere* and the noun *agnitio* to translate Greek ἐπιγιγνώσκει and
ἐπίγνωσις. In his annotation on Rom 1:28 (*et sicut non probaverunt*) LB VI
566C he distinguishes between *agnoscere* 'to acknowledge' and *cognoscere* 'to
come to know' (the verb used by the Vulgate): 'To know (*cognoscere*) is the
act of one who understands, to acknowledge (*agnoscere*) is the act of one
who is grateful and remembers.' It is not only the initial recognition of God
and Jesus, but the continuing acceptance of them that leads to salvation; cf

Bauckham *2 Peter* 188–9, Kelly *Peter and Jude* 298–9, and the paraphrase on 1 Pet 2:1–5. The paraphrase on 1:3 is otherwise largely a development of Bede *Exp 2 Pet* 1:3 CCL 121 261:33–8 and 262:50–7 / Hurst 124–5.

7 'Power' (*virtus*), the word used by the Vulgate in 1:3 to translate both δύναμις 'power' and ἀρετή 'virtue' (NKJ, 'excellence' RSV). Erasmus in his annotation on 1:3 (*propria gloria et virtute*) LB VI 1059D distinguishes between the two meanings of *virtus* and corrects what he assumes to be an error on Bede's part in taking *virtus* in the sense of power in both parts of the verse. The paraphrase otherwise develops the same points made by Bede.

112

8 Cf Bede *Exp 2 Pet* 1:4 CCL 121 262:61–72 / Hurst 125–6, who explains in this way the shift from 'us' in verse 3 to 'you' in verse 4. Cf Bauckham *2 Peter* 176–7 and Kelly *Peter and Jude* 296–7.

9 Cf James 2:20 to which Bede *Exp 2 Pet* 1:5 CCL 121 263:96–7 / Hurst 127 likewise alludes.

10 so that] *ut* 1532. The earlier editions read *et* 'and.'

11 In his annotation on 1:7 (*amorem fraternitatis*) LB VI 1059F Erasmus observes that love (*dilectio*) is a broader and more general feeling than brotherly affection (*fraterna caritas*). Brotherly affection (φιλαδελφία) refers to the love (*amor*) which Christians have for one another; love (*dilectio*, Erasmus' translation here of ἀγάπη) is felt for everyone, even pagans.

113

12 Erasmus is paraphrasing the Vulgate translation of μυωπάζων 'shortsighted' by *manu tentans* 'groping' (DR).

13 'Through your good deeds' is not in the Greek text but comes from the Vulgate.

14 In the paraphrase on 1:5–7

15 by your extended progress ... long time] First in the March 1521 edition. The 1520 editions have the preposition 'in' before the noun 'truth' so that they read 'By your extended progress in godliness you are now well established in the truth' etc. This latter reading is certainly closer to the biblical text of 1:12, 'You ... are established in the present truth' (NKJ).

16 Cf Luke 22:32.

17 Cf Heb 11:13. Nicholas of Lyra likewise refers to Heb 11:13 in his commentary on 2:11.

114

18 The military metaphor occurs in Bede *Exp 2 Pet* 1:14 CCL 121 265:187–266:193 / Hurst 130) and, following him, in the medieval commentaries. In his commentary on 2 Pet 2:14b Hugh of St Cher connects this text with John 21:18 and the *Quo vadis?* story in the *Acts of Peter*; see Edgar Hennecke and Wilhelm Schneemelcher *New Testament Apocrypha* 2 vols (Philadelphia 1965) II 317–18. Bede, Nicholas of Lyra, and Erasmus, however, are silent on the question of how or when Peter received this revelation. Cf Bauckham *2 Peter* 200–1.

19 Erasmus translated the Greek in 1:15: 'I will always be careful to ensure that you have a reminder' rather than (correctly) 'I will be careful to ensure

that you always have a reminder'; hence the repeated reference in the paraphrase to the act of reminding.

20 In his annotation on 1:16 (*non enim indoctas fabulas*) LB VI 1060F Erasmus
comments on the participle σεσοφισμένοις 'cunningly devised': 'Such were
once philosophers' disputations, more wily than salutary, and today some
debates of the theologians.' The medieval commentators, whose Latin Bible
read in 2 Pet 1:16 either *doctas fabulas* 'artificial fables' (DR) or *indoctas fabulas*
'ignorant fables' naturally did not see any allusion to philosophers in these
words. Nor do modern commentators see such an allustion in the Greek
term, though they hold different views about just what it means; cf Bauckham *2 Peter* 213–14 and Kelly *Peter and Jude* 316.

21 Erasmus introduces into the paraphrase on 2 Peter elements from the
accounts of the transfiguration in Matthew and Luke; cf eg Matt 17:2 and
Luke 9:32 and 35. Bauckham *2 Peter* 205–12 provides a detailed comparison
of the biblical texts. Even if Erasmus were aware of the problems posed by
these texts, it would be inappropriate to introduce them into the *Paraphrase*
which assumes that Peter the apostle, who was an eyewitness, is the author
of the epistle.

22 Erasmus has modeled his paraphrase directly on Isa 42:1 rather than on the
citations of it in the NT. Therefore, I have followed the AV and RSV translations of Isaiah rather than the the text of 2 Pet 1:17 and Matt 17:5.

23 Erasmus takes the 'prophetic word' of verse 19 to be the words spoken by
the Father at the transfiguration; see the annotation on 1:19 (*et habemus
firmiorem*) LB VI 1061E and, for a survey of the exegesis of the phrase, Bauckham *2 Peter* 224–5.

24 Bede and Nicholas of Lyra do not identify the 'holy mountain' of 2 Pet 1:18,
but the interlinear *Gloss* and Hugh of St Cher list Tabor along with the
Mount of Olives as possibilities. The first extant reference to the location of
the transfiguration on Tabor occurs in Origen *Selecta in psalmos* (on Ps 88:13)
PG 12 1548. Mt Tabor, which is in Galilee, was venerated as the site of the
transfiguration since the fourth century; see Paul J. Achtemeier ed *Harper's
Bible Dictionary* (San Francisco 1985) 1014–15.

25 Cf the paraphrase on Heb 9:8.

26 so manifest] Added in 1532

115

27 The meaning of the words 'the morning star arises in your hearts' (RSV) in
1:19 is not immediately evident; see Bauckham 2 Peter 226. The meaning of
Erasmus' paraphrase *lucifer ille praedicationis euangelicae* – literally 'that
morning star of evangelical preaching' – is likewise unclear. It could mean
the morning star, which is evangelical preaching – an unusual, possibly
unique interpretation – or the morning star of evangelical preaching; that is,
the subject of evangelical preaching, namely Christ. The latter is the standard explanation; cf Rev 22:16.

28 Erasmus means Jewish exegetes, since in his annotation on 1:19 (*et habemus
firmiorem*) LB VI 1061E he calls this approach to Scripture the 'Jewish custom'
and contrasts it with the 'spiritual' interpretation: 'And this prophetic word
is more certain than that of the prophets whom the Jews venerate – Peter
does not disapprove of this, provided that they understand that the proph-

ecies must be interpreted spiritually.' Cf Erasmus' *Enarratio in primum psalmum*, where he contrasts his own approach with that of the Jews who ineptly twist Psalm 1 to suit the person of King Josiah (ASD V-2 36:88), or the *Commentarius in psalmum* 2 (ASD V-2 102:187–91): 'The majority of the psalms have a double plot-line: a historical one which serves as a kind of foundation and an allegorical or anagogical one which is concealed beneath the covering of historical events. To put the matter better – the second plot-line reveals the story of the gospel or the doctrine of true godliness or the image of eternal felicity. For there is generally no passage of Scripture which cannot be accommodated to tropology.' Cf also the *Ecclesiastes* LB V 825B–826E. A similar contrast between the Jewish literal and the Christian spiritual reading of the Bible, and of the Psalms in particular, is made by Jacques Lefèvre d'Etaples; see Guy Bedouelle *Lefèvre d'Etaples et l'intelligence des Ecritures* (Geneva 1976) 173–89, especially 175–6.

Chapter 2

1 Cf Deut 18:20–2. It is not clear whether Erasmus has specific OT incidents in mind or not. In 2 Pet 3:15–16 Balaam appears as the classic example of a prophet motivated by greed. In 2 Kings 22:5–12 four hundred prophets speak what the king wishes to hear while Micaiah alone opposes their false prophecy. Cf also Jer 23:14–22.

116

2 In place of the word ἀσελγείαις 'licentiousness' (RSV) in 2:2 Erasmus' Greek text reads ἀπωλείαις, which he translated by *exitia*, 'ruin, destruction' (cf AV and NKJ 'destructive ways'). This invented reading subsequently became the reading of the *textus receptus* but appears to have no manuscript support whatsoever. The word ἀπωλεία occurs twice in verse 1 and its employment in verse 2 undoubtedly was an error on the part of the typesetter of the *Novum instrumentum*; see H.J. de Jonge, *Apologia ad annotationes Stunicae*, ASD IX-2 251:418n.

3 would prefer] *mallent*, first in the May 1522 edition, and subsequently in the 1523, 1532, and 1534 editions as well as in LB. The other editions, including 1538 and 1540, read 'will prefer' (*malent*). The future tense (*malent*) suits the context better. The subjunctive (*mallent*) quite likely originated in a typographical error.

4 to prepare] *parare*, 1520–1534. The 1538 and 1540 editions read 'to produce' (*parere*). The change could well have stemmed from Erasmus, but the replacement of *a* by *e* is an easy typographical error.

5 Erasmus understood the Greek οὐκ αργεῖ 'is not idle' in 2:4 to mean 'does not tarry'; the paraphrase expresses this meaning *per contrarium*.

117

6 The author of 2 Peter does not say what sin the angels committed (see Bauckham *2 Peter* 248–9), but pride was the traditional explanation for the rebellion of Lucifer and the other angels. Modern commentators explain 2

Pet 2:5 and Jude 6, on which it depends, differently: Jude 6 alludes to *1 Enoch* 6–19, which is an elaboration of the sin of the 'sons of God' described in Gen 6:1–4; see Bauckham *Jude* 51–3.

7 by crimes] Added in the March 1521 edition

8 he] March 1521. The first and second editions read 'Noah.'

9 Cf the paraphrase on 1 Pet 3:20 and on 3:9 below. The sentence as a whole is a paraphrase on the words 'preacher of righteousness' in 2:5; cf Bede *Exp 2 Pet* 2:5 CCL 121 271:96–103 / Hurst 138.

10 Erasmus apparently means that Sodom and Gomorrah are now covered by the Dead Sea, the water of which exemplifies the annihilation of the sinners. The paraphrase appears to be a reduction of Bede *Exp 2 Pet* 2:6 CCL 121 271:104–8 / Hurst 138: '[Peter's] assertion that the cities were reduced to ashes must be understood in two ways. First, through fire God reduced them, together with the surrounding lands, to ashes, and then, after subsequently covering the place of the fire with the waves of the Dead Sea, he still wanted the surrounding region to preserve the appearance of the ancient punishment through its sulphurous atmosphere and the sterile produce of its ashy soil.'

11 Cf Gen 19:4–9.

12 The paraphrase follows the Vulgate rather than the Greek text. In his annotation on 2 Pet 2:9 (*servare cruciandos*) LB VI 1063C Erasmus observes that in the Greek the particple 'being punished' is in the present tense and implies that the ungodly are being punished while awaiting the Last Judgment (cf the translation 'under punishment' in NKJ, RSV), whereas the translation of the Vulgate (*cruciandos* 'to be tormented') implies a future rather than a present punishment for them. Erasmus evidently preferred this latter interpretation since his Latin version follows the lead of the Vulgate rather than his understanding of the Greek text. Translators and commentators are divided on this issue; see Bauckham *2 Peter* 254.

13 Erasmus understood the words κυριότητος 'authority' (RSV) and δόξας 'the glorious ones' (RSV) in 2:10 to mean pre-eminent human beings rather than angels (similarly in Jude 8); cf his annotation (*sectas non metuunt*) LB VI 1063D. Modern commentators are divided, but generally take the two words to refer to angels; see Bauckham *2 Peter* 255 and 261.

118

14 The past tenses suggest that Erasmus has Satan and the fallen angels of 2:4 in view. See Bauckham *2 Peter* 261–3 for a discussion of the problems posed by 2:11.

15 Cf the paraphrase on Rom 13:13 (CWE 42 76).

16 This peculiar paraphrase is based in part upon a misunderstanding of the syntax of the original Greek of 2:13, 'carousing in their own deceptions while they feast with you' (NKJ). Erasmus construed the dative case of the pronoun 'you' with the participle 'carousing' rather than with the verb 'feast.' When construed with the dative case the Greek verb ἐντρύφω 'carouse' can mean 'treat contemptuously, insult, mock,' and that is how Erasmus translates it in his Latin version. He found support, if not for the grammar, at least for the exegesis in Bede *Exp 2 Pet* 2:13 CCL 121 273:188–90 / Hurst 142, where Bede describes the unrighteous as those who 'blas-

pheme the behaviour of those who live chastely, [and] do not cease from slandering those who savour of wholesomeness.'

17 Bosor, not Beor, is the form of the name in Erasmus' Greek text. See Metzger *Textual Commentary* 704.

18 For the story of Balaam see Num 22, especially 22:7, 17, 18. His characterization in 2 Pet 2:15–16, and in Jude 11, is based upon later Jewish literature; see Bauckham *Jude, 2 Peter* 82 and 268–9. For the theme of corruption cf the paraphrase on 1 Tim 6:5 and Titus 1:11.

119

19 wrap ... error] LB reads 'and wrap error in darkness.'

20 The adjective 'everlasting,' which is not found in 2 Pet 2:17, is introduced from Jude 13.

21 wallowing] *volutationem*, first in March 1521. The first and second editions read 'wallow' (*volutabrum*). In his annotation on 2 Pet 2:22 (*in volutabro luti*) LB VI 1065F, Erasmus comments that the Greek implies a return by the sow to her wallowing, and for this reason he prefers the word *volutatio* (the act of wallowing) to the word *volutabrum* (the wallow, or place of wallowing) which the Vulgate uses to translate the Greek (cf AV and NKJ with RSV).

22 Cf *Adagia* III v 13 and IV iii 62.

Chapter 3

120

1 This description of the scoffers is a comment on the phrase *in deceptione* 'deceitful' found in the Vulgate but not in Erasmus' Greek text; cf AV with DR and RSV. The prohibition against heeding such scoffers appears in Luke 21:8.

2 Cf Bede *Exp 2 Pet* 3:4 ['Where is the promise of his coming' NKJ] CCL 121 276:5–6 / Hurst 146: 'Scoffing, namely, at the faith and hope of Christians in that they promise in vain that there will be a time of resurrection for them.' Cf 1 Cor 15:12–18.

3 The notion that the scoffers are only pretending not to know occurs in the *Gloss* on 2 Pet 3:5, though not in Bede.

4 'At the same time' is inserted to reinforce the reading of the Greek text of 3:5, 'the heavens were of old,' against the text of the Vulgate, which reads 'the heavens were before' (*prius*), a reading which attempts to make the text of 2 Pet 3:5 conform to Gen 1:6–10. See Erasmus' annotation on 2 Pet 3:5 (*caeli erant prius*) LB VI 1066E, and for a discussion of the problems posed by this entire verse, Bauckham *2 Peter* 297–8 and Kelly *Peter and Jude* 357–60.

5 Erasmus translated the Greek prepositional phrase δι'ὕδατος by *per aquam*, which suggests that he understood the preposition to have an instrumental (cf 'by means of water' RSV) rather than a locative meaning (cf 'in the water' NKJ). However, in the paraphrase he takes it in a local sense; see the list of modern commentators in Bauckham *2 Peter* 298 who, following the account in Gen 1:6–7 and 9, understand the Greek in a similar way. Bede *Exp 2 Pet* 3:5 CCL 121 276:22–277:34 / Hurst 147 and the medieval commentators likewise take the preposition in the local sense but give it a quite different interpretation.

6 Ancient and medieval commentators disputed (as do modern) whether the flood destroyed some, all, or none of the heavens as well as the earth. See, eg, Bede *Exp 2 Pet* 3:6–7 CCL 121 277:35–53 / Hurst 147–8. Erasmus is either ignoring this debate or taking the position, without argument or explanation, that 'heavens' in 2 Pet 3:7 refers to the upper sky which, as Nicholas of Lyra remarks in his discussion of these verses, 'revolves each day with the firmament.'

121

7 us] 1532. The editions prior to 1532 follow the text of the NT and read 'you.' The change was evidently made to make the pronoun fit the context of the paraphrase.

8 Erasmus follows his Greek text of 3:10, which has the phrase 'in the night,' introduced, he thought, from Matt 24:43 and Luke 12:39 (he should have said from 1 Thess 5:2); see his annotation (*sicut fur*) LB VI 1066F.

9 Erasmus is paraphrasing the text of the Vulgate, which reads 'hastening to the coming,' rather than the Greek text which reads 'hastening the coming' (NKJ); cf his annotation on 2 Pet 3:12 (*festinantes in adventum*) LB VI 1066F.

10 The concluding clause in this paraphrase on 2:13 arose from the mistaken belief that the antecedent of the relative pronoun ἐν οἷς in the Greek text (*in quibus* in the Vulgate) could be either 'new heavens and earth' or the 'we' implicit in the participle 'looking for.' The paraphrase accommodates both possibilities, although Erasmus thought the second possibility was preferable; see the annotation on 2 Pet 3:13 (*in quibus iusticia*) LB VI 1066F.

11 The antithesis between divine and human judgment occurs in Bede *Exp 2 Pet* 3:14 CCL 121 281:170 / Hurst 153.

122

12 The word 'almost' (*fere*) occurs in Erasmus' Latin translation and is introduced into the paraphrase from there. It has no basis in the Greek text or in the Vulgate.

13 Cf eg Rom 13:12; 1 Cor 1:7, 5:5; 2 Cor 1:14; 1 Thess 5:2; 2 Thess 2:2, 5:2.

14 Cf 1 Thess 5:1–5.

15 Bede *Exp 2 Pet* 3:16 CCL 121 282:219–22 / Hurst 155 suggests as an example 'the grace of God that justifies the ungodly.'

PARAPHRASE ON JUDE

Argument

124

1 The reference is presumably to Paul in 2 Thess 2:5–12 and 1 Tim 4:1, and to Peter in 2 Pet 2:1 and 3:2–4.

Epistle of Jude

125

1 The identification of the author of the Epistle with the apostle Jude Thad-

daeus, the brother of James the Less, which was the common assumption of the medieval church, was based on an interpretation of Luke 6:16 where the name 'Jude of James' was understood to mean 'Jude, the brother of James,' rather than 'Jude, the son of James' (contrast AV and DR with RSV and NKJ; cf also Mark 3:18, Matt 10:3). Jude was also identified with the Lebbaeus mentioned in Matthew's list of the twelve apostles (Matt 10:3) and the Thaddaeus who appears in Mark's list (Mark 3:18). 'Jude, the brother of James' is the name given to the apostle in the paraphrases on Matt 10:3 and on Acts 1:13, but not until the 1534 edition; the earlier editions have 'Jude, the son of James.' However, Jerome *De viris illustribus* 4 and modern commentators prefer to identify the author of the Epistle with Jude, the brother of James the Just; cf Mark 6:3 and Bauckham *Jude* 21–5. In his annotation on Matt 10:3 (*primus Simon*) LB VI 53E Erasmus describes Jude as the son of James (*filius Iacobi*) in the first (1516) through the fourth (1527) editions of the *Novum Testamentum*. Questioned on this point by Noël Béda, Erasmus admitted that he was in error (*Divinationes ad notata Beddae* LB IX 463E), and in the fifth edition of 1535 changed *filius* 'son' to *frater* 'brother.' Cf also the exchange with Ambrosius Pelargus in Allen Epp 2181–2 and 2184–6. Since the *Paraphrases* do not as a rule innovate in such matters, it is likely that Erasmus here means Jude, the brother of James the Less. Luther *Commentary on Peter and Jude*, trans J.N. Lenker (Grand Rapids, Mich 1982) 290 likewise begins his exposition by identifying Jude as the brother of the two apostles James the Less and Simon (the Canaean), but in his comment on verses 17–18 (301) points out that this passage clearly shows that the author was not one of the apostles but 'another pious man ... who had read the epistles of Peter.' Luther does not, however, indicate who he thought this 'pious man' might have been.

2 That is, without requiring them to be circumcised

3 concord] March 1521. The 1520 editions read 'peace.'

4 Toil] *laborate* 1520–1534. The 1538 edition reads, erroneously, the infinitive *laborare* 'to toil.' The 1540 edition corrected the error to read *laboravi* 'I toiled,' which is the reading of LB. The verb 'to toil' is a paraphrase on Erasmus' translation of the Greek verb ἐπιαγωνίζεσθαι 'to contend earnestly' by *ut vestris laboribus adiumento sitis* 'so that you aid through your toils'; cf the annotation on Jude 3 (*deprecans supercertare semel traditae fidei*) LB VI 1089E.

5 The treasure] 1520–1534. The 1538 and 1540 editions, followed by LB, read 'For the treasure.'

6 you] Twice. LB reads 'we' for the first 'you' and 'us' for the second 'you.'

126

7 Cf 2 Pet 2:1 and 1 Tim 4:1.

8 Cf Bede *Exp Iudae* 4 CCL 121 335:18–25 / Hurst 241–2. The harshness of the Mosaic law consisted in the penalties which it prescribed such as stoning and burning; hence it compelled people to obey it through fear of punishment. The law of the gospel, by contrast, is a law of love. Inspired by God's love, its adherents willingly do more than what might be otherwise expected of them; cf the paraphrase on 1 Tim 1:9.

9 adorn] 1520–1538. The 1540 edition and LB read 'ordain.'

10 Cf 1 Cor 15:2.

11 Several of the details of the paraphrase on verse 5 – calling out to God, murmuring against God, hastening toward the promised land – occur in Bede *Exp Iudae* 5 CCL 121 336:50–60 / Hurst 243. Erasmus seems to have consulted Bede rather than the narrative in the OT; cf Exod 14 and Num 14:1–38. Cf also 1 Cor 10:1–12.

12 Erasmus follows the Clementine Vulgate here, which reads 'Jesus' in place of 'the Lord,' the reading of Erasmus' Greek text. Bede *Exp Iudae* 5 CCL 121 336:45–6 / Hurst 243 points out that 'By Jesus [Jude] does not mean the son of Nave [ie Joshua] but our Lord.' Commentators, nevertheless, dispute whether 'Lord' refers to God or to Jesus; cf Bauckham *Jude* 43 nb and 49.

127

13 Erasmus thought that the Greek noun ἀρχή 'domain' (NKJ) in Jude 6 meant 'origin.' In his annotation on Jude 6 (*suum principatum*) LB VI 1089F, Erasmus states that the word 'signifies that first nature in which [the angels] were created.' He then takes the word οἰκητήριον 'habitation' (NKJ), 'dwelling' (RSV) to be a metaphor for the angels' heavenly condition or station.

14 The verbs in the main clauses of this sentence have no explicit subject, but the allusion to Rev 12:9 suggests that it is Jesus who performs these actions. Bede *Exp Iudae* 6 CCL 121 336:66–73 / Hurst 243–4 likewise asserts that it was Jesus who in his pre-existent status as the Son punished the angels.

15 This assumption, for which there is no explicit biblical evidence, is perhaps an inference from Gen 13:10.

16 Cf Gen 19:1–25.

17 Cf Bede *Exp Iudae* 4 CCL 121 337:88–9 / Hurst 244: the fire which destroyed the Sodomites is 'an example of the punishment of those who transfer the grace of our Lord into their own wantonness.'

18 Erasmus was not sure of the meaning of the participle ἐνυπνιαζόμενοι 'in their dreamings' (RSV), but thought it might describe the obscene dreams of dissolute people, by which he presumably means erotic dreams; or the fact that 'lust operates in a dream state when reason is put to sleep'; see his annotation on Jude 8 (*et hi qui carnem*) LB VI 1090D. In his Latin version he translates it 'deluded by dreams,' which may in fact be the meaning of the verb in this context; cf Bauckham *Jude* 55–6 and Kelly *Peter and Jude* 261. The participle is omitted in the Vulgate, though not in the best manuscripts, and hence is not discussed by Bede and the medieval commentators.

19 Cf 2 Pet 2:10 and Erasmus' annotation on Jude 8 (*maiestatem autem*) LB VI 1090E.

20 demon] *daemoni* 1532. The earlier editions read *domino* 'lord.'

21 In patristic and medieval thought Cain is the exemplar of envy. See Augustine *Tractatus in epistulam ad Parthos* 5.8 (on 1 John 3:12) PL 35 2016; Bede *Exp Iudae* 11 CCL 121 338:122–3 / Hurst 245–6; the *Gloss* and Hugh of St Cher on 1 John 3:12. Hugh comments on Jude 11 that those who 'walk in the way of Cain' envy the achievements of others; Nicholas of Lyra likewise states in his commentary on Jude 11 that Cain killed Abel because of envy and hatred.

22 For Cain and Abel, see Gen 4:2–10; for Balaam, Deut 23:4–5 and Josh 24:9–10; for Korah, Num 16:1–33.

23 The paraphrase on Jude 12a seeks to incorporate Erasmus' Greek text which reads ἐν ταῖς ἀγάπαις ὑμῶν – translated 'among your charities' by Erasmus – and the text of the Vulgate which has *in epulis suis* 'in their banquets.' When Erasmus initially translated Jude and when he wrote the *Paraphrase* on it in 1520, he did not know that the word ἀγάπη could mean 'feast.' When Zúñiga pointed out his error – see the *Apologia ad annotationes Stunicae* ASD IX-2 2:260–1 – Erasmus corrected his annotation on this verse (*in epulis suis*) LB VI 1091D but never revised the Latin translation in the *Novum Testamentum* or the *Paraphrase*.

24 Erasmus' Greek text at this point in Jude 12 reads, literally, 'fearlessly shepherding themselves.' He translated the passage 'living by their own guidance and will without fear of anyone,' explaining in his annotation on it (*pascentes*) LB VI 1091E that the participle 'shepherding' implies living in the manner of shepherds and only for themselves: '[Jude] means that they obey no one's command but live as they wish.' Cf Kelly *Peter and Jude* 271.

25 They] 1532. The earlier editions read 'But they.'

128

26 Cf Bede *Exp Iudae* 12 CCL 121 338 155–7 / Hurst 247 for this explanation of the words 'twice dead.' See the paraphrase on 1 Tim 4:16 for a similar explanation of the double destruction caused by false teaching.

27 Cf Bede *Exp Iudae* 13 CCL 121 339:168–71 / Hurst 247–8 for a similar treatment of the brief comparisons in this verse.

28 of the way] *viae*, omitted in the 1540 edition and in LB. These stars are the planets whose light is reflected, not genuine, and whose erratic movements (as seen from earth) are unreliable guides, unlike the fixed stars of the firmament such as the pole-star (cf page 3 above).

29 something novel is happening to you] 1532. The earlier editions read 'this is something novel.'

129

30 Cf 2 Thess 2:5–12 and 2 Pet 3:2–4. Erasmus thought that 2 Peter was written before the Epistle of Jude.

31 Cf Bede *Exp Iudae* 20–1 CCL 121 341:250–3 / Hurst 251 who likewise alludes to 1 Pet 2:5. The explanation, which follows, of faith as belief in the salvation of the godly and the damnation of the ungodly as well as the injunction not to take the punishment of the wicked into one's own hands are recurring themes in the *Paraphrases*.

32 The paraphrase on 22–3 follows Erasmus' Greek text (cf AV, NKJ), which he felt was obscure but, as he explains in his annotation on it (*de igne rapiant*) LB VI 1092E, apparently meant: '[The readers are commanded] to take into account the difference among persons and then to draw some to Christ by kindness, to use fear to deter others from sinning, and to hate not people themselves but their vile emotions, which [Jude] here calls the stained garment of the flesh, that is, whatever pertains in any way to moral vileness.'

130

33 The paraphrase on verse 25 follows the text of the Vulgate, which reads: 'To the only God our Saviour through Jesus Christ our Lord, be glory and

magnificence, empire and power, before all ages, and now, and for all ages of ages' (DR). Erasmus' Greek text reads 'to God who alone is wise' and does not contain the phrases 'through Jesus Christ our Lord,' and 'before all ages.' Similarly, the concluding sentence is a paraphrase on the phrase 'in the coming of our Lord Jesus Christ,' which is found in the Vulgate at the end of verse 24, but not in the Greek text. The Greek text had been criticized by Edward Lee (cf *Responsio ad annotationes Lei* LB IX 245) and Erasmus may have thought it prudent to follow the expanded text of the Vulgate.

PARAPHRASE ON JAMES

Dedicatory Letter

132

1 The dedicatory letter (Ep 1171) is translated by R.A.B. Mynors with minor revisions by JJB. Matthäus Schiner was elected bishop of Sion, in Switzerland, in 1499 and in virtue of this office became count of the Valais. Having lost his possessions in the Duchy of Milan after the French victory at Marignano in September 1515 and having been forced to flee the Valais in August 1517 because of a popular uprising against him, Schiner took up residence in Zürich until removing to Rome after the death of Pope Leo X on 1 December 1521. There he was a firm supporter of Pope Adrian VI and in the spring of 1522 invited Erasmus to join him in Rome, but any decision on Erasmus' part was forestalled by Schiner's death from the plague on 1 October 1522.

In the autumn of 1516 Schiner travelled in disguise to England to persuade Henry VIII to collaborate with the emperor Maximilian in continuing hostile action against the French. He reached Brussels on 4 October and left four days later on the eighth. Erasmus was in Brussels on 6 October (Ep 475) and was in close contact with Cuthbert Tunstall, the English ambassador to Burgundy (Ep 475:15–16). It seems likely that Erasmus was first introduced to Schiner through Tunstall at this time. Since Schiner did not return through the Netherlands, the next opportunity for meeting him would not have occurred until 29 May 1517 when Erasmus dined with Schiner in Antwerp (Ep 584). In September 1520 Schiner joined the court of Charles V, whose election as emperor he had strongly supported, and travelled with it to Aachen for the coronation in November. Erasmus was also in attendance at court at different times and places in late September until its departure from Louvain on 8 October. He thus had several occasions at which he might have renewed his acquaintance with Schiner. At one of them the cardinal encouraged him to paraphrase the Epistles of James and John, just as, a year later, after returning to Brussels with Charles in June 1521, he was to encourage Erasmus to paraphrase the Gospel of Matthew. See CEBR III 221–3 and, for a comprehensive treatment of Schiner's life and activities as both bishop and statesman, Albert Büchi *Kardinal Matthäus Schiner als Staatsmann und Kirchenfürst: Ein Beitrag zur allgemeinen und schweizerischen Geschichte von der Wende des XV.–XVI. Jahrhunderts* In 2 parts *Collectanea Friburgensia* Neue Folge 18 (1923) and 23 (1937).

2 Erasmus says *cum stilo rhetorico verius quam apostolico*, by which he means that the style of Hebrews is different, not so much from the style of Paul in particular as from the 'apostolic simplicity' characteristic of the Gospels and the other Epistles.

133

3 James 2:10. See Augustine Ep 167 CSEL 44 590–607.
4 James 2:17 and 20
5 Rom 4
6 The difficulty of establishing connections from section to section of the Epistle is a recurring complaint in the commentaries; see, for example, Martin Dibelius and Heinrich Greeven *James* (Philadelphia 1975) 2: '*the entire document lacks continuity in thought* [their italics]. There is not only a lack of continuity in thought between individual sayings and other smaller units, but also between larger treatises [within the Epistle].'
7 Erasmus means in contrast to the attacks launched against his edition of the New Testament, and in particular the Latin version included in it. See August Bludau *Die beiden ersten Erasmus – Ausgaben des Neuen Testaments und ihre Gegner* (Freiburg im Breisgau 1902) 482–549, and Rummel *Critics* I.
8 Cf the complaint voiced in the *Responsio ad annotationes Lei* LB IX 283A–B.

134

9 From Horace *Epistles* 1.18.66, which Erasmus explains in *Adagia* I viii 46
10 Thomas Aquinas; for Erasmus' assessment of Thomas' biblical studies see Jean-Paul Massaut 'Erasme et Saint Thomas' in *Colloquia Erasmiana Turonensia* ed J.-C. Margolin 2 vols (Toronto 1972) II 581–611.
11 Erasmus means 'Ambrosiaster,' the name which he was later to give to the author of the commentary on the thirteen Epistles of Paul, but at this date he had not yet distinguished the anonymous commentator from Ambrose, the bishop of Milan. See CWE 42 138 n13.
12 Hugo Carrensis (Hugh of Saint-Cher d 1263) and Nicolaus de Lyra (Nicholas of Lyre, in Normandy, d 1349) were the authors of the two most widely used commentaries on the Bible in the Middle Ages. Hugh's *Postillae* were apparently written either by himself or, more likely, under his direction when he was a professor in the Dominican school of theology at Paris from 1230 to 1235, and were intended to update and supplement the existing *Glossa ordinaria* through the addition of comments on the four senses of the text made by numerous twelfth- and thirteenth-century scholars. See Beryl Smalley *The Study of the Bible in the Middle Ages* 3rd ed (Oxford 1952) 269–75.
Nicholas was a member of the Franciscan order and a master in theology at Paris until his death. His commentary appeared in two parts, a longer *Postilla* on the literal or historical sense, which was extremely influential and is probably the commentary which Erasmus has in mind here, and somewhat later a shorter *Postilla moralis*, a commentary on the allegorical, tropological, and anagogical senses. Nicholas' *Postillae* were the first of the medieval commentaries to appear in print. It and Hugh's commentary were both printed in several editions from the fifteenth through the early eight-

eenth centuries. It is not possible to tell just what edition or editions
Erasmus was using at this time. Later he owned at least parts of the Amer-
bach-Froben edition of the *Gloss* and Nicholas' two *Postillae*. I have, therefore, employed the Basel editions of both Hugh and Nicholas. Their commentaries, as well as that of the *Glossa ordinaria*, are printed adjacent to the
biblical text. Since the Basel editions have no folio or page numbers, citations are keyed to the modern chapter and verse numbers so that readers
may easily locate them in any edition; however, a citation is sometimes
identified by the signature number of the page in the Basel edition.

13 Cf Ep 1155 n4.
14 Cf Ep 1183:131–4.
15 Cf *Adagia* I i 50.
16 Cf *Adagia* I ii 5.
17 A recurrent characterization of Erasmus' critics in his correspondence at this
time; cf CWE Epp 1166:13–17, 1174:6–7, 1191:29–35, 1205:32–6.

Argument

135

1 Jerome *De viris illustribus* 2 states that immediately after the passion of the
Lord the apostles ordained James bishop of Jerusalem.

Chapter 1

136

1 Cf the paraphrase on 1 Pet 1:1. Erasmus' view of the scattering of the Chris-
tian community after the death of Stephen is influenced by Acts 8. Bede *Exp
Iac* 1:1 CCL 121 183:9–13 / Hurst 7 makes the same connection between
James 1:1 and Acts 8:1–4. The *Gloss*, drawing in part upon Bede, states in
the prologue to the Epistle of James: 'We read that after the death of St
Stephen a great persecution was made against the church in Jerusalem and
that all except the apostles were dispersed among the regions of Judaea and
Samaria. Therefore, [James] sends this epistle to these disciples, who suffered for righteousness. He writes also to those who, after having received
the faith of Christ, were not yet making the effort to become perfect
through works, as well as to the elect who persisted in faith.'
2 Erasmus says *prora et puppis*, literally 'the stem and stern'; cf *Adagia* I i 8.

137

3 Cf 1 Cor 1:23.

138

4 Cf the *Enchiridion* CWE 66 39–40, and the *Paraclesis* Holborn 140:17–141:3.
5 what is required] 1532. The earlier editions read 'what is effected.'
6 It is pharisaical ... good and merciful] Added in the 1532 edition. The sentence, 'He takes no notice ... to have trust in him,' was sharply criticized by
Noël Béda and defended by Erasmus *Divinationes ad notata Bedae* LB IX 479D,

where he cites the parable of the Pharisee and the tax collector (Luke 18:9–14) to prove that it is faith, not works, which induces God to hear one's prayer. The paraphrase here is actually on the words of the tax collector in Luke 18:14. The 'pious prayer' contains echoes of Ps 86 and resembles an act of contrition.

7 Erasmus retained the Vulgate's 'with no wavering' ('nothing wavering' DR) in his Latin version but noted the other meaning of the Greek μηδὲν διακρινόμενος 'never doubting' (RSV) in his annotation on James 1:6 (*nihil haesitans*) LB VI 1026C. The paraphrase incorporates both meanings.

8 this person] LB reads *hîc* 'here' for *hic* 'this one.'

9 or the truthfulness of his promises] Added in 1532

139

10 The reference to the kingdom of heaven may be an anticipation of 2:5 or an allusion to Matt 5:3 and Luke 6:20. Cf Bede *Exp Iac* 1:9 CCL 121 185:103–4 / Hurst 11: 'Everyone who endures adversities humbly for the Lord will receive from him proudly the rewards of the kingdom.'

11 just as] Added in 1532

12 Cf Bede *Exp Iac* 1:11 CCL 121 186:116–17 / Hurst 11: 'Yet the elect also flourish, but not like hay. For "the righteous will flourish like a palm tree" [Ps 92:12].' The symbol of the palm tree and its branches is ubiquitous in Christian tradition, but the information that it is an evergreen comes from Pliny *Naturalis historia* 16.33.79.

140

13 See the paraphrase on 1 John 2:16 for the image of the noisy stir of life.

14 Cf Bede *Exp Iac* 1:12 CCL 121 187:154–7 / Hurst 13: 'One ought to rejoice the more in temptations the more it is evident and sure that God often places a heavier burden of temptations on those whom he loves.'

15 Cf 1 Pet 5:4 and 1 Cor 9:25. A garland of oak leaves was awarded a Roman soldier who saved the life of a fellow soldier in action; a garland of laurel was the prize given to the victor in the athletic and other contests held at Delphi in honour of the god Apollo.

141

16 Erasmus repeatedly speaks of sin (*peccatum*) as a vice or flaw (*vitium*). The noun *vitium* and its cognates *vitiosus* 'vicious, flawed' and *vitiare* 'to vitiate, to spoil or render flawed' in some way occur several times in this passage. *Vitium* is a key term in Erasmus' anthropology; see, for example, the *Enchiridion* CWE 66 45. For Erasmus' view of original sin, described here as 'the vice (or defect) of our first parents,' see Erasmus' annotation on Romans 5:12 (*in quo omnes peccaverunt*) LB VI 585B, the paraphrase on Rom 5:12–15 CWE 42 34–6, and Payne *Theology* 42–3.

17 Erasmus follows Aristotelian (and medieval) cosmology. In Aristotle's geocentric universe the region above the orbit of the moon is flawless and perfect; the sublunary region below the moon, which includes the earth, is imperfect and subject to contingency. See D.J. Allan *The Philosophy of Aristotle* chapter 5 (Oxford-London-New York-Toronto 1952) 57–62.

142

18 Cf Bede *Exp Iac* 1:17 CCL 121 189:229–31 / Hurst 16: 'After [James] has taught that the vices by which we are tempted are present in us not from God but from ourselves, he shows on the contrary that whatever good we do we have received as a gift from God.'

19 us] *nos* 'us' is the reading of the 1520, 1521, 1522, and the 1523 octavo editions and is certainly correct. *uos* is the reading of the 1523 folio edition and the 1532 and subsequent editions. The setting of *n* for *u* and *vice versa* is one of the most common forms of typographical error found in sixteenth-century printed books. It is especially frequent in books printed by the Froben firm since, unlike many other printers (and Erasmus in his own orthography), it always used *u*, not *v*, for initial *u*.

20 Erasmus comments in an annotation on James 1:17 (*nec*) LB VI 1028D in language as obscure as the original Greek: 'It [sc *conversionis obumbratio* 'shadow of turning' (NKJ)] signifies that a shadow is cast by this light and that our sun ascends and descends at the solstices.' He refers to Jerome *Adversus Jovinianum* PL 23 266A for support of this interpretation, but Jerome says nothing of the kind in his (allegorical) commentary. James 1:17, together with similar verses in the OT and NT, is cited by Augustine *De civitate Dei* 11.21 and *De natura boni* 24 CSEL 25/2 866:4–11, and Hilary *De Trinitate* 4.8 PL 10 101B for biblical proof of the immutability of God. These and similar patristic texts constitute the tradition behind Erasmus' statement about the unchangeability and self-consistency of God, but the interpretation given here and in the following sentence of the word 'shadow' appears to be Erasmus' own invention.

143

21 Cf John 1:9, though Erasmus doubtless has the language of the Nicene Creed in mind. The light or illumination produced by the gospel is a frequent image in the *Paraphrases* as is the contrast between the dawning day and the light of the gospel with the darkness and shadows of Judaism.

22 For Erasmus' conception of the transforming word see my article 'From Soul to Soul: Persuasion in Erasmus' Paraphrases on the New Testament' *Erasmus in English* 15 (1987–8) 7–9.

23 Cf 2 Cor 5:17.

24 Cf John 1:7–9.

25 Cf Eph 4:22 and Col 3:8–9.

144

26 Matt 13:7 and 22.

27 it from being able] *possit*, the reading of the 1520 and 1521 editions with the singular 'seed' (*semen*) from the preceding sentence as subject. The February 1522 and later editions read *possint* 'them from being able,' which assumes a plural antecedent 'seeds' as the subject. The change from singular to plural is most likely the result of a typographical error since there seems to be no reason for the obfuscating change to the plural.

28 and obstinacy] Added in 1532

29 'In life, not in words' *non in lingua, sed in vita*, which, literally translated, means 'not in the tongue, but in life.' *Vita*, as often in Erasmus means 'way

of life,' so *lingua* here means 'the use of the tongue' in, for example, philosophical disputations. Compare his statement in the *Paraclesis* Holborn 144:35–145:1: 'This kind of philosophy [sc the philosophy of Christ] is grounded in the feelings more truly than in syllogisms, is life more than disputation, inspiration rather than erudition, transformation rather than ratiocination.' Cf also the opening paragraph of the *Paraphrase on Mark* CWE 49 13.

145

30 See the paraphrase on Rom 7:7–12 CWE 42 42–3.
31 Béda criticized this statement which Erasmus defended by saying that he was speaking about the carnal or gross (*crassa*) part of the Law – the so-called law of ceremonies – and was comparing the law of commandments to the law of grace (*Divinationes ad notata Bedae* LB IX 479E). Erasmus offers the same defence in support of the contrast between the two laws in the paraphrase on 4:5 (ibidem 480A). Béda was not satisfied, and the controversy raged on for years.
32 Cf Matt 13:22 (Mark 4:18–19, Luke 8:14).
33 Cf Matt 5:22.
34 Cf Matt 6:19-21.
35 Cf Matt 5:27–28.

146

36 For cloaks and phylacteries see Matt 23:5, for ritual washings Mark 7:2–4, and for long prayers Luke 20:47. 'Discrimination among foods,' Erasmus' term for the sundry prescriptions of Lev 11 about clean and unclean creatures, occurs repeatedly in his lists of Jewish ceremonies.

147

37 Cf Luke 14:13–14.
38 For ... brother] Added in the 1532 edition. Cf Bede *Exp Iac* 1:27 CCL 121 193:353–5 / Hurst 21.

Chapter 2

1 Cf 1 Cor 2:8. Erasmus calls Christ the prince rather than the Lord of glory, presumably because he is the Son of the King of Glory (Ps 24). He passes over his own suggestion, advanced in his annotation on James 2:1 (*Jesu Christi gloria*) LB VI 1029D and adopted in his Latin version, that the Greek noun δόξα in this verse means 'opinion' rather than 'glory' – no one, I think, accepts this suggestion. The meaning of the verse , according to Erasmus, is that we are not to have our faith in our Lord Jesus Christ accompanied by a differentiation of people based on our personal opinion about them, so that instead of considering them simply as Christians, we judge whether they are high-born or low-born, wealthy, or relatives or strangers.
2 Cf Luke 6:20.
3 there] *illic* first in February 1522. The 1520 and 1521 editions read 'here.'

Again there appears to be no reason for the change, which introduces an inelegant repetition and is at variance with the Greek text.

4 Erasmus understood the Greek of the first part of verse 4 to mean 'have you not made a judgment inside yourselves' and consequently the second half of the verse to mean 'and become judges of [your own] wicked thoughts.'

148

5 Cf Augustine Ep 167.18 CSEL 44 605–6 and, following him, Bede *Exp Iac* 2:5 CCL 121 194:32–4 / Hurst 23. They both assume that to be poor is to be virtuous.
6 At baptism, cf Acts 2:38.
7 Bede *Exp Iac* 2:7 CCL 121 194:49 / Hurst 23 refers to Phil 2:9, which may have suggested to Erasmus the allusion to Phil 2:10–11.

149

8 In Lev 19:18
9 'The sum of the whole Law': *summa totius legis*. This phrase is an echo of the paraphrase on Rom 13:9–10 CWE 42 76, where Paul's statement 'love is the fulfilment of the Law' is paraphrased 'love is the sum of all laws' (*summa legum omnium est caritas*). This explanation of the text, both here and in the *Paraphrase on Romans*, appears in Augustine Ep 167 CSEL 44 603–6, parts of which Bede quotes in *Exp Iac* 2:10–11 CCL 121 195:70–82 / Hurst 24–5. Cf also Matt 22:35–40 and the paraphrase on 1 Tim 1:4–9.
10 Cf Matt 5:17–48, though there is no overt reference to this text here.

150

11 Cf Gal 5:13.
12 Cf the paraphrase on 1 Tim 1:9.
13 Alluding to Matt 18:23–35
14 Cf Matt 25:31–46. Erasmus seems also to have in mind the 'plea for mercy' in the art of rhetoric. One of the topics in this plea is to show that one has been gentle and compassionate in the use of one's own power over others; see Cicero *De Inventione* 2.35.107 and the *Rhetorica ad Herennium* 2.17.25.
15 Cf Augustine Ep 167.19 CSEL 44 607: 'Mercy triumphs over judgment because more persons are gathered through mercy,' quoted by Bede *Exp Iac* 2:13 CCL 121 196:125–9 / Hurst 27.
16 Cf Augustine Ep 167.20 CSEL 44 608, cited by Bede *Exp Iac* 2:14 CCL 121 197:135–43 / Hurst 27–8.
17 Cf Gal 5:6.

151

18 Noël Béda criticized this assertion of the intrinsic connection between faith and love on the ground that they are distinct and independent gifts of the Spirit. Erasmus replied that in the present context faith means saving faith. God never gives this faith without at the same time giving love and *vice versa* (*Divinationes ad notata Bedae* LB IX 479E–480A). This dispute too was to go on. See the *Supputatio* LB IX 697D–F, where Erasmus calls the faith under discussion 'justifying faith' and says that it consists of 1/ the acceptance of

everything taught by Sacred Scripture, and 2/ a complete confidence and hope in God's promises. He protests that it would be out of place to incorporate into the *Paraphrase* 'scholastic disputations' about whether faith exists absolutely and is infused alone without love, and becomes a living or a dead faith depending upon the presence or absence of love. The issue was escalated by the faculty of theology at Paris, when it declared Erasmus' view of faith and love heretical and contrary to Paul's explicit statement in 1 Cor 13:2. Erasmus defended himself against this charge on three grounds: first, the faculty had misunderstood the rhetorical nature of Paul's language as well as of his own; secondly, the kinds of questions argued by contemporary theologians would be anachronistic in the *Paraphrase*; thirdly, what he himself says about faith and love is precisely what James says and also numerous other Doctors of the church. Since he is speaking only about justifying faith (*fides justificans et cor purificans*), his statement about faith and love cannot be heretical (*Declarationes ad censuras Lutetiae vulgatas* LB IX 844B–846C).

19 This interpretation of verse 18 has several modern supporters; see, for example, the survey in Martin *James* 86–7. In the 1522 edition of the *Novum Testamentum* Erasmus added to his annotation on this passage (*sine operibus*) LB VI 1031D the statement: 'The language of the Greek text seems somewhat clearer [than that of the Vulgate]. James, in order to teach that neither faith without works nor works without faith are adequate, sets up an exchange with two other persons. It is said to the one who, relying on faith, neglects works: "You have faith and in your view that is sufficient." The other speaker, trusting in works but disregarding faith, replies, "I have deeds; that is enough for me." James rejects both assertions, saying, "On the contrary, what neither of you has is sufficient for salvation. You there who boast of your faith, teach us through your deeds that you have a faith which is not idle. I shall then reveal through my deeds that I have both." Certainly the words "you have faith [alone]" do not square with the character (*persona*) of the apostle, who rejects faith without deeds.'

152

20 Cf Mark 5:7 and Luke 4:41. Bede *Exp Iac* 2:19 CCL 121 197:164–7 / Hurst 29 cites the latter passage in making this same point.

21 Bede *Exp Iac* 2:19 CCL 121 198:182 uses the phrase 'futile faith' (*fides inanis*); cf 1 Cor 15:14 and 17.

22 Cf Rom 4:3 and 16. Erasmus' paraphrase follows the lead of Bede *Exp Iac* 2:21–4 CCL 121 198:194–200:255 / Hurst 30–2, who is concerned to demonstrate that Paul and James do not contradict each other, but only emphasize two different dimensions of Abraham's action – Paul, Abraham's faith in God; James, Abraham's obedience and readiness to act upon that faith: 'For they both knew that Abraham was perfect, both in faith and in works, and therefore each of them has emphasized in preaching on him the virtue which each perceived his hearers needed more.' Since Bede believed that Paul was the author of the Epistle to the Hebrews, he draws upon Heb 11:17–19 as well as upon Romans. Erasmus likewise subtly blends allusions to Hebrews and Rom 4 with the statements of James in order to suggest that there is no real contradiction between James and Paul.

23 Cf Rom 4:18.

24 Cf Rom 4:17 and Heb 11:19.

25 This contention is the starting point of Bede's exegesis *Exp Iac* 2:21 CCL 121 198:206–8 / Hurst 30: 'No one should think [as the Jews do] that he has come to the gift of righteousness, which is in faith, by the merits of his former good deeds.'

26 Cf Gen 15:6.

27 This point also appears in Bede *Exp Iac* 2:21 CCL 121 199:226–9 / Hurst 31: 'Would [Abraham] delay giving a tunic or his own food to the poor for the sake of divine love when he did not delay giving over to death immediately at the order of the Lord the son whom he had received as an heir when he was an old man?'

153

28 The description, 'friend of God,' which is not found in the OT in this form, occurs in Jewish apocryphal literature. See eg *Book of Jubilees* 19:9, 30:20, *4 Ezra* 3:14. Erasmus does not comment on this phrase in his *Annotationes*, nor, it seems, do Bede and the medieval commentators.

29 'Men and women of old' is my translation of *illis priscis*. I assume that, like Bede, Erasmus has in mind the catalogue in Heb 11.

30 Erasmus' language is a little loose and is affected by what is said of Abel in Heb 11:4. Rahab is not explicitly called righteous anywhere in the Bible. Nothing is said about her righteousness in Joshua 2 or 6; James 2:25 says that she 'was justified by works,' while Heb 11:31 says, 'By faith Rahab the harlot did not perish.' Bede *Exp Iac* 2:25 CCL 121 201:288–94 / Hurst 34 makes the point that Rahab was 'an iniquitous woman, a foreign woman. Yet she, by works of mercy, by showing hospitality to the servants of God even at risk to her life, deserved to be made righteous from sins, to be enrolled as a member of the people of Israel, to be included in the list of their royal lineage, to be among the ancestry of the families of our Lord and Saviour himself ... to be rescued from the devastation of her ... homeland, whose perfidy she rejected.'

31 The word 'spies' is taken from Heb 11:31.

32 is cold and no longer loving] *friget ex charitate* first in 1532. The words imply that this faith once had love. The earlier editions read *friget absque charitate* 'is cold without love.' *Absque charitate* is a paraphrase on *absque spiritu* 'without the spirit' in 2:26. The revision probably reflects the theological controversies referred to in n18 above.

Chapter 3

154

1 Here as elsewhere in the *Paraphrase* 'teacher' means 'preacher.' Erasmus identifies this office with that of the bishop. See immediately below and the paraphrase on 1 Tim 3:1.

2 Bede *Exp Iac* 3:1 CCL 121 202:16 / Hurst 35, adapting Phil 1:17, makes this point. Cf the paraphrase on 3:13 below.

3 Bede *Exp Iac* 3:2 CCL 121 203:56–9 / Hurst 37 paraphrases: 'If anyone avoids a slip of the tongue, which is almost unavoidable, this person, by having

made this restraint into a fixed habit, also learns how to keep guard over the other members of his body, which are more easily restrained, so that they do not turn aside from the right way.'

4 For this twofold treatment of speech see the *Lingua* CWE 29 365; and for the underlying assumptions about the power of speech, the paraphrase on John 1:2 CWE 46 16.

5 Bede *Exp Iac* 3:3 CCL 121 203:64–8 / Hurst 37 reports that some manuscripts read *sicut* 'just as' instead of *si* 'if' as the first word of this verse; cf Erasmus' annotation here (*si autem frenos*) LB VI 1031F. The use of a comparison instead of a condition in the paraphrase on 3:3 may thus be a reflection of the reading *sicut*, not simply a rhetorical variation of the original text.

155

6 A summary of the paraphrase on 3:6–13 appears in the *Lingua* CWE 29 366–7. The subject of the abuse of the tongue by clerics, especially for calumny and other forms of slander, is developed at length in this later work; see especially CWE 29 348–62. Erasmus' treatment of the topic is itself part of a long history of such discussions; see CWE 29 251–2 and Mark D. Johnston 'The Treatment of Speech in Medieval Ethical and Courtesy Literature' *Rhetorica* 4 (1986) 21–46.

7 Erasmus found the translation *materia* 'building material, matter' for ὕλη in Jerome *Commentarius in Isaiam* 66:15 PL 22 664A and evidently believed that in James 3:5 the Greek word meant 'timber' or 'matter' (*materia*), not 'forest' (*silva*) as rendered in the Vulgate; cf his annotation on 3:6 (*ecce quantus ignis*) LB VI 1032E and the translation 'matter' in AV. The paraphrase suggests that he had something like lumber or firewood in mind. Modern translators and commentators, however, prefer to translate the Greek by 'forest' or a similar word.

8 The 'anatomy' of the tongue and its teleological implications are elaborated in the *Lingua* CWE 29 265–9.

9 The Greek word κόσμος in 3:6 is translated by *universitas* 'universe, world' in the Vulgate, which is also the meaning preferred in modern translations. The Greek noun does have several other meanings such as arrangement, order, ornament, and the like. Erasmus, therefore, translated it by the Latin word *mundus*, which likewise means 'world' but can also denote a set of equipment and materials used to decorate something or to perform some task. In his annotation on 3:6 (*universitas iniquitatis*) LB VI 1032E Erasmus comments: '*Mundus* sometimes means a pile of things placed together, as in the phrase *mundus muliebris* [a woman's collection of ornaments and toiletries].' In the paraphrase the noun *congeries* 'collection, heap' is used together with *mundus* to indicate the meaning which Erasmus prefers here. He then reinforces this understanding of the Greek with phrases such as 'every evil ... is drawn from the tongue as though it were their storehouse (*mundus*).'

10 This interpretation of an obscure Greek phrase in 3:6 ('the course of nature' AV, 'the cycle of nature' or 'the wheel of birth' RSV) is made by Bede *Exp Iac* 3:6 CCL 121 205:131–3 / Hurst 40: '"The wheel of our birth" [is] the ceaseless advance of our earthly life by which we are continuously moved from the day of our birth right up to death as if by the always turning wheel of a carriage.'

11 The image of evil as a disease is frequent in the *Paraphrases*, but Bede *Exp
Iac* 3:6 CCL 121 205:122–4 / Hurst 39 compares the presence of evil spirits to
a person sick with chills and fever. The comparison may have prompted the
disease imagery here.

156

12 Bede *Exp Iac* 3:7 CCL 121 206:146–51 / Hurst 40 mentions accounts of
trained tigers and asps. Erasmus appears to have had a special interest in
such tales; see the colloquy 'Sympathy' in Thompson *Colloquies* 516–27. The
idea that wild creatures can be trained is a commonplace in classical literature; cf eg Sophocles *Antigone* 349–52, Lucretius *De rerum natura* 5.1297–1307
(horses and elephants), Pliny *Naturalis historia* 8.2 (elephants), 25 and 38
(crocodiles), 10.6 (eagles). Maximus of Tyre *Dissertatio* 8.5 has a remarkable
story about a pet crocodile, but Erasmus may not have known this work.

13 These words are a paraphrase on Erasmus' Greek text, which has
ἀκατάσχετον 'unruly' (AV, NKJ), whereas the Vulgate has *inquietum* 'unquiet'
(DR), which translates the variant reading ἀκατάστατον 'restless' (RSV).

14 The poison or venom produced by the tongue is the opening theme of the
Lingua CWE 29 262. The comparison *a minore* with wild animals likewise
appears there (348).

15 See the *Lingua* CWE 29 353 and 357–9 for similar complaints about the abuse
of the pulpit and the unconscionable employment of slander by clerics.

16 A variation on Matt 25:40

17 See the paraphrase on 5:12 below.

18 Cf Luke 6:28.

157

19 See Ep 948:99–238 for a series of such episodes, which others reported to
Erasmus or at which he himself was present.

20 Erasmus alludes here and in the preceding sentence to Christ's silence on
the cross when mocked and slandered (Matt 27:39–44, Luke 23:35–7). The
slandered benefactor is Erasmus himself; cf the dedicatory letter 133.

21 According to Pliny *Naturalis historia* 27.2.4, aconite is the most swiftly acting
and deadly of all the poisons. Erasmus would doubtless have found the
English name of the plant, monkshood, especially apt.

158

22 It is not clear whether Erasmus is thinking of the congregation assembled in
a church or an audience of students at a scholastic disputation (cf *Ratio*
Holborn 180–1). The members of neither audience have any interest in what
they are hearing but talk among themselves about whatever is on their minds.

23 Evangelical philosophy is here an alternative name for what Erasmus more
often calls the 'philosophy of Christ'; see CWE 66 xxi–xxv. Evangelical philosophy is fundamentally different from a philosophy, or theology, devoted
to questions posed and answered in dialectical debate, the prescription of
rules and regulations, and 'Jewish' ceremonies; cf the description of the
false preachers (theologians) in the paraphrase on 3:15 below.

24 endowed with true knowledge] LB reads 'truly endowed with knowledge.'

25 through pride and a contest in words] The 1540 edition, followed by LB,
reads 'a contest in pride and words.'

26 See Bede *Exp Iac* 3:13 CCL 121 208:217–26 / Hurst 43 for a similar statement.

27 Unlike the *mundus* from which worldly wisdom is drawn. The image of the clean vessel (*sincerum vas*) is more classical than biblical (cf Horace *Satires* 1 3:56 and *Epistles* 1.2.54), but Erasmus may have in mind the use of the word 'vessel' in texts like 1 Thess 4:4. For his view that a pure heart is the fundamental prerequisite for the preacher see his *Ecclesiastes* LB V 774A–776E.

159

28 Cf *Ratio* Holborn 301:10–302:6.

29 Cf Luke 11:46.

30 See John 3:3 where Erasmus, following the Vulgate, likewise takes the adverb ἄνωθεν to mean 'from on high.'

31 Erasmus follows the Vulgate in translating ψυχική by *animalis*. In his annotation on 3:16 (*animalis, diabolica*) LB VI 1033E he comments on this word: '[James] calls human emotions "sensual" to contrast them with spirit.' Later in the same annotation he remarks that this sensual wisdom is called demonic because it comes from the spirit of this world, not from the Spirit of Christ.

32 whose promptings] *qui ea suggerunt*. LB reads *quia ea suggerunt* 'because their promptings.'

33 The words 'what fights ... behaviour' are an instance of double paraphrase. *Inconstantia* is the translation of ἀκαταστασία 'confusion' (NKJ), 'disorder' (RSV) in the Vulgate, which Erasmus retained in his own Latin version. However, in his annotation on this word (*ibi inconstantia*) LB VI 1033E he says (correctly) that the Greek word means 'uproar' and 'civil disorder.' 'Fights' and 'disagreements' paraphrase his understanding of the Greek, 'inconstancy in beliefs and behaviour' the text of the Vulgate.

34 This clause is a paraphrase on the words *bonis consentiens* 'consenting to the good' (DR) transmitted in some manuscripts of the Vulgate, and appears to follow Bede's interpretation of them. In his annotation on 3:17 (*suadibilis*) LB VI 1035F, Erasmus states that he did not find this phrase in either the Greek manuscripts or in the oldest [Latin] manuscript [in the College] of St Donatian [in Bruges], but Bede, he says, reads and comments on it. Bede *Exp Iac* 3:17 CCL 121 210:282–3 / Hurst 46 takes the adjective *bonis* to be masculine gender and hence to mean good people: 'It behooves a wise man to give assent to the persuasion of the good.' Bede's English translator evidently overlooked this comment and took the word *bonis* to be neuter gender and the phrase to mean 'in agreement with what is good.'

35 'Condemns no one' is a paraphrase on the Vulgate translation of ἀδιάκριτος by *non iudicans* 'without judging' (DR). Erasmus' own translations are *absque diiudicatione* in his Latin version and *nihil discernens* in his annotation (*iudicans sine simulatione* LB VI 1033F), both of which mean 'without partiality.'

36 For the deadliness of an unspiritual wisdom see the *Enchiridion* CWE 66 40.

160

37 Cf the paraphrase on Titus 3:11.

Chapter 4

1 'Worldly passions' is a paraphrase on the text of the Vulgate which renders

the Greek ἐκ τῶν ἡδονῶν 'from your pleasures' by *ex concupiscentiis* 'from your desires.' *Concupiscentia* is also the word used in the Vulgate to translate ἐπιθυμία 'desire' in 1:14–15. Commentators following the text of the Vulgate readily connected 4:1 with 1:14, and consequently understood 'wars and quarrels' to be metaphors both for conflicts raised in the soul by desires or passions and for dissensions in the community. Cf Bede *Exp Iac* 4:1–2 CCL 121 211:1–19 / Hurst 47–8.

2 *Pugnae* 'battles' is Erasmus' translation of the Greek μάχαι; *lites* 'contentions' is the translation in the Vulgate.

3 Cf Col 3:9–10.

4 The notion of envy, developed here in the paraphrase on 4:2, is not in the transmitted Greek text; however, Erasmus proposed emending the verb φονεύετε 'you kill,' which did not seem to him to fit the context, to φθονεῖτε 'you envy.' He is thus paraphrasing his own emendation, which he accepted in his Latin version. Modern scholars still debate the text; cf eg Martin Dibelius and Heinrich Greeven *James* (Philadelphia 1975) 217–18, who support the emendation, with Davids *James* 158–9 and Martin *James* 140–1, who do not.

5 nor] March 1521. The 1520 edition reads 'and.'

6 The illustration is used by Bede *Exp Iac* 4:3 CCL 121 211:24–212:27 / Hurst 48: 'He ... asks wrongly who, having lost the love of things above, seeks only to obtain the lowest goods, and these not for the support of human frailty but for the superfluity of unnecessary pleasure.'

161

7 Cf Eph 5:26.

8 Erasmus is probably anticipating 4:5, but may be alluding to 2 Cor 11:2.

9 Cf *Adagia* III vi 84: 'A mind leaning in two directions,' which, Erasmus says, is equivalent to 'being lame in both feet,' and applies to a person of uncertain faith and loyalty. Several of the phrases used in the paraphrase on James 4:4 occur in the *Enchiridion* CWE 66 57, which suggests that both texts draw upon one of Erasmus' theological *loci* (see *Ratio* Holborn 291).

10 See Matt 6:24 and Luke 16:13, and the reference to the *Enchiridion* in n9 above.

11 Cf 2 Cor 6:15–16.

12 Erasmus combines here the NT image of the bride of Christ with the OT image of Israel as God's unfaithful wife (cf eg Ezek 16:8–14 and Hos 2); however, the details of his imagery do not correspond to any one biblical text.

13 'Sacred scrolls': *sacris voluminibus*. The quotation which follows is not found in the OT, as Erasmus knew. It is not clear then whether by 'sacred scrolls' he means Sacred Scripture or simply holy books of some kind. In the paraphrase on Acts 17:28 LB VII 737B the phrase *sacra volumina* 'sacred scrolls' clearly means the Bible.

14 Erasmus retains with slight modification the translation of the Vulgate. I have used Knox here rather than DR since the language of the latter is too archaic ('To envy doth the spirit covet which dwelleth in you'). Erasmus' Greek text and his Latin version both have 'in us' (cf AV), not 'in you,' which is the reading of the early editions of the Vulgate. In his annotation

on 4:5 (*ad invidiam spiritus concupiscit*) LB VI 1034E Erasmus explains the meaning of 4:5 and 6: 'In my own view the most likely meaning is that the spirit of a person devoted to the world begrudges itself but the bounty of the grace which God imparts [to us] exceeds our power to desire.' In other words, grace overcomes the concupiscence inherent in human nature; see Martin *James* 150–1 for the arguments both in favor of and against this interpretation. In the paraphrase Erasmus adduces a congeries of NT texts to support his interpretation; cf Luke 18:29, Matt 10:37–9, 1 Cor 3:16, 2 Cor 6:16–7:1.

15 In so far ... act] Added in 1532
16 Cf 2 Cor 6:16–7:1.

162

17 Cf the paraphrase on 1 John 2:15.
18 Only let us] March 1521 and subsequent editions. The 1520 edition reads *tantum ut* 'provided that we' but prints the clause as though it were an independent sentence.
19 Cf Proverbs 3:34 LXX. In his annotation on 4:6 (*maiorem autem dat*) LB VI 1034F Erasmus observes that the term 'humble' in this verse refers to social status, not to mental attitude. He also believed that the quotation from Proverbs was a gloss introduced into the text of James from 1 Pet 5:5, but this view does not affect the paraphrase.
20 Bede *Exp Iac* 4:8 CCL 121 214:100–6 / Hurst 51 likewise interprets nearness to God in terms of moral disposition (*affectus*): he who pursues virtue is near to God, he who is awash in filthy vice is far from God.
21 That is, in this world; cf Bede *Exp Iac* 4:9–10 CCL 121 214:123–9 / Hurst 52 who likewise develops this double antithesis: misery vs. vain happiness in this life; true happiness vs. eternal misery in the next.

163

22 Erasmus evidently understood the command, 'Do not speak evil against one another' in 4:11 to imply mutual or reciprocated abuse and slander.
23 This paraphrase on the word 'judges' appears to rest on Erasmus' understanding of Matt 7:1, which he translates, 'Do not condemn, lest you be condemned.'
24 us] *nos*. The 1540 edition and LB read *quos* 'anyone.'
25 Cf Matt 7:1–5, Luke 6:37, Rom 2:1–2 and 14:4, 1 Cor 4:5 and 5:12–13, all of which are alluded to at one point or another in the paraphrase on 4:11–2. Bede *Exp Iac* 4:11 CCL 121 215:133–6 / Hurst 52 by contrast assumes that the Law is the Mosaic law and refers to Lev 19:16–18. Modern scholars are likewise divided over the law which James has in mind. Cf Davids *James* 169–70 with Martin *James* 163. For Erasmus' conception of evangelical law or the *lex Christi* as he calls it, see C.D. McCullough 'The Concept of Law in the Thought of Erasmus' *Erasmus of Rotterdam Society Yearbook One* (1981) 89–112.
26 and yet we] The 1540 edition and LB read 'and to' for 'and yet we,' thus construing the verb 'indulge' with 'condemn.'

164

27 Cf Rom 14:4.

28 Cf Matt 7:33–4 and Luke 6:41–2.

29 Cf Bede *Exp Iac* 4:13 CCL 121 215:154–8 / Hurst 53: '[James] notes that there is a manifold folly in this kind of arrangement, obviously because they are both making plans about increasing their profits and thinking that they will live a long time while asserting that where they will live for a year is within their own power.'

30 The paraphrase on 4:14 follows the text of the Vulgate, 'we shall go into that city,' rather than Erasmus' Greek text which reads 'let us go into this city.' Erasmus does not comment in his *Annotationes* on this difference between the two texts; however, he does comment on the similar difference in readings in verse 15, where he states that he believes the Greek text is corrupt and needs to be emended (*si dominus voluerit*) LB VI 1035E. His choice of the text of the Vulgate in place of the Greek text of 4:14 is thus probably deliberate.

165

31 Cf Bede *Exp Iac* 4:14 CCL 121 215:164–216:171 / Hurst 54 who, after quoting Wisd 2:2–3, comments on 4:16: 'For the people who reached these conclusions [in Wisd] believed that there was no life except this one, saying with Epicurus, "After life there is nothing, and death itself is nothing."'

32 Cf Rom 7:15–20 and the *Enchiridion* CWE 66 41–3. The conflict between knowing what is good but doing what is wrong is a frequent topic in classical literature; cf eg the well-known words of Ovid's Medea (*Metamorphoses* 7.19–21):

A strange power draws me against my will:
I desire one thing, reason urges another.
I see and approve the better course, I follow the worse.

Chapter 5

166

1 The motif of the heir is imported from classical literature. However, Erasmus inverts the customary contrast of the thrifty father and the wastrel heir; cf eg Horace *Satires* 2.3.118–28, *Odes* 4.7.17–20, *Epistles* 2.2.190–4.

2 Cf Bede *Exp Iac* 5:3 CCL 121 217:25–9 / Hurst 56. The notion that the word 'flesh' means the corrosive desire of wealth in the soul occurs in Bede who, influenced by Luke 16:25, says ibidem 217:16–20 / Hurst 55, 'By the word "flesh" can also be understood those fleshly delights which the corrosion that is wealth eats up like fire while the raging flame tortures the dissolute soul outwardly and the piercing sorrow of its obstinacy accuses it no less inwardly.'

3 This sentence is a paraphrase on the text of the Vulgate: 'You have stored up for yourselves wrath against the last days' (DR). The words 'wrath for yourselves' do not occur in the Greek text.

4 I have paraphrased rather than literally translated Erasmus' sentence which reads, 'the harvester ... cries aloud such that their voice' etc. The illogical

plural 'their' is probably an unconscious recollection of the plural in the NT
text.

5 whom you too ought to fear] Added in the March 1521 edition. Cf Bede
Exp Iac 5:4 CCL 121 217:39–41 / Hurst 56–7: '[James] calls him the Lord of
Sabaoth, that is, the Lord of hosts, to terrify those who think the poor have
no protector.' The contrast between the wretched poor and the self-indulgent rich is the central focus of Bede's commentary on 5:4–5 ibidem
218:45–54 / Hurst 56–7.

6 'Their teeth were clenched': *ringebantur.* Erasmus may be creating a variation on the biblical idiom of grinding or gnashing the teeth as a gesture of
hostility (cf Job 16:10, Ps 35:16, Acts 7:54) or one of pain and regret (Matt
8:12, 13:42, 25:30). However, in the physiognomy of Erasmus' time such a
grimace would be a sign of mental distress just as the smile which might
appear on the faces of the self-indulgent rich would be evidence of their
folly. See Harry Vredeveld '"That Familiar Proverb": Folly As the Elixir of
Youth in Erasmus' *Moriae Encomium*' *Renaissance Quarterly* 42 (1989) 88–90.

7 This interpretation of the phrase 'as in a day of slaughter' (NKJ) is advanced
without further comment in the annotation on 5:5 (*in die occisionis*) LB VI
1036D. Bede *Exp Iac* 5:5–6 CCL 121 218:55–219:77 / Hurst 57–8, followed by
the medieval commentators, read this phrase with verse 6 – 'You have
condemned and murdered the righteous one' – and inferred that 'the righteous one' was Jesus and the 'day of slaughter' was the day of his crucifixion. Modern scholars would for the most part agree with Erasmus in rejecting Bede's interpretation, but prefer to see in the phrase a reference to the
eschatological Day of Wrath rather than to some holiday feast.

8 did] March 1521 and subsequent editions. The 1520 edition reads 'do.'

9 This metaphorical interpretation of 'you have murdered' is supported by
some modern scholars; cf Davids *James* 179–80. Others, such as Martin *James*
181–2, take the language literally and speak of judicial murder. The adroit
paraphraser manages to have it both ways!

10 Cf the story of the rich man and Lazarus in Luke 16:19–26.

167

11 Cf Erasmus' annotation on 5:7 (*donec accipiat temporaneum et serotinum*) LB VI
1036E. Commentators from Augustine onward were unsure about the meaning of 5:7. Erasmus believed that James had Deut 11:14 in mind and therefore he correctly understood the two rains as belonging to two different
seasons of the year, but being unfamiliar with the climate of the eastern
Mediterranean he takes them to be the spring and summer rains of his
north European experience. However, in the contrast which follows between the transitory harvest of the farmer and the harvest of immortality of
the faithful he also incorporates in the paraphrase on 5:8 the medieval allegorical interpretation of the 'early' as the present life and the 'later' as the
future life; cf Bede *Exp Iac* 5:7 CCL 121 219:89–94 / Hurst 58.

12 Cf the paraphrase on 2 Tim 4:8.

13 Erasmus appears to mean that envy at the good fortune of others and
distrust in the impartiality of God can lead to the unforgivable sin of
despair.

14 such grumblings ... despair] March 1521 and the subsequent editions. The

1520 edition reads 'such grumblings in the mind are the opening notes of despair.'

15 Cf Matt 23:29–35.

168

16 Erasmus appears to have Heb 11:36–7 in mind.

17 contesting] *certantem.* The 1540 edition and LB read 'you watched his contest' (*certamen*).

18 Cf Job 1:12–2:7 and 42:10.

19 Erasmus silently rejects the view of Augustine and Bede that the words, in 5:11, 'you have seen the end of the Lord,' refer to the passion and ascension of Jesus.

20 'Your speech': *sermo vester.* These two words are taken from the text of the Vulgate (where they are imported from Matt 5:37); they are not found in the Greek text of James 5:12.

21 'Disciples of truth': *veritatis discipuli.* This phrase should perhaps be translated 'disciples of the truth' as in John 14:6.

22 Magical incantations, both oral or written, to cure mental distress or disorders as well as physical diseases were ubiquitous in the ancient Mediterranean world and in Erasmus' own world. Likewise hot and cold baths were a normal part of medical therapy. For the sixteenth-century belief in the therapeutic power of rings and gems see George Frederick Kunz *Rings for the Finger* (Philadelphia-London 1917) 336–54 and his *The Curious Lore of Precious Stones* (Philadelphia-London 1913) 367–91.

23 lift up] March 1521 and subsequent editions. The 1520 edition reads 'turn.'

169

24 Erasmus had a jaundiced view of physicians; see the colloquy 'The Funeral' in Thompson *Colloquies* (Chicago-London 1965) 360. But Mark 5:26 offers a biblical instance of the failure of physicians compared to the healing power of Jesus.

25 Erasmus writes *seniores* – which can mean either 'older men,' or, if used as a title, 'elders' – both here in 5:14 and in 5:15 below. The Vulgate has *presbyteros,* a transliteration of the original Greek, which Erasmus retained in his Latin version. This term was understood to mean 'priest' (cf DR) and the present verse was one of the two scriptural bases for the sacrament of extreme unction, the other being Mark 6:13. Consequently, Hugh of St Cher and Nicholas of Lyra in their commentaries on 5:14 discuss the actions of anointing and praying in terms of the administration of the sacrament of extreme unction. Hugh in particular is more concerned with questions – such as, for example, what were the necessary qualifications of the priest for administering the sacrament – than he is with explicating the actual text. In paraphrasing *presbyteros* by *seniores* Erasmus may be following Bede *Exp Iac* 5:14 CCL 121 221:162–5 / Hurst 61, who takes the word *presbyteros* to mean older men, adding the comment that the sick person 'should not report the cause of his infirmity to the younger [*iuniores*] and less learned men lest perchance he receive from them some harmful advice or counsel.' Bede to be sure may be thinking of older and younger priests since the 'cause of the infirmity' may be some sin which has to be confessed.

Although Erasmus avers that he never questioned the institution of the sacrament of extreme unction (LB IX 389D–E), his use of *seniores* in the paraphrase might seem to call into question the sacramental interpretation of this verse as in the later controversy between William Tyndale and Thomas More, for which see Heinz Holeczek *Humanistische Bibelphilologie als Reformproblem bei Erasmus von Rotterdam, Thomas More und William Tyndale* Studies in the History of Christian Thought 9 (Leiden 1975) 323–31. The interpretation 'older men' is explicitly repudiated by the Council of Trent, session XIV, On the Sacrament of Extreme Unction, chapter 3, and anyone who upholds it is declared anathema in canon IV; see J[ames] Waterworth *The Canons and Decrees of the Sacred and Oecumenical Council of Trent* etc (London 1848) 106 and 111.

26 This contrast between the efficacy of prayer and the futility of magic may be only an instance of rhetorical paraphrase through contrast; or like the passing hit at physicians, it may also be an oblique criticism of the 'magical' actions that surrounded the act of dying in Erasmus' time; see eg 'The Funeral' (n24 above). Invoking the name of Jesus in such a situation is a Lucan theme; cf Luke 10:17, Acts 3:6, 4:10 and 30.

27 Both Hugh of St Cher and Nicholas of Lyra make the same observation: Christ will alleviate the illness if it is to the sick person's advantage. The phrase which Erasmus employs here, *siquidem expediat*, is equivalent to a formula; cf Thomas Aquinas *Summa contra gentiles* 4.73. It is used by the Council of Trent in the decree on extreme unction, session 14, chapter 2: 'The sick ... at times obtains bodily health, when expedient for the welfare of the soul' (J[ames] Waterworth *The Canons and Decrees of the Sacred and Oecumenical Council of Trent* etc [London 1848] 106).

28 Bede *Exp Iac* 5:15 CCL 121 221:176–7 / Hurst 62 makes this same assertion and quotes 1 Cor 11:30 to support it; cf Erasmus' paraphrase on 1 Cor 11:30 (LB VII 897D–E). In the paraphrase on Mark 6:13 (CWE 49 80) Erasmus distinguishes between the visible oil which contributes to the healing of the body and the (invisible) oil of evangelical grace which has to be put on the soul by Jesus to heal it of the diseases of its vices. This same distinction between the functions of the anointing with oil and the prayer and invocation of Christ appears to be in Erasmus' mind here in the paraphrase on James 5:14–15 though less clearly stated. As Payne *Theology* 217 observes, 'Erasmus repudiates a merely fleshly, formalistic, magical understanding and usage [of the sacraments].'

29 'Slight trespasses' (*levibus offensis*) and 'offence' (*delictum*) below are renderings of the Greek word παραπτώματα 'faults' (AV) in 5:16, which is the reading of Erasmus' Greek text. In his annotation on 5:16 (*peccata vestra*) LB VI 1037D Erasmus comments, 'παραπτώματα means mistakes rather than sins, as if one were to speak of slips. James has in view the daily offences which Christians commit among themselves. God wants them to make up with one another without delay. If James had meant that confession [to a priest] which we consider part of the sacrament of penance, he would not have added ἀλλήλοις, that is, "to one another," but [would have said] "to priests."' In the 1522 edition of the *Novum Testamentum* Erasmus added to this annotation a reference to Bede *Exp Iac* 5:16 CCL 121 222:186–7 / Hurst 62: 'We confess our daily and minor sins to one another as peers and

believe that we are saved by their daily prayer.' Bede, however, is careful to point out that more serious sins must be confessed to a priest.

30 Cf Matt 21:22 and John 14:12–14.

31 This description of Elijah, together with the epithet 'godly' below, neither of which terms is used of him in the Bible, is probably a paraphrase on the word 'righteous' in 5:16. Erasmus would thus be identifying the 'righteous man' of verse 16 with Elijah. Modern commentators prefer to separate 5:16 from 5:17 and to take the 'righteous man' of 16 to be someone different from Elijah; see eg Martin *James* 211–12.

32 This antithesis between one and many occurs in Bede *Exp Iac* 5:18 CCL 121 222:201–3 / Hurst 63, though in somewhat different form: 'The one man Elijah obtained just as much as the several prayers of very many righteous persons can obtain.'

33 Cf Bede *Exp Iac* 5:19–20 CCL 121 223:225–7 / Hurst 64: 'For if it is very rewarding to rescue from death the flesh, which is going to die sometime, how much more meritorious is it to free from death the soul which is going to live without end in its heavenly homeland?'

170

34 his own] *sua*. The possessive adjective is omitted in the 1540 edition and in LB so that their text reads: 'Christ in turn will forgive the sins ... of him who has called a brother back' etc.

35 It is not clear from the Greek text of 5:20 just whose soul is saved, the soul of the sinner or of the one who turns him from error, and the interpretation of this verse is much vexed (cf eg the commentaries of Davids and Martin on it). Bede, however, believed that the sins of both persons were 'covered' and the souls of both saved through the action of the brother who 'cures his neighbour' (*Exp Iac* 5:20 CCL 121 223:233–6 / Hurst 64). Although Erasmus leaves the question open in his Latin version, the paraphrase in the manner of Bede compasses both possibilities.

PARAPHRASE ON 1 JOHN

Dedicatory Letter

172

1 Ep 1179, translated by R.A.B. Mynors, with revisions by JJB. The year date, omitted in the letter, is 1521.

2 Erasmus does not indicate anywhere what this business might have been, but he probably has in mind activities connected with the diet that was to open in Worms on 27 January; see Ep 1179 n1 (CWE 8 397) and Ep 1197 introduction (CWE 8 194–5).

Argument

173

1 See Jerome *De viris illustribus* 9 and Erasmus' annotation on 3 John 9 (*testimonium redditur*) LB VI 1088C.

Chapter 1

174

1 Though the identification of the 'word of life' with the Son was traditional, Erasmus appears to be following Augustine *Tract in 1 Ioannem* 1.1 PL 35 1978–9. Augustine makes the same points found in Erasmus: the Word existed from eternity, it became flesh through the Virgin Mary and was manifested so that it could be seen by the eyes of the body and not just the eyes of the mind, and the Word became flesh so that we might be healed. Augustine ibidem PL 35 1980 also introduces the reference to 'doubting' Thomas; see the next note.

2 See John 20:24–9; Luke 24:36–43.

3 See John 20:29.

4 The term herald (*praeco* in Latin, κῆρυξ in Greek) and its cognates are not found in the Johannine Gospel and Epistles. Whether or not done with this intention, Erasmus, by introducing such words and even quotations from the synoptic Gospels as well as from the Pauline Epistles, assimilates the Johannine texts to the other parts of the New Testament.

175

5 At Jesus' baptism and at the transfiguration; cf Mark 1:11 (Matt 3:17, Luke 3:22) and 9:7 (Matt 17:5, Luke 9:35). Neither event occurs in the Gospel of John.

6 Cf Mark 16:14, Matt 28:17, Luke 24:11–12; by contrast, in John 20:8, the Beloved Disciple believes immediately.

7 Cf Rom 5:14 and 17.

8 Erasmus means in philosophy.

9 escapes death] 1532. The earlier editions read 'truly escapes.'

176

10 Erasmus' Greek text of 1:4 has the second person pronoun as does the text of the Vulgate. However, he also knows about the alternative reading with the first person pronoun (cf AV with RSV), which he says in his annotation on this passage (*ut gaudeatis*) LB VI 1071F he would prefer if the Greek manuscripts were not against it; cf Metzger *Textual Commentary* 708. The subsequent explication with the first person 'we' may be intended to accommodate this alternative reading, just as the paraphrase 'you may rejoice' for 'your joy may be' is intended to accommodate the text of the Vulgate which reads 'that you may rejoice, and your joy may be full.' The verb 'you may rejoice' (*gaudeatis*) is not found in the Greek manuscripts.

11 The light ... darkness is sin] 1532. The punctuation of all the editions through 1523 places the genitive 'of the soul' with the noun 'darkness' rather than with 'light': 'The light is truth and innocence, darkness of the soul is sin' etc.

177

12 Erasmus shifts from the indicative of the preceding sentence to the subjunctive without any apparent reason since the two sentences are otherwise grammatically identical.

13 For Erasmus pride is the source of sin; self-effacement or humility is the necessary first step toward contrition and confession. See *Exomologesis* LB V 147C–150A.
14 Cf Matt 6:14–15.
15 Erasmus' Latin can be read as I have translated it in keeping with the allusion to Matt 18:21–35, or it may be translated 'the Lord's mercy,' which might seem to fit the immediate context better.
16 Cf Rom 3:24–6.
17 recalls] 1532. The earlier editions read 'reckons.'

178
18 Cf Matt 6:14–15 and Luke 6:37, which Erasmus is about to cite.
19 This particular trio of sins may be fortuitous, but Erasmus may have had in mind a view held in the early church that the decree of the Council of Jerusalem (see Acts 15:20) prohibited these specific actions; cf eg Tertullian *De pudicitia* 12.4–5; Robert M. Grant *Augustine to Constantine: The Rise and Triumph of Christianity in the Roman World* (San Francisco 1990) 58–9. A similar trio, though based on the Decalogue, appears in Rom 2:21–2.
20 Erasmus quotes the text of his own Latin version rather than the Vulgate.
21 Erasmus apparently means through the sacrament of confession; see 'The Whole Duty of Youth' in Thompson *Colloquies* 38–9 and Payne *Theology* 191–216.
22 Erasmus seems to be alluding to the parable of the Pharisee and the tax collector in Luke 18:9–14. See the paraphrase on Luke 18:13 (LB VII 422E) and on James 1:5.
23 The reference is not immediately evident. Erasmus could be referring to any number of OT texts (cf Brown *Epistles* 211–12; Bede *Exp 1 Ioannis* 1:10 CCL 121 288:164–5 / Hurst 165 cites Eccles 7:21), but he may have specifically in mind Pss 14:1–3 and 53:1–3 as employed by Paul in Rom 3:9–11.

Chapter 2

179
1 See the paraphrase on Rom 6:15 CWE 42 38–9.
2 Cf Gal 5:14, Rom 13:8–10.
3 Cf James 2:17–26.
4 Cf Matt 16:24. Bede *Exp 1 Ioannis* 2:6 CCL 121 291:73–4 / Hurst 169 cites this verse (Hurst erroneously attributes the citation to Luke 9:23) to support his interpretation of 1 John 2:6: to walk like Christ is to pray for one's enemies, to despise the good things of this world, to endure mockery and insult.
5 The syntax of Erasmus' Latin is ambiguous. The participle 'walking' could modify either 'the disciple' or the pronoun 'him.' Christ, who gave his life for others, walked in the path of perfect love; on the other hand, the disciple who follows Christ is likewise walking in the path of perfect love. The latter seems to be what Erasmus intends to say.

180
6 See Luke 23:34.

7 See Lev 19:18.
8 Erasmus is quoting from Matt 22:38–9, not from the OT.
9 Cf Matt 6:14–15.

181

10 Cf 1 Cor 13:7.
11 Cf chapter 1 n19. Usury was forbidden in Lev 25:36–7 and Deut 23:19–20, but there seems to be no apparent reason for the present reference to this particular sin unless Erasmus considers usury to be a form of theft.
12 Cf Bede *Exp 1 Ioannis* 2:13 CCL 121 292:123–30 / Hurst 171: 'He calls them fathers as being older and mature in wisdom, not in age ... For it is the duty of fathers to recall and know the past and to reveal it to the younger generation ... And therefore he properly calls those fathers who learned to know him who is from the beginning, that is, the Lord Christ, together with the Father and the Holy Spirit, and to preach him faithfully to their hearers.'
13 Cf Bede ibidem 292:131–7 / Hurst 171: 'Adolescence is a difficult time because of the urgings of the body, but it is also apt for contests because of the strength inherent in this time of life. Hence John is writing to those young men who have overcome the temptations of bodily pleasures through love of the word of God. He is writing also to those who, when faced with persecution on account of the word of God, because of their greater perfection have bravely rejected all the tricks of the malicious enemy.'

182

14 Cf the paraphrase on 2 Tim 3:6.
15 'The pride and noise of life': *fastus strepitusque vitae*. Erasmus uses the word *strepitus* (literally 'noise, din') elsewhere as an image of the pomp and stir of wealth, but he may have employed it here because he thought that the Greek word ἀλαζονία 'pride, boastfulness,' which John employs in 2:16, was cognate with the verb ἀλαλάζω 'shout, cry aloud'; cf his annotation on this verse (*superbia vitae*) LB VI 1074E. He also notes in the same annotation that the Greek word βίος in this verse means 'livelihood,' that is, the material resources of life, not simply life; see Brown *Epistles* 311–12.

183

16 Erasmus seems to have Rev 20:1–3 in mind.
17 Paul in particular; see 2 Thess 2:3–12.

184

18 'Storm' is perhaps a brachyology for the storm of persecutions which are to afflict the faithful in the last days; cf Matt 24:4–14. Alternatively, the word may be a metaphor for the cataclysmic drama of the last days to which the sufferings of the faithful and the appearance of false Christs are the preludes; cf Matt 24:20–9 and parallels.
19 you] LB reads 'us.'
20 Cf Bede *Exp 1 Ioannis* 2:19 CCL 121 295:239–41 / Hurst 176: 'It appeared that we should weep as though over a loss when we heard, "They went out

from us," but consolation is immediately offered through the addition of
the words, "But they were not from us."'

21 Cf Augustine *Tract in 1 Ioannem* 3.4 PL 35 1999 and Bede *Exp 1 Ioannis* 2:19
CCL 121 295:239–296:241 / Hurst 176–7. They make the same point that
Christians are tested by their response to temptation and they compare the
departure of the schismatics to the relief of the body from evil humours.
They likewise state that not all who are baptized, confess Christ, and par-
take of the sacraments are true Christians.

22 The word *Christos* means 'The Anointed One,' so the term 'Christian' could
conceivably mean a person who is anointed. The (false) etymology is
tailored to the context.

23 Erasmus seems to have 1 Cor 2:15 in mind, but he may also be alluding to
1 John 4:1.

24 departure] *secessu* 'secession, departure' is the reading of the three 1521 editions. The February 1522 edition introduced the reading *successu* 'success'
which is retained in the 1532 and later editions. *Successu* looks like a typographical error – the February 1522 edition contains scores of similar errors
– and while it appears to make some sense does not really fit the context. I
have retained, therefore, the reading of the 1521 editions.

185

25 Cf the paraphrase on 2 Pet 1:21. The inference that the 'antichrists' referred
to in 1 John 2:22 were Jews, though made by Bede *Exp 1 Ioannis* 2:22 CCL
121 297:294–5 / Hurst 178, has no basis in the text; cf Brown *Epistles* 352.

26 Cf Augustine *Tract in 1 Ioannem* 3.8 PL 35 2002: 'A greater liar is the person
who confesses aloud that Jesus is the Christ, but denies him by his deeds.'
However, the reference to the Beatitudes and the antithetical elaboration of
the idea are due to Erasmus.

27 Cf Matt 5:3; and in what follows, 5:6, 5:5, 5:4, 5:7, 5:11.

28 Cf Matt 16:24.

29 Cf John 16:33.

186

30 Cf John 12:44–50.

31 Cf Col 1:18 and 24.

32 Augustine *Tract in 1 Ioannem* 3.11 PL 35 2003 develops at some length this
contrast between the promise of eternal life and the goods of this world; see
also 3.12 PL 35 2003–4.

33 This interpretation of the words 'the anointing' in 2:27 is given by
Augustine *Tract in 1 Ioannem* 4.2 PL 35 2005; see on 2:20 above.

34 Cf John 14:26 and 15:16–17.

35 'Truthful': *verax*. Erasmus used this adjective to translate ἀληθές 'true,' in
his Latin version of 2:27, whereas the Vulgate has *verum* 'truth' (DR). The
translation in Augustine *Tract in 1 Ioannem* 4.2 PL 35 2005 is likewise *Et
verax est* 'it is truthful.'

36 Bede *Exp 1 Ioannis* 2:27 CCL 121 299:360–75 / Hurst 181 makes the same
point about the need to adhere to orthodox doctrine. It is one of the major
themes of his commentary on the Epistles of John.

37 That is, in the teaching of the Spirit. Erasmus follows Augustine *Tract in 1*

Ioannem 4.2 PL 35 2005 in understanding the pronoun αὐτῷ, which could mean either 'him' or 'it' in 2:27, to be neuter and to refer to the noun χρῖσμα 'anointing'; see his annotations (*sicut unctio eius* and *manete in eo*) LB VI 1075E. However, in his Latin version he uses the masculine *eo* 'him' to translate the pronoun in 2:28, although in the *Paraphrase* he clearly takes it again to be neuter. The Vulgate takes the pronoun to be masculine, 'abide in him' (DR), in both occurrences, as does Bede *Exp 1 Ioannis* 2:27–8 CCL 121 298:369–80 / Hurst 181–2, though Bede is also aware of the reading in Augustine. See Brown *Epistles* 361 for a discussion of this ambiguity in the Greek.

38 Augustine *Tract in 1 Ioannem* 4.2 PL 35 2005 links verse 27 to the thought of verse 28 in this way.

187

39 Erasmus thought (erroneously) that the Greek of 2:28 could mean either 'he is not ashamed of us' or 'we are not ashamed before him'; see his annotation on 2:28 (*non confundamur ab illo*) LB VI 1075F. The paraphrase includes both possibilities.

40 Cf John 13:13–14.

41 Cf Matt 7:22–3, and for the 'I do not know you' (*nescio vos*) Matt 25:12.

Chapter 3

1 See John 15:14–15; the epithet 'faithful' (*fideles*) comes from Matt 25:21.

2 The words, 'and are,' paraphrase the clause, 'and we are,' which the Vulgate adds to the end of this sentence. It is not found in Erasmus' Greek text and is omitted from his Latin version. See Metzger *Textual Commentary* 710–11.

3 Erasmus' Greek text and his Latin version have 'you'; 'us' is the reading of the Vulgate.

4 Cf Rom 8:15 and Gal 4:6. The notion that we should rejoice at being children of God is also Pauline; see Phil 2:17–18.

188

5 Cf Augustine *Tract in 1 Ioannem* 3.2 (on 1 John 3:2) PL 35 2008, who makes this same antithesis between majesty and humiliation, harking back to 1:1.

6 Cf Phil 3:21. I have taken the noun *animis* in Erasmus' sentence to be the ablative plural of *animus* 'mind', but it could equally well be the plural of *anima* 'soul.' In either case the phrase is a rhetorical way of saying that the whole person will be transformed into the likeness of Christ. Erasmus does not mean that the soul or mind will be transformed in the same way as the body, but that the condition of the soul will be or has to be made pure and innocent, 'justified,' if it is going to be like Christ and 'see' God as he is. That process, as he emphasizes repeatedly in the *Paraphrases* and elsewhere, begins on earth. Cf eg the paraphrase on 1 Cor 13:11: 'But when I became a man, I rejected childish things and I now keep pushing my mind toward better things until I am brought step by step to the highest things. But if this goal is not attained in this life, nevertheless, it must be practised here in order that it may be attained in the future' (LB VII 901D); and the para-

phrase on 1 Cor 15:48–58, where the need to 'practise immortality' in this life is emphasized (LB VII 911). In CWE 66 introduction xxiii the author notes that Erasmus has transformed the *meditatio mortis* of medieval piety into a *meditatio beatae vitae futurae*. In other words, the only true objective of human life is salvation, and godliness (*pietas*) is the standard by which to measure all thought and action.

7 Cf Eph 5:1–5 and Bede *Exp 1 Ioannis* 3:3 CCL 121 302:75–80 / Hurst 187: 'He who is eager to strive vigorously to perform good actions gives clear evidence thereby of his hope from on high, being convinced that no one will arrive at the likeness of God in the future except by making himself holy with the holiness of God in the present, that is, unless he imitate [this holiness] by rejecting "wickedness and worldly desires" and, on the contrary, by living "righteously and godly" [Titus 2:12].'

8 Augustine *Tract in 1 Ioannem* 4.6 (on 1 John 3:2) PL 35 2009 compares the Christian to a jar which has to be scrubbed clean in order to receive the honey which God will pour into it.

9 Although Erasmus recasts the thought in his own language, he is essentially following Bede *Exp 1 Ioannis* 3:4 CCL 121 303:97–105 / Hurst 188. After pointing out that the Greek word for 'iniquity' is ἀνομία 'lawlessness,' Bede argues that by calling sin iniquity John 'clearly suggests that by every single sin we commit we act against the law of God.' While for Bede the 'law of God' comprises both the precepts of the Mosaic law and 'the natural law which we all received in the first-created man,' for Erasmus evangelical law is primarily the 'law of love,' articulated in the statements of Christ in the Gospels, especially in the Sermon on the Mount (Matt 5–7), and only secondarily the law of Moses 'spiritually understood.'

189

10 Cf Augustine *Tract in 1 Ioannem* 4.10 (on 1 John 3:8) PL 35 2011: '"Is of the devil" – you know what he means: by imitating the devil. The devil made no one, brought no one into existence, created no one, but whoever imitates the devil is, as it were, born from him and becomes the devil's son by imitating him.'

11 Augustine *Tract in 1 Ioannem* 4.11 PL 35 2011 makes the same contrast between human descent from Adam and spiritual rebirth but he develops it in terms of original sin and baptism, an understanding of the text which Erasmus would prefer to ignore (cf the paraphrase on Romans 5:12–19 CWE 42 34–6) in order to place the emphasis on the role of the gospel (*evangelica doctrina*) in regeneration. However, the general course of the paraphrase on verses 9–11 follows Augustine *Tract in 1 Ioannem* 5.1–7 PL 35 2012–16, either directly or in Bede's abridgment of Augustine *Exp 1 Ioannis* 3:9–11 CCL 121 305:175–91 / Hurst 191–2.

12 Cf Bede *Exp 1 Ioannis* 3:9 CCL 305:177–80 / Hurst 191: '[John] says this ... about violating charity which he, who has within himself the seed of God – that is, the word of God through which he is reborn – cannot do'; and on 3:10 ibidem 183–5 / Hurst 191: 'Love alone, therefore, distinguishes between the children of God and the children of the devil. Those who have charity are born of God; those who do not have it are not born of God.'

190

13 The *Gloss* on Gen 1:3, in a discussion of the reasons why the devil fell from his original state of beatitude, states that 'The devil fell because he envied human beings who were created in the image of God,' although the author qualifies this explanation by arguing that envy is the consequence of pride (*superbia*). Cf Wisd 2:24–5: 'But by the envy of the devil, death came into the world and they follow him that are of his side'; and John 8:44: '[The devil] was a murderer from the beginning.' Underlying such texts is the assumption, which Erasmus encapsulates in the paraphrase on 1 John 3:11–12, that the temptation of Eve was tantamount to the murder of humanity. Cf Rom 5:12 and Brown *Epistles* 442–3, though one should not assume that Erasmus was familiar with all the sources which Brown adduces. For example, Erasmus either did not know or chose to ignore the tradition that the serpent impregnated Eve and was the father of Cain while Adam was the father of Abel.

14 Augustine *Tract in 1 Ioannem* 5.8 (on 1 John 3:12) PL 35 2016 begins his explication of the reference to Cain with the maxim (quoted by Bede *Exp 1 Ioannis* CCL 121 306:195–6 / Hurst 192), 'Where there is envy, there cannot be brotherly love.' Cf the paraphrase on Jude 11.

15 The idea that the word 'world' in 3:13 means people devoted to the world (*homines mundo dediti*) is developed emphatically and at length by Augustine *Tract in 1 Ioannem* 4.9 PL 35 2017. Cf the paraphrase on 4:5.

16 Erasmus' Greek text has the word 'brother' here (cf AV), which is omitted in the Vulgate and in the better Greek manuscripts. The word 'neighbour' then is a paraphrase on the word 'brother' in Erasmus' Greek text.

17 Public distortion of his own writings and person was very much on Erasmus' mind at this time; see the dedicatory letter to the *Paraphrase on James* 133–4. In the *Apologia de loco 'Omnes quidem'* LB IX 440F–441A almost identical language to that in the paraphrase on 1 John 3:15 is employed in a scathing criticism of the Carmelite prior Nicolaas Baechem (Egmondanus). These reflections on the 'poisoned tongue' were to receive extended development five years later in the *Lingua* (CWE 29 255–6).

18 Cf Matt 5:22; and also the paraphrase on James 4:1–2.

19 Augustine *Tract in 1 Ioannem* 5.10 PL 35 2018, quoted by Bede *Exp 1 Ioannis* 3:15 CCL 121 307:228–32 / Hurst 193, makes this equivalence between hate and death, but the conceit that the hater murders himself seems to be Erasmus' own contribution to the thought.

191

20 Cf John 10:11.

21 Cf John 21:15–19. The reference occurs in Bede *Exp 1 Ioannis* 3:16 CCL 121 307:247–53 / Hurst 194, though Bede is actually quoting from Augustine *Tract in 1 Ioannem* 5.11 PL 35 2018 rather than directly from John.

22 Augustine *Tract in 1 Ioannem* 5.12 (on 1 John 3:16–18) PL 35 2018–19 employs this same kind of second-person address, a feature of the so-called diatribe style, in his commentary on these verses. Although there is almost no verbal similarity between Erasmus' paraphrase and Augustine's commentary, the latter's example may have moved Erasmus to use it at this point.

23 Cf Luke 11:41. Augustine *Tract in 1 Ioannem* 5:12 PL 35 2018 speaks only of material aid; however, Bede *Exp 1 Ioannis* 3:18 CCL 121 308:267–8 / Hurst 195 adds the comment, 'likewise when we behold them in need of spiritual gifts.' For 'comfort, teaching, and admonition' cf 1 Thess 5:14.

24 The future tense appears to be accidental and is not evidence that Erasmus knew the reading with the future (cf RSV 'we will know'). His Greek text and Latin version have, with the Vulgate, the present tense 'we know' (cf NKJ).

25 Cf Bede *Exp 1 Ioannis* 3:18 CCL 121 308:269–74 / Hurst 195: '[He adds] "in truth" so that we bestow these benefits on them with a simple intention [that is, without ulterior motive] and not for the sake of human praise, not through vainglory, not to the prejudice of others who, though endowed with greater means, do not do anything of this sort. For the purity of truth cannot dwell in any mind tainted with such warts, although it appears to perform the deeds of love for its neighbours.'

26 The idea that the word 'heart' in 3:19 refers to the conscience is found in Augustine *Tract in 1 Ioannem* 6.3 PL 35 2020–1 and Bede *Exp 1 Ioannis* 3:20 CCL 121 308:295–300 / Hurst 196. Both commentators also emphasize the fact that no one can hide from God.

27 Cf Matt 6:2.

28 'Open': *simplex*. The term occurs in Bede in the passage quoted in n25 above. For Erasmus 'openness' or 'simpleness' (*simplicitas*) denotes a condition or state of mind in which actions are performed without ulterior motives or not under the influence of some impure emotion. 'Simplicity' is the contrary of 'duplicity'; cf the paraphrase on James 1:8.

192

29 Bede *Exp 1 Ioannis* 3:21 CCL 121 309:305–6 / Hurst 196–7 likewise alludes to the Lord's Prayer and quotes Matt 6:12

30 'Welfare' (*salus*) is perhaps equivalent to 'salvation' in the present context. Cf the paraphrase on Matt 6:11 where 'daily bread' is interpreted as both physical and spiritual nourishment (LB VII 37C).

31 Cf Matt 6:14–15.

32 The reference of the third person singular pronouns in 1 John 3:23–4 is ambiguous and disputed; see the next note. Erasmus, however, clearly thinks of Christ as the primary subject of the verbs in the two verses, although he also works all three Persons of the Trinity into the paraphrase.

33 Though Augustine *Tract in 1 Ioannem* 6.10 (on 1 John 3:23) PL 35 2025 similarly refers to the body of Christ in this context, he, and the great majority of modern scholars, refer the third person pronouns in this verse to God, not to Christ; see Brown *Epistles* 464. In what follows Erasmus identifies the Spirit in verse 24 with the Spirit of Christ, probably because he saw in verse 23 a direct reference to John 15:12.

34 In his paraphrase on Acts 8:16–17 (LB VII 699E) Erasmus comments: 'This power [that is, of baptizing with water] was delegated to deacons but the imposition of hands through which the Holy Spirit was conferred was reserved to the apostles alone and their representatives.' See Payne *Theology* 165–6 on Erasmus' tendency to associate the gift of the Holy Spirit with the sacrament of baptism rather than of confirmation.

193

35 Erasmus follows the view of Augustine, Bede, and Theophylact, all of
   whom understand 'spirit' in 3:24 to be the equivalent of 'love' – that is, the
   gift of the Spirit is the gift of love (cf the paraphrase on James 2:26 n32) –
   and join verse 24 directly to verse 23. See Brown *Epistles* 465–6 for a discussion of the various opinions about the meaning of 'spirit' in this verse.

Chapter 4

1 Cf Bede *Exp 1 Ioannis* 4:3 CCL 121 311:38–49 / Hurst 200–1, who quotes
  Augustine *Tract in 1 Ioannem* 6.13 (on 1 John 4:2) PL 35 2028 to the effect
  that the false spirits deny Christ by their deeds. Augustine and Bede, however, are mainly concerned with identifying the antichrists with individual
  heresiarchs of later times.
2 This sentence is a paraphrase on the text of the Clementine Vulgate which
  in 4:3 reads 'every spirit that dissolves (*qui solvit*) Jesus' for 'every spirit
  that does not confess.' Modern scholars assume that the Vulgate contains a
  translation of a Greek variant λύει 'does away with, dissolves' for the
  ὁμολογεῖ 'does not confess' of the extant Greek manuscripts; see Brown
  Epistles 494–6, Metzger *Textual Commentary* 713. Erasmus, however, thought
  that the Vulgate version of the sentence was invented to combat heretical
  teachings about the dual nature of Christ; cf his annotation on 1 John 4:3 (*Et
  omnis spiritus qui solvit Iesum ex deo non est*) LB VI 1077E. Consequently, the
  paraphrase treats it as a further idea in the development of John's argument. Following Bede *Exp 1 Ioannis* 4:3 CCL 121 311:26–45 / Hurst 200–1,
  Erasmus understands the verb *solvit* to mean to dissolve or divide the es-
  sential unity of the incarnate Son through rejecting one or the other of his
  two natures. In the *Annotationes* Erasmus leaves the choice between the two
  readings to the reader; in the *Paraphrase* he includes both readings.
3 Erasmus considered the present tense of the Greek verb in this clause in 4:3
  to have a future meaning and therefore translated it as a future in his Latin
  version; cf his annotation on it (*de quo audistis quum venit*) LB VI 1078D. The
  paraphrase follows this translation.

194

4 'Through it' (the Spirit) or perhaps 'through him' (the Father). Erasmus'
  pronoun here, *illum*, could refer either to the Father or to the Spirit.
5 Just as Christ has a body, consisting of those who believe in him, so the
  devil too has a body whose members are all who oppose and reject Christ.
6 The antithesis between 'attacks' and 'protects' occurs in Bede *Exp 1 Ioannis*
  4:4 CCL 121 312:61–5 / Hurst 201–2: '[John] teaches them always to have
  confidence and the hope of overcoming in the midst of adversities, keeping
  in mind that the Lord is stronger in protecting them than the devil in attacking them.'
7 The language which Erasmus employs here, *mundum sapiunt*, may be influenced by Bede's description of the antichrists as people who smack of
  worldly things (*mundana sapiunt*) in *Exp 1 Ioannis* 4:5 CCL 121 312:69 / Hurst
  202. But cf the paraphrase on James 3:15, where the same image is used,

NOTES TO PAGES 194–7

and Phil 3:19c, which the Vulgate translates *terrena sapiunt* 'smack of earthly things.'

8 For these teachings cf eg (casting away riches) Matt 6:19, Luke 12:33; (spurning pleasure) Luke 8:14, 16:19–25; (suffering) Matt 16:24, Luke 6:22–3; (holding life cheap compared to following Christ) Matt 10:38–9, Luke 14:27; (seeking a reward in heaven) Matt 6:1, Luke 14:14.

9 Cf John 15:13.

10 Erasmus takes the word 'first' in 4:10 from the Vulgate; cf his annotation on 4:10 (*quoniam ipse prior*) LB VI 1978E.

195

11 This interpretation is made by Augustine *Tract in 1 Ioannem* 7.9 (on 1 John 4:10) PL 35 2033 and, following him, Bede *Exp 1 Ioannis* CCL 121 313:125–8 / Hurst 204. They understand the word *propitiatio* in the Latin text of 4:10 to mean 'sacrifice.' Erasmus combines in the paraphrase two different interpretations of the Greek term ἱλασμόν – sacrifice (expiation) and propitiation. See Brown *Epistles* 217–22 for a review of the meaning of the Greek word and the question whether the atonement is an expiation or a propitiation.

12 That is, to the 'rule of true godliness'; cf the paraphrase on 1 Tim 3:16.

196

13 treats] *prosequatur*, 1521–1534. The 1538 and 1540 editions and LB read *persequatur* 'persecutes.'

14 The animal comparison occurs in Augustine *Tract in 1 Ioannem* 9.1 (on 1 John 4:17) PL 35 2045.

15 Erasmus observes in his annotation on 4:20 (*quem videt, deum quem non videt*) LB VI 1078F that the Greek has the perfect tense while the Vulgate has the present tense. However, the variation in the paraphrase between 'has seen' and 'does see' is probably rhetorical rather than an effort to accommodate the present tense of the Vulgate.

197

16 The example of Caesar, that is, the Roman emperor, is used by Augustine *Tract in 1 Ioannem* 9.11 (on 1 John 4:20) PL 35 2053, though not by Bede.

17 The motive of conversion is advanced by Augustine *Tract in 1 Ioannem* 8.10 PL 35 2041–2042: 'Why should you love your enemy? ... Pray for him to have eternal life with you; pray for him to be your brother. If, in loving your enemy, you pray that he be your brother, you are loving your brother when you love him. For you do not love what is actually in him but what you want to be there.'

Chapter 5

1 Cf Matt 11:30.

2 Cf Heb 11:36–8.

3 Bede *Exp 1 Ioannis* 5:4 CCL 121 320:52–5 / Hurst 215–6 illustrates this passage by quoting Gal 5:6, 'faith working through love,' and John 16:33, 'In the world you shall have distress: but have confidence, I have overcome the world' [DR].

4 Cf Matt 19:21 (Mark 10:21, Luke 18:22) and the paraphrase on 2 Tim 4:8.
5 Cf Phil 3:20.
6 The view that in 5:6 'water' refers to the baptism of Christ, 'blood' to his passion and death occurs in Bede *Exp 1 Ioannis* CCL 121 320:64–321:69 / Hurst 216. Bede also sees in these words a reference to the sacraments of baptism and the Eucharist. See Brown *Epistles* 572–8 for a survey of the various interpretations of the words 'through water and blood.'

198

7 That Jesus, who was without sin, submitted to a baptism of repentance posed a problem both in the early church and subsequently. See eg Robert H. Gundry *Matthew: A Commentary on His Literary and Theological Art* (Grand Rapids, Mich 1982) 50–1 on Matt 3:14, and C.E.B. Cranfield *The Gospel According to Saint Mark* (Cambridge 1985) 51–2. The latter quotes Calvin's view that Jesus allowed himself to be baptized so 'that He might consecrate baptism in His own body, that we might have it in common with him.' Erasmus' own solution of the problem may be found in the paraphrase on Matt 3:14–15 (LB VII 17A–D), where he argues that everything that Jesus submitted to during his life – circumcision, purification in the Temple, baptism, the scourging, crucifixion – he did not for himself but for us: to impart his innocence [ie righteousness] to us and to provide us with an example to follow. The idea that Jesus' life is an example for believers is patristic; cf CWE 46 118 n74, 145 n38, 207 n6. Both explanations occur repeatedly in the *Paraphrases* on the Epistles.
8 Cf Matt 3:16, Mark 1:10, Luke 3:22, and John 1:32, though in the Fourth Gospel it is John the Baptist who testifies. Bede *Exp 1 Ioannis* 5:6 CCL 121 321:70–4 / Hurst 216 refers the mention of the Spirit in this verse to the descent of the dove at Jesus' baptism. Cf Brown *Epistles* 579–80.
9 The Greek manuscripts which Erasmus used in preparing the first two editions of the *Novum Testamentum* (Basel 1516 and 1519) did not contain the following passage in 5:7–8: '... in heaven: the Father, the Word, and the Holy Spirit; and these three are one. And there are three that bear witness on earth...' This passage was known only from Latin manuscripts until the Codex Montfortianus (no 61 in the list of codices in NTGL) was produced containing a Greek text of it; see Brown *Epistles* 775–87 for the history of the passage. When informed of the existence of the Codex Montfortianus and the Greek text in it, Erasmus added the Greek text together with a Latin version to his third edition of the *Novum Testamentum* (Basel 1522). The inclusion of the passage in the *Paraphrase on 1 John* suggests that Erasmus had already received a copy of the Greek text by December 1520, unless he is simply paraphrasing the text of the Vulgate as he often does elsewhere. For a discussion of the entire matter see H.J. de Jonge, 'Erasmus and the Comma Johanneum' *Ephemerides Theologicae Lovanienses* 56 (1980) 381–9 and Rummel *Annotations* 40 and 132–4.
10 At Jesus' baptism (Matt 3:17, Mark 1:11, Luke 3:22) and transfiguration (Matt 17:5, Mark 9:7, Luke 9:35; cf also 2 Pet 1:17)
11 Cf Matt 3:16 and the parallel passages in Mark 1:10, Luke 3:22, and John 1:32.
12 Cf Acts 2:2–3. Erasmus' language in the paraphrase is reminiscent of the

description of descents of divinities from the sky found in Roman literature; cf eg Martial 8.32.1 or Virgil *Aeneid* 7.620.

13 Cf John 19:30 and 34. Bede *Exp 1 Ioannis* 5:7–8 CCL 121 321:85–99 / Hurst 217, whose text of 1 John did not contain the words about the three witnesses in heaven, assumes that the water and blood mentioned in verse 8 refer to the blood and water which flowed – miraculously according to Bede – from Jesus' side and 'bear witness that Jesus is truth because this could not have happened if Jesus did not have the true nature of flesh.' Bede, however, believes that the spirit is here the Holy Spirit who descended on Jesus after baptism, which also seems to be the view of all other commentators. In referring all three witnesses – the spirit as well as the water and blood – to Jesus' death on the cross Erasmus may be follow- ing Augustine who says in his *Collatio cum Maximino* 2.22.3 PL 42 794–5: 'We know that three things issued from the body of the Lord when he was hanging on the cross: first, the spirit – hence it is written "And bowing his head, he gave up his spirit" [John 19:30]; secondly, when his side was pierced by the lance, blood and water [issued].' Augustine goes on to con- sider the three physical witnesses of spirit, water, and blood to be an alle- gory of the Trinity. Erasmus ignored this allegorical interpretation of the text and was censured in 1527 by a committee of Spanish monks who accused him of defending [Greek] manuscripts which in their view were corrupt because they did not contain the passage about the heavenly witnesses, of impugning the authority of Jerome because he rejected the authenticity of a text which in their view Jerome had translated, of sustain- ing the cause of Arianism, and of waging inexorable war against the testi- mony of the three divine witnesses, rejecting censure and heaping up frivol- ous arguments from all sides against the text. See the *Apologia adversus monachos* LB IX 1029E–F, and for the history of this controversy, Rummel *Critics* II 81–105.

14 The sentence – 'and these three agree' (RSV) – in 5:8 is omitted in the Codex Montfortianus, which led Erasmus to believe that its Greek text about the three heavenly witnesses was a translation of the Vulgate; see his *Apologia ad annotationes Stunicae* ASD IX-2 258:538–40 and his annotation on 1 John 5:7 (*tres sunt qui testimonium dant in caelo*) LB VI 1079B–1081F, especially 1080D.

15 Bede *Exp 1 Ioannis* 5:7–8 CCL 121 32:85–105 / Hurst 217–8 makes the same point that the three witnesses – Holy Spirit, blood and water – testify to the dual nature of Christ, true God and true human.

16 John the Baptist; cf John 1:15, 19–34.

199

17 This statement seems to combine John 17:20–6 and 12:28–9. Bede *Exp 1 Ioannis* 5:10 CCL 121 323:146–54 / Hurst 219–20 cites Luke 3:22 and John 12:28–9 as testimonies of the Father, but in John 12:29 the voice of the Father is compared to thunder, not to a trumpet. Erasmus was working on the *Paraphrase on Hebrews* at the time he was writing the *Paraphrase on 1 John*, and may have confused the thunder in John 12:29 with the trumpet mentioned in Heb 12:19, or with the trumpet-like voices from heaven in Rev 1:10 and 4:1. That there is a link between the Johannine statements about testimony with the account of the transfiguration in the synoptic

Gospels has also been suggested by some modern scholars; see Raymond E. Brown *The Gospel according to John I–XII* (Garden City, NY 1966) 476.

18 The image of the earnest or pledge occurs in 2 Cor 1:22 and 5:5, and in Eph 1:14, where Paul calls the Spirit 'the guarantee of our inheritance until the redemption of the purchased possession' (NKJ). See the paraphrase on Eph 1:14 (LB VII 947E), where Erasmus says, 'The inheritance in which we have been included will not be given in its entirety until the general resurrection. In the meantime God imparts to us his Spirit like a pledge and guarantee of the promised inheritance. From this sign we are certain that God considers us as his children and that he will claim as his own those whom he has redeemed by the death of his Son.' In his annotation on Eph 1:14 (*qui est pignus*) LB VI 834E, Erasmus, following Jerome's commentary on this verse (PL 26 457B), distinguishes between a deposit – a guarantee to pay the full price in a sales transaction (*arrabo* 'an earnest') – and a pledge – the pawn or collateral put up for a loan (*pignus*, the word used in the Vulgate to translate the Greek ἀρραβών): 'An *arrabo* is given in a contract of sale in order to confirm the obligation. If the deposit which God gives to his own is so great, how great will be the property which he will give in his own time?' The indwelling of the Spirit is thus both the guarantee that God will fulfil his part of the covenant at the resurrection and a proof to the Christian that he or she is a child of God and will in due course come into the rightful inheritance of immortal life and a share in the kingdom of heaven.

19 Cf the paraphrase on Rom 8:15 and Gal 4:6 (CWE 42 47 and 115–16).

20 The combination of the term 'legal right' (*ius*) and the term 'earnest' (*arra*), neither of which actually occur in the text of 5:13, suggests a certain confusion in Erasmus' mind between the right of ownership in the law of sale and the right of an heir to take possession of a legacy. Though Erasmus was familiar with the language of Roman law, there is no reason to believe that he had any special knowledge of the law or that he thought through the implications of the legal metaphors which he employs. For instance, the right of an heir in Roman law is quite different from that in ancient Greek law or in English common law. In Roman law the right to inherit exists from birth rather than from the death of the person from whom the inheritance comes. From the perspective of Roman law the Christian becomes an heir from the moment of his or her rebirth in Christ and cannot be deprived of that right to inherit except through formal disinheritance; see Francis Lyall *Slaves, Citizens, Sons: Legal Metaphors in the Epistles* (Grand Rapids, Mich 1984) 106–17. God 'acknowledges' the faithful Christian as a legitimate child but 'disowns' the sinner. Legal imagery is pervasive in the *Paraphrases* but it is difficult to decide whether it is theologically significant or simply ornamental as seems to be the case in this paraphrase on 5:13.

21 Erasmus is paraphrasing his Greek text which reads 'and that you may continue to believe in the name of the Son of God' (NKJ). However, he believed, correctly, that the Greek text was corrupt compared to the text of the Vulgate in which this clause is omitted; see his annotation on 1 John 5:13 (*haec describo*) LB VI 1082C and Metzger *Textual Commentary* 717.

22 Cf John 14:13–14 and 16:23.

23 Cf Rom 8:26, which is cited by Bede *Exp 1 Ioannis* 3:14 CCL 121 324:203–7 / Hurst 222.

24 Cf John 14:13.

200

25 Cf Bede *Exp 1 Ioannis* 5:16 CCL 121 325:237–41 / Hurst 223, who observes
that a '"sin leading to death" ... occurs when anyone, after the recognition
of God, which has been given through the grace of our Lord Jesus Christ,
opposes the brotherhood and is aroused by the torches of envy against the
very grace by which he has been reconciled to God.'

26 See Brown *Epistles* 612–19 for a survey of the interpretations of this much
discussed text. Brown agrees essentially with Erasmus that the persons
committing the deadly sin are the secessionists, though Erasmus generalizes
the situation to cover any apostate, including Satan.

27 Bede *Exp 1 Ioannis* 5:16 CCL 121 325:248–326:57 / Hurst 224 adduces Alexander the coppersmith (2 Tim 4:14) as an example of one who 'sinned from
envy by opposing brotherhood' and, therefore, was not prayed for by Paul.

28 Cf 2 Tim 4:15.

29 'Capital crime': *capitale crimen*. The phrase means literally 'a charge carrying
the death penalty.' It is classicizing language for 'mortal sin,' just as 'misdeed' means 'venial sin'; see CWE 42 xxxvi.

30 Cf the paraphrase on Heb 10:26.

31 Cf Matt 13:19–22.

201

32 Erasmus' Latin here, *verum illum deum*, is a fusion of the text of the Vulgate
verum deum 'true God' with his own translation of the Greek text *illum qui
verus est* 'him that is true' (cf NKJ). See Metzger *Textual Commentary* 718 and
Erasmus' *Apologia ad annotationes Stunicae*, ASD IX-2 260:548–9.

33 Cf John 14:20.

34 Bede *Exp 1 Ioannis* 5:20 CCL 121 328:342–7 / Hurst 227–8 took the pronoun *hic*
'this, he,' (οὗτος, the first word of the concluding sentence in verse 20) to refer
to the Son, Jesus Christ, in the preceding sentence, and asserted that John is
calling Jesus true God as he often did; see Brown *Epistles* 625 for a list of commentators from the fourth century to the twentieth who take this view. But as
Brown points out ibidem 625–6, the antecedent of the Greek pronoun is by no
means certain. Erasmus in his annotation on this verse (*deum verum*) LB VI
1084B argues that the words 'He (this) is the true God' can be referred to the
Father. The paraphrase likewise begins with *hic*, so that it is not immediately
clear whether the reference is to the Father or to the Son, but I assume from
the annotation that it is intended to refer to the Father. It is also possible that
Erasmus intends a distinction here, predicating 'true God' of the Father and
'eternal life' of the Son, in which case he would mean that one can come to the
Father only through the Son (cf John 14:6).

35 This sentence is a paraphrase of the Amen which is found at the end of the
Epistle in the Vulgate and in Erasmus' Greek manuscripts.

PARAPHRASE ON 2 JOHN

204

1 in us] 1521–1538. The 1540 edition and LB read 'in you.'

2 DR translates verse 3: 'Grace be with you, mercy, and peace from God the Father, and from Christ Jesus the Son of the Father.' The subjunctive rather than the future indicative is the reading of the Clementine Vulgate – *sit* instead of *erit*, the reading in modern editions of the Vulgate and in Erasmus' Latin version. Erasmus thus takes the wish form of verse 3 from the Vulgate as he knew it.

3 'You' is the reading of the Vulgate; the Greek text and Erasmus' Latin version have 'us.'

4 The words 'the Lord' come from the Greek text; they are not in the Vulgate.

5 we need only] First in July 1521. The first edition and the March 1521 edition read 'Only let us continue' and begin a new sentence with these words.

6 Erasmus means the commandment to love one another; see John 13:34.

7 Erasmus is paraphrasing the clause, 'you should walk in it,' in verse 6. He thought the pronoun 'it' in the Greek referred to the noun 'commandment' rather than to the noun 'love' as modern commentators prefer to understand the text.

8 Cf AV: 'Many deceivers are entered into the world.' This is the reading of Erasmus' Greek text. The Vulgate and other Greek manuscripts read 'have gone out' (cf NKJ and RSV).

205

9 Cf Matt 10:22.

10 Cf 1 Cor 15:33, which Erasmus quotes in a slightly modified version of the text of the Vulgate.

11 impostor] 1532. The earlier editions read the plural, 'impostors.'

12 The first edition and the March 1521 edition have 'Amen' at the conclusion of the Epistle, as in Erasmus' Greek text. This Amen is omitted in the July 1521 and later editions of the *Paraphrase*. Erasmus may have felt that it was not congruent with the private nature of the letter. There is likewise no Amen at the end of 3 John. See Metzger *Textual Commentary* 720 and 722.

PARAPHRASE ON 3 JOHN

208

1 You would] First in July 1521. The first edition and the March 1521 edition read the indicative 'You will.'

2 Cf the paraphrase on Titus 3:14.

3 Bede, *Exp 3 Ioannis* 7 CCL 121 332:36–9 / Hurst 236 advances as one possible explanation of the words 'for His name's sake' the view that the men came 'to preach his name of their own free will.' To travel abroad on business is criticized in the paraphrase on James 4:13, which may have suggested the contrast between the two motives here.

4 Cf the paraphrase in 1 Tim 6:5.

5 Bede *Exp 3 Ioannis* 8 CCL 121 333:49–51 / Hurst 237 quotes Gregory the Great *Homily on the Gospel of John* 1.20.12 PL 76 1166A–B: 'Anyone who bestows temporal means on those who have spiritual gifts is a fellow-worker in those very spiritual gifts.'

6 Cf Matt 10:41, quoted by Bede *Exp 3 Ioannis* 8 CCL 121 333:54–6 / Hurst 237.

209

7 Bede *Exp 3 Ioannis* 9 CCL 121 333:58–62 / Hurst 237 comments: 'Diotrephes, it seems, was some heresiarch of that time, proud and insolent, preferring to usurp the first place in knowledge for himself by teaching new doctrines rather than to obey humbly the ancient commandments of the Church which John was preaching.'

8 does not ... see] LB has the perfect 'has not ... seen.' The Greek text in 11b, Erasmus' Latin version, and the Clementine Vulgate have the perfect tense 'has not seen God.' But some early editions of the Vulgate have the present tense 'does not see.' Erasmus may be following such a text and not simply adjusting the perfect tense of the Greek text to the context of the paraphrase.

9 Cf Bede *Exp 3 Ioannis* 12 CCL 121 334:78–80 / Hurst 238: 'He proposes him as a model to be imitated by Gaius in order that he too in a similar way can be worthy of everyone's praise.'

10 The plural 'you' is the reading of Erasmus' Greek text in 12; cf AV 'ye know.'

11 Brown *Epistles* 725 (on verse 13a) doubts the need for such 'psychological hypotheses,' but the insecurity of correspondence is a recurring topic in ancient epistolography. Letter carriers were not reliable, as Erasmus well knew from the example of his Ep 1033.

12 The End] January 1521 and 1532. The intervening editions have a more elaborate formula, 'The End of the Paraphrase on the Canonical Epistles of John authored by Erasmus of Rotterdam.'

PARAPHRASE ON HEBREWS

Dedicatory Letter

212

1 The translation of the dedicatory letter (Ep 1181) is by R.A.B. Mynors with minor revisions by JJB.

Silvestro Gigli died on 18 April 1521 and may never have known about this dedication. Erasmus had received several favours from Gigli in the past and felt indebted to him; see Epp 447, 521, 567, and especially 1079 and 1080. The dedication of the *Paraphrase on Hebrews* may have been intended to fulfil the promise made in Ep 1079, that if Erasmus lived one more year he would provide Gigli with tangible evidence of his devotion and gratitude to him. See CEBR II 97–8. The letter was omitted from the 1532 edition, but there is no evidence to indicate whether the omission was accidental or deliberate.

2 In the preface to his *Res rusticae*; cf *Adagia* II iii 48 / CWE 33 156.

3 Here and in the Argument Erasmus accepts the ascription to Paul. In the *Annotationes* to the *Novum Testamentum*, in a note appended to the concluding annotation on Heb 13:24 (*de Italia fratres*) LB VI 1023C, and elsewhere Erasmus argued strongly against Pauline authorship; see eg Ep 1171 to Cardinal Schiner 132 above, the *Apologia ad Fabrum* LB IX 53B–57F, and the responses to Noël Béda and to the faculty of theology in Paris, LB IX 497B and 863D–866F.

213

4 vehement] *grauiter*; first in March 1521. The first edition reads *gnauiter* 'active,' which Allen retained and is the reading translated in the CWE edition of the Letters.

Argument

214

1 Kenneth Hagen, *Hebrews Commenting from Erasmus to Bèze 1516–1598* Beiträge zur Geschichte der biblischen Exegese 23 (Tübingen n d) 4–8 believes that Erasmus is following the medieval consensus on the inveterate hostility of the Jews toward Christians and towards Paul in particular. To be more exact, Erasmus takes most of the points in this sentence and in what follows from the Argument prefixed to Chrysostom's *Homilies on Hebrews* PG 63 12–14 / NPNF 363–5. Jewish 'hatred' of gentiles was a stock theme of non-Christian authors also; see eg Tacitus *Historiae* 5.5.

2 Cf Rom 11:13.

3 Cf Acts 21:21.

4 Cf Heb 10:32–4.

Chapter 1

215

1 In his annotation on Heb 1:1 (*in prophetis, in filio*) LB VI 983C (added in 1522) Erasmus notes that Chrysostom *Hom in Heb* 1 (on Heb 1:2) PG 63 15 / NPNF 368b understood the preposition ἐν 'in' in this verse to mean 'through'; cf the translation 'by' in AV, RSV.

2 The *Gloss* on 1:1, followed by Hugh of St Cher, Nicholas of Lyra, and Aquinas, distinguishes three basic modes of divine communication with humans: dreams, open speech (*vox aperta*), and interior or hidden inspiration; cf Num 12:6–8. The commentators subdivide the basic three categories into various sub-groups. Hugh, for example, catalogues fifteen different modes of divine appearance and speech in the Old Testament, including the use of natural objects such as clouds, fire, stones. None of these commentators, however, mention the wind as a mode of divine communication. Erasmus has in mind 1 Kings 19:12 which reads, in the Vulgate, *et post ignem sibilus aurae tenuis*, 'and after the fire, the whistling of a gentle breeze' (Knox).

3 Presumably Pss 2 and 110

4 Aquinas *Exp in epist ad Heb* c 1 lect 1 (on Heb 1:2 'through whom he also created the worlds') 670b–671a demonstrates that the words 'through whom' do not imply that the Son is inferior to the Father, but that on the contrary the power (*virtus*) of both is the same. Chrysostom *Hom in Heb* 2 PG 63 21 / NPNF 372–3 makes the same point but in an argument directed against various heresies.

5 Aquinas *Exp in epist ad Heb* c 1 lect 1 (on Heb 1:2) 669b–670a, after citing Ps 82:6 and John 1:12, explains that the Son, who is the heir and through

whom the universe was created, is uniquely different from all other 'sons.'
Cf also Chrysostom *Hom in Heb* 2 (on Heb 1:5) PG 63 24 / NPNF 373b.

6 Erasmus understood the word ἀπαύγασμα ('brightness' NKJ) to mean reful-
gence or reflected light in the sense that the words 'light from light' have in
the Nicene Creed; cf his annotation on Heb 1:3 (*splendor gloriae*) LB VI 983C.

7 Erasmus retains the translation *substantiae* 'substance' (DR) from the Vulgate,
but in his annotation on 1:3 (*et figura*) LB VI 983D he observes that the Greek
word ὑπόστασις (*substantia*) means 'person' rather than 'essence'; cf AV and
NKJ. However, the meaning 'person' arose only in later theological disputation; see Spicq *Hébreux* II 9.

8 Aquinas *Exp in epist ad Heb* c 1 lect 2 (on Heb 1:3) 673a concludes that in
the language of verse 3 Paul is stating that the Son is co-eternal, co-equal,
and consubstantial with the Father.

9 Cf the words *ex patre natum* in the Nicene Creed.

10 In an annotation on 1:3 (*portansque omnia verbo virtutis suae*) LB VI 983D
Erasmus states: 'In my judgment φέρων in this passage does not have the
meaning of *portans* ['carrying'] or *baiulans* ['bearing'] but rather the meaning
of *agens* ['driving'] or *movens ac moderans* ['moving and governing']. Cf
Chrysostom *Hom in Heb* 2 (on Heb 1:3) PG 63 23 / NPNF 372b who likewise
says that the participle φέρων means 'moving' rather than 'carrying' or 'up-
holding.'

216

11 Cf Aquinas *Exp in epist ad Heb* c 1 lect 3 (on Heb 1:4) 674b: 'The proper
name of the angels is *angelus* because the word *angelus* means *nuntius* ['messenger']; however, the proper name of Christ is *Filius Dei* ['Son of God'] ...
The names are infinitely different.'

12 For the meaning of the epithet 'mystical' see the Prologue to Nicholas of
Lyra's *Postilla moralis*, where he states that after he had completed his exposition of Sacred Scripture according to the literal meaning (*sensus literalis*),
he now proposes to expound this same Scripture according to the 'mystical
sense' (*sensus mysticus*). Elsewhere, and more commonly, Erasmus speaks of
the 'spiritual' meaning. A 'mystical' psalm is one which must be read or
interpreted in its spiritual sense and specifically in its Christological significance. In this respect Erasmus' approach to the interpretation of the Old
Testament is similar to that of Jacques Lefèvre d'Etaples; cf Guy Bedouelle
Lefèvre D'Etaples et l'Intelligence des Ecritures (Genève 1976) chapter 4, 173–89.
For Erasmus' own reading of certain psalms see ASD V-9 *Enarrationes in
Psalmos: Pars prior*.

13 Cf Chrysostom *Hom in Heb* 3 (on Heb 1:7–8) PG 63 28 / NPNF 375b: 'Behold,
the greatest difference! that they are created, but He uncreated.' Lefèvre
Comm in Heb 231r likewise notes that God is not the begetter (*genitor*) but
the maker (*factor*) of the angels.

14 Aquinas *Exp in epist ad Heb* c 1 lect 3 (on Heb 1:7) 676b observes that fire is
the most active of the four elements and thus a symbol of the mobility and
speed appropriate to messengers. Referring to Song of Sol 8:6, he also
observes that fire connotes love. Nicholas of Lyra, commenting on the
words 'flame of fire' in Ps 104:4 says that 'angels burn with love and are
ever ready to execute the divine will.'

15 Cf Chrysostom *Hom in Heb* 3 (on Heb 1:8) PG 63 29 / NPNF 376b and Erasmus' annotation (*thronus tuus, deus*) LB VI 984D, added in 1522.

217

16 'In a special way': *peculiarius*. With this term Erasmus avoids the dispute in patristic and medieval commentaries over whether the anointing referred to in Heb 1:9 (Ps 45:7), which was in any case spiritual, pertained to the divine or to the human nature of the Son. Cf Theodoret *Comm in Heb* PG 82 685–8, Theophylact *Exp in Heb* PG 125 200, Aquinas *Exp in epist ad Heb* c 1 lect 4 677–8.

17 Erasmus' Greek text and Latin translation, and consequently the paraphrase on 1:10, erroneously incorporate the connector 'and' into the quotation from the psalm.

18 *circumvolves* is Erasmus' translation of ἐλίξεις in 1:12. He believed the Greek verb meant to roll (*volvere*) or to turn (*vertere*), and considered the former to be more apt when speaking of the heavens or a garment than the verb *mutare* employed in the Vulgate; see his annotation (*mutabis eos*) LB VI 984E. *Circumvolvere*, however, means either 'to revolve,' or 'to twine or wrap around,' so that it is not entirely clear whether Erasmus understands the metaphor to mean, 'to turn the heavens around as one might reverse a cloak,' or, 'to roll or fold them up' (RSV and NKJ). The addition of the adverb 'suddenly' (*subito*, perhaps from 1 Cor 15:52 or 2 Pet 3:10) seems to suggest a quick reversal rather than a rolling up. The medieval commentaries, which, however, read 'you will change' (*mutabis* in their text of the Vulgate), not 'you will fold or turn,' explicate this verse from the description of the new world in Rev 21.

19 *ut adsint*, that is, to aid and protect, as the medieval commentaries explain this ministering function of angels, citing Ps 90:11. But again Erasmus seems to be choosing a vague term in order to pass over in silence the extended discussions of just how and why the angels serve the needs of the elect.

Chapter 2

1 Cf Luke 16:31. The mention of the prophets in the paraphrase on 2:1 and 2 implies that 'word' (AV) in verse 2 denotes more than just the Pentateuch or the Mosaic law. Cf Chrysostom *Hom in Heb* 3 (on Heb 2:2) PG 63 32 / NPNF 378b and Aquinas *Exp in epist ad Heb* c 2 lect 1 684a.

2 Cf Gal 3:19 and Acts 7:38 and 53. The belief that angels brought the Law from God to Moses appears in Jewish apocrypha (eg *Book of Jubilees* 1:27) and other Jewish literature more or less contemporaneous with the NT; see Spicq *Hébreux* II 54–5.

3 Cf Chrysostom *Hom in Heb* 3 (on Heb 2:2) PG 63 33 / NPNF 379a: 'How then was it confirmed? What if those who heard were forgers? saith some one. This objection then he overthrows, and shows that the grace was not human.'

218

4 Cf 1 John 1:1.

5 Cf 1 Cor 12:4–11.

6 Erasmus partly quotes and partly paraphrases his Latin version of the Greek text of 2:7. His translation *Fecisti eum paulisper inferiorem angelis* 'you made him for a little while lower than the angels' was attacked by Lefèvre as blasphemous because the words 'you made' detracted from the divine nature of Christ and as incorrect because the Greek adverbial phrase βραχύ τι in this verse meant little in degree, not little in time. The paraphrase *demisisti illum paulisper infra angelos*, literally 'you sent him down for a little while below the angels,' avoids the accusation that Christ was inferior to the angels while still holding to the view that the author of Hebrews was referring to the period of Christ's life on earth. See Erasmus' lengthy annotation on 2:7 (*minuisti eum paulo minus ab angelis*) LB VI 985C–991D, the article on Lefèvre in CEBR II 315–18 with the bibliography cited on the controversy, and Rummel *Critics* I 49–51. As a glance at modern translations and commentaries will show, the question is still disputed though the majority of modern scholars appear to agree with Erasmus.

7 then follows] First in the March 1521 edition. The punctuation of the first edition makes the words *et mox*, literally, 'and then,' a part of the biblical citation: 'You lowered him for a little while ... and then you crowned,' as though the 'and then' and the 'for a little while' were being contrasted. The quotation is repunctuated in the March 1521 edition to show that *et mox* is not part of the citation.

8 too] Added in the March 1521 edition

9 Cf Aquinas *Exp in epist ad Heb* c 2 lect 2 (on Heb 2:8) 688b: 'When [Paul] says, "we do not yet see everything in subjection to them," he shows that this has not yet been fulfilled because infidels, sinners, and demons are not yet subject to him ... Sinners are not subject to Christ through the rebellion of their will.' Cf Rom 10:16, which Aquinas cites in this context.

10 The contrast between the passion and death of the Son and the impassibility of angels occurs in Theophylact *Exp in Heb* (on Heb 2:9) PG 125 209A.

219

11 Cf the paraphrase on Rom 5:16 (CWE 42 35).

12 Modern scholars assume that the reference here is to Isa 8:17 LXX. Medieval commentators knew that Chrysostom referred to Isa 8:18 at this point, but since the translation of 8:17 in the Vulgate, 'I will wait for (*expectabo*) the Lord,' is quite different from that in LXX, they, and apparently Erasmus too, were puzzled by the reference to Isaiah.

13 Erasmus employs in the paraphrase on 2:16 the Vulgate translation *semen Abrahae apprehendit*, although in his Latin version he uses the verb *assumit* 'assume' to translate the two occurrences of ἐπιλαμβάνεται in this verse. The verb form *apprehendit* can be either present or past tense. In the NT it is present, but since in the paraphrase Erasmus has replaced the present tense by the past in the preceding sentence – 'Christ held' – I have translated *apprehendit* as a past tense. The phrase 'seed of Abraham' is generally thought to be an allusion to Isa 41:8, but the addition of the words 'in accordance with the divine promise' in the paraphrase suggests that Erasmus is thinking of Gen 22:17–18 and Gal 3:16–18.

Chapter 3

220

1 'Established' (*constitutus*) is Erasmus' translation of the verb ποιήσαντι in 3:2 ('appointed' RSV; *fecit* 'made' Vulg) to avoid the implication that the Son was created. See note 33 on 2:7 above and Spicq *Hébreux* II 65–6.

221

2 Ps 95:7–11. Erasmus partly quotes the text, marked by the insertion of 'he says' twice, and partly paraphrases it. The paraphrase retains the single long sentence of the biblical text, but I have divided it into four separate sentences to make it more readable.

3 Cf Exod 16:3.

222

4 See Num 14:30–1, where Caleb, Joshua, and the children then under twenty years of age are exempted from death in the wilderness.

Chapter 4

1 lest] 1532. The earlier editions read 'and.'

223

2 Nave, which occurs in Sir 46:1, is a common alternative to Nun for the name of Joshua's father in patristic and medieval commentaries.

3 Cf Chrysostom *Hom in Heb* 6 (on Heb 4:9) PG 63 57 / NPNF 395b.

4 The last clause appears to be a faint echo of Isa 35:10; cf Chrysostom *Hom in Heb* 6 (on Heb 4:10) PG 63 58–9 / NPNF 396b–397a.

5 This identification of 'the word of God' in 4:12 with the incarnate Word or Jesus Christ appears in Chrysostom *Hom in Heb* 7 PG 63 60 / NPNF 398a, and in numerous patristic and medieval commentators; see Spicq *Hébreux* II 87. It is rejected by modern commentators.

6 'Laid open for scrutiny' is my paraphrase of the participle *resupinata* (literally, 'laid on the back'), which Erasmus employed to translate the Greek participle τετραχηλισμένα, the meaning of which is in any case obscure in this verse (see Spicq *Hébreux* II 90–1). Erasmus thought (erroneously) that the Latin verb *resupinare* described the action of a person lying on his back to study a ceiling or similar object, and hence could be a metaphor for the act of examining or scrutinizing; see his annotation on 4:13 (*et aperta*) LB VI 996E.

224

7 The verb 'to find,' which occurs in the original Greek, the Vulgate, and Erasmus' Latin version of 4:16, is omitted, probably inadvertently, in the paraphrase.

Chapter 5

225

1 Cf Exod 28:1.

2 The meaning of the phrase ἀπὸ τῆς εὐλαβείας in 5:7 has been discussed since the time of the church Fathers; see Spicq *Hébreux* II 114–17. It was translated *pro sua reverentia* 'in keeping with his reverence' in the Vulgate. Erasmus retained this translation in his Latin version, but omitted the *sua* 'his' which has no equivalent in the Greek. Lefèvre *Comm in Heb* 238 argued that εὐλάβεια in this verse means piety or devotion (*pietas*), not reverence or godly fear, and that it designates the Son's attitude toward the Father. Erasmus accepts this view about the meaning of the Greek but prefers to believe that the term describes the reciprocal devotion of the Father and the Son to each other; see his annotation on 5:7 (*pro sua reverentia*) LB VI 997E and Chrysostom *Hom in Heb* 8 (on Heb 5:8) PG 63 70 / NPNF 404.

3 Cf Chrysostom *Hom in Heb* 8 (on Heb 5:8) PG 63 69–70 / NPNF 404, and Theophylact *Exp in Heb* PG 125 244B.

4 For Erasmus' view of the totally human agony which Christ felt in the garden see the *De taedio Iesu* LB V 1263–92, and his correspondence with John Colet on this subject, Epp 108–111.

226

5 Cf the paraphrase on Galatians 4:21–31 (CWE 42 119–21) for an example of what Erasmus means by allegory in this context. Lefèvre *Comm in Heb* 237v was perhaps the first commentator to take 'milk' as a metaphor for the literal meaning of Scripture and 'solid food' as a metaphor for the spiritual meaning: 'All who are fixated on the literal meaning are slack and weak when it comes to understanding the spiritual meaning which is the solid food.' This interpretation of the text does not seem to occur in the patristic and medieval Latin commentaries; they prefer to distinguish between the milk of the catechism and the solid food of theology. See eg Aquinas *Exp in epist ad Heb* c 5 lect 2 (on Heb 5:12) 711–13. But as the paraphrase on 6:1 indicates, for Erasmus theology means a deeper insight into the meaning of Scripture.

Chapter 6

227

1 thereafter] LB reads 'but.'

2 Heb 6:2 speaks of the laying on or imposition of the hands (plural), which is the usual formula in the NT. Precisely what Erasmus has in mind with the use of the singular 'hand' is not clear (cf the phrase 'the priest's hand' in the paraphrase on 6:4 below). He may be thinking of the rite of confirmation in which the bishop places only one hand upon the head of the person being confirmed.

3 Cf 1 Cor 3:12.

4 Cf the paraphrase on 1 Pet 2:2–5 and Chrysostom *Hom in Heb* 9 (on Heb 6:1) PG 63 77 / NPNF 409b.

5 Aquinas *Exp in epist ad Heb* c 6 lect 1 (on Heb 6:5) 715b explains that the 'word of God' is called 'good' because it is the 'word of eternal life.' He illustrates his explanation by citing John 6:68: 'Lord to whom can we go? You have the words of eternal life.'

6 Spicq *Hébreux* II 153–4 has a list of commentators, patristic (eg Chrysostom *Hom in Heb* 9 (on Heb 6:6) PG 63 79 / NPNF 410–11), medieval (eg Aquinas *Exp in epist ad Heb* c 6 lect 1 716b), sixteenth-century and modern, who have taken the prefix ἀνα in the verb ἀνασταυροῦντας to mean 'again' and have inferred from this meaning that this clause denied the possibility of a second baptism. See Rom 6:2–11, though it is doubtful that the Pauline conception of baptism as a dying and rising with Christ is to be found in the Epistle to the Hebrews in the way that Erasmus employs it in the paraphrase here on verses 4 and 5.

228
7 Cf the paraphrase on 3:13 above.
8 This observation is made by Chrysostom *Hom in Heb* 11 (on Heb 7:15–16) PG 63 91 / NPNF 419a.

229
9 Cf Gen 13:14–17, 15:4–6, 17:15–20.

Chapter 7

1 Gen 14:1 and 9 speak of four kings, not three.
2 Abraham gave Melchisedek a tenth of the spoils taken from the four kings, but Erasmus may have inferred from Gen 14:20 (*Et dedit ei decimas ex omnibus* Vulg) that Abram gave Melchizedek a tenth of all that he owned. The *Gloss* on Gen 14:20 states that 'Abram gave Melchizedek a tenth of his property after the blessing just as according to the Law the people give a tithe to the priests who bless them.'

230
3 Erasmus means that in respect to his divine nature Christ had neither a human father nor a human mother. In respect to his human nature he has a human mother but a divine father.
4 Erasmus means his divine genealogy in the Trinity; cf Aquinas *Exp in epist ad Heb* c 7 lect 1 (on Heb 1:3) 722b, who, citing Isa 53:8, comments: 'The generation of Christ is ineffable.'
5 Cf Num 18:21–4.
6 Cf Exod 4:14.
7 Ps 110:4, cf Heb 5:6 above.

231
8 Aquinas *Exp in epist ad Heb* c 7 lect 3 (on Heb 7:11–12) 727a explains that a new priest needs a new law because the Old Testament 'is a carnal commandment since it had carnal observances such as circumcision and carnal purifications and likewise promised carnal punishments and rewards, whereas the New Testament ... is not dispensed through carnal things but consists in spiritual ones. It has a spiritual power which generates everlast-

ing life in us, and the goods and punishments which it promises are everlasting.' Patristic and modern commentators prefer to locate the contrast in
the qualities of the two priests, not in the difference between the two laws;
that is, in the powerless, mortal Levite compared to the omnipotent, immortal Christ. See eg Spicq *Hébreux* II 193.

9 Cf Chrysostom *Hom in Heb* 13 (on Heb 7:20) PG 63 105 / NPNF 429a.

10 'Crude': *crassa*. This adjective when applied to material things means 'thick,
dense, gross,' and, applied to the mind, 'dull, insensitive.' It is repeatedly
used by Erasmus to characterize the rituals of the Mosaic law, especially
animal sacrifice, and is often combined with the adjective *carnalis* 'carnal,'
as just above in the paraphrase on verse 16, to describe the materialistic
nature of the Mosaic law in contrast to the spirituality of the law of the
gospel (cf CWE 42 141 n9 on Rom 1:19). The adjective thus emphasizes the
materialism and this-worldly dimension of the Mosaic law (and of later
Christian practices which in Erasmus' view revive the attitudes the spiritual
law of the gospel had abrogated).

11 A Platonizing interpretation of the import of 1 Cor 2:10–16, and of texts like
Rom 10:4, Gal 3:24; see Payne *Theology* 35–9.

12 Cf Exod 20:13 and 15, Lev 5:6–13.

232

13 Cf 9:7 below.

14 'Representative' (*legatus*), a word with numerous English equivalents, including envoy or ambassador. Christ is our ambassador (or apostle; cf 3:1)
to the court of God the Father. For Christ as the Head of the church see Col
1:18. The Pauline image of the body of Christ does not actually occur in
Hebrews, but Erasmus' introduction of it into the paraphrase on 7:19 is
consonant with the assumption that Paul is the author of the Epistle and
the writer of the *Paraphrase* on it.

15 Twice each year; see the commentaries on Luke 1:8–9. The reference to this
practice as a possible explanation of 7:23 apparently originated with
Erasmus. Though generally rejected, it has left its mark in the commentary
tradition. Patristic, medieval, and modern commentators adopt the second
reason given here: the continuity of the (high) priesthood is interrupted by
death.

16 The repeated change ... brings with it] This is the reading of the first edition. In the March 1521 edition the main clause is changed into a subordinate clause 'as the repeated change ... brings with it' by changing the conjunction *et* 'also' to *ut* 'as.' The indicative verb was then emended in the
1534 and later editions to the subjunctive to make the clause read 'so that
the repeated change' etc. But both of these emendations, whether made by
Erasmus or a corrector at the press, leave the sentence without a main
clause. I have, therefore, translated the text of the first edition which is,
presumably, what Erasmus originally wrote.

17 Cf Rom 8:34.

18 'Godly' (*pius*) and 'without guile' (*expers doli*; cf 1 Pet 2:22) are Erasmus'
translations of ὅσιος 'holy' and ἄκακος 'innocent' (DR), 'harmless' (AV) in
7:26. For the view that ἄκακος means 'without guile' see Chrysostom *Hom
in Heb* 13 (on Heb 7:26–8) PG 63 106 / NPNF 430a.

Chapter 8

233

1 For this contrast between the reality in heaven and the image on earth see
8:5 below and 10:1. For Erasmus' essentially Platonic view of the relationship between idea (the reality in heaven) and image (the copy or shadow
on earth) see Payne *Theology* 34–5.

234

2 Cf Aquinas *Exp in epist ad Heb* c 8 lect 2 (on Heb 8:6) 731b: '[In the old
covenant] some things are said which pertain to the worship of God, and
these are ceremonial; some things are said which pertain to right living, and
these are moral commands. The latter continue in force, but the former do
not. In the new covenant spiritual content, which is given to the perfect
who are capable of understanding spiritual things, is added to the commands of the old covenant. Thus the same commands remain, but the
promises are different.'

3 Lefèvre *Comm in Heb* 246 likewise takes the covenant rather than the people
to be the object of God's fault finding. In his Latin version of 8:8 Erasmus,
following the Vulgate (*vituperans ... eos*), translates 'blaming them' (*incusans
eos*), but in his annotation (*vituperans enim*) LB VI 1004F, he explains that
there was reprehension 'because God himself complains about it' (*eo*, ie
testamento 'the covenant').

4 Jer 31:31–4. Erasmus partly quotes, partly paraphrases the quotation of this
text in Hebrews. Hence the omission of the 'and' ('when' in RSV) in 8:8 and
the words 'after those days' in 8:10 may be deliberate, though I suspect that
both omissions were accidental. See the next two notes.

5 Lord, I] The two clauses 'Behold ... coming' and 'I will make ... with the
house of Judah' are connected in the Greek text by καί, translated by *et*
'and' in the Vulgate and in Erasmus' Latin version, by 'when' in RSV. The *et*
is omitted in the paraphrase, probably by accident.

6 Israel] The phrase 'after those days' is included in the paraphrase on these
verses from Jeremiah in 10:16 below, but omitted here. There seems to be
no particular reason for omitting them here, and I suspect that the omission
was an oversight on Erasmus' part. But in the phrase 'out of the land of
Egypt' in 8:9, the words 'the land of' are omitted in Erasmus' Latin version
and consequently in the paraphrase.

7 Nicholas of Lyra says toward the end of his comment on 8:13: 'The Old
Law, which ... consisted in sensible signs, was first written on stone tablets,
but the New Law, as more perfect, was first written not with ink but by the
spirit of the living God on the tablets of the heart (cf 2 Cor 3:3).'

8 Cf Theophylact *Exp in Heb* (on Heb 8:11) PG 125 296A: 'The Jewish Law was
shut up in one corner [of the world] and few knew it, but the voice of the
apostles went out to every land.' Nicholas of Lyra likewise explains that the
truth about God will be disseminated by the apostles and by Paul in particular (cf Gal 1:11–12), but the prevalent view in the *Gloss*, Hugh of St
Cher, and Aquinas (*Exp in epist ad Heb* c 8 lect 3 734a) is that Jeremiah and
Hebrews are referring to the knowledge of God that will be obtained
through the beatific vision.

9 If Erasmus is here following Theophylact *Exp in Heb* (on Heb 8:12) PG 125 296B, he means the forgiveness of sins through baptism.

Chapter 9

235

1 ceremonies ... tabernacle was such] First in 1532. The earlier editions read 'ceremonies the observance of which was to give the appearance of right-eousness. It had a certain holiness, but of a worldly kind, grounded in external and visible things. Even the gentiles place a value upon this kind of holiness. But the structure of the Temple was such' etc. The revision was most likely caused by a dispute with Noël Béda; see *Elenchus in N. Bedae censuras* LB IX 512C–513C. For the details about the temple service and its arrangements cf Chrysostom *Hom in Heb* 15 (on Heb 9:1–5) PG 63 117 / NPNF 438a and Theophylact *Exp in Heb* PG 125 296D–297A.

2 This clause is an explanation of the meaning of the words *iustificationes cultus* 'justifications of divine service' (DR), which the Clementine Vulgate uses to translate δικαιώματα λατρείας 'regulations for worship' (RSV) in 9:1.

3 The Vulgate translates the adjective κοσμικόν in 9:1 by *saeculare* 'pertaining to the age, secular.' Erasmus translated it by *mundanum* 'worldly,' which is the term he employs here in the paraphrase. The medieval commentators interpreted the term 'secular' to mean either man-made and temporary (the *Gloss*, Hugh of St Cher, Aquinas *Exp in epist ad Heb* c 9 lect 1 735), or earthly and dedicated to corporal activities (Hugh of St Cher as an alterna-tive interpretation and Nicholas of Lyra). Hugh also records Chrysostom's explanation (*Hom in Heb* 15 PG 63 117 / NPNF 738b) that Paul calls the sanc-tuary 'cosmic' because it was accessible to all the people. Modern commen-tators for the most part assume that the adjective means 'worldly' in the sense of belonging to the visible world in contrast to the phrase 'not of this creation' in 9:11; see eg Spicq *Hébreux* II 248.

4 Cf Erasmus' comment in his annotation on 9:2 (*candelabra*) LB VI 1005F: 'λυχνία means lampstand but I translate it as lights because the one lampstand supported several lights.'

5 There were twelve loaves of bread; see Lev 24:5–9.

6 Aquinas *Exp in epist ad Heb* c 9 lect 1 (on Heb 9:4) 736a observes that all the objects in the ark of the covenant were preserved in memory of an event.

7 Censer (*thuribulum*) is the translation in the Vulgate. Erasmus notes in his annotation on 9:4 (*thuribulum*) LB VI 1006E that the Greek word θυμιατήριον also means incense-altar. All the references to the incense-altar in the OT and other Jewish sources place it in the Holy Place, not in the Holy of Holies. This and other inconsistencies between the OT and Heb 9:4 were explained away in medieval commentaries through various allegorical treat-ments of the texts; cf eg the *Gloss* on 9:4 and Aquinas *Exp in epist ad Heb* c 9 lect 1 736b. For modern treatments of these questions see Spicq *Hébreux* II 250–1. Erasmus simply ignores the entire problem.

8 Following the Vulgate, Erasmus uses the word *testamentum* 'testament' to translate the Greek noun διαθήκη throughout Hebrews. In secular Greek the word usually had the meaning 'will' or 'testament,' but it was used in

LXX to translate Hebrew *b'rith* 'covenant.' Erasmus knew from Jerome *Comm in Ier* 31:31–2 PL 24 884A that the Hebrew word *b'rith* never means 'last will and testament' but only 'covenant' or, as the Vulgate commonly translates the Hebrew in the OT, 'pact, agreement' (*pactum*). Cf Erasmus' annotations on Gal 3:17 (*testamentum confirmatum a deo*) LB VI 815E and especially on Heb 9:16 (*ubi enim testamentum*) LB VI 1007E, where he observes that the argument advanced in 9:16 is evidence that the author of this Epistle did not know Hebrew [that is, that the author could not have been Paul]. Jerome remarks in his note on Jeremiah that 'it is correct to call a covenant a testament because it contains the wishes of its maker and the attestation of those who make the covenant.' Leaving aside the problems connected with the meaning of Heb 9:16–17, I have followed Erasmus' lead and have rendered his Latin *testamentum* by English 'testament.'

9 Cf Exod 16.

10 Cf Num 17:8. The detail about cutting the rod from its trunk is not in Scripture. Cf Homer *Iliad* 1.235.

11 Cf Deut 10:1–5.

12 Cf Hugh of St Cher, for example, who devotes over two and one-half folio pages (P4r–P6r) to this task, or the more succinct but still lengthy list in Lefèvre *Comm in Heb* 247–8.

13 Spicq *Hébreux* II 252 presents a modern statement of this view.

14 Cf Lev 16.

236

15 Cf Chrysostom *Hom in Heb* 15 (on Heb 9:5) PG 63 117 / NPNF 439a; also *Hom* 25 (on Heb 11:19) PG 63 174. 'Riddle' (*aenigma*) is another term which, like shadow, Erasmus employs to indicate that events and objects described in the Old Testament are to be interpreted spiritually and accommodated in one way or another to Christ, the gospel, or the Church. The word riddle carries the additional nuance that the reader of the Old Testament, and in some places of the New, is being challenged to search for the underlying spiritual meaning of the text. Cf the *Paraphrase on John* 4:10, CWE 46 55 and n16 with the reference to Cyril of Alexandria *Commentarium in evangelium Ioannis* PG 73 296C–D.

16 The text of Hebrews 9:9 is ambiguous here. The phrase 'the time present' can be understood as 'the time then present,' which is how Erasmus and the AV translate the Greek, or 'the time now present,' which is the way Lefèvre and the majority of modern commentators and translators understand the phrase.

17 Cf Matt 15:10–11 and parallels.

18 As in 9:1 above, Erasmus is paraphrasing in 9:10 the Vulgate translation *iustificationes* 'justifications.' In Erasmus' Greek text of this verse the participle 'imposed' (which he took to mean 'located' or 'situated in') modifies the nouns 'gifts and sacrifices' rather than the noun 'regulations' (cf RSV). Consequently, he translated verses 9–10: '... which was a similitude for that present time in which gifts and sacrifices were offered which could not make the worshipper perfect in conscience, situated as they were only in food and drink, and in various ablutions and justifications, until the time of reformation.' Thus he understood the sentence to mean that the rituals of

the Jewish religion were concerned only with matters of food and drink, with ablutions, and justifications of the flesh. In this respect he is within the medieval understanding of Judaism. Aquinas, for example, *Exp in epist ad Heb* c 9 lect 1 735 commenting on the words 'worldly sanctuary' in 9:1 and citing Gal 4:9, says: 'Here one sees the difference between the New Testament and the Old. Although both are corporal, nevertheless, the New contains grace and is sacred. Divine power works salvation more securely in it under the cover of visible actions. This power was not in the Old Testament because it contained in itself no grace.' Cf Nicholas of Lyra's commentary on Heb 10:4, where he denies that the rituals of the Old Law conferred grace and argues that only the sacraments of the New Law confer justifying grace because they have received this power from the passion and death of Christ.

19 Cf the paraphrase on Gal 3:23–5 CWE 42 113–4.

20 The word κτίσις can mean 'building' or 'structure' in late Greek, though the Vulgate and modern translations prefer the translation 'creation' in 9:11. Erasmus does not annotate his translation *structura*. He may be following Lefèvre *Comm in Heb* 248r who translates κτίσις at one point by *aedificatio* 'building' and at another by *structio* 'construction,' and refers the 'structure' to the man-made tent of Moses and the temple of Solomon.

21 Lefèvre *Comm in Heb* 248v, commenting on 9:13, emphasizes the contrast between the 'irrational animals' which humans offer and the 'spotless rational victim which the Holy Spirit offers to God.'

237

22 LB punctuates this sentence as a question. The first edition and the Basel editions punctuate the sentence as a statement.

23 Erasmus means the fire which reduced the red heifer to ashes (see Num 19:1–10), if, that is, he is here following Theophylact *Exp in Heb* (on Heb 9:14) PG 125 305D, who makes this connection between the OT rite and the text of Heb 9:14.

24 Lefèvre *Comm in Heb* 248v makes this same statement and quotes Zech 9:11 where the Vulgate has *in sanguine testamenti tui* rather than *pacti tui* (cf RSV 'because of the blood of my covenant with you').

25 Exod 24:4–8

26 The notion that the blood was mixed with the water is found in Hugh of St Cher on 9:19 and Aquinas. The latter *Exp in epist ad Heb* c 9 lect 4 (on Heb 9:19) 742b adds an allegorical explanation: 'The blood is mixed with water because baptism receives its efficacy from the blood of Christ.' The author of Hebrews appears in any case to be conflating several different rituals; see Spicq *Hébreux* II 264–5.

27 Chrysostom *Hom in Heb* 16 (on Heb 9:15) PG 63 123 / NPNF 443a observes that a testament had to be witnessed and cites John 8:18 for the fact that Christ himself is a witness. The medieval commentators understood the verb 'dedicated' in Heb 9:18 to mean 'confirmed' or 'ratified.' They thus call the blood the *confirmator* 'confirmer, ratifier' of the testament; see eg Aquinas *Exp in epist ad Heb* c 9 lect 4 (on Heb 9:20) 742: '"This is the blood" ... that is, the ratifier of the testament ... For this blood is a figure of the blood of Christ through which the new testament was ratified, and there-

fore Christ used those words [of Moses], "This is the blood of the new testament" [Matt 26:28], that is, blood that ratifies.' There is some ambiguity in Erasmus' language in the paraphrase on Heb 9:20. In his Latin version he translates the Greek *hic est sanguis testamenti*, adding from Exod 24:8 (Vulg) or Matt 26:28 the verb *est*, which is omitted in the original Greek and in the Vulgate in Heb 9:20. The paraphrase has *hic est sanguis testis, et confirmator* without punctuation before *testis* or after *confirmator*. Hence it could be translated as I have done it or 'This is the blood, the witness and ratifier,' etc.

238

28 Nothing is said or implied about possible profanation of the sanctuary in the text of Heb 9:24. Erasmus may have in mind actions such as those of Antiochus Epiphanes (cf 1 Macc 1:54, 59), Pompey the Great, who is said to have actually entered the Holy of Holies, or the effort of the emperor Gaius to have his statue placed in the temple (Josephus *Jewish Antiquities* 14.72 and 18.261–2).
29 That is, with the angels; see the paraphrase on 1:7 above.
30 Erasmus presumably means the annual expiation of sins on the Day of Atonement.
31 The *Gloss*, Hugh of St Cher, Aquinas *Exp in epist ad Heb* c 9 lect 5 745b, and Nicholas of Lyra on 9:28 explain that the words 'a second time without sin' (I translate the Greek and the Vulgate literally) mean either that Christ in his first appearance in the incarnation assumed the likeness of sinful flesh and was crucified as a criminal (Hugh adds this point) but in his second appearance will be in his glorified flesh (*caro gloriosa*); or that Christ in his first appearance was the victim of judgment but in his second appearance will be the Judge of all. The variations in modern translations, which are really paraphrases of the original Greek (eg 'apart from sin' NKJ, 'not to deal with sin' RSV, 'sin done away with' NEB), likewise suggest that the meaning of the phrase remains problematic. Lefèvre's solution *Comm in Heb* 250r was to construe the phrase with the clause 'those who wait' rather than with the verb 'appear.' Erasmus seems to offer both possibilities: the description of Christ in the previous sentence, 'like a criminal deserving punishment,' picks up Hugh's variation on the medieval answer that Christ was born in the likeness of sinful flesh, while 'those who have persevered in a life of innocence' presents Lefèvre's suggestion.

239

32 Cf Theophylact *Exp in Heb* PG 125 317A who similarly concludes his commentary on Heb 9:28 with a reference to the Last Judgment.

Chapter 10

1 did not have the same power] *idem valuerit* 1532. The earlier editions read *idem voluerit* 'did not want the same thing' [that Christ wanted – to take away the sins of many and to be seen in glory (9:28)].
2 Chrysostom *Hom in Heb* 17 (on Heb 10:3) PG 63 130 / NPNF 448 and Theophylact *Exp in Heb* PG 125 321A, following him, use the image of disease.

3 Erasmus retained in his Latin version of Heb 10:7 the Vulgate translation *in capite libri* 'in the head of the book' (DR) of the Greek ἐν κεφαλίδι βιβλίου – the meaning of which is in any case uncertain – without indicating exactly what he thought this phrase meant other than that it referred to a part of a book; see his annotation on Heb 10:7 (*hostiam et oblationem noluisti*) LB VI 1009D. The paraphrase, in taking the Latin *caput* 'head' in its literal sense, resembles the kind of explanation found in Aquinas *Exp in epist ad Heb* c 10 lect 1 (on Heb 10:7) 747a: '"In the head of the book," that is, in the ordinance of God, who is the head of Christ, who is the book; "it is written" that the Son of God must become flesh and die.'

240

4 Though included in the quotation, the words 'and to offer ... to your mind' are not in the biblical text. They are typical of the way in which the paraphrase expands a text by negating the opposite of what it says.
5 The inference that the words 'once for all' in 10:10 mean that blood sacrifices have been abolished is made by Chrysostom *Hom in Heb* 18 PG 63 135 / NPNF 451b.
6 Cf Ps 110:1 and Heb 1:13 above.
7 Or] *aut* in all editions. The 'or' may be a stylistic variation in place of 'and,' or a misreading – either on the part of Erasmus or of the typesetter of the first edition – of *atque* 'and,' the conjunction which Erasmus uses at this point in his Latin version.
8 Jer 31:33–4
9 'Confidence' (*fiducia*) is the Vulgate translation of παρρησία 'boldness' in 10:19; in his Latin version Erasmus translates the word by 'freedom' (*libertas*). Chrysostom *Hom in Heb* 19 PG 63 139 / NPNF 454b, after observing that sins bring with them a feeling of shame, states that the remission of all our sins, and the fact that we have become heirs and have obtained so much love produces this boldness in us.
10 Cf Aquinas *Exp in epist ad Heb* c 10 lect 2 (on Heb 10:20) 749a: 'Just as the high priest entered the Holy of Holies through the veil, so we, if we wish to enter the sanctuary of glory, must enter through the flesh of Christ, which was the veil of his deity ... For faith about the deity [of Christ] is insufficient unless there is also faith about the incarnation.' Cf also Chrysostom *Hom in Heb* 15 (on Heb 9:1) PG 63 117 / NPNF 438 and *Hom in Heb* 15 (on Heb 10:20) PG 63 139 / NPNF 455a.
11 Chrysostom *Hom in Heb* 19 (on Heb 10:20) PG 63 139 / NPNF 455a and, following him, Theophylact *Exp in Heb* PG 125 329A make this point.

241

12 Cf 3:5–6 above. Aquinas *Exp in epist ad Heb* c 10 lect 2 (on Heb 10:21) 749b likewise sees in the mention of the 'house of God' an allusion to this earlier passage as well as to 1 Tim 3:15.
13 Cf Theophylact *Exp in Heb* (on Heb 10:14) PG 125 325D, where he states that all who are baptized are sanctified in the blood of Christ, and Aquinas *Exp in epist ad Heb* c 10 lect 2 (on Heb 10:22) 749, who observes that two things are necessary, faith and the sacrament of faith, baptism. Cf the paraphrase on 10:4 above.

14 Theophylact *Exp in Heb* (on Heb 10:23) PG 125 332A likewise takes the word 'confession' to refer to the promises made at baptism.

15 Cf Matt 24:13.

16 expect] *expectandum* 1521–1538. The 1540 edition, followed by LB, reads *expetendum* 'seek.'

17 Theophylact *Exp in Heb* (on Heb 10:26) PG 125 333A speaks of mortal sins in the plural. Most modern commentators believe the author is referring in 10:26 only to the sin of apostasy; see eg Spicq *Hébreux* II 321–3.

242

18 Chrysostom *Hom in Heb* 20 (on Heb 10:26) PG 63 143 / NPNF 457b and Theophylact *Exp in Heb* (on Heb 10:26) PG 125 333A argue that verse 26 prohibits a second baptism. Cf Erasmus' annotation on Heb 10:27 (*quae consumptura est*) LB VI 1010F.

19 Lefèvre *Comm in Heb* 251v makes this same point.

20 The prohibition against eating pork is found in Lev 11:7–8 and Deut 14:8. No specific penalty was prescribed in the OT for eating unclean food and the statement that this act was punishable by death is incorrect.

21 Cf Deut 19:15.

22 Cf 1 Cor 3:16 and 6:19–20: a person's body is the temple of the Holy Spirit.

23 Theophylact *Exp in Heb* (on Heb 10:30) PG 125 336C makes a similar contrast between human and divine judgment. Cf also Aquinas *Exp in epist ad Heb* c 10 lect 3 (on Heb 10:31) 753b.

24 That the clause 'those who were so treated' in 10:33 referred to the apostles is the view of Chrysostom *Hom in Heb* 21 PG 63 149 / NPNF 461b and Theophylact *Exp in Heb* PG 125 337B. It was reinforced for them by the reading 'my chains' in their text of 10:34 (cf NKJ), which seemed to confirm the Pauline authorship of the Epistle.

243

25 Cf Matt 6:19–20; Luke 12:33–4, 14:13–14; and Col 1:5. Aquinas *Exp in epist ad Heb* c 10 lect 4 (on Heb 10:34b) 754b likewise notes that heavenly riches are increased by the removal of earthly wealth. Cf also Mark 10:21 and parallels.

26 Cf 2 Tim 4:8. The image from athletic contests is used at this point by Chrysostom *Hom in Heb* 21 (on Heb 10:36) PG 63 150 / NPNF 462b, but he makes no reference to 2 Tim.

27 who ... again] I have adopted the text of the 1540 edition, which may go back to a correction made by Erasmus. The 1532 edition reads 'for he was about to ascend into heaven, having promised that he would return to us again.' This text, though grammatically construable, is more awkwardly written than one would expect from Erasmus.

28 Erasmus seems to have conflated the promise made by the two angels in Acts 1:11, which occurred after the ascension, with the promise made by Jesus before the passion in texts such as Matt 24:30, Luke 21:27, or John 14:3.

29 Erasmus quotes the Vulgate text of Hab 2:4. In his annotation on Rom 1:17 (*ex fide vivit*) LB VI 563B, he observes that the preposition used with the noun 'faith' (Greek ἐκ, Latin *ex*) denotes source; hence I have translated 'from faith' rather than the more usual 'by faith.'

30 The words 'my soul ... in him' come from the first half of the Septuagint version of Habakkuk 2:4 as quoted by the author of Hebrews in 10:38. The order of the two parts of the verse in Habakkuk are reversed in Heb 10:38; see Spicq *Hébreux* II 332. Since in Habakkuk it is the Lord who speaks these words, 'my soul' is a circumlocution for 'I the Lord.'

31 Isaiah is a mistake for Habakkuk, presumably made by Erasmus himself. It appears in the first edition and is not corrected until LB.

Chapter 11

1 'Confidence': *fiducia*. In his Latin version of 11:1 Erasmus, following the Vulgate, renders πίστις by *fides* 'faith.' In his annotation on this verse (*sperandarum substantia*) LB VI 1012D, Erasmus comments, 'in this passage "faith" is not used in its strict sense for that through which we believe what ought to be believed, but for that through which we hope, that is, through confidence itself.'

244

2 Erasmus takes the term ὑπόστασις (*substantia* in the Vulgate) in 11:1 in its literal meaning of support or underpinning, and understands it to be a metaphor for certitude; see his annotation (*sperandarum substantia*) LB VI 1012D.

3 The comparison with the belief of philosophers that God is uncreated is made by Chrysostom *Hom in Heb* 22 (on Heb 11:3) PG 63 154 / NPNF 465b, but Erasmus adds the idea that the universe itself is uncreated. He probably has Aristotle in mind; cf Aristotle's *Physica* 8.1.

4 Chrysostom *Hom in Heb* 22 (on Heb 11:4) PG 63 155 / NPNF 466a makes this point, which is repeated by Theophylact *Exp in Heb* PG 125 341D: 'Who could be a model of sinlessness? His parents? His brother?'

5 No reason is given in the Bible for God's acceptance of Abel's sacrifice and his rejection of Cain's (Gen 4:3–4). For the explanation given by Erasmus cf Josephus *Jewish Antiquities* 1.54.

6 This explanation of the statement that God bore witness to Abel by sending fire from heaven to consume his sacrifice appears in Chrysostom *Hom in Heb* 22 (on Heb 11:4) PG 63 155 / NPNF 466a, Jerome *Liber hebraicarum quaestionum in Genesim* CSEL 72 6–7, and with varying detail in the medieval commentaries. Spicq *Hébreux* II 342–3 gives the history of this 'Jewish legend,' as he calls it.

245

7 This interpretation of the words 'he still speaks' in 11:4c is offered by Chrysostom *Hom in Heb* 22 PG 63 155 / NPNF 466b and is followed by the *Gloss*, Hugh of St Cher, and Nicholas of Lyra. Aquinas, however, *Exp in epist ad Heb* c 11 lect 2 (on Heb 11:4) 759b considers the interpretation presented in Erasmus' next sentence to be the correct one.

8 The *Gloss* on Jude 14 likewise confuses Enoch son of Jared (Gen 5:18–24) with Enoch son of Cain (Gen 4:17).

9 This sentence appears to be a paraphrase on the statement 'Enoch walked with God' in Gen 5:22.

10 Cf Chrysostom's exposition of 11:6 (*Hom in Heb* 22 PG 63 157 / NPNF 467a), which contains several of the details found in the paraphrase.

11 See Gen 6:13.

12 Cf Matt 24:37-9 (Luke 17:26-7). Chrysostom *Hom in Heb* 23 (on Heb 11:7) PG 63 159 / NPNF 469 and Theophylact *Exp in Heb* PG 125 345A-B cite the Lucan text.

246

13 For the paraphrase on 11:8-10 see Theophylact *Exp in Heb* PG 125 345-8, who was himself abridging Chrysostom *Hom in Heb* 23 PG 63 160-2 / NPNF 469-71.

14 See for Abraham Gen 14, for Isaac Gen 26, and for Jacob Gen 27:41-5 and 33:18-19. Nicholas of Lyra in his commentary on the phrase 'living in tents with Isaac and Jacob' in Heb 11:9 demonstrates that all these events took place during Abraham's lifetime.

15 The subject of the verb in the causal clause at the end of 11:11 is not explicit in the original Greek, and consequently it could be translated either 'she considered' (RSV) or 'he trusted' (NEB). Aquinas *Exp in epist ad Heb* c 11 lect 3 762b contemplated both possibilities in his comment on the phrase 'by faith' at the beginning of verse 11: 'Namely her own or Abraham's, because in the order of nature it was impossible for a ninety-year-old woman to be impregnated by a hundred-year-old man. However, each believed God, for whom nothing is difficult.' The paraphrase likewise accommodates both possibilities: Sarah was convinced that God could not lie while Abraham refused to heed nature and put his trust in God. For an argument in support of this interpretation of the text see Philip Edgecombe Hughes *A Commentary on the Epistle to the Hebrews* (Grand Rapids, Mich 1977) 471-6.

247

16 Cf Rom 9:8, which Aquinas *Exp in epist ad Heb* c 11 lect 3 (on Heb 11:12) 763a likewise cites.

17 The 'true-born descendants' are the Hebrews and specifically Isaac and Jacob. Theophylact *Exp in Heb* (on Heb 11:13) PG 125 349D and modern scholars prefer to take the words 'all these' in 11:13 to refer to all the patriarchs from Abel onward. Erasmus may have been influenced by the comment of Aquinas *Exp in epist ad Heb* c 11 lect 4 (on Heb 11:13) 763a: '"All these," that is, Abraham, Isaac, and Jacob. This view is better since the promise was made only to them, not to Abel, Enoch, and Noah.'

18 Ps 39:12

19 See Judg 1.

20 See Deut 3:27 and 34:1-4. This obvious example does not seem to occur in the patristic and medieval commentaries.

21 Theophylact *Exp in Heb* (on Heb 11:16) PG 125 352B-C makes this contrast between God, who created and rules the entire universe, and his special designation as the God of Abraham, Isaac, and Jacob (in Exod 3:6 [quoted in Mark 12:26 and parallels], 15, 16 etc). Cf Erasmus' annotation on 11:16 (*et siquidem illius meminisset*) LB VI 1014E, where he states that 'their' in the words 'God was not ashamed to be called their God' must refer to the patriarchs Abraham, Isaac, and Jacob.

248

22 Chrysostom *Hom in Heb* 25 (on Heb 11:19) PG 63 173 / NPNF 478b, Theophylact *Exp in Heb* (on Heb 11:17) PG 125 353A and Aquinas *Exp in epist ad Heb* c 11 lect 4 (on Heb 11:17) 765a all explain Abraham's faith as his belief that God can bring the dead back to life.

23 Cf Chrysostom *Hom in Heb* 25 (on Heb 11:19b) PG 63 174 / NPNF 479a: 'For since the sacrifice had been completed, and Isaac slain in intention, therefore [God] gave him to the Patriarch.'

24 Cf Aquinas *Exp in epist ad Heb* c 11 lect 4 (on Heb 11:19b) 765b: '"He received him," namely Isaac, "for a parable," that is, a figure of Christ who was to be crucified and sacrificed.'

25 was on the point of death] First in 1523. The 1521 and 1522 editions read 'when Isaac was dead.'

26 See Gen 48:14. This detail is also mentioned by Theophylact *Exp in Heb* (on Heb 11:21a) PG 125 353D.

27 This explanation of Jacob's action is one of numerous allegorical interpretations of 11:21; cf eg Aquinas *Exp in epist ad Heb* c 11 lect 5 765: Jacob was moved to adore the staff of Joseph 'from a consideration of the power of Christ which Joseph's own power prefigured. For as the governor of Egypt he carried a staff, a sign of the power of Christ.' Despite its appearance in the paraphrase Erasmus himself did not believe this particular interpretation of Joseph's staff; see his annotation on Heb 11:21 (*et adoravit fastigium virgae illius*) LB VI 1015D.

28 See Gen 50:25.

29 See Exod 2:1–3.

249

30 Cf Theophylact *Exp in Heb* (on Heb 11:25) PG 125 357A, who comments: 'By "the passing pleasures of sin" [Paul] means participation in the luxurious life of the palace.'

31 Cf Theophylact ibidem 357A–B: 'As those who received benefits from Christ afterwards insulted him and fastened him to the cross, so long ago those on whom Moses had conferred benefits branded him with ignominy. For that Hebrew whom Moses had freed from the Egyptian said to him the very next day, "Who made you a prince and judge over us? Do you intend to kill me as you killed the Egyptian?" [Exod 2:14].'

32 Chrysostom and Theophylact believe, as do many modern commentators (see Spicq *Hébreux* II 359), that the reference is to Moses' flight to Midian after the murder of the Egyptian (Exod 2:11–16). The *Gloss* on Heb 11:27, Nicholas of Lyra, Erasmus, and some modern commentators (Westcott, for example) prefer a reference to the exodus because Hebrews 11:27 contradicts the statement in Exod 2:14–15 that Moses was afraid of Pharoah. Aquinas *Exp in epist ad Heb* c 11 lect 6 767a leaves the question open.

33 Erasmus seems to have inferred (mistakenly) from the Vulgate text of Exod 12:22 that the *limen*, which he evidently took to mean 'threshold,' was also sprinkled with blood. According to Exod 12:7 only the lintel and two doorposts were.

34 See Exod 14:13–29.

35 See Josh 2:1–21, 6:12–25.

250

36 See Judg 7:16–22. The phrase 'miracle of the lamps' in the paraphrase on
11:32 reflects an allegorical interpretation of the lamps such as that in the
Gloss on Judg 7:16: the lamps (torches) prefigure the shining miracles of
later Christian martyrs.

37 See Judg 4:6–24. Erasmus confuses the fate of Sisera, who was killed when
Jael drove a tent peg into his head, with that of Jabin.

38 See Judg 14 to 16.

39 See Judg 11:1–2 and 32–3.

40 See 1 Sam 17:37–50. Nicholas of Lyra in his commentary on 11:32 likewise
selects the victory over Goliath as David's distinctive exploit, but he makes
no mention of the reason why David decided to fight with only his sling.

251

41 Erasmus may have in view the contrast between the integrity and simplicity
of Samuel's administration (1 Sam 7:15–17) and the excesses of his sons (1 Sam
8:11–13), but his language suggests that he is thinking rather of the practices
of princes and prelates in his own day. Cf his annotation on 2 Tim 4:13 (*et membranas*) LB VI 962D, where he contrasts the simple belongings of Paul with the
retinues of modern prelates: 'O the belongings of an apostle! A cloak to ward
off the rain and a few books – no doubt holy ones. Nowadays, what a train
of horses, of cannons, and other things which I have no desire to mention!'

42 Commentators have generally seen in Heb 11:33–8 a summary of the various afflictions suffered by the faithful, as recorded in the Old Testament, in
the Apocrypha, and in other Jewish literature. They thus tend to offer in
their commentaries a congeries of individuals and incidents; cf eg Spicq
Hébreux II 364–7. Erasmus, however, appears to believe that Paul is continuing to proceed in chronological order from Samuel and David down to the
Maccabean martyrs and even – if Erasmus is following Chrysostom as he
seems to be (see the paraphrase on 12:1 and n1) – to John the Baptist and
the first Christian martyrs. Consequently, his explanation of 11:33 is unique
in taking the antecedent of the relative pronoun 'who' at the beginning of
this verse to be the noun 'prophets' in verse 32. All the commentaries –
patristic, medieval, and modern – which I have seen take the relative pronoun and the first three clauses of 11:33 – subdued kingdoms, worked
righteousness, obtained promises – to refer to the patriarchs mentioned in
verse 32 and earlier. Erasmus, however, appears to be referring to prophets
like Elijah and Micaiah, who counted as nothing the threats of tyrants such
as Ahab (1 Kings 17–22). The 'men renowned for their religious devotion'
are still later figures: the three friends of Daniel who were placed in the
fiery furnace (Dan 3), possibly Daniel himself if he is not counted as a
prophet, and the priest Eleazar and the seven brothers of 2 Maccabees 6
and 7. The exception in this chronological sequence are the 'mothers who
saw their children called back to life' (11:35). The author of Hebrews says
merely that 'women received their dead' with no indication of the circumstances, but ancient, medieval, and modern commentators assume that he is
referring to the miracles performed by Elijah (1 Kings 17:17–24) and Elisha
(2 Kings 4:20–37).

43 See Dan 6:22.

44 See Dan 3:24–7.

45 As Aquinas remarks *Exp in epist ad Heb* c 11 lect 7 (on Heb 11:34) 770, to escape death and to repel enemies was the fortune of several OT heroes. But Erasmus clearly takes these statements in Hebrews 11:34 to belong together and to refer to some specific conflict, most likely the wars of the Maccabees with the kingdom of Syria; cf 1 Macc 2–4 and 2 Macc 7, 9 and 14.

46 The paraphrase 'their dead children' suggests that Erasmus has in mind 1 Kings 17:17–24 and 2 Kings 4:20–37, the only passages in the OT where children are brought back to life.

47 If the reference is to 2 Macc 6:18 and 7:1, as seems to be the case, the command was 'to eat swine's flesh' (DR).

48 Nicholas of Lyra on Heb 11:36 refers to Samson (Judg 16:25), to Job (19:2–3), and to Tobit 2, but the addition of the phrase 'as madmen and criminals' in Erasmus' paraphrase points rather to the events recorded in 1 and 2 Macc. See in particular 1 Macc 7:33 and 9:26.

252

49 There is a legend, found in several early Jewish and Christian texts (see Spicq *Hébreux* II 366) and particularly in Jerome *Commentarius in Isaiam* 15:57 PL 24 546–7, that King Manassah ordered Isaiah to be cut in two with a wooden saw. Hugh of St Cher, Aquinas *Exp in epist ad Heb* c 11 lect 8 (on Heb 11:37) 771b, and Nicholas of Lyra refer to this execution of Isaiah to explain the verb 'sawn in two' (RSV) in 11:37. Lyra also mentions in this context the deaths of the seven brothers in 2 Macc 7. Erasmus was certainly familiar with the story of Isaiah from Jerome (cf the paraphrase on Acts 8:34 LB VII 701C), but his annotation on Heb 11:37 (*secti sunt*) LB VI 1017D indicates that he did not think that the verb ἐπρίσθησαν in 11:37 necessarily meant *sawn* apart. The language of the paraphrase suggests that he has in mind only the execution of the seven brothers.

50 Though found both in his Greek manuscripts and in the Vulgate, Erasmus believed that the clause 'and were tempted' was an interpolation; see his annotation on Heb 11:37 (*tentati sunt*) LB VI 1017D and Metzger *Textual Commentary* 674.

51 The meaning of the 'something better' in 11:40 which God has in store for the faithful has posed a difficulty to commentators from patristic to modern times. Spicq *Hébreux* II 368–9 distinguishes four different interpretations of these words and identifies the commentators who held them. The issue was further complicated for medieval theologians, who wondered if the statement made in verse 40 did not imply that, contrary to Luke 23:43 and 2 Cor 5:1, the soul of the faithful departed did not enter heaven immediately after death. The answer Aquinas gives to both of these problems is the one Erasmus proposes in the paraphrase on 11:40: the something better which all must await is the resurrection of the body and the final union with Christ; see Aquinas *Exp in epist ad Heb* c 11 lect 8 (on Heb 11:40) 772b.

52 Chrysostom *Hom in Heb* 28 (on Heb 11:40) PG 63 192 / NPNF 492 comments: 'For the righteous are also worthy of admiration in this, that they rejoice in the welfare of their brethren, as in their own. So that for themselves also, this is according to their wish, to be crowned along with their own members. To be glorified all together, is a great delight.'

Chapter 12

1 Chrysostom *Hom in Heb* 28 (on Heb 11:37–8) PG 63 187 and 191 / NPNF
  488–92 and Theophylact *Exp in Heb* PG 125 364B–C believed that the martyrs
  referred to in 11:37–8 included John the Baptist and the martyrs of the first
  generation of Christians. Hence in their commentaries on 12:1 they took the
  'cloud of witnesses' to include the martyrs of both the Old and the New
  Testaments; see Chrysostom *Hom in Heb* 28 (on Heb 12:1) PG 63 193 / NPNF
  492b and Theophylact *Exp in Heb* PG 125 368B.
2 Theophylact *Exp in Heb* (on Heb 12:1) PG 125 368B states that the word
  'weight' in 12:1 refers to material goods and desires.
3 The clause 'which ... sides' is a paraphrase on the obscure Greek word
  εὐπερίστατον in 12:1, which the Vulgate translates by *circumstans nos* 'surrounding us,' which may well be the correct meaning of the word; see
  James Moffat *A Critical and Exegetical Commentary on the Epistle to the
  Hebrews* (New York 1924) 166–7. Aquinas *Exp in epist ad Heb* c 12 lect 1 775b
  offers several possible explanations of the participle *circumstans* – that it
  denotes the occasions of sin in the world such as the flesh, the neighbour,
  the demon; or the temptations presented by the enemies surrounding us
  (idolatry would be the prime example in the context of the NT); or the carnal emotions which arise from the flesh. In his annotation on this word (*circumstans nos*) LB VI 1018C, Erasmus explains that the Greek means 'that
  which easily surrounds and clings to and embraces as though unwilling to
  be cast off. Therefore, I have translated it *tenaciter inhaerente peccato* ['the
  tenaciously clinging sin,' cf RSV 'the sin that clings so closely']. Whether
  Aquinas' interpretation fits the text – he explains the "surrounding sin" as
  the "occasion of sin" – I leave to others to examine.'

253
4 For the expression 'to be far from sin' in this context see Chrysostom *Hom
  in Heb* 28 (on Heb 12:2) PG 63 194 / NPNF 493a, who cites 1 Pet 2:22, or
  Theophylact *Exp in Heb* PG 125 369A.
5 begin to think] *arbitrabimini* is found first in February 1522. The three 1521
  editions read the present tense *arbitramini* 'think.'
6 Cf Prov 3:11 and 3:12.
7 Cf the Eighth Rule in the *Enchiridion* CWE 66 105–6.

254
8 By 'spirits' Erasmus probably means souls; cf his paraphrase of the language employed by the faculty of theology at Paris in a criticism of his
  view of ceremonies – *qui dominus est corporum sicut et spirituum* 'who is Lord
  of bodies as of spirits' – which he restates by *qui corporum pariter atque ani-
  marum dominus est* 'who is Lord of bodies as well as of souls' in *Declarationes ad censuras Lutetiae vulgatas* LB IX 890E. Aquinas *Exp in epist ad Heb* c
  12 lect 1 (on Heb 12:9) 776a comments: 'God is our father in a superior
  way, that is, in respect to the soul of which he is the immediate creator.'
  The 'Father of spirits' is an OT title of God; cf Num 16:22 and 27:16: 'the
  God of the spirits of all flesh.' Other commentators have understood the
  word 'spirits' in this phrase to refer to the angels (cf Spicq *Hébreux* II 394),

and Erasmus' Latin could be translated in this sense: 'who is the creator not only of bodies but also of spirits,' but it is more likely that he is following the view of Aquinas.

9 Cf Aquinas *Exp in epist ad Heb* c 12 lect 1 (on Heb 12:11) 776 who bases his interpretation of the term 'peaceable' on the contrast between the physical pain and mental remorse of this life with the peace and serenity of the conscience in the life to come. Theophylact *Exp in Heb* PG 125 373D likewise understands 'peaceable' to mean mental calm.

10 Cf the paraphrase on 1 Tim 6:12.

255

11 See Gen 25:29–34. Patristic and medieval commentators offer a different argument: Esau was unsuccessful either because his repentance was feigned or because it was motivated by the wrong reasons. See eg Chrysostom *Hom in Heb* 21 (on Heb 12:17) PG 63 214 / NPNF 506, Theophylact *Exp in Heb* PG 380B–C, Aquinas *Exp in epist ad Heb* c 12 lect 3 779. For these commentators Esau is the exemplar of all the base emotions listed in the next sentence in the paraphrase.

12 Erasmus retained in his Latin version the Vulgate translation of γνόφῳ 'darkness' by *turbinem* 'whirlwind.'

256

13 Cf Exod 20:18–19.

14 Theophylact *Exp in Heb* PG 125 381 repeatedly observes in his commentary on Hebrews 12 that the various events from the OT mentioned in it are types or shadows of NT realities.

15 The detail 'struck down with a javelin' (*aut jaculo configeretur*) is added from Exod 19:13, where the Vulgate has *aut confodietur jaculis* 'or is pierced with javelins.' The Latin word *iacula* can denote any kind of thrown missile but usually means javelins. The Hebrew says only that the animal is to be stoned or shot.

16 Cf 7:2. Jerome *Liber interpretationis hebraicorum nominum* CCL 72 121 (Lagarde 50:9–10) says 'Jerusalem' means 'vision of peace.'

17 'Assistants' (*assessores*) or 'assessors' is a term used in Roman law to denote coadjutors or assistants to a judge or other magistrate. Augustine *Sermones* 58.1 PL 38 393 uses it of Christ's own session at the right hand of the Father. The *Gloss* on 12:23, followed by the other medieval commentators, identified the 'first-born who are enrolled in heaven' with the apostles; cf eg Aquinas *Exp in epist ad Heb* c 12 lect 4 (on Heb 12:23) 781a. Erasmus, however, appears to identify them with the righteous ones of the Old and New Testaments (see Spicq *Hébreux* II 407 for a list of commentators who so identify the 'first-born'). In Matt 19:28 (Luke 22:30) Jesus tells the apostles that in his kingdom they will sit on thrones, judging the twelve tribes of Israel. Erasmus evidently felt that the apostles had to be included somewhere in this heavenly assemblage, and the texts of Matthew and Luke gave him the handle for doing this.

18 According to Theophylact *Exp in Heb* (on Heb 12:24) PG 125 384D, Cyril of Alexandria had said that the blood of Abel cries out against his murderer, but the blood of Christ speaks to his Father on our behalf. Aquinas *Exp in*

epist ad Heb c 12 lect 4 781b comments: '[Abel's blood] cries for vengeance, but the blood of Christ calls there [ie in heaven] for forgiveness.' Cf Erasmus' annotation on this part of 12:24 (*melius loquentem quam Abel*) LB VI 1020F.

19 Theophylact *Exp in Heb* (on Heb 12:25) PG 125 385A, following Chrysostom, takes 'him who speaks' to be Christ and 'him who speaks on earth' to be Moses, or rather, to be God who issued his oracle on earth through Moses at Sinai. Cf Spicq *Hébreux* II 410–11.

257

20 Erasmus means, let us remain in the state of grace conferred through baptism. The Greek commentators took the words ἔχωμεν χάριν in 12:28 to mean 'let us be thankful'; the Latin commentators took the meaning of what they read in the Vulgate versions *habeamus* or *habemus gratiam* to be 'let us have grace,' or alternatively, reading the verb in the indicative, 'we have grace,' though they also discuss the meaning 'let us be thankful.' Both the original Greek and the Latin of the Vulgate are in any case ambiguous; cf AV and DR with RSV.

Chapter 13

1 Lefèvre *Comm in Heb* 260r begins his commentary on chapter 13 with a miniature sermon on the theme that all who are regenerated in Christ are brothers. Hospitality and aiding the imprisoned or the afflicted are examples of brotherly love at work.

2 Cf Gen 18:1–9. This explication of 13:2b occurs in Chrysostom *Hom in Heb* 33 PG 63 225 / NPNF 514b, Theophylact *Exp in Heb* PG 125 389A, and Aquinas *Exp in epist ad Heb* c 13 lect 1 784a. Cf Erasmus' annotation *placuerunt quidam* LB VI 1021E.

3 Theophylact *Exp in Heb* (on Heb 13:3) PG 125 389B makes the point that as human beings we are all subject to evils, but Erasmus seems to be the first commentator to see a reference to the Mystical Body in the word 'body' in this verse (cf 1 Cor 12:24–7). Brooke Foss Westcott *The Epistle to the Hebrews* (Grand Rapids, Mich 1984) 431, though without mentioning Erasmus, calls it a beautiful but inadmissible interpretation.

4 In his annotation on Heb 13:4 (*honorabile connubium in omnibus*) LB VI 1022F, Erasmus comments on the phrase *in omnibus* 'in all' in this verse: 'Theophylact [*Exp in Heb* (on Heb 13:4) PG 125 389B–C] interprets "in all" to mean variously "in all respects, in every period of life, in every circumstance, or by all persons." I prefer the last alternative inasmuch as marriage is held in honour even among pagans because of its public benefit.' Modern commentators are likewise divided over whether the adjective πᾶσι is masculine ('among all persons') or neuter ('in every respect'). Modern translators seem to prefer the meaning 'all persons' though, unlike Erasmus, restricting the 'all' to Christians alone; cf eg AV, NKJ, RSV, NEB.

5 Cf Matt 6:31, a text which Aquinas *Exp in epist ad Heb* c 13 lect 1 (on Heb 13:5) 784b cites to show that 'anxiety' (*sollicitudo*, the word Erasmus uses here), that is, a concern about material things, is the ground of covetousness (*avaritia*).

6 Cf Josh 1:5. The present tenses in Erasmus' translation of this verse are not a paraphrase to suggest the continuing effect of God's promise (though he may well have believed this) but arise from his mistaken belief that the verbs in the Greek are present indicatives; see his annotation on Heb 13:5 (*non te deseram nec relinquam*) LB VI 1022F.

258

7 Erasmus evidently interprets the injunction to remember their leaders in 13:7 in the light of texts such as 1 Tim 5:17–18, 1 Cor 9:14, and Gal 6:6.

8 Chrysostom *Hom in Heb* 33 (on Heb 13:7) PG 63 226 / NPNF 515a says that by 'faith' Paul here means steadfastness. Hugh of St Cher on 13:7 takes the word 'end' (*exitus*) in this verse to refer to the deaths of the leaders 'who died in Christ or for Christ.' Aquinas *Exp in epist ad Heb* c 13 lect 1 (on Heb 13:17) 785a, followed by Nicholas of Lyra on 13:7, distinguishes between leaders – or prelates as Lyra calls them – who are dead (13:7) and those who are alive (13:17).

9 Theophylact *Exp in Heb* (on Heb 13:8–9) PG 125 392C–393A likewise takes 13:8 in close connection with 13:9 and identifies the strange teachings in 13:9 with Jewish beliefs and practices. The medieval commentators on the other hand took the various and strange doctrines mentioned in 13:9 to be heresies of one kind or another. Theophylact *Exp in Heb* (on Heb 13:10) PG 125 394B–C also introduces a similar contrast between the shadow of the Mosaic law and the reality of the gospel. The medieval commentators on the other hand, who do not consider the Old Law to be abrogated or replaced by the New Law, employ the concept of shadow or prefigurement in order to demonstrate that the Old Law is consistent with the New.

10 See the paraphrase on 1 Tim 4:1–7 and 2 Tim 2:14–19.

11 Chrysostom *Hom in Heb* 33 (on Heb 13:9) PG 63 229 / NPNF 516b and Theophylact *Exp in Heb* PG 125 393A–B take the words 'strengthened by grace' in this verse to mean to be made steadfast in faith.

12 See the paraphrase on 13:11 below.

13 See Lev 16:27.

259

14 Theophylact *Exp in Heb* (on Heb 13:13) PG 125 395A comments: 'Because Christ suffered outside the gate, let us too go out to him outside the gate, that is, the world, "bearing his reproach" [13:13], that is, suffering the same things he did. He was crucified outside like a condemned man and thief. Therefore, let us not be ashamed to go out from the world and its splendours even though this seems to be ignominious.'

15 Theophylact *Exp in Heb* (on Heb 13:15) PG 125 396C makes the same comparison between Christians and Jews but the reason he gives for the exclusion of the Jews is their disbelief in the gospel. Erasmus, characteristically, finds the reason for their exclusion in their commitment to externals, to the flesh as opposed to the spirit.

16 The reference is obscure but Erasmus probably means the various kinds of sin-offering; see eg Lev 4:27–35, 6:1–8. By 'neglect of a brother' (*fratre neglecto*) he presumably means a violation of the commandment to love one's neighbour (Lev 19:18).

17 Cf Theophylact *Exp in Heb* (on Heb 13:17) PG 125 397A, who distinguishes between 'wicked' in matters of faith – such a person must be avoided – and 'wicked' in morals – the latter must be obeyed. Chrysostom *Hom in Heb* 34 (on Heb 13:17) PG 63 231 / NPNF 518–20, who is responsible for introducing this notion into the commentary tradition, carries on at great length about it.

18 compliant and obedient] 1521–1534. The 1538 and later editions read 'both compliant and obedient.'

19 Cf Chrysostom *Hom in Heb* 34 (on Heb 13:18) PG 63 233 / NPNF 520a and Theophylact *Exp in Heb* PG 125 397C–400A. Since they believe that Paul is writing this letter to Jews, they assume that he is defending himself against false allegations such as those in Acts 21:21. Erasmus seems to have in mind Paul's defence of himself in 1 Cor 2 and 3.

260

20 Meanwhile I in turn pray for you] This clause is omitted in the 1540 edition and in LB.

21 'Supreme': *summus*. Erasmus heightens the positive degree of the adjective 'the great' in 13:20 to suggest that Jesus is distinct from any other shepherd. Theophylact *Exp in Heb* PG 125 400C and the medieval commentators note that the epithet 'great' in this verse implies that all other pastors are less than Christ, or, as Aquinas *Exp in epist ad Heb* c 13 lect 3 (on Heb 13:20) 789a puts it, they are only his vicars: he feeds his own sheep; they feed his.

22 Erasmus' interpretation of 13:22b seems to be unique. Patristic and medieval commentators, followed by all modern commentators that I know – some of whom also believe that the author is employing a literary convention – treat this statement as a form of meiosis, though with a variety of nuances: I could have written at great length on this subject, but I did not want to abuse your patience and have therefore written a short account.

23 This explanation occurs in Primasius *Commentaria in epistolas S Pauli* (on Heb. 13:23) PL 68 793B, who states that Paul had dispatched Timothy on a preaching mission. Primasius ibidem 794A also advances the view that Timothy had been set free from prison, which is the commonly accepted interpretation: Timothy has been released from prison and Paul wishes to inform the recipients of the letter of this event.

24 'Favour' is Erasmus' standard gloss on the word grace; cf CWE 42 89 and 140.

25 The title 'Professor of Theology' appears at this point in the first edition of the *Paraphrase on Hebrews* and thus at the conclusion of the complete set of *Paraphrases* on the Epistles in the March 1521 and subsequent editions. Compare the title of Erasmus' commentary on Psalm 1, the first of his own works on the Bible to be published (in 1515): *Enarratio Primi Psalmi ... Auctore Erasmo Roterodamo, Sacrae Theologiae Professore*. This claim to be a professor of theology, inserted here at the end of the collected edition of the *Paraphrases on the Apostolic Epistles,* may be intended to imply that the *Paraphrases* constitute an introductory course in true theology. A similar description, with perhaps similar intentions, appears in the salutation of Ep 396, the dedicatory letter for Erasmus' edition of the works of St Jerome (Basel 1516); see the reproduction in CWE 61 4.

THE SEQUENCE AND DATES OF THE PUBLICATION OF THE PARAPHRASES

EDITIONS OF THE PARAPHRASES CITED BY DATE OF PUBLICATION IN THE NOTES

WORKS FREQUENTLY CITED

SHORT-TITLE FORMS FOR ERASMUS' WORKS

INDEX OF SCRIPTURAL PASSAGES CITED

INDEX OF GREEK AND LATIN WORDS CITED

GENERAL INDEX

The indexes refer primarily to the preface, the translator's note, the dedicatory letter, and the notes. An index of all the names and theological terms in the paraphrase itself is beyond the scope of this volume.

THE SEQUENCE AND DATES OF THE PUBLICATION
OF THE PARAPHRASES

The Epistles

Romans	November 1517
Corinthians 1 and 2	February 1519
Galatians	May 1519
Timothy 1 and 2, Titus, Philemon	November/December 1519
Ephesians, Philippians, Colossians, and Thessalonians 1 and 2	January/February 1520
Peter 1 and 2, Jude	June/July 1520
James	December 1520
John 1–3, Hebrews	January 1521

Gospels and Acts

Matthew	March 1522
John	February 1523
Luke	August 1523
Mark	December 1523/February 1524
Acts	February 1524

The Epistles were originally published by Dirk Martens in Louvain, except for Timothy, Titus, and Philemon which were published by Michaël Hillen in Antwerp. The Gospels and Acts were all originally published by Johann Froben in Basel.

EDITIONS OF THE PARAPHRASES CITED BY DATE OF PUBLICATION IN THE NOTES

1519 — *Paraphrases in epistolas Pauli ad Timotheum duas, ad Titum vnam, & ad Philemonem vnam, per Des. Erasmum Roterodamum recens ab illo conscriptae, & nunc primum typis excusae, ad Christum Paulique gloriam* (Antwerp: Michaël Hillen n d)

March 1520 — *Paraphrases in Epistolas Pauli, ad Timotheum duas, ad Titum unam, & ad Philemonem unam, per Des. Erasmum Roterodamum recens ab illo conscriptae, & nunc primum typis excusae, ad Christum Paulique gloriam* (Basel: Johann Froben, March 1520). Issued separately in roman and italic type

1520 — *Paraphrases in duas Epistolas Petri apostolorum principis, & in vnam Iudae, per Erasmum Roterodamum, quas antehac nullus excudit* (Louvain: Dirk Martens n d)

January 1521 — *Paraphrases in Duas Epistolas Petri apostolorum principis, & in unam Iudae, per Erasmum Roterodamum* (Basel: Johann Froben, January 1521 [1520 on title page])

December 1520 — *In Epistolam Iacobi Episcopi Hierosolymitani Paraphrasis, per Erasmum Roterodamum* (Louvain: Dirk Martens, December 1520)

January 1521 — *Paraphrasis in Treis Epistolas Canonicas Ioannis apostoli, per Erasmum Roterodamum* (Louvain: Dirk Martens, January 1521)

January 1521 — *In Epistolam Pauli Apostoli ad Hebraeos paraphrasis per Erasmum Roterodamum extrema* (Louvain: Dirk Martens, January 1521)

March 1521 — *Paraphrases Erasmi Roterodami in omnes Epistolas Pauli germanas, & in omnes Canonicas, diligenter ab autore recognitae, ac marginalibus indicibus illustratae* (Basel: Johann Froben, March 1521)

July 1521 — *Paraphrases Erasmi Roterodami in omnes epistolas Pauli apostoli germanas, & in eam quae est ad Hebraeos incerti autoris, cum iis quae canonicae uocantur rursus ab eo recognitae absolutaeque: postremo a nobis accuratius excusae, digestaeque per tomos, ut cuique secare in formam enchiridii, si uelit, liberum sit* (Basel: Johann Froben, July 1521)

February 1522 — *Io[hannes] Frob[enius] Lectori S.D. In universas epistolas ab ecclesia receptas, hoc est Pauli quatuordecim, Petri duas, Iudae unam, Iacobi unam, Ioannis treis, paraphrasis, hoc est liberior ac dilucidior interpretatio, per Erasmum Roterodamum ex archetypis primis diligenter ab ipso recognitis. Cuius diligentiae nostra quoque cura non defuit. Tuum erit optime lector dare operam, ne uel ille Christi gloriae, uel nos tuae commoditati frustra sudasse uideamur. Vale.* (Basel: Johann Froben, February 1522)

May 1522   Idem (Basel: Johann Froben, May 1522)

1523 folio   *Tomus Secundus Continens Paraphrasim Desiderii Erasmi Roterodami*
                  In omneis epistolas apostolicas, summa cura recognitam, & ex arche-
                  typis & eruditorum animaduersione, ita ut accuratius fieri uix
                  potuerit. Caetera cognosces lector, inuersa pagina (Basel: Johann
                  Froben 1523)

1523 octavo   *Tomus Secundus Continens Paraphrasim D. Erasmi Rot. In omneis*
                  epistolas apostolicas, summa cura recognitam, & ex archetypis &
                  eruditorum animaduersio, ita ut accuratius fieri uix potuerit. Caetera
                  cognosces lector, inuersa pagella (Basel: Johann Froben 1523)

1532   *Tomus Secundus Continens Paraphrasim D. Erasmi Roterodami In*
                  omneis epistolas apostolicas, summa cura denuo ab ipso autore rec-
                  ognitam, emendatamque, tum ex archetypis, tum eruditorum ani-
                  maduersione, ita ut accuratius uix potuerit. Caetera cognosces lector,
                  inuersa pagina (Basel: Hieronymus Froben and Nicholaus Epi-
                  scopius 1532)

1534   *Tomus Secundus Continens Paraphrasim D. Erasmi Roterodami In*
                  omneis epistolas apostolicas, summa cura denuo ab ipso autore rec-
                  ognitam, emendatamque, tum ex archetypis, tum eruditorum anima-
                  duersione, ita ut accuratius uix potuerit. Caetera cognosces lector,
                  inuersa pagina (Basel: Hieronymus Froben and Nicholaus Epis-
                  copius 1534)

1538   *Tomus Secundus Continens Paraphrasin* [sic] *D. Erasmi Roterodami*
                  In omneis epistolas apostolicas, summa cura denuo ab ipso autore
                  recognitam, emendatamque, tum ex archetypis, tum eruditorum anim-
                  aduersione, ita ut accuratius uix potuerit. Caetera cognosces lector,
                  inuersa pagina (Basel: Hieronymus Froben and Nicholaus Epis-
                  copius 1538)

1540   *Opera Omnia* VII (Basel: Hieronymus Froben and Nicholaus Epi-
                  scopius 1540)

WORKS FREQUENTLY CITED

This list provides bibliographical information for publications referred to in short-title form in introductions and notes. For Erasmus' writings see the short-title list following.

Allen	P.S. Allen, H.M. Allen, and H.W. Garrod eds *Opus epistolarum Des. Erasmi Roterodami* (Oxford 1906–58) 11 vols and index
Ambrosiaster *Comm in 1 Tim* etc	*Ambrosiastri qui dicitur Commentarius in Epistolas Paulinas Pars Tertia ...* ed H.I. Vogels CSEL 81/3 (Vienna 1969)
Aquinas *Exp in epist 1 ad Tim* etc	*Expositio in omnes S. Pauli epistolas* in *Sancti Thomae Aquinatis Doctoris Angelici Ordinis Praedicatorum Opera Omnia* 2nd impression (Parma 1852–73; repr New York 1949) vol XIII
ASD	*Opera omnia Desiderii Erasmi Roterodami* (Amsterdam-New York-Oxford 1969–)
Augustine *Tract in 1 Ioannem*	S. Aurelii Augustini *In Epistolam Ioannis ad Parthos Tractatus decem* PL 35 1977–2062
AV	*The Holy Bible containing the Old and New Testaments* (London 1873)
Bauckham *Jude*	Richard J. Bauckham *Jude, 2 Peter* Word Biblical Commentary 50 (Waco, Texas 1983)
Bauckham *2 Peter*	Richard J. Bauckham *Jude, 2 Peter* Word Biblical Commentary 50 (Waco, Texas 1983)
Bede *Exp Iac* etc	*Bedae Venerabilis Opera*, Pars II, Opera Exegetica 4 *In Epistolas VII Catholicas* CCL 121 (Turnhout 1983)
Brown *Epistles*	*The Epistles of John* translated with introduction, notes, and commentary by Raymond E. Brown SS, Anchor Bible 30 (Garden City, NY 1982)
CCL	*Corpus christianorum, series latina* (Turnhout 1953–)
CEBR	Peter G. Bietenholz and Thomas B. Deutscher eds *Contemporaries of Erasmus: A Biographical Register of the Renaissance and the Reformation* 3 vols (Toronto-Buffalo-London 1985–7)
CSEL	*Corpus Scriptorum Ecclesiasticorum Latinorum* (Vienna 1866–)

Chrysostom *Hom in*   Johannes Chrysostomus *Opera omnia quae extant* XI PG 62
    1 Tim etc   (Paris 1862) 501–720 and XII PG 63 (Paris 1862) 9–236

Chrysostom NPNF   A Select Library of the Nicene and Post-Nicene Fathers of
                          the Christian Church edited by Philip Schaff (Grand
                          Rapids, Mich 1976) first series, XIII and XIV

CWE   *Collected Works of Erasmus* (Toronto-Buffalo-London
                          1974–)

Davids *James*   Peter Davids *The Epistle of James* (Exeter 1982)

DR   *The Holy Bible translated from the Latin Vulgate* (New York
                          1914)

Fee *1 Tim* etc   Gordon D. Fee *1 and 2 Timothy, Titus* New International
                          Biblical Commentary (Peabody, Mass 1988)

Gloss   [Biblia Latina] *Sexta pars biblie cum glosa ordinaria et exposi-
                          tione [L]yre litterali et morali: necnon additionibus ac replicis*
                          (Basel 1498)

Holborn   *Desiderius Erasmus Roterodamus Ausgewählte Werke* ed Hajo
                          Holborn with Annemarie Holborn (Munich 1933)

Hugh of St Cher   *Biblia Latina cum postillis Hugonis de Sancto Charo* (Basel
                          1498–1503) VII

Hurst   *The Commentary on the Seven Catholic Epistles of Bede the
                          Venerable* trans David Hurst, Cistercian Studies Series 82
                          (Kalamazoo, Mich 1985)

Jerome *Comm in*   S. Eusebius Hieronymus Stridensis *Commentariorum in Epi-
    Titum   stolam ad Titum liber unus* PL 26 (Paris 1845) 555–600

Jerome *Comm in*   *Commentariorum in Epistolam ad Philemonem liber unus* PL 26
    Philem   (Paris 1845) 600–616

Kelly *Pastoral Epistles* J.N.D. Kelly *A Commentary on the Pastoral Epistles* I Timothy
                          II Timothy Titus (London 1978)

Kelly *Peter and Jude*   J.N.D. Kelly *A Commentary on the Epistles of Peter and Jude*
                          (London 1982)

Knox   *The Holy Bible: A Translation from the Latin Vulgate in the
                          Light of the Hebrew and Greek Originals* (New York 1954)

LB   J. Leclerc ed *Desiderii Erasmi Roterodami opera omnia*
                          (Leiden 1703–6) 10 vols

Lefèvre *Comm*	Jacobus Faber Stapulensis *Commentarii in Pauli epistolas* (Paris 1512)
LXX	*Septuaginta: id est Vetus Testamentum graece iuxta LXX interpretes* ed Alfred Rahlfs 2 vols (Stuttgart 1982)
Martin *James*	Ralph P. Martin *James* Word Biblical Commentary 48 (Waco, Texas 1988)
Metzger *Textual Commentary*	Bruce M. Metzger *A Textual Commentary on the Greek New Testament* (London-New York 1975)
Michaels *1 Peter*	J. Ramsey Michaels *1 Peter* Word Biblical Commentary 49 (Waco, Texas 1988)
Nestle-Aland NTGL	*Novum Testamentum Graece et Latine* Textum Graecum post Eberhard Nestle et Erwin Nestle communiter ediderunt Kurt Aland Matthew Black Carlo M. Martini Bruce M. Metzger Allen Wikgren – Textus Latinus Novae Vulgatae Bibliorum Sacrorum Editioni debetur; utriusque textus apparatum criticum recensuerunt et editionem novis curis elaboraverunt Kurt Aland et Barbara Aland una cum Instituto studiorum textus Novi Testamenti Monasteriensi (Westphalia) (Stuttgart 1984)
NEB	*New English Bible* (Oxford-Cambridge 1970)
Nicholas of Lyra	[Biblia Latina] *Sexta pars biblie cum glosa ordinaria et expositione [L]yre litterali et morali, necnon additionibus ac replicis* (Basel 1498)
NKJ	*Holy Bible: The New King James Version containing the Old and New Testaments* (Nashville 1979)
NPNF	See Chrysostom
Opuscula	Wallace K. Ferguson *Erasmi Opuscula* (The Hague 1933)
Payne *Theology*	John B. Payne *Erasmus: His Theology of the Sacraments* (Richmond, Va 1970)
PG	J.P. Migne ed *Patrologiae cursus completus ... series graeca* (Paris 1857–86) 162 vols
PL	J.P. Migne ed *Patrologiae cursus completus ... series latina* (Paris 1844–66) 221 vols
Rummel *Annotations*	Erika Rummel *Erasmus' 'Annotations' on the New Testament* (Toronto-Buffalo-London 1986)

Rummel *Critics*   Erika Rummel *Erasmus and His Catholic Critics* 2 vols
                          (Nieuwkoop 1989)

RSV   *The New Oxford Annotated Bible: The Holy Bible, Revised
                          Standard Version containing the Old and New Testaments*
                          (New York 1973)

Selwyn *First Peter*   Edward Gordon Selwyn *The First Epistle of St. Peter* 2nd
                          edition (Grand Rapids, Mich 1983)

Spicq *Epîtres pastorales* C. Spicq OP *Saint Paul Les epîtres pastorales* 4th edition
                          (Paris 1969) 2 vols

Spicq *Hébreux*   C. Spicq OP *L'Epître aux Hébreux* 3rd edition (Paris 1953)
                          2 vols

Theophylact *Exp in   Theophylactus *Expositiones in epistolas Pauli ad Timotheum,
  1 Tim* etc   Titum, Philemonem, Hebraeos* PG (Paris 1864) 125 9–404

Thompson *Colloquies*   Craig R. Thompson *The Colloquies of Erasmus* (Chicago-
                          London 1965)

Vulg   [OT] *Biblia Sacra Vulgatae Editionis Sixti V. et Clementis VIII.*
                          (London n d); [NT] *Novum Testamentum Graece et Latine ...*
                          ed Augustinus Merk SJ 6th edition (Rome 1948)

SHORT-TITLE FORMS FOR ERASMUS' WORKS

Titles following colons are longer versions of the same, or are alternative titles. Items entirely enclosed in square brackets are of doubtful authorship. For abbreviations, see Works Frequently Cited.

Acta: Acta Academia Lovaniensis contra Lutherum *Opuscula* / CWE 71

Adagia: Adagiorum chiliades 1508, etc (Adagiorum collectanea for the primitive form, when required) LB II / ASD II-4, 5, 6 / CWE 30–6

Admonitio adversus mendacium: Admonitio adversus mendacium et obtrectationem LB X

Annotationes in Novum Testamentum LB VI

Antibarbari LB IX / ASD I-1 / CWE 23

Apologia ad Caranzam: Apologia ad Sanctium Caranzam, or Apologia de tribus locis, or Responsio ad annotationem Stunicae ... a Sanctio Caranza defensam LB IX

Apologia ad Fabrum: Apologia ad Iacobum Fabrum Stapulensem LB IX

Apologia adversus monachos: Apologia adversus monachos quosdam hispanos LB IX

Apologia adversus Petrum Sutorem: Apologia adversus debacchationes Petri Sutoris LB IX

Apologia adversus rhapsodias Alberti Pii: Apologia ad viginti et quattuor libros A. Pii LB IX

Apologia contra Latomi dialogum: Apologia contra Iacobi Latomi dialogum de tribus linguis LB IX / CWE 71

Apologiae contra Stunicam: Apologiae contra Lopidem Stunicam LB IX / ASD IX-2

Apologia de 'In principio erat sermo' LB IX

Apologia de laude matrimonii: Apologia pro declamatione de laude matrimonii LB IX / CWE 71

Apologia de loco 'Omnes quidem': Apologia de loco 'Omnes quidem resurgemus' LB IX

Apologia qua respondet invectivis Lei: Apologia qua respondet duabus invectivis Eduardi Lei *Opuscula*

Apophthegmata LB IV

Appendix respondens ad Sutorem LB IX

Argumenta: Argumenta in omnes epistolas apostolicas nova (with Paraphrases)

Axiomata pro causa Lutheri: Axiomata pro causa Martini Lutheri *Opuscula* / CWE 71

Carmina LB I, IV, V, VIII / CWE 85–6

Catalogus lucubrationum LB I

Christiani hominis institutum, carmen LB V

Ciceronianus: Dialogus Ciceronianus LB I / ASD I-2 / CWE 28

Colloquia LB I / ASD I-3

Compendium vitae Allen I / CWE 4

[Consilium: Consilium cuiusdam ex animo cupientis esse consultum] *Opuscula* / CWE 71

De bello turcico: Consultatio de bello turcico (in Psalmi)

De civilitate: De civilitate morum puerilium LB I / CWE 25

Declamatio de morte LB IV

Declamatiuncula LB IV

Declarationes ad censuras Lutetiae vulgatas: Declarationes ad censuras Lutetiae vulgatas sub nomine facultatis theologiae Parisiensis LB IX

De concordia: De sarcienda ecclesiae concordia, or De amabili ecclesiae concordia (in Psalmi)

De conscribendis epistolis LB I / ASD I-2 / CWE 25

De constructione: De constructione octo partium orationis, or Syntaxis LB I / ASD I-4

De contemptu mundi: Epistola de contemptu mundi LB V / ASD V-1 / CWE 66

De copia: De duplici copia verborum ac rerum LB I / ASD I-6 / CWE 24

De immensa Dei misericordia: Concio de immensa Dei misericordia LB V

De libero arbitrio: De libero arbitrio diatribe LB IX

De praeparatione: De praeparatione ad mortem LB V / ASD V-1

De pueris instituendis: De pueris statim ac liberaliter instituendis LB I / ASD I-2 / CWE 26

De puero Iesu: Concio de puero Iesu LB V / CWE 29

De puritate tabernaculi: De puritate tabernaculi sive ecclesiae christianae (in Psalmi)

De ratione studii LB I / ASD I-2 / CWE 24

De recta pronuntiatione: De recta latini graecique sermonis pronuntiatione LB I / ASD I-4 / CWE 26

Detectio praestigiarum: Detectio praestigiarum cuiusdam libelli germanice scripti LB X / ASD IX-1

De taedio Iesu: Disputatiuncula de taedio, pavore, tristicia Iesu LB V

De vidua christiana LB V / CWE 66

De virtute amplectenda: Oratio de virtute amplectenda LB V / CWE 29

[Dialogus bilinguium ac trilinguium: Chonradi Nastadiensis dialogus bilinguium ac trilinguium] Opuscula / CWE 7

Dilutio: Dilutio eorum quae Iodocus Clithoveus scripsit adversus declamationem suasoriam matrimonii

Divinationes ad notata Bedae LB IX

Ecclesiastes: Ecclesiastes sive de ratione concionandi LB V

Elenchus in N. Bedae censuras LB IX

Enchiridion: Enchiridion militis christiani LB V / CWE 66

Encomium matrimonii (in De conscribendis epistolis)

Encomium medicinae: Declamatio in laudem artis medicae LB I / ASD I-4 / CWE 29

Epistola ad Dorpium LB IX / CWE 3 / CWE 71

Epistola ad fratres Inferioris Germaniae: Responsio ad fratres Germaniae Inferioris ad epistolam apologeticam incerto autore proditam LB X / ASD IX-1

Epistola ad graculos: Epistola ad quosdam imprudentissimos graculos LB X

Epistola apologetica de Termino LB X

Epistola consolatoria: Epistola consolatoria virginibus sacris LB V

Epistola contra pseudevangelicos: Epistola contra quosdam qui se falso iactant evangelicos LB X / ASD IX-1

Epistola de esu carnium: Epistola apologetica ad Christophorum episcopum Basiliensem de interdicto esu carnium LB IX / ASD IX-1

Exomologesis: Exomologesis sive modus confitendi LB V

Explanatio symboli: Explanatio symboli apostolorum sive catechismus LB V / ASD V-1

Expositio concionalis (in Psalmi)

Expostulatio Iesu LB V

Formula: Conficiendarum epistolarum formula (see De conscribendis epistolis)

Hyperaspistes LB X

In Nucem Ovidii commentarius LB I / ASD I-1 / CWE 29
In Prudentium: Commentarius in duos hymnos Prudentii LB V / CWE 29
Institutio christiani matrimonii LB V
Institutio principis christiani LB IV / ASD IV-1 / CWE 27

[Julius exclusus: Dialogus Julius exclusus e coelis] Opuscula / CWE 27

Lingua LB IV / ASD IV-1A / CWE 29
Liturgia Virginis Matris: Virginis Matris apud Lauretum cultae liturgia LB V /
   ASD V-1

Manifesta mendacia CWE 71
Methodus (see Ratio)
Modus orandi Deum LB V / ASD V-1
Moria: Moriae encomium LB IV / ASD IV-3 / CWE 27

Novum Testamentum: Novum Testamentum 1519 and later (Novum instrumentum
   for the first edition, 1516, when required) LB VI

Obsecratio ad Virginem Mariam: Obsecratio sive oratio ad Virginem Mariam in
   rebus adversis LB V
Oratio de pace: Oratio de pace et discordia LB VIII
Oratio funebris: Oratio funebris Berthae de Heyen LB VIII / CWE 29

Paean Virgini Matri: Paean Virgini Matri dicendus LB V
Panegyricus: Panegyricus ad Philippum Austriae ducem LB IV / ASD IV-1 / CWE 27
Parabolae: Parabolae sive similia LB I / ASD I-5 / CWE 23
Paraclesis LB V, VI
Paraphrasis in Elegantias Vallae: Paraphrasis in Elegantias Laurentii Vallae LB I /
   ASD I-4
Paraphrasis in Matthaeum, etc (in Paraphrasis in Novum Testamentum)
Paraphrasis in Novum Testamentum LB VII / CWE 42–50
Peregrinatio apostolorum: Peregrinatio apostolorum Petri et Pauli LB VI, VII
Precatio ad Virginis filium Iesum LB V
Precatio dominica LB V
Precationes LB V
Precatio pro pace ecclesiae: Precatio ad Iesum pro pace ecclesiae LB IV, V
Progymnasmata: Progymnasmata quaedam primae adolescentiae Erasmi LB VIII
Psalmi: Psalmi, or Enarrationes sive commentarii in psalmos LB V / ASD V-2, 3
Purgatio adversus epistolam Lutheri: Purgatio adversus epistolam non sobriam
   Lutheri LB IX / ASD IX-1

Querela pacis LB IV / ASD IV-2 / CWE 27

Ratio: Ratio seu Methodus compendio perveniendi ad veram theologiam (Methodus

for the shorter version originally published in the Novum instrumentum of 1516)
LB V, VI

Responsio ad annotationes Lei: Liber quo respondet annotationibus Lei LB IX

Responsio ad collationes: Responsio ad collationes cuiusdam iuvenis gerontodi-
dascali LB IX

Responsio ad disputationem de divortio: Responsio ad disputationem cuiusdam
Phimostomi de divortio LB IX

Responsio ad epistolam Pii: Responsio ad epistolam paraeneticam Albert Pii, or
Responsio ad exhortationem Pii LB IX

Responsio ad notulas Bedaicas LB X

Responsio ad Petri Cursii defensionem: Epistola de apologia Cursii LB X

Responsio adversus febricitantis libellum: Apologia monasticae religionis LB X

Spongia: Spongia adversus aspergines Hutteni LB X / ASD IX-1
Supputatio: Supputatio calumniarum Natalis Bedae LB IX

Tyrannicida: Tyrannicida, declamatio Lucianicae respondens LB I / CWE 29

Virginis et martyris comparatio LB V
Vita Hieronymi: Vita divi Hieronymi Stridonensis *Opuscula*

Index of Scriptural Passages Cited

Index of Greek and Latin Words Cited

General Index

Aaron's robe and rod 22 n13

Abel 127 nn21, 22, 153 n30; offers a sacrifice accepted by God 244 nn5, 6; blood of 256 n18. *See also* Cain

Abraham: faith of 152 n22, 246 n15, 248 n22; model of charity 152 n27; history of 246 n14, 247 n17; God of 247 n21. *See also* Sarah

abuse, prohibition of 163 n22

aconite 157 n2

Acts of Paul and Thecla 47 n10

Acts of Peter 114 n18

Adam: allegory for rational part of the soul 17 n27. *See also* Eve

Adolph of Burgundy 2 n1

Adrian VI, Pope 132 n6

allegorical interpretation 17 n27, 22 n13, 115 n28, 167 n11, 198 n13, 235 n7, 237 n26, 239 n3, 248 n27, 250 nn36, 40

allegory 17 n27, 226 n5. *See also* Adam, Eve

Ambrose, bishop of Milan 134 n11

Ambrosiaster xv, 42 n6
- *Comm in 2 Thess* 38 n18
- *Comm in 1 Tim* (1) 5 n4, 7 nn16, 17, 8 n18, 9 nn23, 26; (2) 14 n9, 15 n12, 15 n13, 16 n18; (5) 27 n2, 28 n6, 29 n12, 30 n13, 31 n18, 33 nn23, 24; (6) 34 n2, 35 n7, 37 n13
- *Comm in 2 Tim* (Argument) 40 n1; (1) 41 n3, 42 nn4, 6, 43 nn7, 8, 10; (2) 46 n5, 47 n10; (3) 49 n4, 50 n10; (4) 52 n3, 53 n12
- *Comm in Titum* (1) 60 n18; (2) 62

n14, 63 nn17, 18; (3) 65 nn9, 11, 66 n15, 67 n22
- *Comm in Philem* 71 n1

Amen: 'liturgical' 38 n21; paraphrases 201 n35; omitted 205 n12

anagogical interpretation 115 n28

angels 117 n13; as spectators of salvation history 86 n26; sin of 117 n6, 118 n14; nature of 126 n13; Law brought to Moses by 217 n2; as ministers to humans 217 n19, 235 n29; impassibility of 218 n10

animals, wild as pets or domesticated 156 nn12, 14

Anna, model for widows 28 n6

Apollos 67 nn22, 23

apostasy, sin of 200 n26, 241 n17

apostles as judges of Israel 256 n17. *See also* James the Less, Jude, Thomas

Aquinas, Thomas xv, 134 n10; *Exp in epist ad 1 Tim* 5 n7, 29 n8, 37 n13; *2 Tim* 46 n5; *Titum* 60 n16, 67 n25; *Philem* 71 n5; *Heb* (1) 215 nn2, 4, 5, 8, 216 nn11, 14, 16; (2) 217 n1; (5) 226 n5; (6) 227 nn5, 6; (7) 230 n4, 231 n8; (8) 234 nn2, 8; (9) 235 nn3, 6, 7, 236 n18, 237 nn26, 27, 238 n31; (10) 239 n3, 240 n10, 241 nn12, 13, 242 n23, 243 n25; (11) 245 n7, 246 n15, 247 nn16, 17, 248 nn22, 24, 27, 249 n32, 251 n45, 252 nn49, 51; (12) 252 n3, 254 nn8, 9, 255 n11, 256 nn17, 18; (13) 257 nn2, 5, 258 n8, 260 n21; *Summa contra gentiles* 169 n27

Chrysostom, John ix, xv–xvi, 58 n5;
  Hom in Macc et matrem 37 n12; *Hom
  in 1 Thess* 16 n21
– *Hom in 1 Tim* (1) 5 nn2, 3, 7 nn14,
  15, 16, 9 nn25, 27, 29, 11 n32, 12
  n35; (2) 13 nn2, 8, 15 nn14, 16, 17,
  17 nn23, 25, 27, 18 nn28, 29, 30; (3)
  19 n4, 20 n6, 22 nn12, 14; (6) 34 n1,
  35 n4, 37 n13
– *Hom in 2 Tim* (1) 42 n5, 43 nn11,
  14; (2) 46 nn4, 5, 6, 47 n11, 48 n14;
  (3) 49 n4, 50 n6; (4) 52 n5, 53 nn6,
  7, 8
– *Hom in Titum* (Argument) 56 n2;
  (1) 58 n5, 59 n9, 60 nn16, 20; (2) 61
  nn2, 5, 62 nn9, 10, 13; (3) 63 n1, 67
  nn21, 22
– *Hom in Philem* 70 n3, 71 nn5, 7, 72
  n11, 73 n18, 74 n23
– *Hom in Heb* (Argument) 214 n1; (1)
  215 nn1, 4, 5, 10, 216 nn13, 15; (2)
  217 nn1, 3, 218 n9; (3) 223 nn3, 4, 5;
  (5) 225 nn2, 3; (6) 227 nn4, 6, 228
  n8; (7) 231 n9, 232 n18; (9) 235 nn1,
  3, 236 n15, 237 n27; (10) 239 nn2, 5,
  240 nn9, 10, 11, 242 nn18, 24; (11)
  243 n1, 244 nn3, 4, 6, 245 nn7, 10,
  12, 246 n13, 248 nn22, 23, 249 n32,
  252 n52; (12) 252 n1, 253 n4, 255
  n11, 256 n19; (13) 257 n2, 258 nn8,
  11, 259 nn17, 19
church, governance of 22 n11;
  militant 44 n2; as bride of
  Christ 161 n12. *See also* house
  church, Index of Latin Words, sv
  'congregatio,' 'ecclesia'
Cicero xvii, 67 n24, 150 n14
Clement, John 78 n22
clergy: support of by the laity 31 n18,
  61 n25; effect of behaviour on
  laity 63 n2
Comma Johanneum. See Johannine
  Comma
confession 169 n29, 177 n13. *See also*
  penance
contrition 177 n13
controversies xiv, 63 n17, 65 n9, 153
  n32. *See also* critics
critics of Erasmus xiv, 62 n14, 66 n16,

134 n17. *See also* Baechem, Nicolaas;
  Béda, Noël; Lee, Edward; Lefèvre
  d'Etaples, Jacques; López, Diego
  Zúñiga; Paris, faculty of theology
  at; Pelargus, Ambrosius; Spanish
  monks
Cyprian 107 n12
Cyril of Alexandria 256 n18

Daniel 251 n41
David, and Goliath 250 n40
David of Burgundy 2 n1
Dead Sea Scrolls 24 n2
despair, sin of 167 n13
devil, children of 189 n10, 194 n5; as
  murderer of humankind 190 n13;
  fall of 190 n13
diatribe style 191 n22
Diotrephes the heresiarch 209 n7
disputations: practice of criticized ix,
  46 n8, 114 n20. *See also* questions
double paraphrase. *See* paraphrase,
  features of
dowry, provision of an act of
  charity 31 n16

earnest 199 n18
Egmondanus. *See* Baechem, Nicolaas
elder. *See* bishop
Eleazar the priest 251 n41
Elijah 169 nn31, 32, 251 n41
Elisha 251 n41
enigma 22 n13, 236 n15
Enoch 77 n14, 245 n8. *See also 1 Enoch*
envy, sin of 160 n4, 167 n13, 190 n13,
  200 n27. *See also* Cain
Epimenides 60 n16
Erasmus: theological commonplace
  book xvi; last will and testament 31 n16; criticisms of contemporary prelates 53 n9, 251 n41, 258
  n8; attitude toward Jews 60 n20;
  misunderstands Greek text of
  NT 77 n20, 118 n16, 121 n10, 187
  n39, 257 n6; novel explanation of
  NT 147 nn1, 4, 232 n15, 251 n42,
  260 n22; view of faith declared
  heretical 151 n18; emendation of
  Greek text of NT 160 n4; controver-

piety, ironic view of 29 n8. *See also* godliness

planets. *See* stars, wandering

Plato 87 n37

platonizing interpretation of Scripture 231 n11, 233 n1

play on words 8 n21, 72 n12, 74 n21

Pliny the Elder 24 n2, 139 n12, 156 n12, 157 n21

Pliny the Younger 91 n21, 104 n18

pope, primacy of 80 n3

prayer 16 n18; Christian and Jewish contrasted 16 n17; efficacy of contrasted to use of magic 169 n26

presbytery 26 n9

pride as source of sin 177 n13

priest, office of 11 n34, 22 n10

Primasius 260 n23

Prudentius 14 n11

pulpit, abuse of 155 nn6, 15

puns. *See* play on words

purple color as symbol of wealth 94 n1

questions ix, 66 n15. *See also* disputations

Rahab 153 n30

redemption 90 n16

regeneration 82 n9, 189 n11

religious dress and titles 49 n2

repentance 13 n5

resurrection of the body: heretical view of 47 n10; awaited with joy by the faithful departed 252 n51

Rhetorica ad Herennium 150 n14

riddle. *See* enigma

righteousness x, xvii, 52 n4. *See also* innocence, Index of Latin Words, sv 'innocentia,' 'iustitia'

rings, therapeutic power of 168 n22

Roman emperor 91 n24, 197 n16

salvation, economy of x; obtained through faith, not descent 7 n17; lost through one's own fault 15 n12; contrasted with material wealth 37 n13, 186 n32; as goal 89 n2, 188 n6

Sarah, faith of 246 n15

Samson 251 n48

Samuel and his sons 251 n41

Satan 118 n14. *See also* devil

satire, topics from 16 n21

Schiner, Matthäus xiii, xv, 132 n1

second baptism, denial of 227 n6, 242 n18

Seneca xvii

servants, portrayal of 62 n12

seven brothers, martyrdom of the 251 n41, 252 n49

shadows. *See* law of Moses, type

shewbread, erroneous statement about 235 n5

sin 29 n8, 92 n26, 178 n19, 188 n9; original x, 141 n16, 189 n11; terms for xvii, 141 n16, 200 n29; seven deadly 89 n10; venial 169 n29; occasions of 252 n3. *See also* apostasy, despair, envy, pride, vindictiveness

Sisera. *See* Jabin

Sodom 117 n10, 127 n17

Son, second person of the Trinity 215 nn4, 5, 8, 218 n10

Sophocles 156 n12

Spanish monks 63 n17, 198 n13

speaking in tongues 85 n24

spirit: demonic 159 n31; gift of 193 n35; earnest of heavenly inheritance 199 n18; as term for soul 254 n8. *See also* Holy Spirit

Spirit of Christ 159 n31, 192 n33

spiritual interpretation 115 n28, 216 n12, 226 n5. *See also* mystical interpretation

spiritual torpor 89 n10

stars: morning star as symbol of Jesus 115 n28; wandering 128 n28

Stunica. *See* López Zúñiga, Diego

Suetonius 87 n37, 91 n21

Sylvanus 77 n20

Tabor, Mount 114 n24

Tacitus 81 n2, 91 n21, 214 n1

teacher 154 n1

temple, contrasted with church 22 n12. *See also* Holy of Holies, Holy Place

This book

was designed by

ANTJE LINGNER

based on the series design by

ALLAN FLEMING

and was printed by

University

of Toronto

Press